Ran and the Gray World 7

Story and Art by **Aki Irie**

Contents

Character Introduction ⋯⋯⋯⋯⋯⋯⋯⋯ 7

Bonus Story: **Shizuka's Vagabond Diaries** ⋯⋯ 31

Bonus Story: **Hibi's Heart Isn't in It** ⋯⋯⋯⋯ 39

Chapter 38: **The Final Transformation** ⋯⋯⋯ 47

Chapter 39: **Torn to Pieces** ⋯⋯⋯⋯⋯⋯⋯ 75

Chapter 40: **New Year's Cleaning in Haimachi** ⋯⋯ 119

Chapter 41: **Ran Departs and the Rain Is Soft** ⋯⋯ 143

Chapter 42: **A Parting Gift and a Path to Spring (Part 1)** ⸱⸱⸱⸱⸱ 171

Chapter 43: **A Parting Gift and a Path to Spring (Part 2)** ⸱⸱⸱⸱⸱ 195

Chapter 44: **A Parting Gift and a Path to Spring (Part 3)** ⸱⸱⸱⸱⸱ 219

Chapter 45: **The Land of New Leaves** ⸱⸱⸱⸱⸱⸱⸱⸱⸱⸱⸱⸱⸱⸱⸱⸱⸱⸱⸱⸱⸱⸱⸱⸱⸱⸱⸱⸱⸱⸱⸱⸱⸱⸱ 247

Final Chapter: **Into the Clouds** ⸱⸱⸱ 271

Afterword ⸱⸱ 295

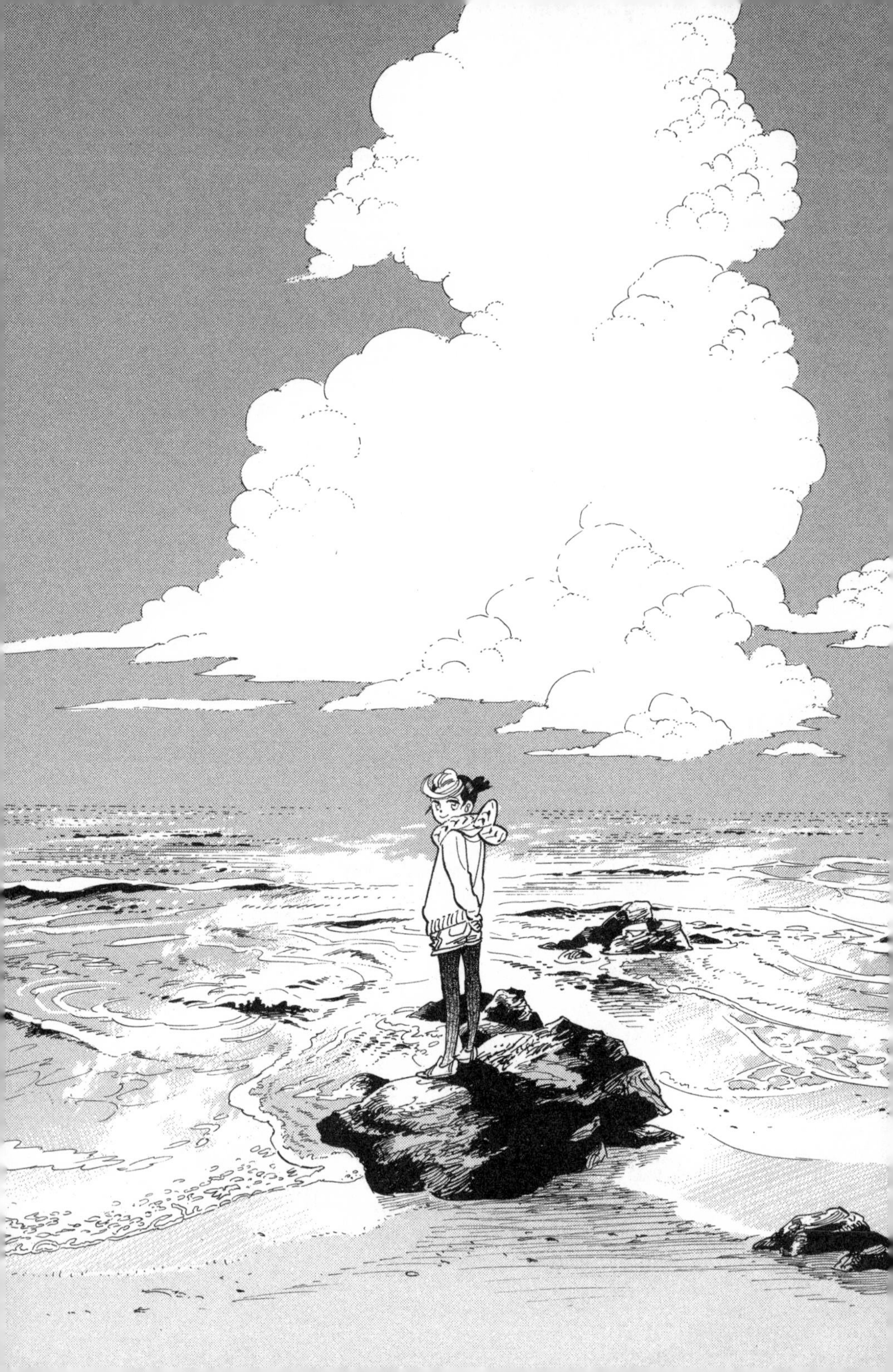

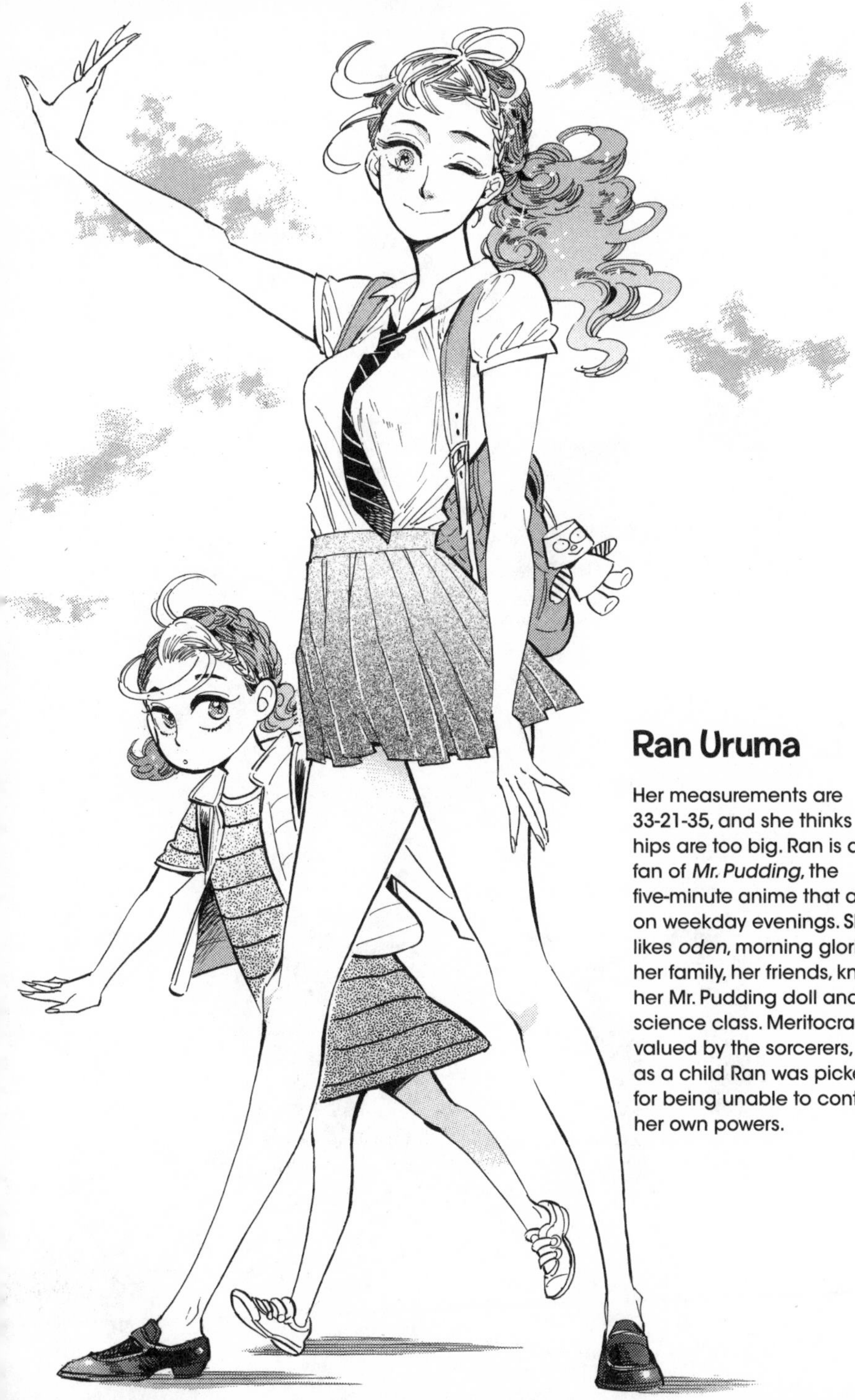

Ran Uruma

Her measurements are 33-21-35, and she thinks her hips are too big. Ran is a big fan of *Mr. Pudding*, the five-minute anime that airs on weekday evenings. She likes *oden*, morning glories, her family, her friends, knitting, her Mr. Pudding doll and her science class. Meritocracy is valued by the sorcerers, and as a child Ran was picked on for being unable to control her own powers.

Shizuka Uruma

The most powerful sorceress in history. She was stillborn as a child and had been laid to rest when an elder sorceress took her in and raised her with love and care. Shizuka's magic is controlled by her emotions rather than logic or theory, and it doesn't bother her that this style is becoming obsolete. Her family is her reason for living.

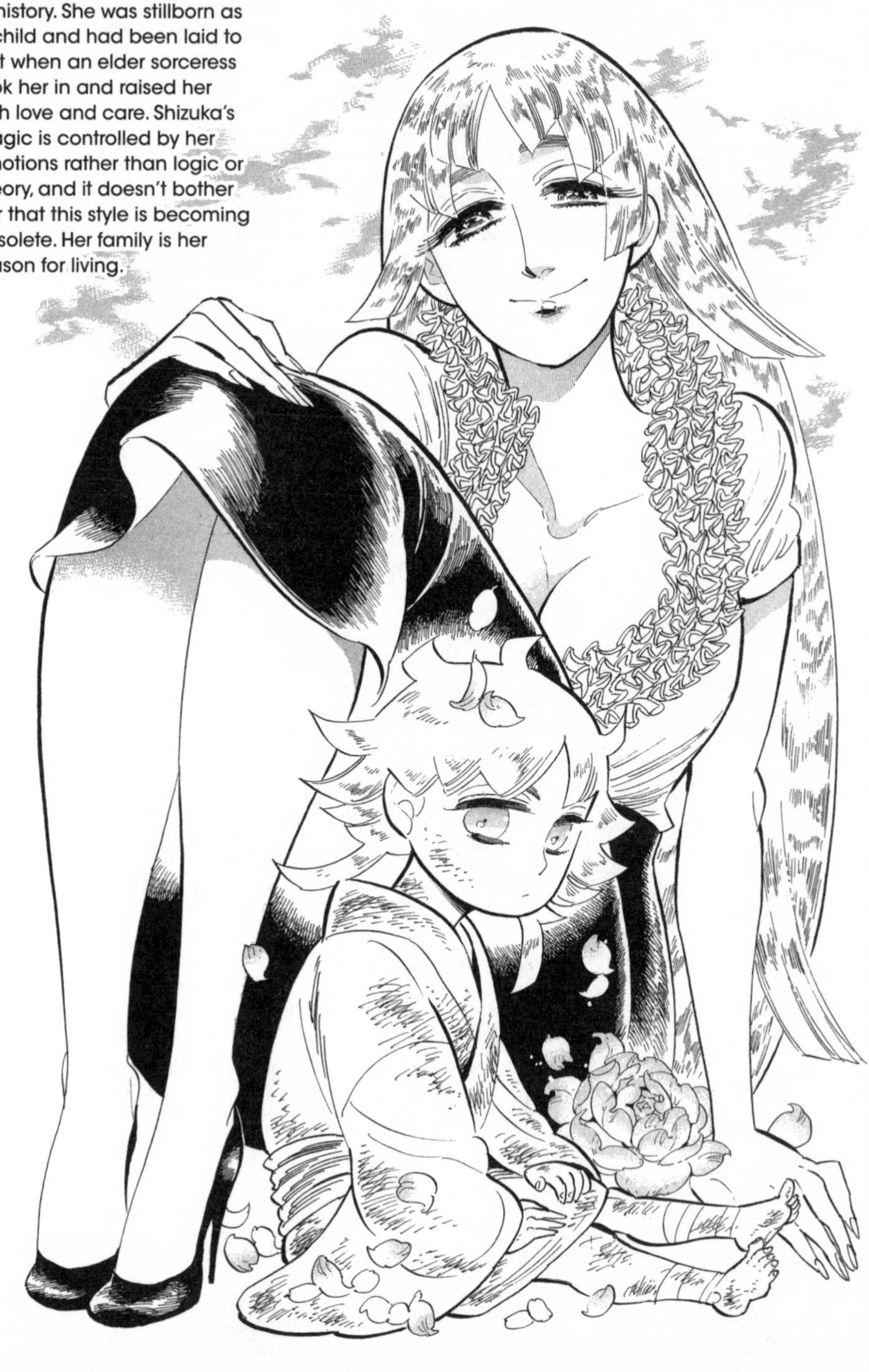

Zen Uruma

Leader of the sorcerers and head of the Black Crows. As a child, he was a small but powerful troublemaker, and he was the youngest to be admitted to the Black Crow Army. He trained under the leader at the time but fled after numerous run-ins. He later returned to the Crows and got married. Zen's broad connections and the insights cultivated during his youth led him to became the most popular person in the village. He worries about not spending enough time with his family. He likes miso oden, *kotatsu*, plum wine, bonsai, the smell of ink and collecting hydrangea blossoms.

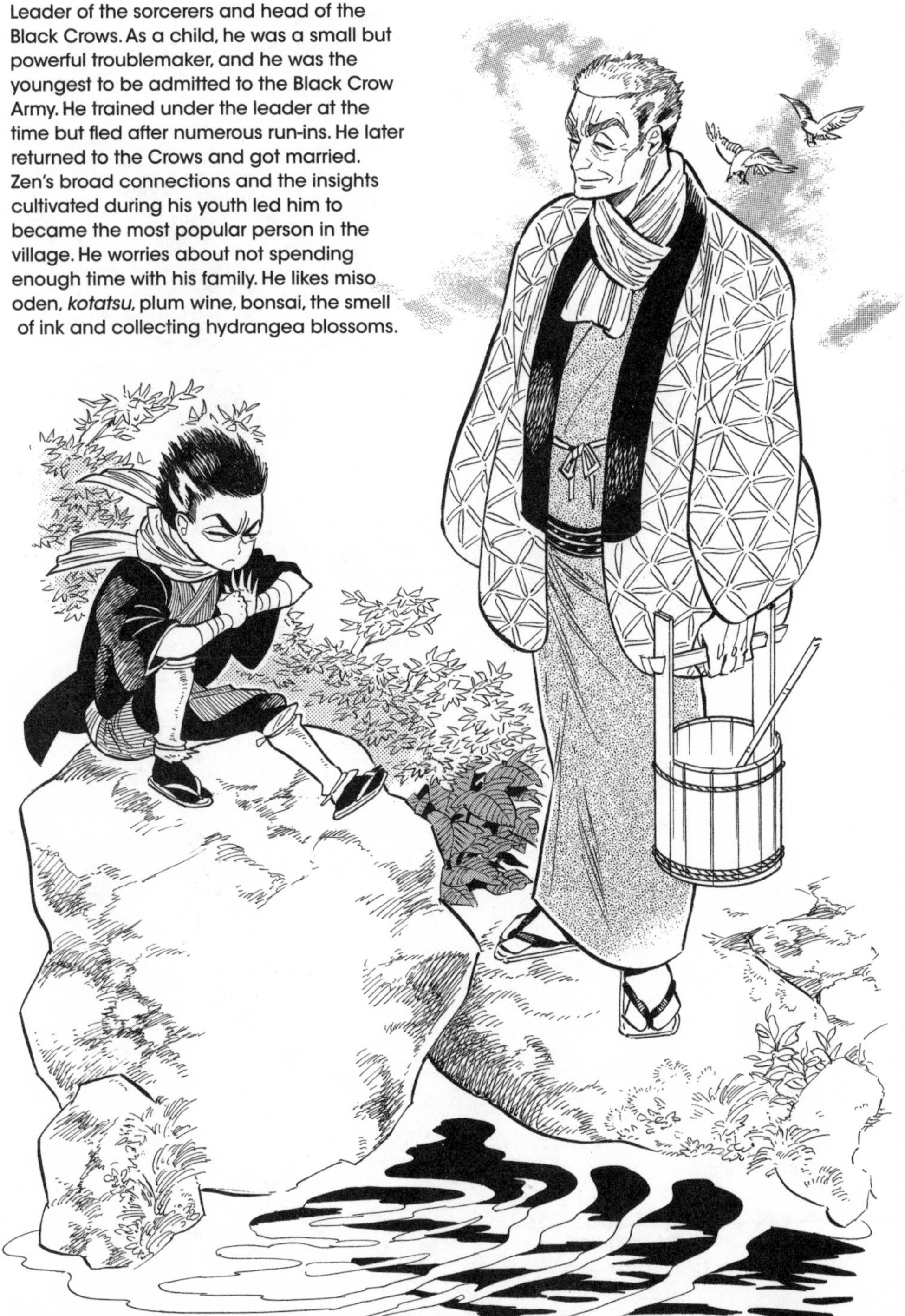

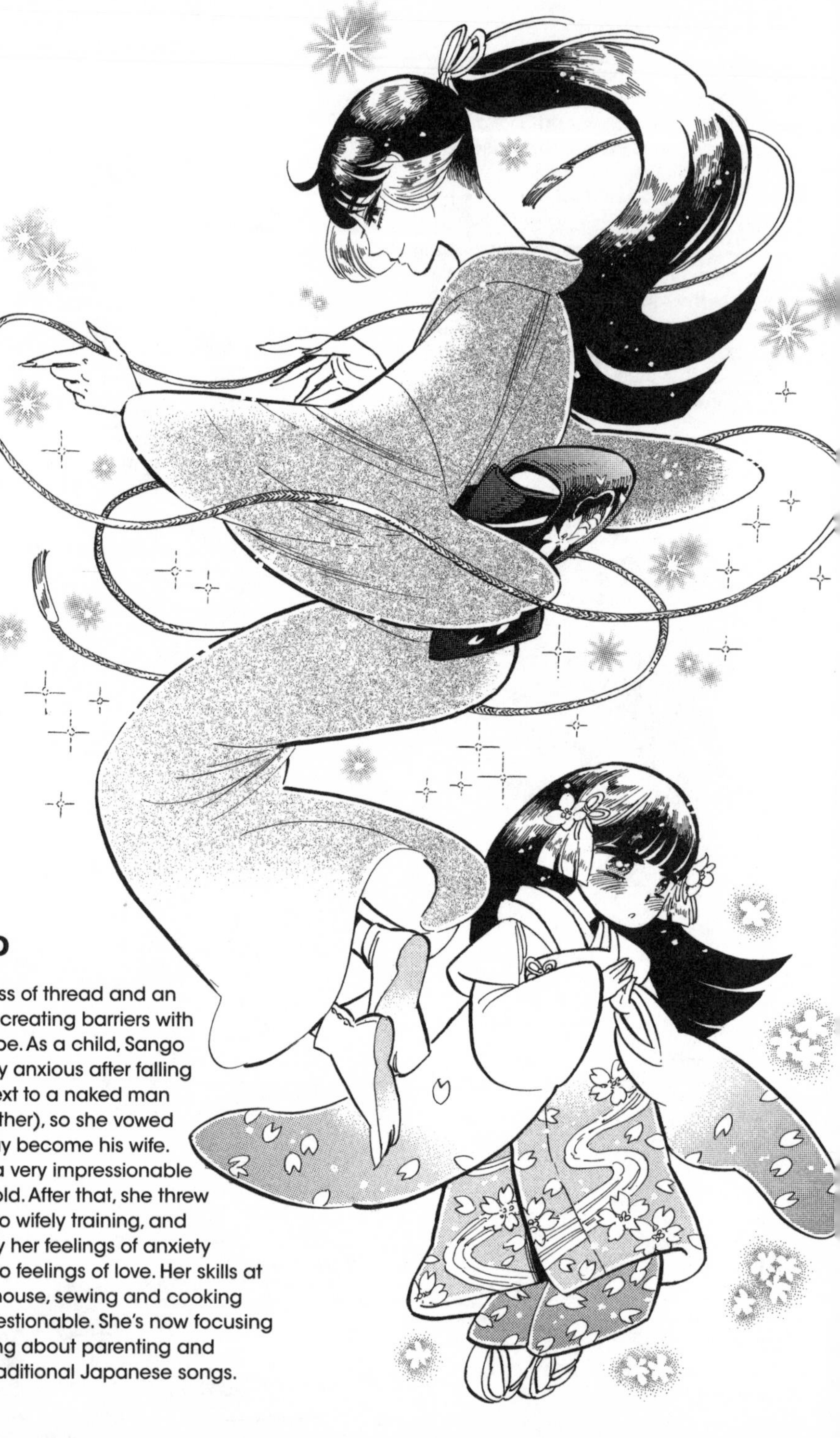

Sango

A sorceress of thread and an expert at creating barriers with woven rope. As a child, Sango felt deeply anxious after falling asleep next to a naked man (a boy, rather), so she vowed to one day become his wife. She was a very impressionable five-year-old. After that, she threw herself into wifely training, and eventually her feelings of anxiety turned into feelings of love. Her skills at keeping house, sewing and cooking are unquestionable. She's now focusing on learning about parenting and singing traditional Japanese songs.

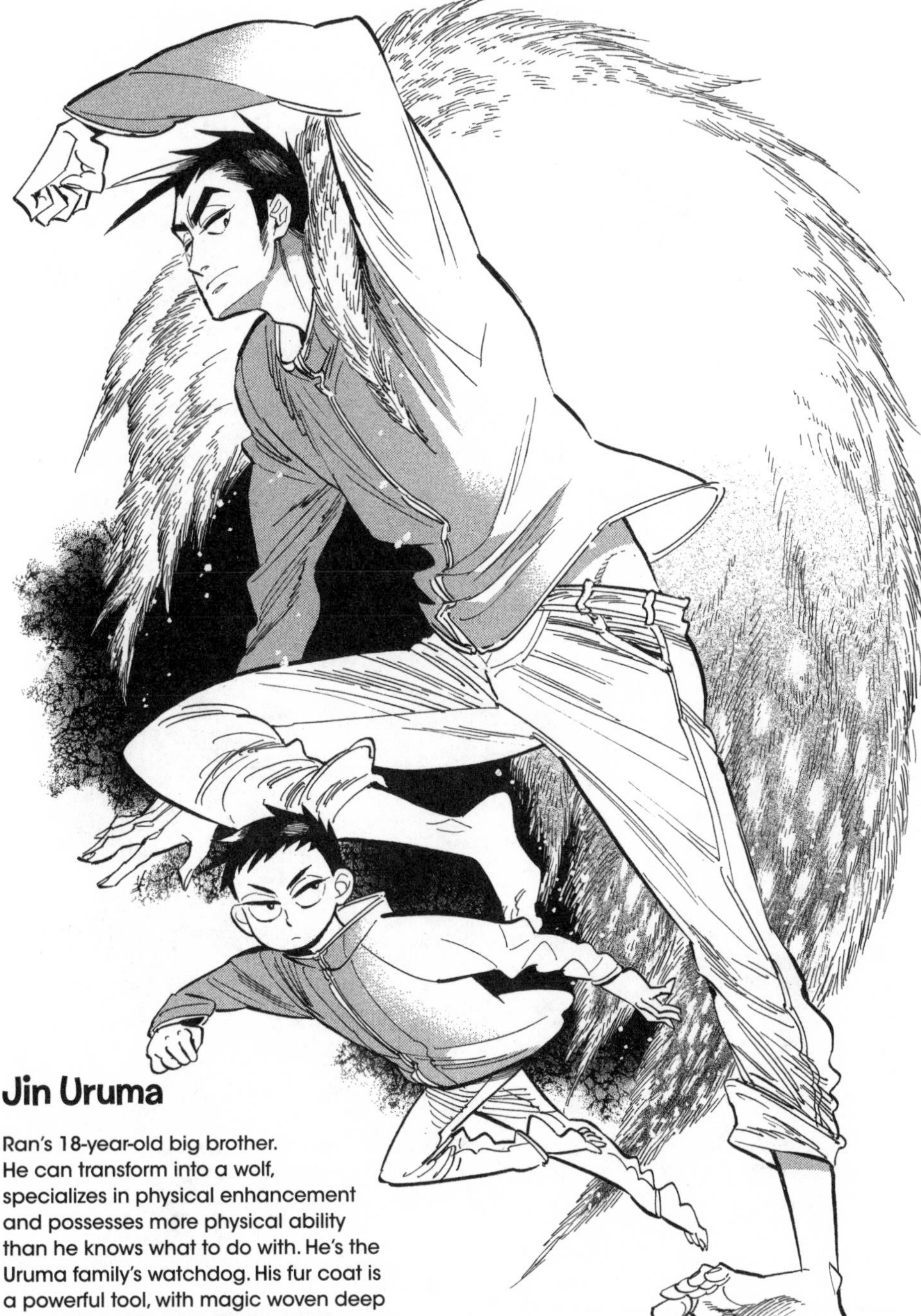

Jin Uruma

Ran's 18-year-old big brother. He can transform into a wolf, specializes in physical enhancement and possesses more physical ability than he knows what to do with. He's the Uruma family's watchdog. His fur coat is a powerful tool, with magic woven deep into it. Jin wants to battle the big guys but is forbidden to do so by order of his boss (Zen).

Tamao Tachibana

A leading authority on both magic and the research of magic. Though Tamao was born a sorceress, she possesses no magical power and was once deemed worthless and consequently abandoned. It was her physical strength as a sorceress that helped her survive and thrive. As a child, the first powerful sorcerer she met was Zen Uruma. She was blown away by his powerful magic, which gave meaning to her life. She likes magic, sake, sushi, futons, Master Zen, powerful magic, and sorceresses and sorcerers who are wise.

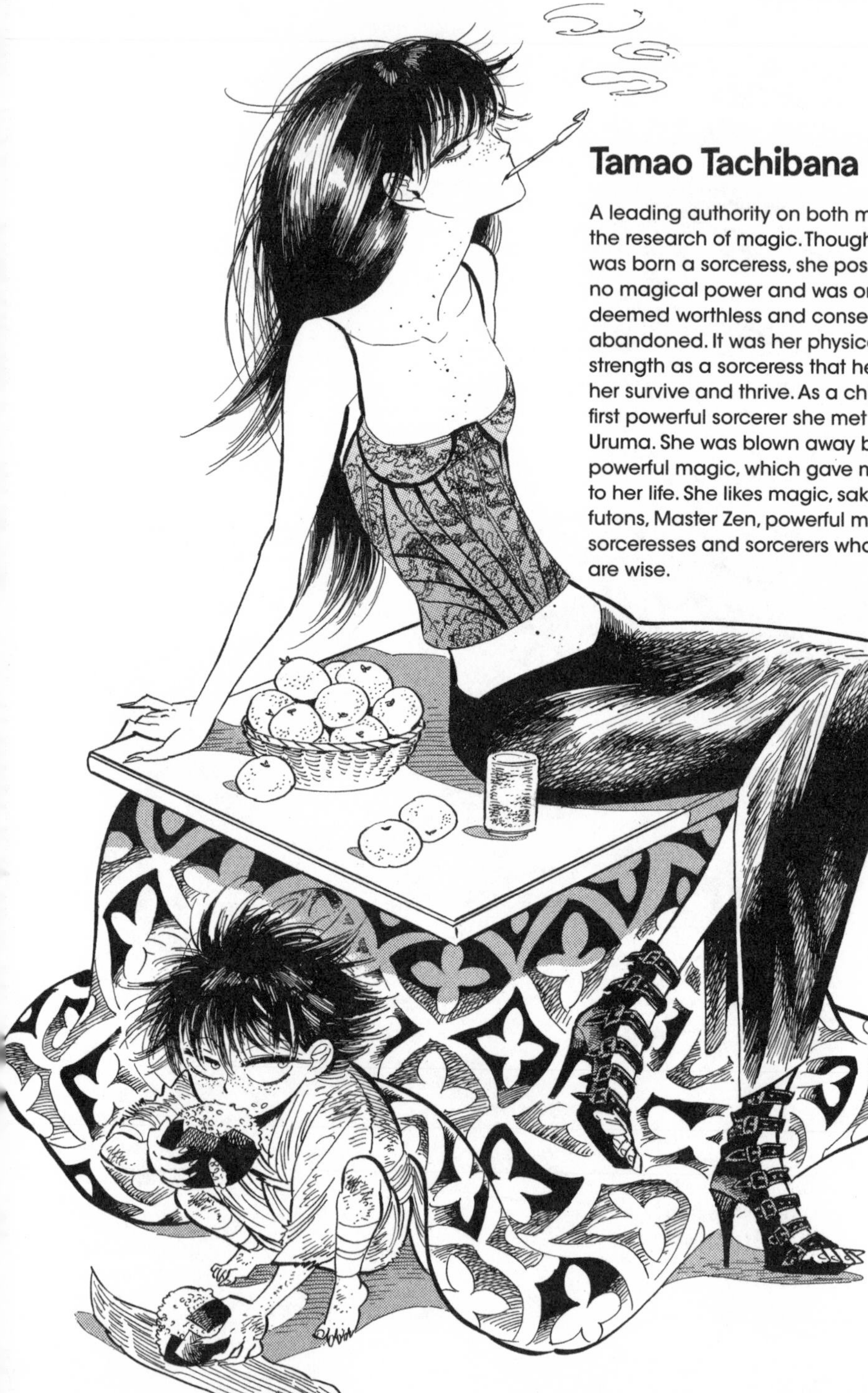

Nio Gekkoin

Even as a young sorceress, Nio could control her magic as well as an adult. Her mother Gekko's training ensured that Nio's magic and daily life were both disciplined and beautiful. Though traditional magic has long been handed down through the Gekkoin family, Nio is more interested in theoretical magic. She feels somewhat burdened by her mother.

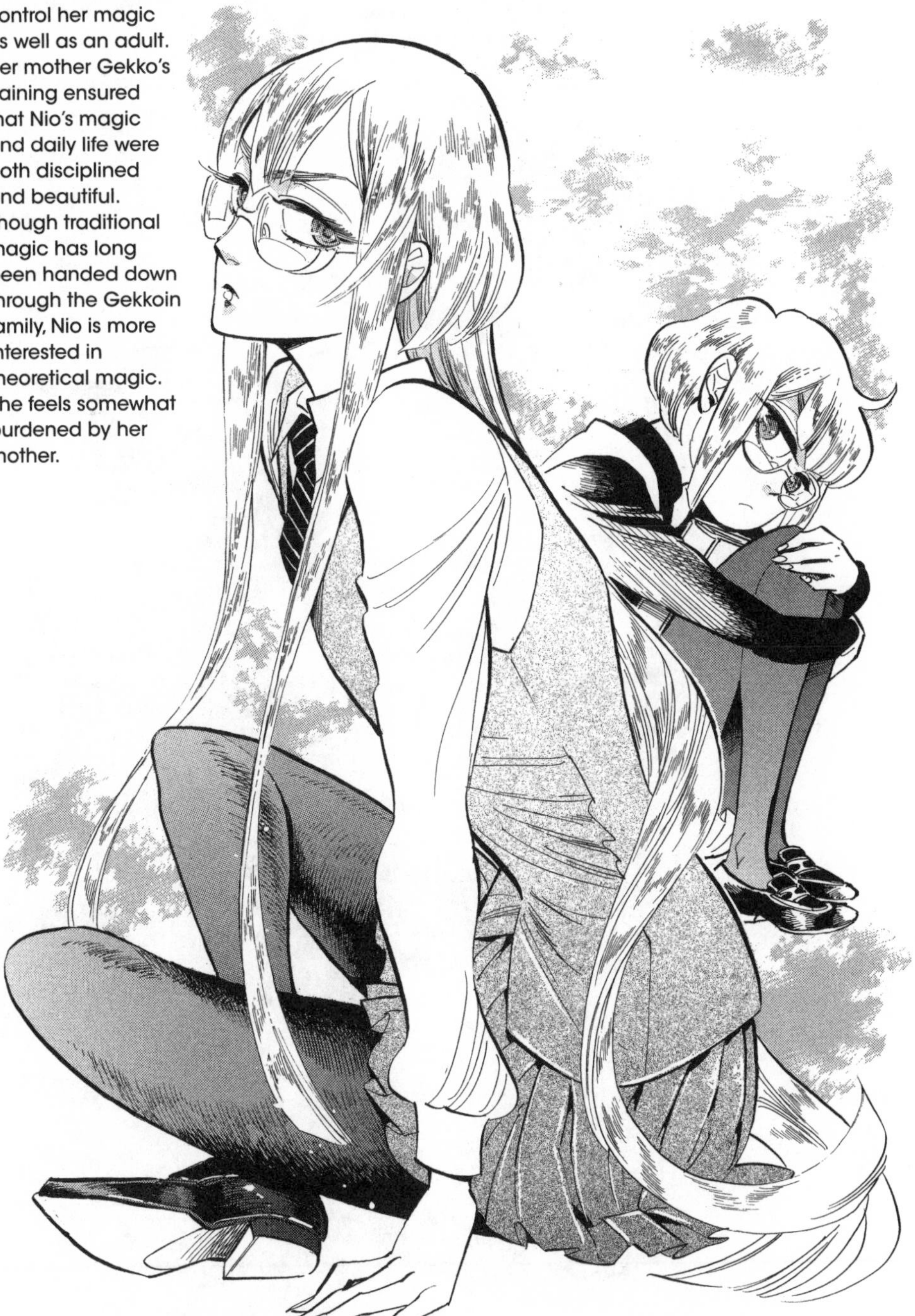

Otaro Mikado

Throughout high school, his life consisted of school, family and studies. In college, he dabbled in a range of activities, never realizing that the reason he found them boring lay within himself. He likes Ran, silk linen, cheese, tree shade and the unexpected. At the end of his life, he tries to become an adult for young Ran. His tolerance and childlike purity live on in Ran's heart.

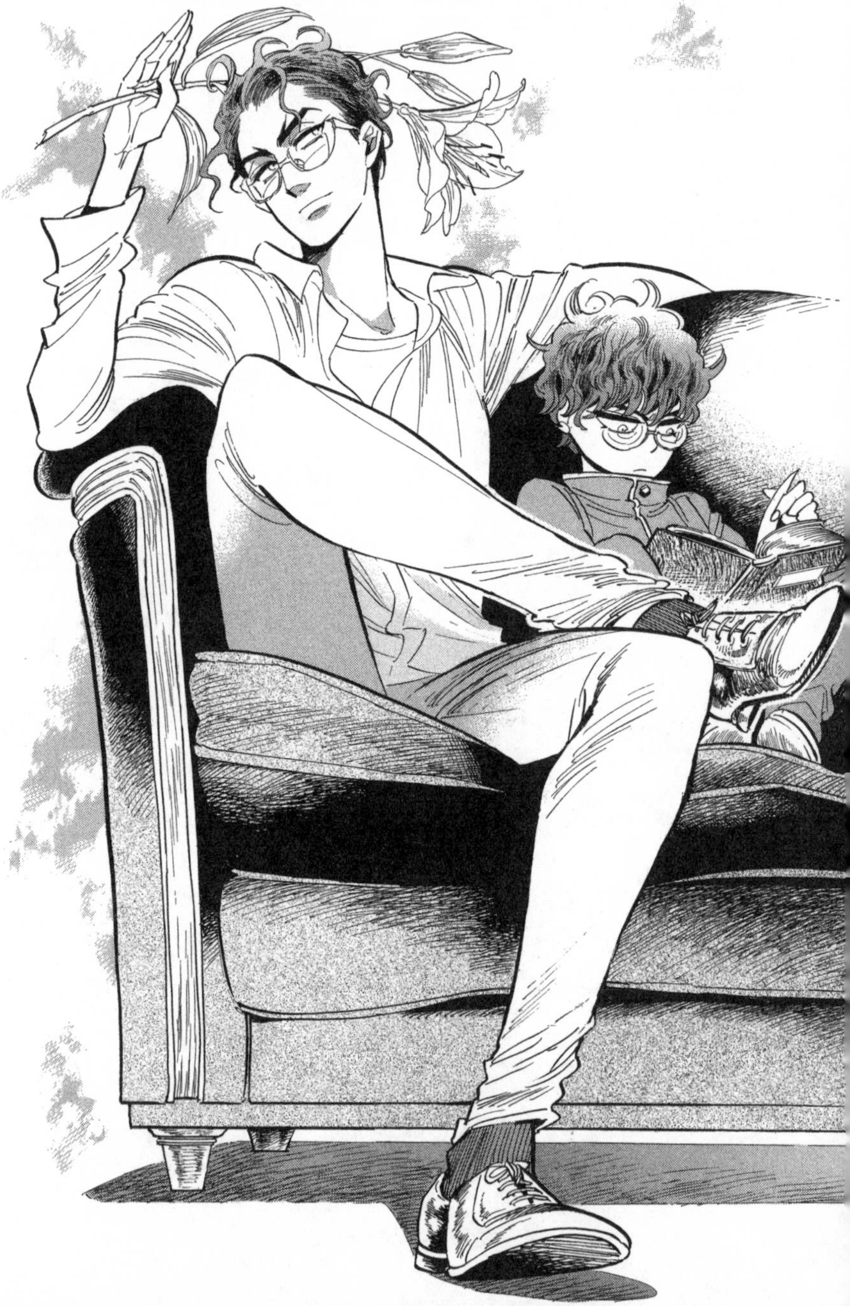

Makoto Hibi

The only son of owners of a flower shop.
His parents have many friends,
so he grew up surrounded by adults.
Hibi knows the names of flowers well.
He has to work in the store for his
allowance, and right now he wants
a skateboard.

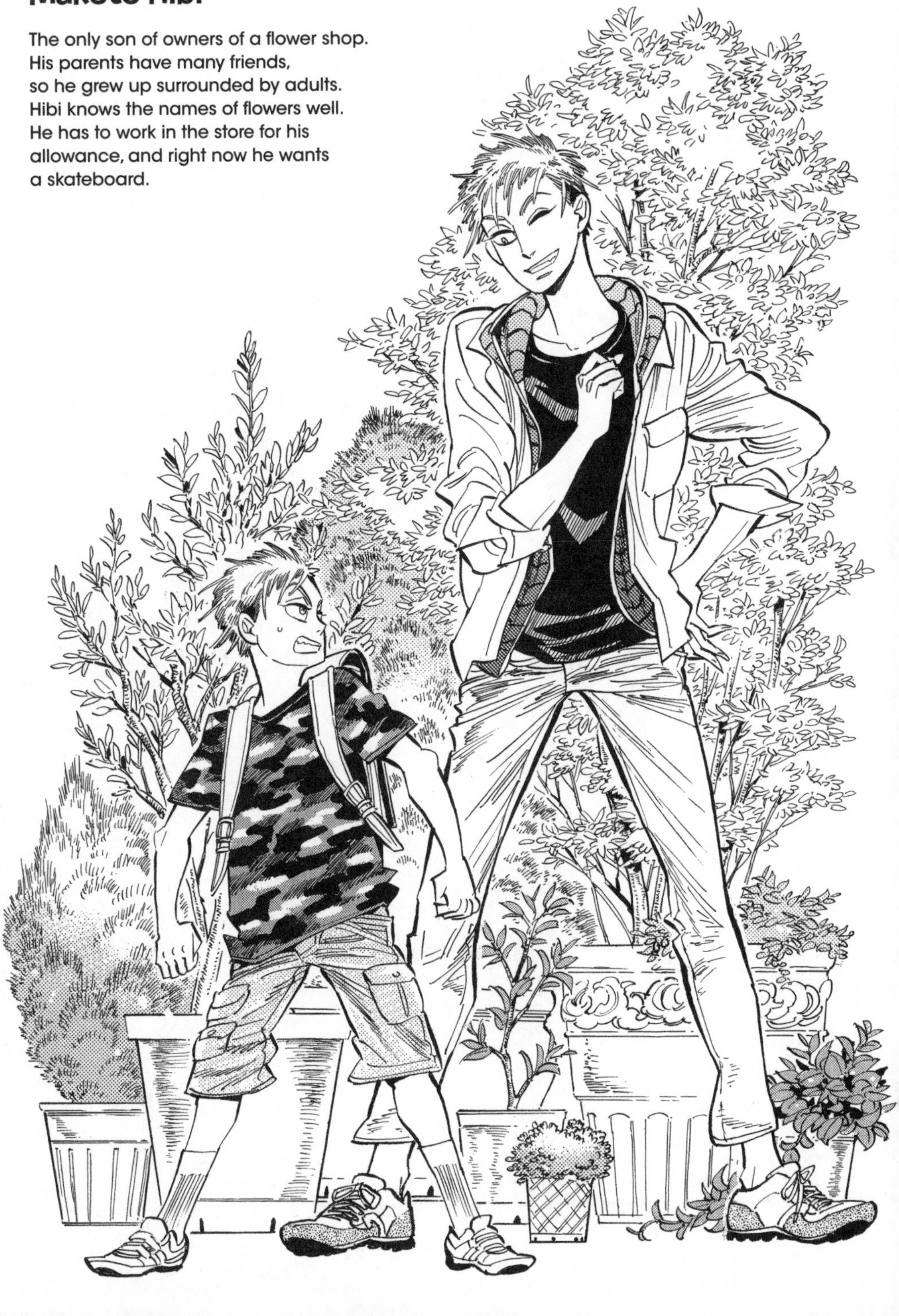

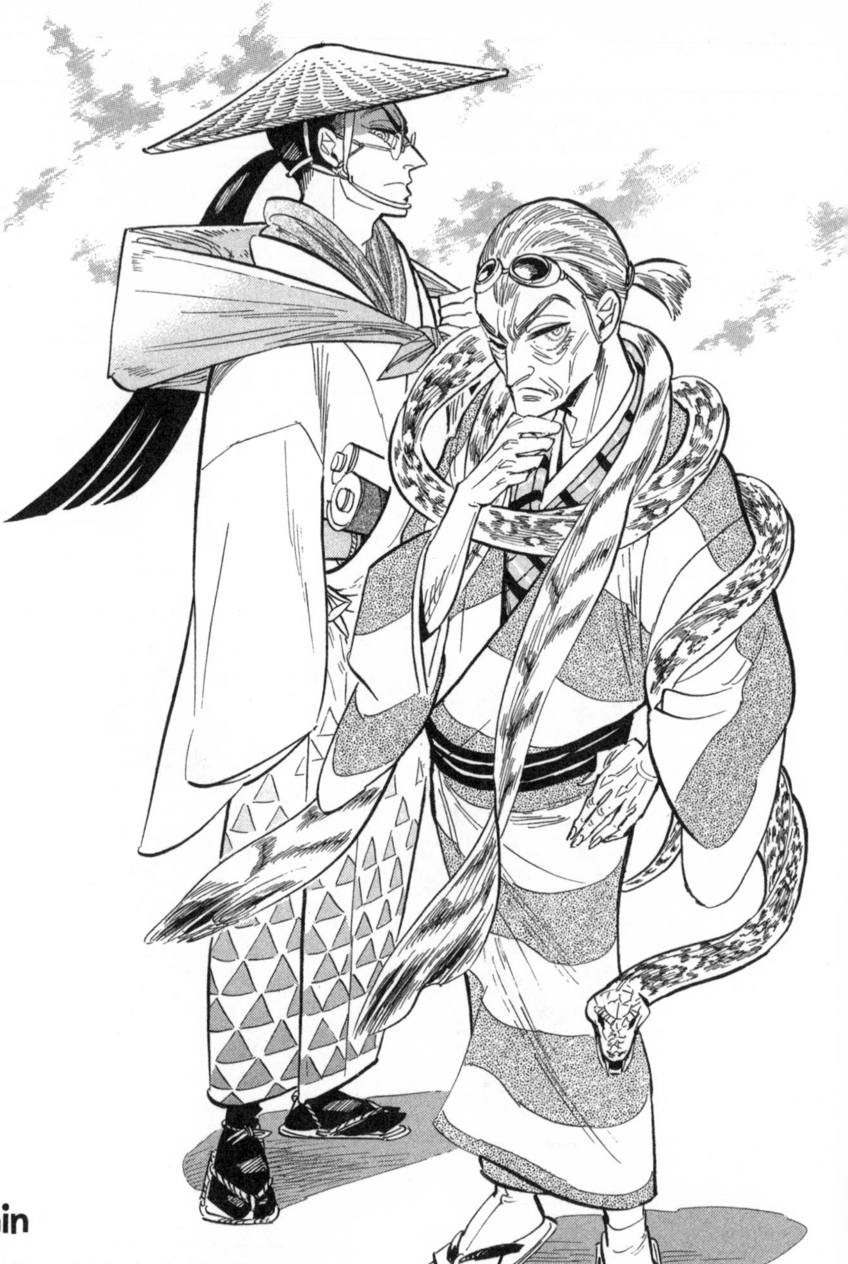

Becchin

He can see through physical objects, which is convenient as it allows him to see diseases within a body. The nurses that he takes around with him aren't his lovers, they're just nurses. When he was young, he wandered the country investigating different types of illnesses and folk remedies. He's always been popular with the ladies. He uses snakeskin patterns to ward off evil.

Muan

A 19-year-old who's always gotten by on his looks. He can see magic. When he was young, Becchin took him in as an apprentice. Though Muan is one of the least powerful sorcerers, he's established himself through his unique skills. He wanders the country collecting magic samples. Because he borrowed money to finance the tools for his journey, he is constantly on the run. His favorite things are Japanese sweets, money and girls with money.

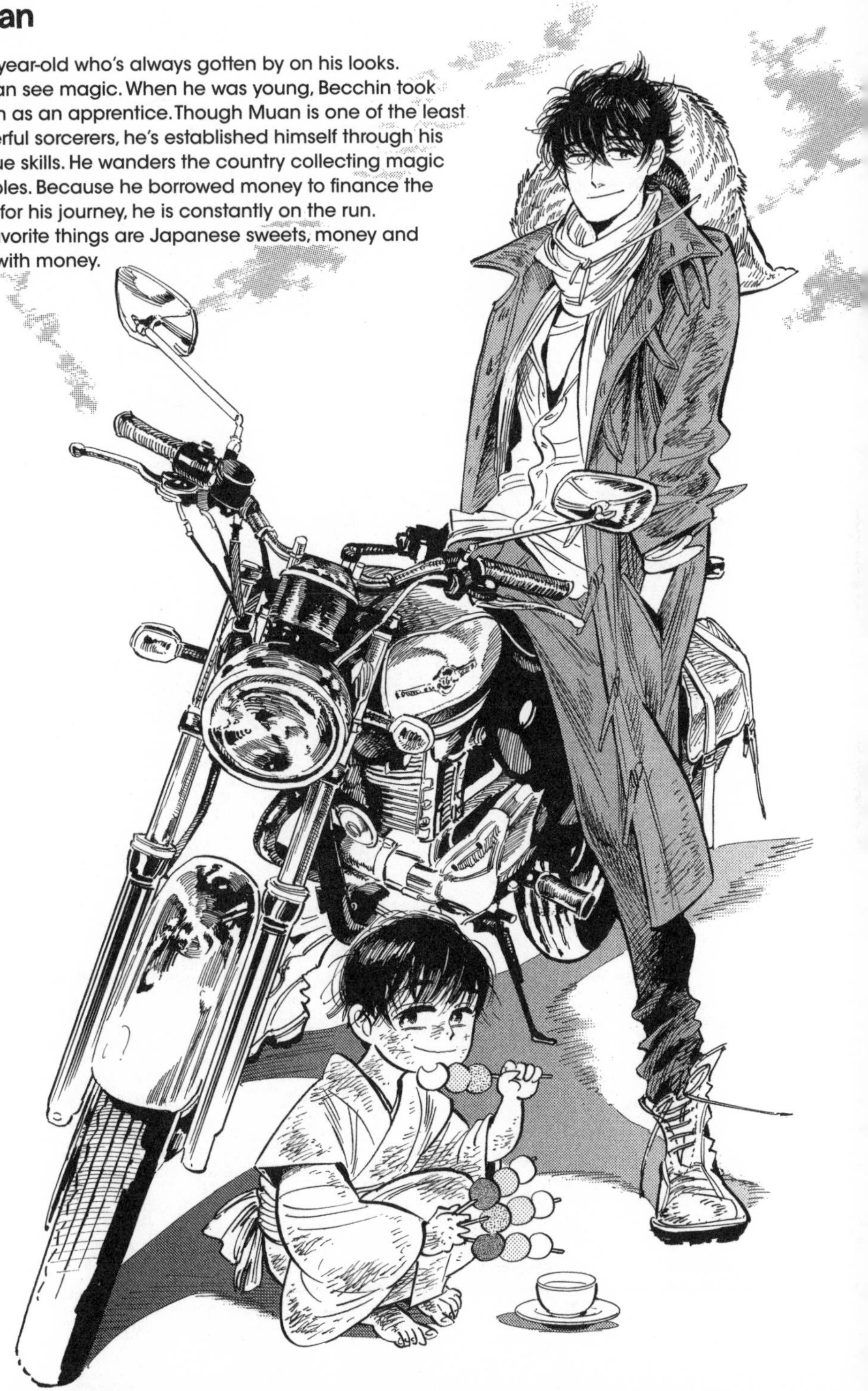

Suzuro

He was born in the sorcerers' village, but his wild nature led him to join the White Dogs. The fierce intensity of their admissions process and their training was just right for him. Only strength mattered. He became their leader at a young age. His taste buds have been destroyed. To him, everything is delicious. He loves mayo, hates baths, can't swim and is looking for a wife.

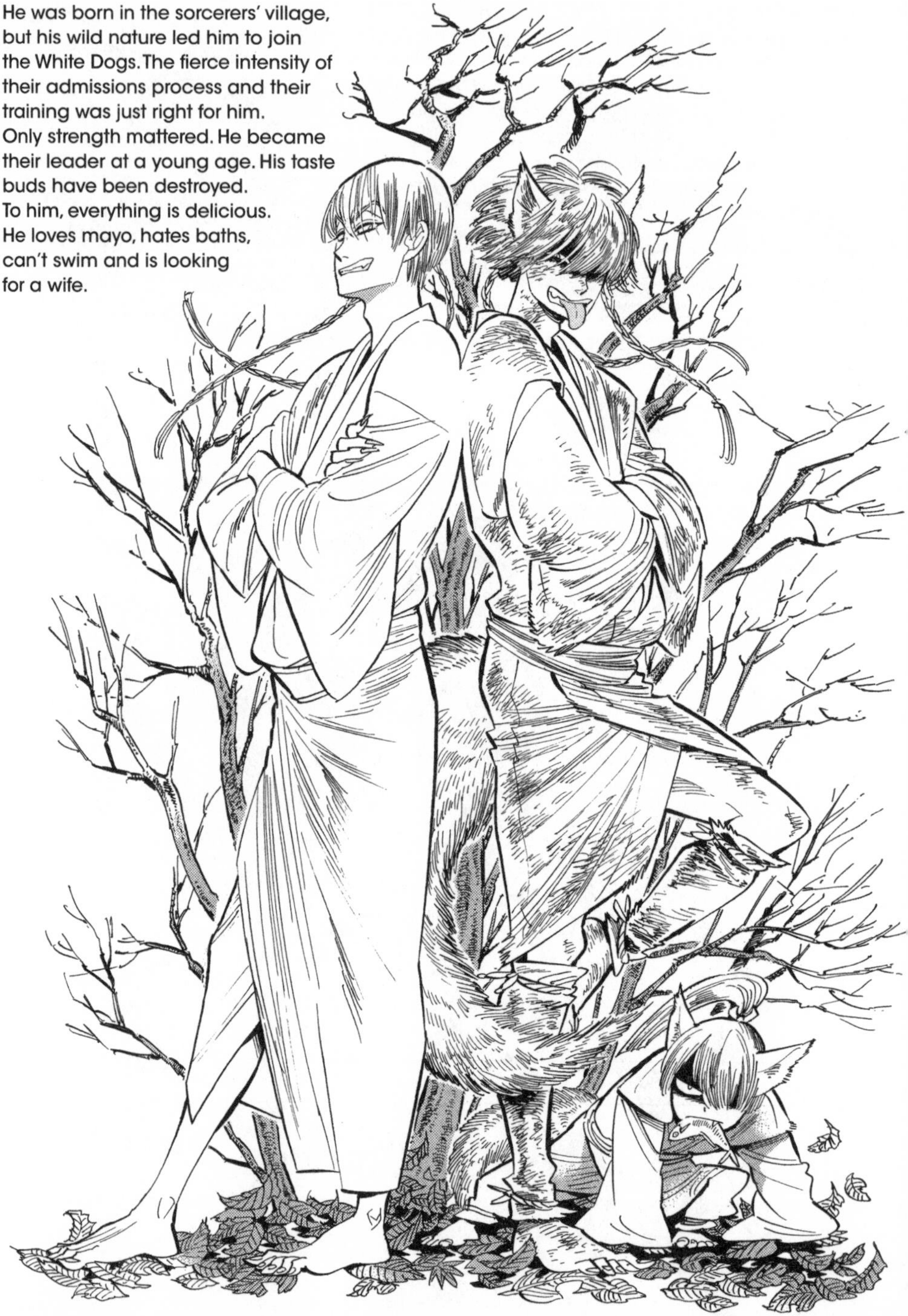

The Black Crows

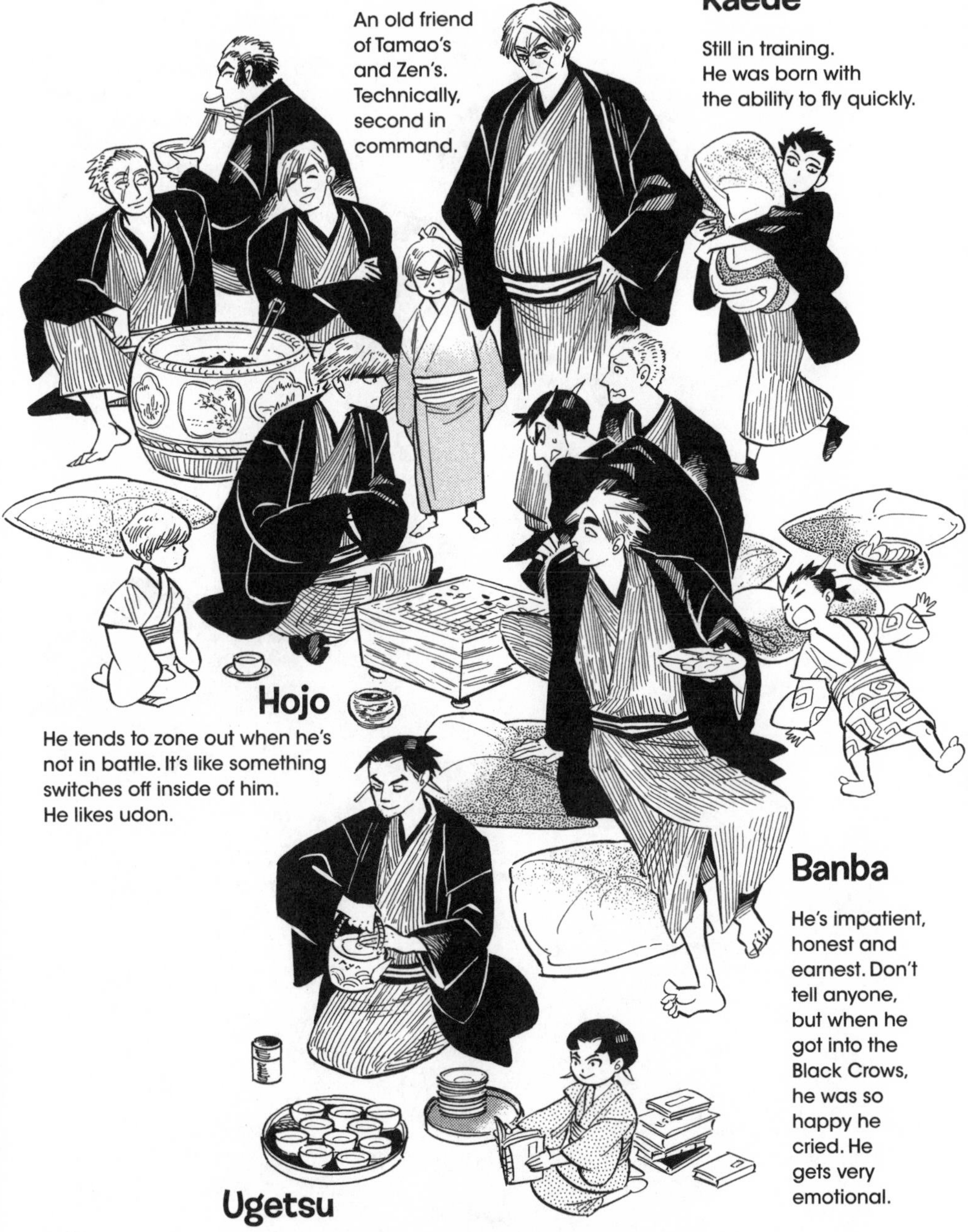

Zazanza

An old friend of Tamao's and Zen's. Technically, second in command.

Kaede

Still in training.
He was born with the ability to fly quickly.

Hojo

He tends to zone out when he's not in battle. It's like something switches off inside of him.
He likes udon.

Banba

He's impatient, honest and earnest. Don't tell anyone, but when he got into the Black Crows, he was so happy he cried. He gets very emotional.

Ugetsu

When he was unable to fight in battle, he spent time in the break room and perfected his tea-making skills.
He later quit the Black Crows and opened a tea shop that became massively successful.

Kohaku

One of the four Sumeragi sisters. Fourteen years old. She has two magic powers: the rather modest ability to burn things with charcoal and the ability to warm people from deep within their bodies. She likes working and cleaning. Though she thinks of herself as dowdy, everyone loves her personality. She's the kind of person you want to have around you during hard times. She loves mushrooms.

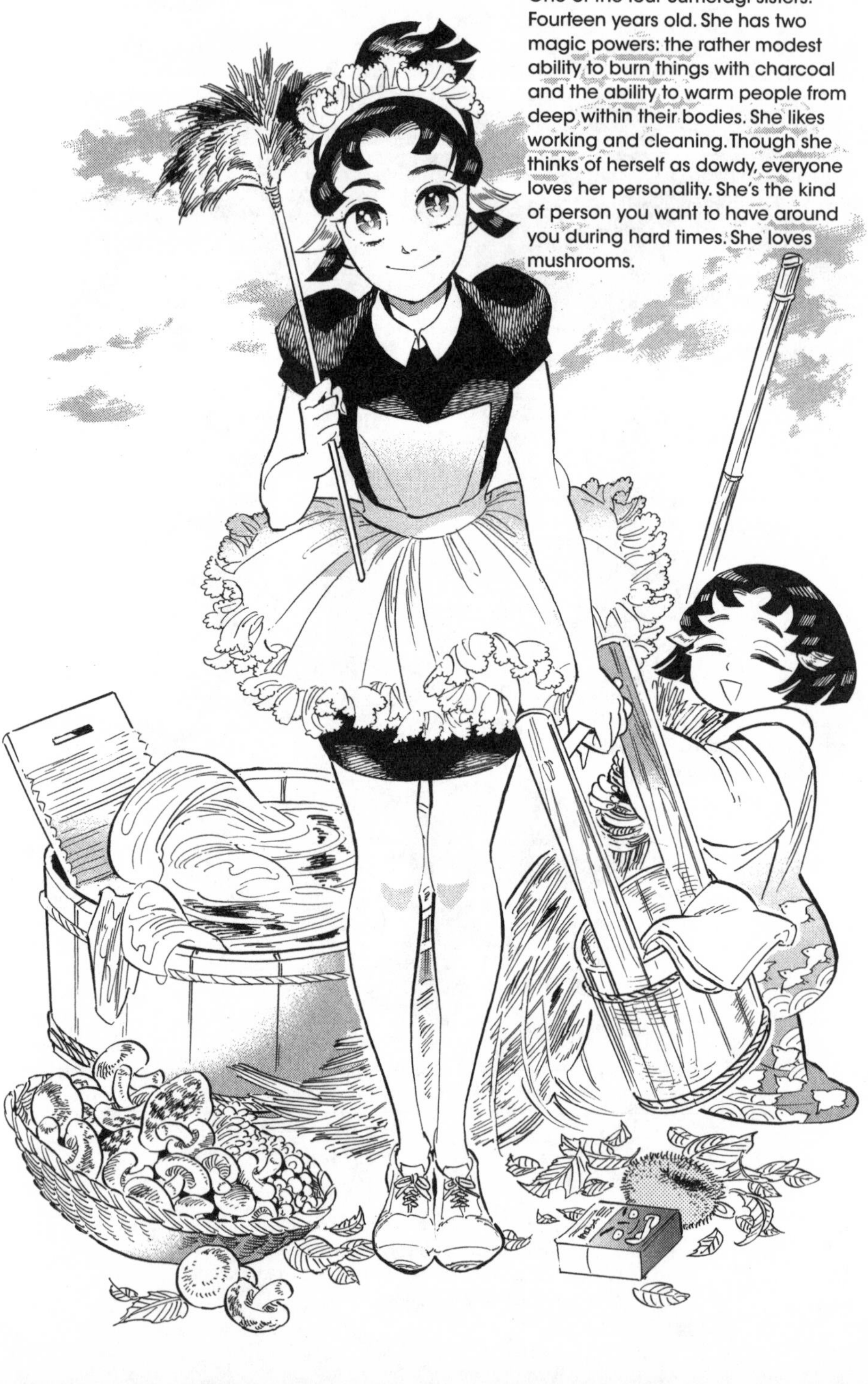

Meno

One of the four Sumeragi sisters. Twenty-one years old. A sorceress of ice. Generally, men tend to be skilled at attack magic and women at protective magic, and few are skilled at both. Her favorite things are her sisters, *hoto* soup, *mizu manju* sweets, plum blossoms, matcha and grated daikon radish. She's kind, but if you cross Meno, she'll completely transform and become quite masculine. That's when it rains blood and ice.

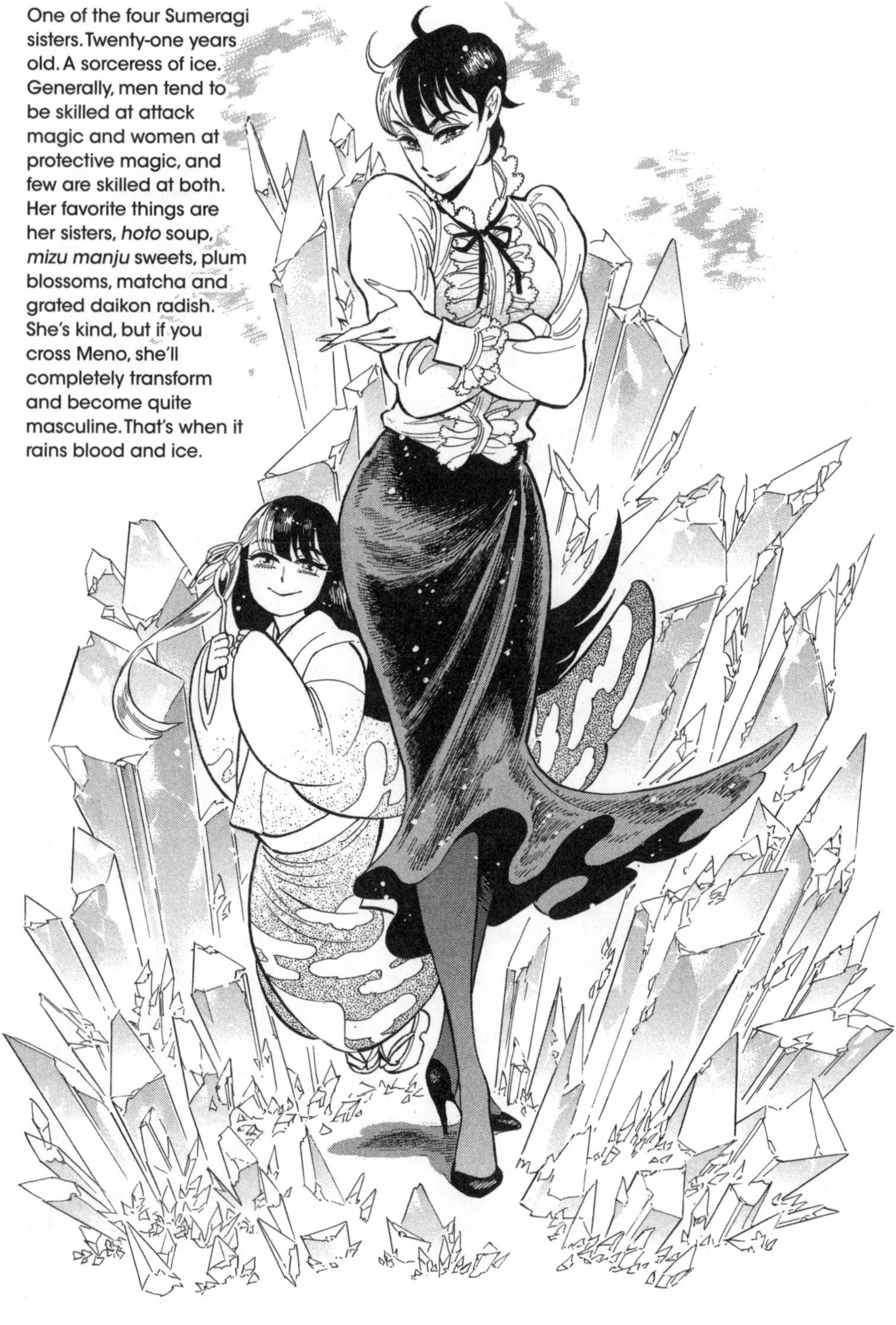

Shinobu Jo

The Jo household is wealthy and established like the Mikado family. Shinobu is the fifth son and has been friends with Otaro since before they were a year old. He eventually made other friends as an adult. Shinobu's hobby is clothing design, and he has a boutique where he sells his own designs.
On his days off, he visits textile factories and studios as well as batting centers. He can often be found hanging out by the river. He has plans to hire more boutique staff.

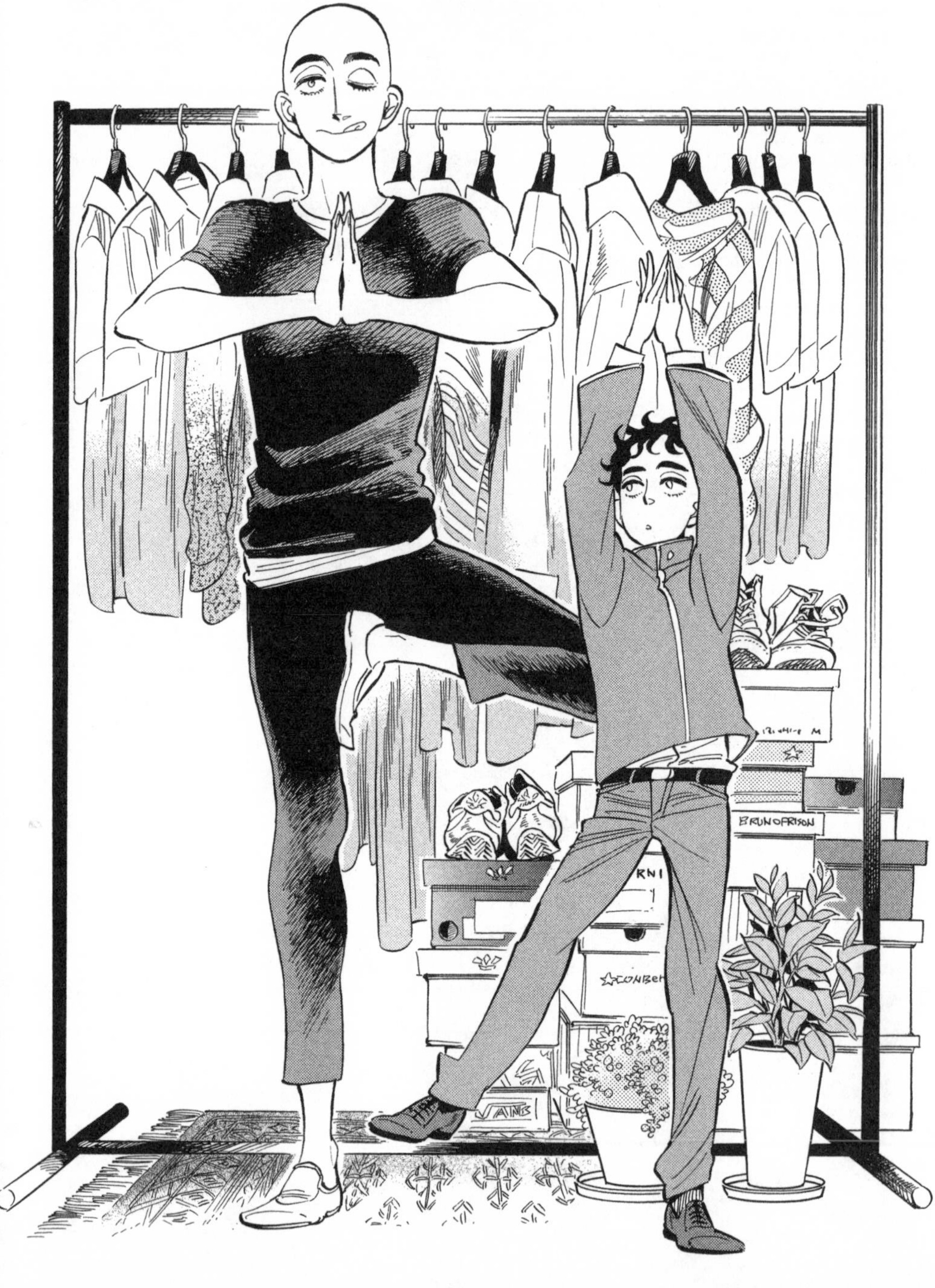

Plum Peach Cherry

Pork buns are her specialty. She's known as the Guardian Deity of Reconstruction and Youth and is massively popular. Peach Plum is bombarded by client bookings but makes sure to take breaks.

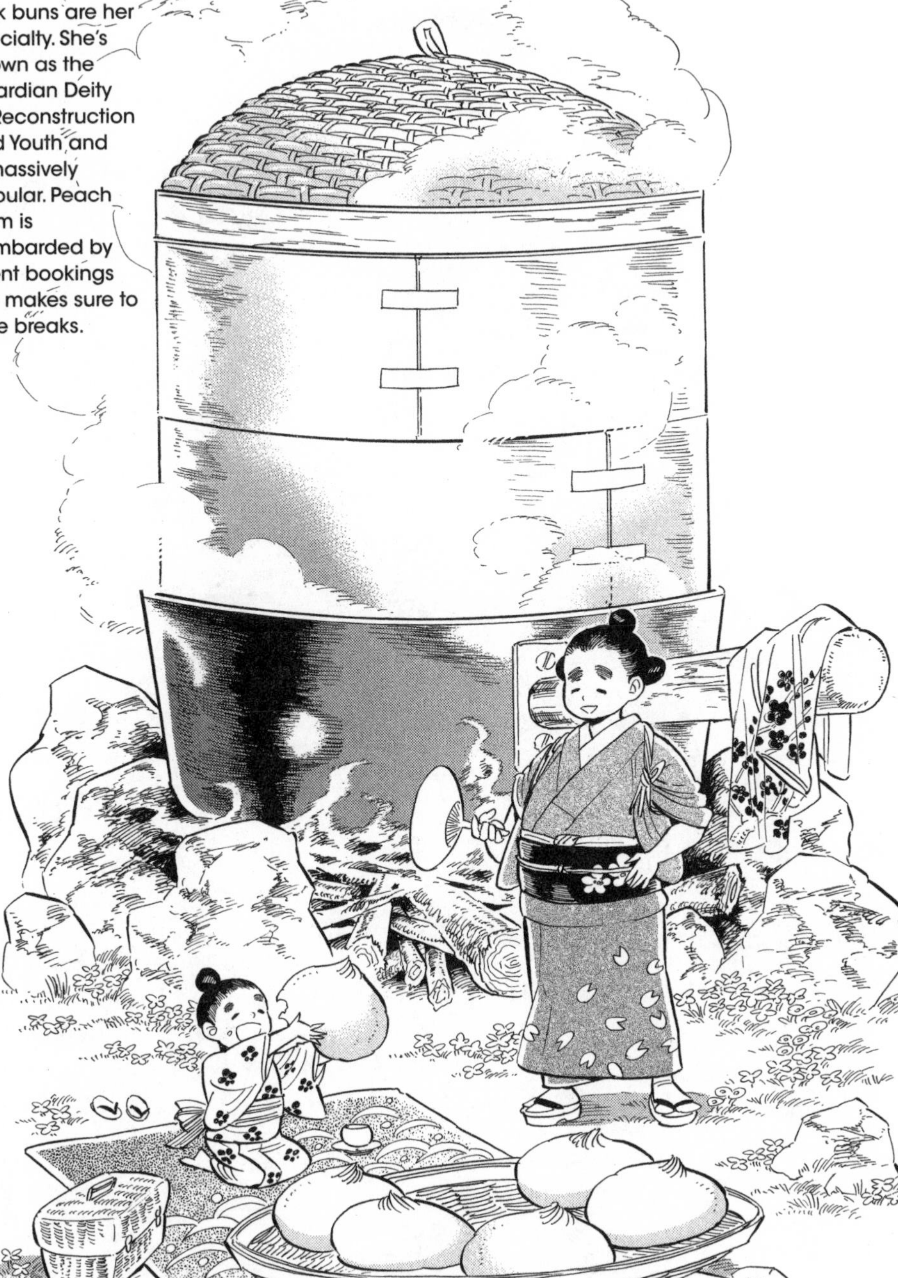

Ippongi Family

The Uruma's next-door neighbors. They're in it for the long haul.

Yoshie

Mistakenly thinks her family is normal and suffers for it. Continues to feel a bit awkward and uncomfortable.

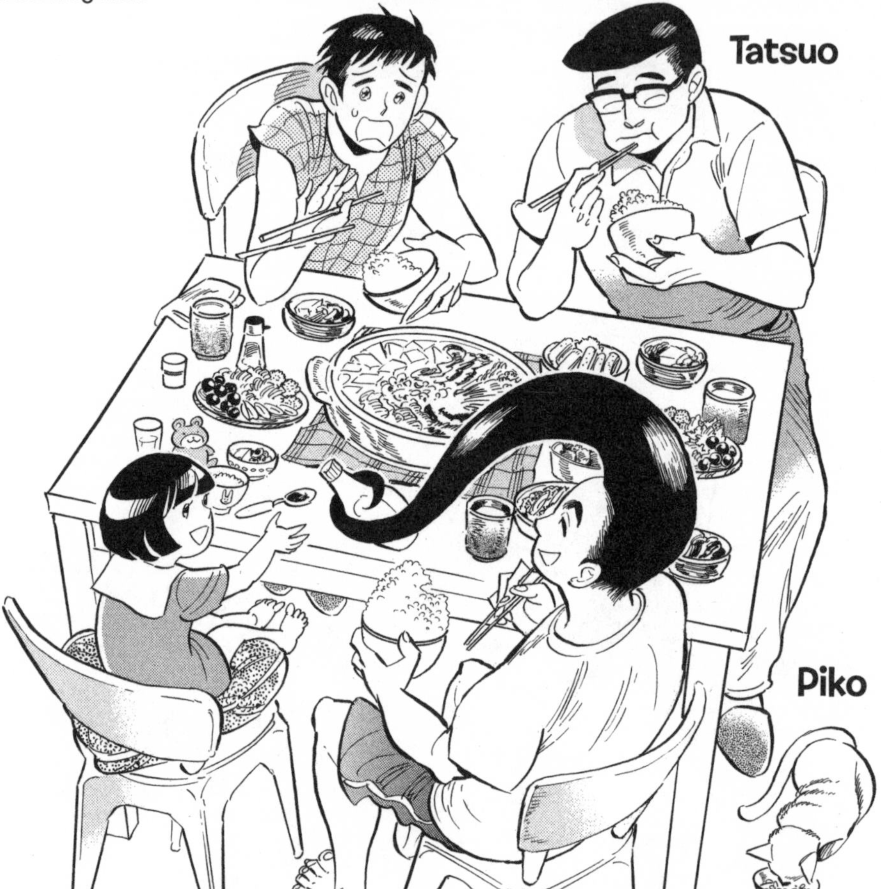

Tatsuo

Piko

Mie

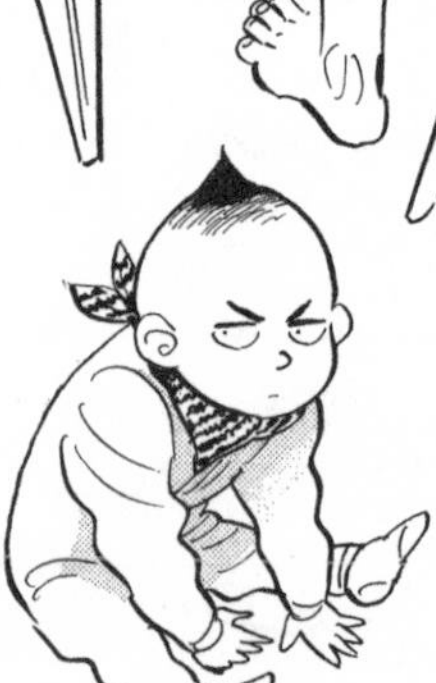

Ryu

He comes up with tricks using his beloved hair. Ryu brainwashed Ran into thinking that he's cool. For the past two years, he's had a crush on his best friend Yamato Tennoji's big sister.

Sasa

In charge of medicinal herbs, and she treasures herb fields. She's easily moved to tears.

Nogiku

She's in charge of sutures, but she can't sew fabric. She loves zombie movies.

Ruri

Second of the Sumeragi sisters. In charge of blades. She loves blades. She also loves sashimi.

Velvet

Becchin's daughter. She can transform into a snake and is in charge of anesthesia. She researches poisons and wishes her dad would give her a raise.

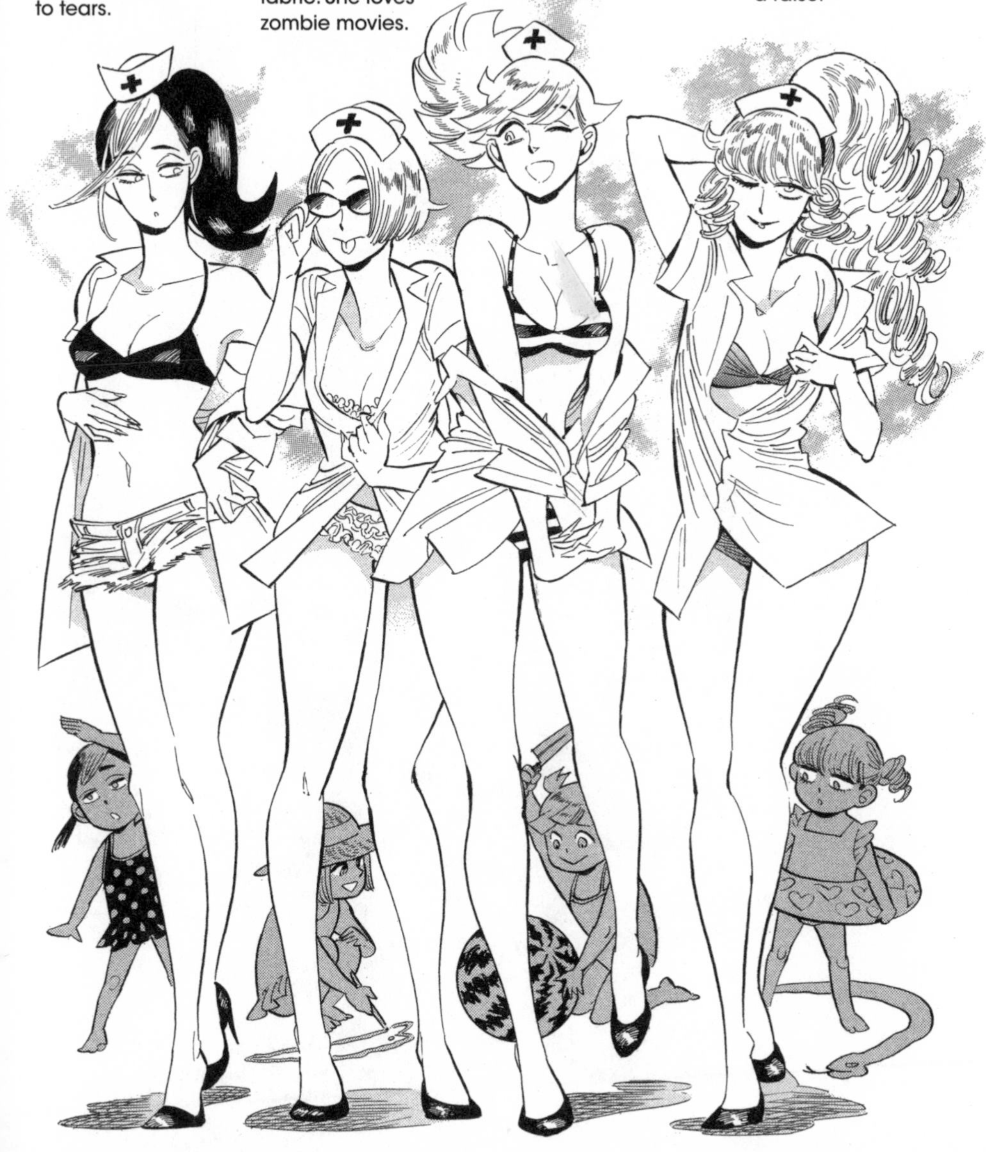

Ryoko Tennoji

She threw herself into her studies after being rejected by Jin, but she quickly finished everything and ended up with time on her hands. She spends each day thinking about how to get revenge so that she can move forward. She's a hard worker who always reaches her goals. Her younger brother gets better grades than she does. She used to be chubby.

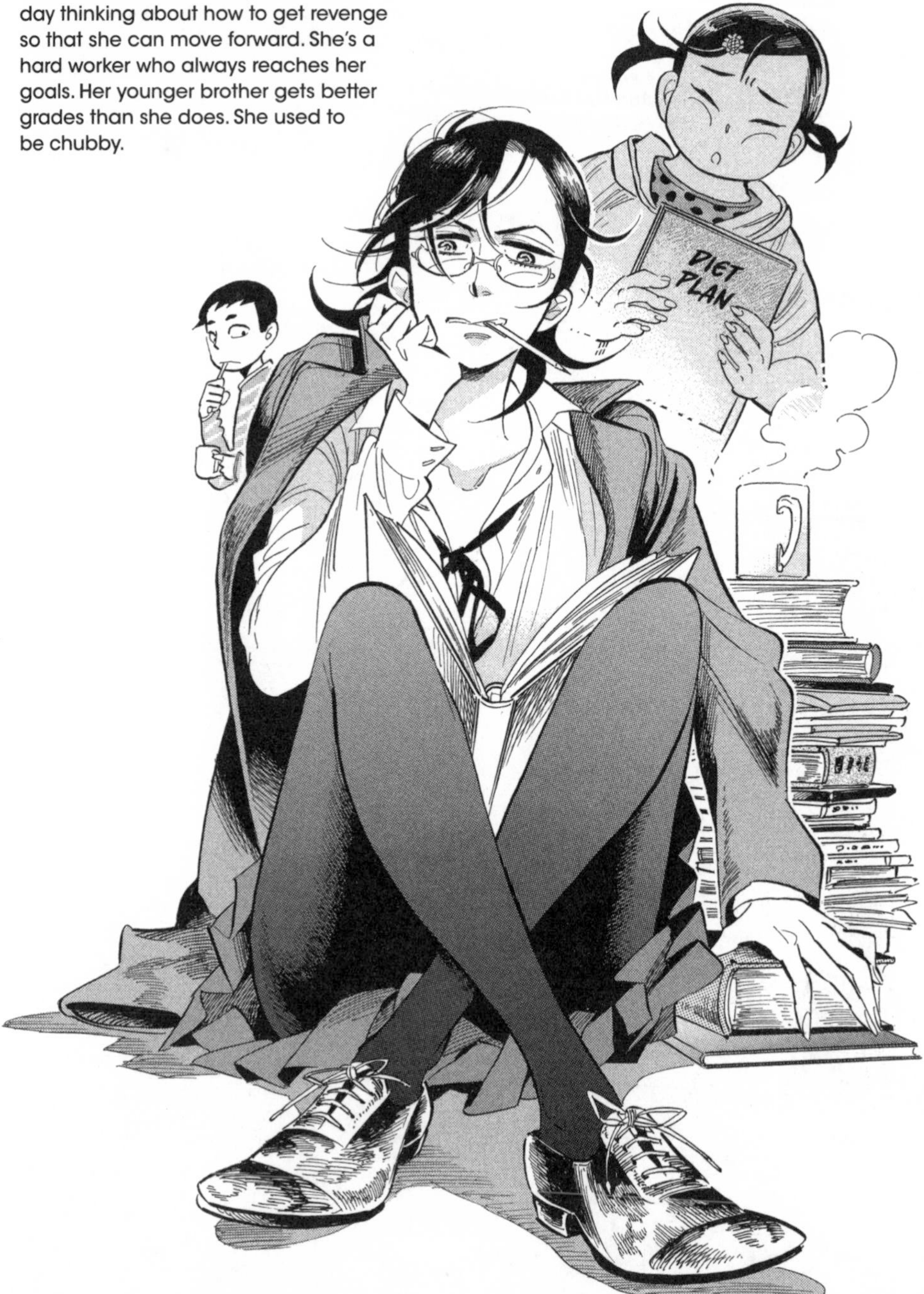
DIET PLAN

Kanta

He was raised as if he was good-looking, but people think he's gross. He means no harm. He's good at cheap magic.

Oe

Hooked on games. Has fun every day.

Umihiko

Loves people who do their best. He can make any-thing become light.

Samihiko

Hates people who don't do their best. He can make anything become heavy.

Jun

Knows a lot about what can be used as poison or medicine. Good at putting on makeup.

Akane

Likes fire. Dreams of living in a home behind a furnace.

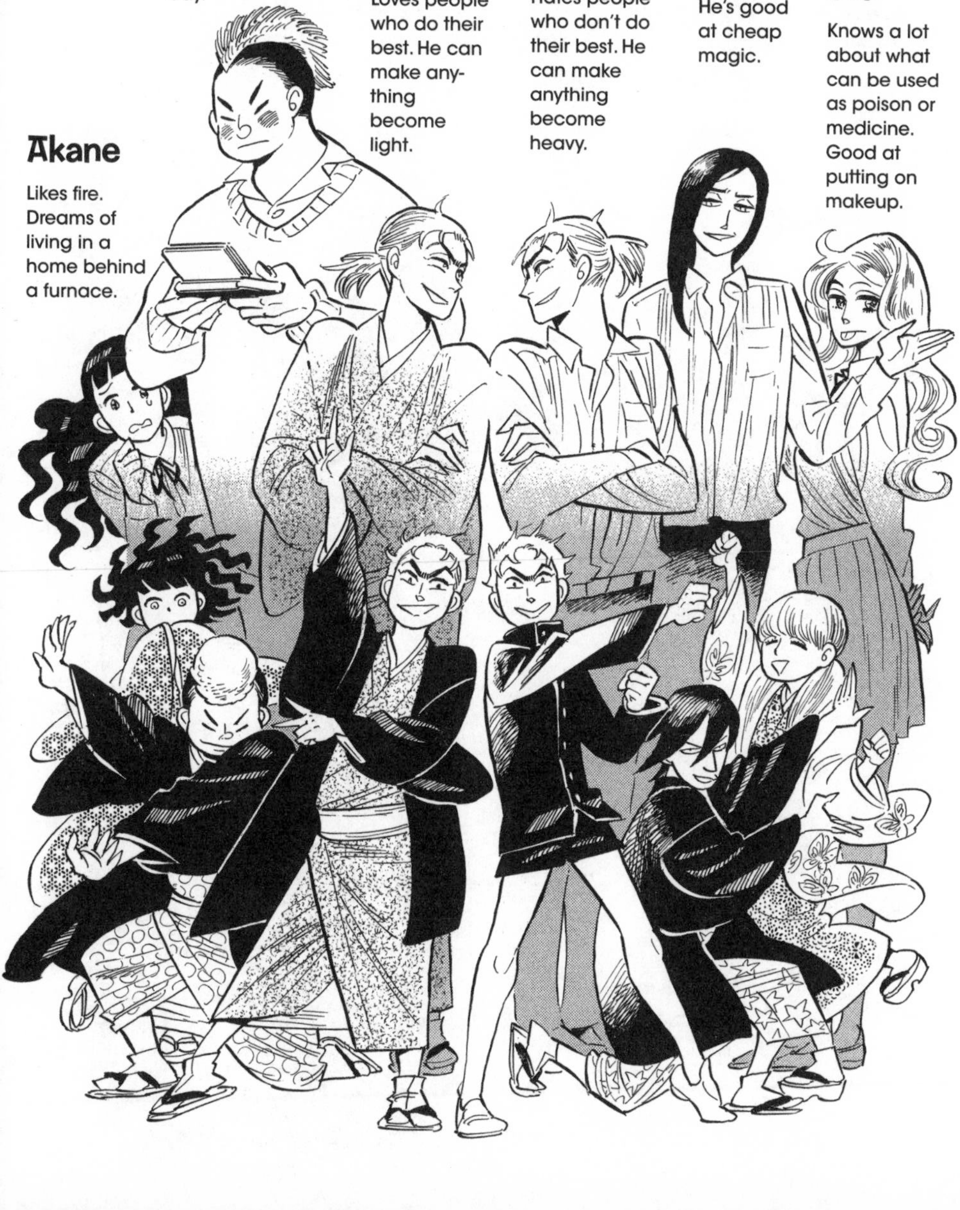

Ogi Mikado

Mayor of Haimachi. Head of the Mikado family, which owns real estate across Haimachi. She lost her sight during her teenage years. She's the inspiration for the Haimachi City mascot, "Haimachi Komachi Ogi." She lives her life for other people and for the world. Her noble airs caused a rift between her son and herself.

Kuniyoshi Gogo

Asked by Ogi to look after Otaro. He's cared for Otaro since he was a toddler and thinks that raising children is fascinating. Not only does he cook, but he keeps house, gardens, flies helicopters, has a sailing license and can hunt. He is very responsible and very skilled.

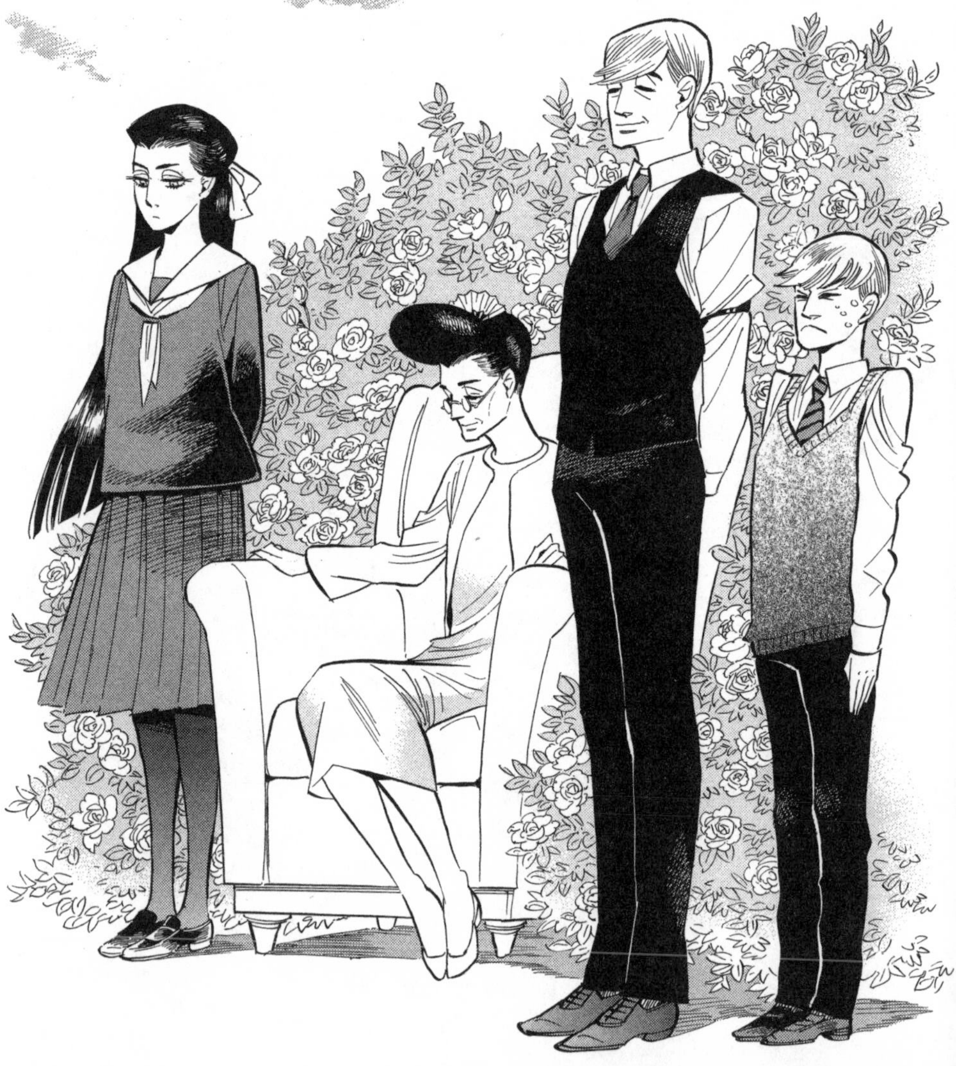

Daichi Asayama

He loves dogs and is still waiting for his puppy to come back to him. He thinks his friend Jin Uruma is rather doglike.

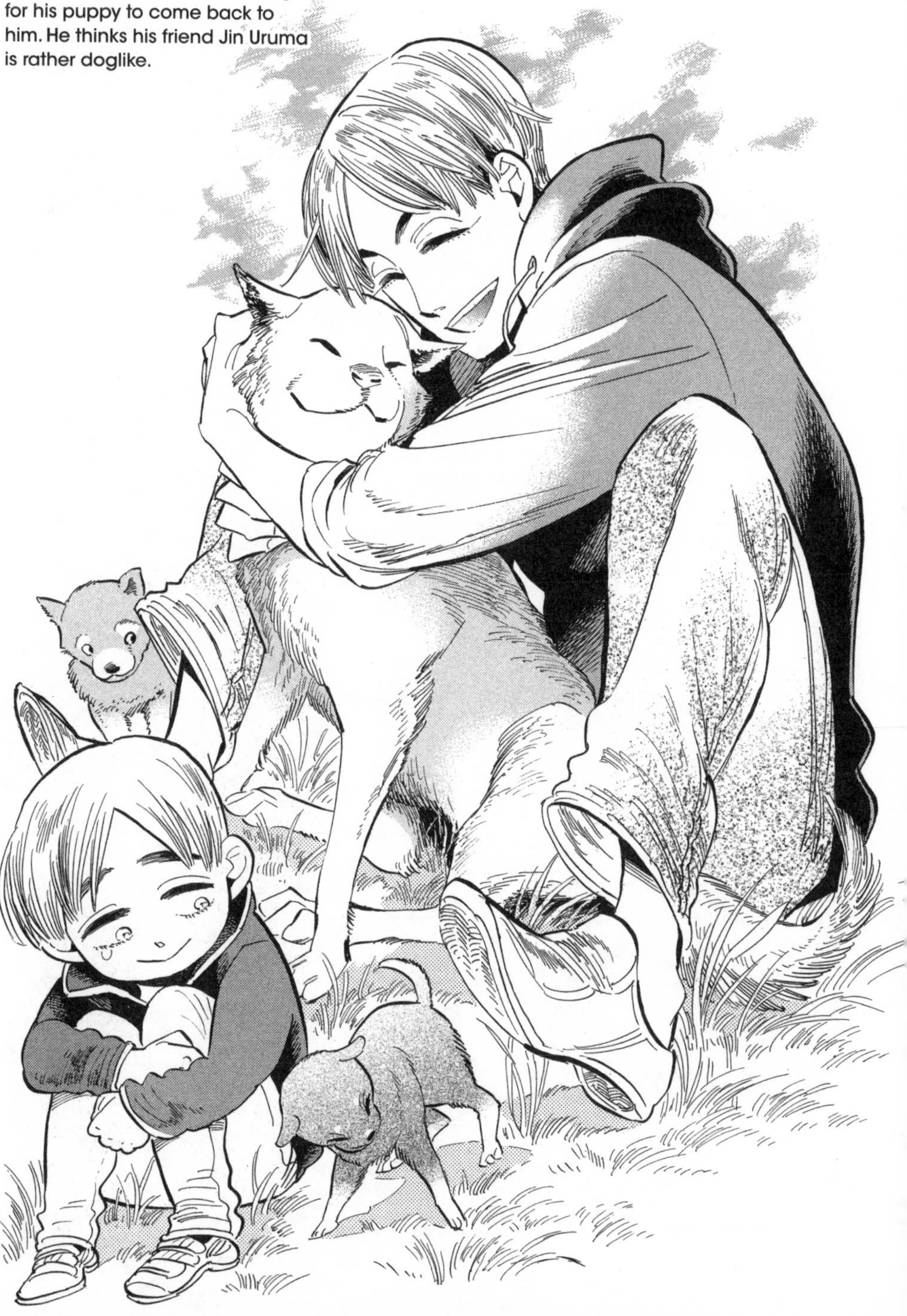

Toshikazu Hirota

Teaches the fourth grade class in room 3. Truthfully, he didn't want to work all that hard, but his colleagues strung him along, and now he's doing his best as a teacher. He's a strong blade of grass billowing in the wind.

Tetsuo Sekiguchi

Ran's teacher. He believes education is the greatest asset for any child. He's a seed sower.

Hana Aoki

Teaches the fourth grade class in room 2 at Haimachi Elementary. A stern look from her can quiet down the class in an instant. She's known as the Exploding Sunflower of Haimachi Elementary.

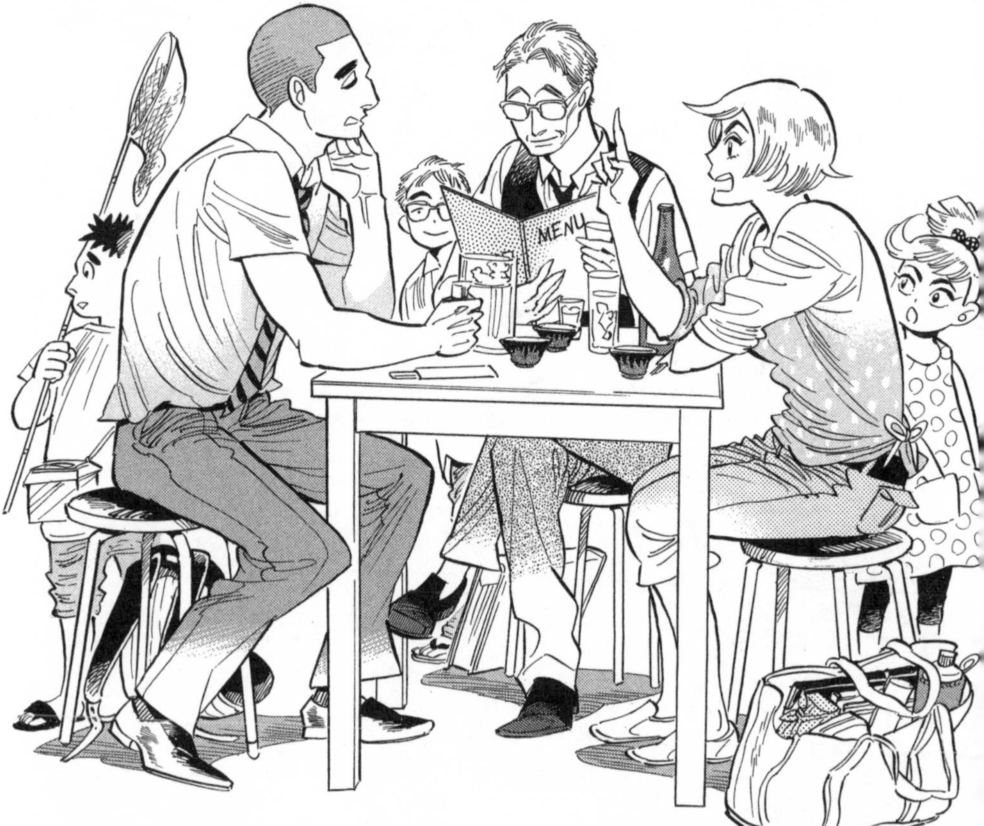
MENU

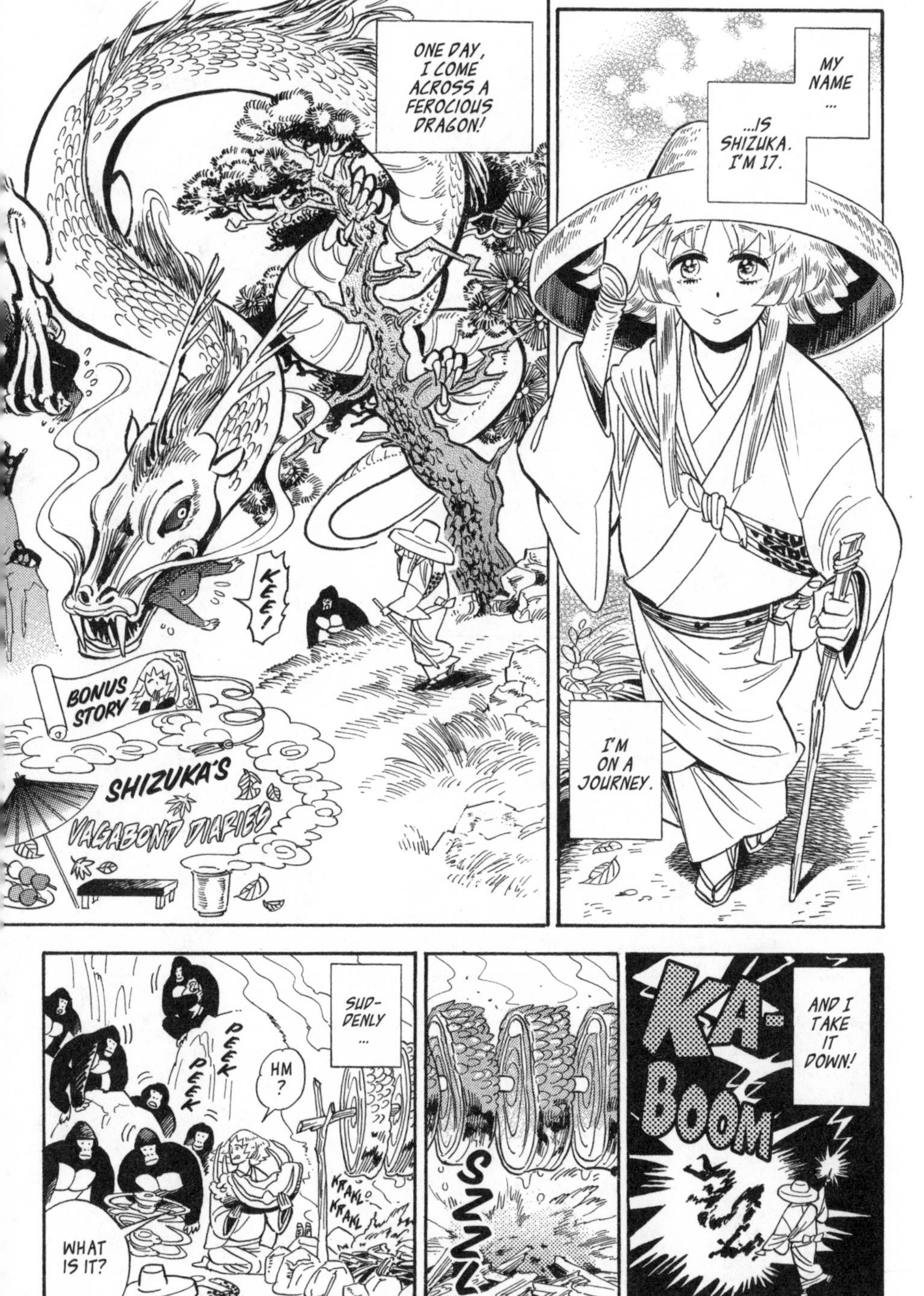
MY NAME ...
...IS SHIZUKA. I'M 17.
I'M ON A JOURNEY.
ONE DAY, I COME ACROSS A FEROCIOUS DRAGON!
KEE!
BONUS STORY
SHIZUKA'S VAGABOND DIARIES
KA-BOOM
AND I TAKE IT DOWN!
SZZZ
SUD-DENLY ...
HM?
PEEK PEEK
KRAKL KRAKL
WHAT IS IT?

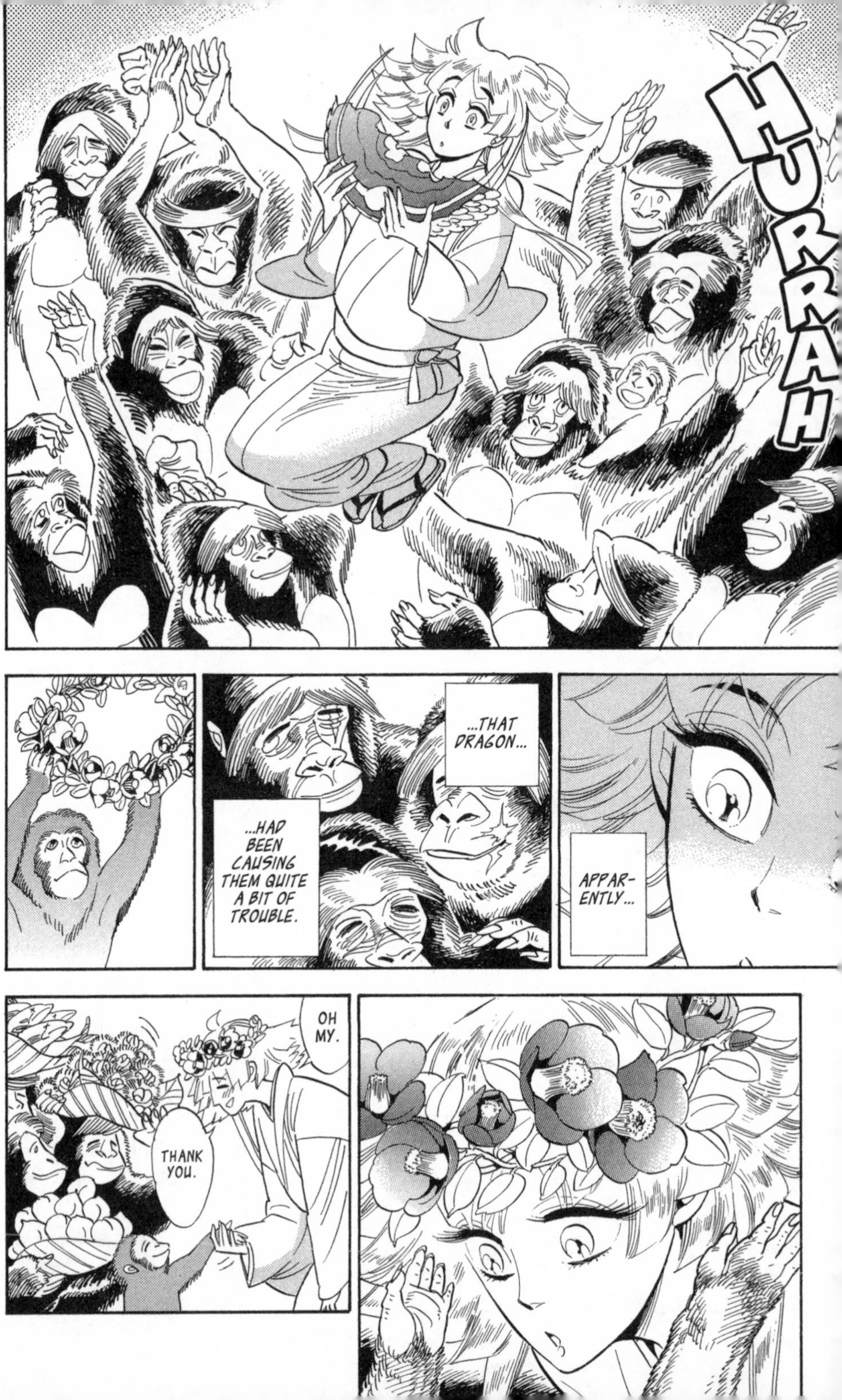
HURRAH
APPAR-
ENTLY...
...THAT
DRAGON...
...HAD
BEEN
CAUSING
THEM QUITE
A BIT OF
TROUBLE.
OH
MY.
THANK
YOU.

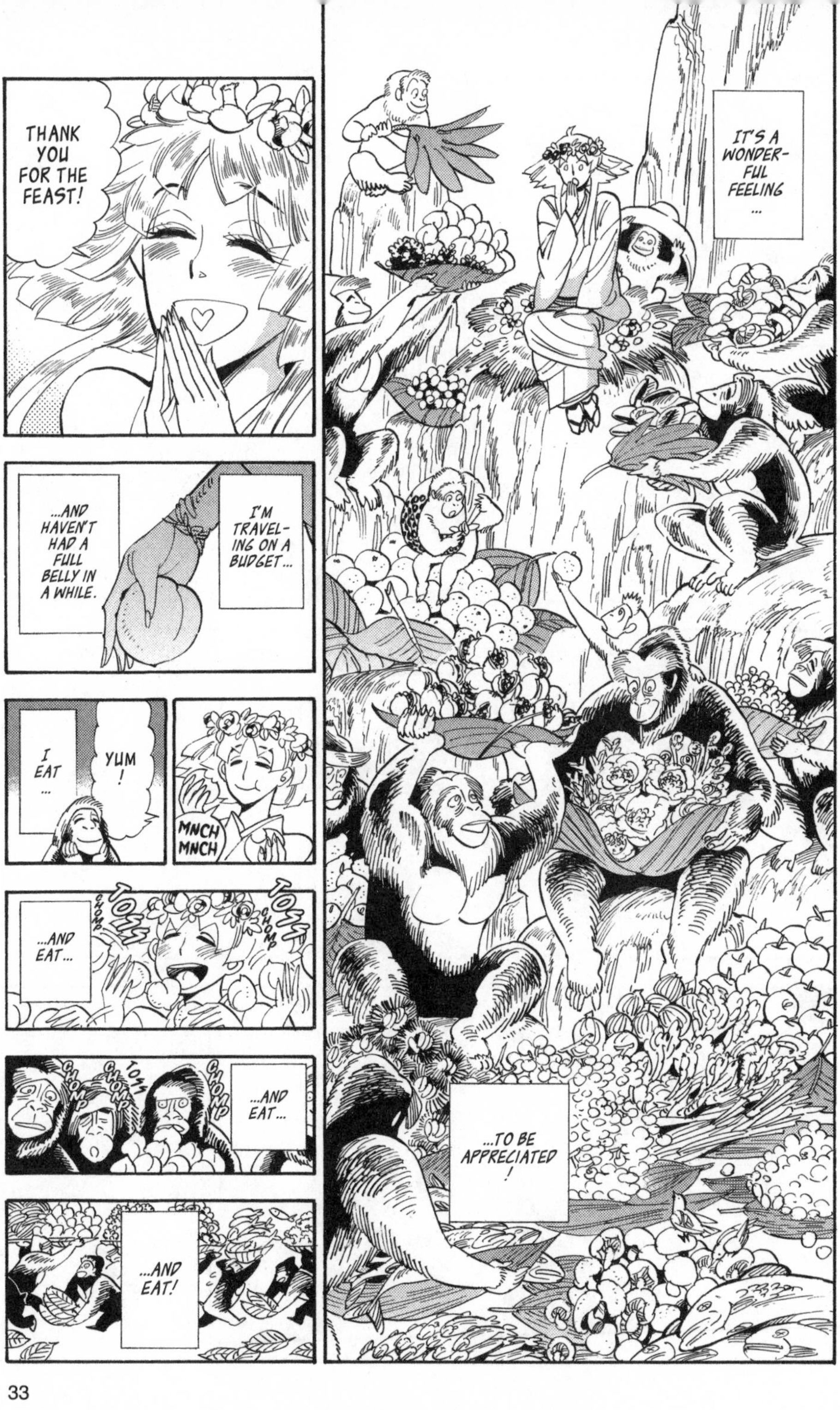
IT'S A WONDERFUL FEELING ...
...TO BE APPRECIATED!
THANK YOU FOR THE FEAST!
I'M TRAVELING ON A BUDGET...
...AND HAVEN'T HAD A FULL BELLY IN A WHILE.
MNCH MNCH
YUM!
I EAT...
TOM CHOMP
TOM CHOMP
...AND EAT...
...AND EAT...
CHOMP
TOM CHOMP
CHOMP
...AND EAT!

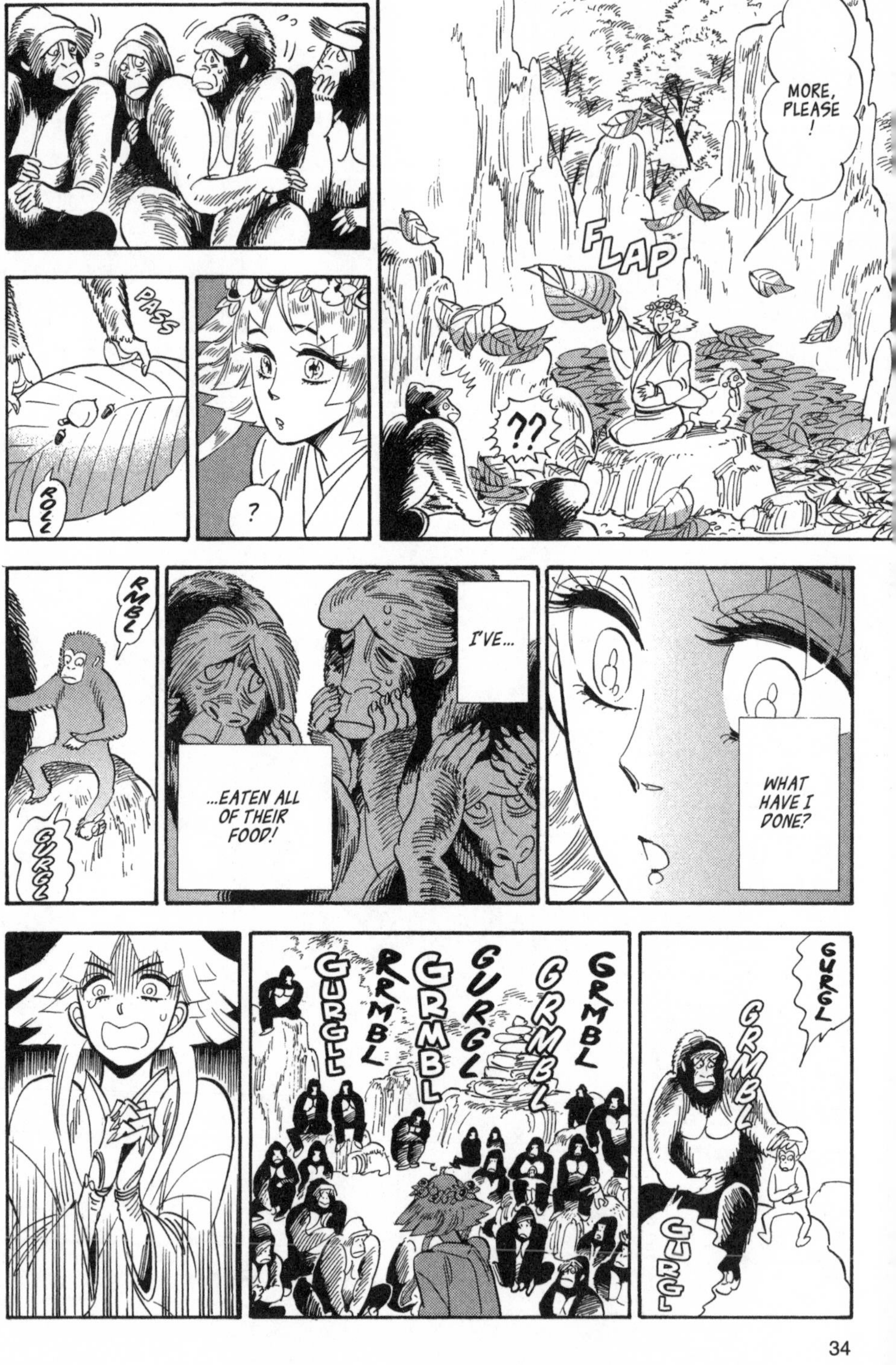
MORE, PLEASE!
FLAP
??
?
PASS
ROLL
WHAT HAVE I DONE?
I'VE...
...EATEN ALL OF THEIR FOOD!
RMBL
GURGL
GURGL
GRMBL
GURGL
GRMBL
GRMBL
GURGL
GRMBL
RRMBL
GURGL

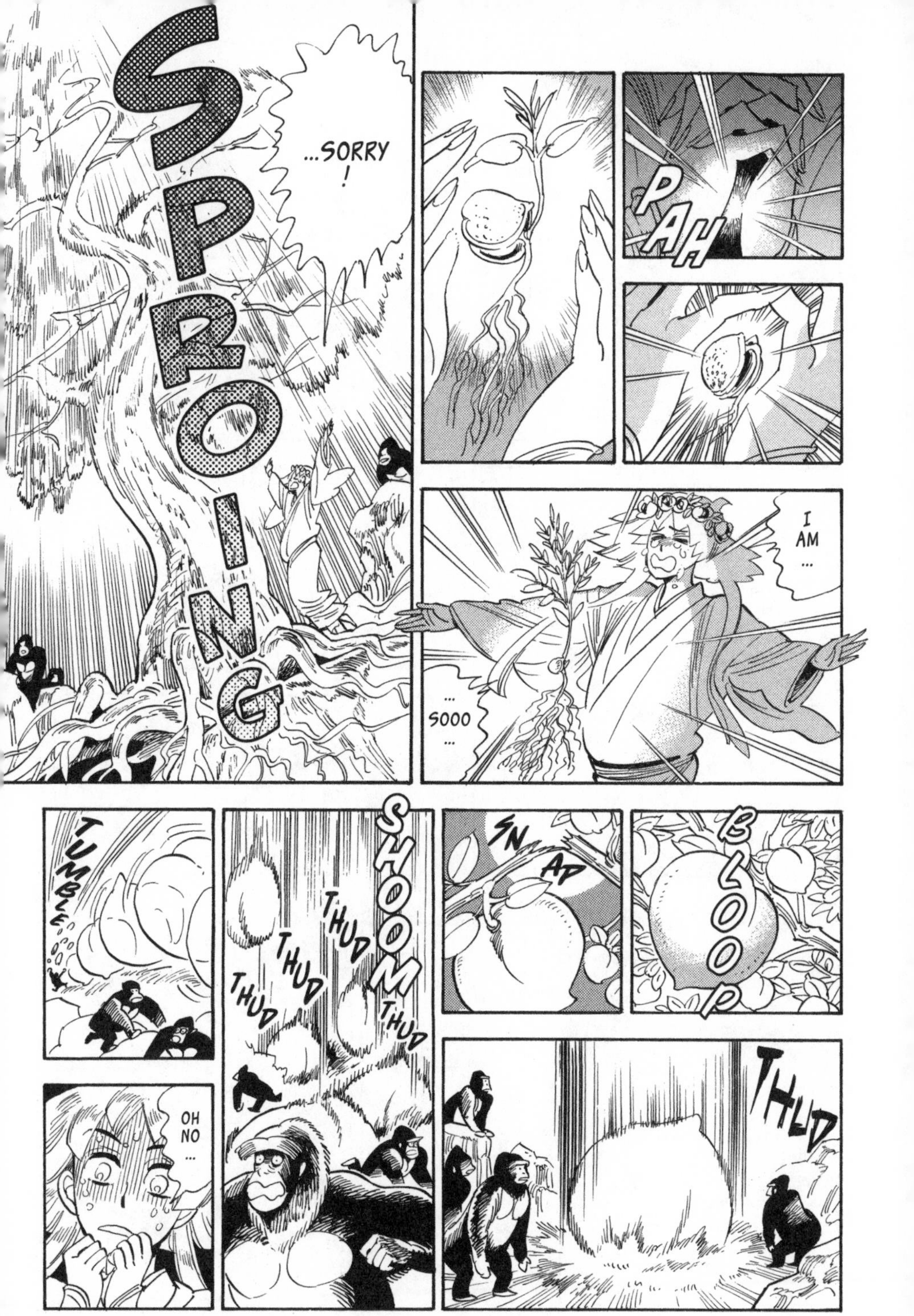
PAH
I AM ...
... SOOO ...
SPROING
...SORRY!
BLOOP
SNAP
THUD
SHOOM
THUD
THUD
THUD
THUD
TUMBLE
OH NO ...

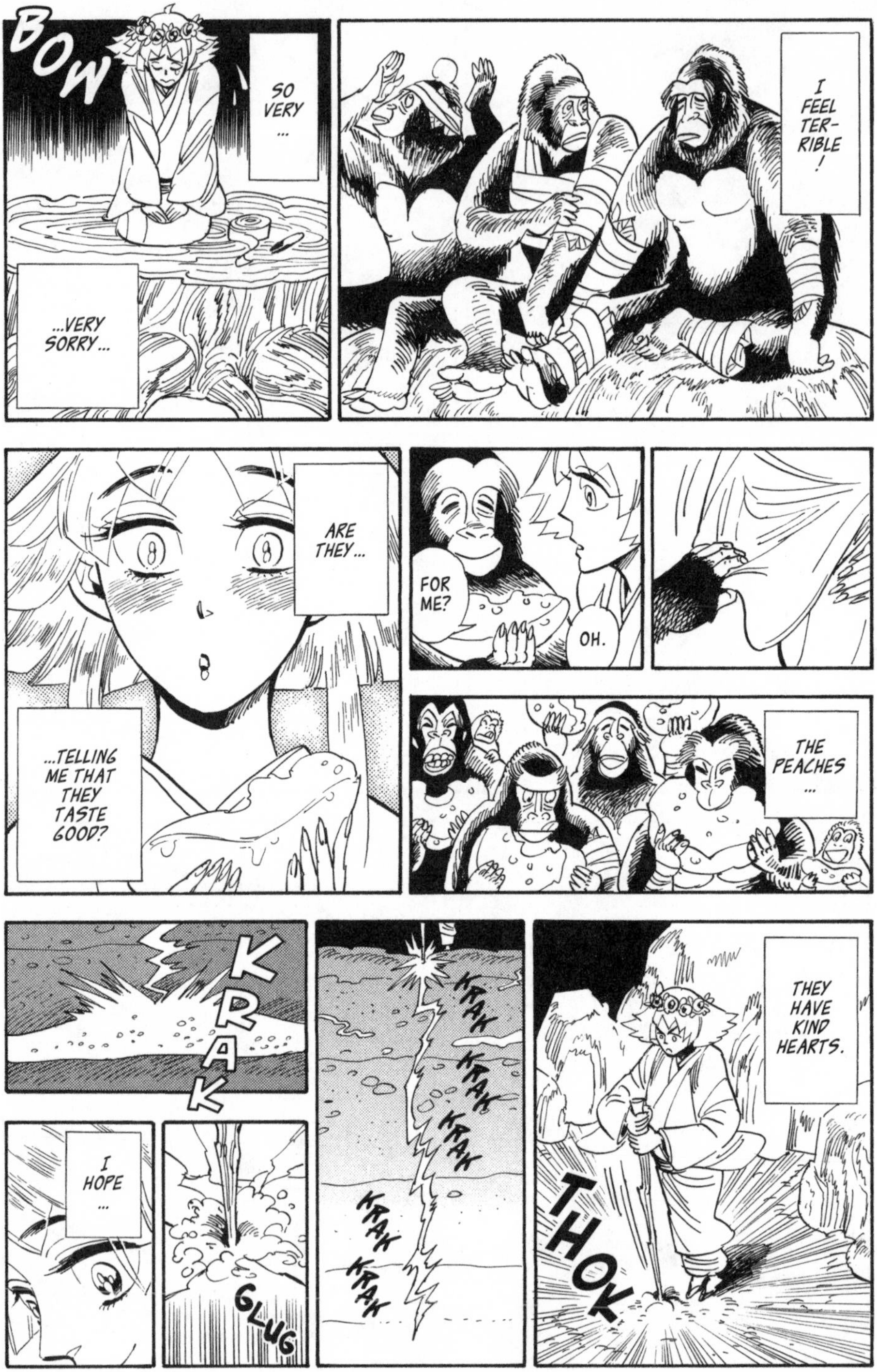
I FEEL TER-RIBLE!
BOW
SO VERY ...
...VERY SORRY...
FOR ME?
OH.
THE PEACHES ...
ARE THEY...
...TELLING ME THAT THEY TASTE GOOD?
THEY HAVE KIND HEARTS.
THOK
KRAK KRAK KRAK KRAK KRAK KRAK
KRAK
GLUG
I HOPE ...

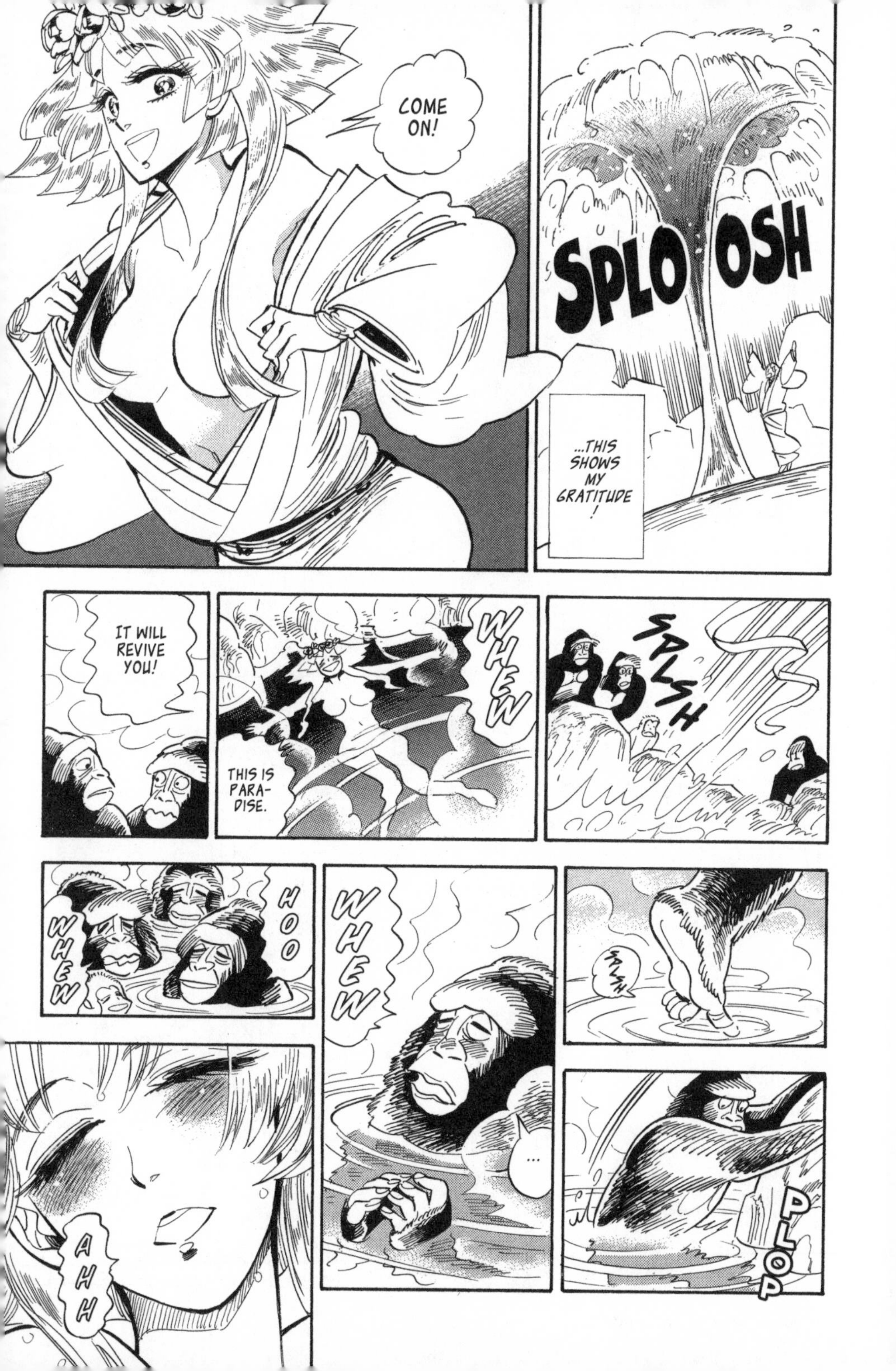
SPLOOSH
...THIS SHOWS MY GRATITUDE!
COME ON!
SPLSH
WHEW
THIS IS PARA-DISE.
IT WILL REVIVE YOU!
SPLSH
PLOP
WHEW
...
HOO
WHEW
AHH

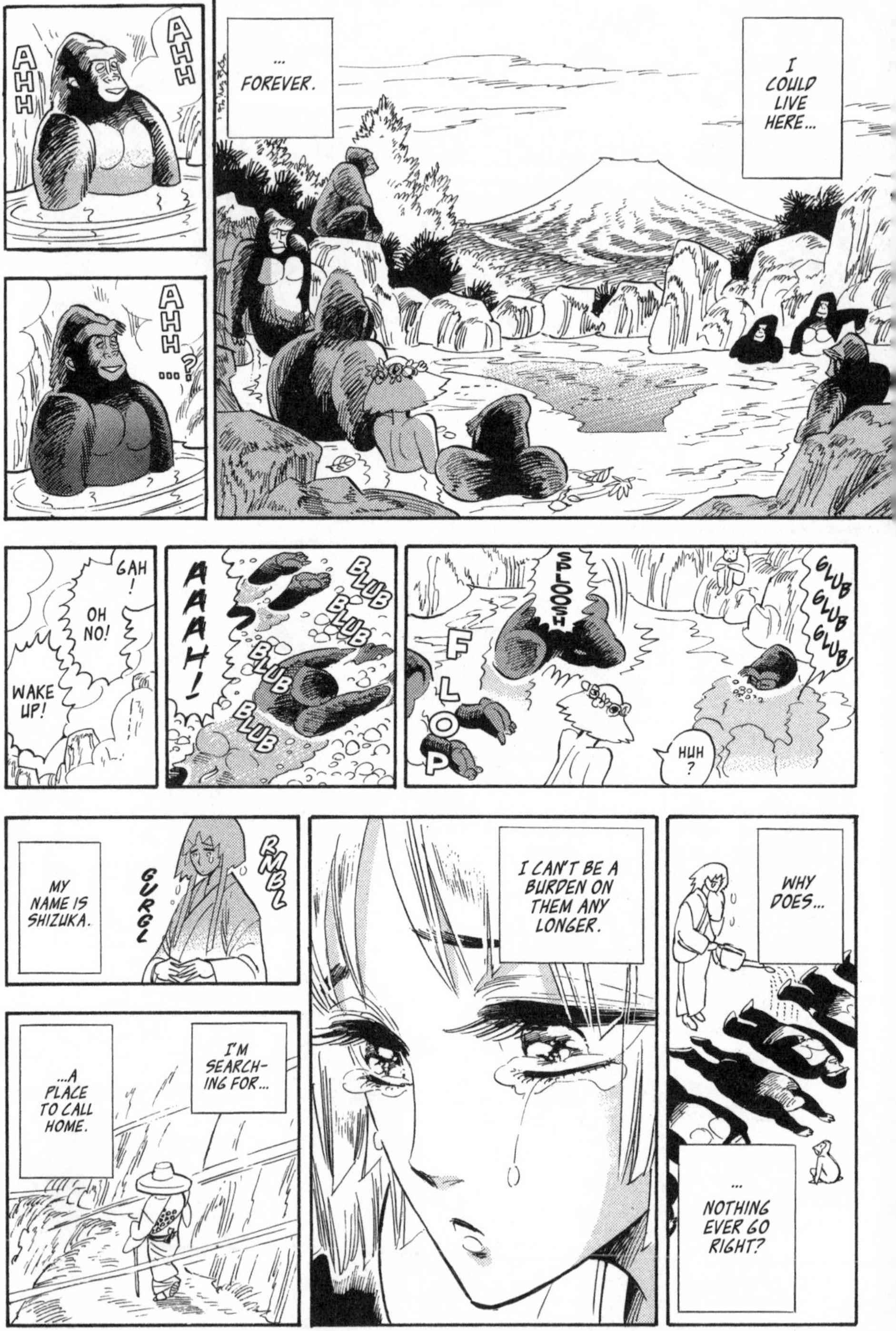
I COULD LIVE HERE...
... FOREVER.
AHH AHH
AHH ...?
SPLOOSH
GLUB GLUB GLUB
FLOP
HUH?
AAAAH!
BLUB BLUB BLUB BLUB
GAH!
OH NO!
WAKE UP!
WHY DOES...
... NOTHING EVER GO RIGHT?
I CAN'T BE A BURDEN ON THEM ANY LONGER.
RMBL
GURGL
MY NAME IS SHIZUKA.
I'M SEARCHING FOR...
...A PLACE TO CALL HOME.

Bonus Story / The End

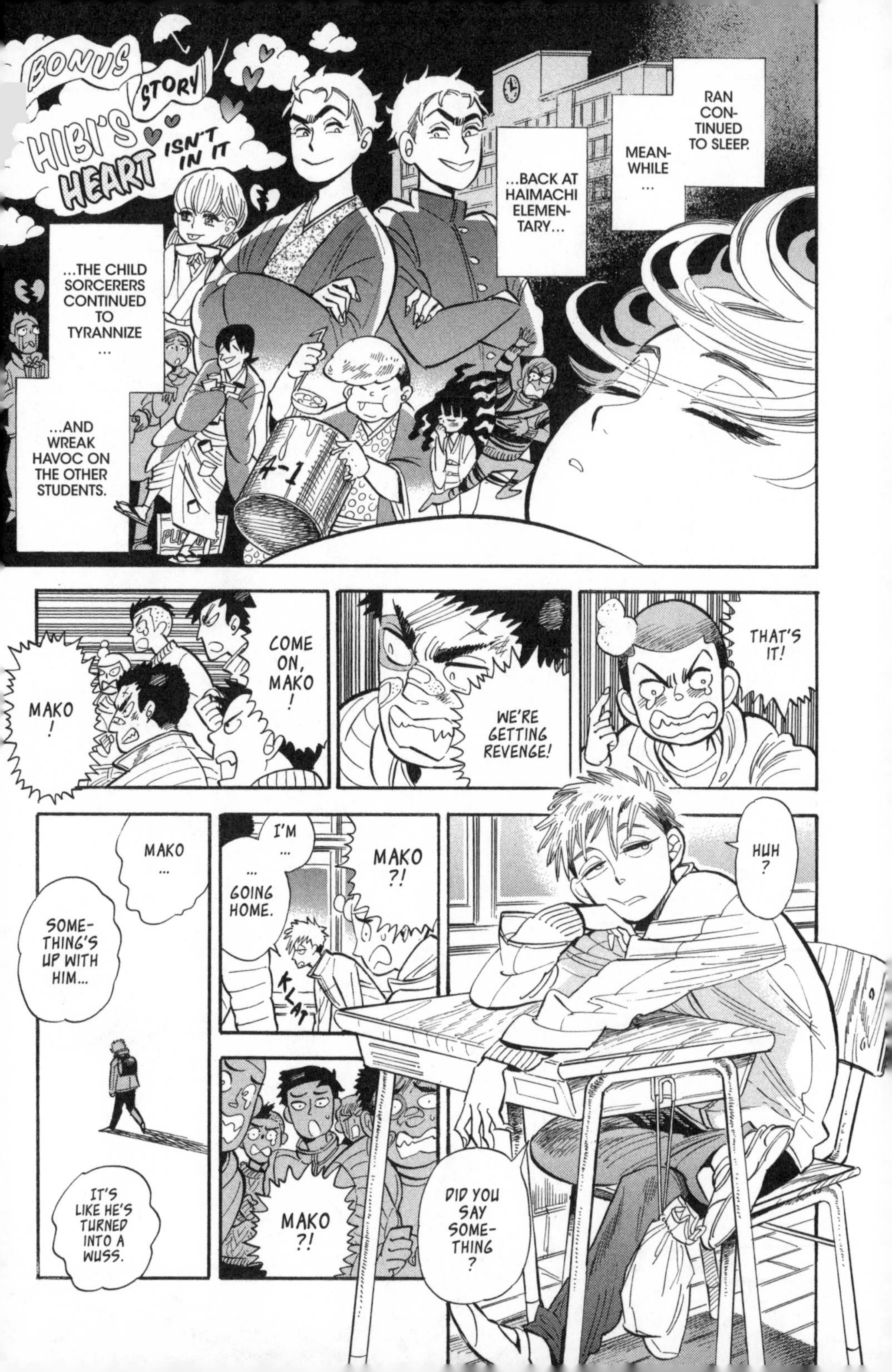
RAN CONTINUED TO SLEEP.
MEANWHILE...
...BACK AT HAIMACHI ELEMENTARY...
BONUS STORY
HIBI'S HEART ISN'T IN IT
...THE CHILD SORCERERS CONTINUED TO TYRANNIZE...
...AND WREAK HAVOC ON THE OTHER STUDENTS.
THAT'S IT!
WE'RE GETTING REVENGE!
COME ON, MAKO!
MAKO!
HUH?
DID YOU SAY SOMETHING?
MAKO?!
I'M...
...GOING HOME.
KLAT
MAKO?!
MAKO...
SOMETHING'S UP WITH HIM...
IT'S LIKE HE'S TURNED INTO A WUSS.

OH.

THAT'S OKAY. I'LL COME BACK.

I'M SORRY.

MISS RAN IS STILL RESTING ...

HEY, YOU!

YOU'RE MAKOTO HIBI.

RIGHT ?

...

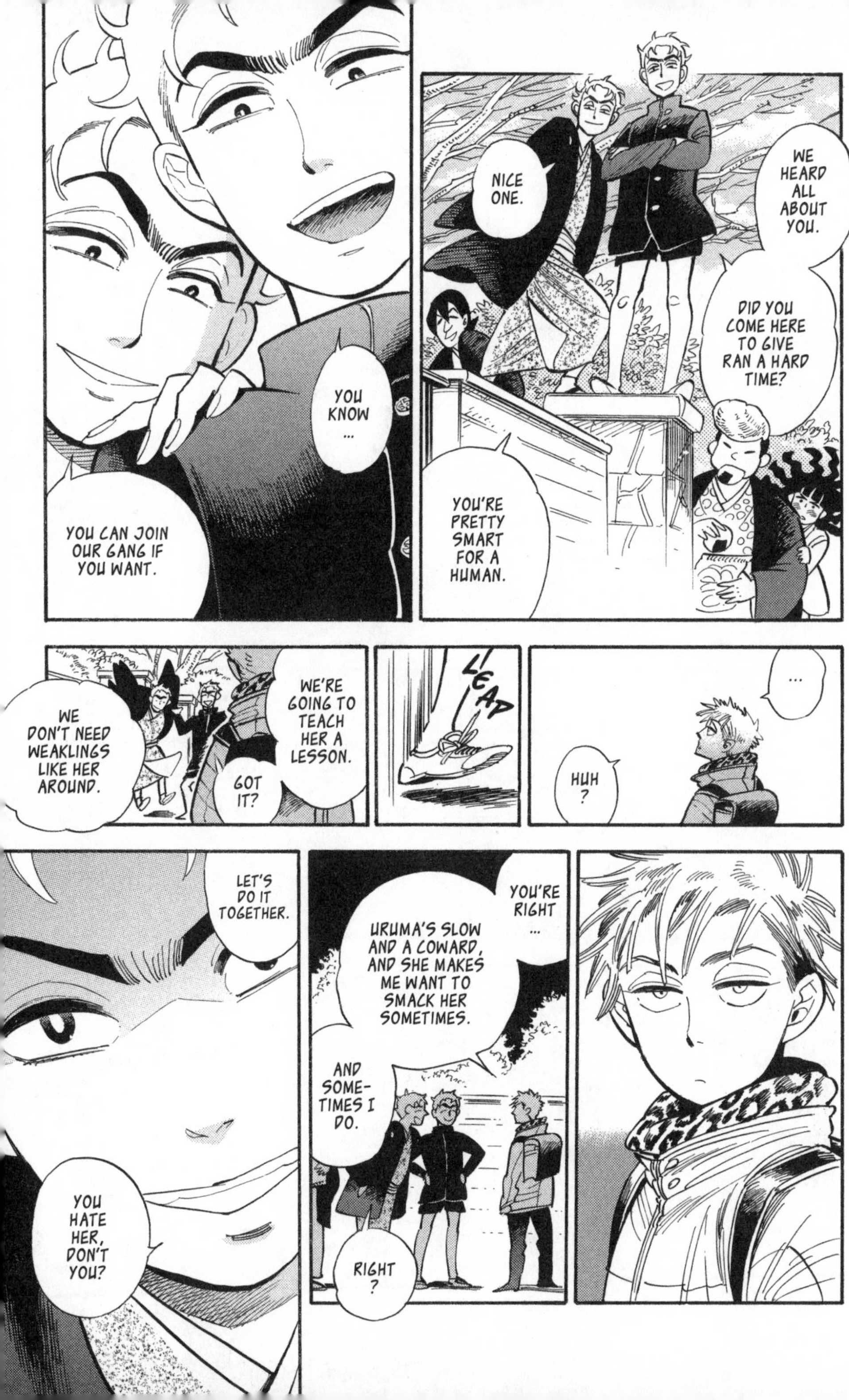
WE HEARD ALL ABOUT YOU.
NICE ONE.
DID YOU COME HERE TO GIVE RAN A HARD TIME?
YOU'RE PRETTY SMART FOR A HUMAN.
YOU KNOW ...
YOU CAN JOIN OUR GANG IF YOU WANT.
...
HUH?
LEAP
WE'RE GOING TO TEACH HER A LESSON.
GOT IT?
WE DON'T NEED WEAKLINGS LIKE HER AROUND.
YOU'RE RIGHT ...
URUMA'S SLOW AND A COWARD, AND SHE MAKES ME WANT TO SMACK HER SOMETIMES.
AND SOMETIMES I DO.
RIGHT?
LET'S DO IT TOGETHER.
YOU HATE HER, DON'T YOU?

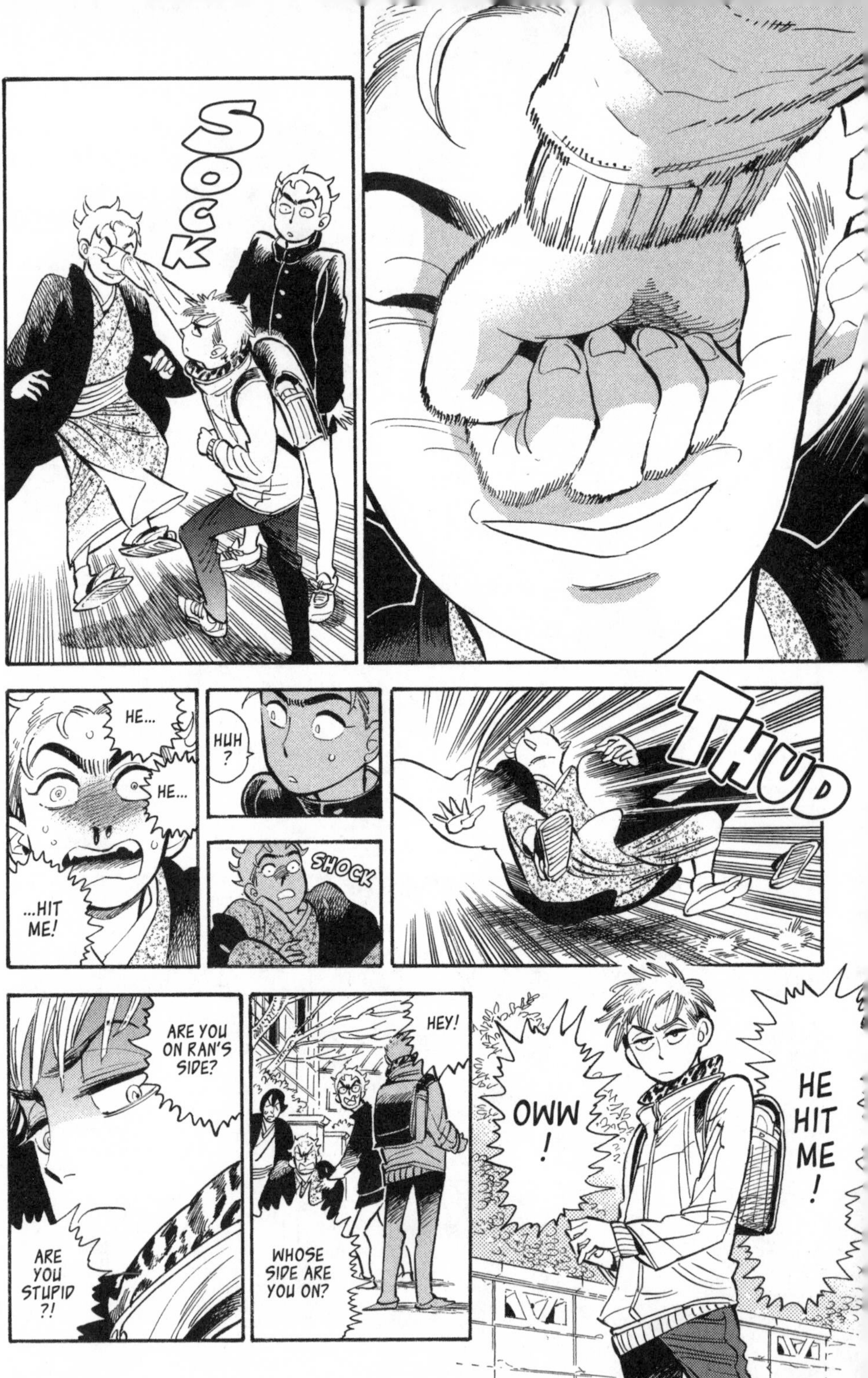
SOCK
THUD
HUH?
SHOCK
HE...
HE...
...HIT ME!
HE HIT ME!
OWW!
HEY!
WHOSE SIDE ARE YOU ON?
ARE YOU ON RAN'S SIDE?
ARE YOU STUPID?!

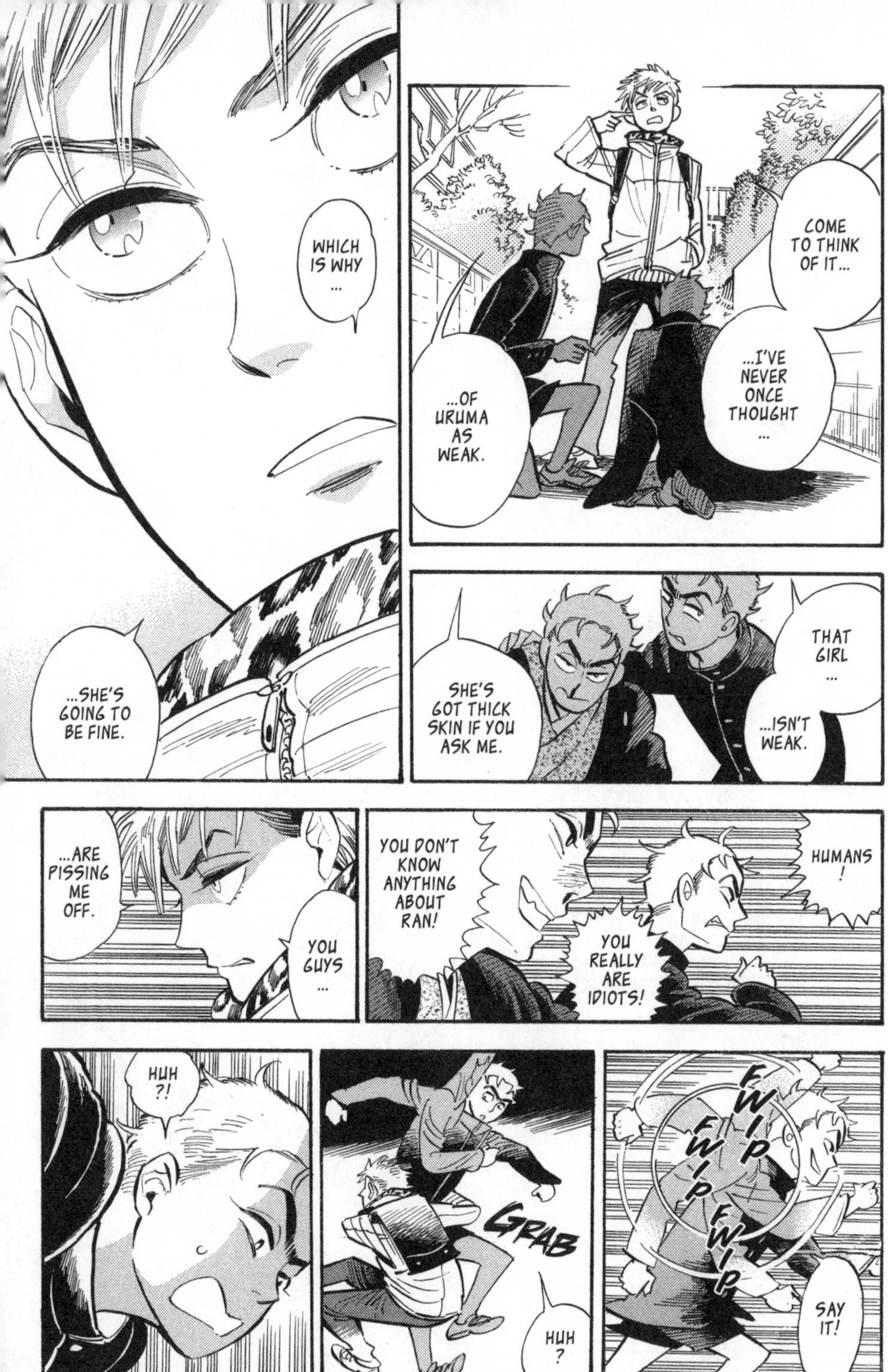
COME TO THINK OF IT...
...I'VE NEVER ONCE THOUGHT...
...OF URUMA AS WEAK.
THAT GIRL...
...ISN'T WEAK.
SHE'S GOT THICK SKIN IF YOU ASK ME.
WHICH IS WHY...
...SHE'S GOING TO BE FINE.
HUMANS!
YOU REALLY ARE IDIOTS!
YOU DON'T KNOW ANYTHING ABOUT RAN!
YOU GUYS...
...ARE PISSING ME OFF.
FWIP FWIP FWIP FWIP
SAY IT!
GRAB
HUH?
HUH?!

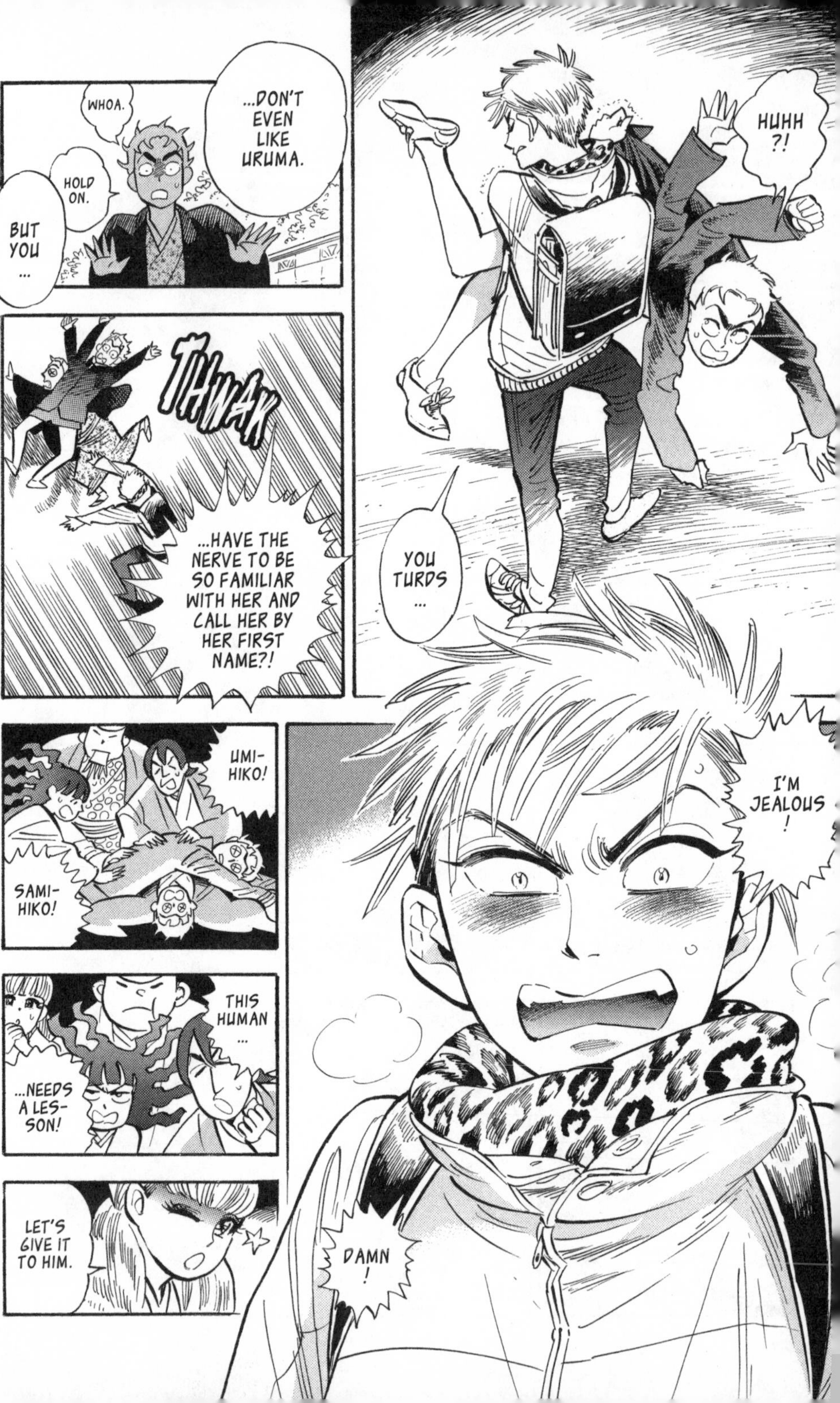
HUHH?!
YOU TURDS...
...DON'T EVEN LIKE URUMA.
WHOA.
HOLD ON.
BUT YOU...
THWAK
...HAVE THE NERVE TO BE SO FAMILIAR WITH HER AND CALL HER BY HER FIRST NAME?!
I'M JEALOUS!
DAMN!
UMI-HIKO!
SAMI-HIKO!
THIS HUMAN...
...NEEDS A LES-SON!
LET'S GIVE IT TO HIM.

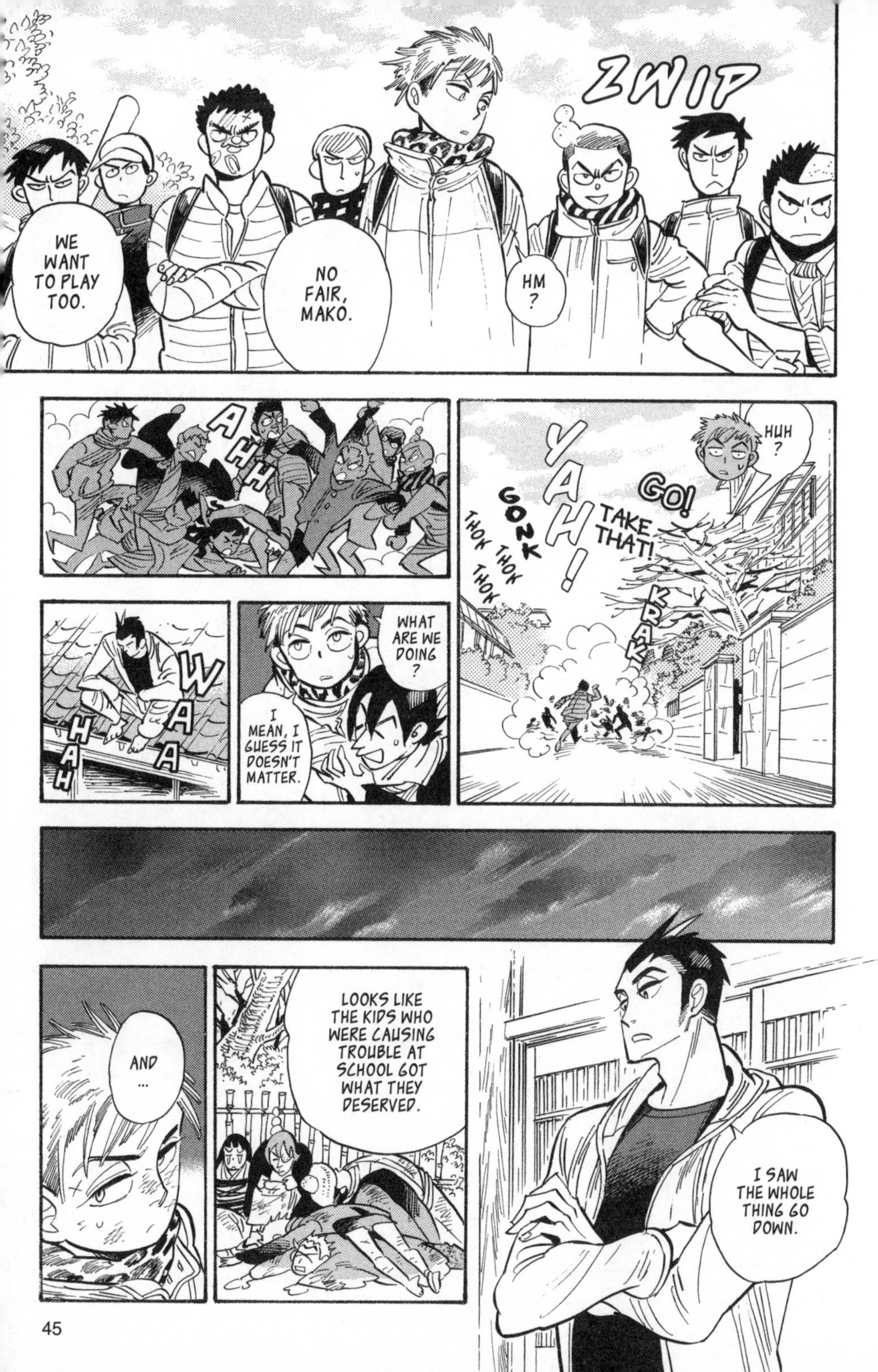
ZWIP
HM?
NO FAIR, MAKO.
WE WANT TO PLAY TOO.
HUH?
GO!
TAKE THAT!
YAH!
GONK
THOK THOK THOK
KRAK
AHHH
WHAT ARE WE DOING?
I MEAN, I GUESS IT DOESN'T MATTER.
WAAA
HAH
I SAW THE WHOLE THING GO DOWN.
LOOKS LIKE THE KIDS WHO WERE CAUSING TROUBLE AT SCHOOL GOT WHAT THEY DESERVED.
AND ...

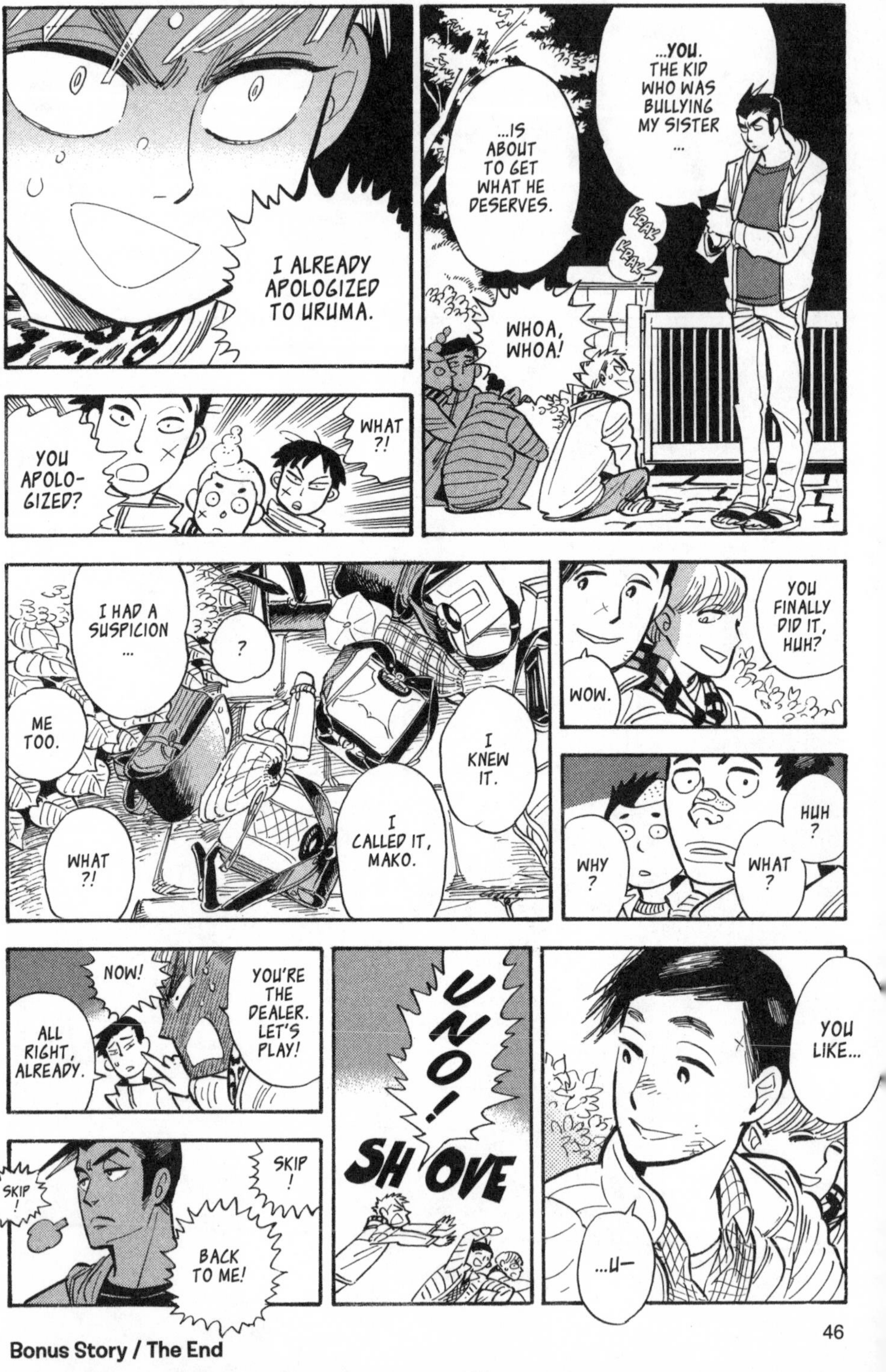
...YOU. THE KID WHO WAS BULLYING MY SISTER ...
...IS ABOUT TO GET WHAT HE DESERVES.
KRAK
KRAK
WHOA, WHOA!
I ALREADY APOLOGIZED TO URUMA.
WHAT ?!
YOU APOLO-GIZED?
YOU FINALLY DID IT, HUH?
WOW.
HUH ?
WHAT ?
WHY ?
I HAD A SUSPICION ...
?
I KNEW IT.
ME TOO.
I CALLED IT, MAKO.
WHAT ?!
YOU LIKE...
...U—
UNO!
SHOVE
YOU'RE THE DEALER. LET'S PLAY!
NOW!
ALL RIGHT, ALREADY.
SKIP !
BACK TO ME!
SKIP !

Bonus Story / The End

Chapter 38
The Final Transformation

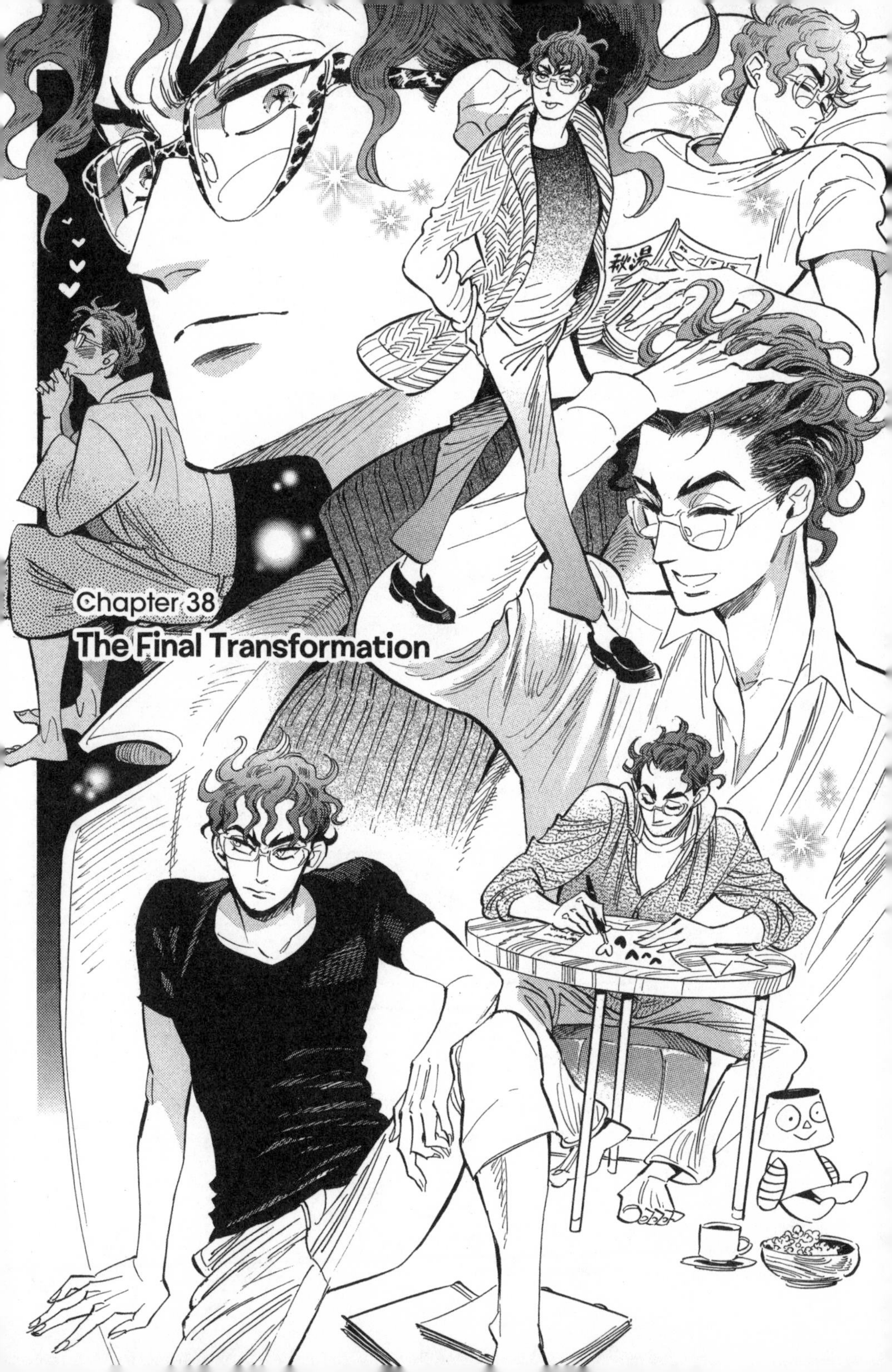

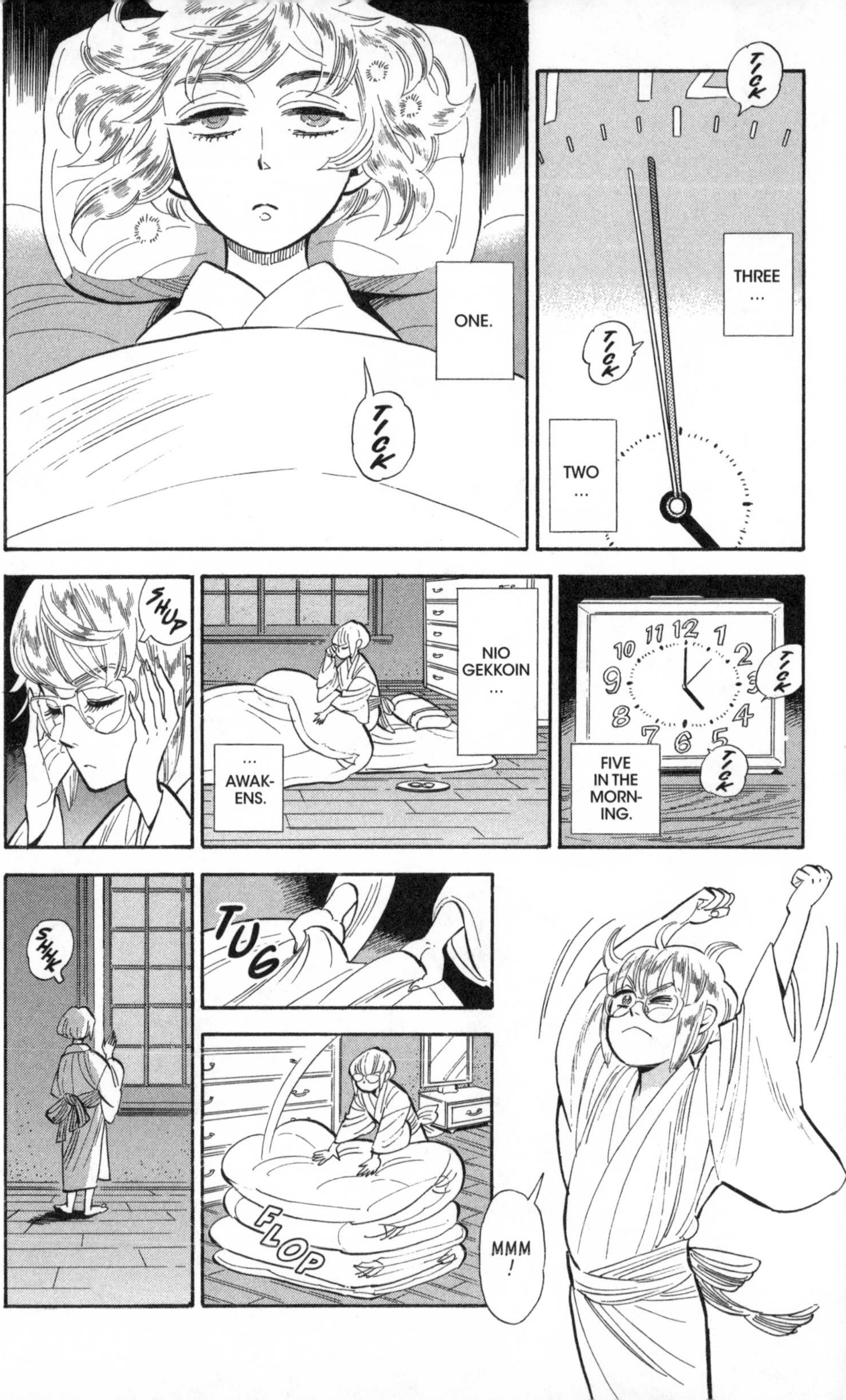
TICK
THREE ...
TICK
TWO ...
ONE.
TICK
TICK
FIVE IN THE MORN- ING.
TICK
NIO GEKKOIN ...
... AWAK- ENS.
SHUP
MMM !
TUG
FLOP
SHHK

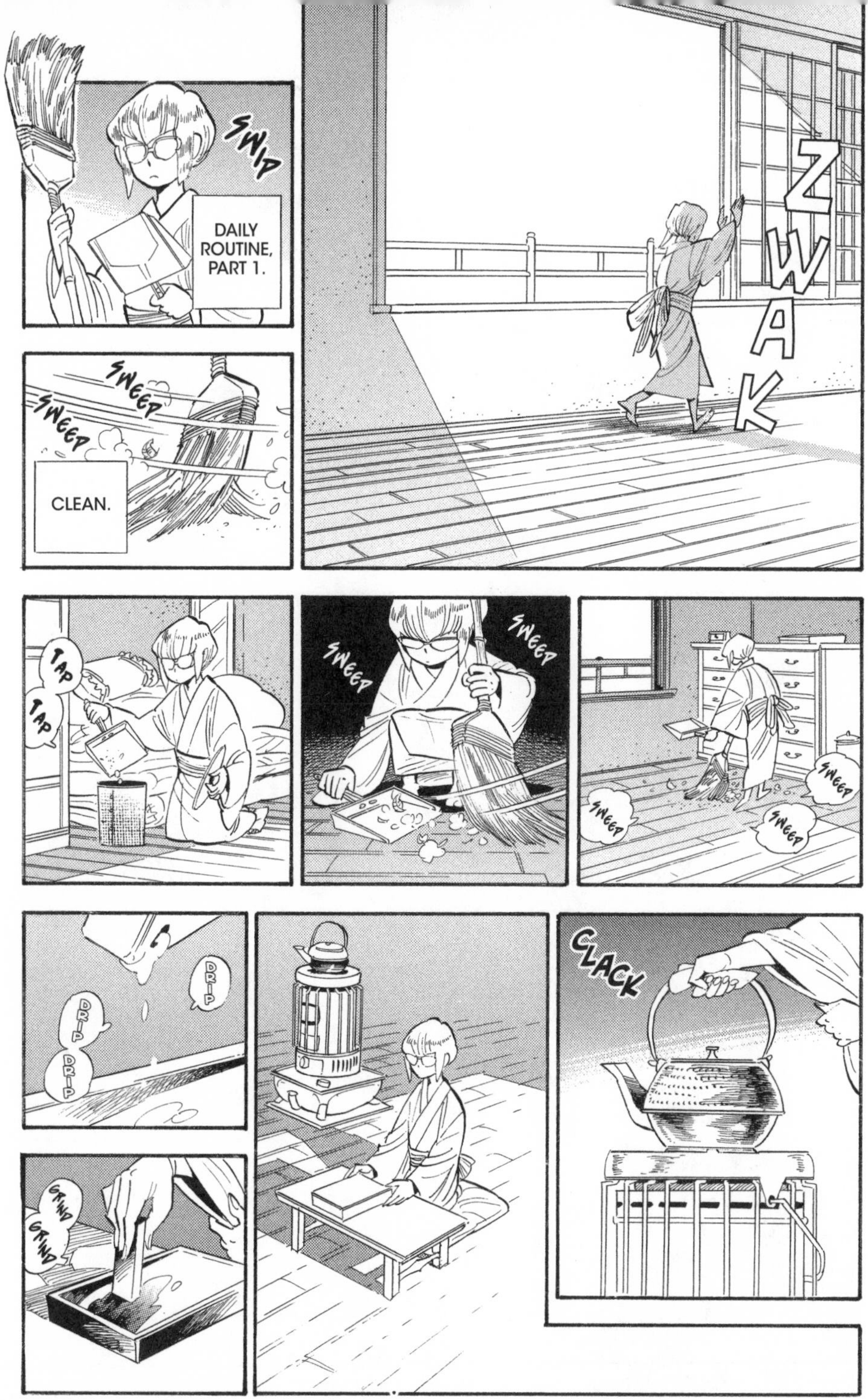

ZWAK
SWIP
DAILY ROUTINE, PART 1.
SWEEP
SWEEP
CLEAN.
SWEEP
SWEEP
SWEEP
SWEEP
SWEEP
TAP
TAP
CLACK
DRIP
DRIP
DRIP
GRIND
GRIND

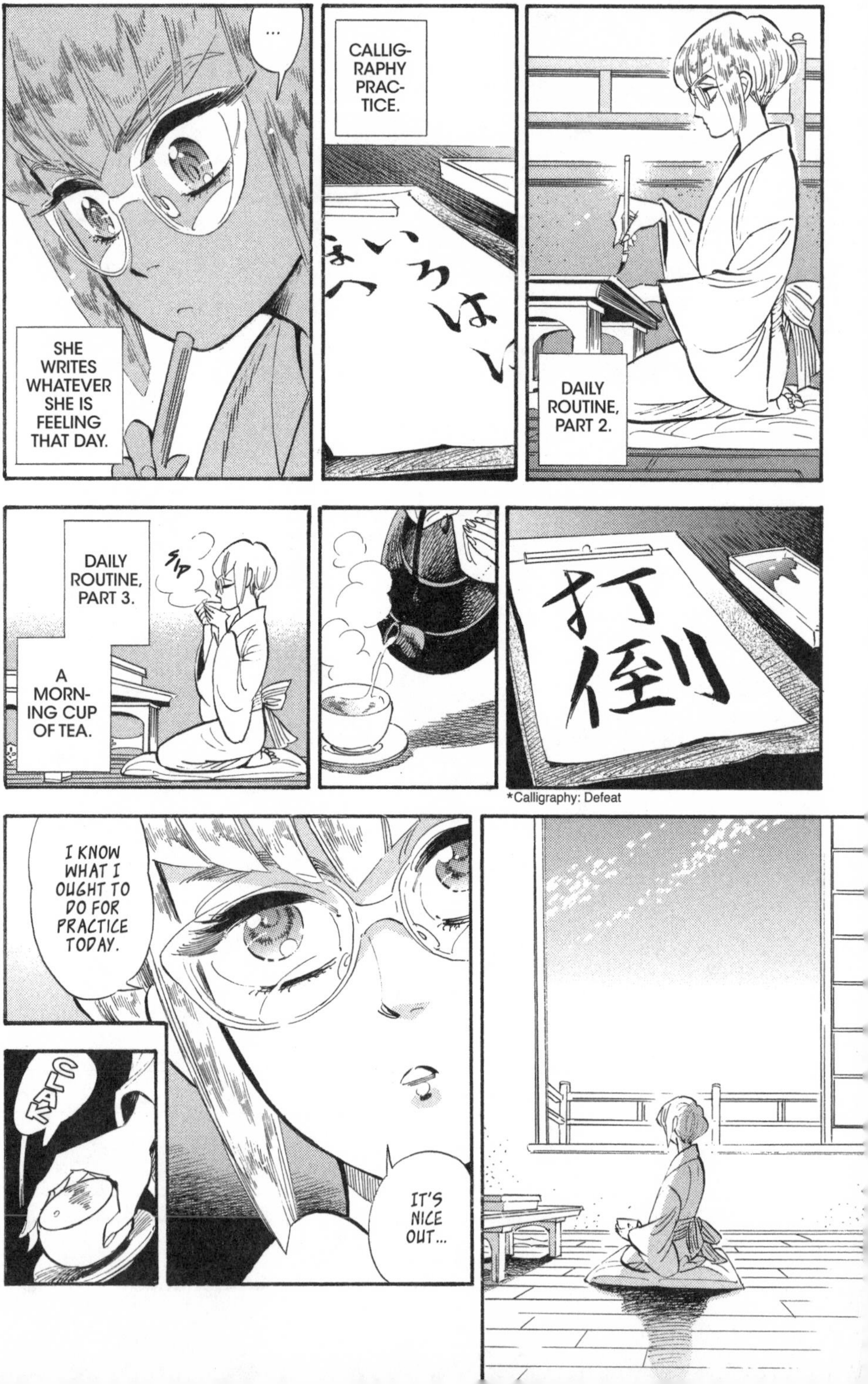
DAILY ROUTINE, PART 2.
CALLIG-RAPHY PRAC-TICE.
...
SHE WRITES WHATEVER SHE IS FEELING THAT DAY.
打倒
*Calligraphy: Defeat
DAILY ROUTINE, PART 3.
SIP
A MORNING CUP OF TEA.
I KNOW WHAT I OUGHT TO DO FOR PRACTICE TODAY.
IT'S NICE OUT...
CLAK

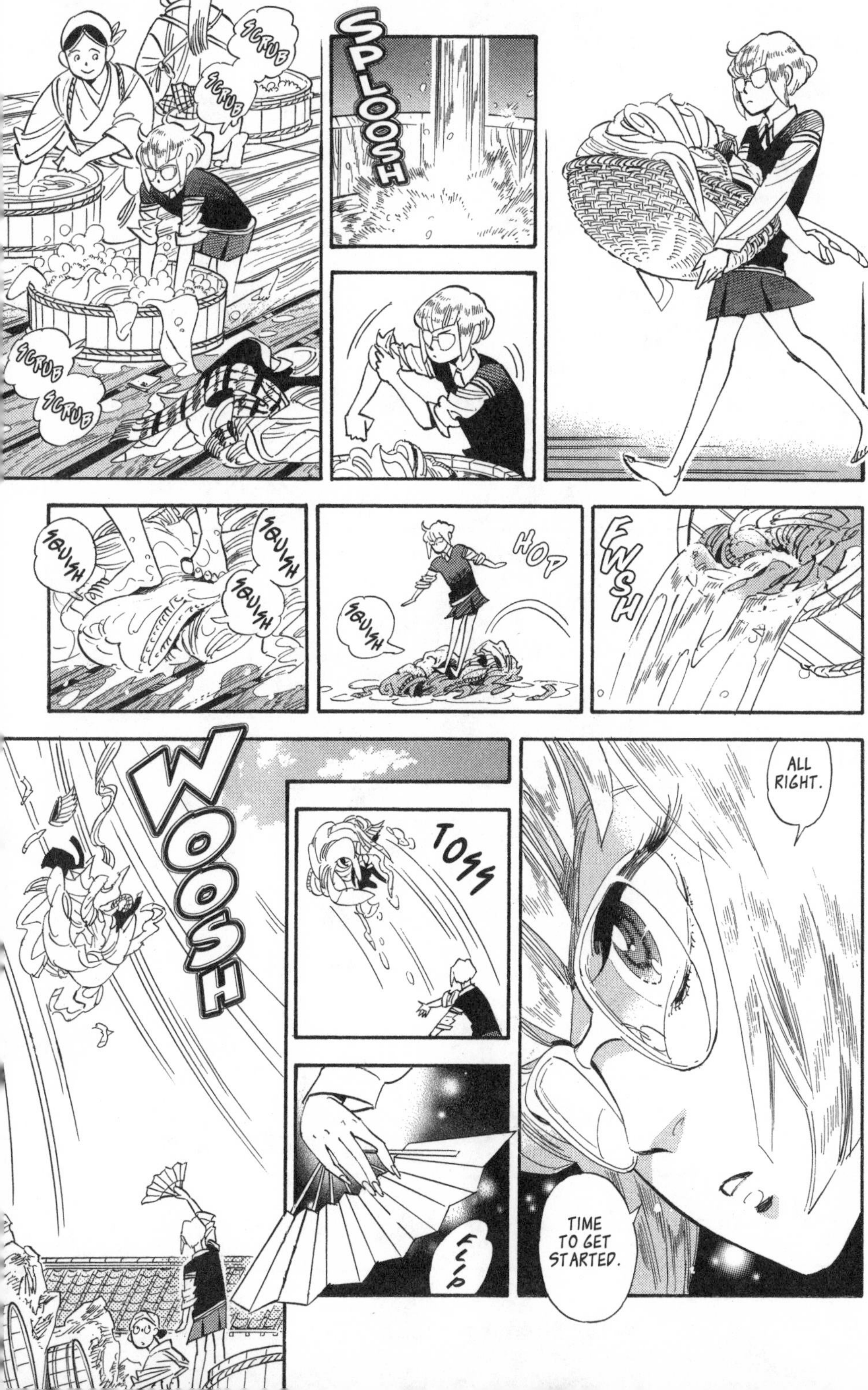

SPLOOSH
SCRUB
SCRUB
SCRUB
SCRUB
FWSH
HOP
SQUISH
SQUISH
SQUISH
SQUISH
ALL RIGHT.
TIME TO GET STARTED.
TOSS
FLIP
WOOSH

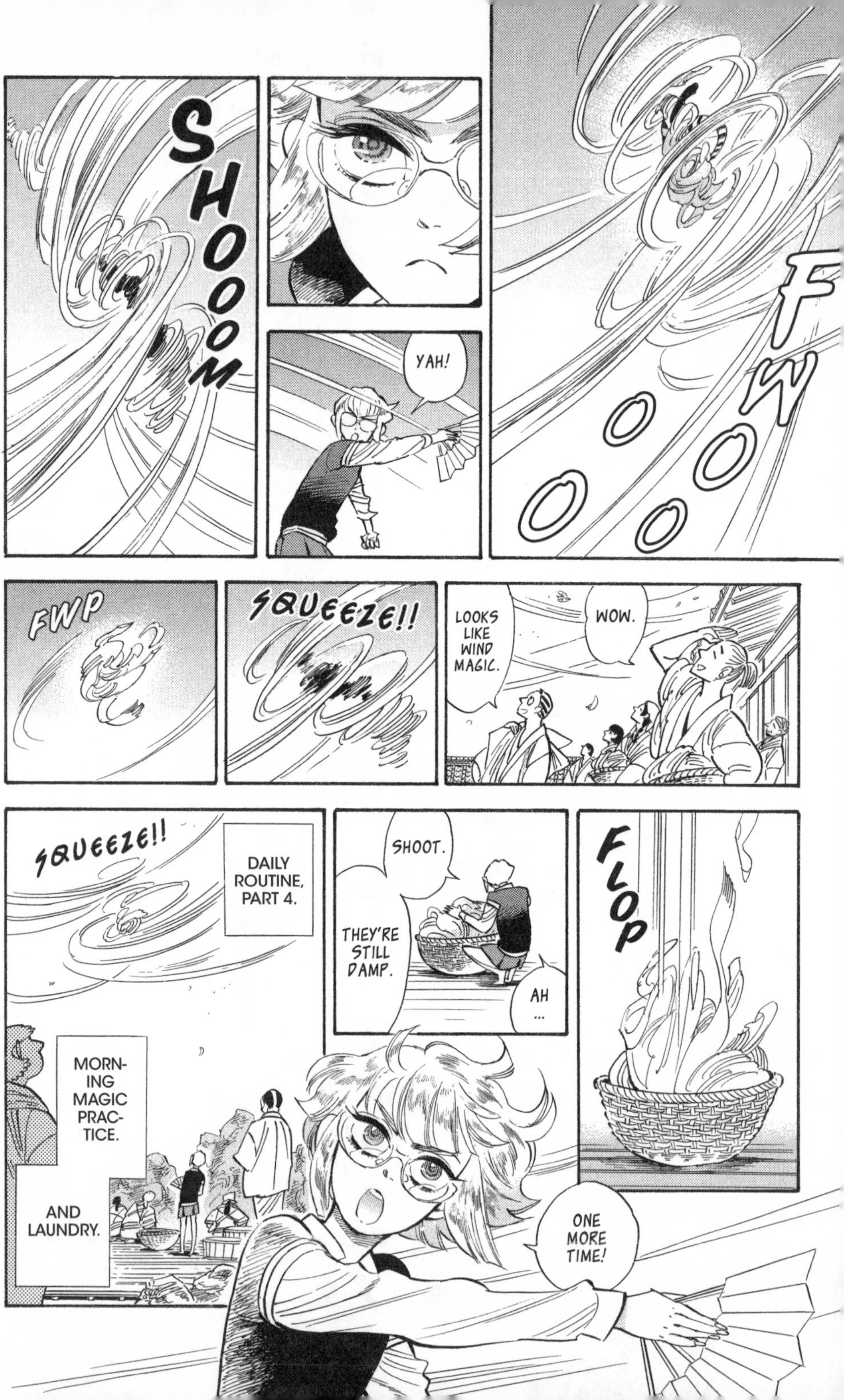
FWOOOOO
YAH!
SHOOOOM
WOW.
LOOKS LIKE WIND MAGIC.
SQUEEZE!!
FWP
FLOP
SHOOT.
THEY'RE STILL DAMP.
AH ...
SQUEEZE!!
DAILY ROUTINE, PART 4.
ONE MORE TIME!
MORNING MAGIC PRACTICE.
AND LAUNDRY.

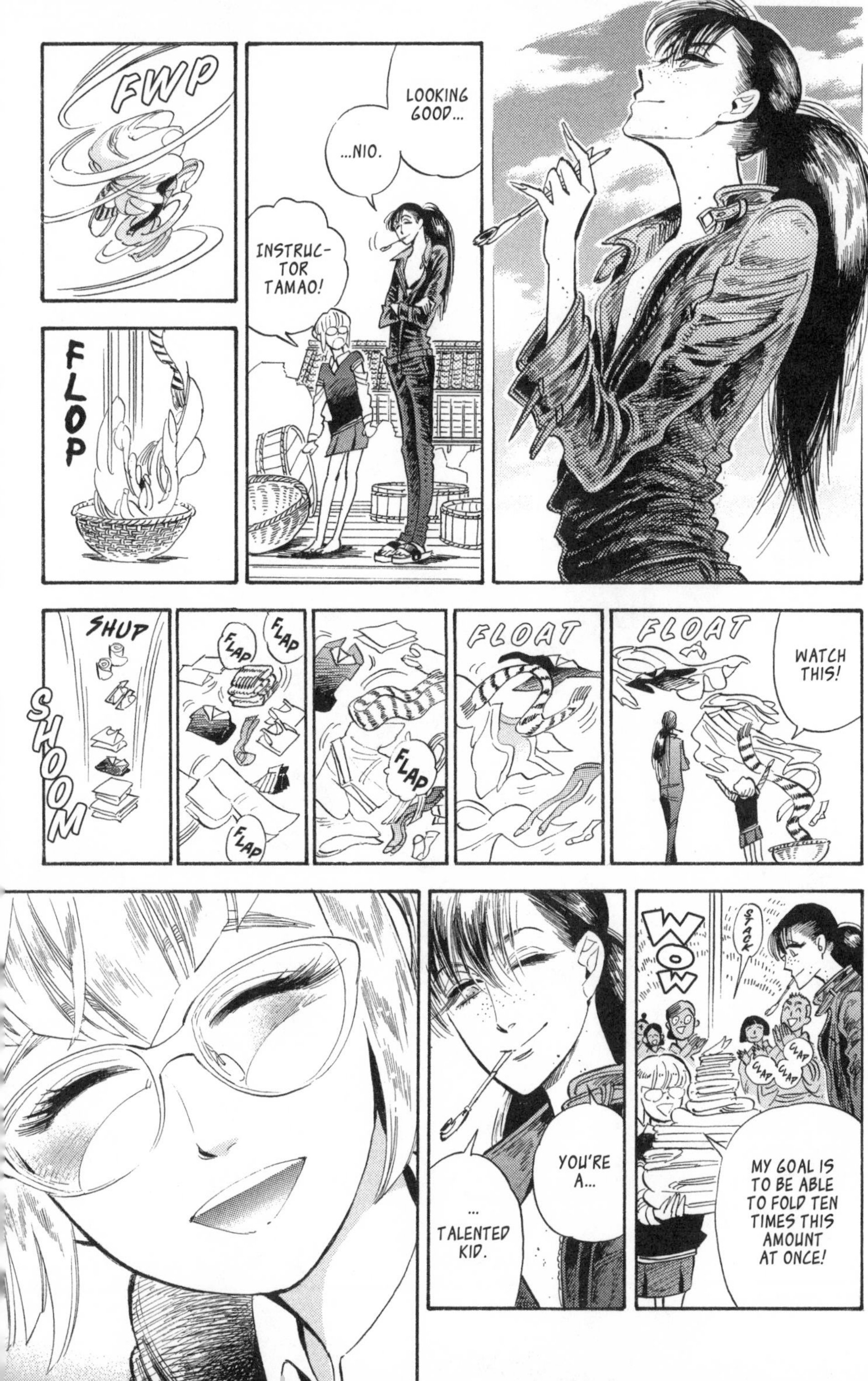
LOOKING GOOD...
...NIO.
INSTRUCTOR TAMAO!
FWP
FLOP
FLOAT
WATCH THIS!
FLOAT
FLAP
FLAP
FLAP
FLAP
SHUP
SHOOM
WOW
STACK
CLAP
CLAP
CLAP
CLAP
MY GOAL IS TO BE ABLE TO FOLD TEN TIMES THIS AMOUNT AT ONCE!
YOU'RE A...
... TALENTED KID.

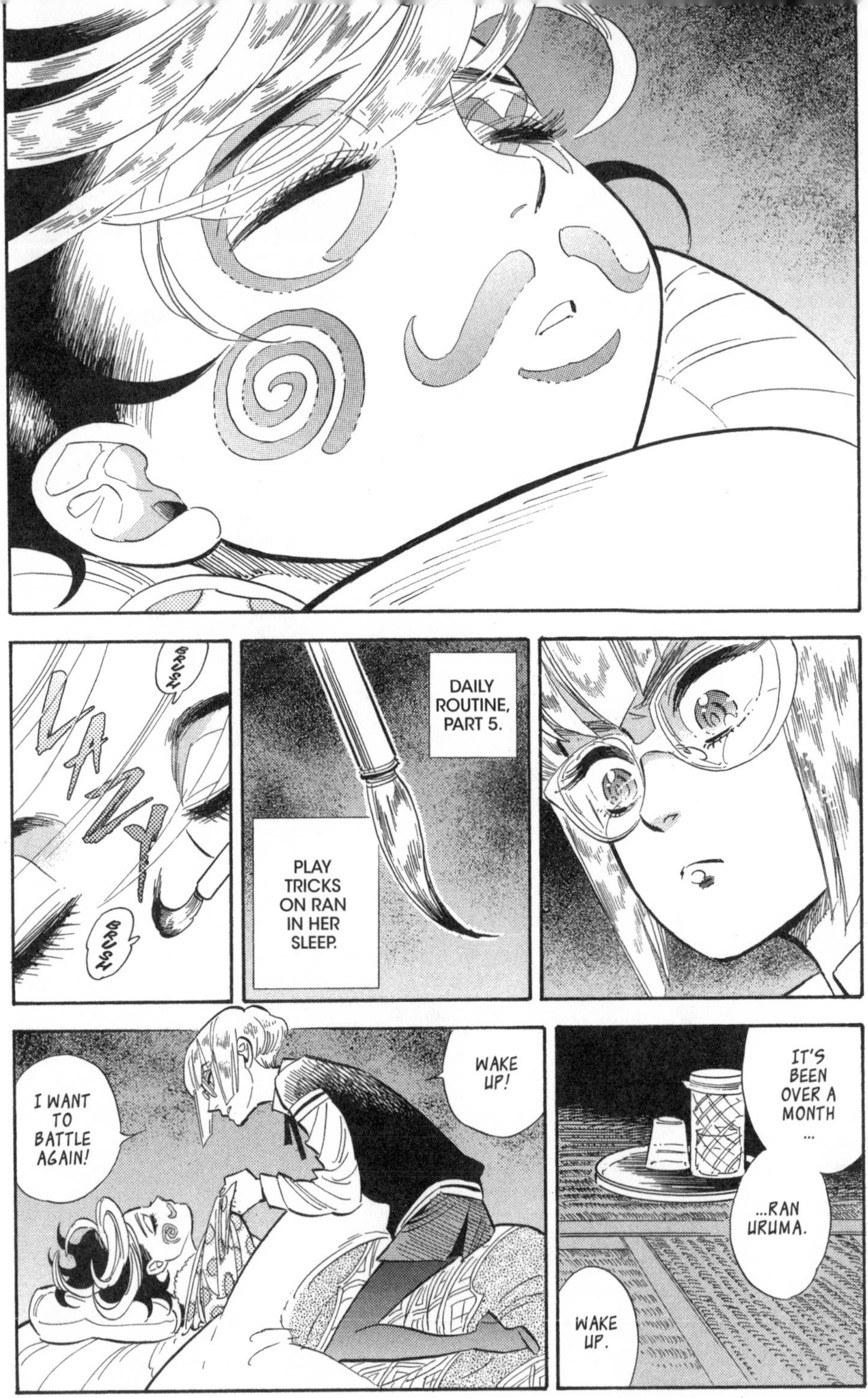
DAILY ROUTINE, PART 5.
PLAY TRICKS ON RAN IN HER SLEEP.
BRUSH
LAZY
BRUSH
IT'S BEEN OVER A MONTH ...
...RAN URUMA.
WAKE UP.
WAKE UP!
I WANT TO BATTLE AGAIN!

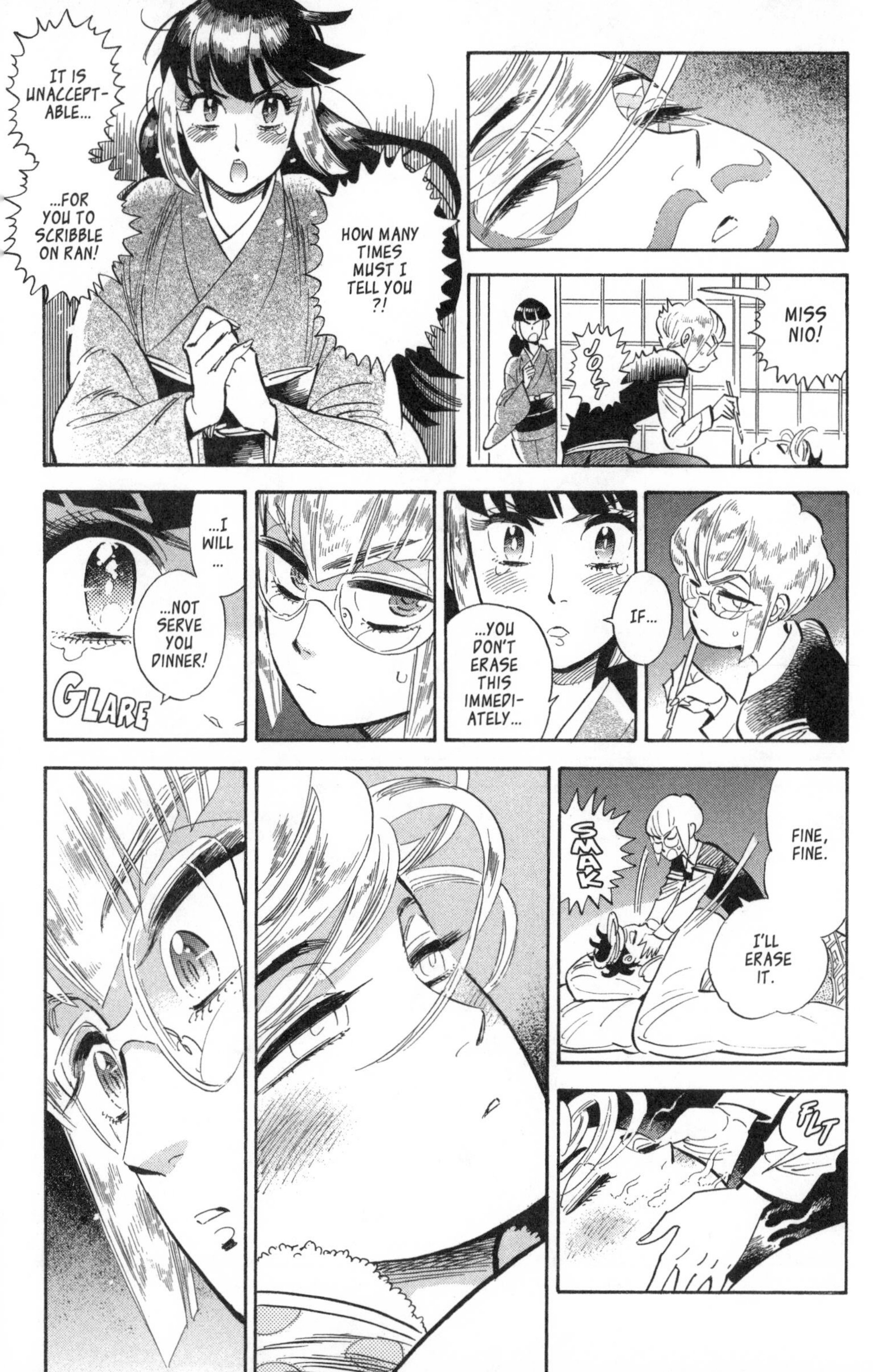
MISS NIO!
JOLT
HOW MANY TIMES MUST I TELL YOU ?!
IT IS UNACCEPTABLE...
...FOR YOU TO SCRIBBLE ON RAN!
IF...
...YOU DON'T ERASE THIS IMMEDIATELY...
...I WILL ...
...NOT SERVE YOU DINNER!
GLARE
FINE, FINE.
I'LL ERASE IT.
SMAK
FLT

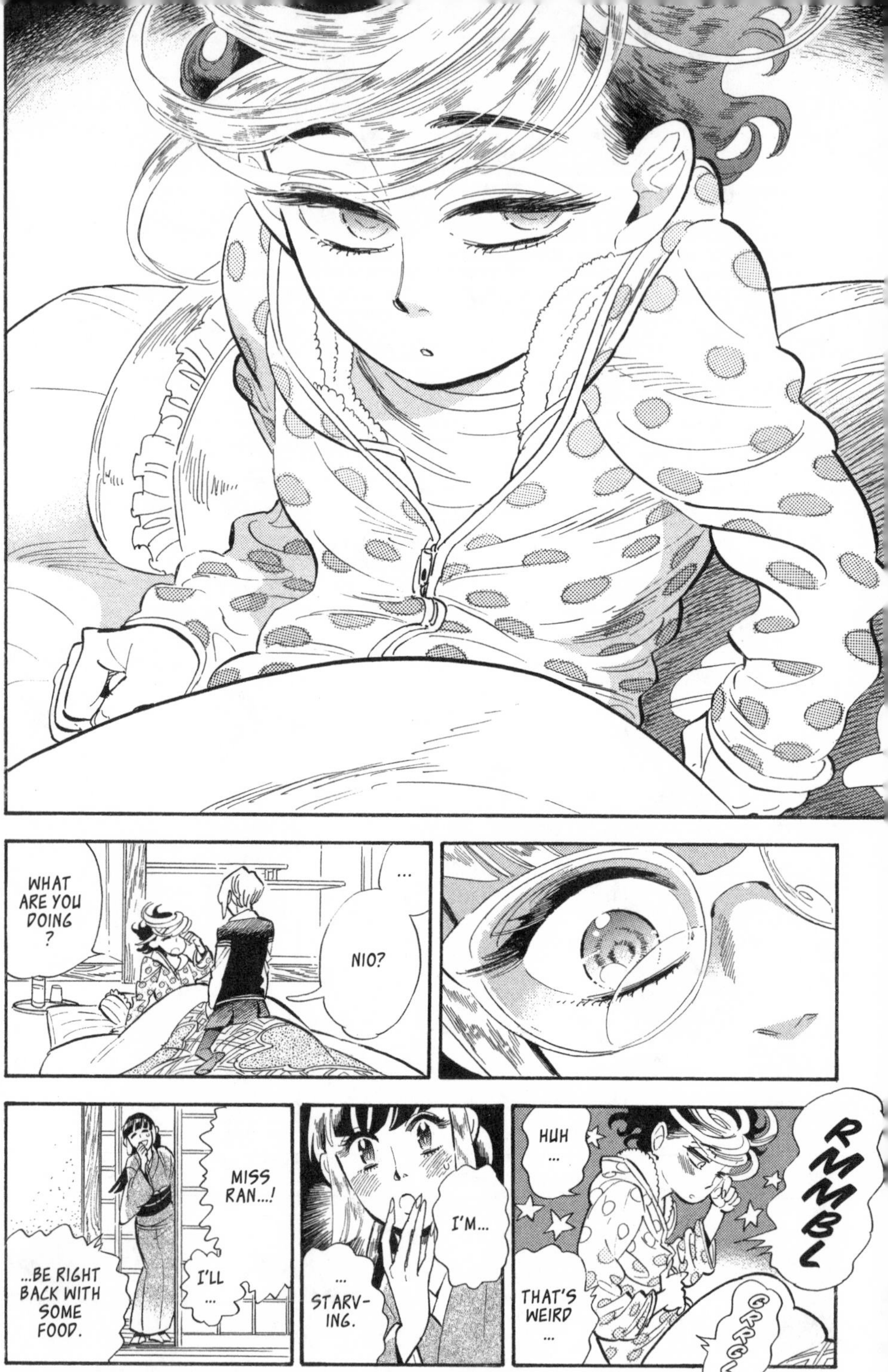
... NIO?
WHAT ARE YOU DOING?
RMMBL
HUH ...
THAT'S WEIRD ...
GRRGL
I'M...
... STARV-ING.
MISS RAN...!
I'LL ...
...BE RIGHT BACK WITH SOME FOOD.

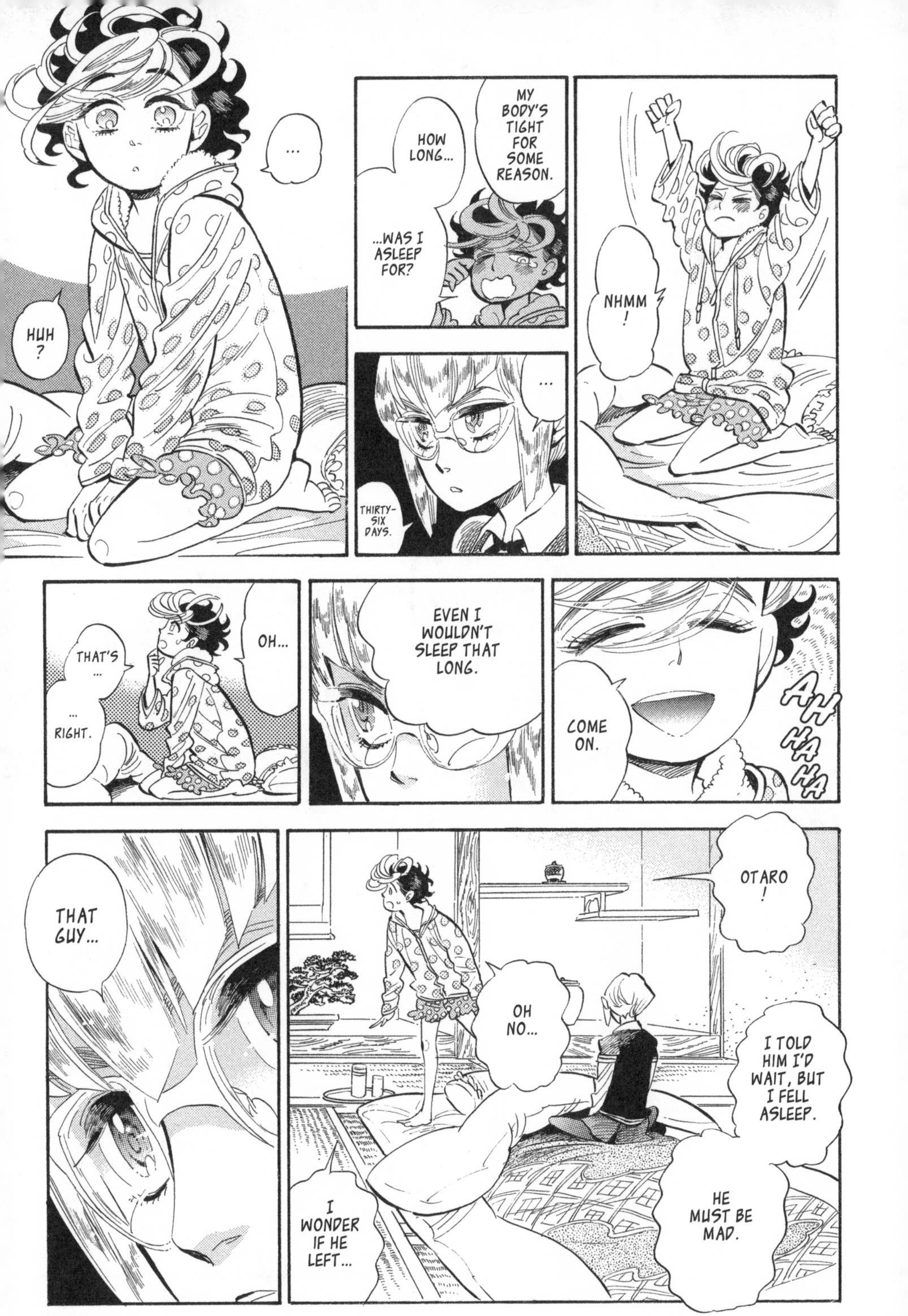

NHMM!
MY BODY'S TIGHT FOR SOME REASON.
HOW LONG...
...WAS I ASLEEP FOR?
...
THIRTY-SIX DAYS.
...
HUH?
AH HA HA HA
COME ON.
EVEN I WOULDN'T SLEEP THAT LONG.
OH...
THAT'S...
...RIGHT.
OTARO!
I TOLD HIM I'D WAIT, BUT I FELL ASLEEP.
OH NO...
HE MUST BE MAD.
I WONDER IF HE LEFT...
THAT GUY...

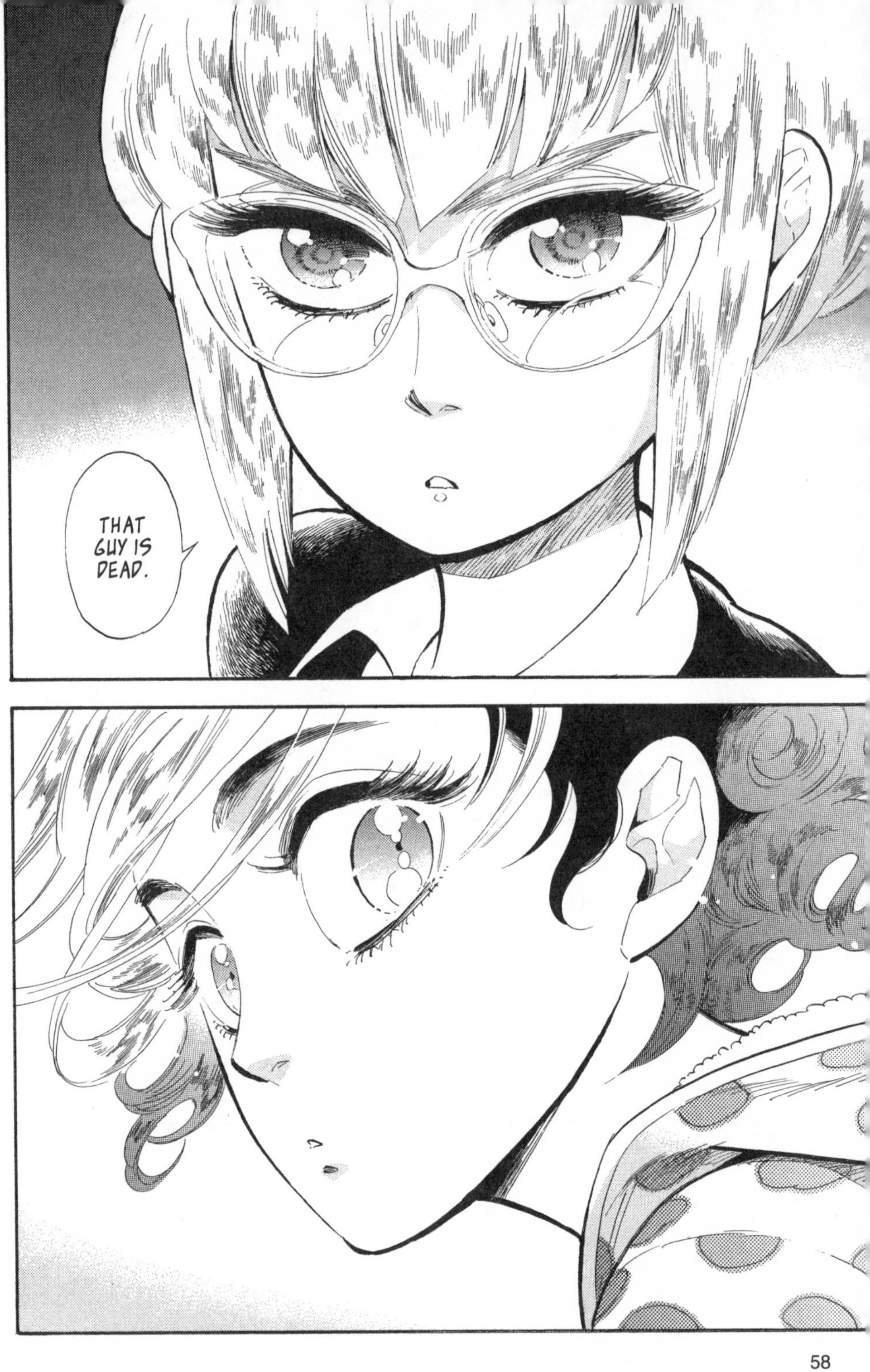
THAT GUY IS DEAD.

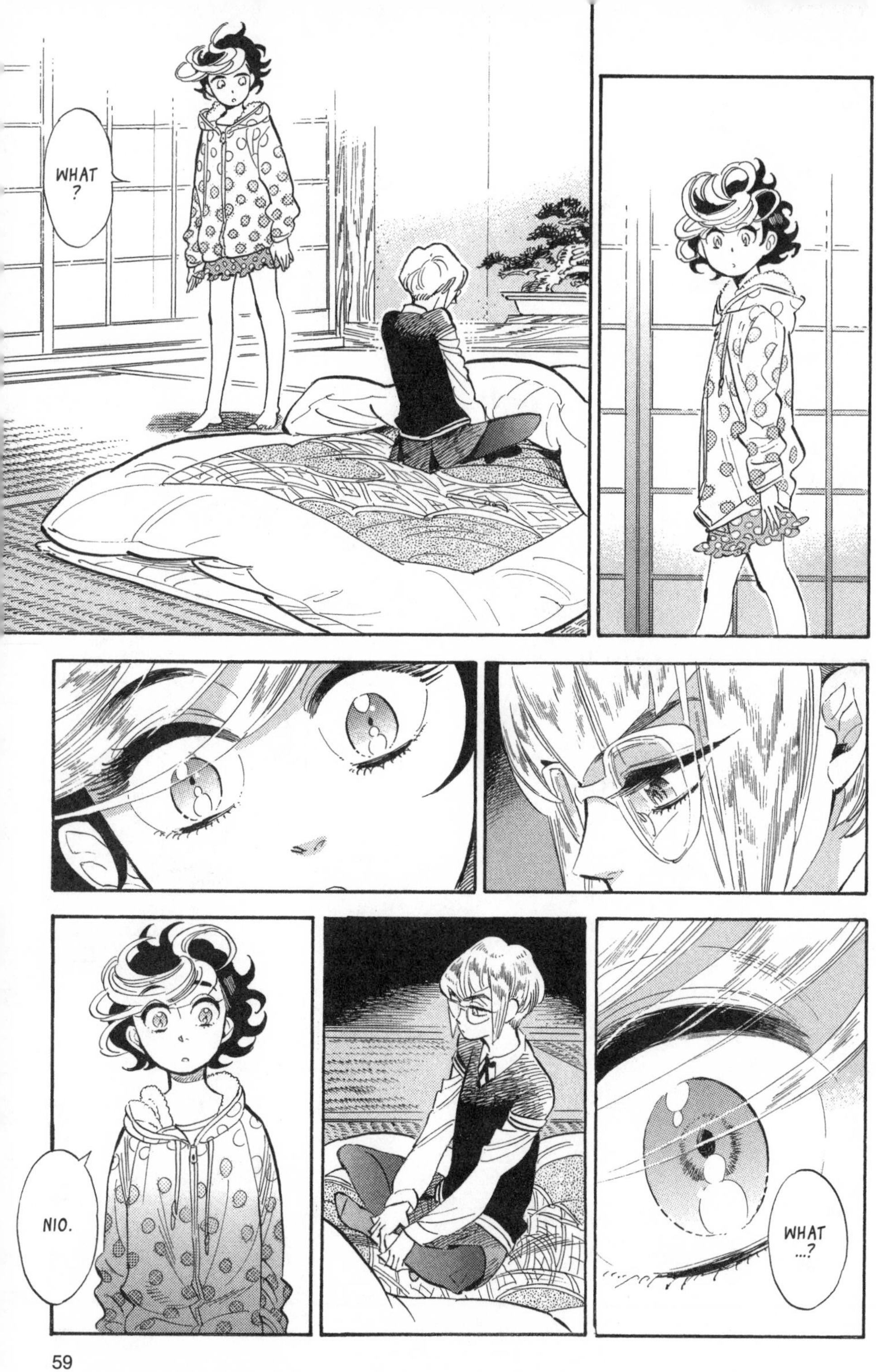
WHAT ?
WHAT ...?
NIO.

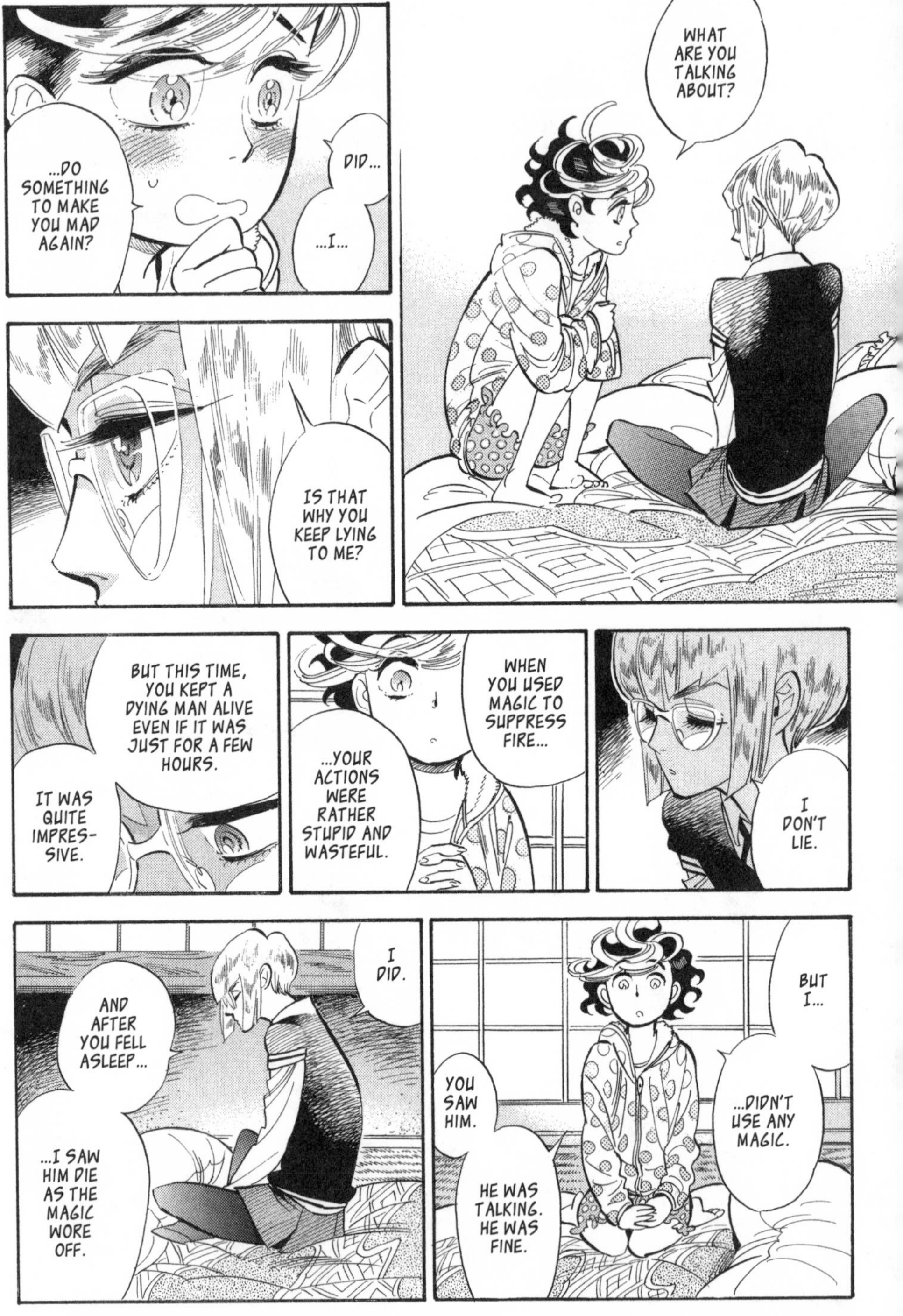
WHAT ARE YOU TALKING ABOUT?
DID... ...I...
...DO SOMETHING TO MAKE YOU MAD AGAIN?
IS THAT WHY YOU KEEP LYING TO ME?
I DON'T LIE.
WHEN YOU USED MAGIC TO SUPPRESS FIRE...
...YOUR ACTIONS WERE RATHER STUPID AND WASTEFUL.
BUT THIS TIME, YOU KEPT A DYING MAN ALIVE EVEN IF IT WAS JUST FOR A FEW HOURS.
IT WAS QUITE IMPRESSIVE.
BUT I...
...DIDN'T USE ANY MAGIC.
YOU SAW HIM.
HE WAS TALKING. HE WAS FINE.
I DID.
AND AFTER YOU FELL ASLEEP...
...I SAW HIM DIE AS THE MAGIC WORE OFF.

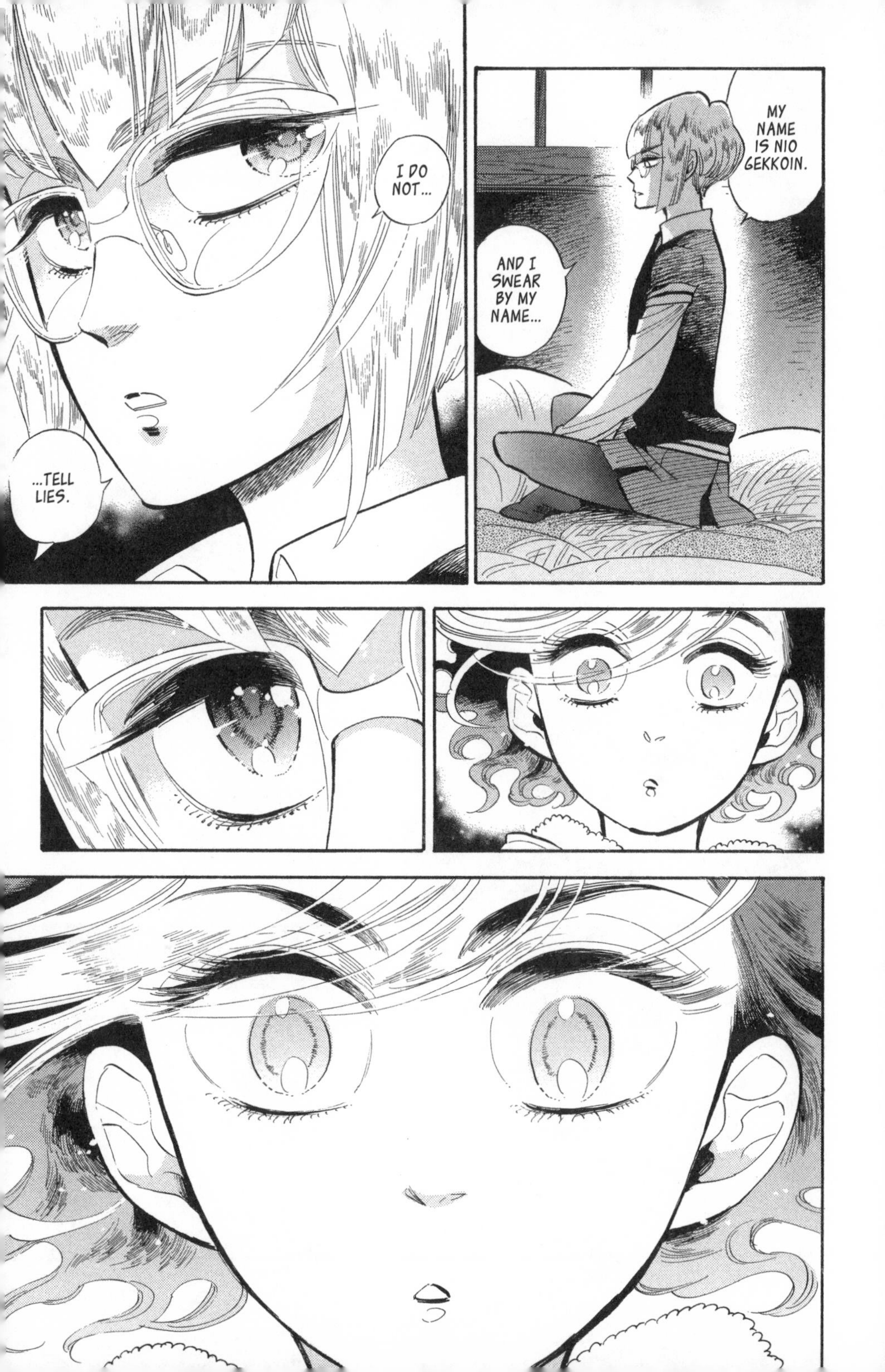
MY NAME IS NIO GEKKOIN.
AND I SWEAR BY MY NAME...
I DO NOT...
...TELL LIES.

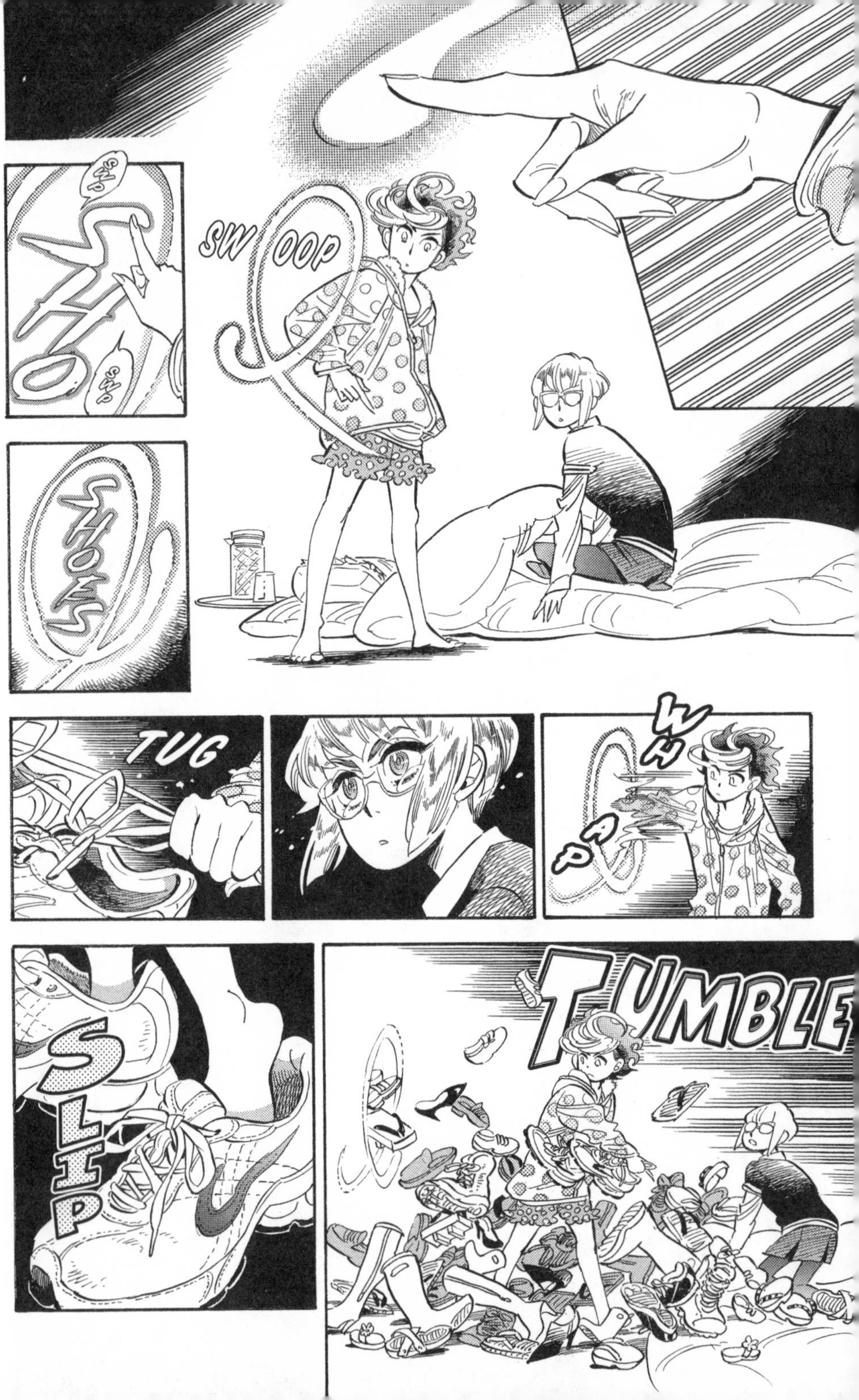
SW OOP
SNIP
SHO
snip
SHOES
WHAP
TUG
TUMBLE
SLIP

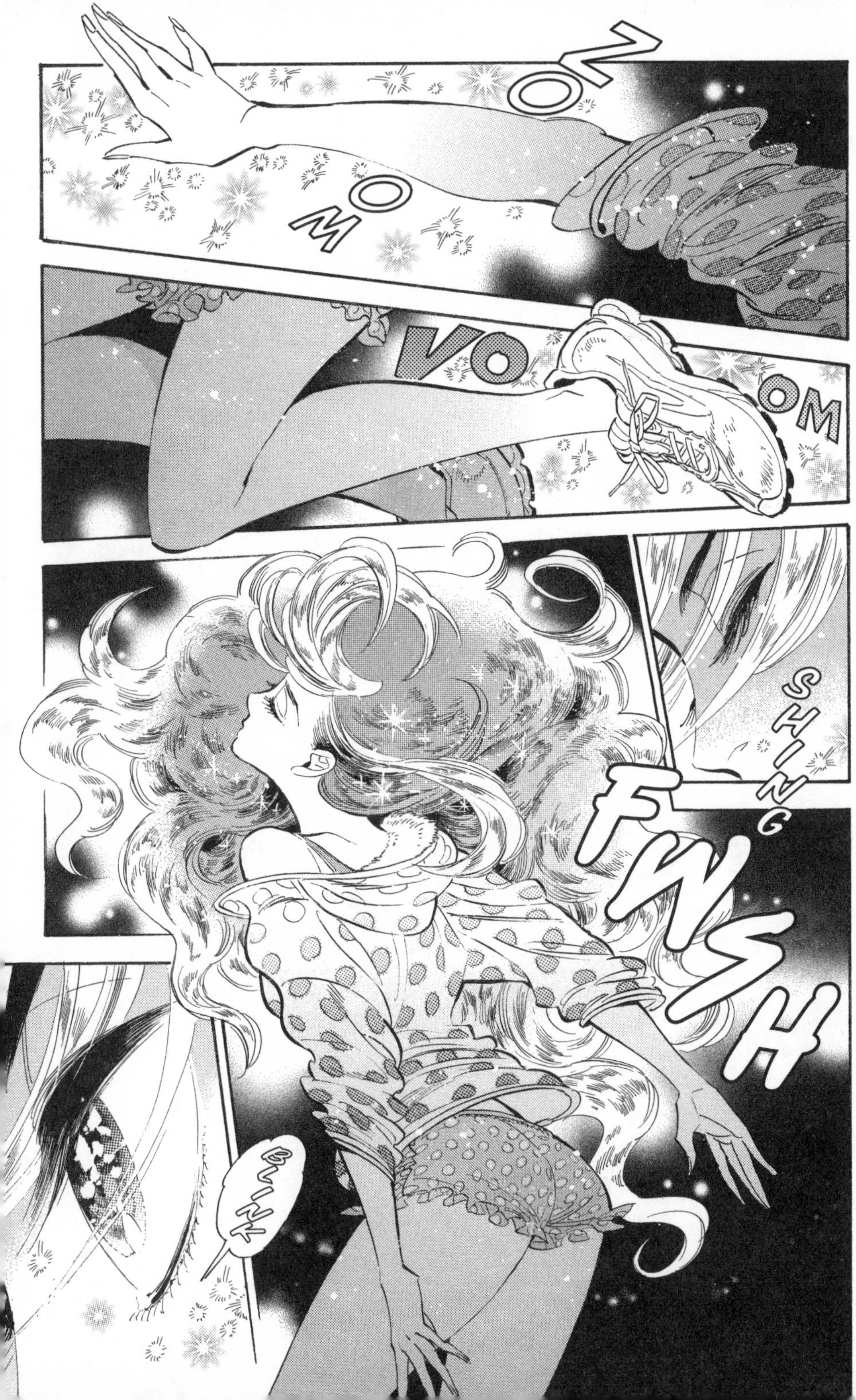
ZOOM
VO
OM
SHING
FWSH
BLINK

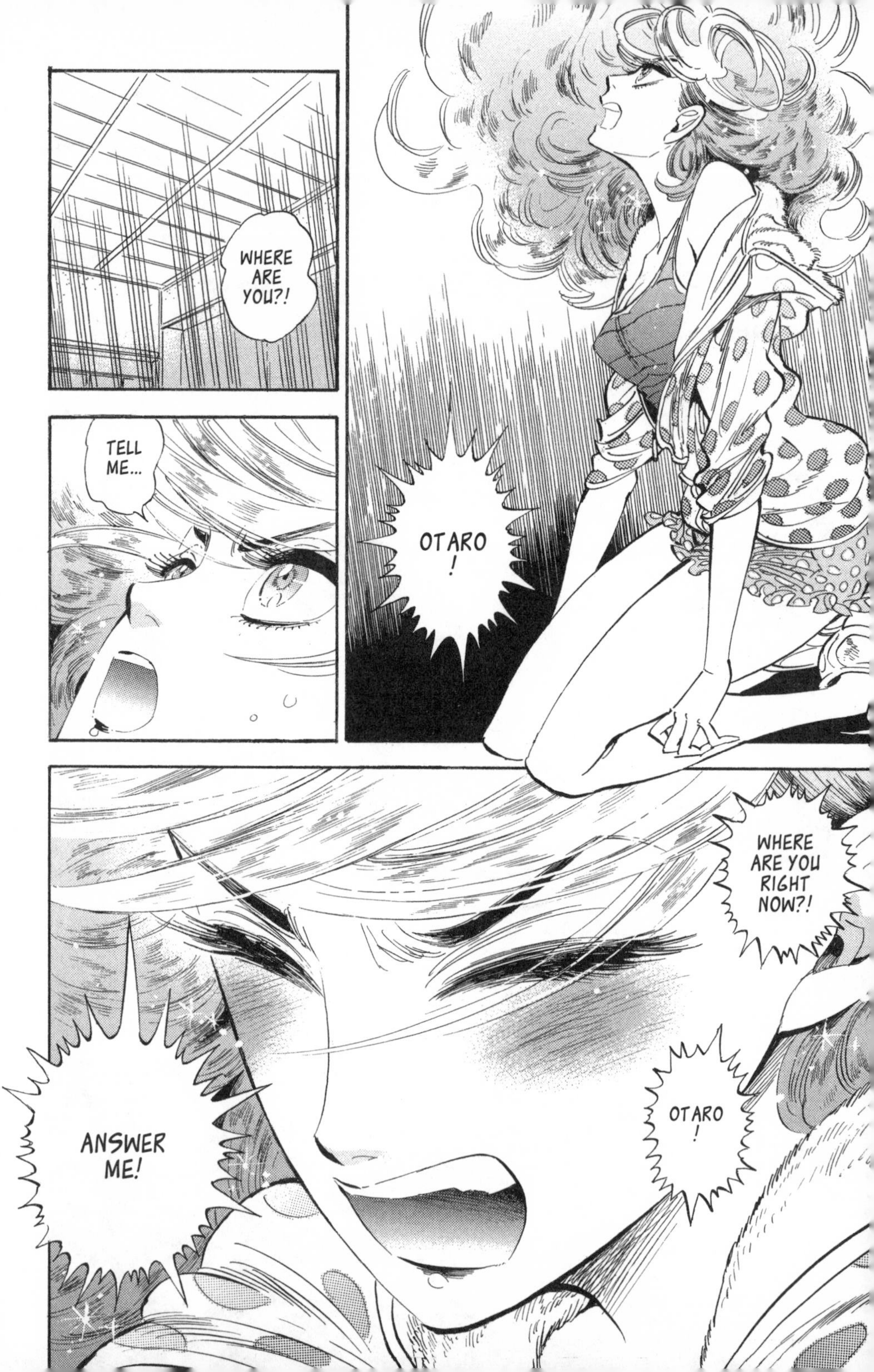
OTARO!
WHERE ARE YOU?!
TELL ME...
WHERE ARE YOU RIGHT NOW?!
OTARO!
ANSWER ME!

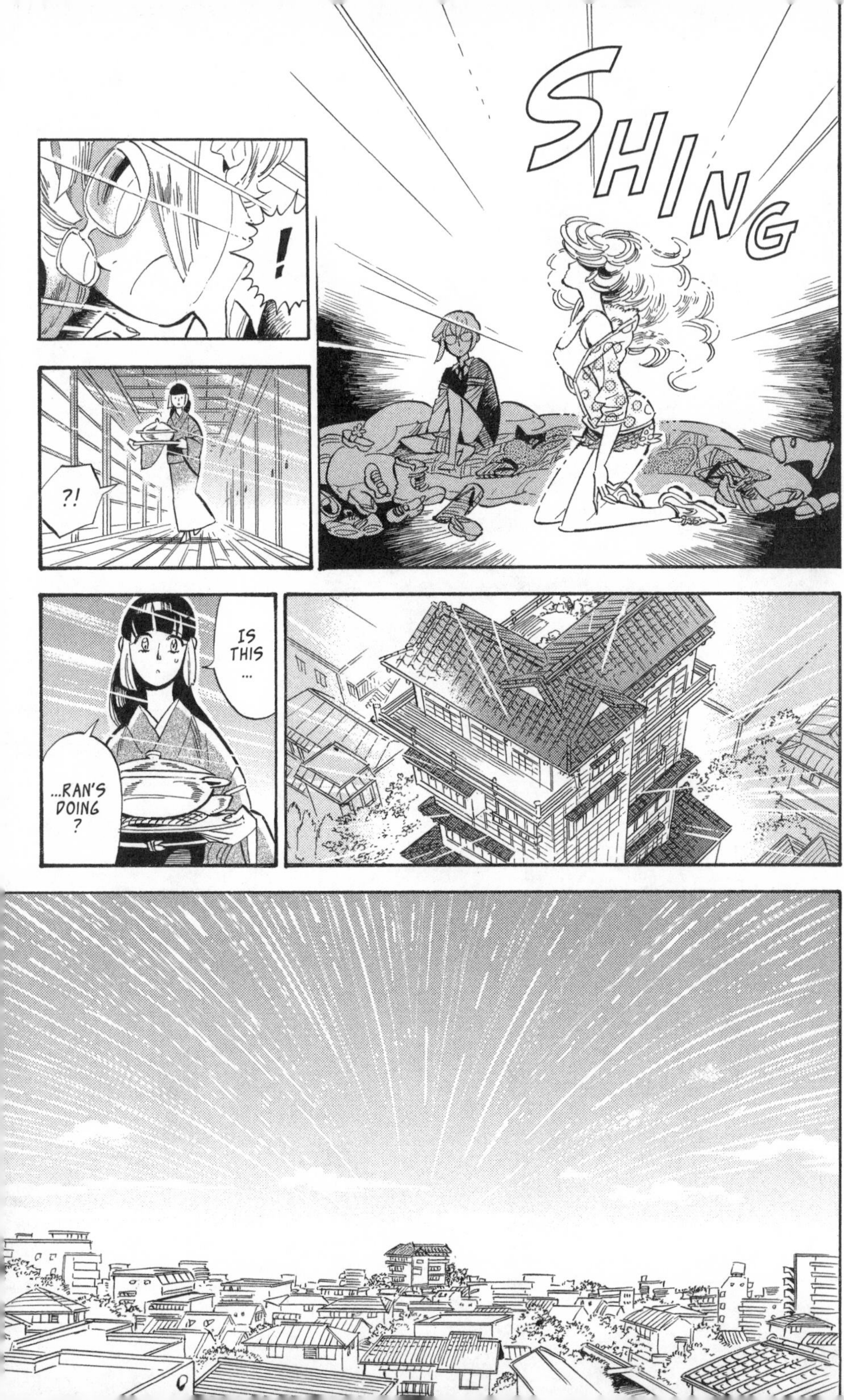
SHING
!
?!
IS THIS ...
...RAN'S DOING ?

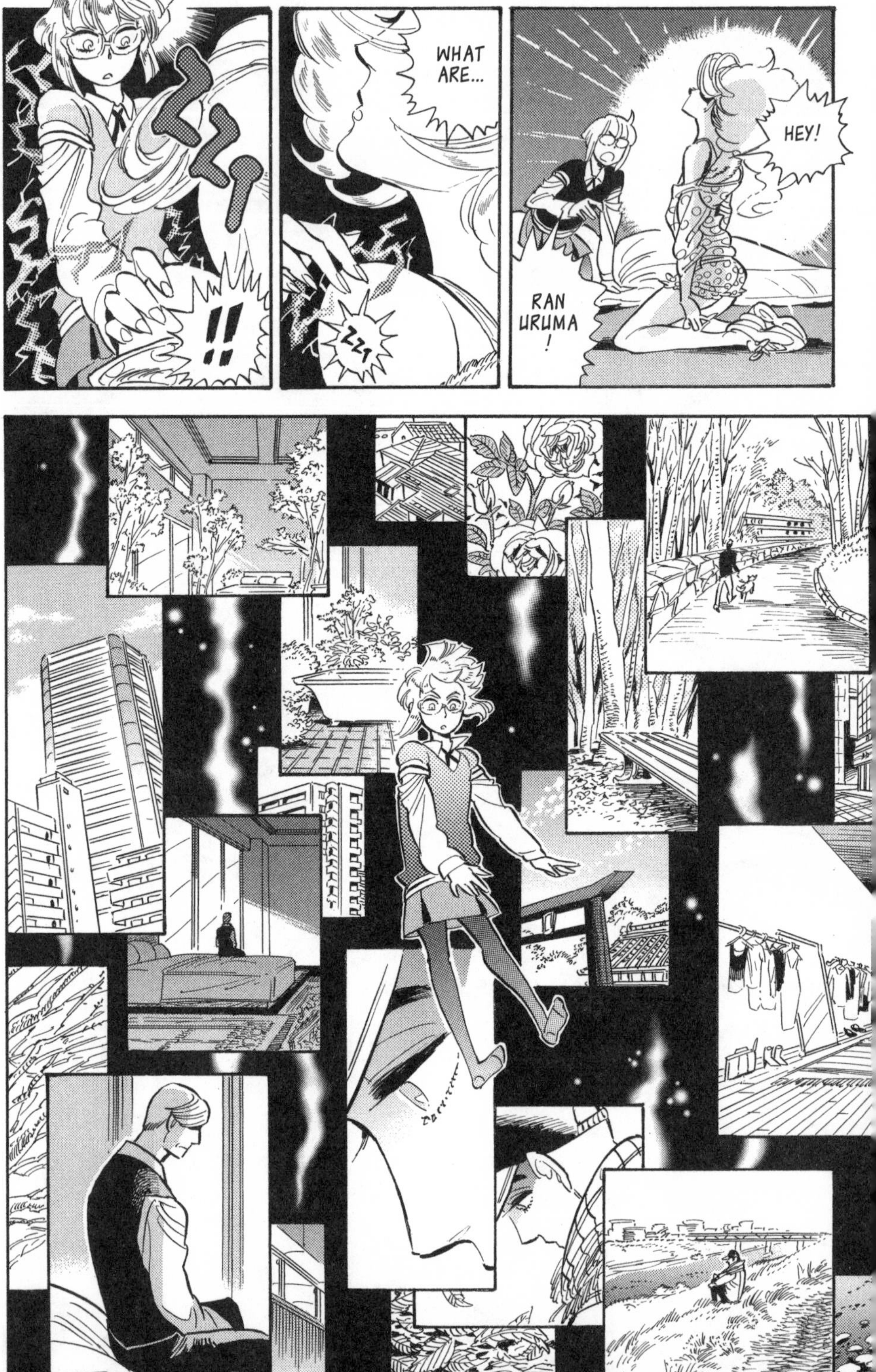
HEY!
RAN URUMA!
WHAT ARE...
ZZZ
!!

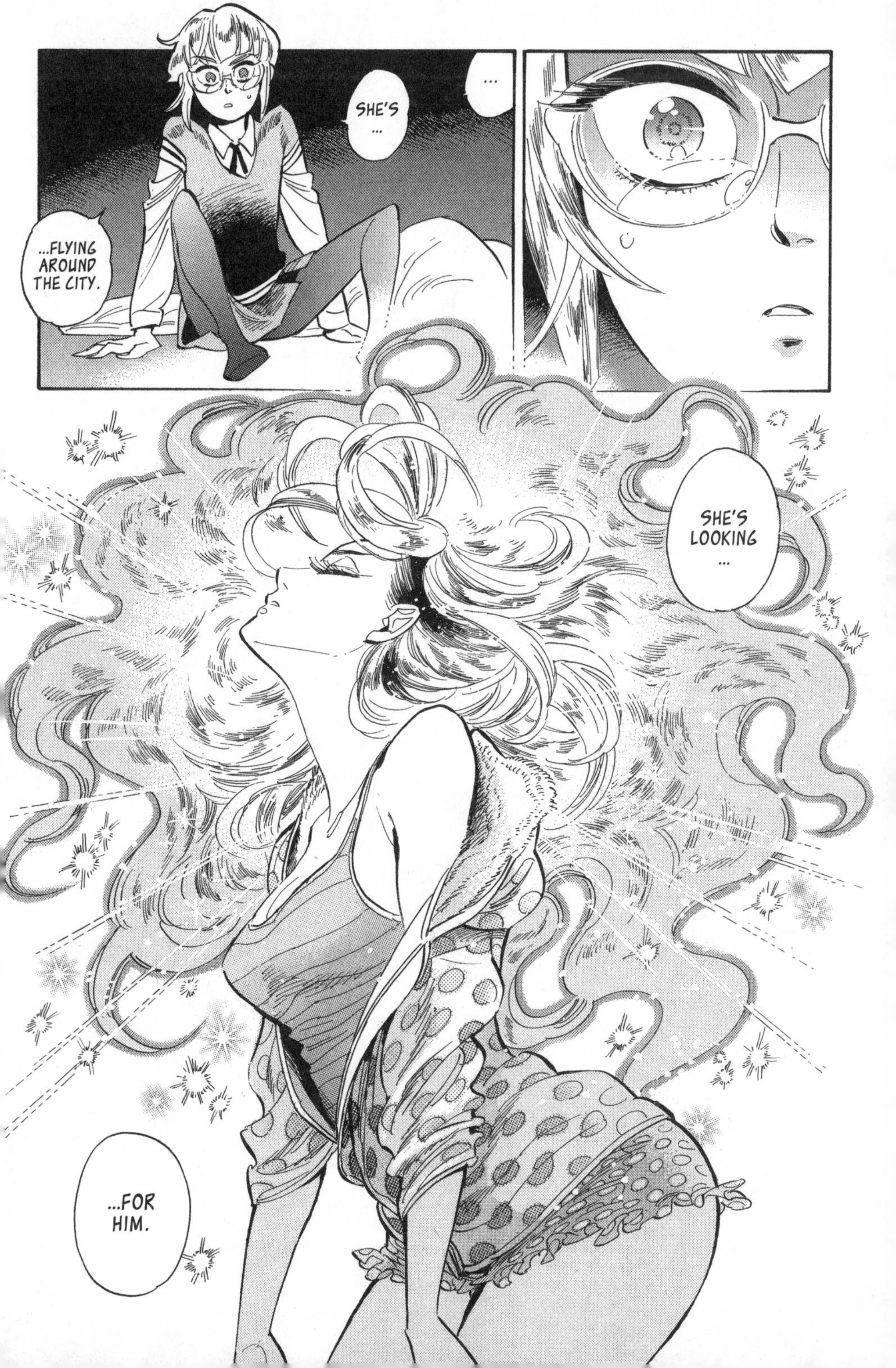
...
SHE'S ...
...FLYING AROUND THE CITY.
SHE'S LOOKING ...
...FOR HIM.

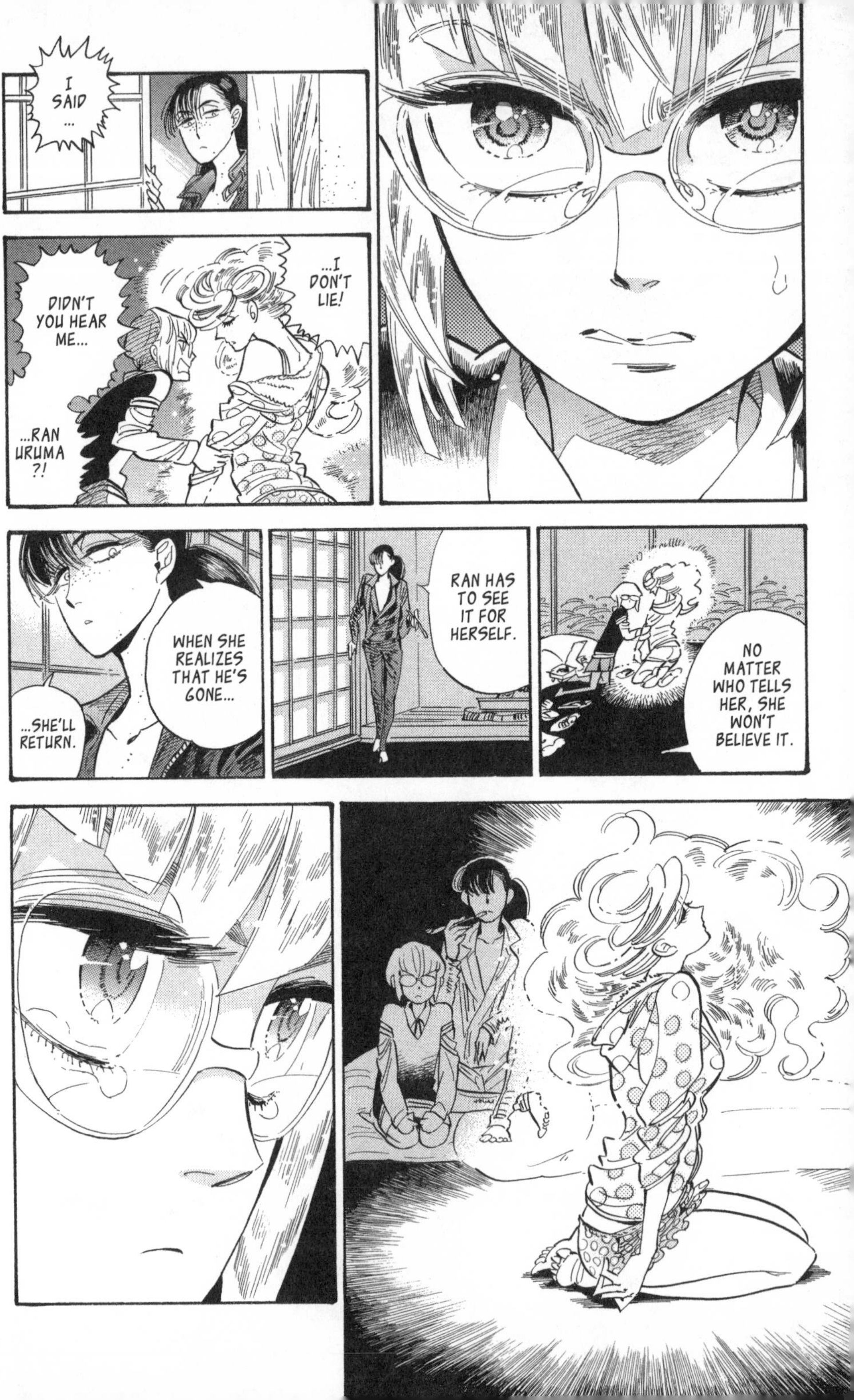
I SAID ...
...I DON'T LIE!
DIDN'T YOU HEAR ME...
...RAN URUMA ?!
NO MATTER WHO TELLS HER, SHE WON'T BELIEVE IT.
RAN HAS TO SEE IT FOR HERSELF.
WHEN SHE REALIZES THAT HE'S GONE...
...SHE'LL RETURN.

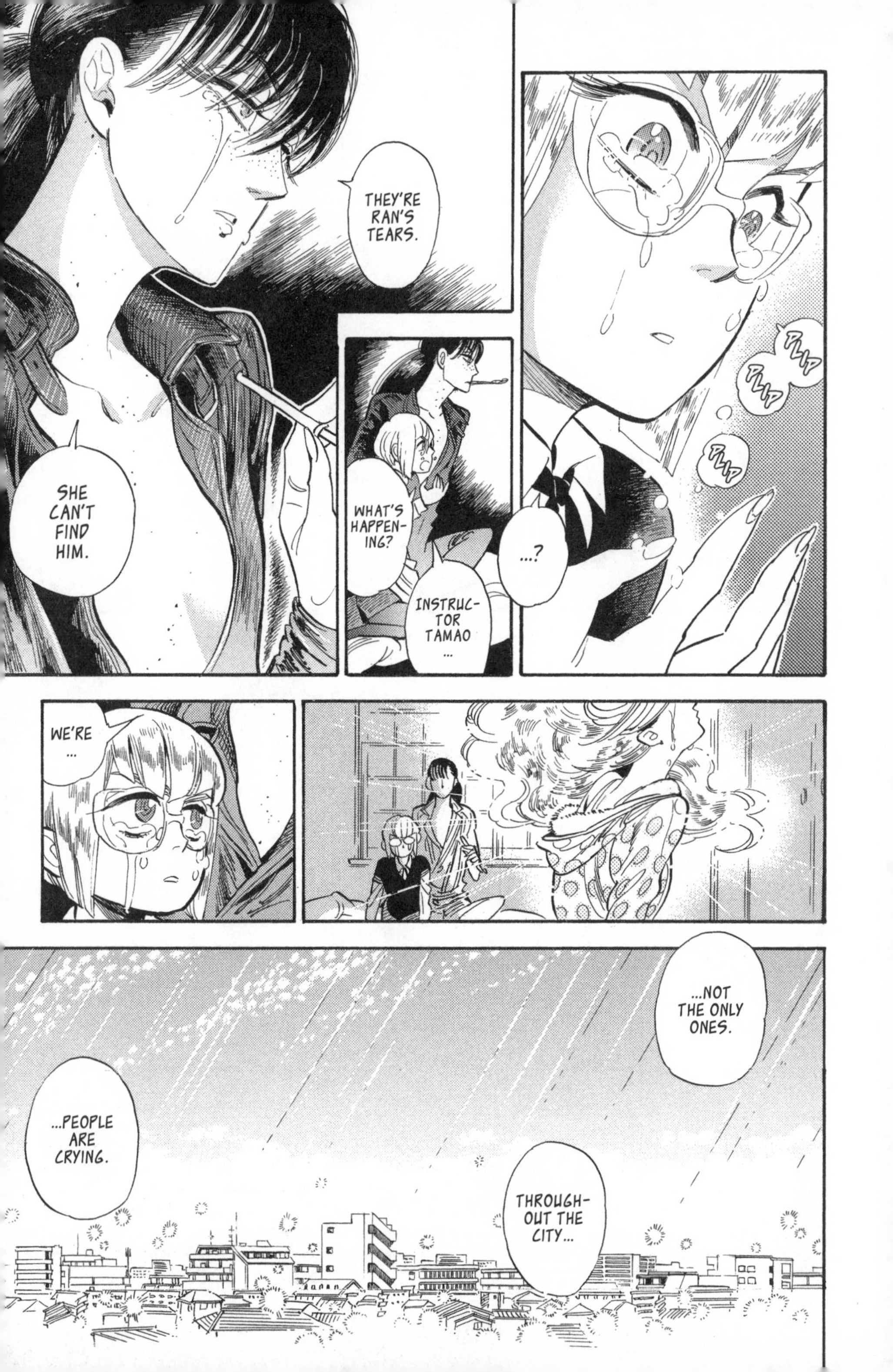
PLIP
PLIP
PLIP
...?
INSTRUCTOR TAMAO ...
WHAT'S HAPPENING?
THEY'RE RAN'S TEARS.
SHE CAN'T FIND HIM.
WE'RE ...
...NOT THE ONLY ONES.
THROUGH-OUT THE CITY...
...PEOPLE ARE CRYING.

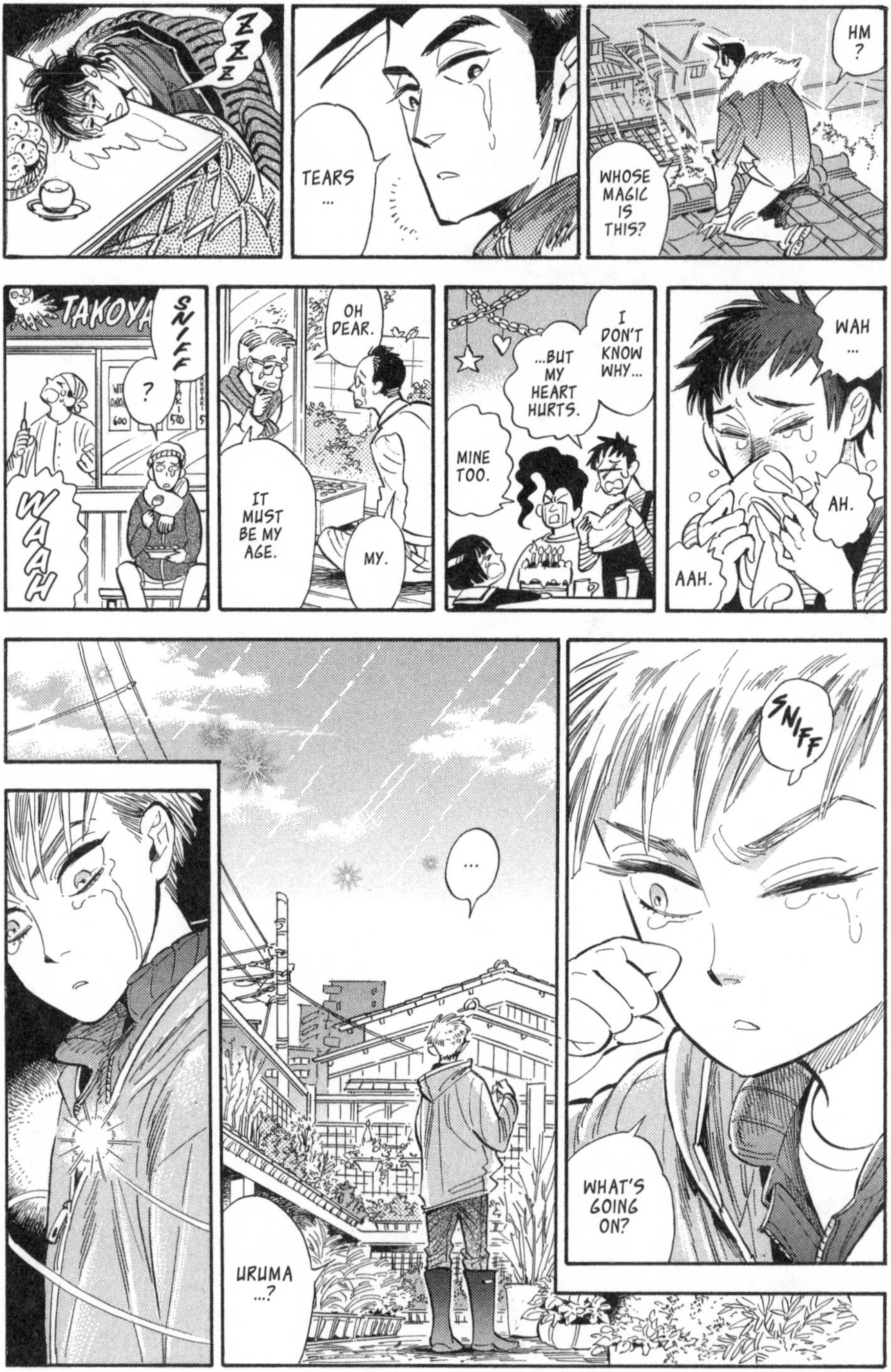
HM?
WHOSE MAGIC IS THIS?
TEARS...
ZZZ
WAH...
AH.
AAH.
I DON'T KNOW WHY...
...BUT MY HEART HURTS.
MINE TOO.
OH DEAR.
IT MUST BE MY AGE.
MY.
TAKOYA
SNIFF
?
WAAH
SNIFF
WHAT'S GOING ON?
...
URUMA...?

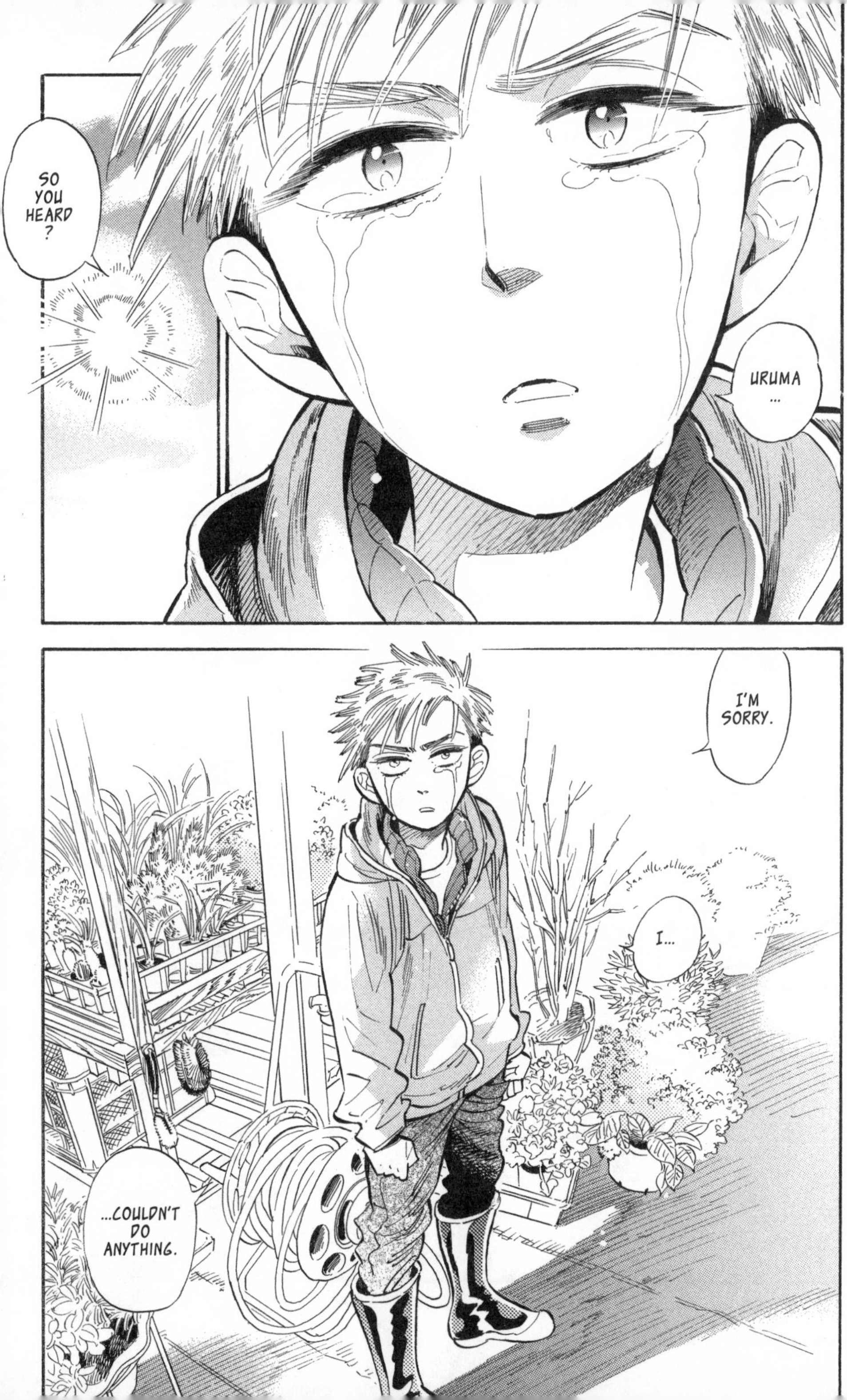
URUMA ...
SO YOU HEARD ?
I'M SORRY.
I...
...COULDN'T DO ANYTHING.

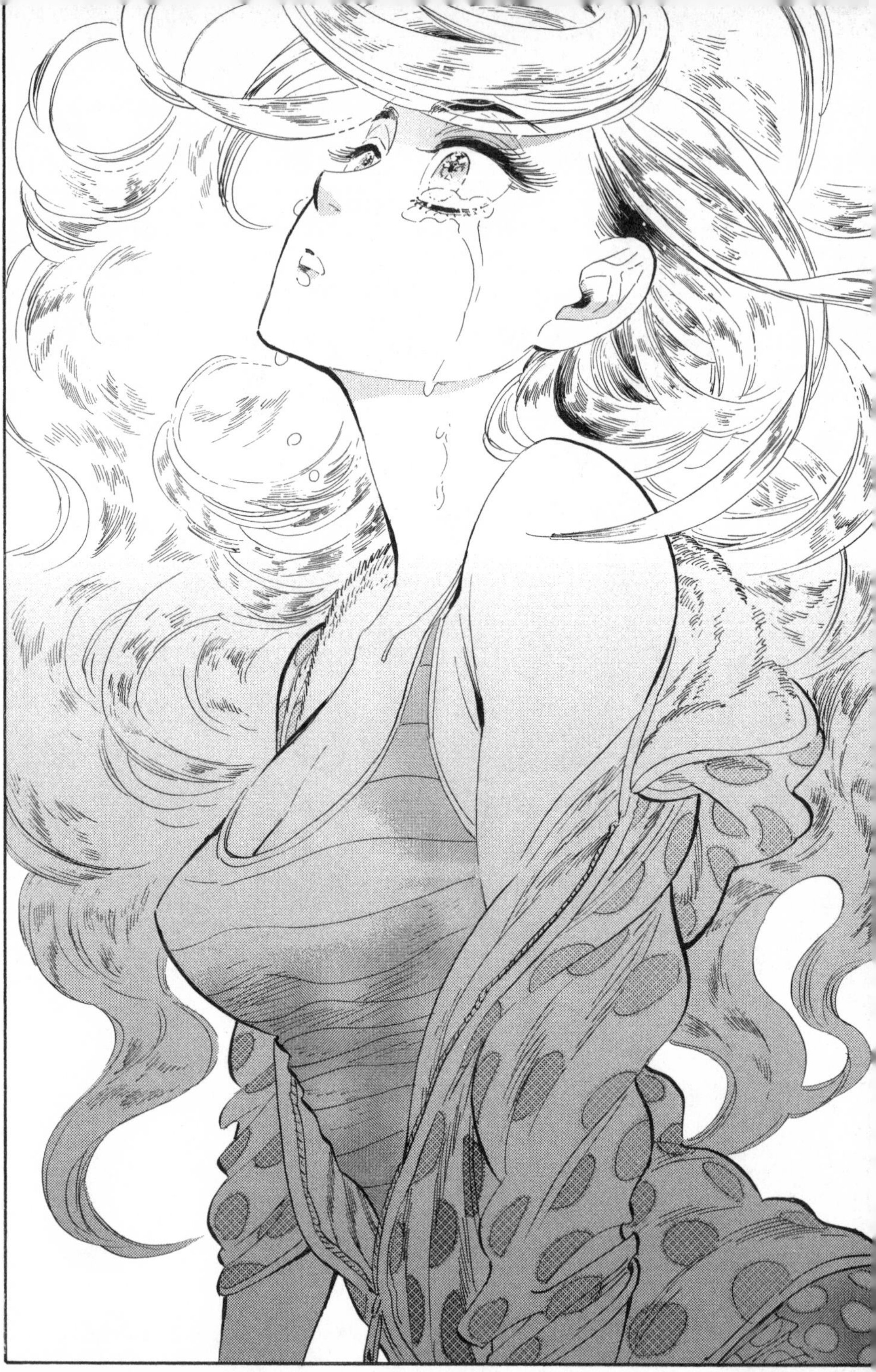

Chapter 38 / The End

Chapter 39
Torn to Pieces

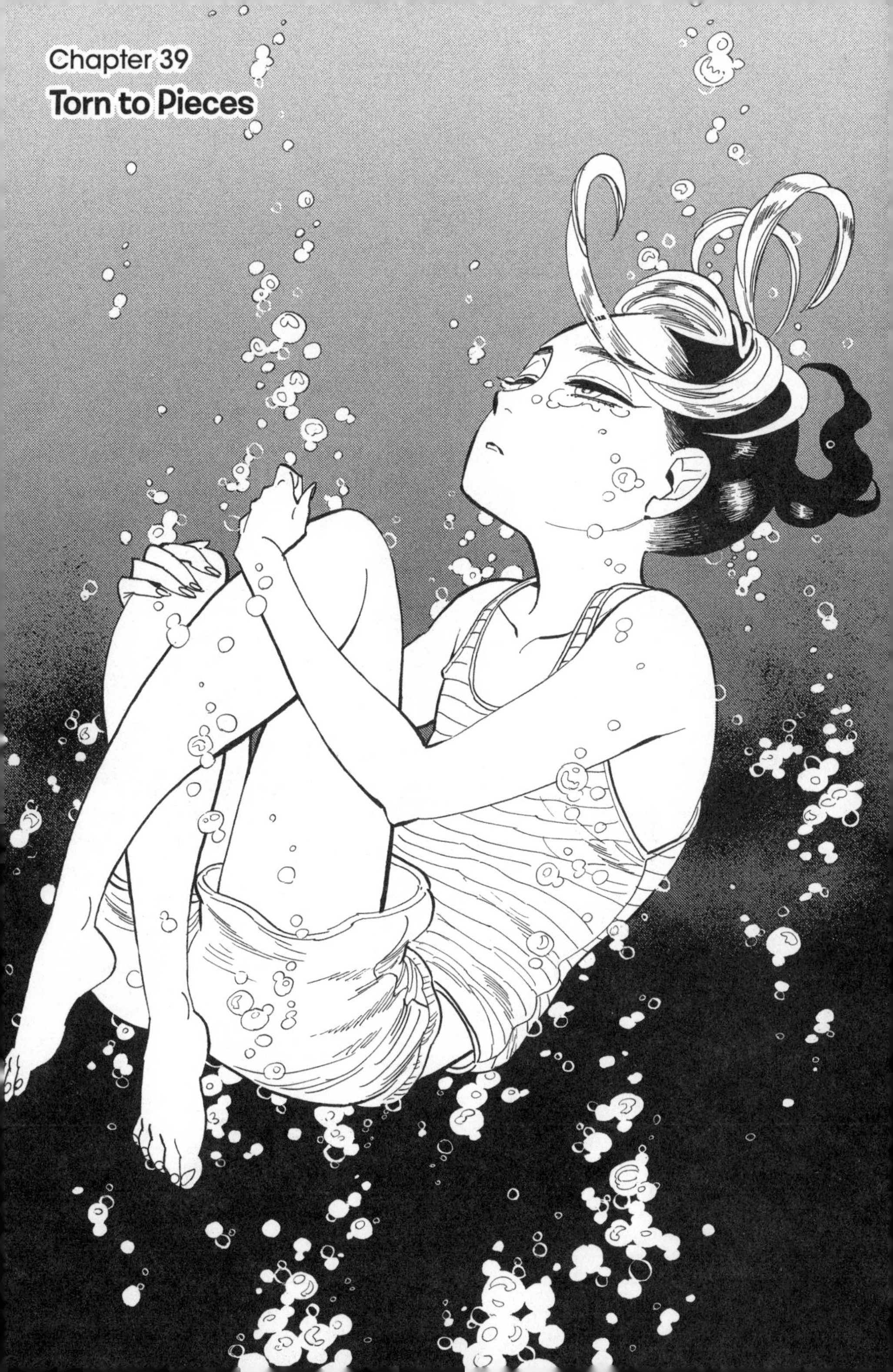

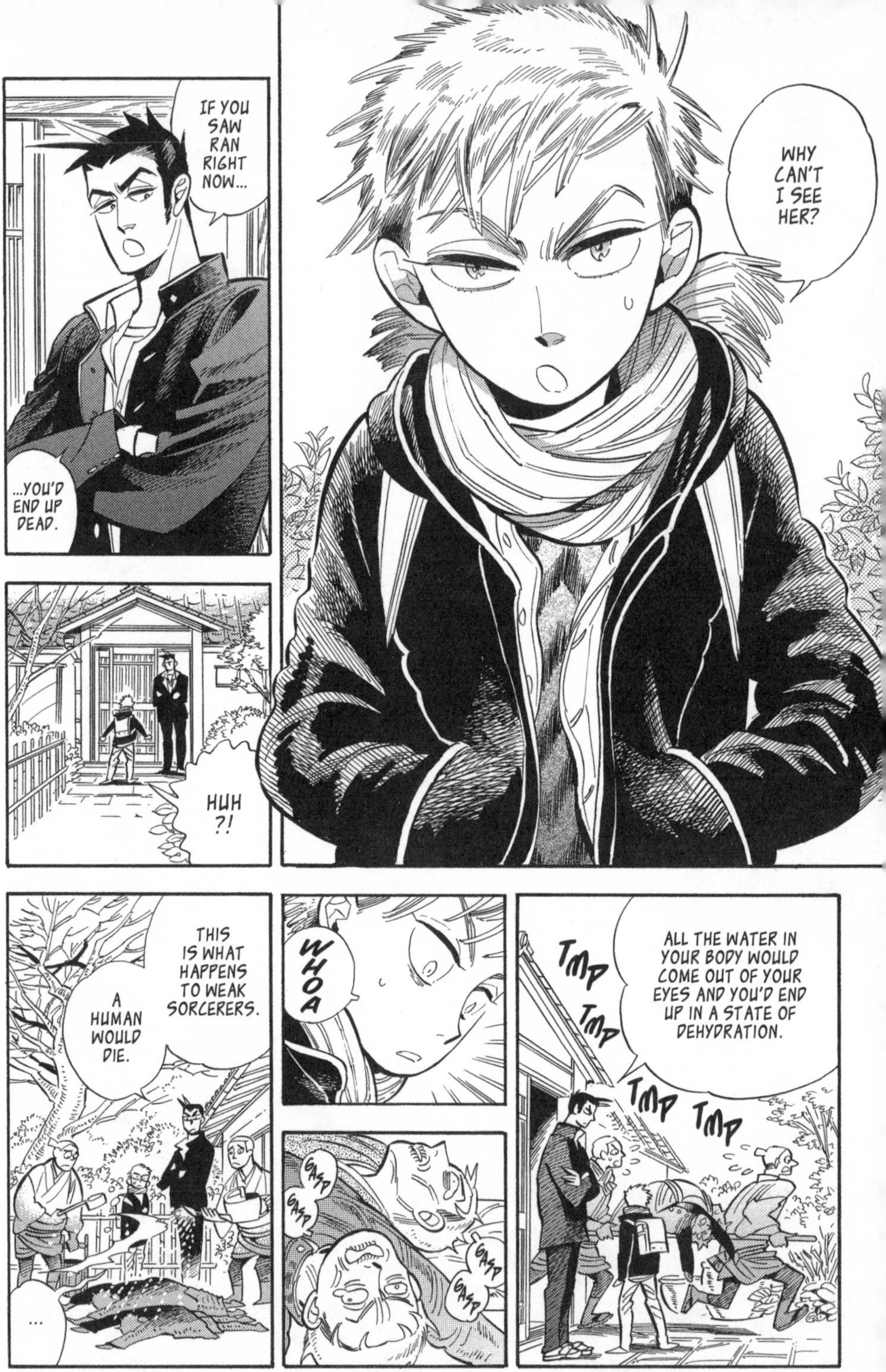
WHY CAN'T I SEE HER?
IF YOU SAW RAN RIGHT NOW...
...YOU'D END UP DEAD.
HUH?!
ALL THE WATER IN YOUR BODY WOULD COME OUT OF YOUR EYES AND YOU'D END UP IN A STATE OF DEHYDRATION.
TMP TMP
TMP TMP
WHOA
GASP GASP
GASP GASP
THIS IS WHAT HAPPENS TO WEAK SORCERERS.
A HUMAN WOULD DIE.
...

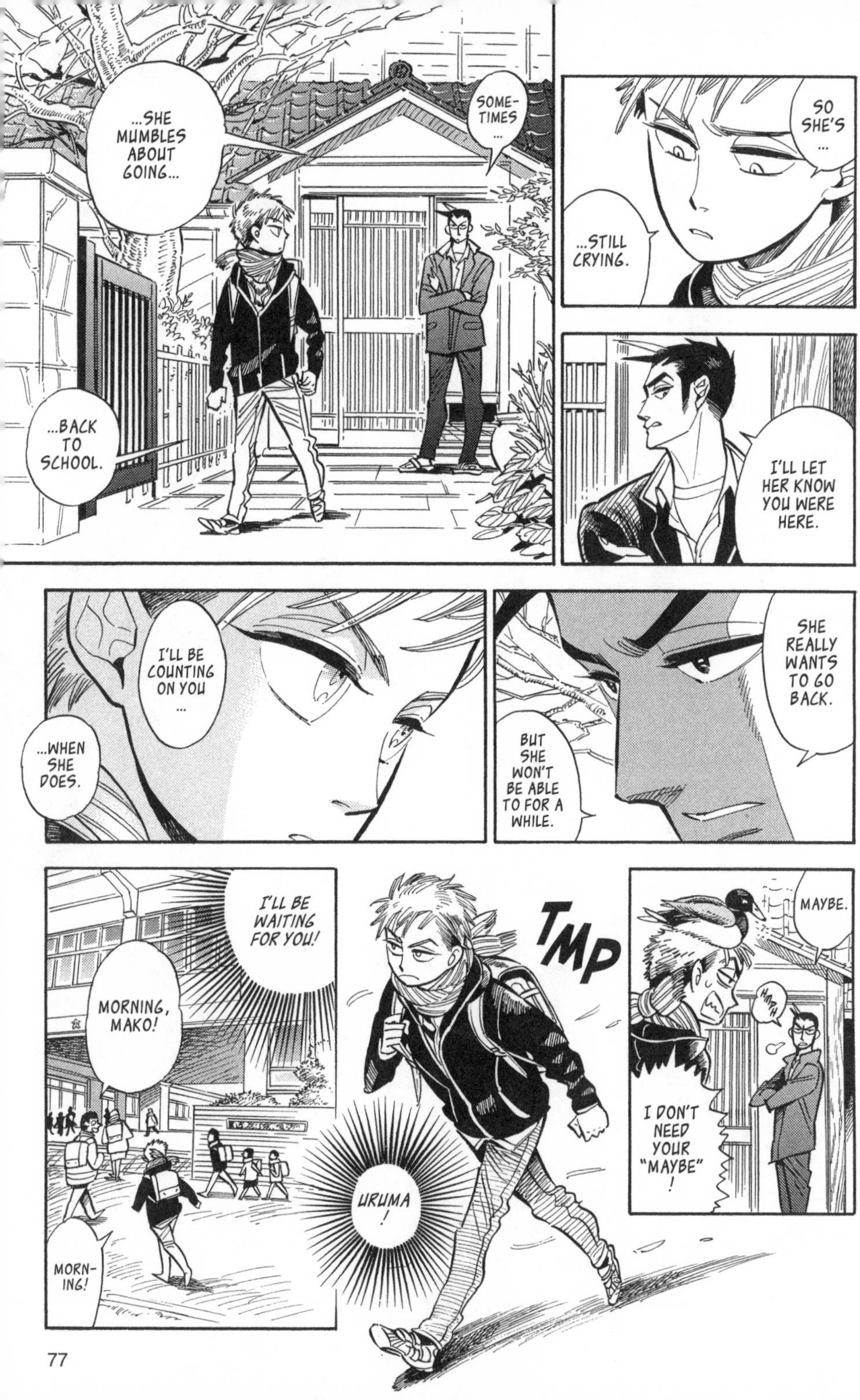
SO SHE'S ...
...STILL CRYING.
I'LL LET HER KNOW YOU WERE HERE.
SOME-TIMES ...
...SHE MUMBLES ABOUT GOING...
...BACK TO SCHOOL.
SHE REALLY WANTS TO GO BACK.
BUT SHE WON'T BE ABLE TO FOR A WHILE.
I'LL BE COUNTING ON YOU ...
...WHEN SHE DOES.
MAYBE.
HMPH
I DON'T NEED YOUR "MAYBE" !
TMP
URUMA !
I'LL BE WAITING FOR YOU!
MORNING, MAKO!
MORN-ING!

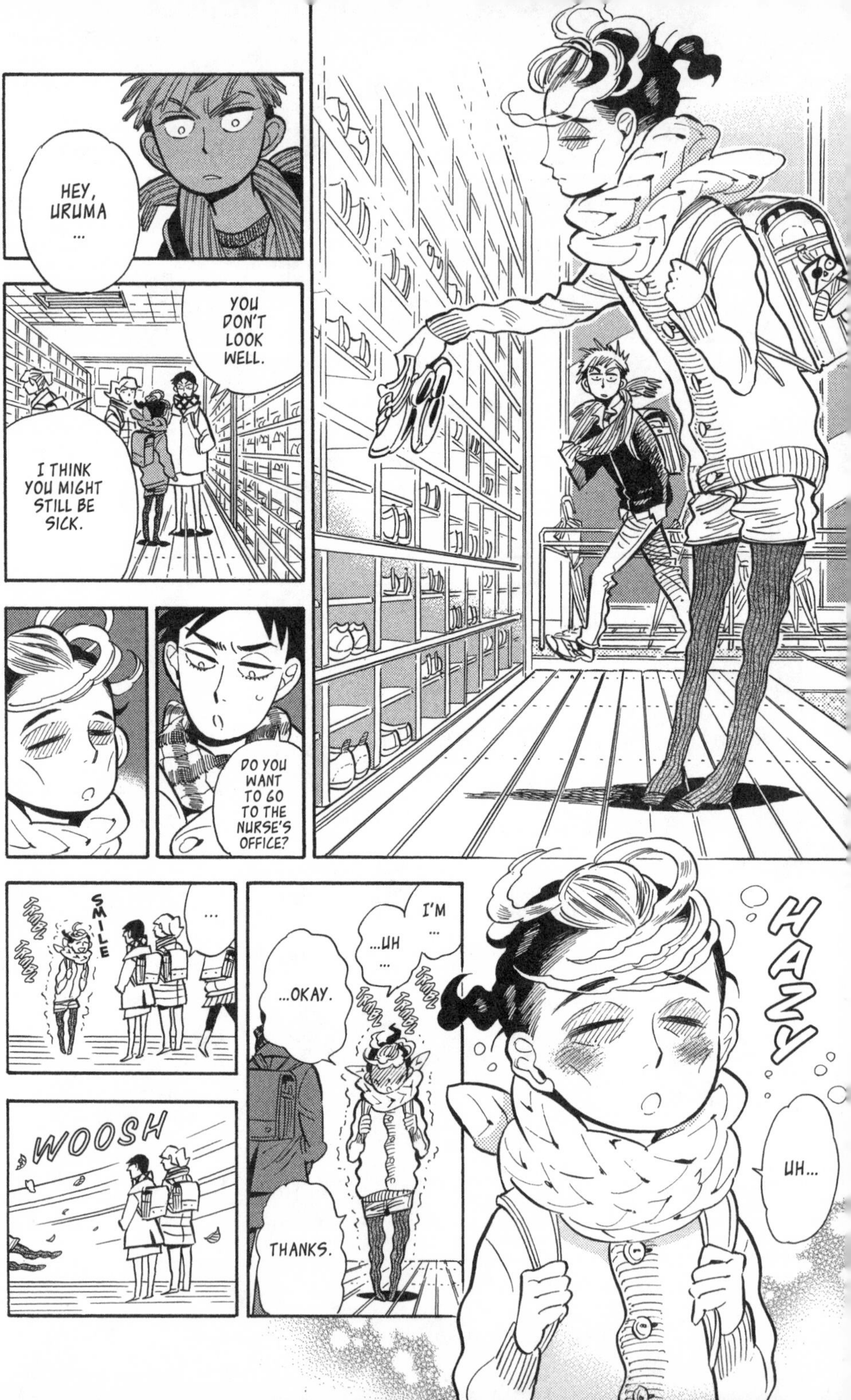
HEY, URUMA ...
YOU DON'T LOOK WELL.
I THINK YOU MIGHT STILL BE SICK.
DO YOU WANT TO GO TO THE NURSE'S OFFICE?
HAZY
UH...
I'M ...
...UH ...
...OKAY.
THANKS.
SMILE
...
WOOSH

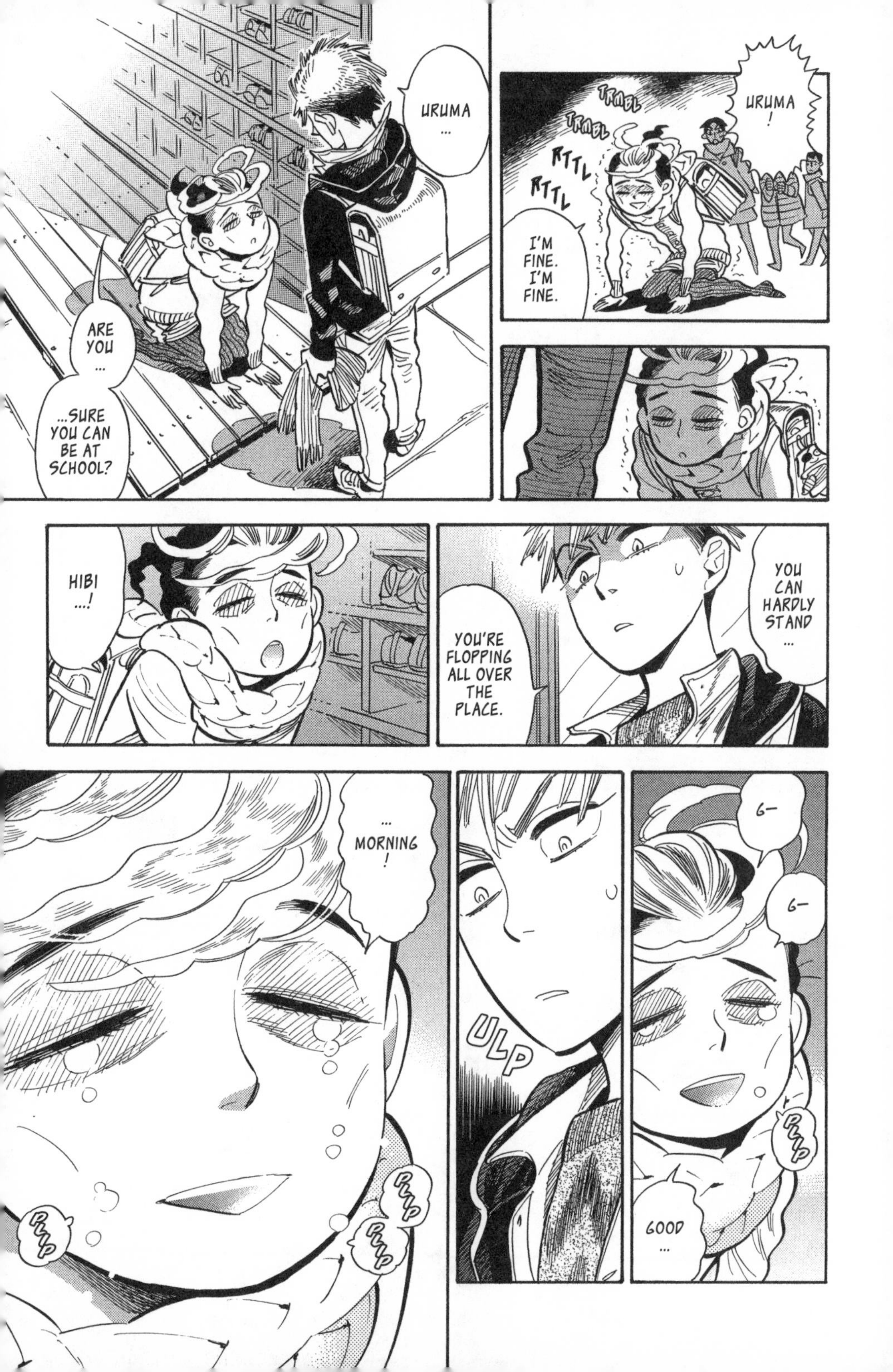
URUMA!
TRMBL
TRMBL
RTTL
RTTL
I'M FINE. I'M FINE.
URUMA...
ARE YOU...
...SURE YOU CAN BE AT SCHOOL?
YOU CAN HARDLY STAND...
YOU'RE FLOPPING ALL OVER THE PLACE.
HIBI...!
G–
G–
PLIP
GOOD...
ULP
...MORNING!
PLIP
PLIP
PLIP

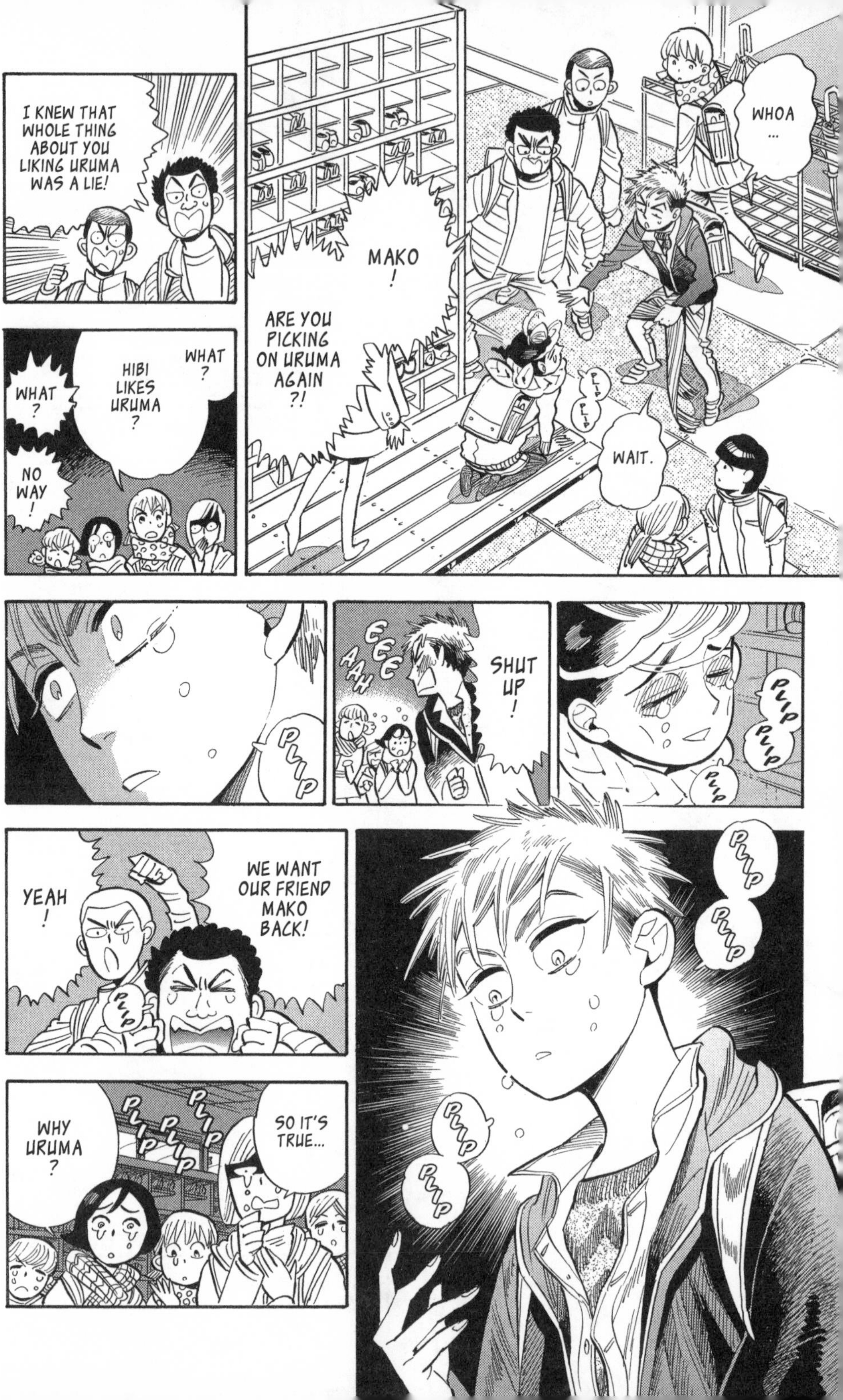
WHOA ...
MAKO!
ARE YOU PICKING ON URUMA AGAIN?!
PLIP PLIP
WAIT.
I KNEW THAT WHOLE THING ABOUT YOU LIKING URUMA WAS A LIE!
WHAT?
HIBI LIKES URUMA?
WHAT?
NO WAY!
PLIP PLIP PLIP
SHUT UP!
EEEAAAH
PLIP
PLIP PLIP
PLIP PLIP
WE WANT OUR FRIEND MAKO BACK!
YEAH!
PLIP
SO IT'S TRUE...
PLIP PLIP PLIP
WHY URUMA?

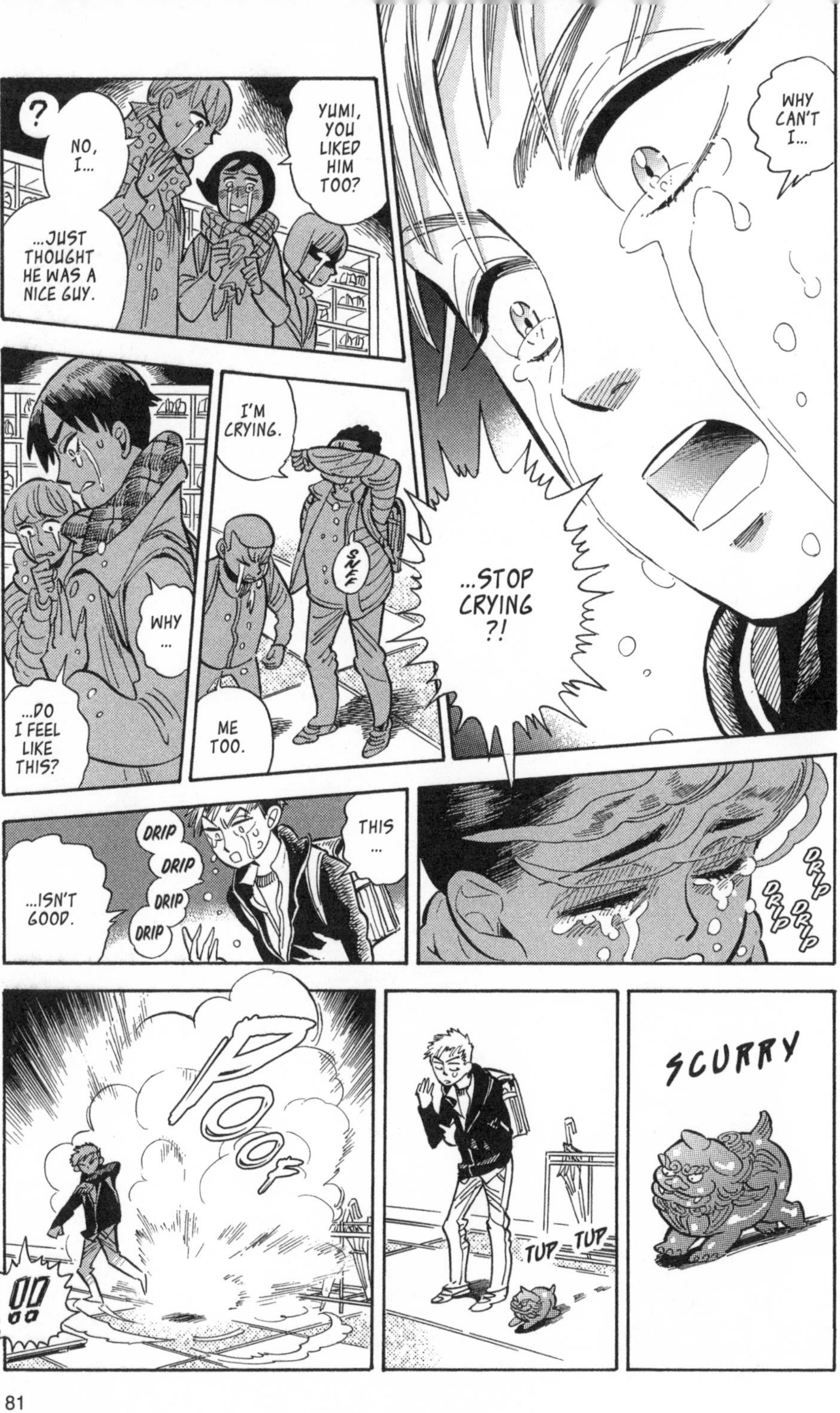
WHY CAN'T I...
...STOP CRYING?!
YUMI, YOU LIKED HIM TOO?
?
NO, I...
...JUST THOUGHT HE WAS A NICE GUY.
I'M CRYING.
SNFF
ME TOO.
WHY...
...DO I FEEL LIKE THIS?
DRIP DRIP DRIP DRIP
THIS...
DRIP DRIP DRIP DRIP
...ISN'T GOOD.
SCURRY
TUP TUP
POOF
!!

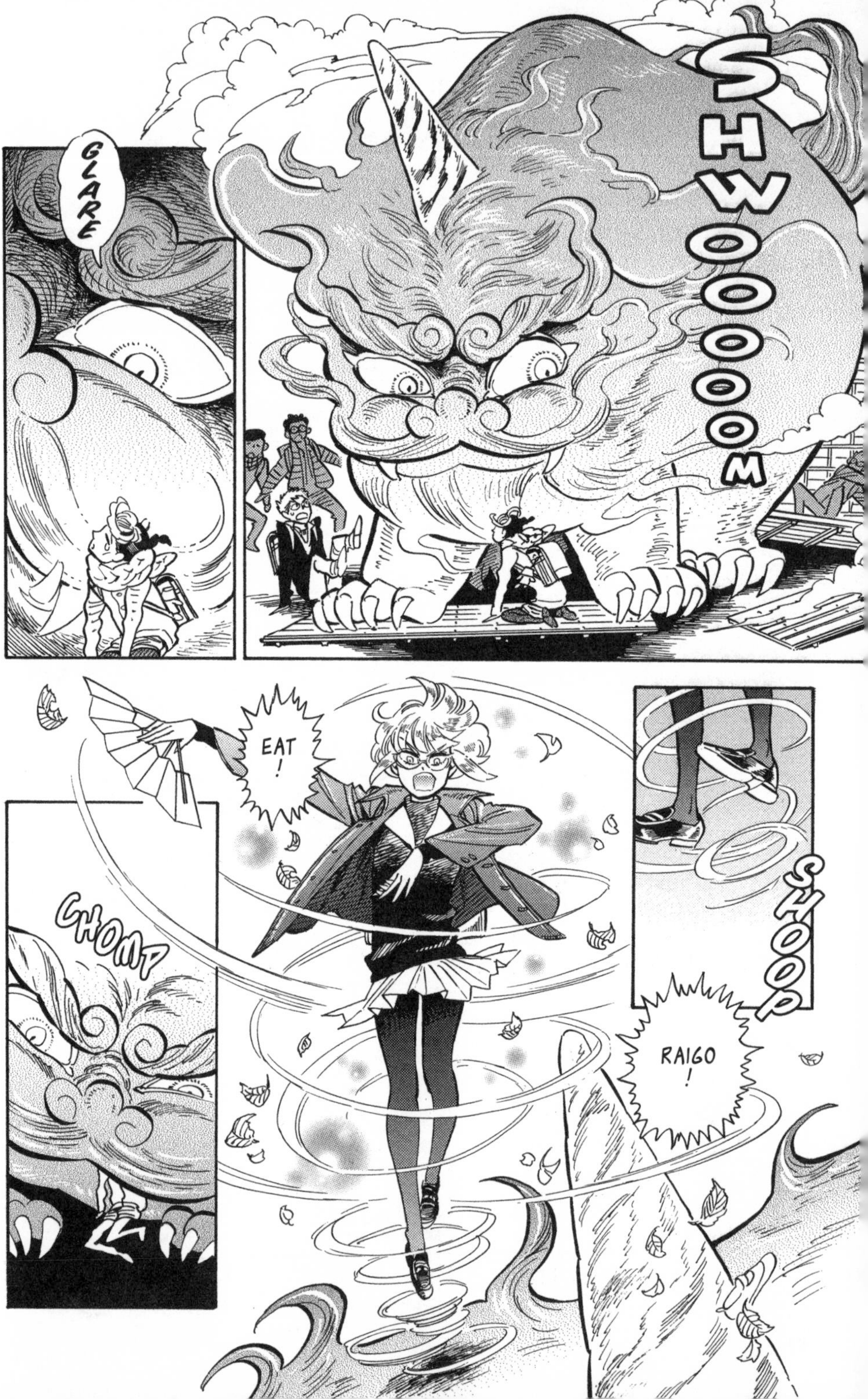
SHWOOOOOOM
GLARE
SHOOP
RAIGO!
EAT!
CHOMP

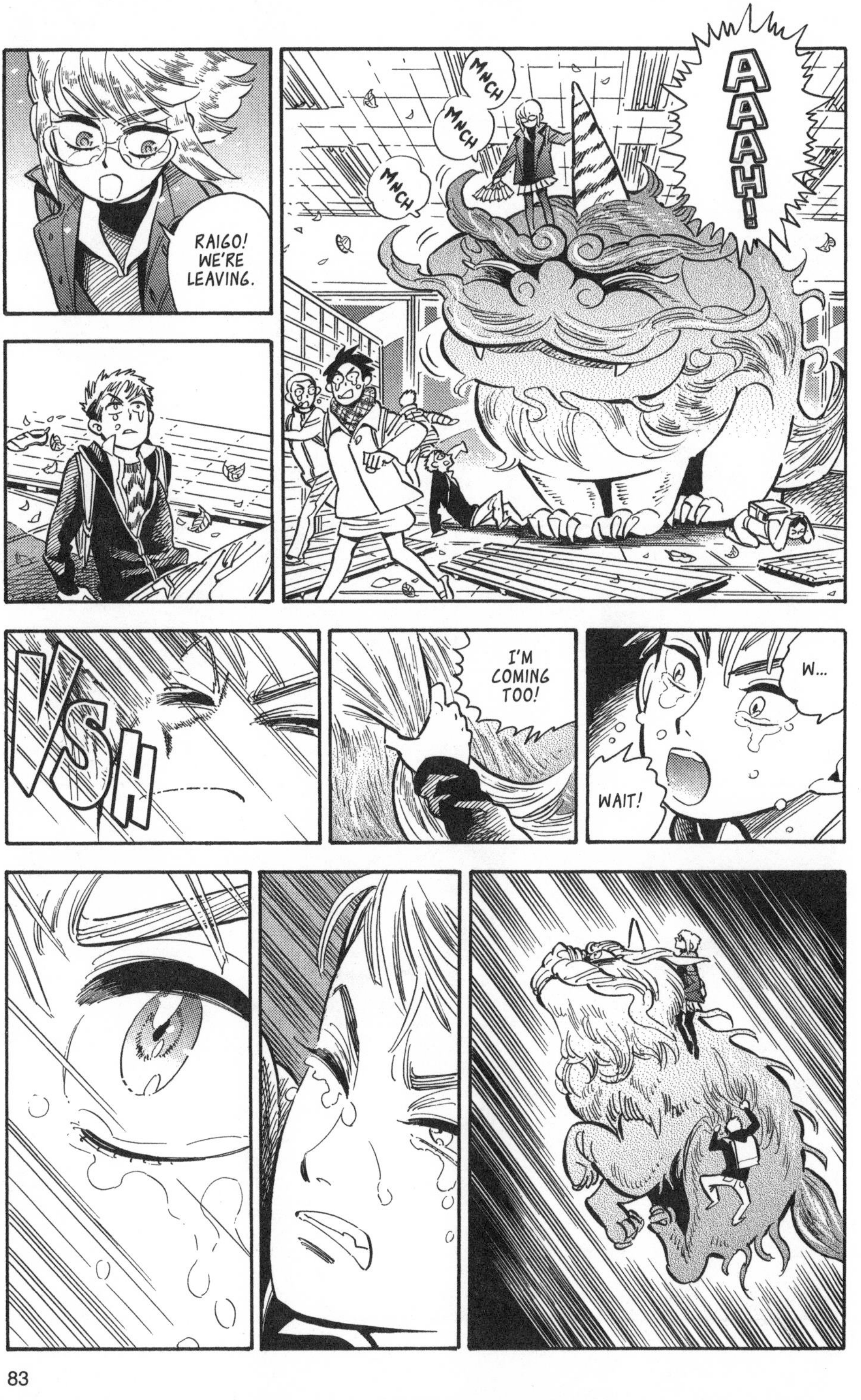
AAAAH!
MNCH
MNCH
MNCH
RAIGO! WE'RE LEAVING.
W...
WAIT!
I'M COMING TOO!
VSH

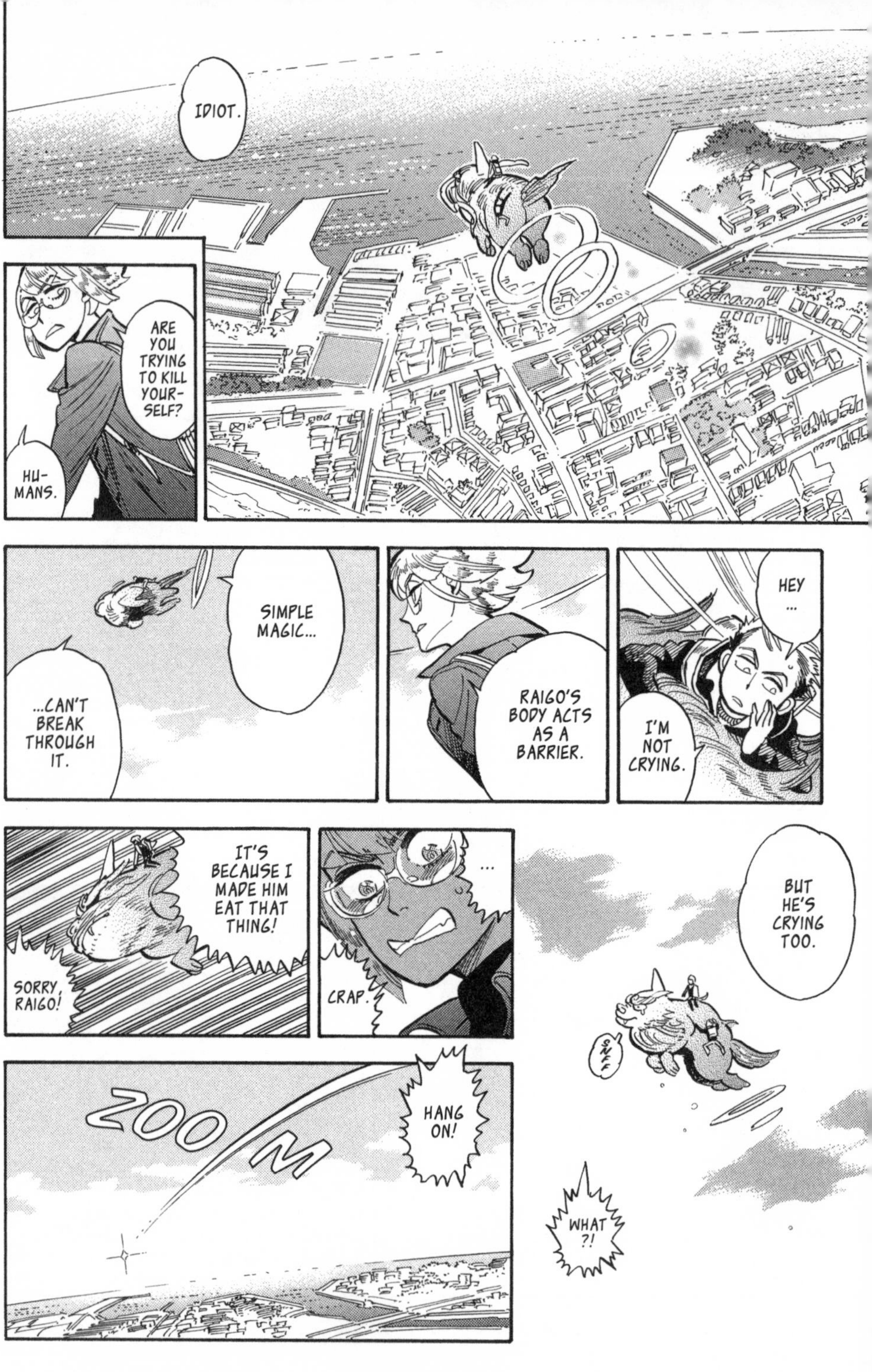
IDIOT.
ARE YOU TRYING TO KILL YOUR-SELF?
HU-MANS.
HEY...
I'M NOT CRYING.
RAIGO'S BODY ACTS AS A BARRIER.
SIMPLE MAGIC...
...CAN'T BREAK THROUGH IT.
BUT HE'S CRYING TOO.
SNIFF
...
CRAP.
IT'S BECAUSE I MADE HIM EAT THAT THING!
SORRY, RAIGO!
HANG ON!
ZOOM
WHAT?!

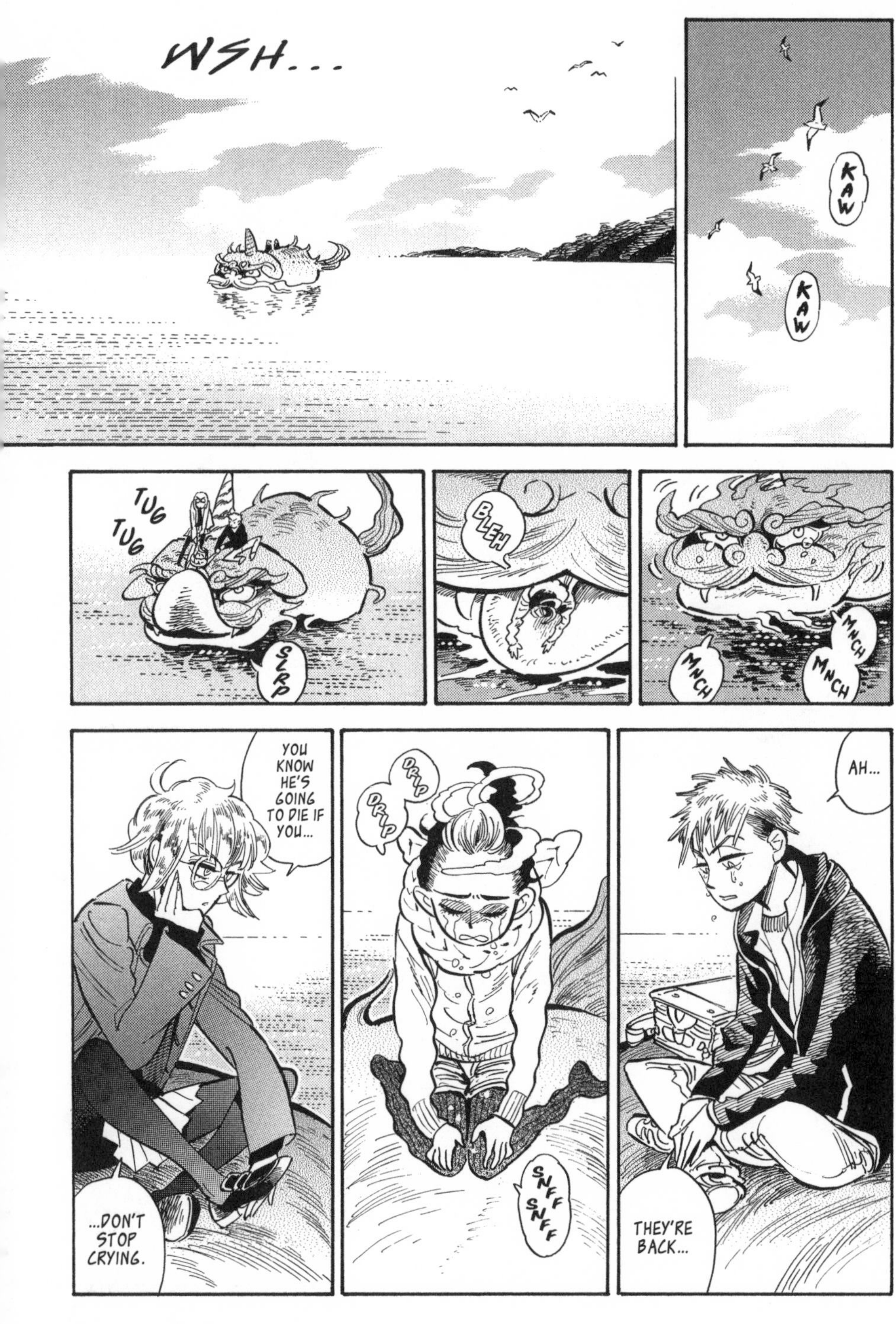
KAW
KAW
WSH...
MNCH
MNCH
MNCH
BLEH
TUG TUG
SLRP
AH...
THEY'RE BACK...
DRIP
DRIP
SNFF SNFF
YOU KNOW HE'S GOING TO DIE IF YOU...
...DON'T STOP CRYING.

I'M SORRY, HIBI...

I CAN'T STOP.

I...

HIC

URUMA...

...IT ALL CAME RUSHING BACK...

HIC

I WANTED TO SEE YOU, HIBI...

...BUT WHEN I SAW YOUR FACE...

I'M...

I'M SORRY...

...SORRY...

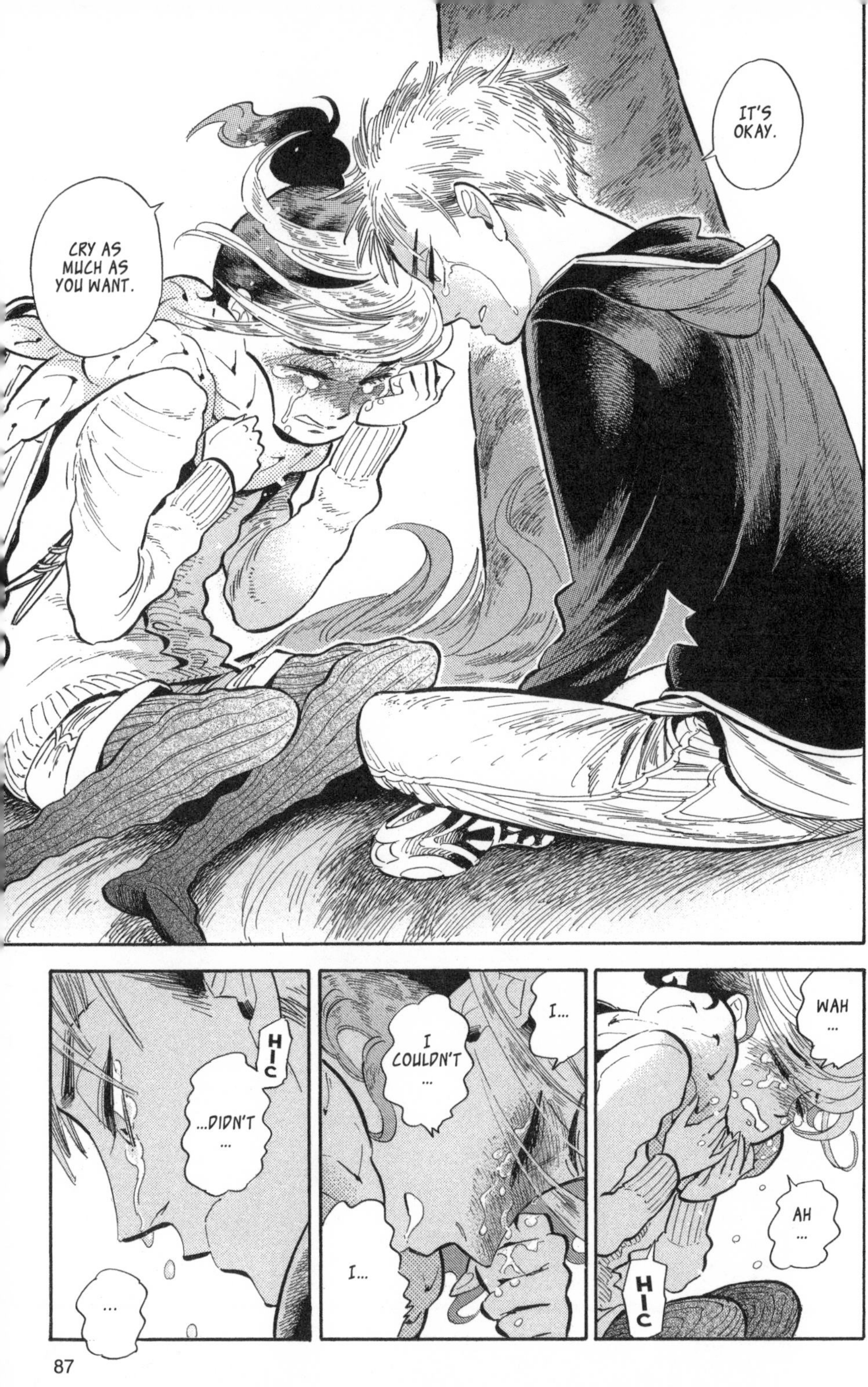
IT'S OKAY.
CRY AS MUCH AS YOU WANT.
WAH ...
AH ...
HIC
I...
I COULDN'T ...
I...
HIC
...DIDN'T ...
...

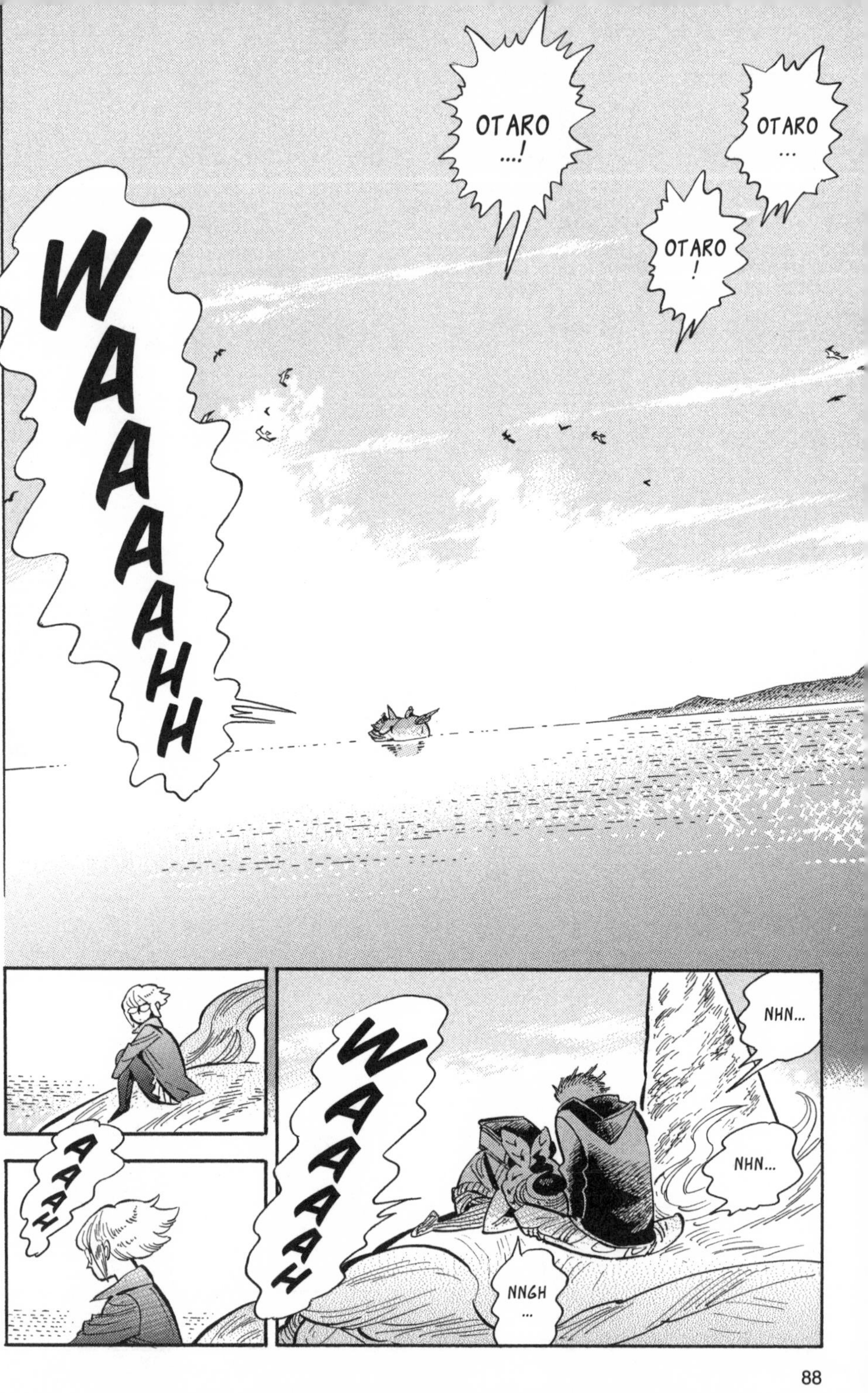
OTARO
...
OTARO
!
OTARO
...!
WAAAAAHH
NHN...
NHN...
WAAAAAH
NNGH
...
AAAAH

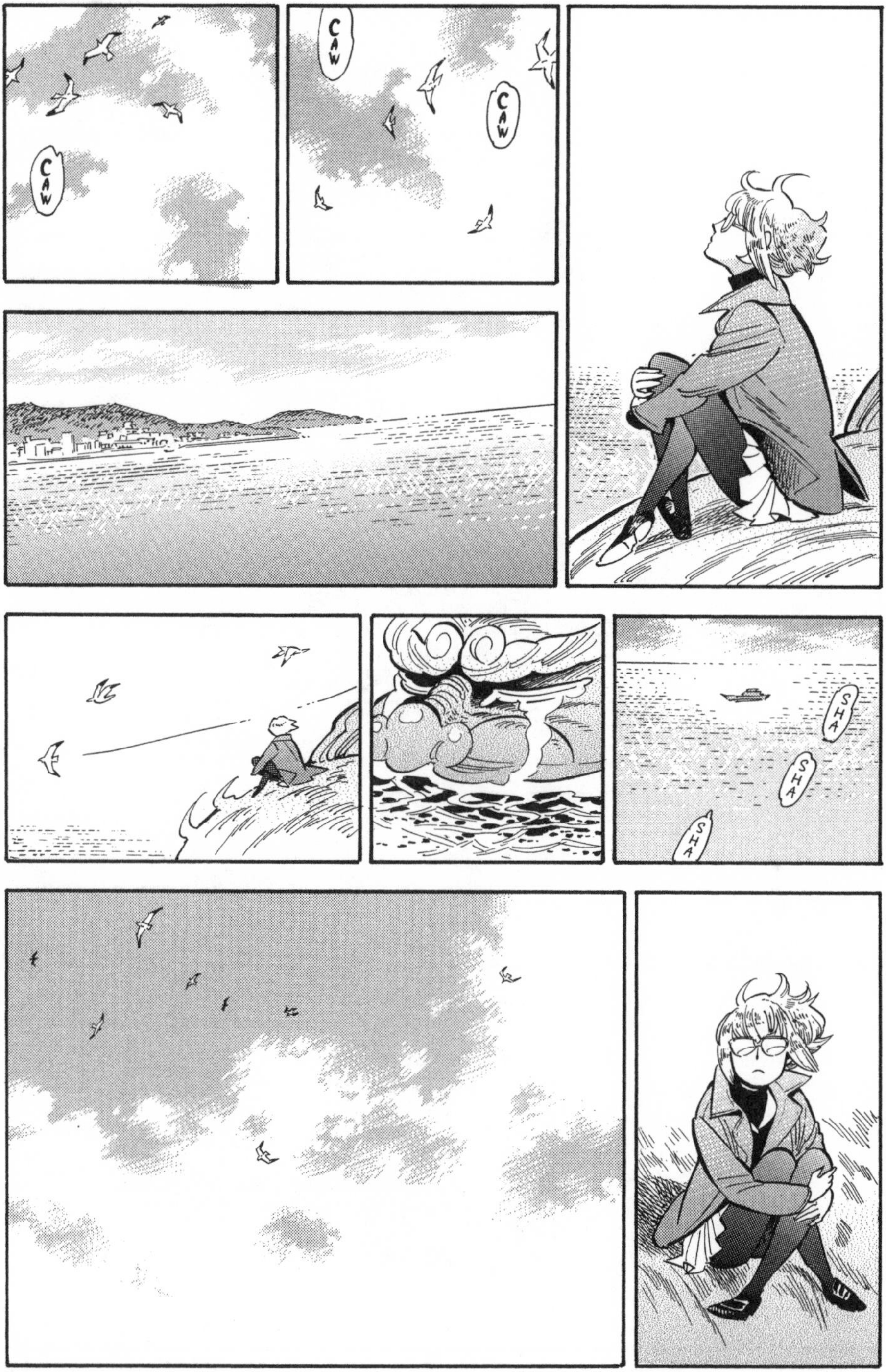
CAW
CAW
CAW
SHA
SHA
SHA

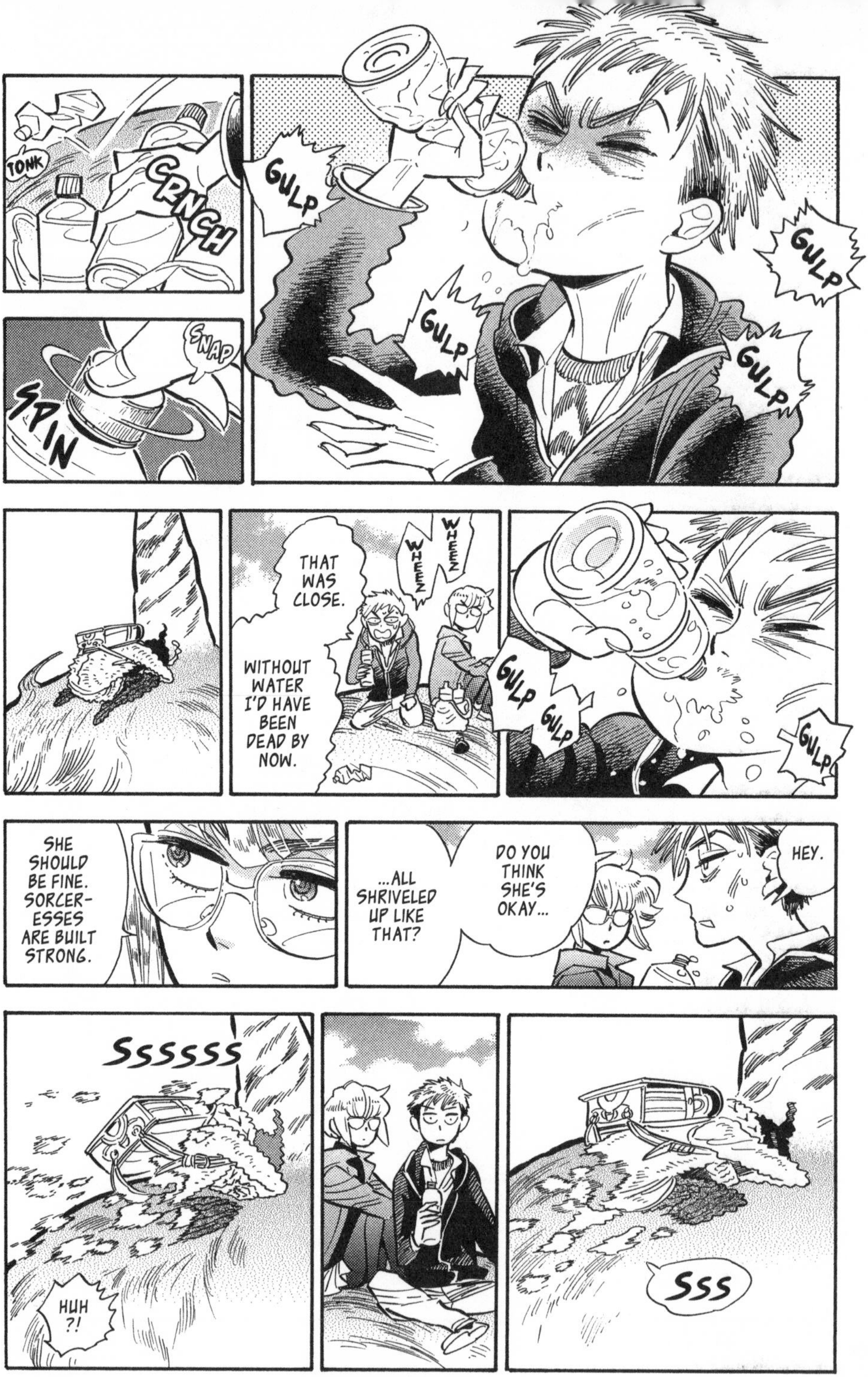

GULP
GULP
GULP
GULP
TONK
CRNCH
SNAP
SPIN
GULP
GULP
GULP
WHEEZ
WHEEZ
THAT WAS CLOSE.
WITHOUT WATER I'D HAVE BEEN DEAD BY NOW.
HEY.
DO YOU THINK SHE'S OKAY...
...ALL SHRIVELED UP LIKE THAT?
SHE SHOULD BE FINE. SORCER-ESSES ARE BUILT STRONG.
SSS
SSSSSS
HUH?!

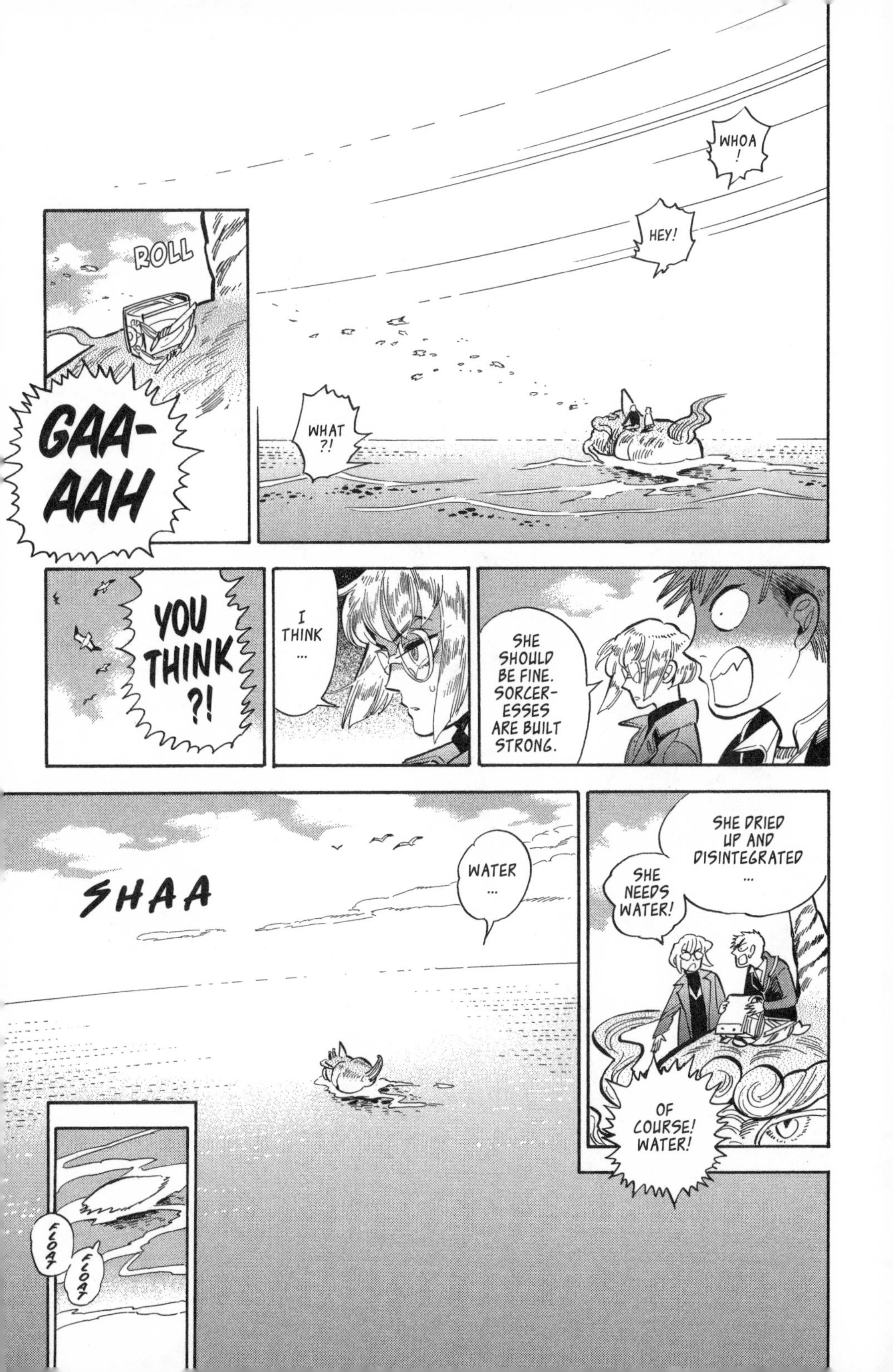
WHOA!
HEY!
WHAT?!
ROLL
GAA-AAH
SHE SHOULD BE FINE. SORCER-ESSES ARE BUILT STRONG.
I THINK...
YOU THINK?!
SHE DRIED UP AND DISINTEGRATED...
SHE NEEDS WATER!
OF COURSE! WATER!
WATER...
SHAA
FLOAT
FLOAT

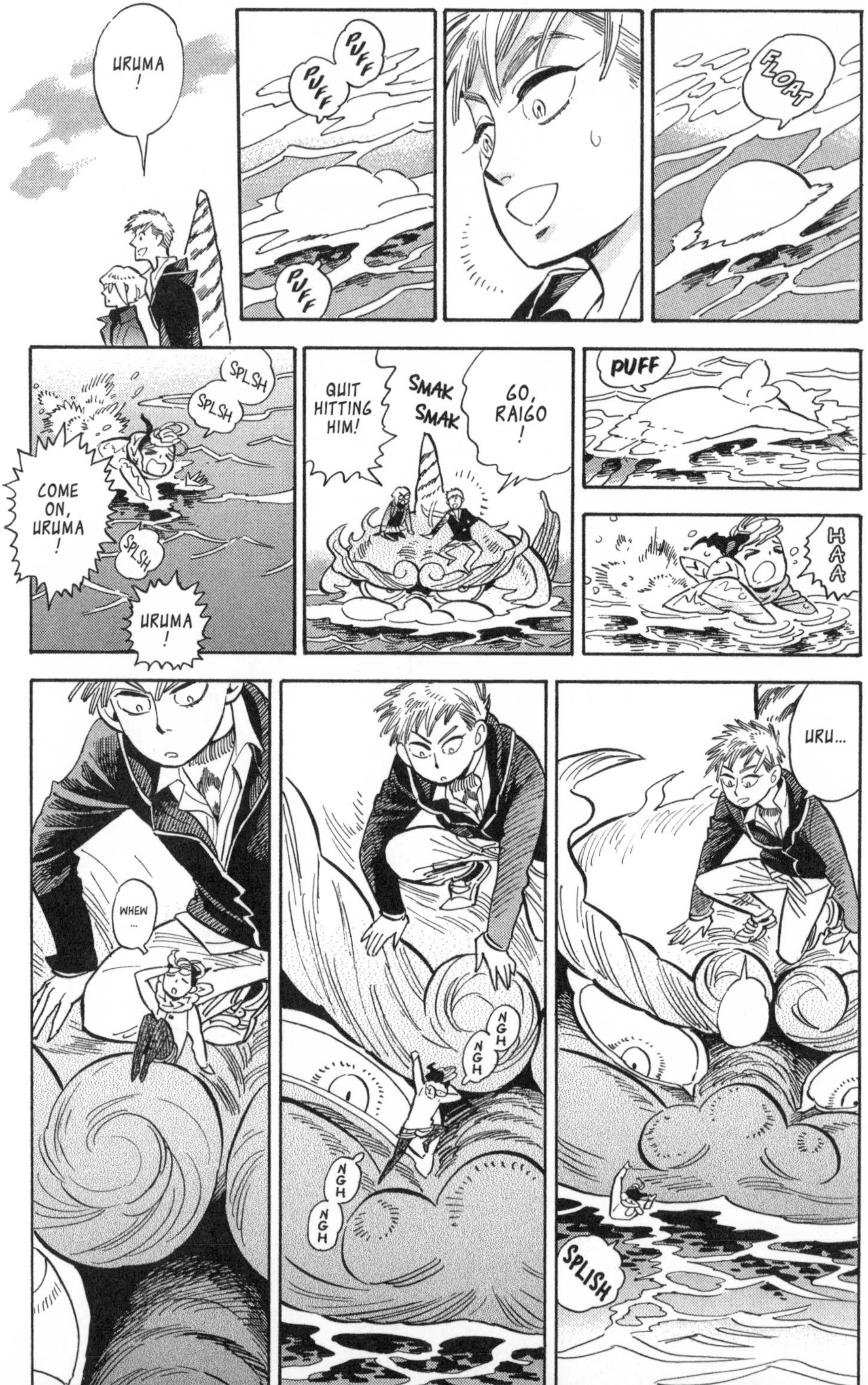
FLOAT
PUFF PUFF
PUFF
URUMA!
PUFF
HAAA
GO, RAIGO!
SMAK SMAK
QUIT HITTING HIM!
SPLSH SPLSH
COME ON, URUMA!
SPLSH
URUMA!
URU...
SPLISH
NGH NGH
NGH NGH
WHEW...

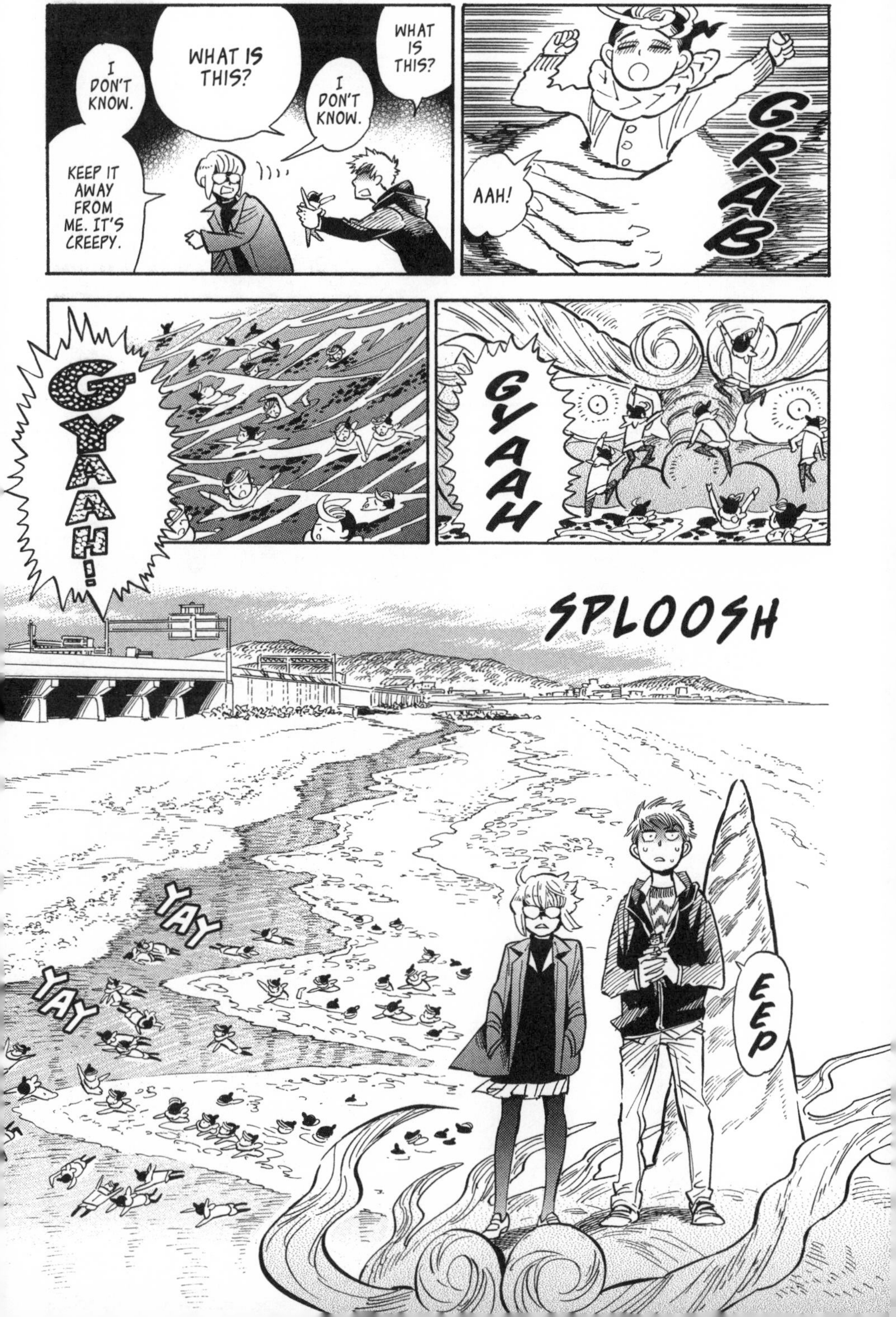

AAH!
GRAB
WHAT IS THIS?
I DON'T KNOW.
WHAT IS THIS?
I DON'T KNOW.
KEEP IT AWAY FROM ME. IT'S CREEPY.
GYAAH
GYAAAH!
SPLOOSH
EEP
YAY
YAY

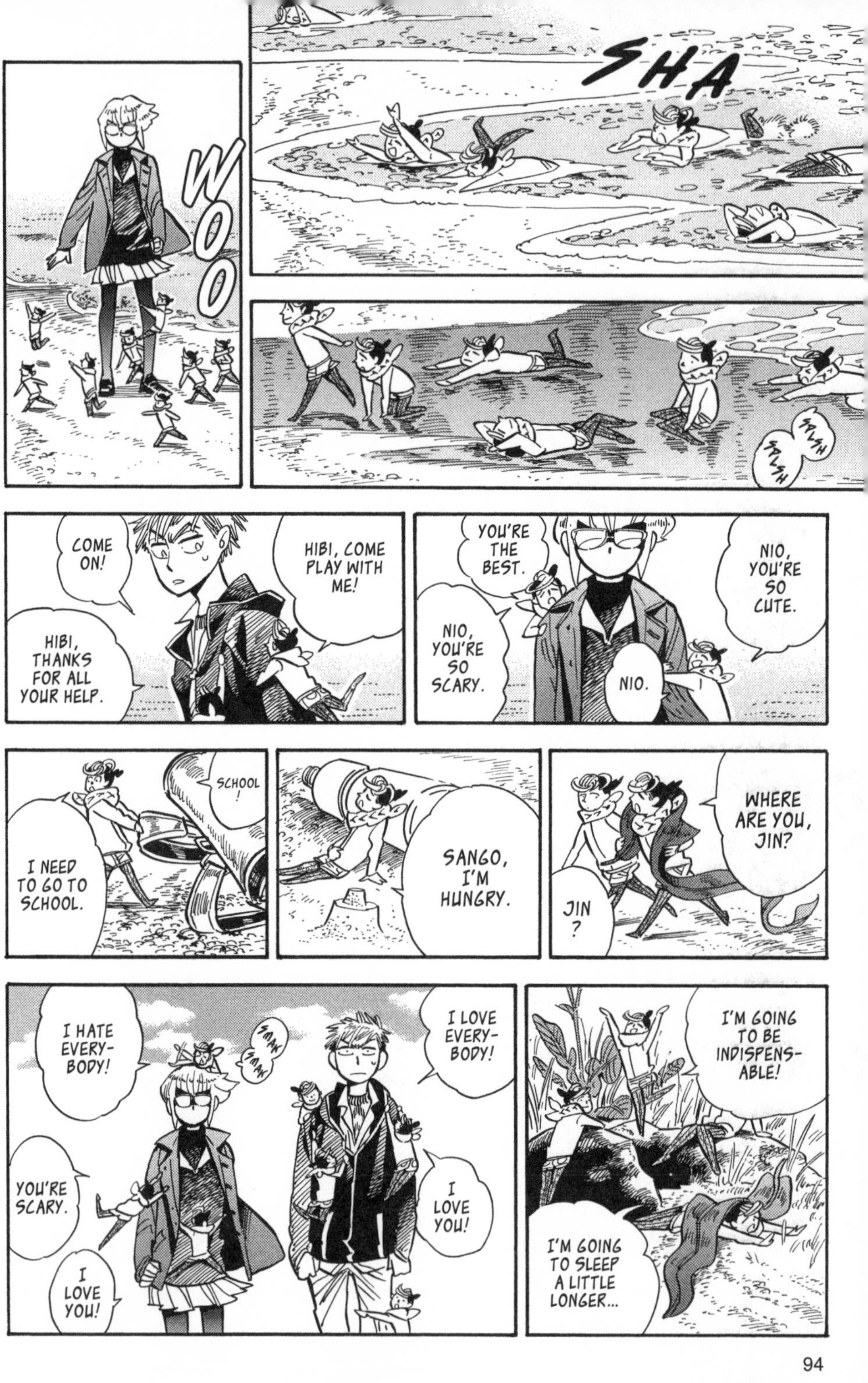
SHA
SPLASH SPLASH
WOO
NIO, YOU'RE SO CUTE.
YOU'RE THE BEST.
NIO, YOU'RE SO SCARY.
NIO.
HIBI, COME PLAY WITH ME!
COME ON!
HIBI, THANKS FOR ALL YOUR HELP.
WHERE ARE YOU, JIN?
JIN?
SANGO, I'M HUNGRY.
SCHOOL!
I NEED TO GO TO SCHOOL.
I'M GOING TO BE INDISPENS-ABLE!
I'M GOING TO SLEEP A LITTLE LONGER...
I LOVE EVERY-BODY!
SMAK SMAK
I HATE EVERY-BODY!
I LOVE YOU!
YOU'RE SCARY.
I LOVE YOU!

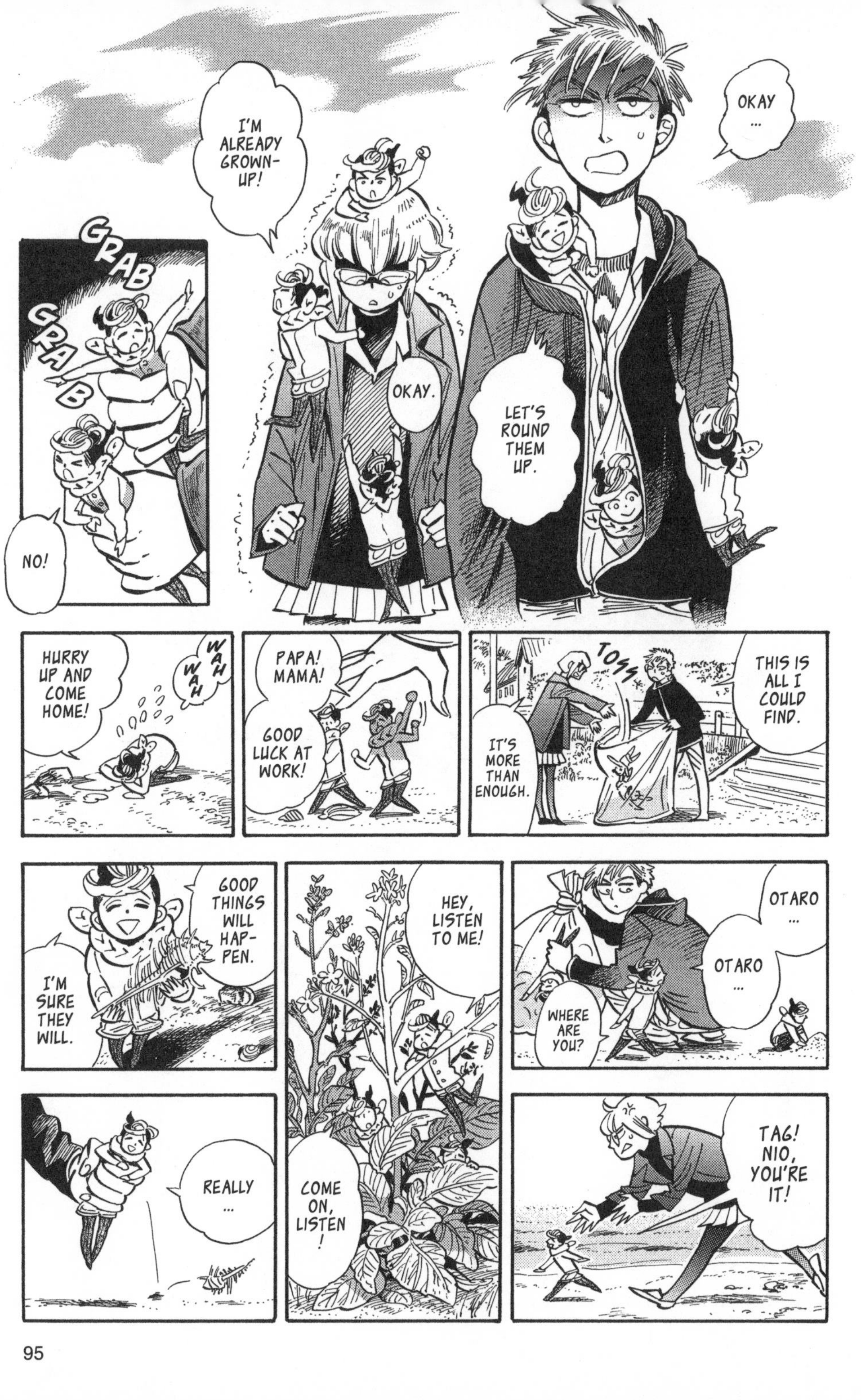

OKAY ...
I'M ALREADY GROWN-UP!
LET'S ROUND THEM UP.
OKAY.
GRAB GRAB
NO!
TOSS
THIS IS ALL I COULD FIND.
IT'S MORE THAN ENOUGH.
PAPA! MAMA!
GOOD LUCK AT WORK!
WAH WAH
HURRY UP AND COME HOME!
OTARO ...
OTARO ...
WHERE ARE YOU?
TAG! NIO, YOU'RE IT!
HEY, LISTEN TO ME!
COME ON, LISTEN!
GOOD THINGS WILL HAP-PEN.
I'M SURE THEY WILL.
REALLY ...

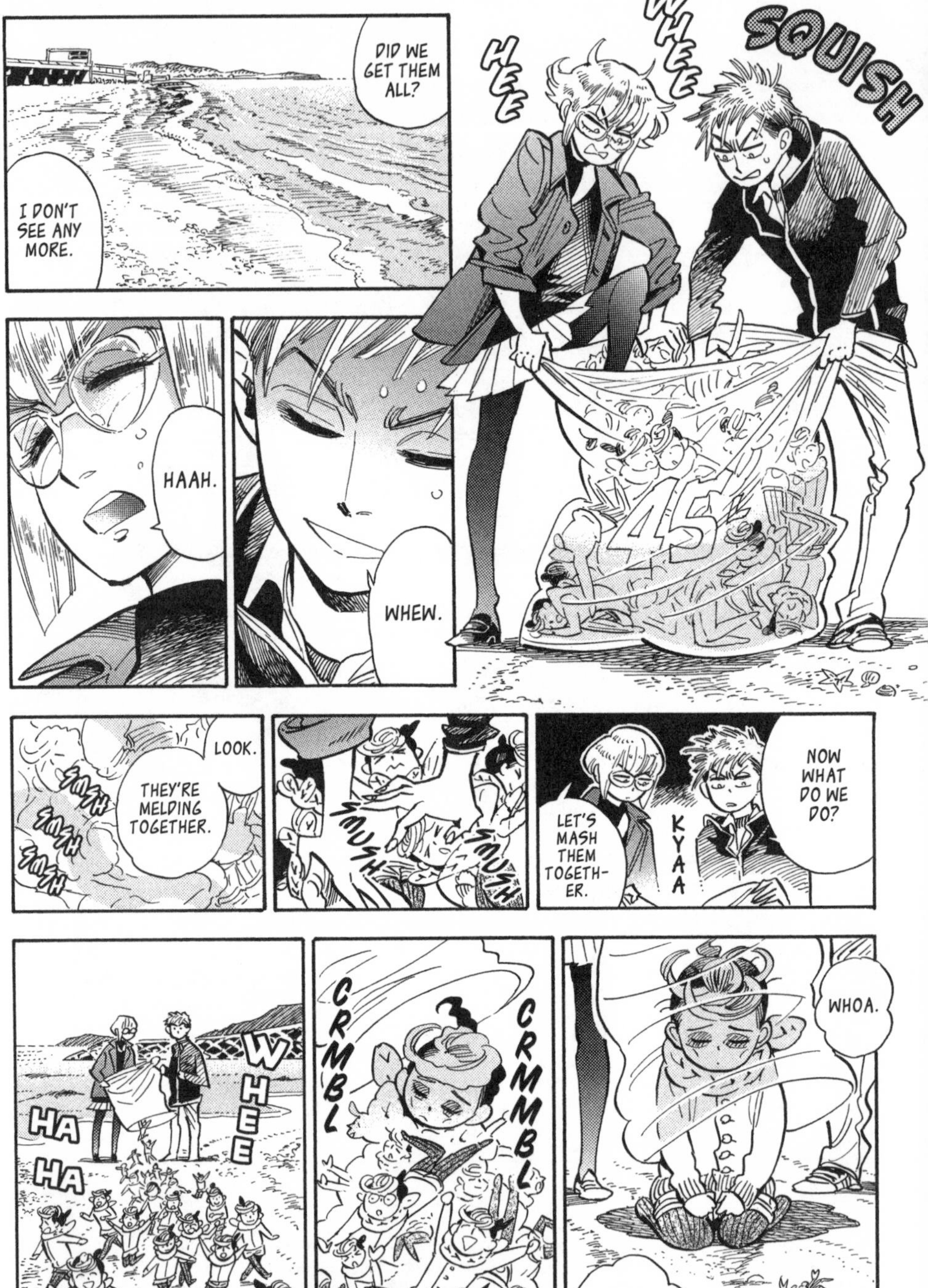
HEE
WHEE
SQUISH
45
DID WE GET THEM ALL?
I DON'T SEE ANY MORE.
WHEW.
HAAH.
NOW WHAT DO WE DO?
KYAA
LET'S MASH THEM TOGETH-ER.
SMUSH
SMUSH
LOOK.
THEY'RE MELDING TOGETHER.
SMSH
SMSH
SMSH
WHOA.
WE DID IT.
CRMBL
CRMMBL
WHEE
HA
HA

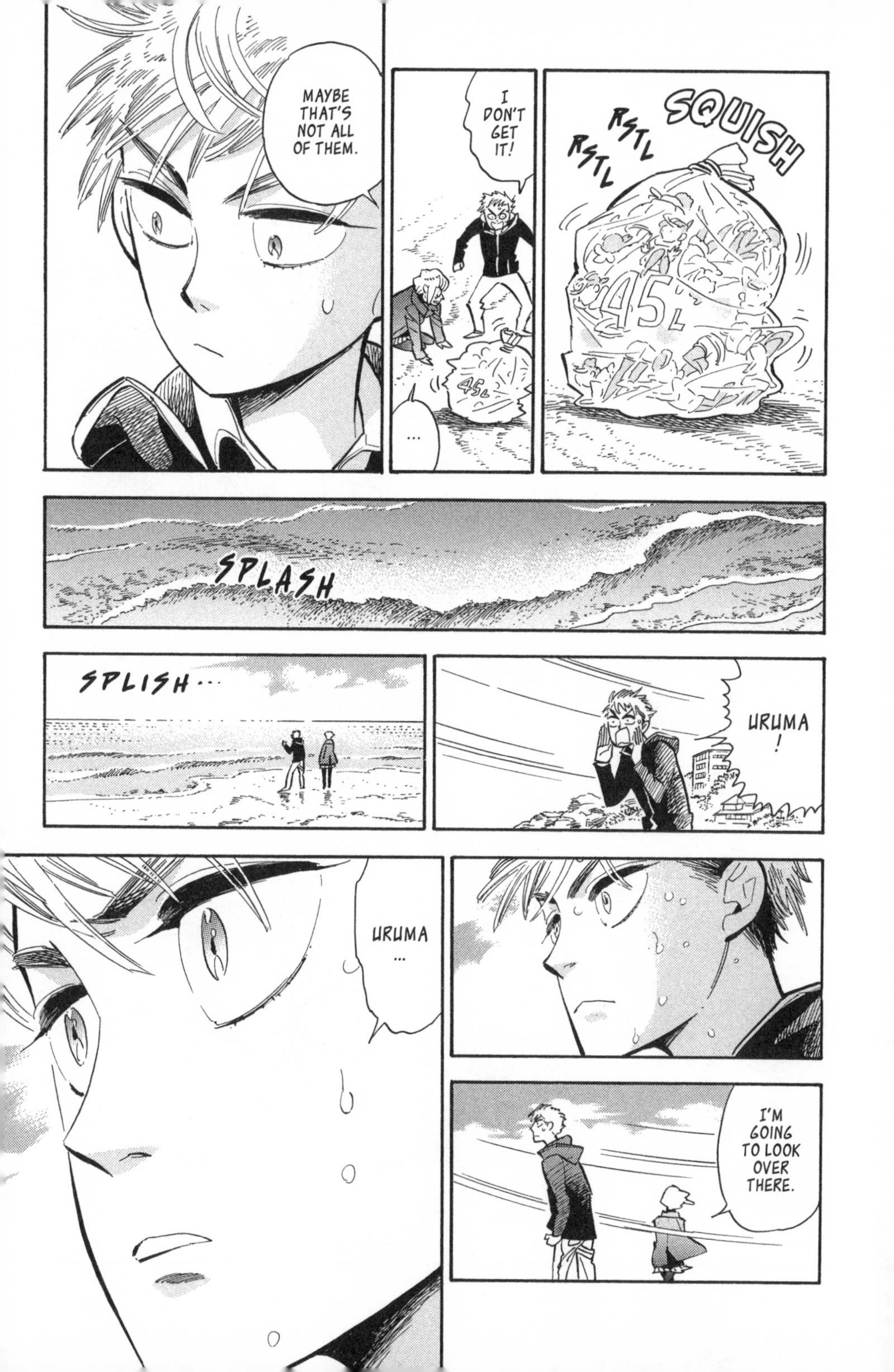
RSTL
RSTL
SQUISH
I DON'T GET IT!
...
MAYBE THAT'S NOT ALL OF THEM.
SPLASH
URUMA!
SPLISH...
I'M GOING TO LOOK OVER THERE.
URUMA...

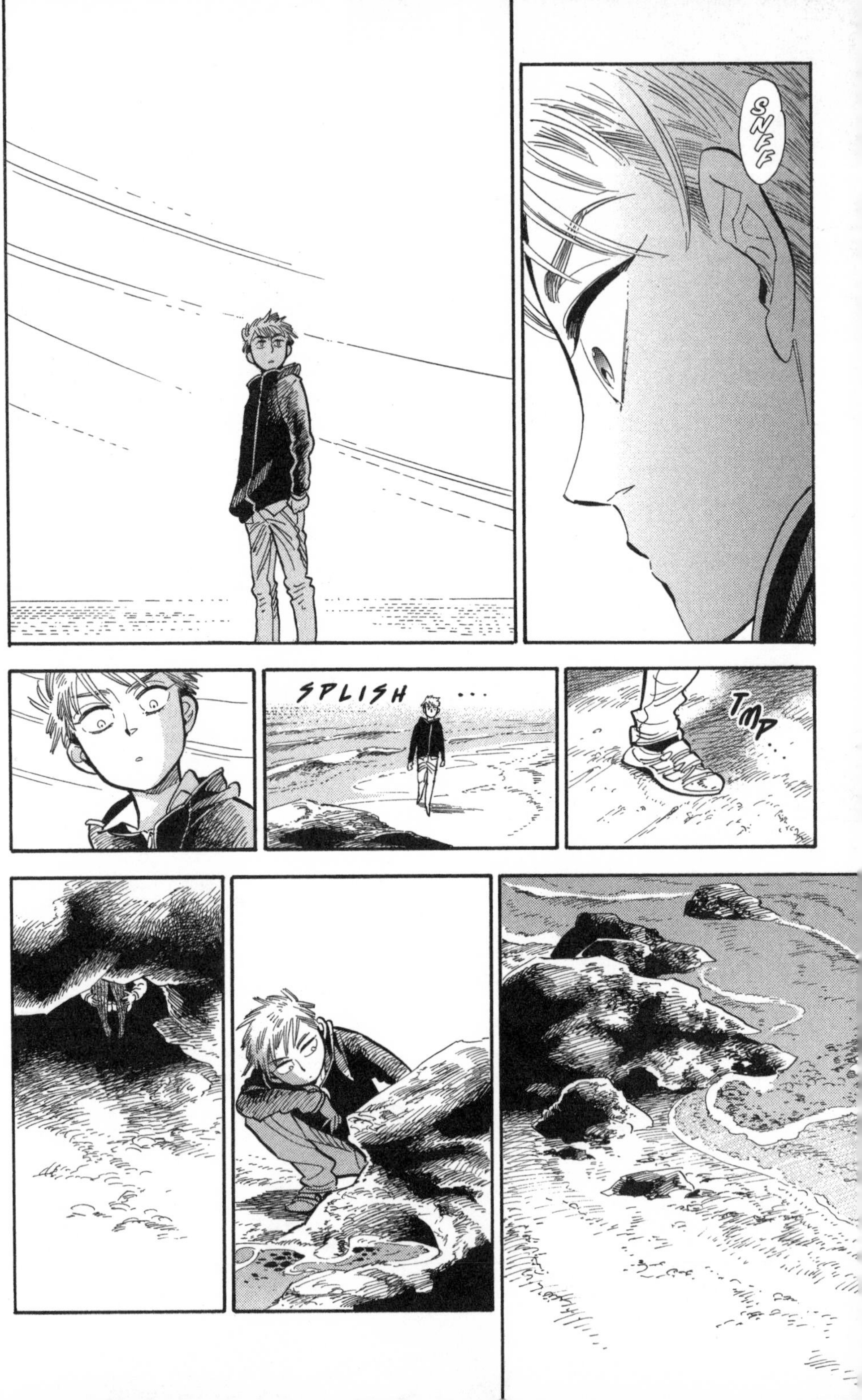
SNFF
TMP...
SPLISH...

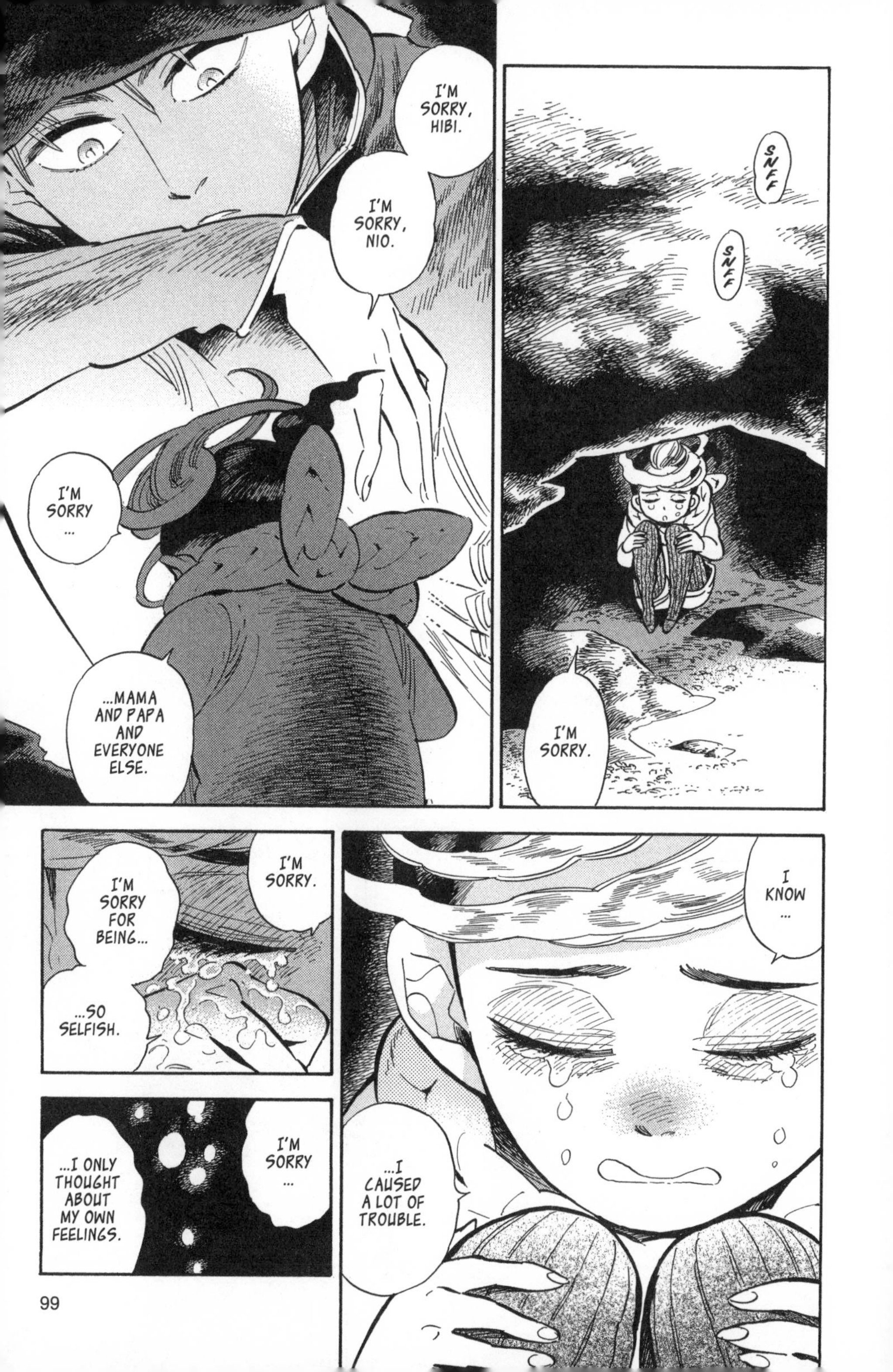
SNFF
SNFF
I'M SORRY.
I'M SORRY, HIBI.
I'M SORRY, NIO.
I'M SORRY ...
...MAMA AND PAPA AND EVERYONE ELSE.
I KNOW ...
...I CAUSED A LOT OF TROUBLE.
I'M SORRY.
I'M SORRY FOR BEING...
...SO SELFISH.
I'M SORRY ...
...I ONLY THOUGHT ABOUT MY OWN FEELINGS.

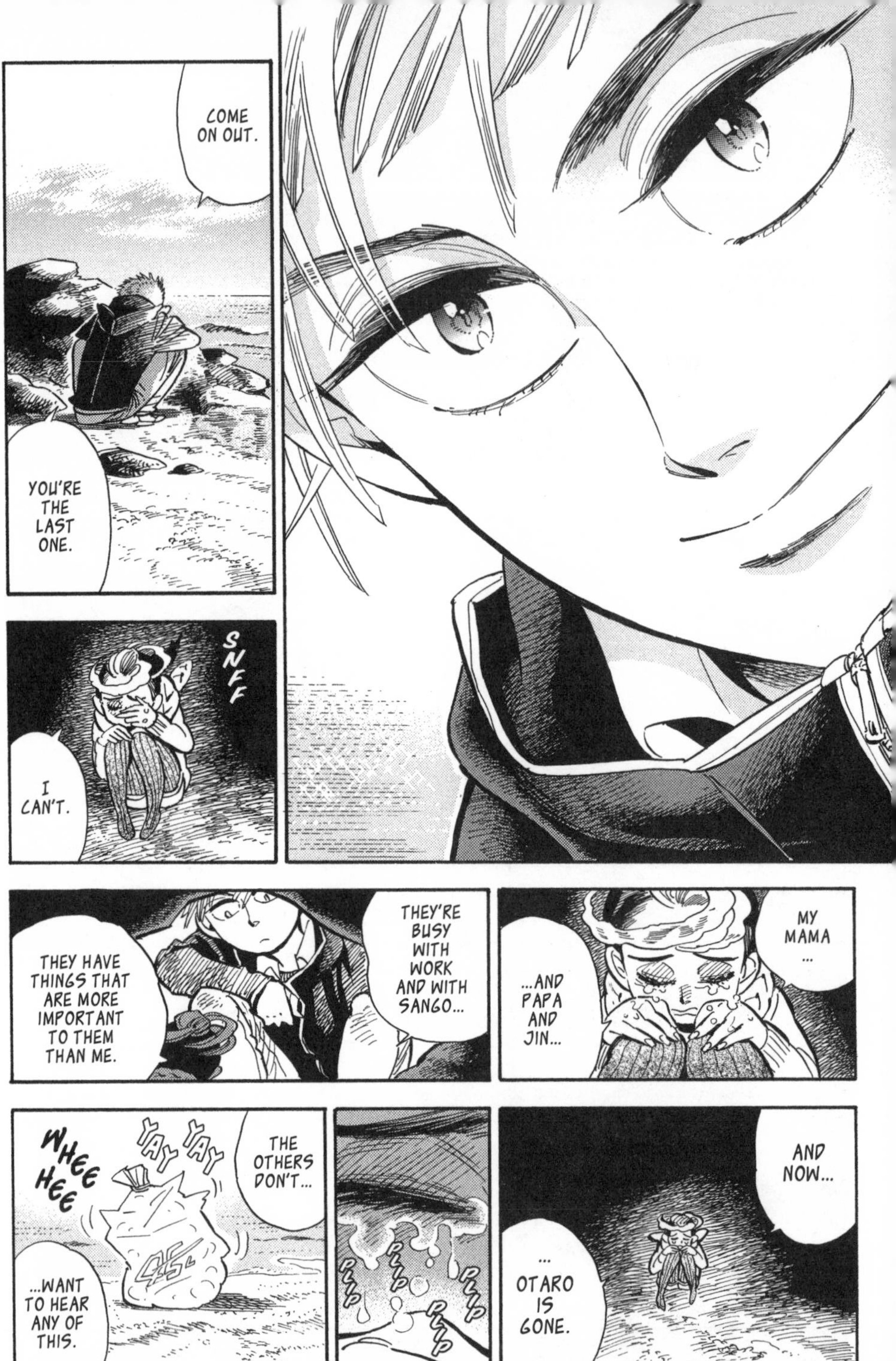
COME ON OUT.
YOU'RE THE LAST ONE.
SNFF
I CAN'T.
MY MAMA...
...AND PAPA AND JIN...
THEY'RE BUSY WITH WORK AND WITH SANGO...
THEY HAVE THINGS THAT ARE MORE IMPORTANT TO THEM THAN ME.
AND NOW...
...OTARO IS GONE.
PLIP
PLIP
PLIP
PLIP
PLIP
THE OTHERS DON'T...
YAY YAY
WHEE HEE
...WANT TO HEAR ANY OF THIS.

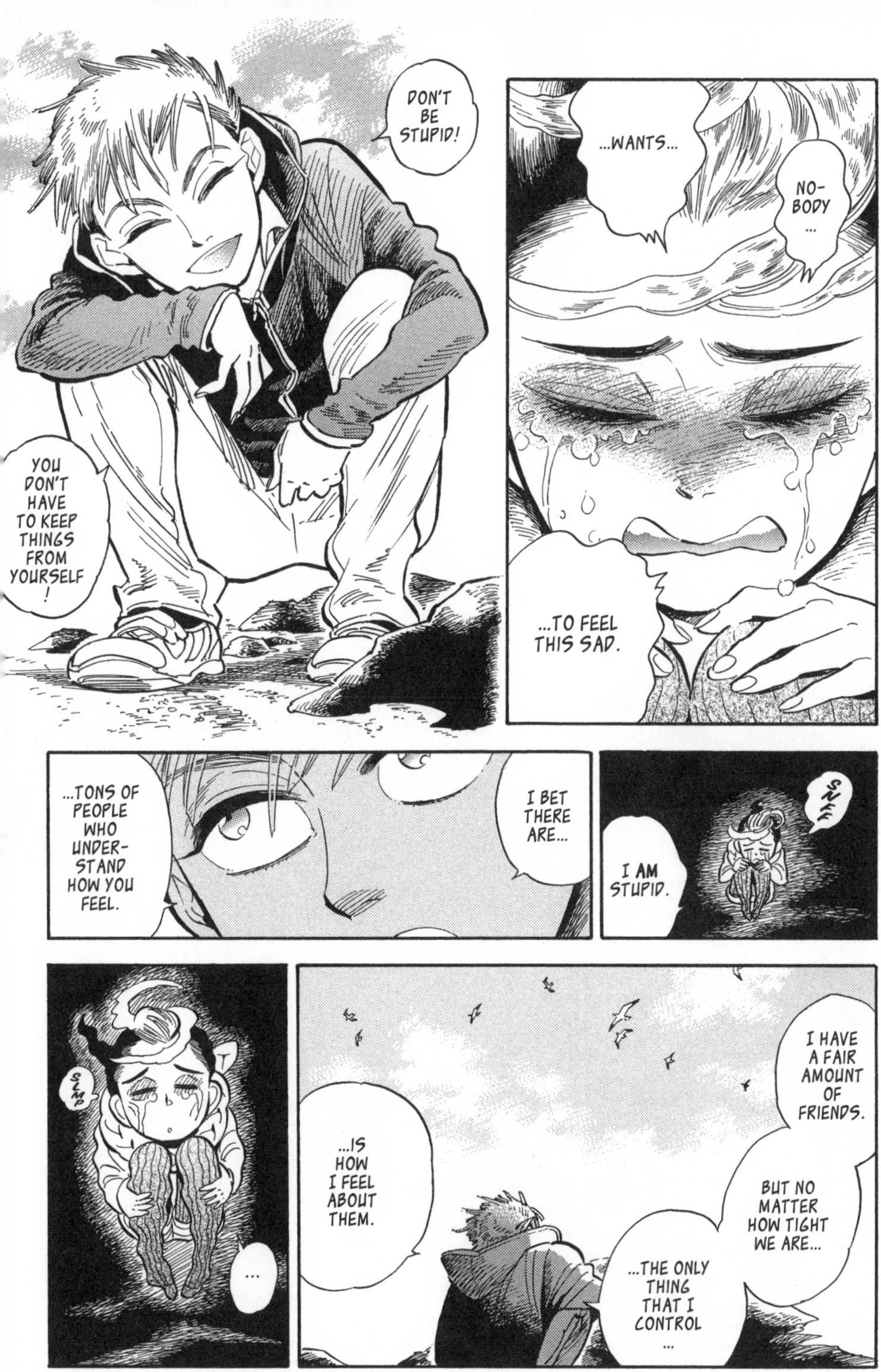
NO-BODY ...
...WANTS...
...TO FEEL THIS SAD.
DON'T BE STUPID!
YOU DON'T HAVE TO KEEP THINGS FROM YOURSELF!
SNFF
I AM STUPID.
I BET THERE ARE...
...TONS OF PEOPLE WHO UNDER-STAND HOW YOU FEEL.
I HAVE A FAIR AMOUNT OF FRIENDS.
BUT NO MATTER HOW TIGHT WE ARE...
...THE ONLY THING THAT I CONTROL ...
...IS HOW I FEEL ABOUT THEM.
SLMP
...

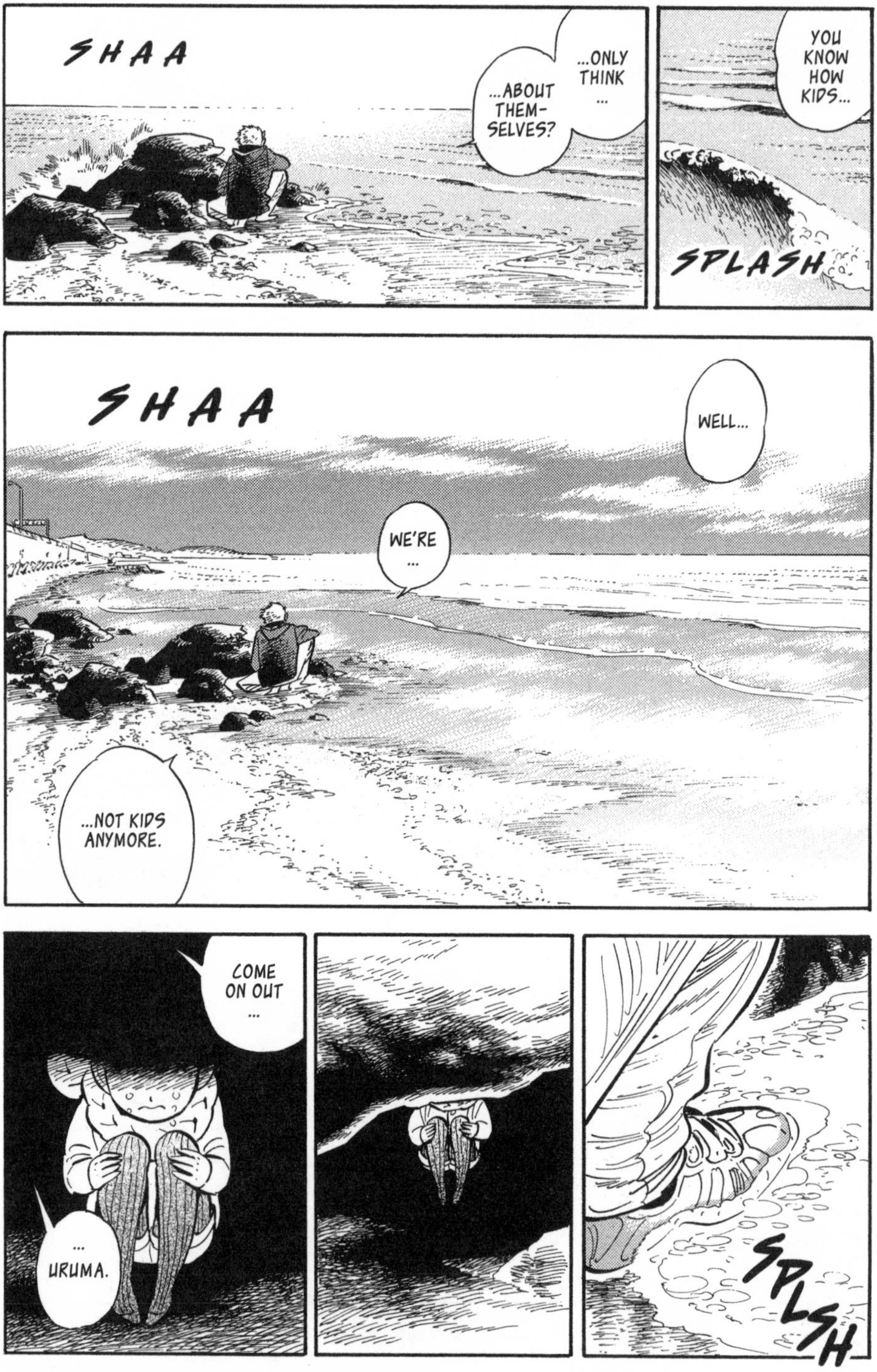
YOU KNOW HOW KIDS...
SPLASH
...ONLY THINK ...
...ABOUT THEM-SELVES?
SHAA
WELL...
SHAA
WE'RE ...
...NOT KIDS ANYMORE.
SPLSH
COME ON OUT ...
... URUMA.

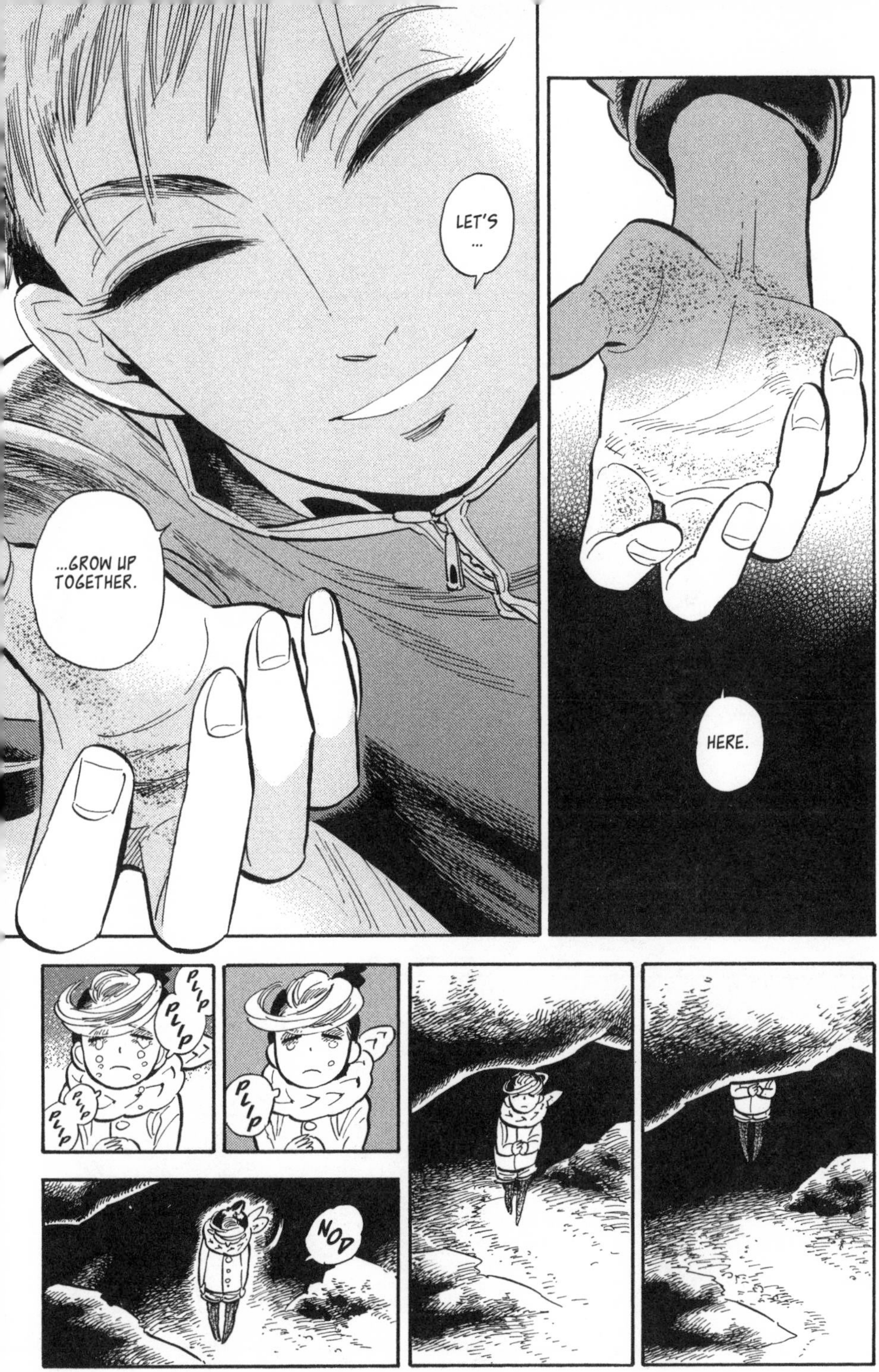
HERE.
LET'S ...
...GROW UP TOGETHER.
PLIP
PLIP PLIP
PLIP PLIP
NOD

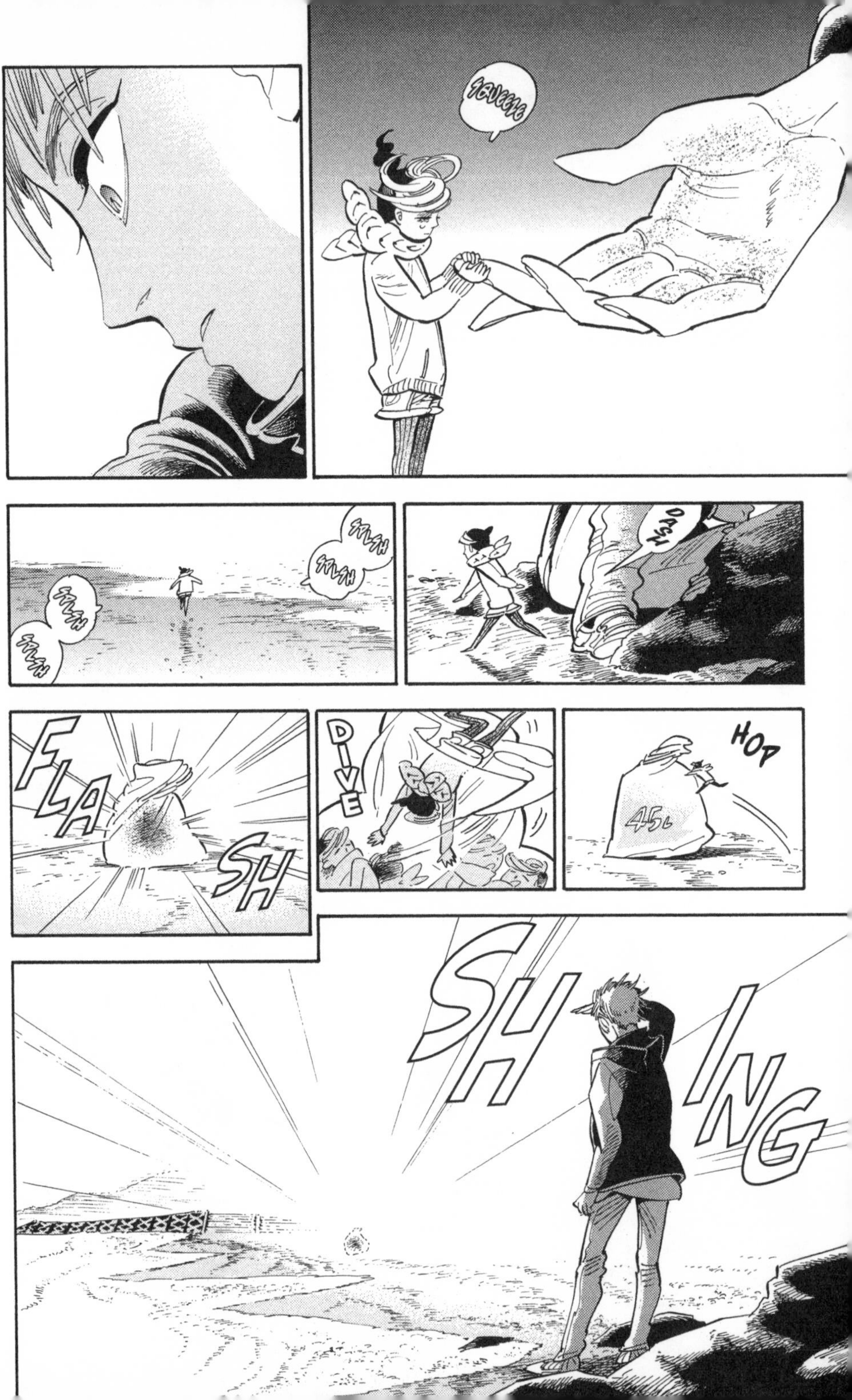
SQUEEZE
DASH
SPLSH
SPLSH
SPLSH
SPLSH
HOP
45L
DIVE
FLASH
SHING

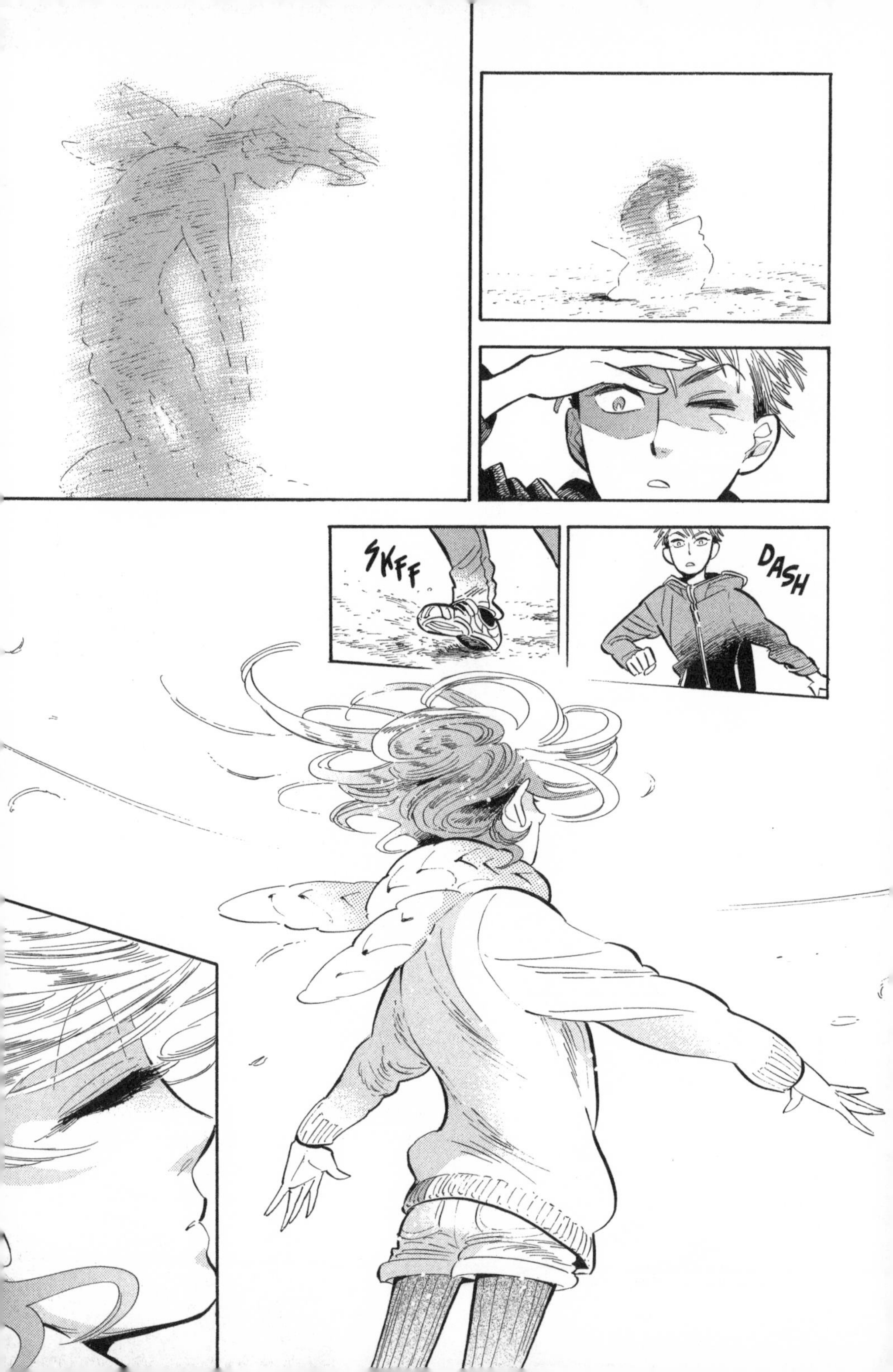
DASH
SKFF

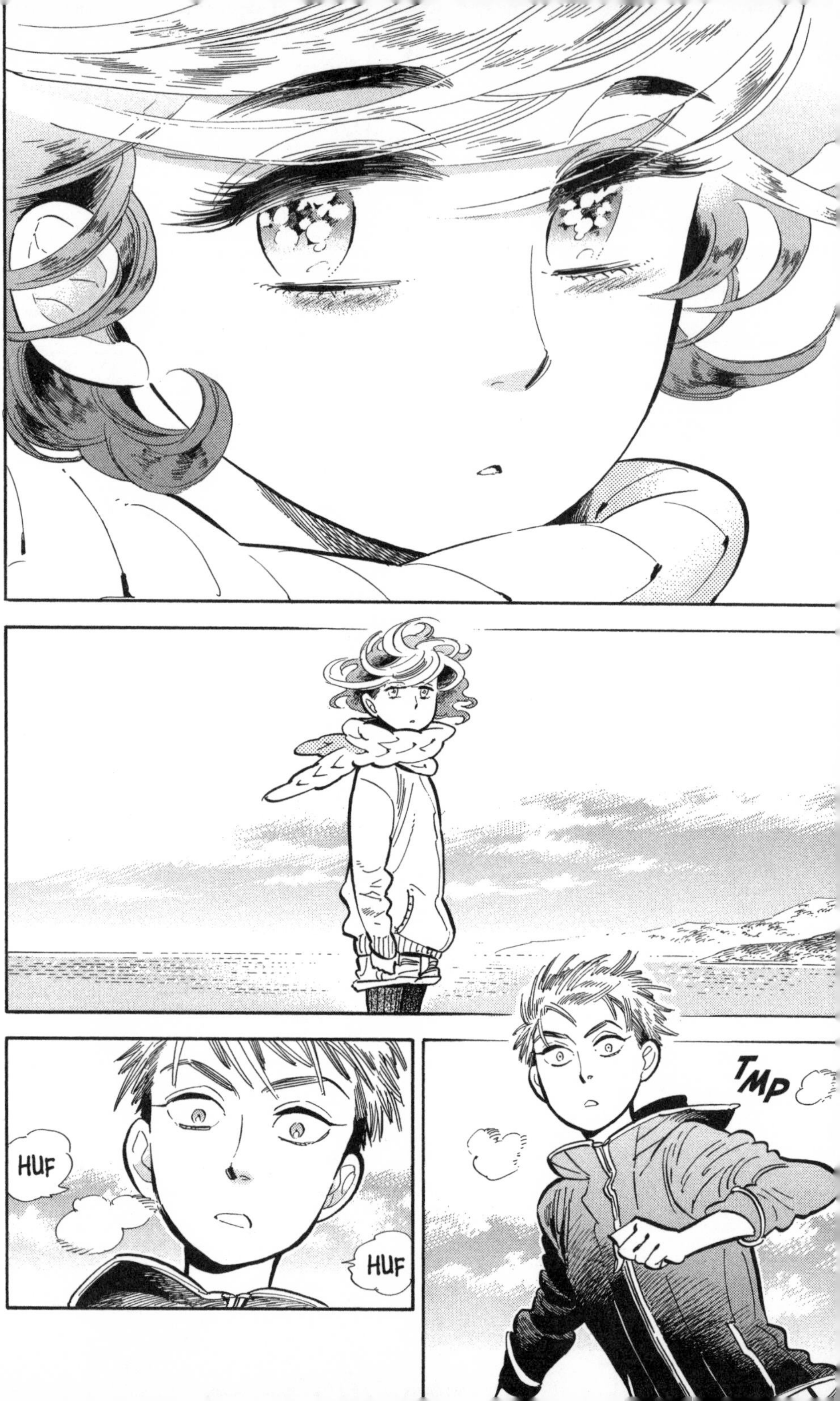
TMP
HUF
HUF

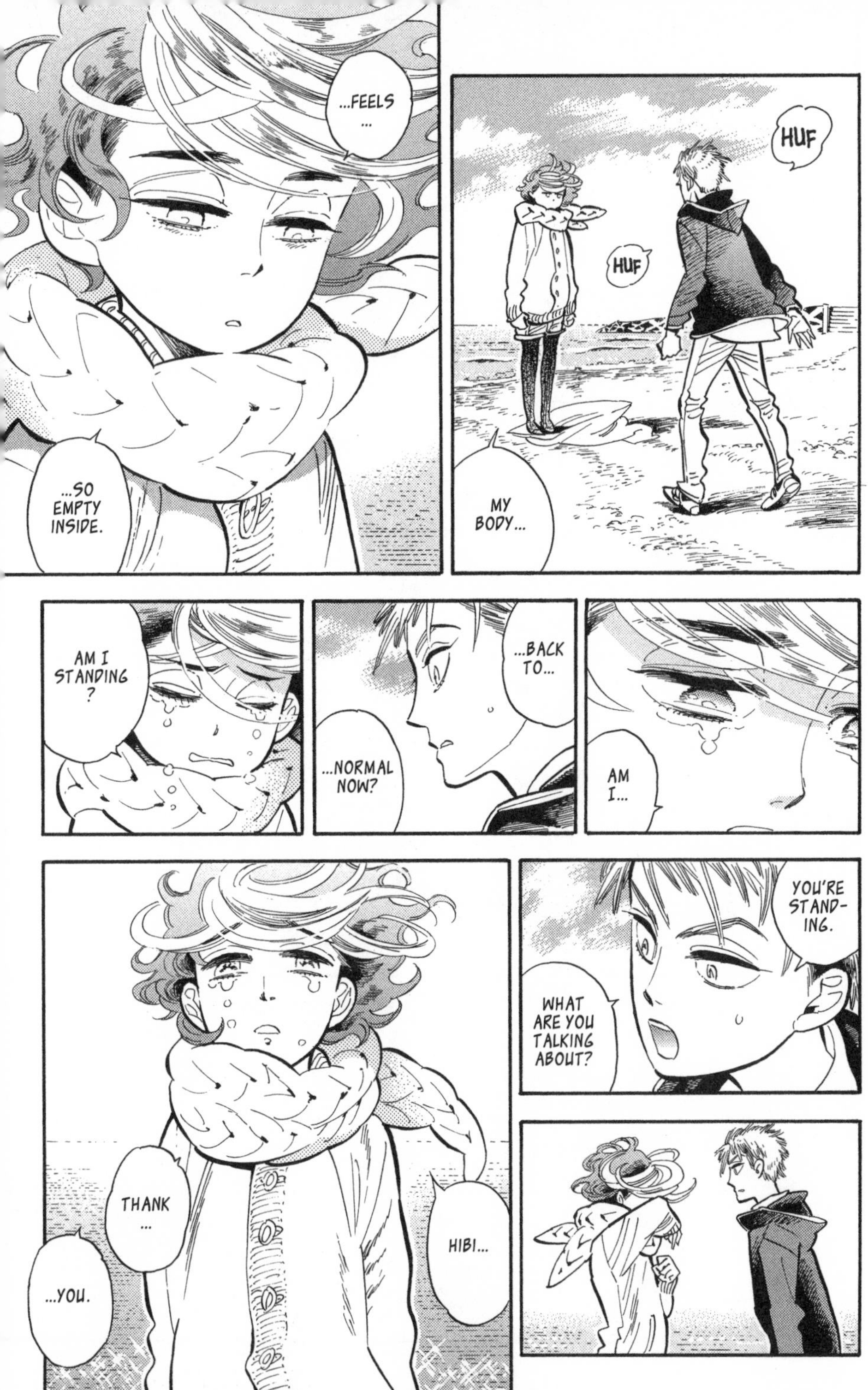
HUF
HUF
MY BODY...
...FEELS ...
...SO EMPTY INSIDE.
AM I...
...BACK TO...
...NORMAL NOW?
AM I STANDING ?
YOU'RE STAND-ING.
WHAT ARE YOU TALKING ABOUT?
HIBI...
THANK ...
...YOU.

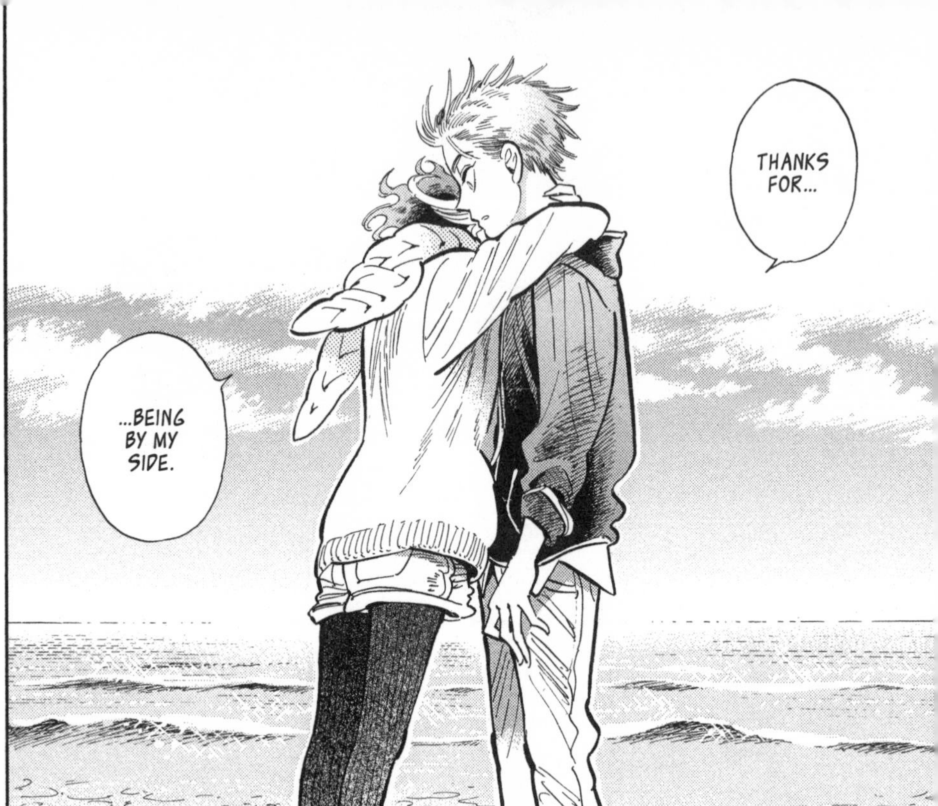
THANKS FOR...
...BEING BY MY SIDE.

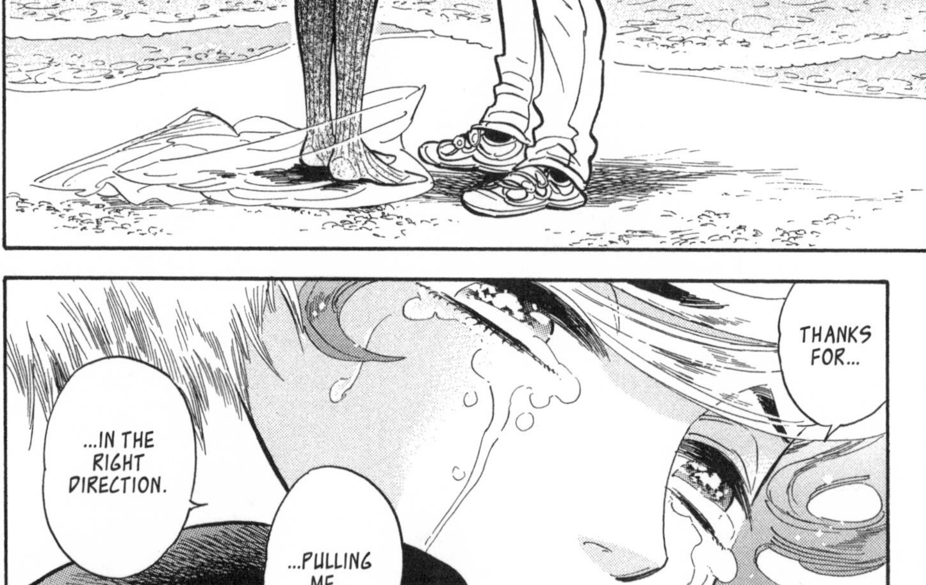
THANKS FOR...
...PULLING ME...
...IN THE RIGHT DIRECTION.

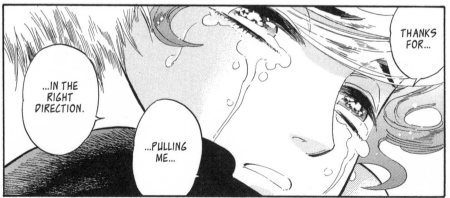

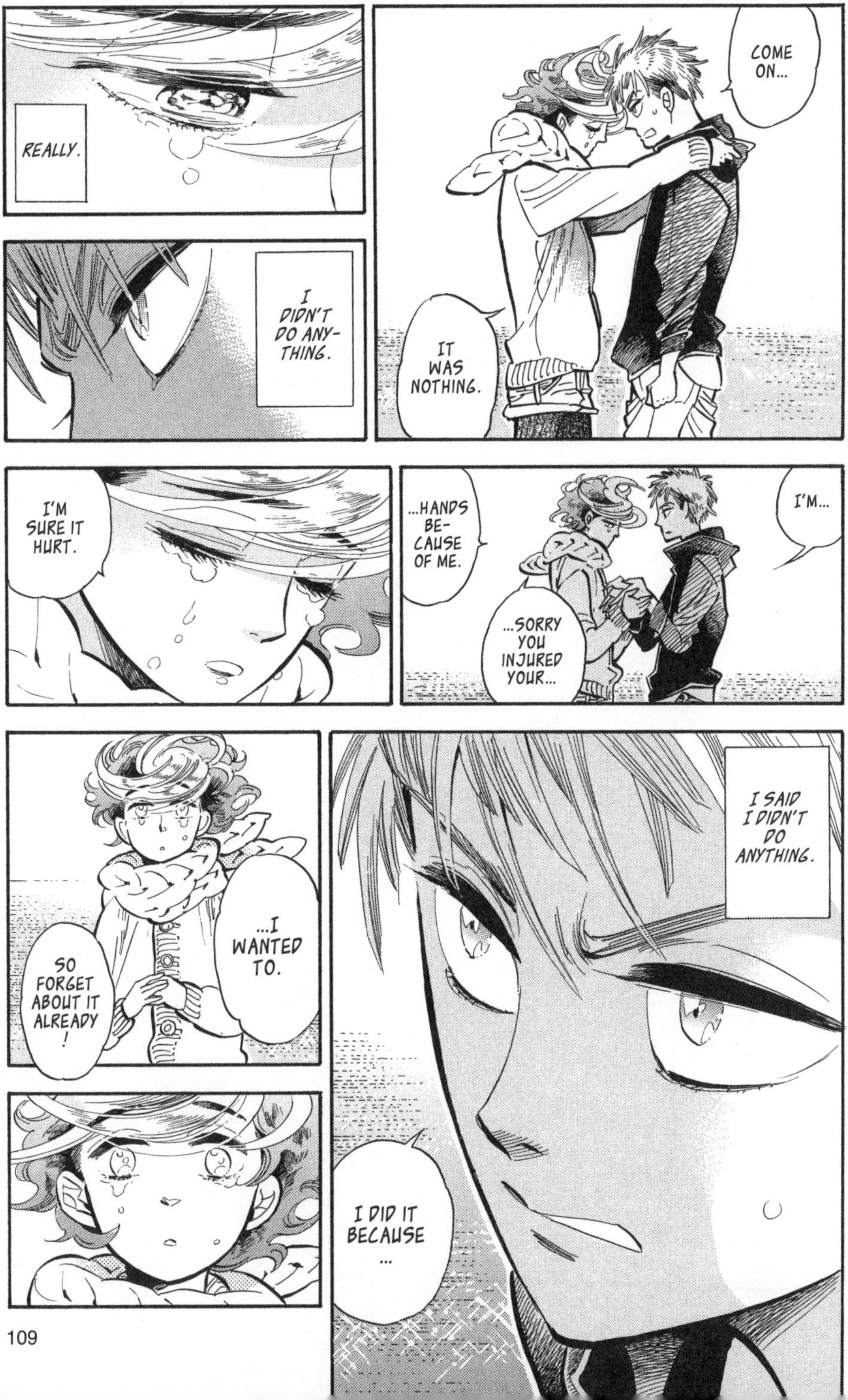
COME ON...
IT WAS NOTHING.
REALLY.
I DIDN'T DO ANY-THING.
I'M...
...SORRY YOU INJURED YOUR...
...HANDS BE-CAUSE OF ME.
I'M SURE IT HURT.
I SAID I DIDN'T DO ANYTHING.
I DID IT BECAUSE ...
...I WANTED TO.
SO FORGET ABOUT IT ALREADY !

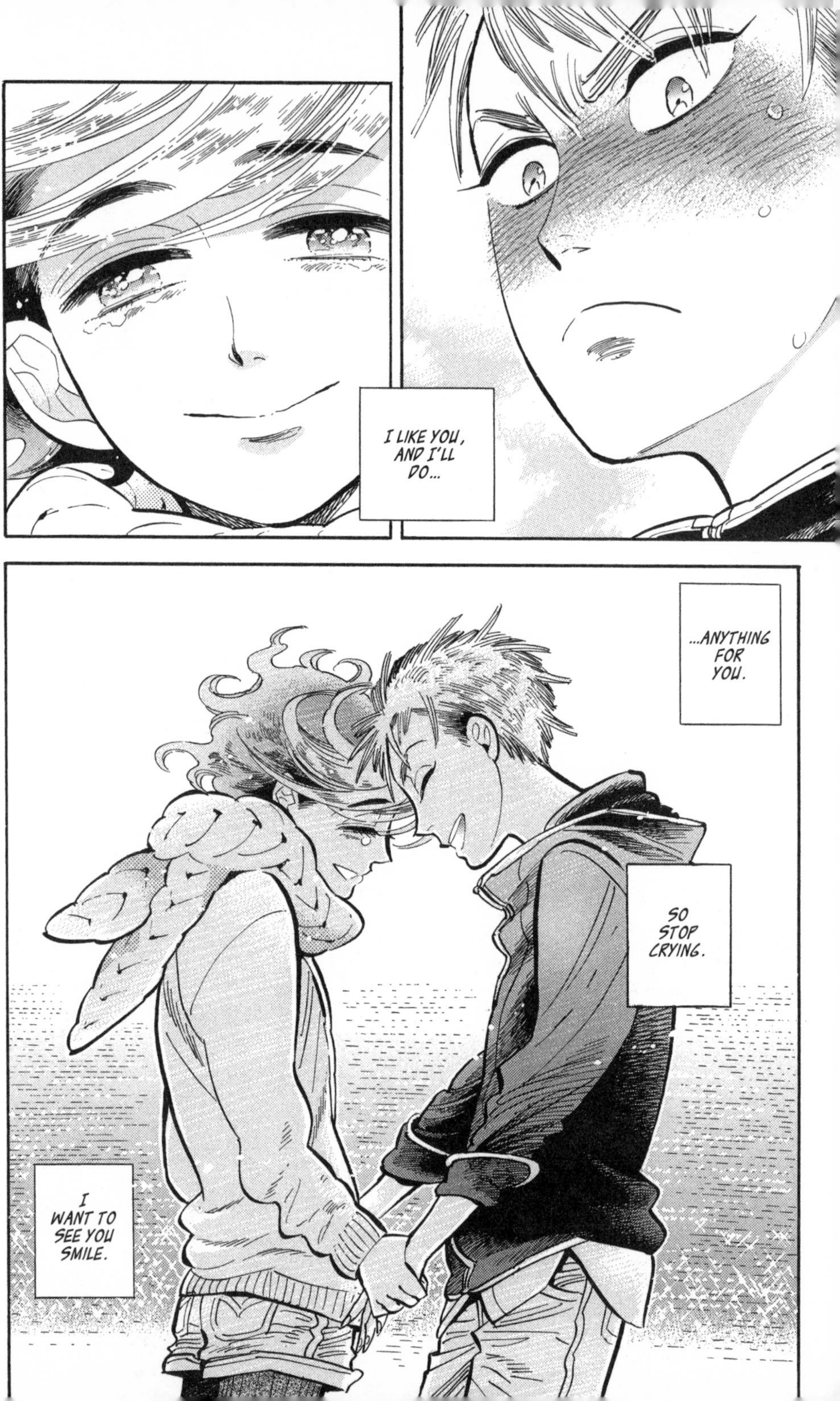
I LIKE YOU, AND I'LL DO...
...ANYTHING FOR YOU.
SO STOP CRYING.
I WANT TO SEE YOU SMILE.

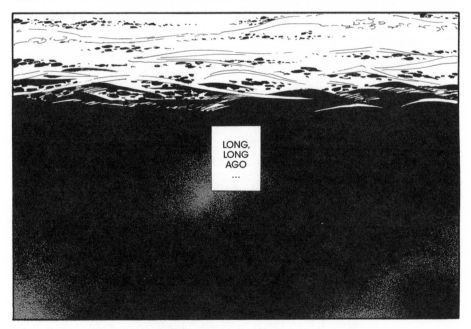

LONG,
LONG
AGO
...

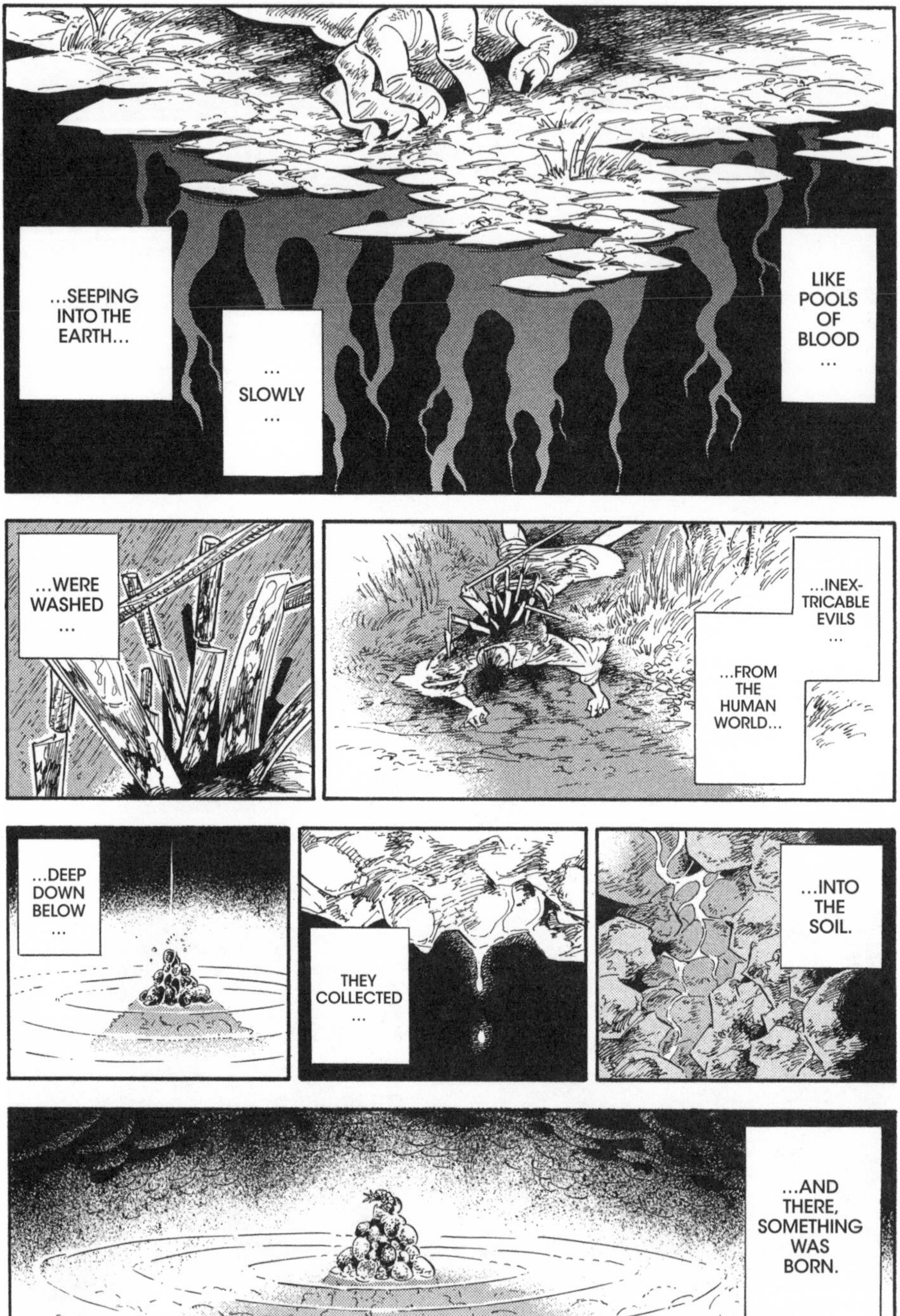
LIKE POOLS OF BLOOD ...
... SLOWLY ...
...SEEPING INTO THE EARTH...
...INEX-TRICABLE EVILS ...
...FROM THE HUMAN WORLD...
...WERE WASHED ...
...INTO THE SOIL.
THEY COLLECTED ...
...DEEP DOWN BELOW ...
...AND THERE, SOMETHING WAS BORN.

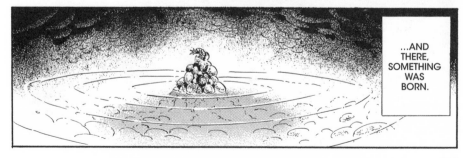

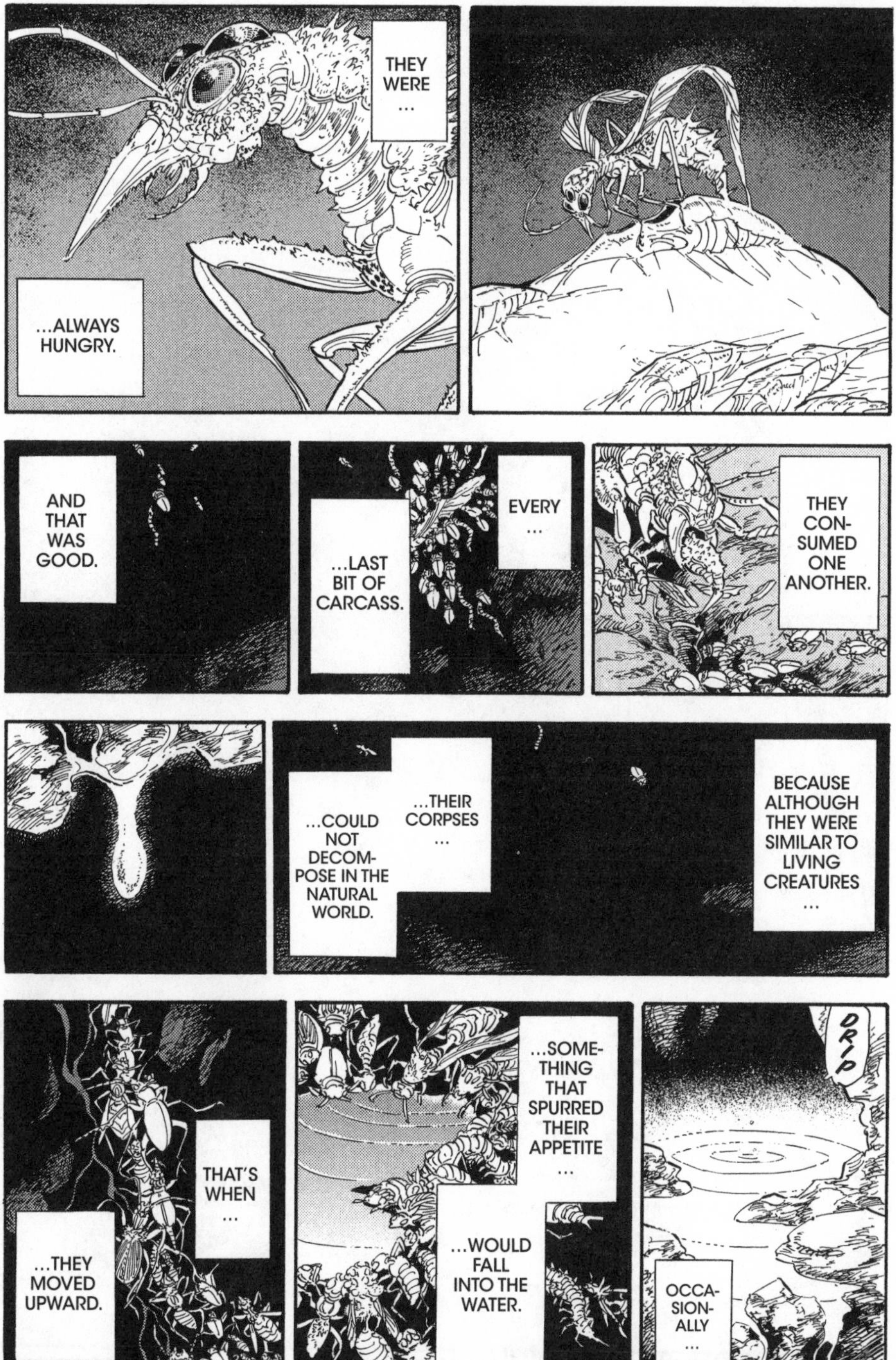
THEY WERE ...
...ALWAYS HUNGRY.
THEY CONSUMED ONE ANOTHER.
EVERY ...
...LAST BIT OF CARCASS.
AND THAT WAS GOOD.
BECAUSE ALTHOUGH THEY WERE SIMILAR TO LIVING CREATURES ...
...THEIR CORPSES ...
...COULD NOT DECOMPOSE IN THE NATURAL WORLD.
DRIP
OCCASIONALLY ...
...SOMETHING THAT SPURRED THEIR APPETITE ...
...WOULD FALL INTO THE WATER.
THAT'S WHEN ...
...THEY MOVED UPWARD.

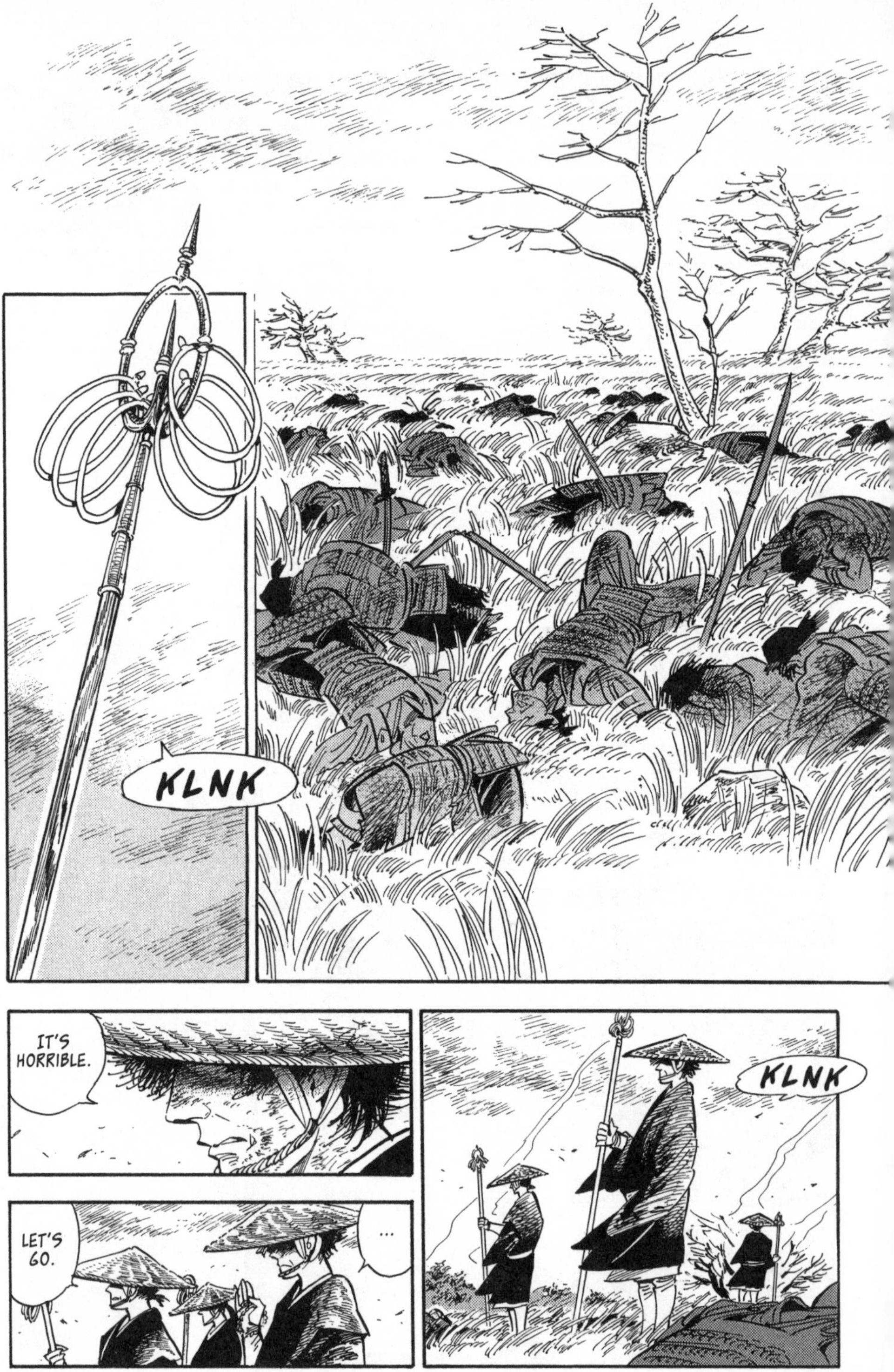
KLNK
KLNK
IT'S HORRIBLE.
...
LET'S GO.

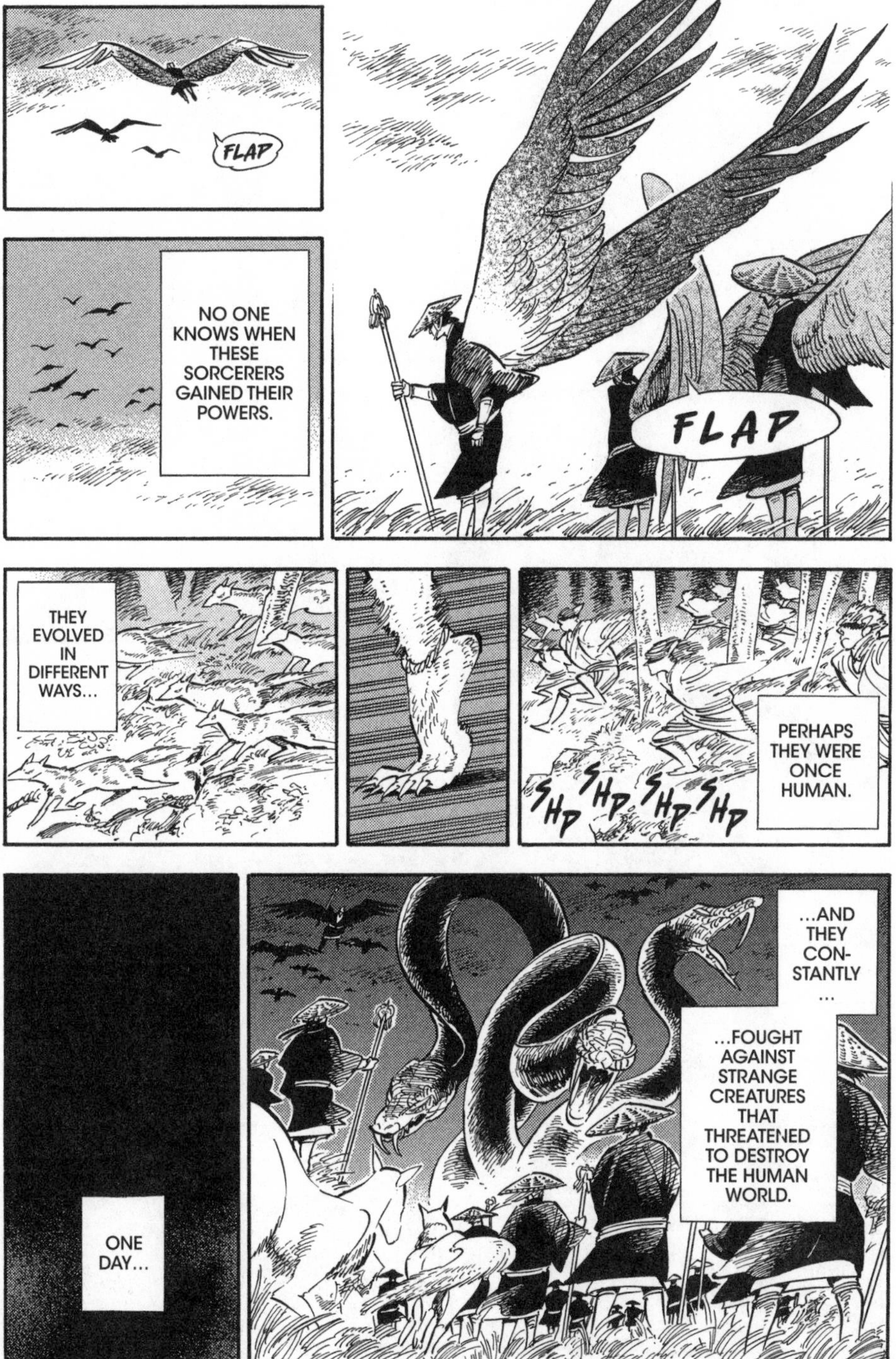
FLAP
FLAP
NO ONE KNOWS WHEN THESE SORCERERS GAINED THEIR POWERS.
SHP SHP SHP SHP
PERHAPS THEY WERE ONCE HUMAN.
THEY EVOLVED IN DIFFERENT WAYS...
...AND THEY CON-STANTLY ...
...FOUGHT AGAINST STRANGE CREATURES THAT THREATENED TO DESTROY THE HUMAN WORLD.
ONE DAY...

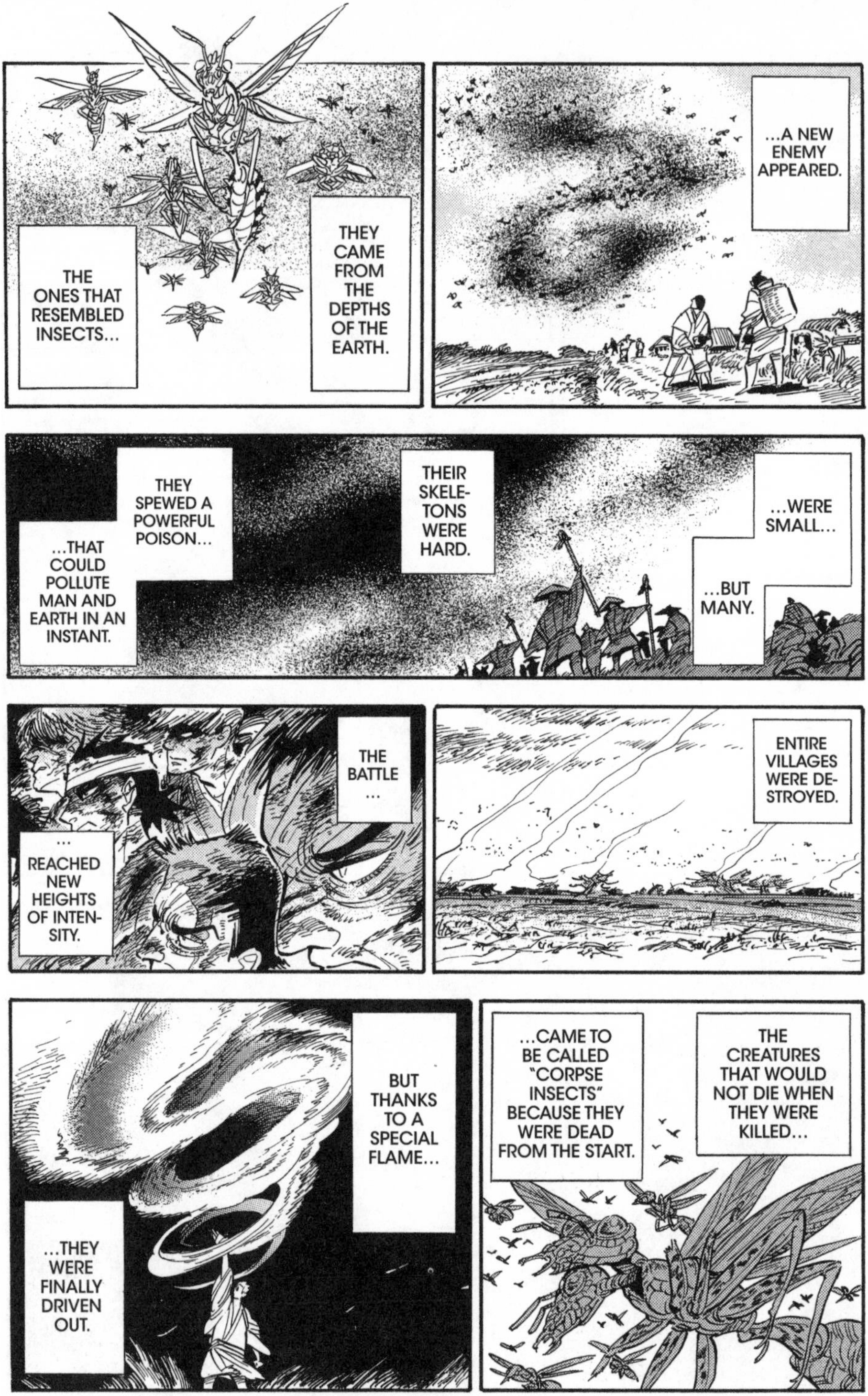
...A NEW ENEMY APPEARED.
THEY CAME FROM THE DEPTHS OF THE EARTH.
THE ONES THAT RESEMBLED INSECTS...
...WERE SMALL...
...BUT MANY.
THEIR SKELETONS WERE HARD.
THEY SPEWED A POWERFUL POISON...
...THAT COULD POLLUTE MAN AND EARTH IN AN INSTANT.
ENTIRE VILLAGES WERE DESTROYED.
THE BATTLE ...
... REACHED NEW HEIGHTS OF INTENSITY.
THE CREATURES THAT WOULD NOT DIE WHEN THEY WERE KILLED...
...CAME TO BE CALLED "CORPSE INSECTS" BECAUSE THEY WERE DEAD FROM THE START.
BUT THANKS TO A SPECIAL FLAME...
...THEY WERE FINALLY DRIVEN OUT.

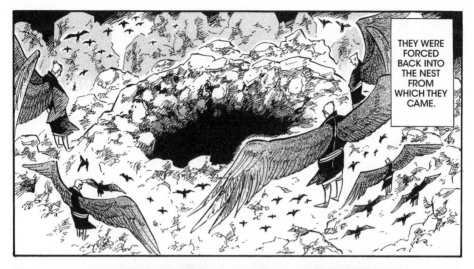

THEY WERE FORCED BACK INTO THE NEST FROM WHICH THEY CAME.
THE INJURED SORCERERS...
...WERE CARED FOR...
...BY THE HUMANS WHO LIVED ON THAT LAND.
THE SORCERERS PROMISED TO WATCH OVER THE LAND...
...FOREVER.
THE ENTRANCE TO THE...
...INSECTS' NEST WAS SEALED AND PLACED UNDER WATCH.
AFTER THAT...
...THE SORCERERS DEVELOPED NEW WAYS...
...TO SEAL THE BUGS AWAY. THEY STRENGTHENED THEIR MAGIC SKILLS...
...IN ANTICIPATION OF THE NEXT BATTLE.
THEY...
...WAITED FOR THE DAY.

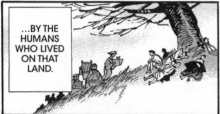

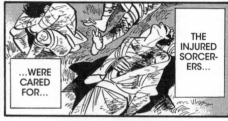

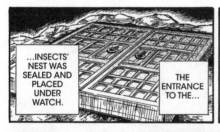

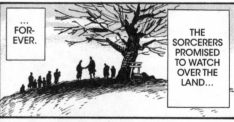

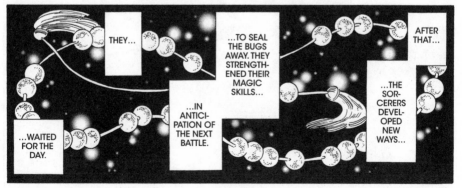

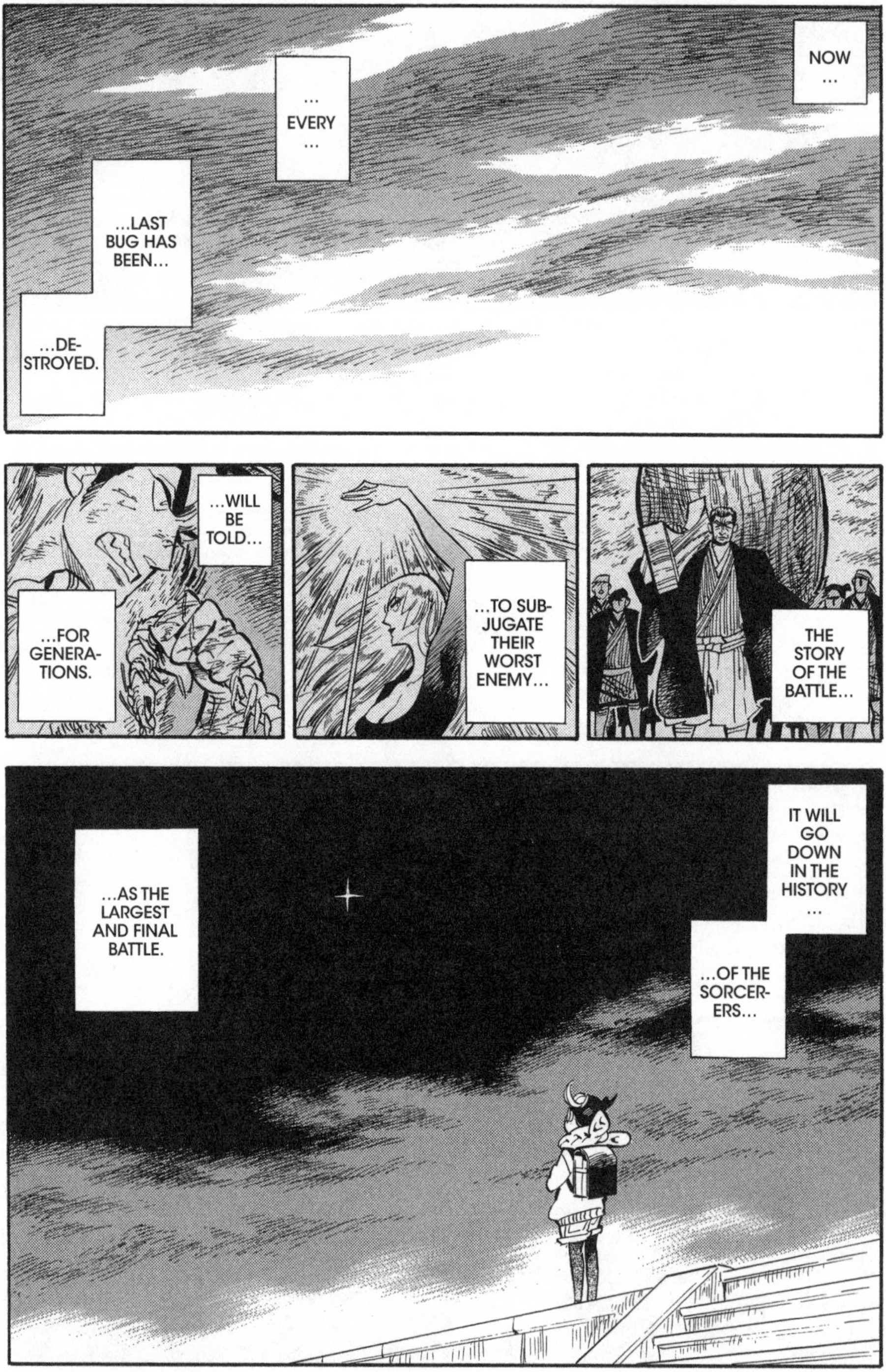
NOW...
...EVERY...
...LAST BUG HAS BEEN...
...DESTROYED.
THE STORY OF THE BATTLE...
...TO SUBJUGATE THEIR WORST ENEMY...
...WILL BE TOLD...
...FOR GENERATIONS.
IT WILL GO DOWN IN THE HISTORY...
...OF THE SORCERERS...
...AS THE LARGEST AND FINAL BATTLE.

Chapter 39 / The End

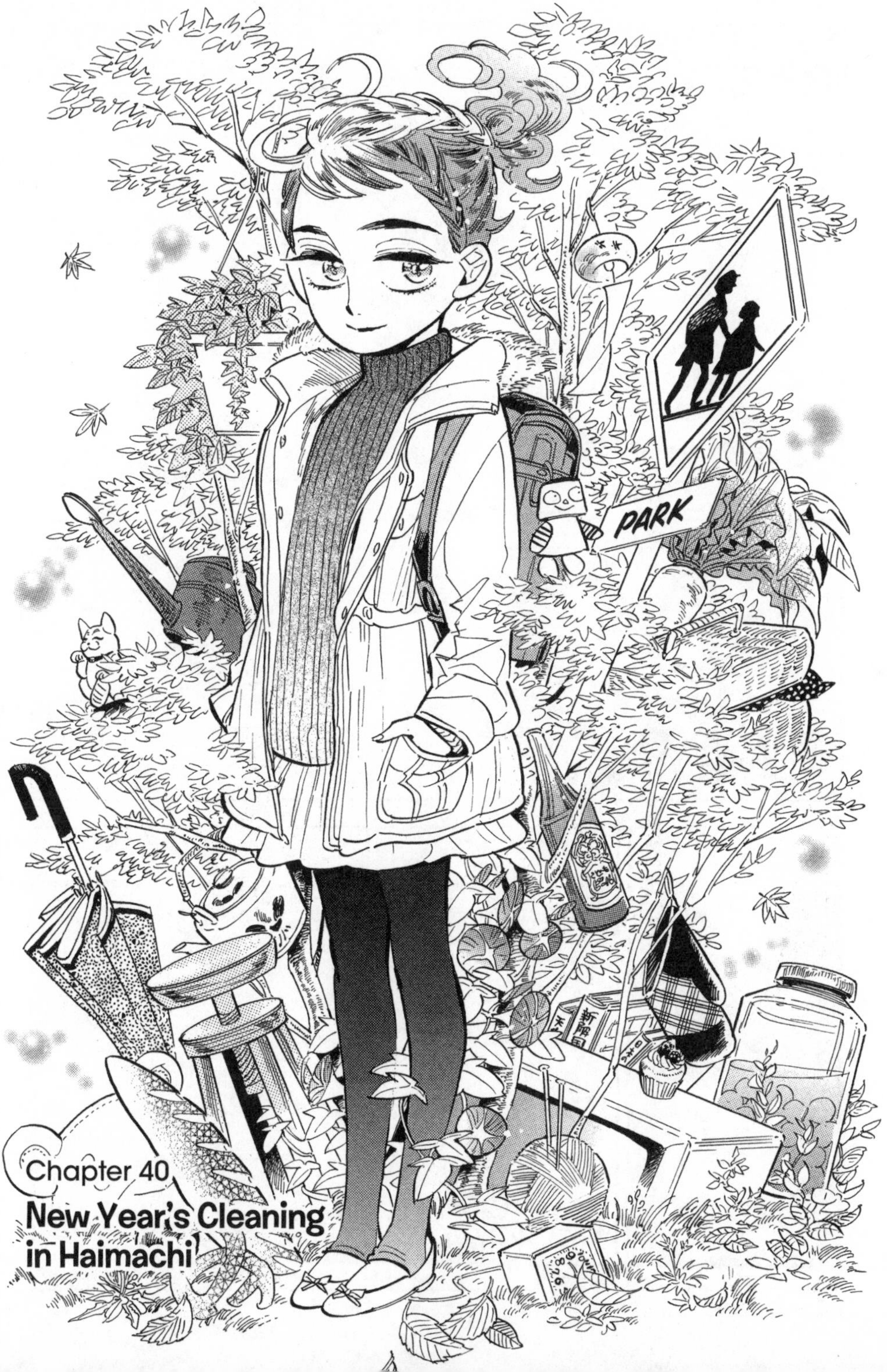
PARK

Chapter 40

New Year's Cleaning in Haimachi

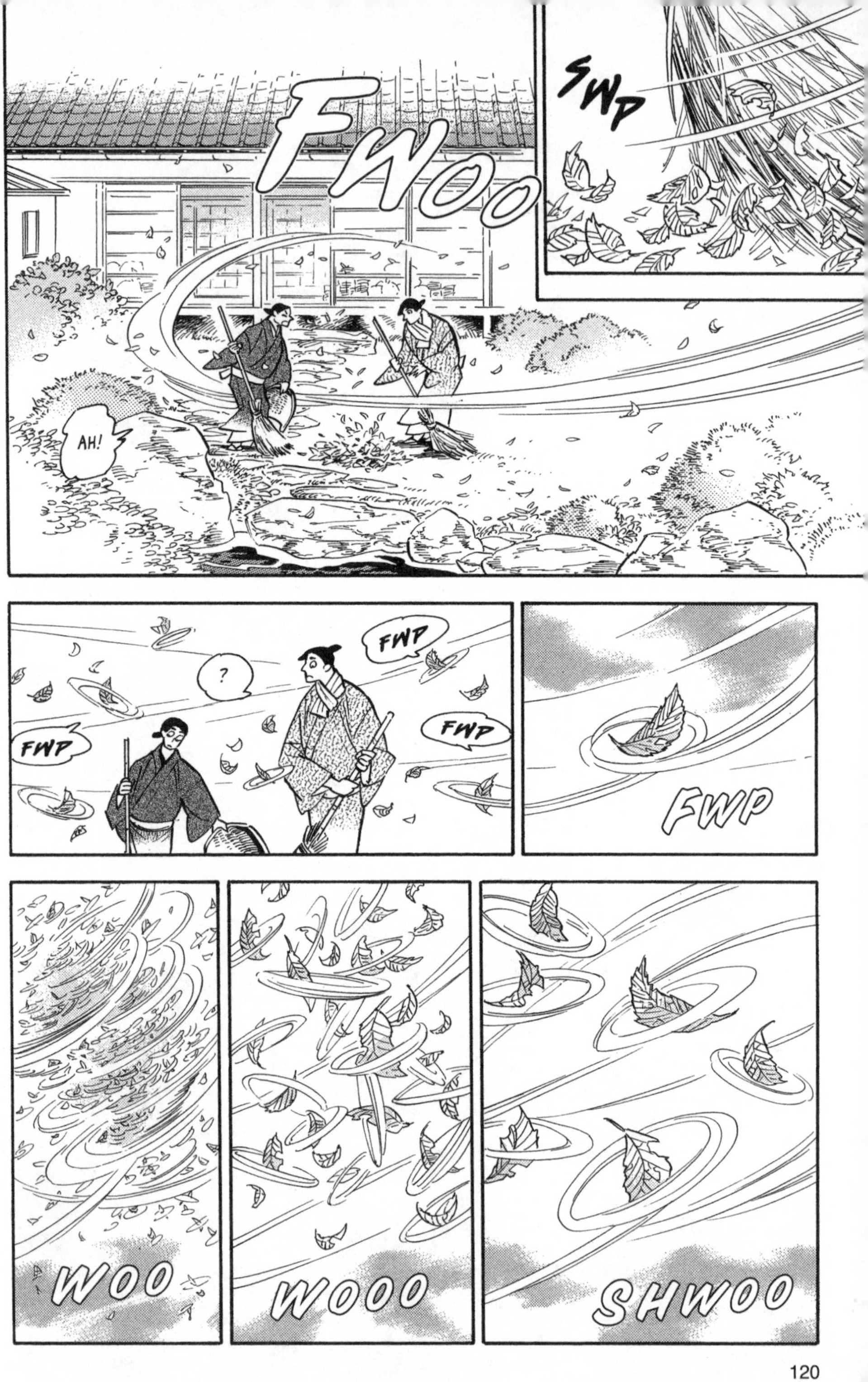
SWP
FWOO
AH!
FWP
FWP
FWP
?
FWP
SHWOO
WOOO
WOO

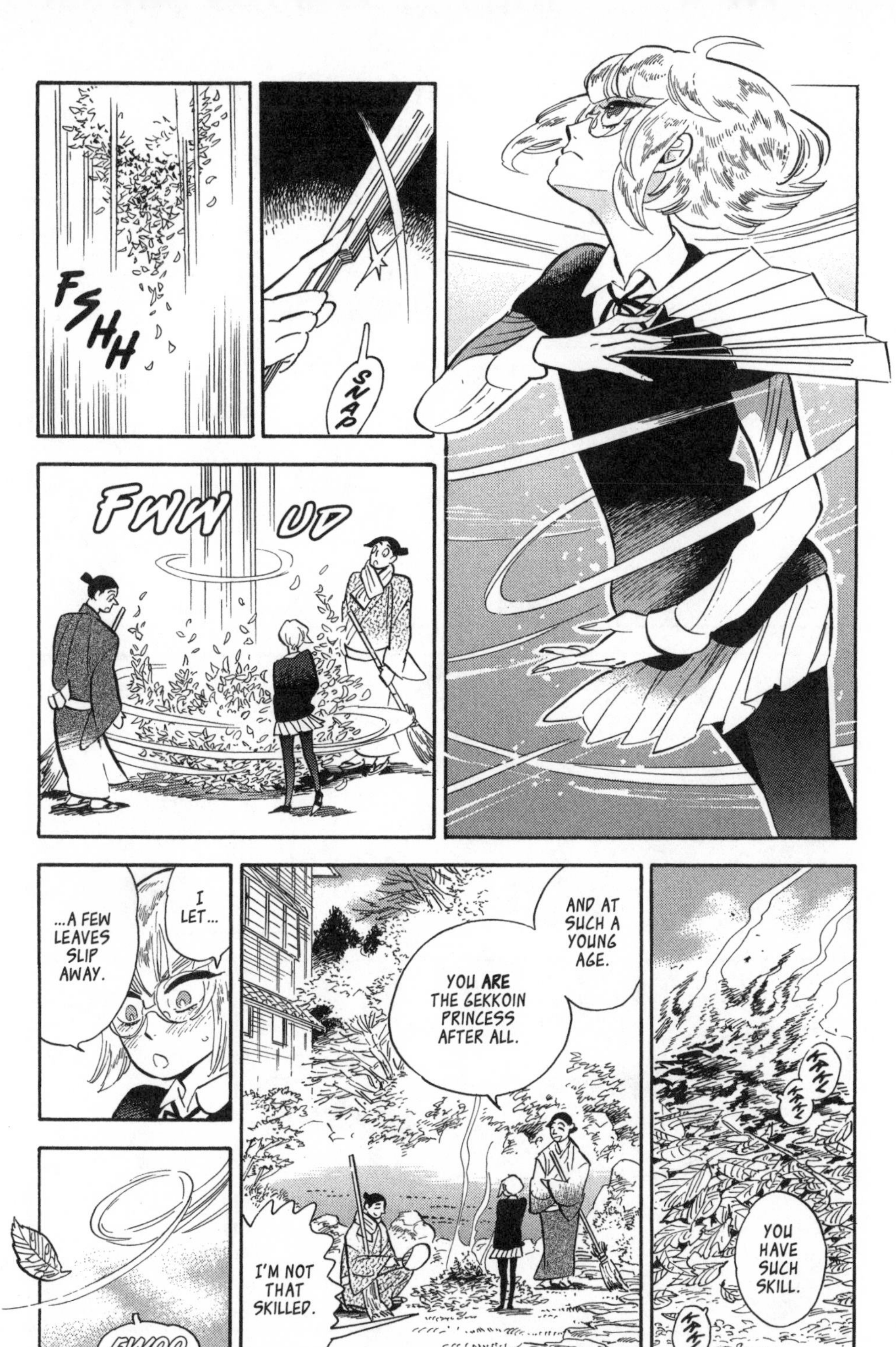
SNAP
FSHH
FWW UD
KRKK
KRKK
YOU HAVE SUCH SKILL.
KRKK
AND AT SUCH A YOUNG AGE.
YOU ARE THE GEKKOIN PRINCESS AFTER ALL.
I'M NOT THAT SKILLED.
I LET...
...A FEW LEAVES SLIP AWAY.
FWOO

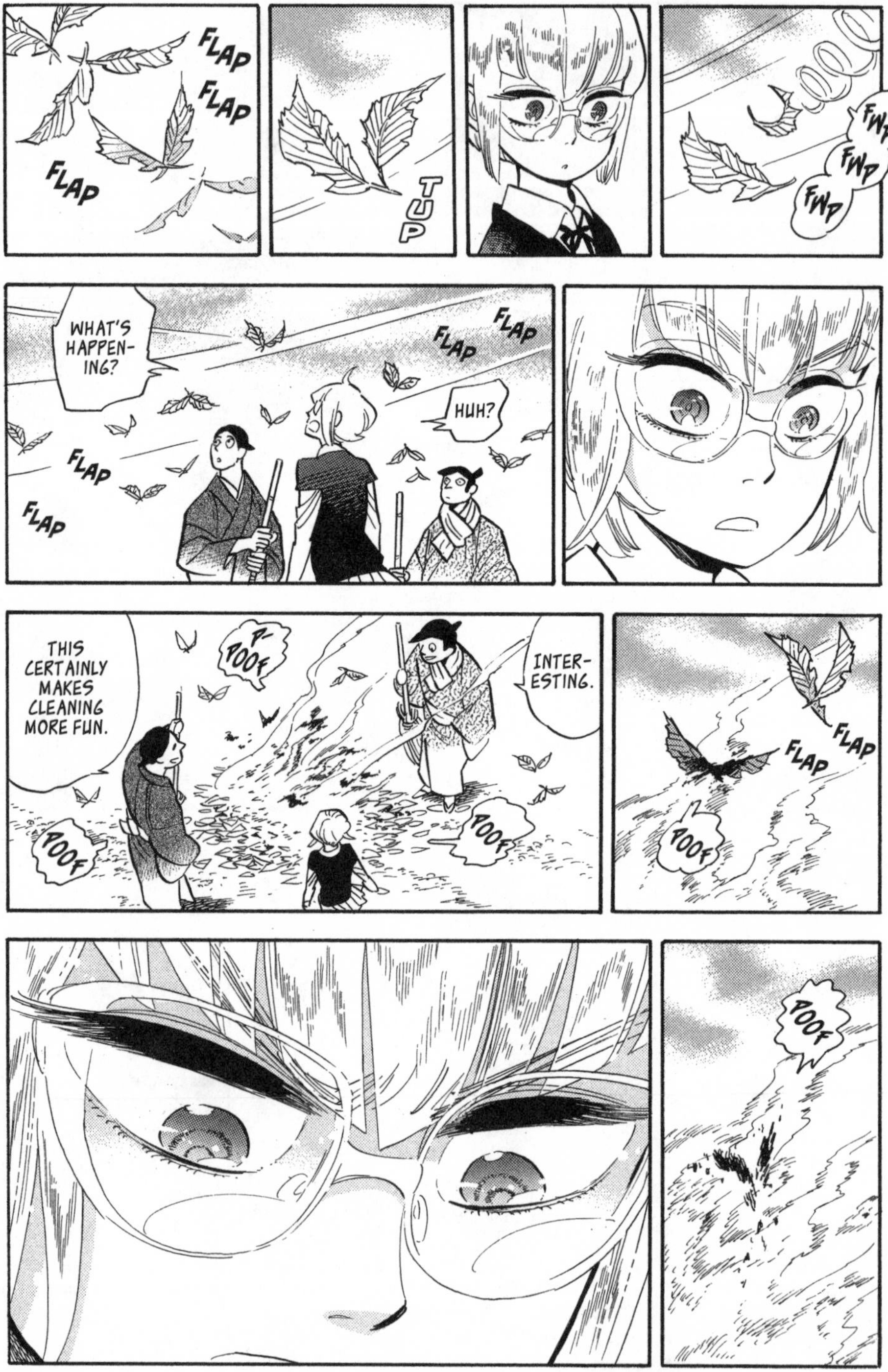
FWP
FWP
FWP
TUP
FLAP
FLAP
FLAP
FLAP
FLAP
HUH?
WHAT'S HAPPEN-ING?
FLAP
FLAP
FLAP
FLAP
POOF
INTER-ESTING.
P-POOF
POOF
THIS CERTAINLY MAKES CLEANING MORE FUN.
POOF
POOF

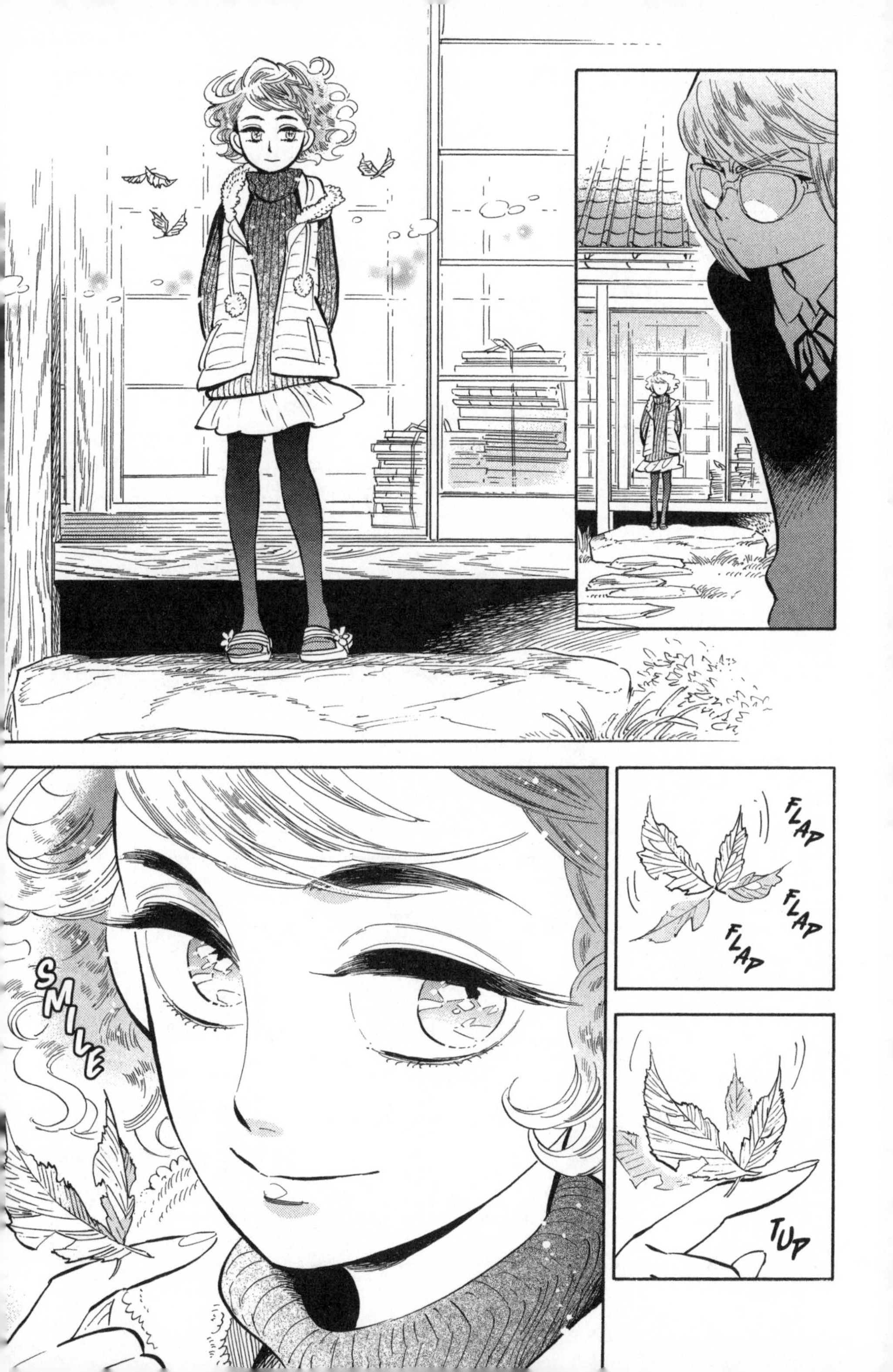
FLAP
FLAP
FLAP
TUP
SMILE

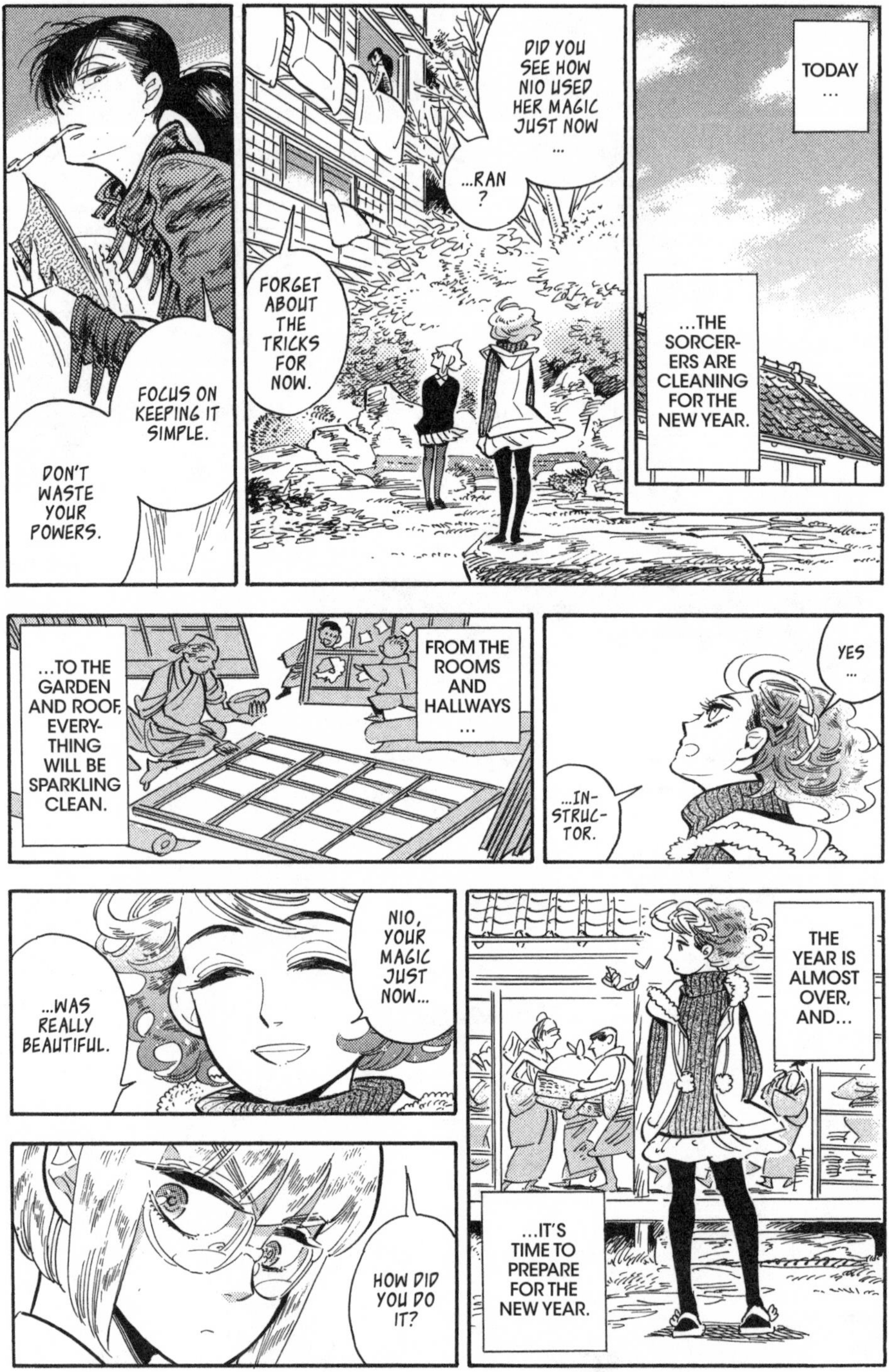
TODAY...
...THE SORCERERS ARE CLEANING FOR THE NEW YEAR.
DID YOU SEE HOW NIO USED HER MAGIC JUST NOW...
...RAN?
FORGET ABOUT THE TRICKS FOR NOW.
FOCUS ON KEEPING IT SIMPLE.
DON'T WASTE YOUR POWERS.
YES...
...INSTRUCTOR.
FROM THE ROOMS AND HALLWAYS...
...TO THE GARDEN AND ROOF, EVERYTHING WILL BE SPARKLING CLEAN.
THE YEAR IS ALMOST OVER, AND...
...IT'S TIME TO PREPARE FOR THE NEW YEAR.
NIO, YOUR MAGIC JUST NOW...
...WAS REALLY BEAUTIFUL.
HOW DID YOU DO IT?

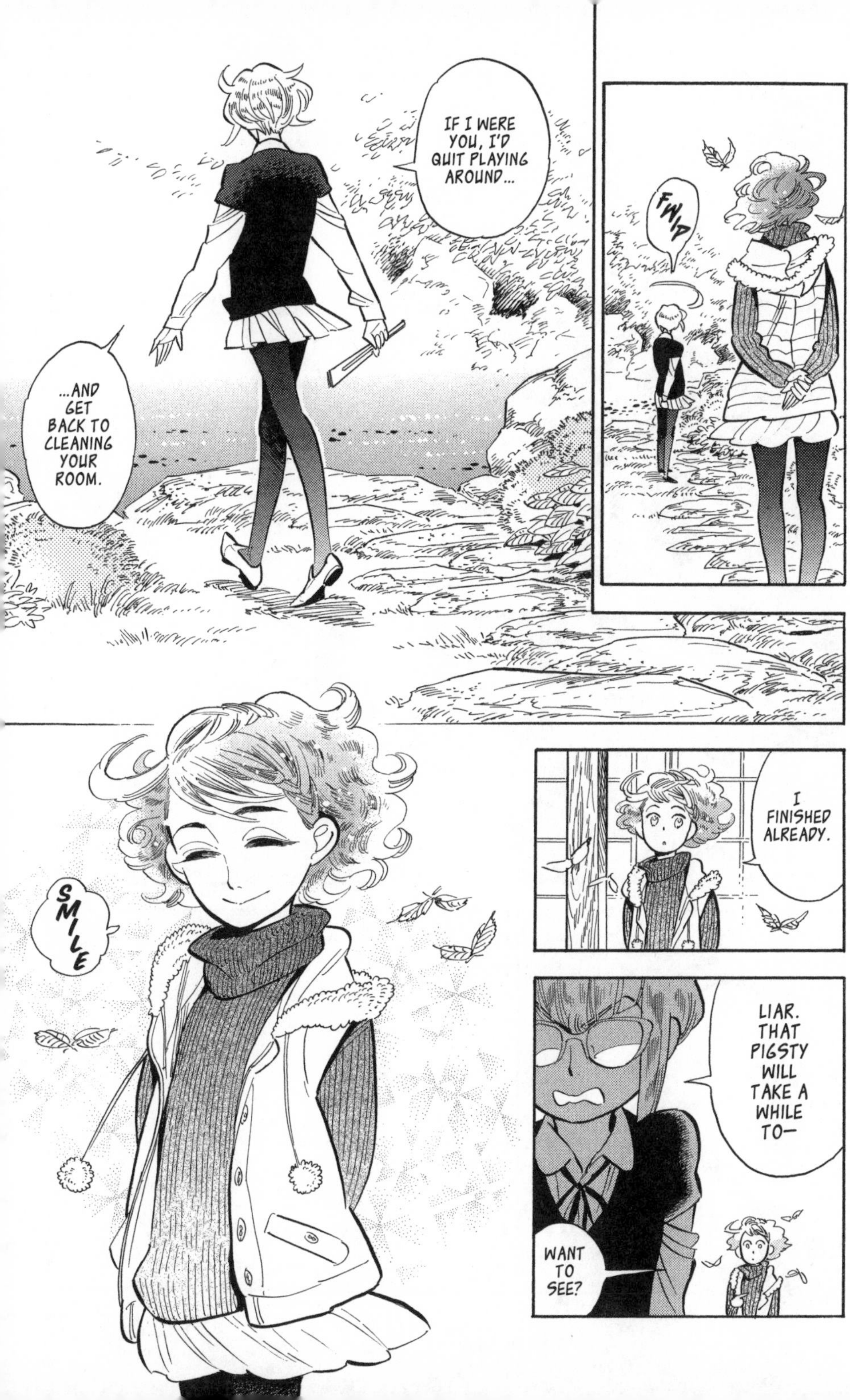
FWIP
IF I WERE YOU, I'D QUIT PLAYING AROUND...
...AND GET BACK TO CLEANING YOUR ROOM.
I FINISHED ALREADY.
LIAR. THAT PIGSTY WILL TAKE A WHILE TO—
WANT TO SEE?
SMILE

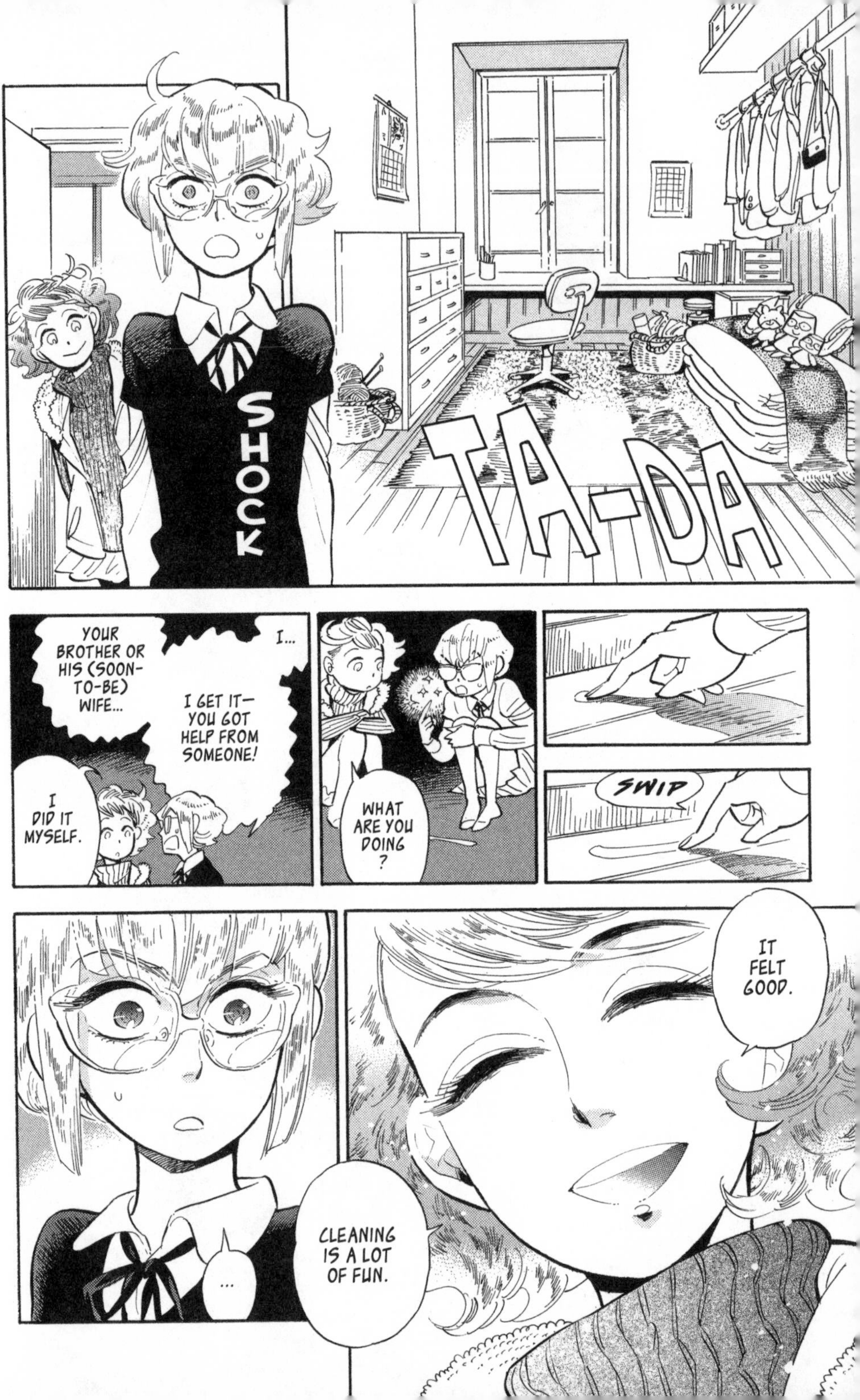
TA-DA
SHOCK
SWIP
WHAT ARE YOU DOING ?
I...
I GET IT—YOU GOT HELP FROM SOMEONE!
YOUR BROTHER OR HIS (SOON-TO-BE) WIFE...
I DID IT MYSELF.
IT FELT GOOD.
CLEANING IS A LOT OF FUN.
...

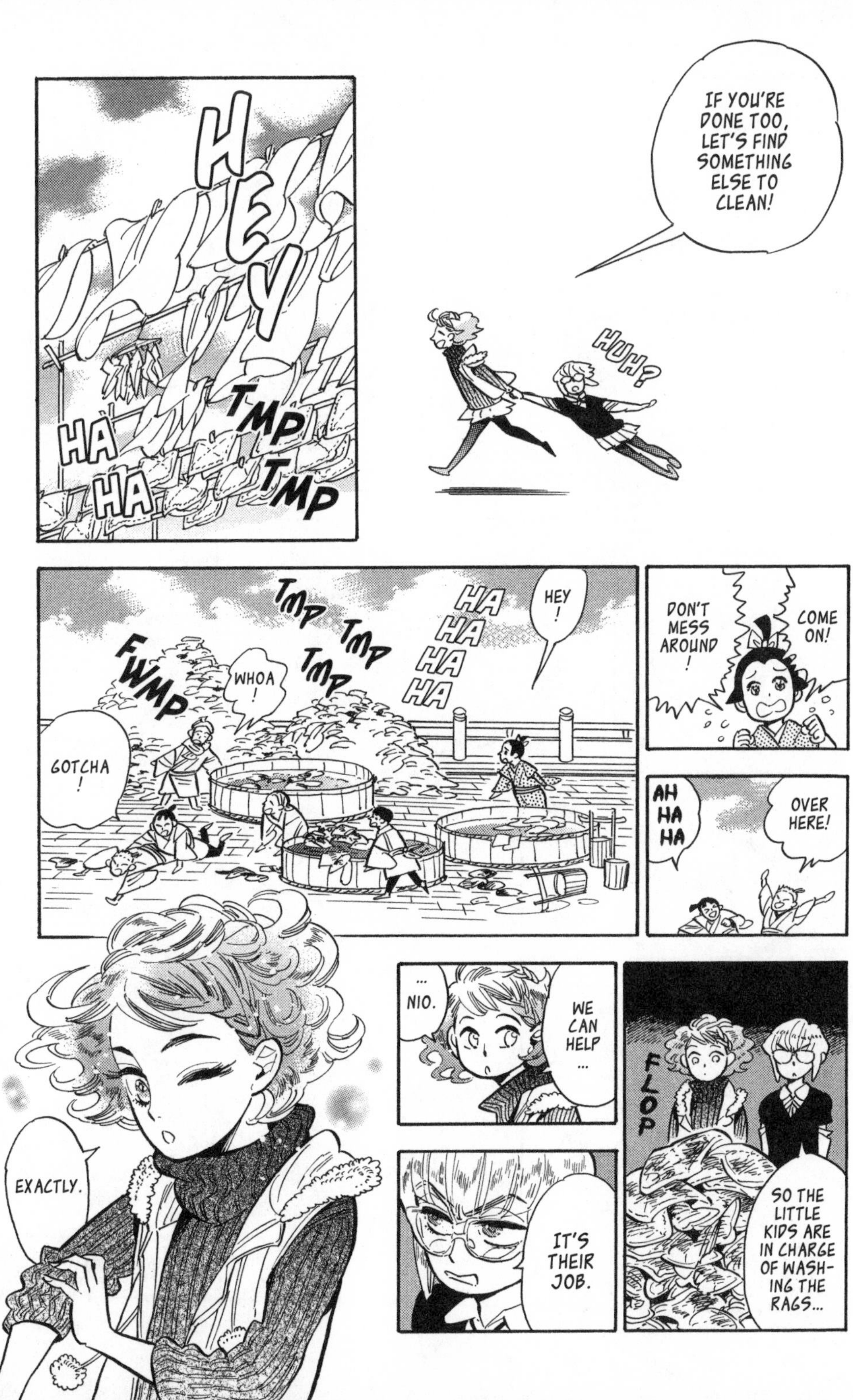
IF YOU'RE DONE TOO, LET'S FIND SOMETHING ELSE TO CLEAN!
HUH?
HEY
HA HA
TMP TMP
COME ON!
DON'T MESS AROUND!
OVER HERE!
AH HA HA
HEY!
HA HA HA HA
TMP TMP TMP
WHOA!
FWMP
GOTCHA!
SO THE LITTLE KIDS ARE IN CHARGE OF WASHING THE RAGS...
FLOP
WE CAN HELP...
...NIO.
IT'S THEIR JOB.
EXACTLY.

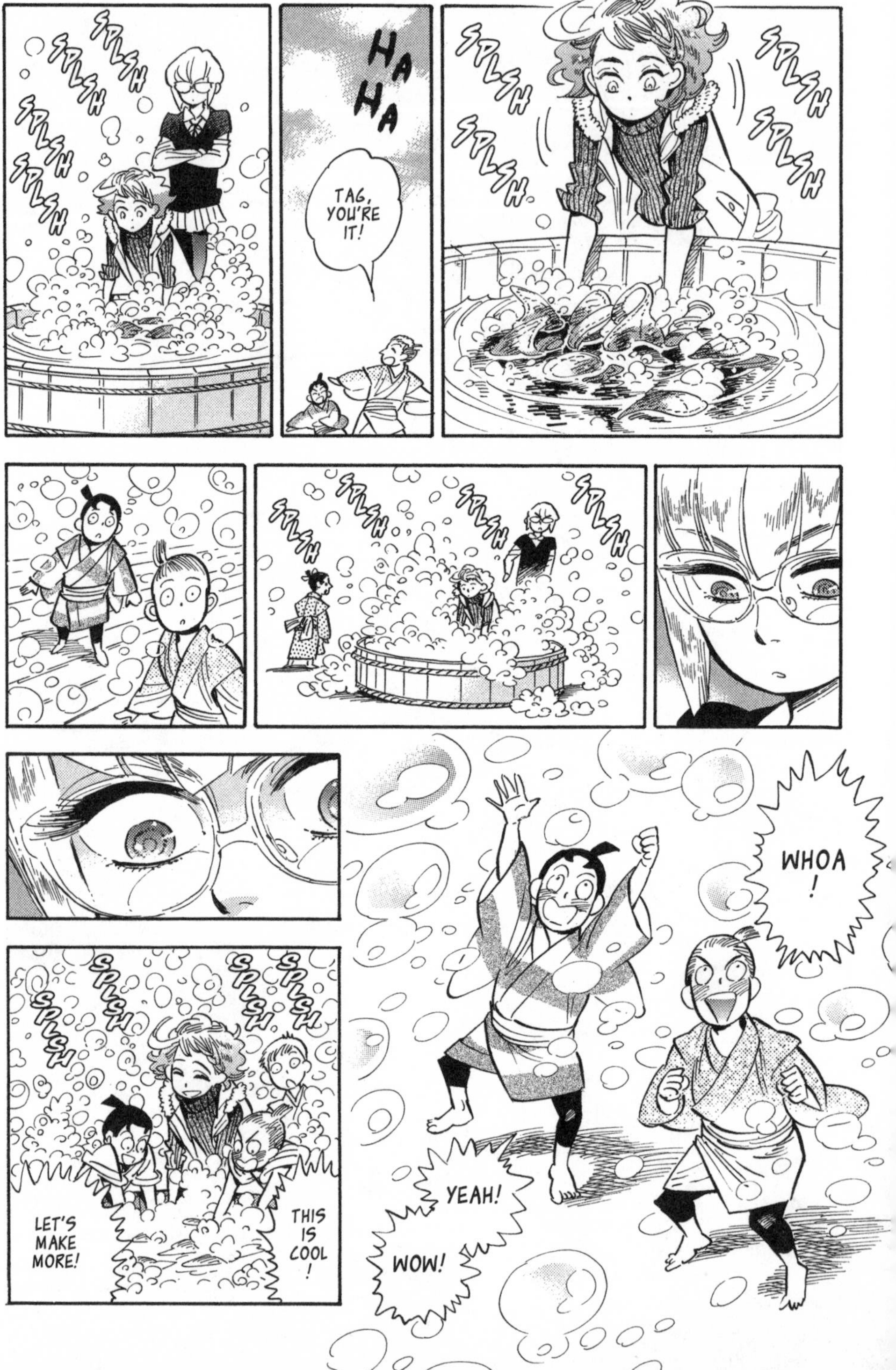

SPLSH
SPLSH
SPLSH
SPLSH
HA HA
TAG, YOU'RE IT!
SPLSH
SPLSH
SPLSH
SPLSH
SPLSH
SPLSH
SPLSH
WHOA!
YEAH!
WOW!
SPLSH
SPLSH
SPLSH
SPLSH
THIS IS COOL!
LET'S MAKE MORE!

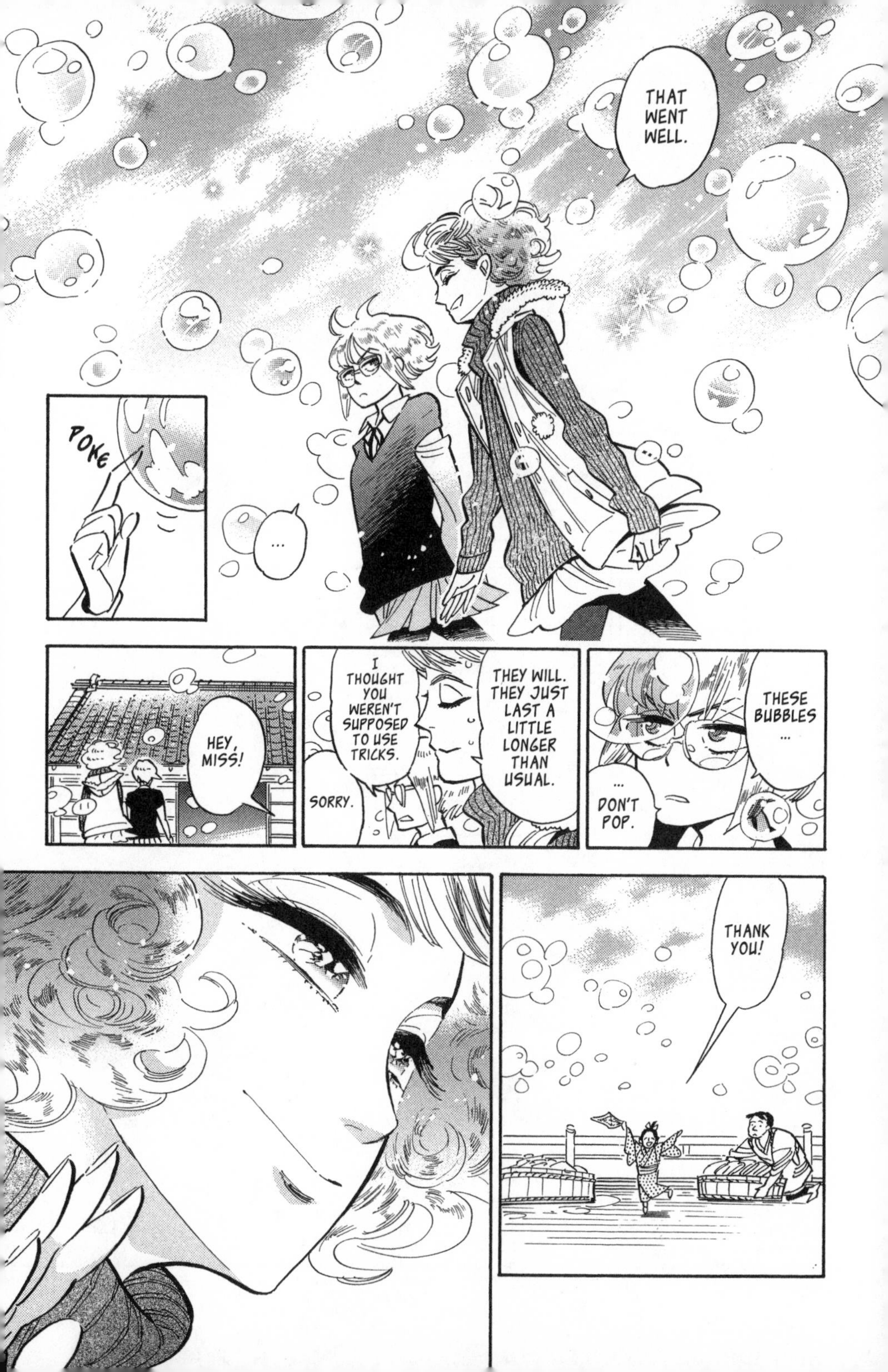
THAT WENT WELL.
...
POKE
THESE BUBBLES ...
... DON'T POP.
THEY WILL. THEY JUST LAST A LITTLE LONGER THAN USUAL.
I THOUGHT YOU WEREN'T SUPPOSED TO USE TRICKS.
SORRY.
HEY, MISS!
THANK YOU!

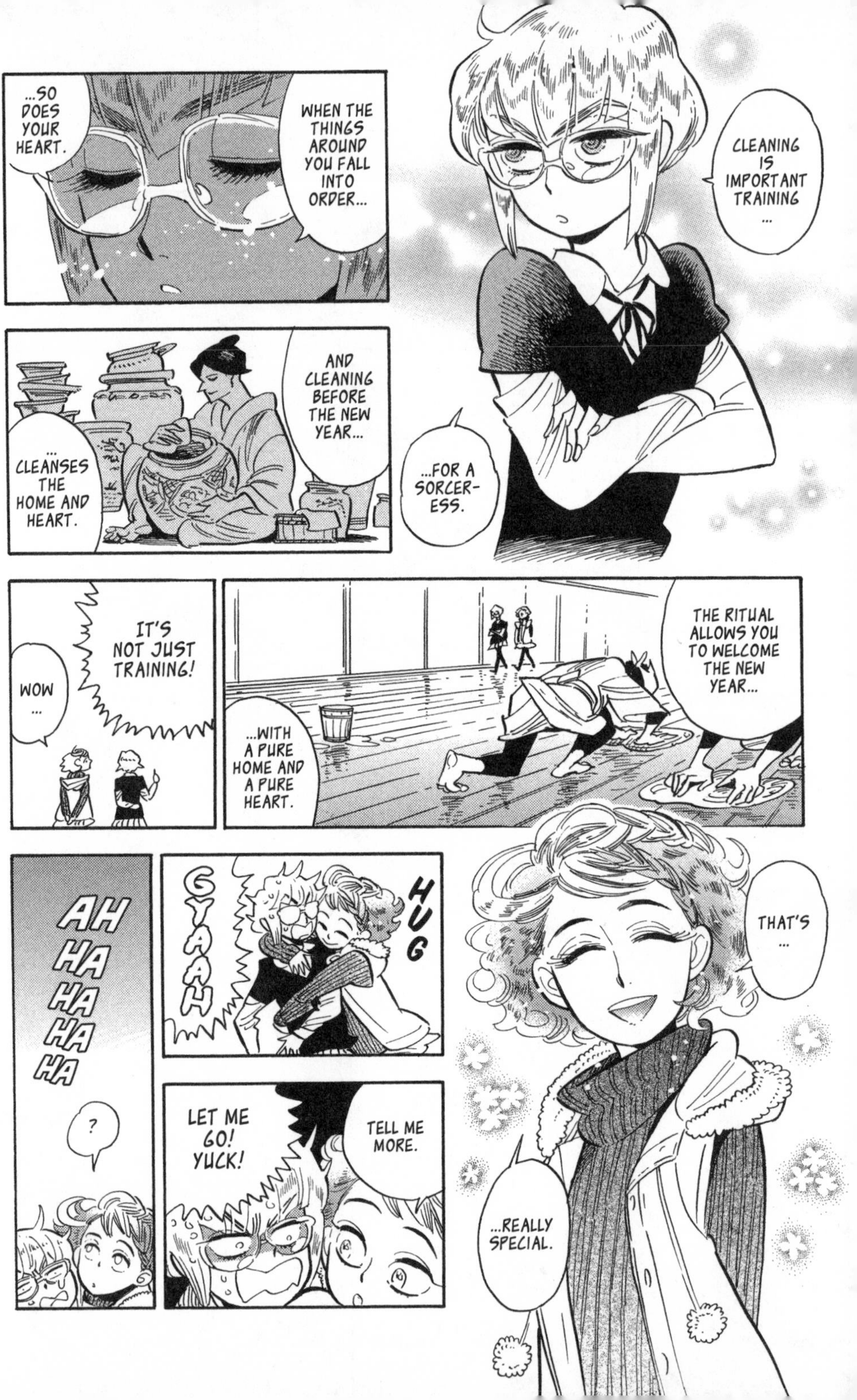
CLEANING IS IMPORTANT TRAINING ...
...FOR A SORCER-ESS.
WHEN THE THINGS AROUND YOU FALL INTO ORDER...
...SO DOES YOUR HEART.
AND CLEANING BEFORE THE NEW YEAR...
... CLEANSES THE HOME AND HEART.
THE RITUAL ALLOWS YOU TO WELCOME THE NEW YEAR...
...WITH A PURE HOME AND A PURE HEART.
IT'S NOT JUST TRAINING!
WOW ...
THAT'S ...
...REALLY SPECIAL.
HUG
GYAAAH
TELL ME MORE.
LET ME GO! YUCK!
AH HA HA HA HA HA
?

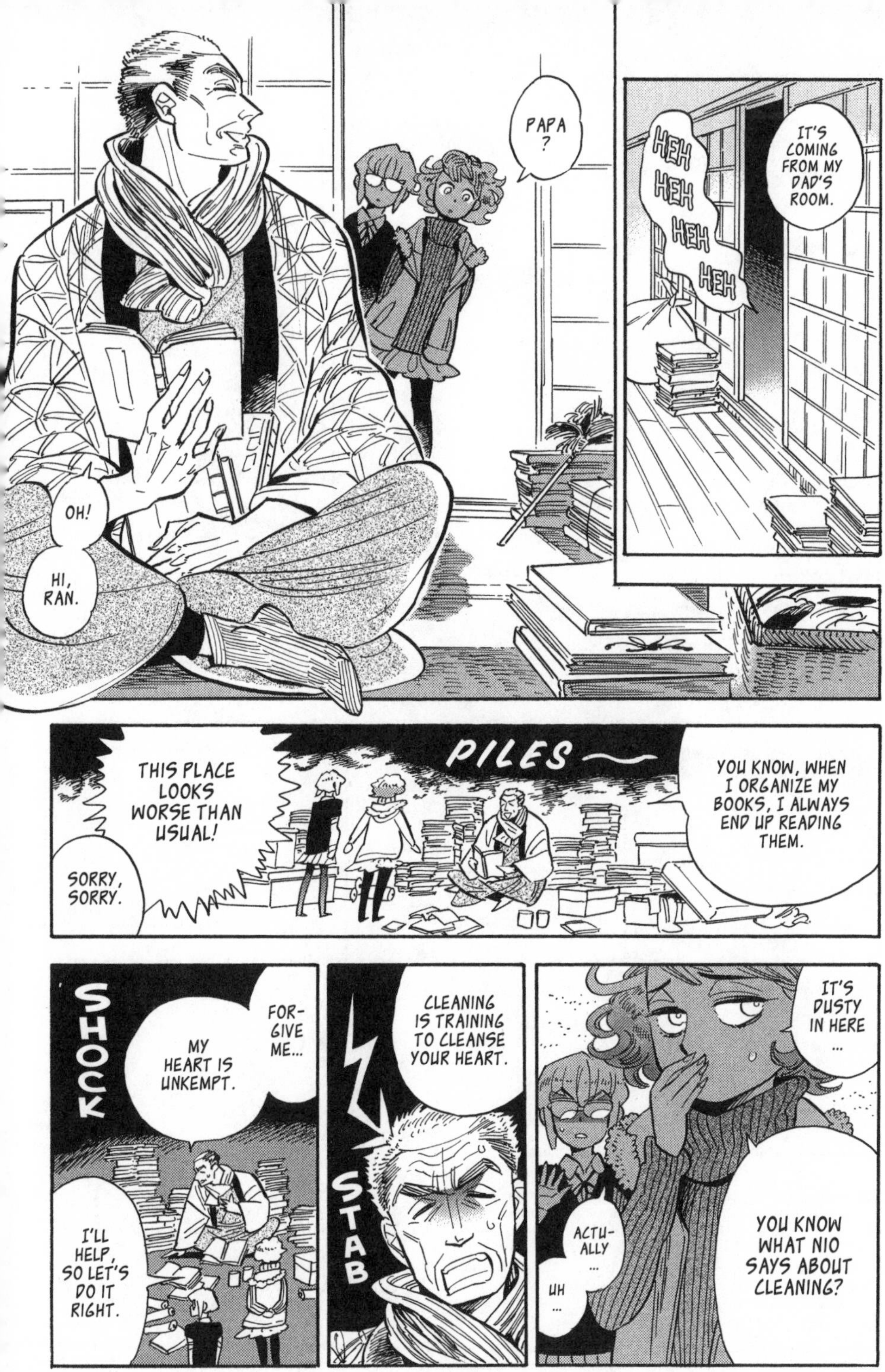
HEH HEH HEH HEH
IT'S COMING FROM MY DAD'S ROOM.
PAPA ?
OH!
HI, RAN.
PILES
THIS PLACE LOOKS WORSE THAN USUAL!
SORRY, SORRY.
YOU KNOW, WHEN I ORGANIZE MY BOOKS, I ALWAYS END UP READING THEM.
IT'S DUSTY IN HERE ...
ACTU- ALLY ...
UH ...
YOU KNOW WHAT NIO SAYS ABOUT CLEANING?
CLEANING IS TRAINING TO CLEANSE YOUR HEART.
STAB
SHOCK
FOR- GIVE ME...
MY HEART IS UNKEMPT.
I'LL HELP, SO LET'S DO IT RIGHT.

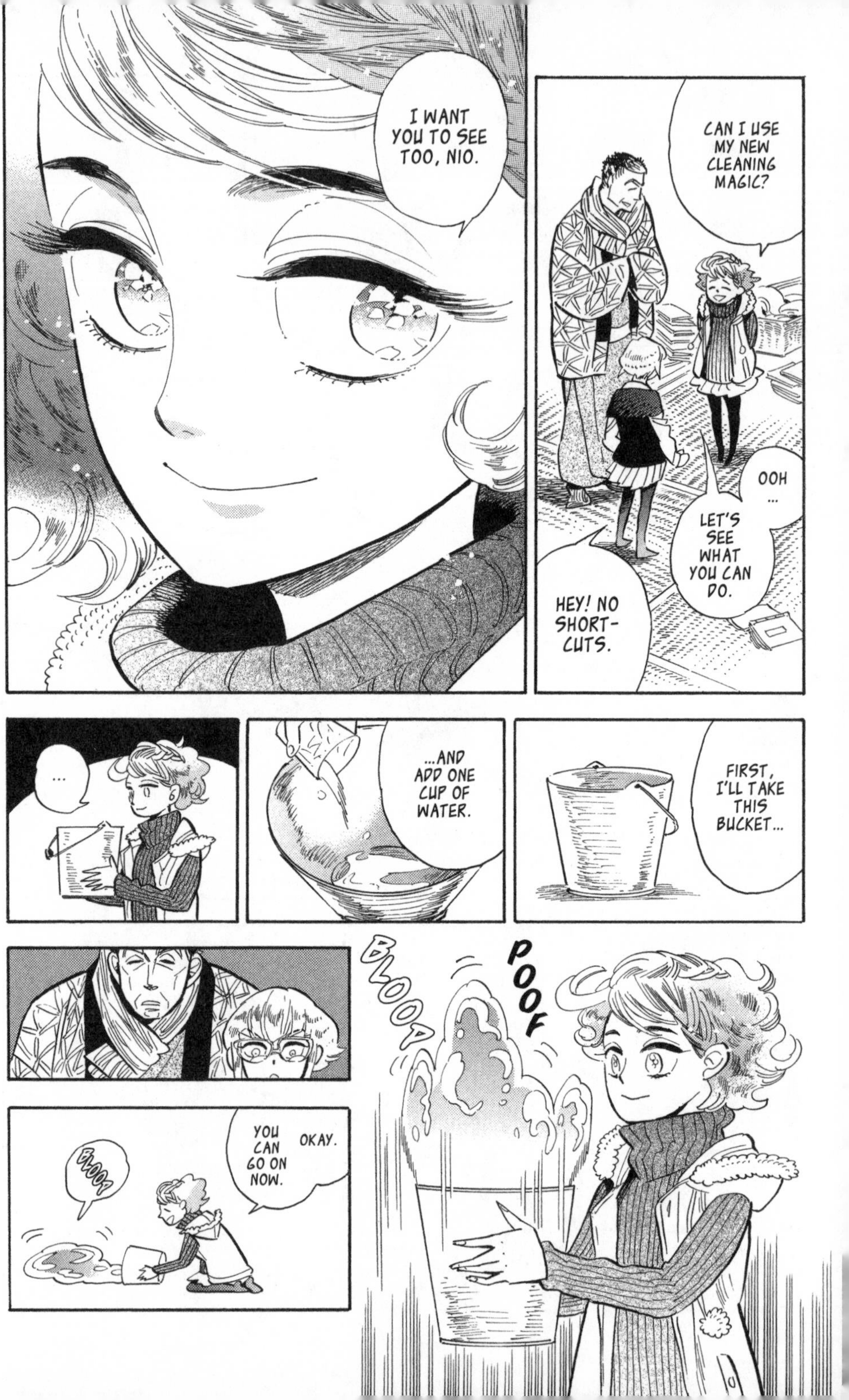
CAN I USE MY NEW CLEANING MAGIC?
OOH ...
LET'S SEE WHAT YOU CAN DO.
HEY! NO SHORT-CUTS.
I WANT YOU TO SEE TOO, NIO.
FIRST, I'LL TAKE THIS BUCKET...
...AND ADD ONE CUP OF WATER.
...
POOF
BLOOP
OKAY.
YOU CAN GO ON NOW.
BLOOP

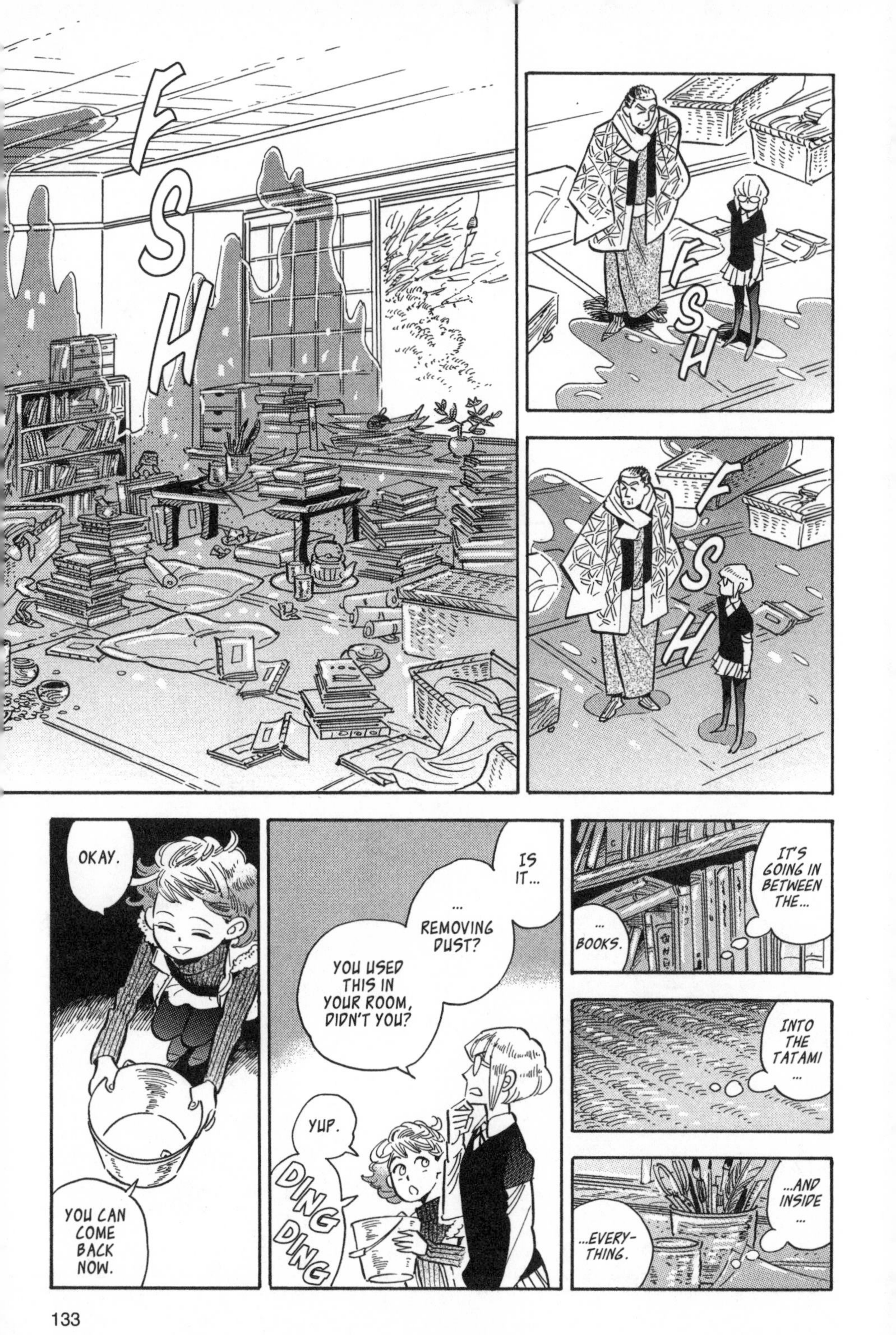
FSH
FSH
FSH
IT'S GOING IN BETWEEN THE...
...BOOKS.
INTO THE TATAMI...
...AND INSIDE...
...EVERY-THING.
IS IT...
...REMOVING DUST?
YOU USED THIS IN YOUR ROOM, DIDN'T YOU?
YUP.
DING DING
OKAY.
YOU CAN COME BACK NOW.

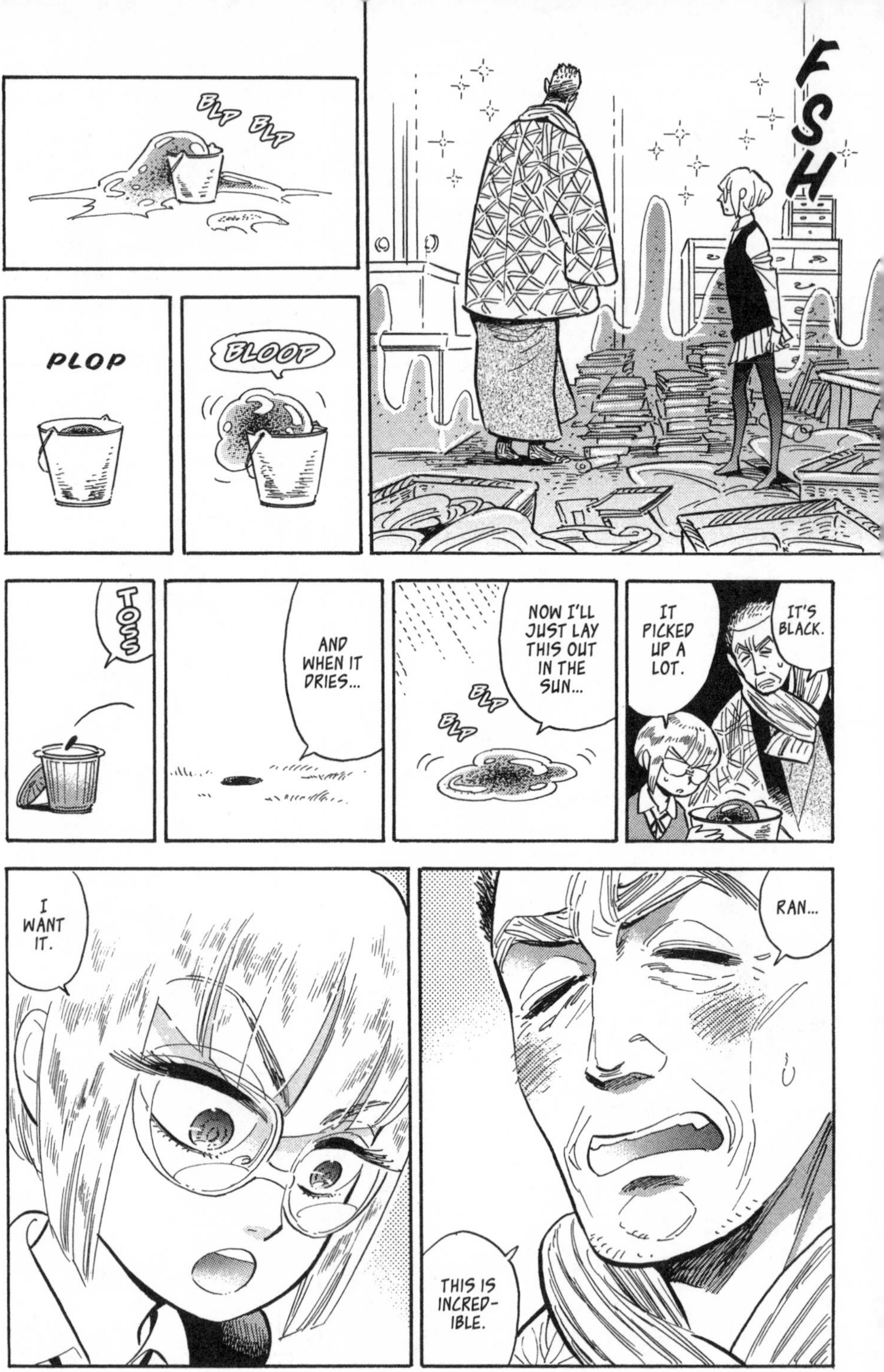
FSH
BLP BLP
BLOOP
PLOP
IT'S BLACK.
IT PICKED UP A LOT.
NOW I'LL JUST LAY THIS OUT IN THE SUN...
BLP
BLP
AND WHEN IT DRIES...
TOSS
RAN...
THIS IS INCRED-IBLE.
I WANT IT.

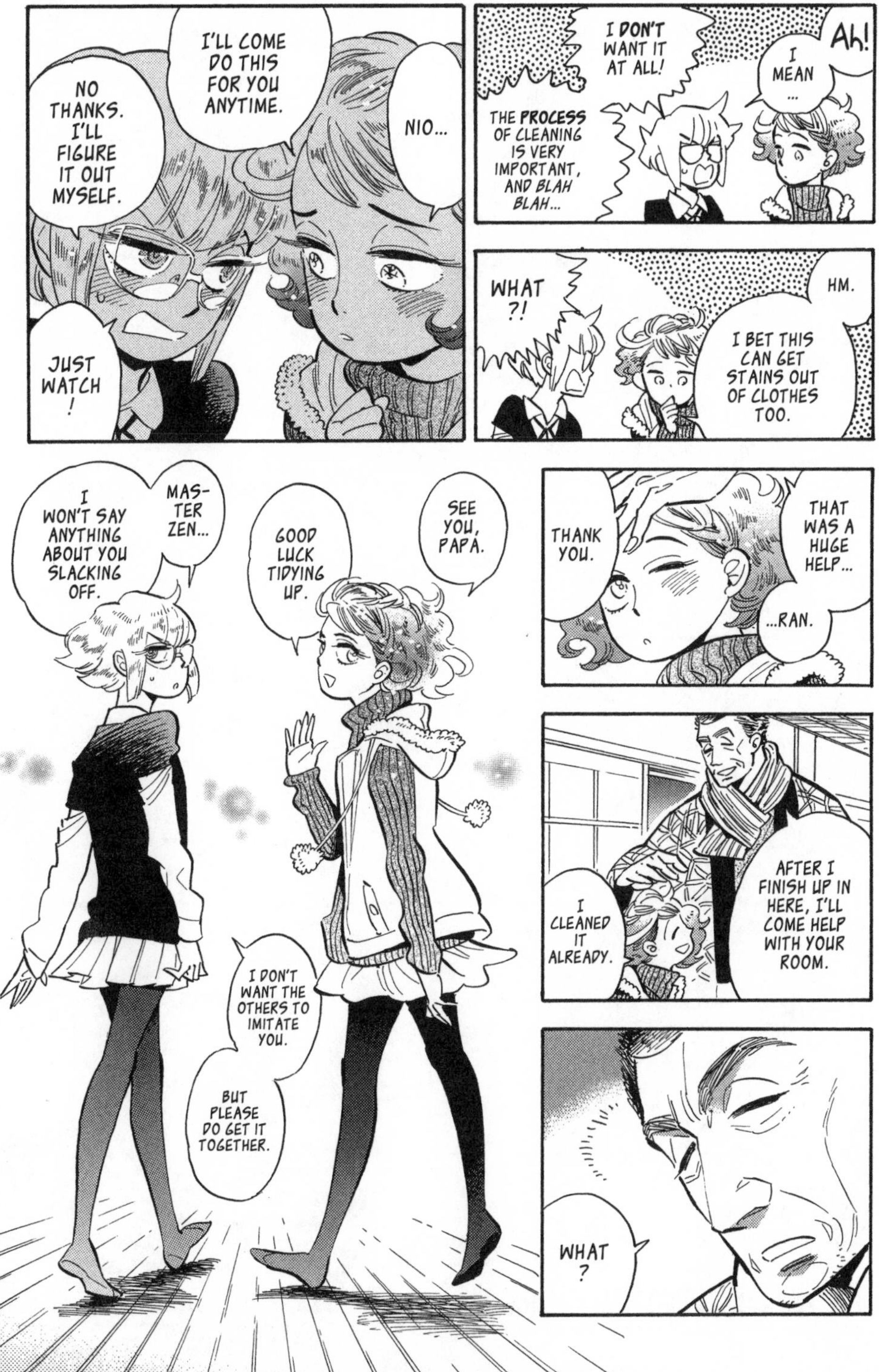
Ah!
I MEAN ...
I DON'T WANT IT AT ALL!
THE **PROCESS** OF CLEANING IS VERY IMPORTANT, AND *BLAH BLAH*...
HM.
I BET THIS CAN GET STAINS OUT OF CLOTHES TOO.
WHAT ?!
NIO...
I'LL COME DO THIS FOR YOU ANYTIME.
NO THANKS. I'LL FIGURE IT OUT MYSELF.
JUST WATCH!
THAT WAS A HUGE HELP...
...RAN.
THANK YOU.
AFTER I FINISH UP IN HERE, I'LL COME HELP WITH YOUR ROOM.
I CLEANED IT ALREADY.
WHAT?
SEE YOU, PAPA.
GOOD LUCK TIDYING UP.
MASTER ZEN...
I WON'T SAY ANYTHING ABOUT YOU SLACKING OFF.
I DON'T WANT THE OTHERS TO IMITATE YOU.
BUT PLEASE DO GET IT TOGETHER.

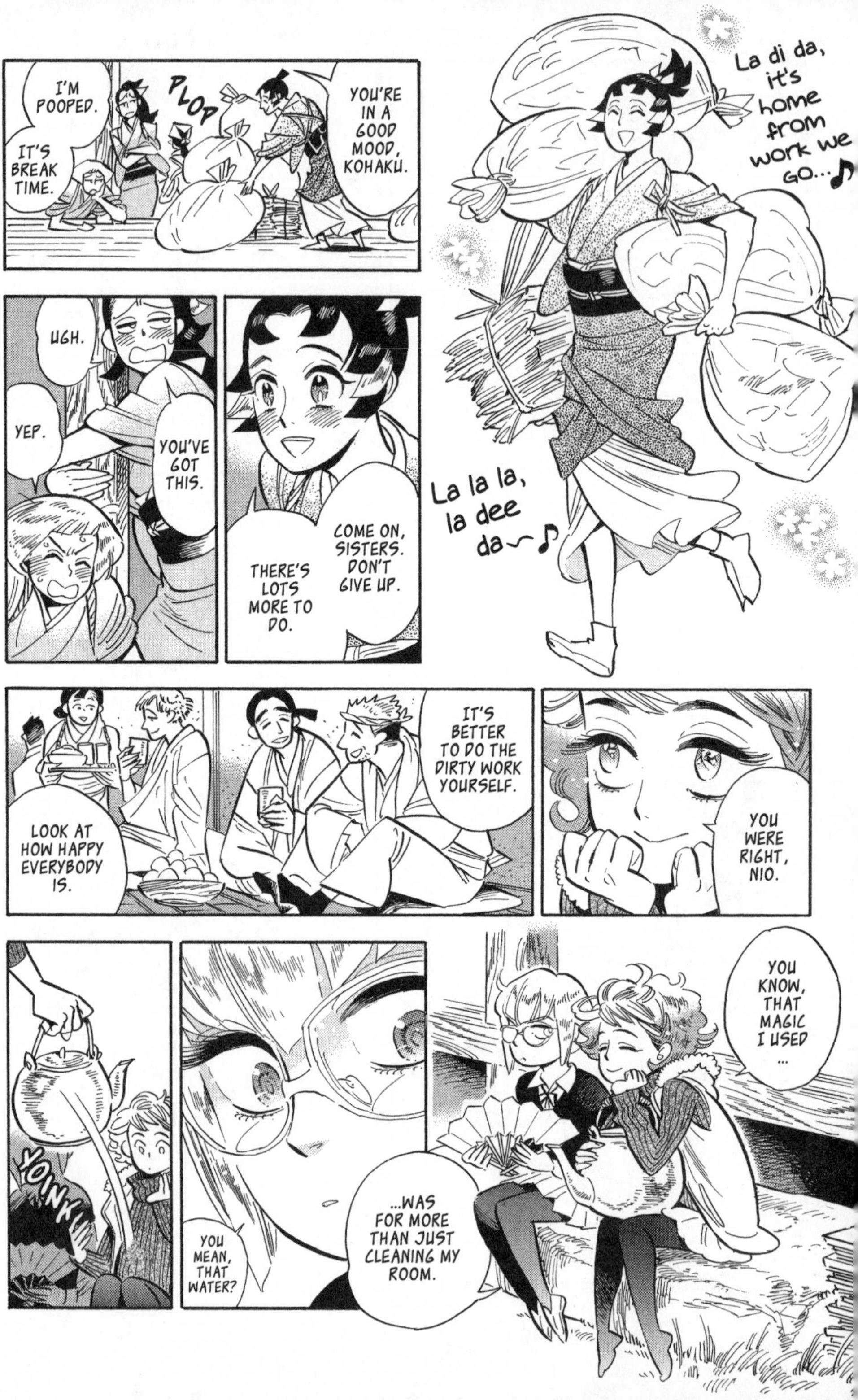
La di da, it's home from work we go...♪
La la la, la dee da~♪
YOU'RE IN A GOOD MOOD, KOHAKU.
PLOP
I'M POOPED.
IT'S BREAK TIME.
COME ON, SISTERS. DON'T GIVE UP.
THERE'S LOTS MORE TO DO.
UGH.
YOU'VE GOT THIS.
YEP.
YOU WERE RIGHT, NIO.
IT'S BETTER TO DO THE DIRTY WORK YOURSELF.
LOOK AT HOW HAPPY EVERYBODY IS.
YOU KNOW, THAT MAGIC I USED ...
...WAS FOR MORE THAN JUST CLEANING MY ROOM.
YOU MEAN, THAT WATER?
YOINK

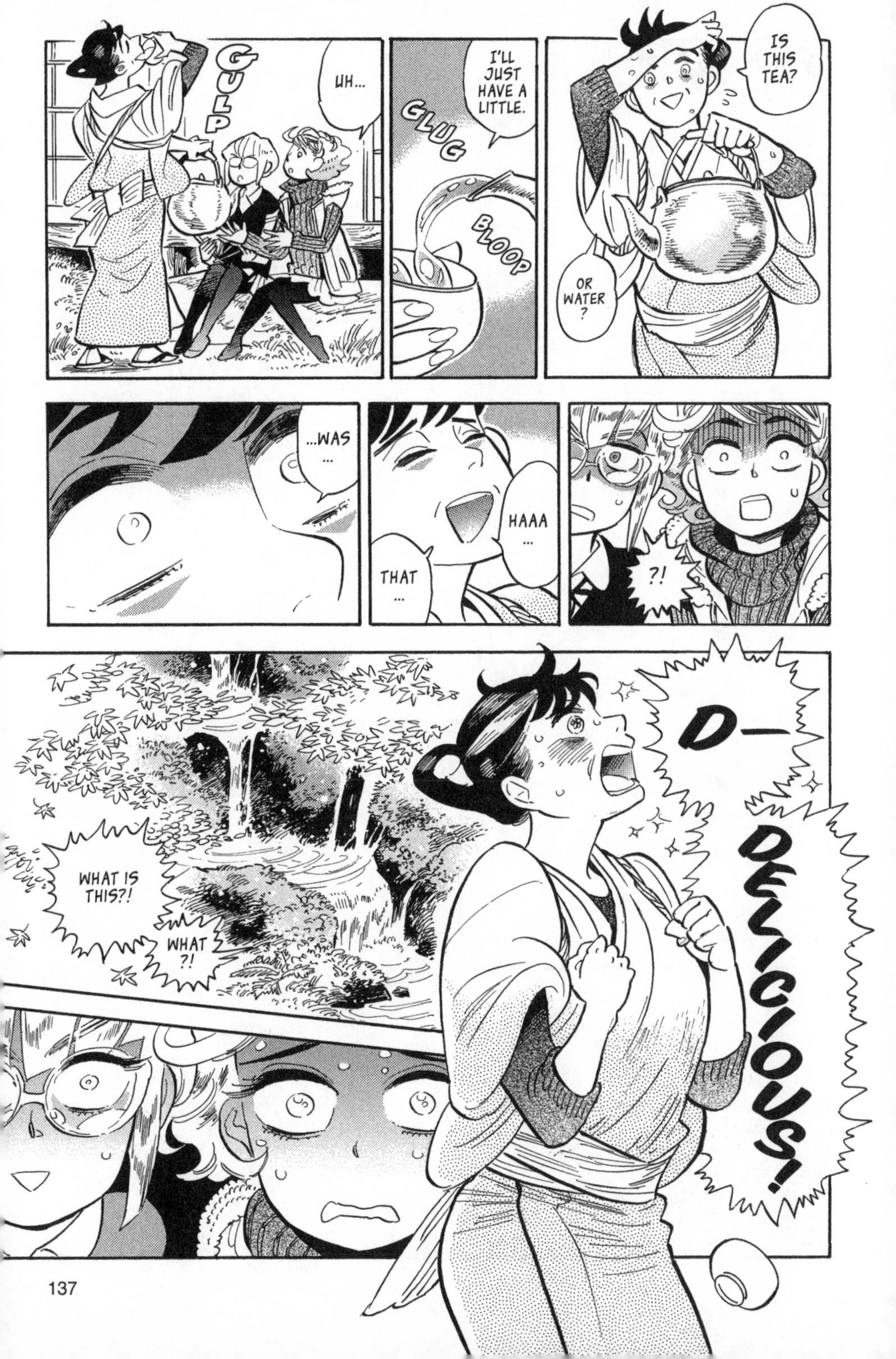
IS THIS TEA?
OR WATER?
I'LL JUST HAVE A LITTLE.
GLUG
BLOOP
UH...
GULP
?!
HAAA...
THAT...
...WAS...
D— DELICIOUS!
WHAT IS THIS?!
WHAT?!

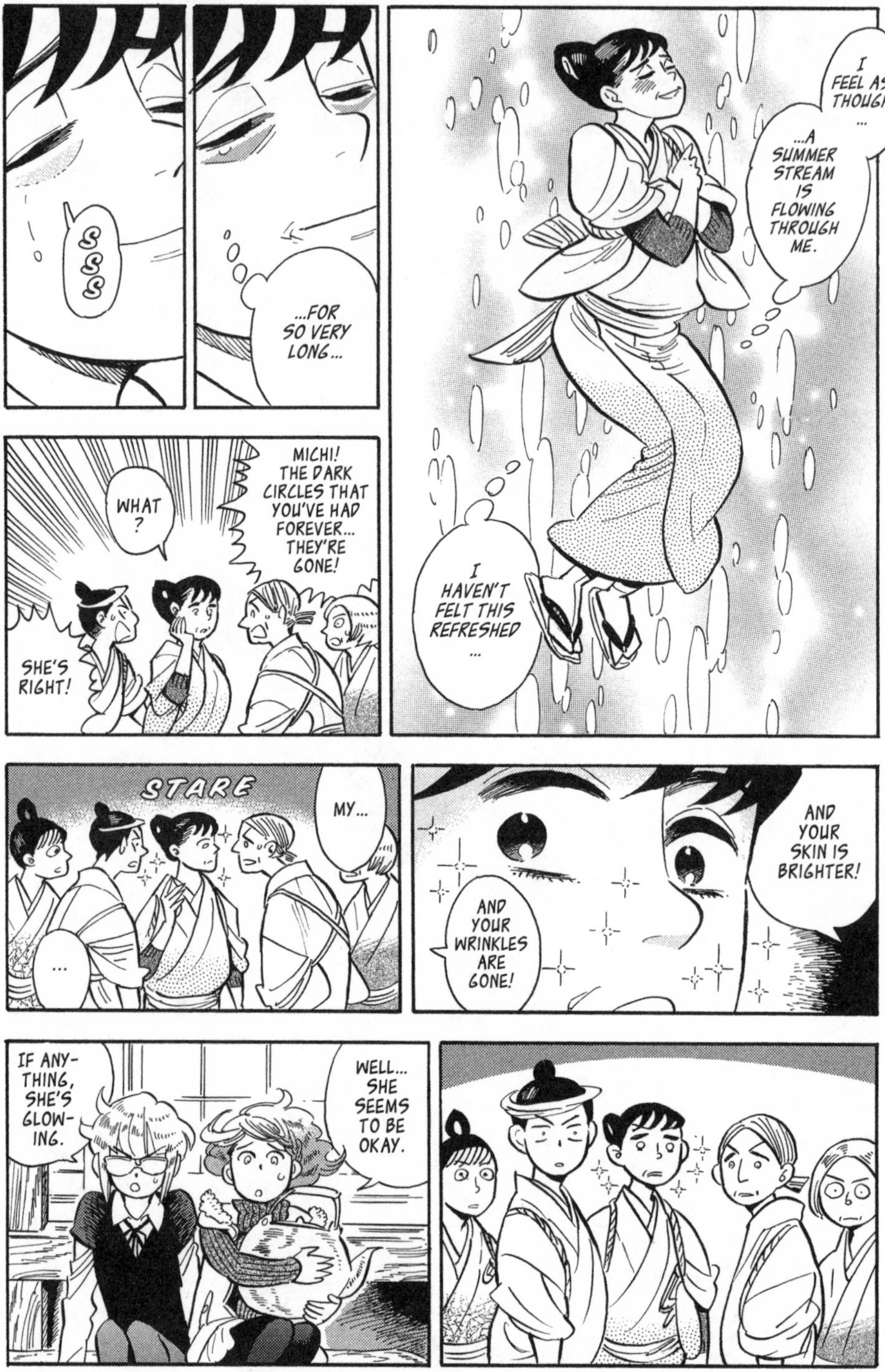

I FEEL AS THOUGH...
...A SUMMER STREAM IS FLOWING THROUGH ME.
I HAVEN'T FELT THIS REFRESHED...
...FOR SO VERY LONG...
SSS
MICHI! THE DARK CIRCLES THAT YOU'VE HAD FOREVER... THEY'RE GONE!
WHAT?
SHE'S RIGHT!
AND YOUR SKIN IS BRIGHTER!
AND YOUR WRINKLES ARE GONE!
STARE
MY...
...
WELL... SHE SEEMS TO BE OKAY.
IF ANY-THING, SHE'S GLOW-ING.

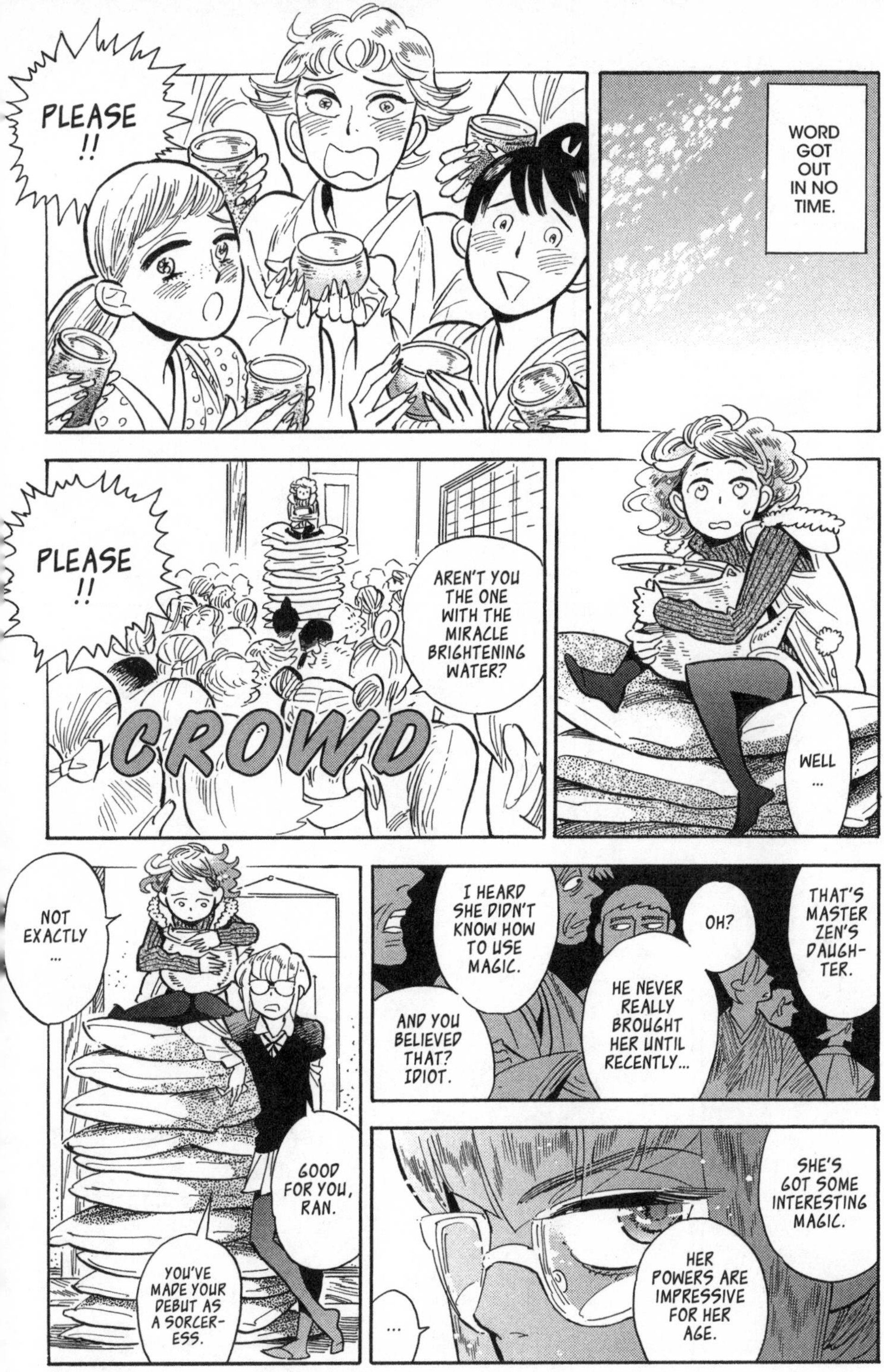
WORD GOT OUT IN NO TIME.
PLEASE!!
WELL...
AREN'T YOU THE ONE WITH THE MIRACLE BRIGHTENING WATER?
PLEASE!!
CROWD
THAT'S MASTER ZEN'S DAUGHTER.
OH?
I HEARD SHE DIDN'T KNOW HOW TO USE MAGIC.
HE NEVER REALLY BROUGHT HER UNTIL RECENTLY...
AND YOU BELIEVED THAT? IDIOT.
SHE'S GOT SOME INTERESTING MAGIC.
HER POWERS ARE IMPRESSIVE FOR HER AGE.
...
NOT EXACTLY...
GOOD FOR YOU, RAN.
YOU'VE MADE YOUR DEBUT AS A SORCERESS.

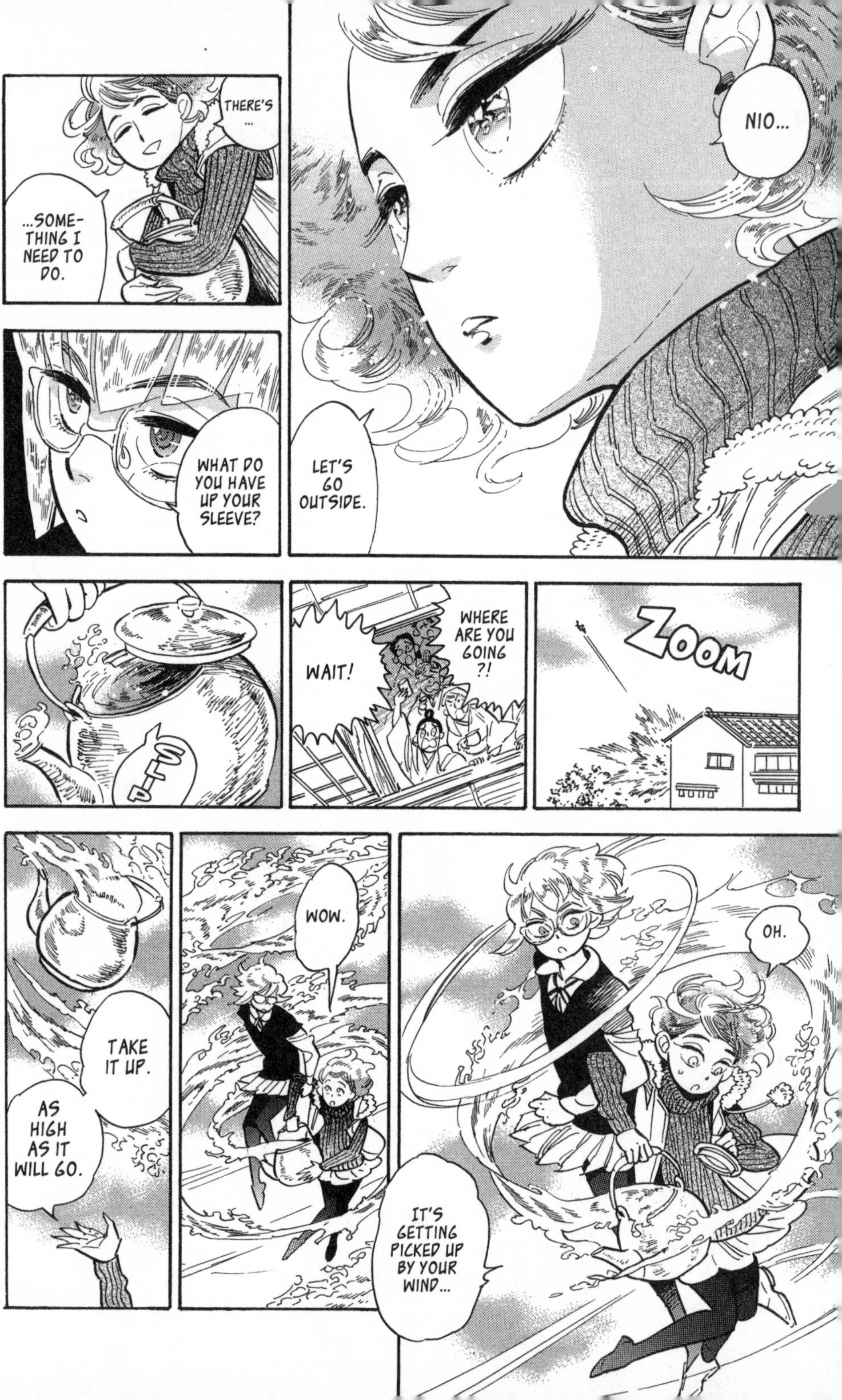
NIO...
LET'S GO OUTSIDE.
THERE'S ...
...SOMETHING I NEED TO DO.
WHAT DO YOU HAVE UP YOUR SLEEVE?
ZOOM
WHERE ARE YOU GOING ?!
WAIT!
SLIP
OH.
IT'S GETTING PICKED UP BY YOUR WIND...
WOW.
TAKE IT UP.
AS HIGH AS IT WILL GO.

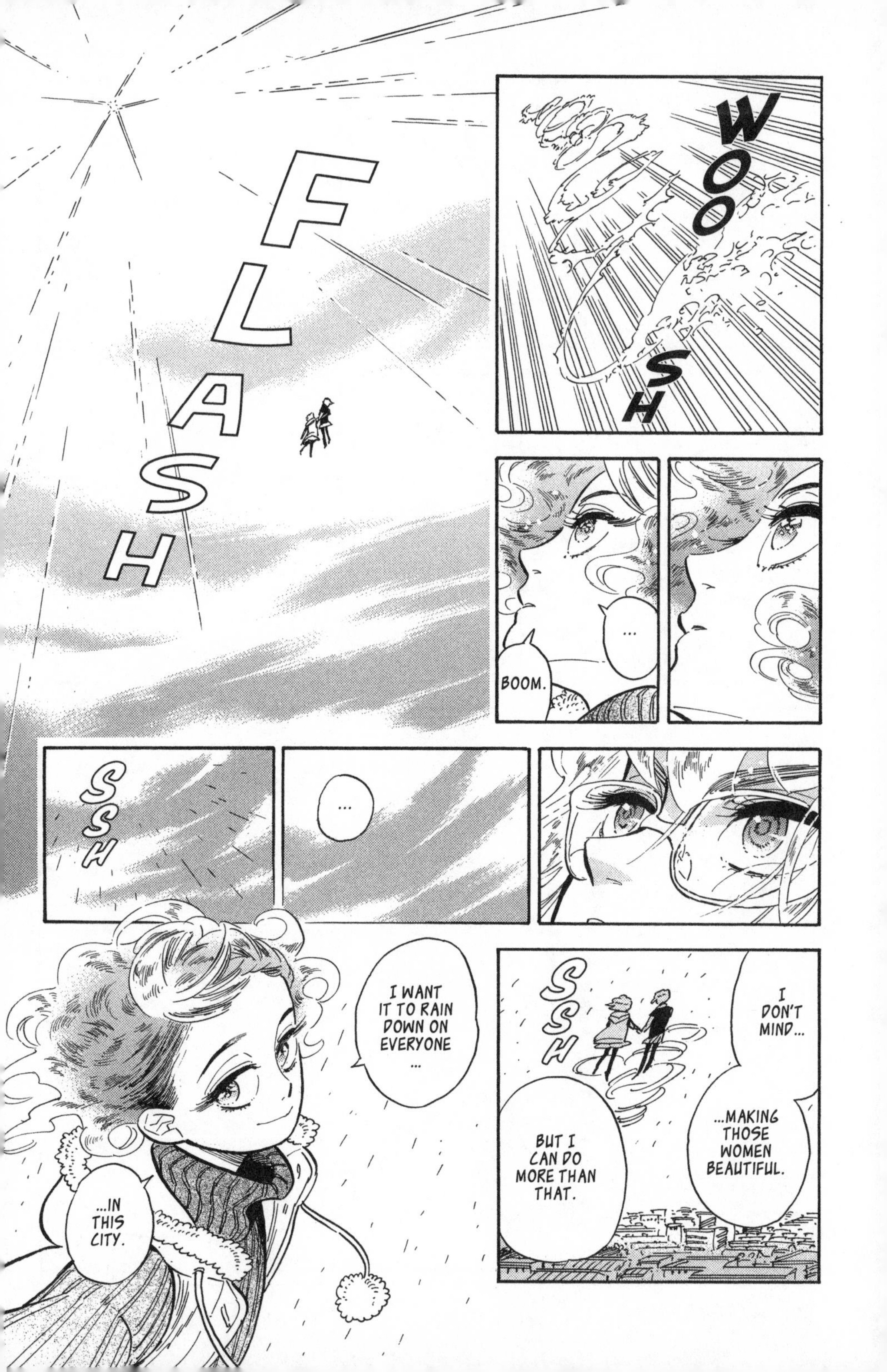
WOOSH
FLASH
...
BOOM.
SSH
...
I DON'T MIND...
...MAKING THOSE WOMEN BEAUTIFUL.
BUT I CAN DO MORE THAN THAT.
SSH
I WANT IT TO RAIN DOWN ON EVERYONE ...
...IN THIS CITY.

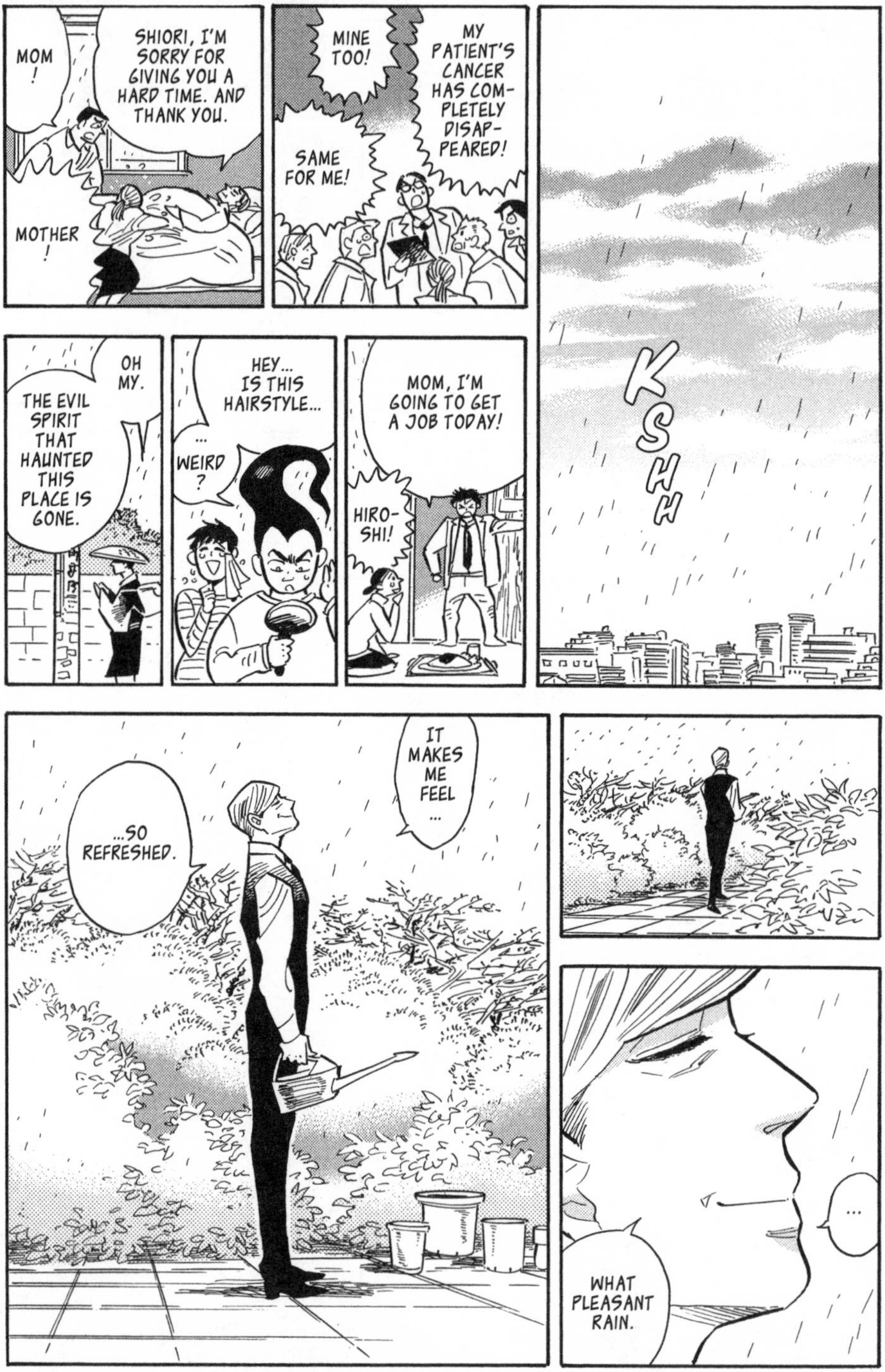
KSHH
MY PATIENT'S CANCER HAS COMPLETELY DISAPPEARED!
MINE TOO!
SAME FOR ME!
SHIORI, I'M SORRY FOR GIVING YOU A HARD TIME. AND THANK YOU.
MOM!
MOTHER!
MOM, I'M GOING TO GET A JOB TODAY!
HIROSHI!
HEY... IS THIS HAIRSTYLE...
...WEIRD?
OH MY.
THE EVIL SPIRIT THAT HAUNTED THIS PLACE IS GONE.
...
WHAT PLEASANT RAIN.
IT MAKES ME FEEL...
...SO REFRESHED.

Chapter 40 / The End

Chapter 41
Ran Departs and the Rain Is Soft

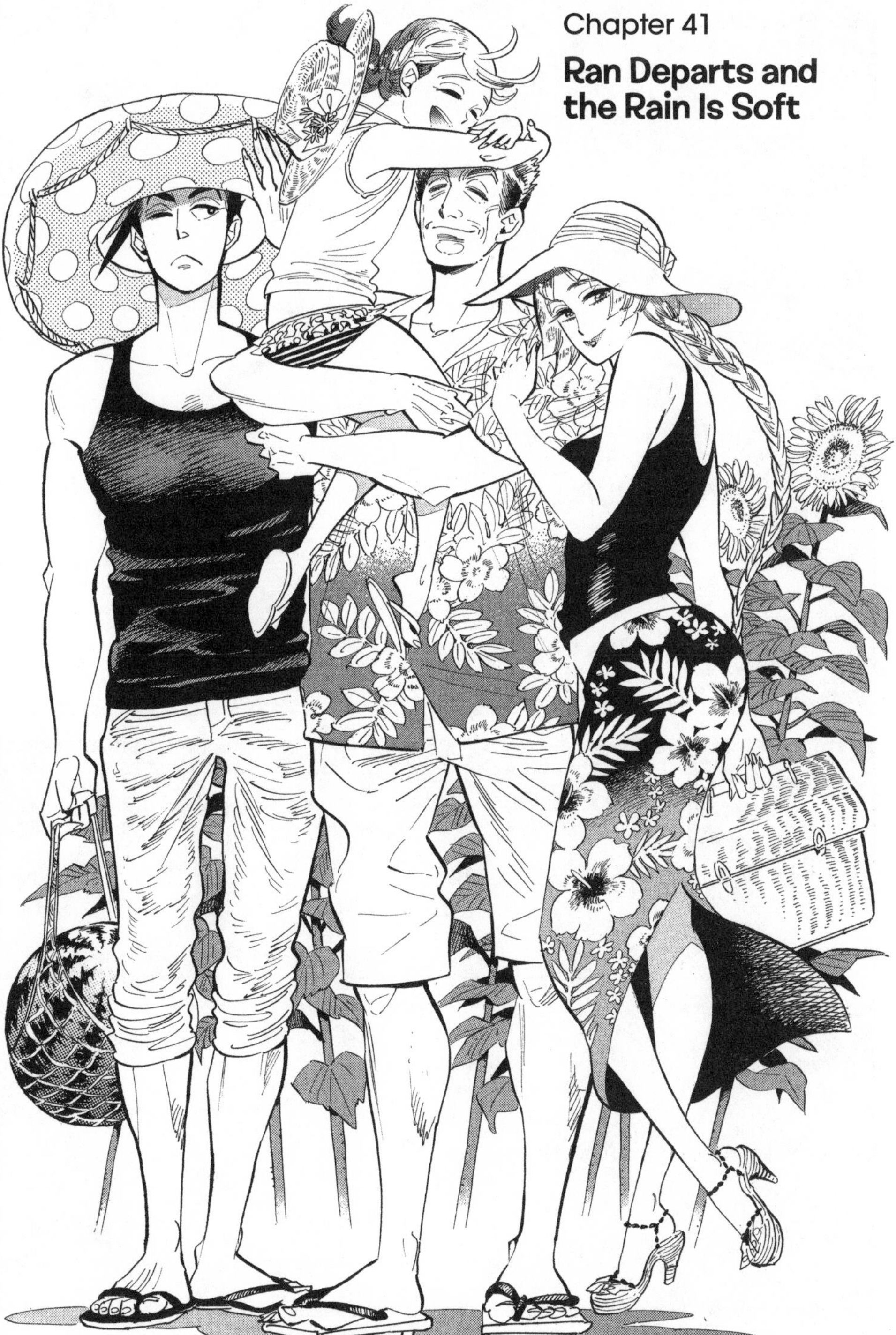

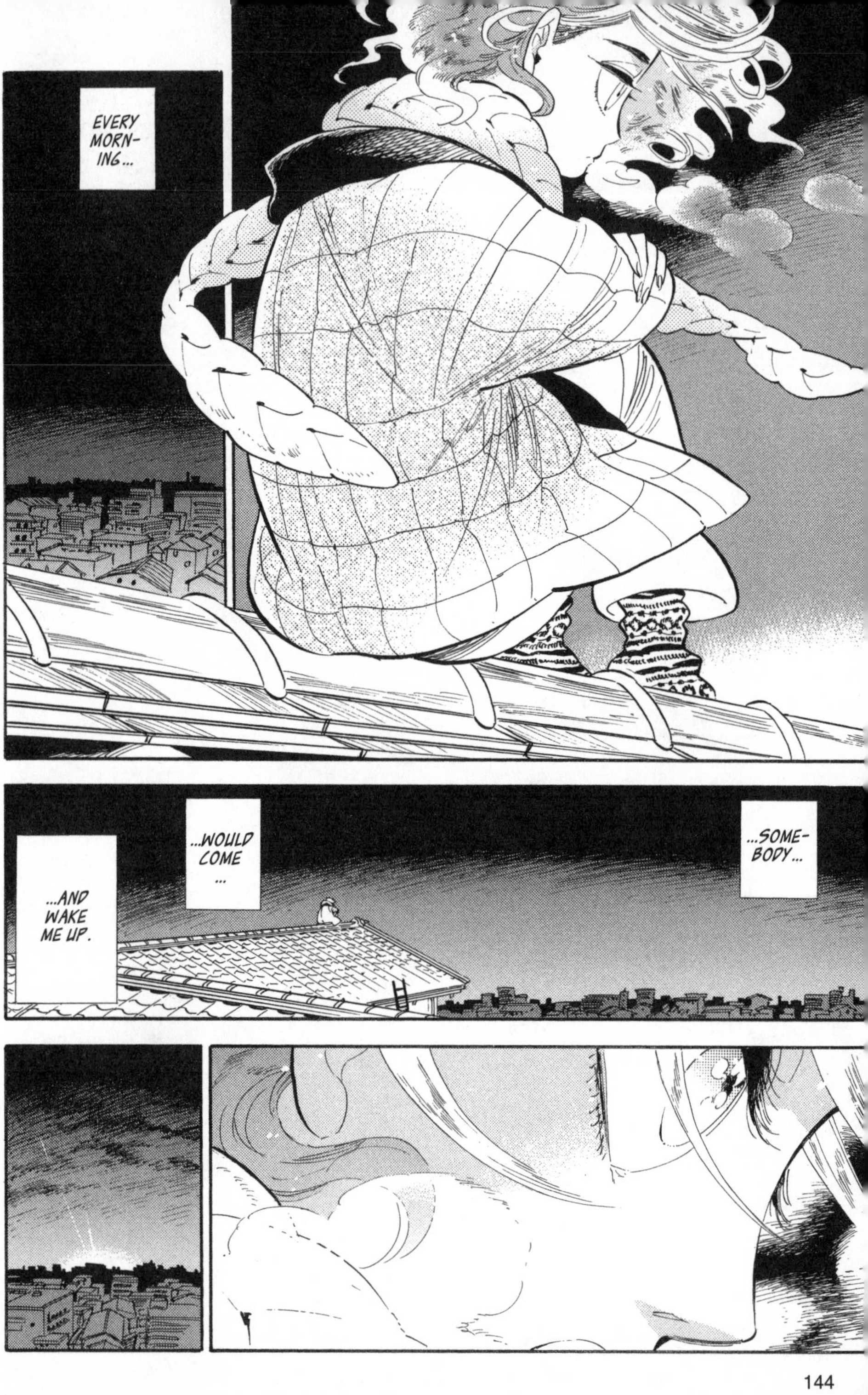
EVERY MORNING...
...SOMEBODY...
...WOULD COME...
...AND WAKE ME UP.

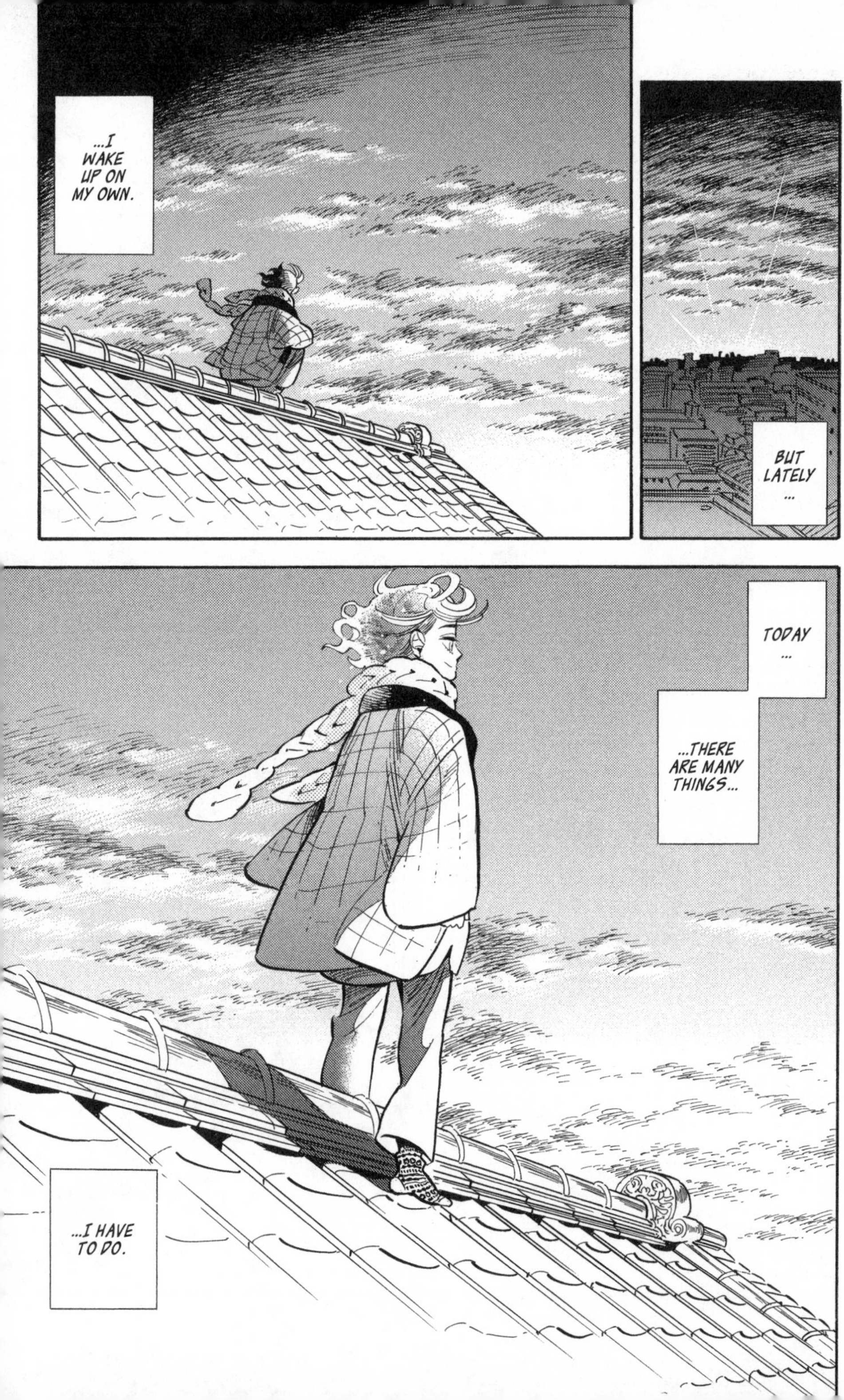
BUT LATELY ...
...I WAKE UP ON MY OWN.
TODAY ...
...THERE ARE MANY THINGS...
...I HAVE TO DO.

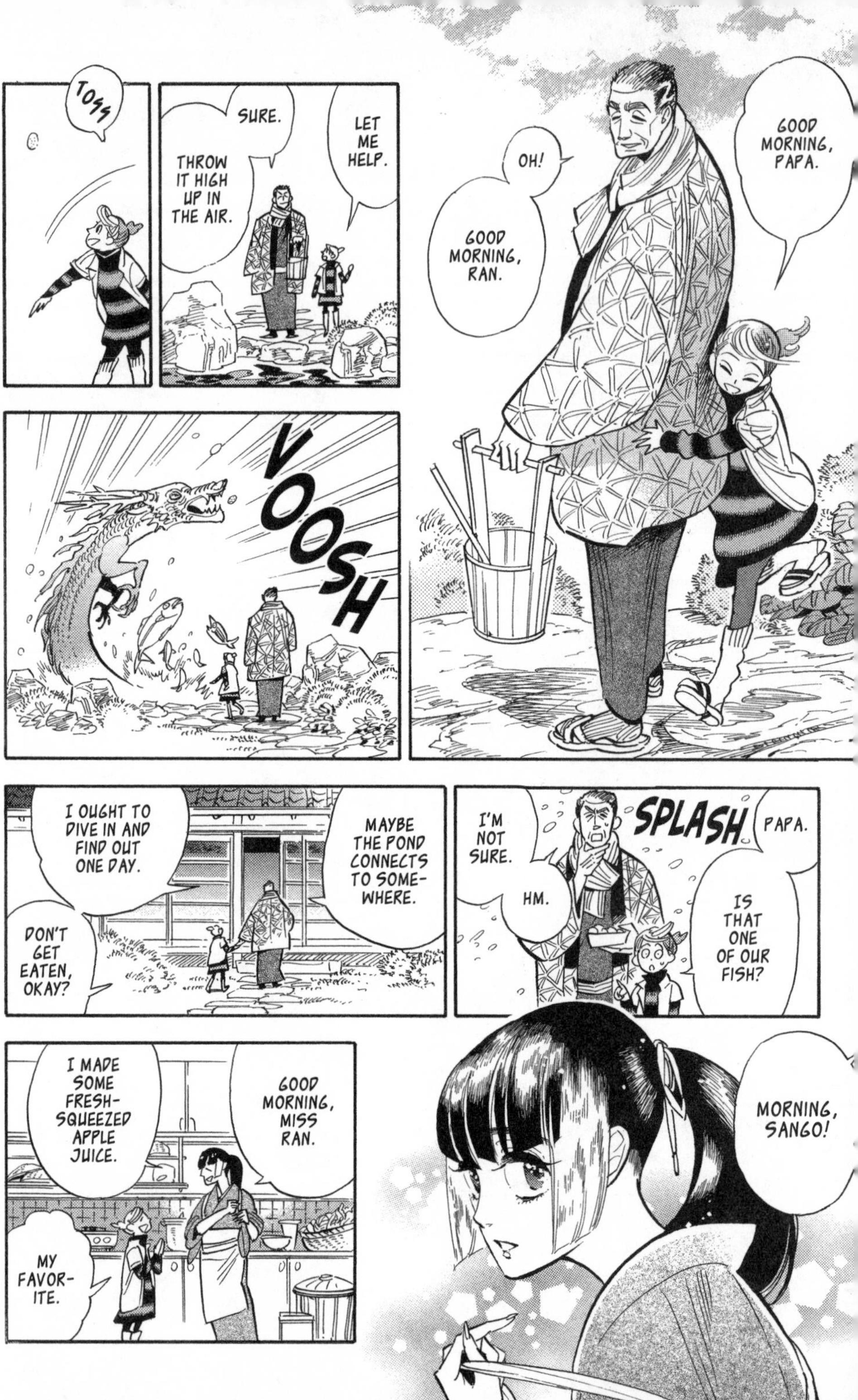
GOOD MORNING, PAPA.
OH!
GOOD MORNING, RAN.
LET ME HELP.
SURE.
THROW IT HIGH UP IN THE AIR.
TOSS
VOOSH
PAPA.
SPLASH
IS THAT ONE OF OUR FISH?
I'M NOT SURE.
HM.
MAYBE THE POND CONNECTS TO SOME-WHERE.
I OUGHT TO DIVE IN AND FIND OUT ONE DAY.
DON'T GET EATEN, OKAY?
MORNING, SANGO!
GOOD MORNING, MISS RAN.
I MADE SOME FRESH-SQUEEZED APPLE JUICE.
MY FAVOR-ITE.

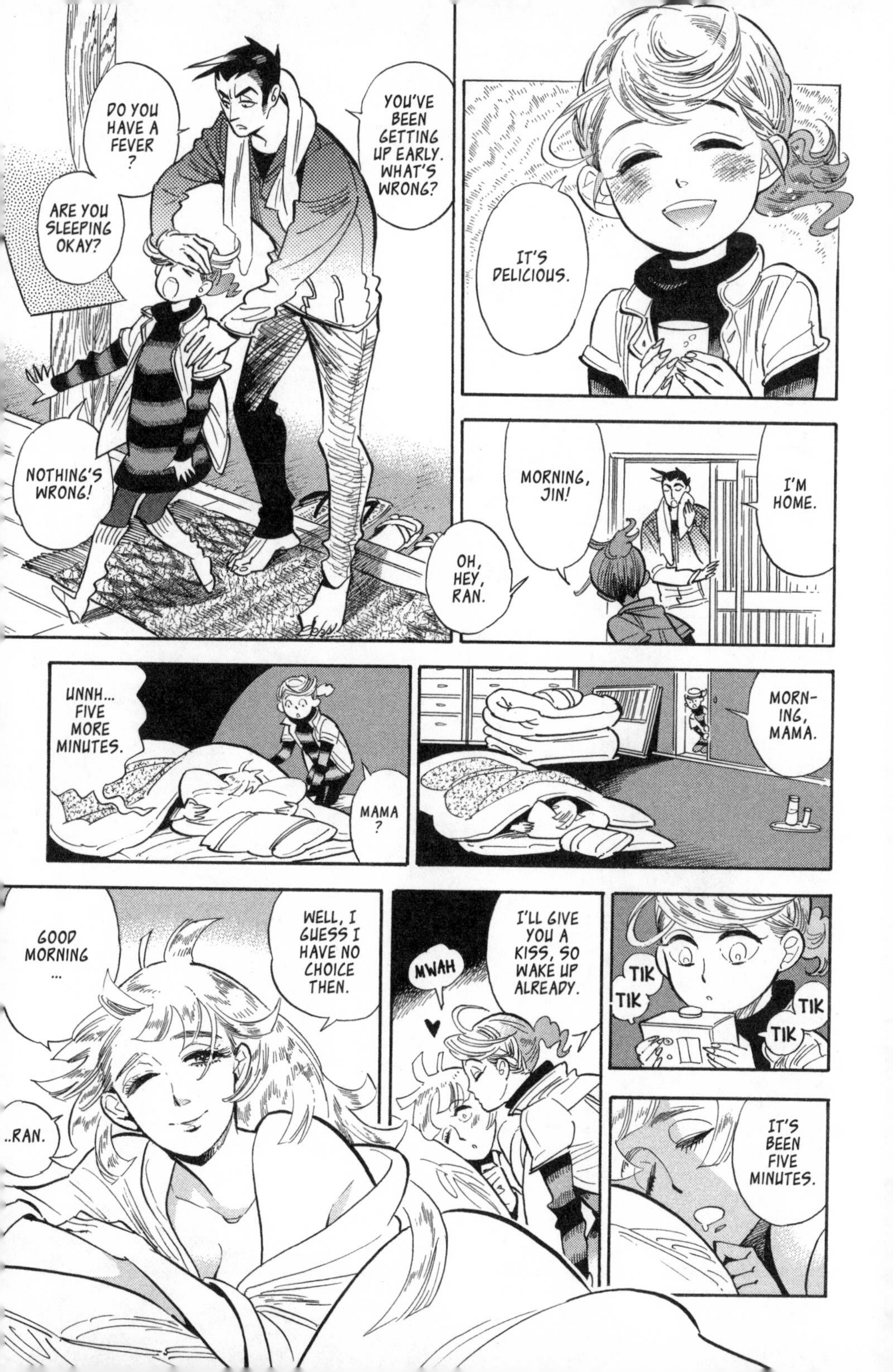
IT'S DELICIOUS.
I'M HOME.
MORNING, JIN!
OH, HEY, RAN.
YOU'VE BEEN GETTING UP EARLY. WHAT'S WRONG?
DO YOU HAVE A FEVER?
ARE YOU SLEEPING OKAY?
NOTHING'S WRONG!
MORN-ING, MAMA.
MAMA?
UNNH... FIVE MORE MINUTES.
TIK
TIK
TIK
TIK
IT'S BEEN FIVE MINUTES.
I'LL GIVE YOU A KISS, SO WAKE UP ALREADY.
MWAH
WELL, I GUESS I HAVE NO CHOICE THEN.
GOOD MORNING ...
..RAN.

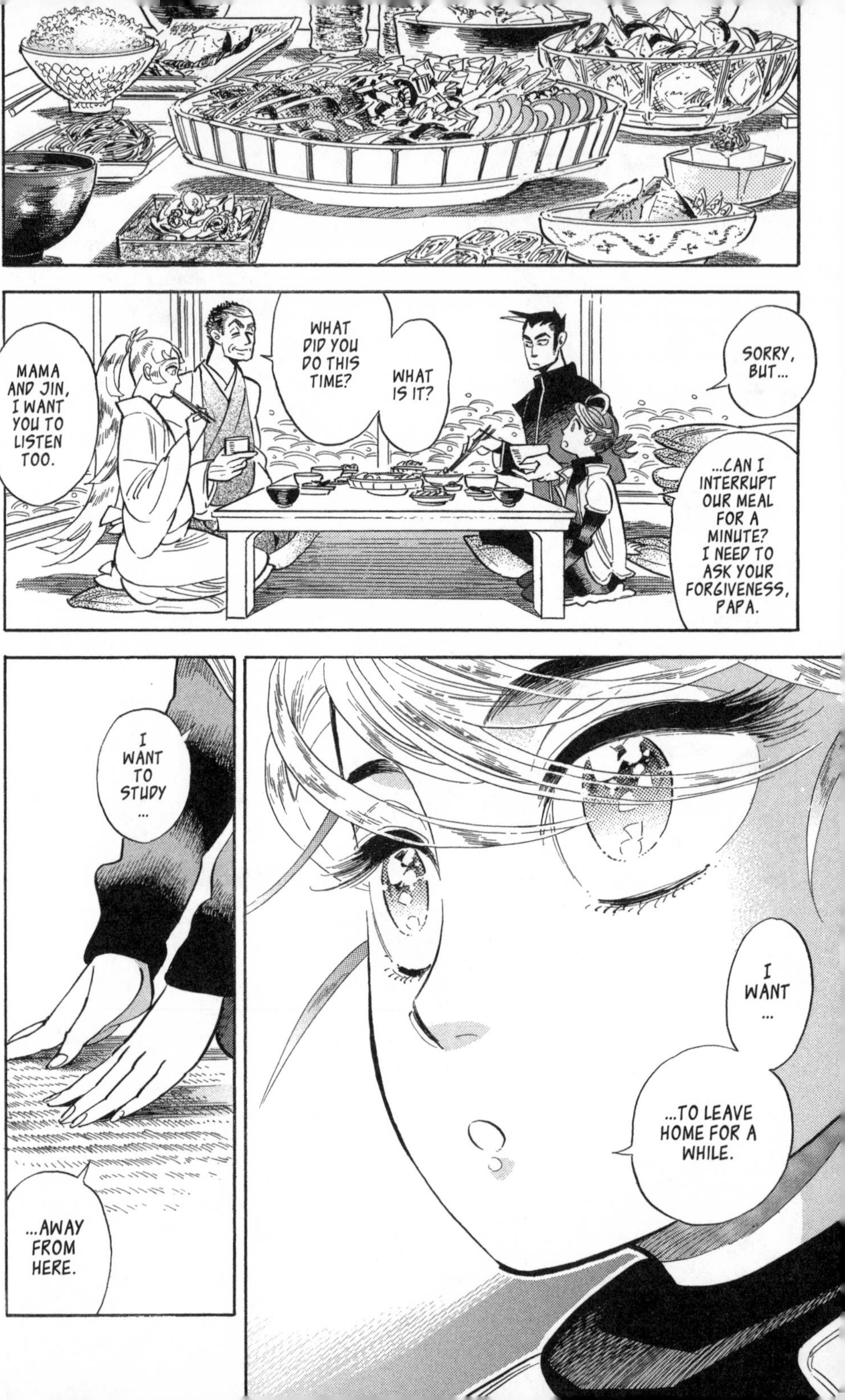
SORRY, BUT...
...CAN I INTERRUPT OUR MEAL FOR A MINUTE? I NEED TO ASK YOUR FORGIVENESS, PAPA.
WHAT IS IT?
WHAT DID YOU DO THIS TIME?
MAMA AND JIN, I WANT YOU TO LISTEN TOO.
I WANT...
...TO LEAVE HOME FOR A WHILE.
I WANT TO STUDY...
...AWAY FROM HERE.

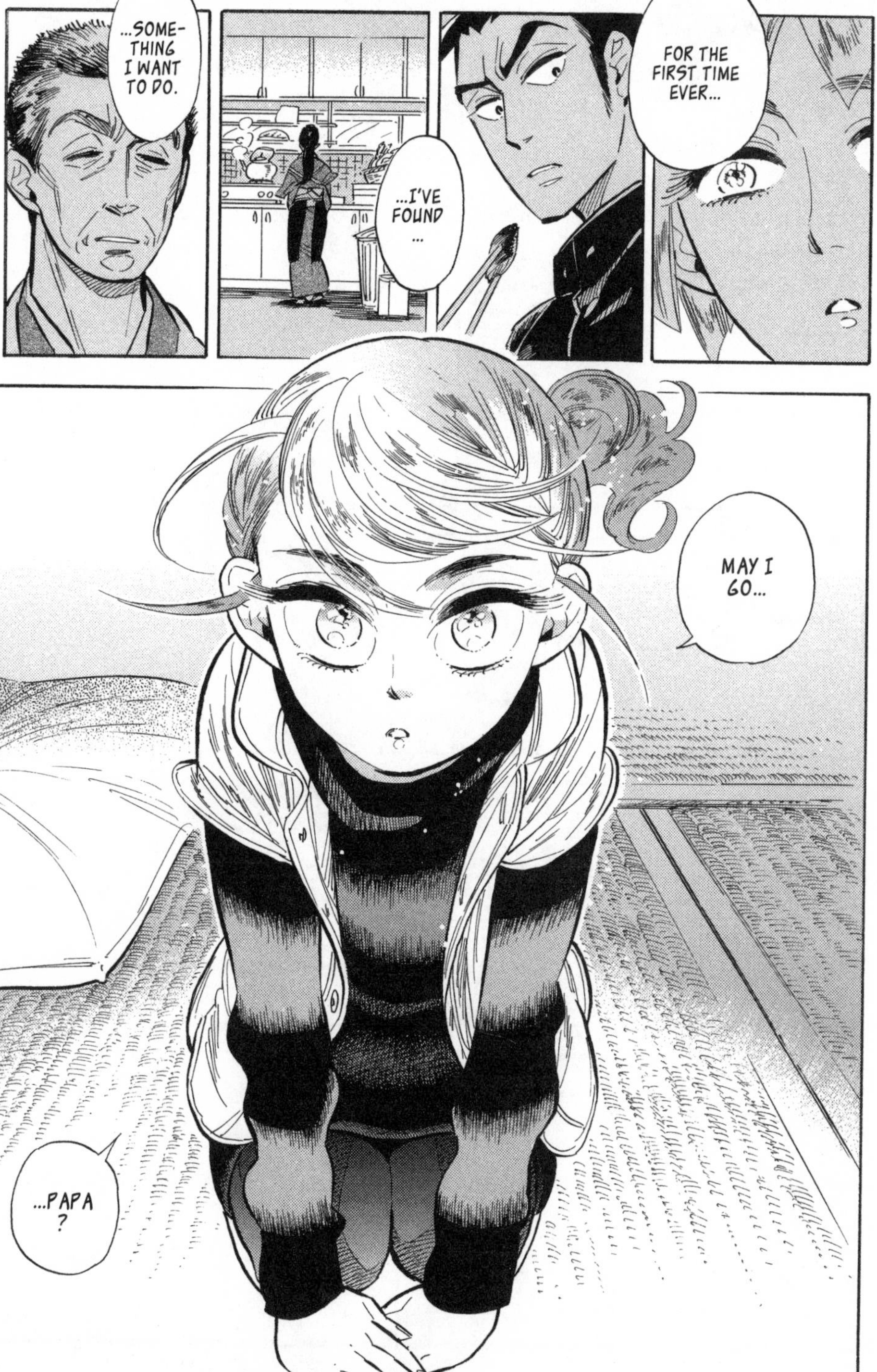
FOR THE FIRST TIME EVER...
...I'VE FOUND ...
...SOME-THING I WANT TO DO.
MAY I GO...
...PAPA ?

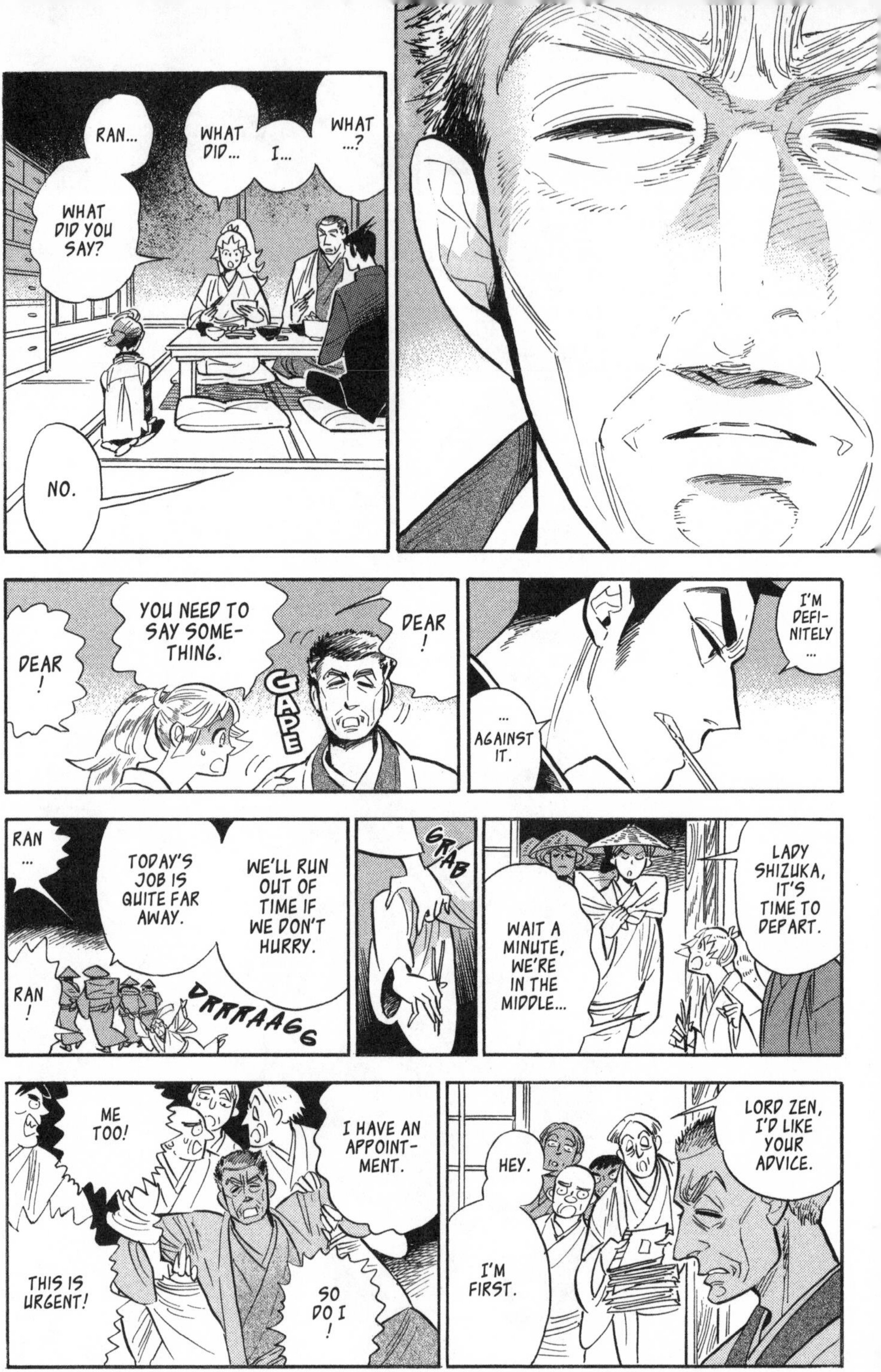
WHAT ...?
I...
WHAT DID...
RAN...
WHAT DID YOU SAY?
NO.
I'M DEFINITELY ...
... AGAINST IT.
DEAR!
YOU NEED TO SAY SOMETHING.
GAPE
DEAR!
LADY SHIZUKA, IT'S TIME TO DEPART.
WAIT A MINUTE, WE'RE IN THE MIDDLE...
GRAB
WE'LL RUN OUT OF TIME IF WE DON'T HURRY.
TODAY'S JOB IS QUITE FAR AWAY.
RAN ...
DRRRAAGG
RAN!
LORD ZEN, I'D LIKE YOUR ADVICE.
HEY.
I'M FIRST.
I HAVE AN APPOINTMENT.
ME TOO!
SO DO I!
THIS IS URGENT!

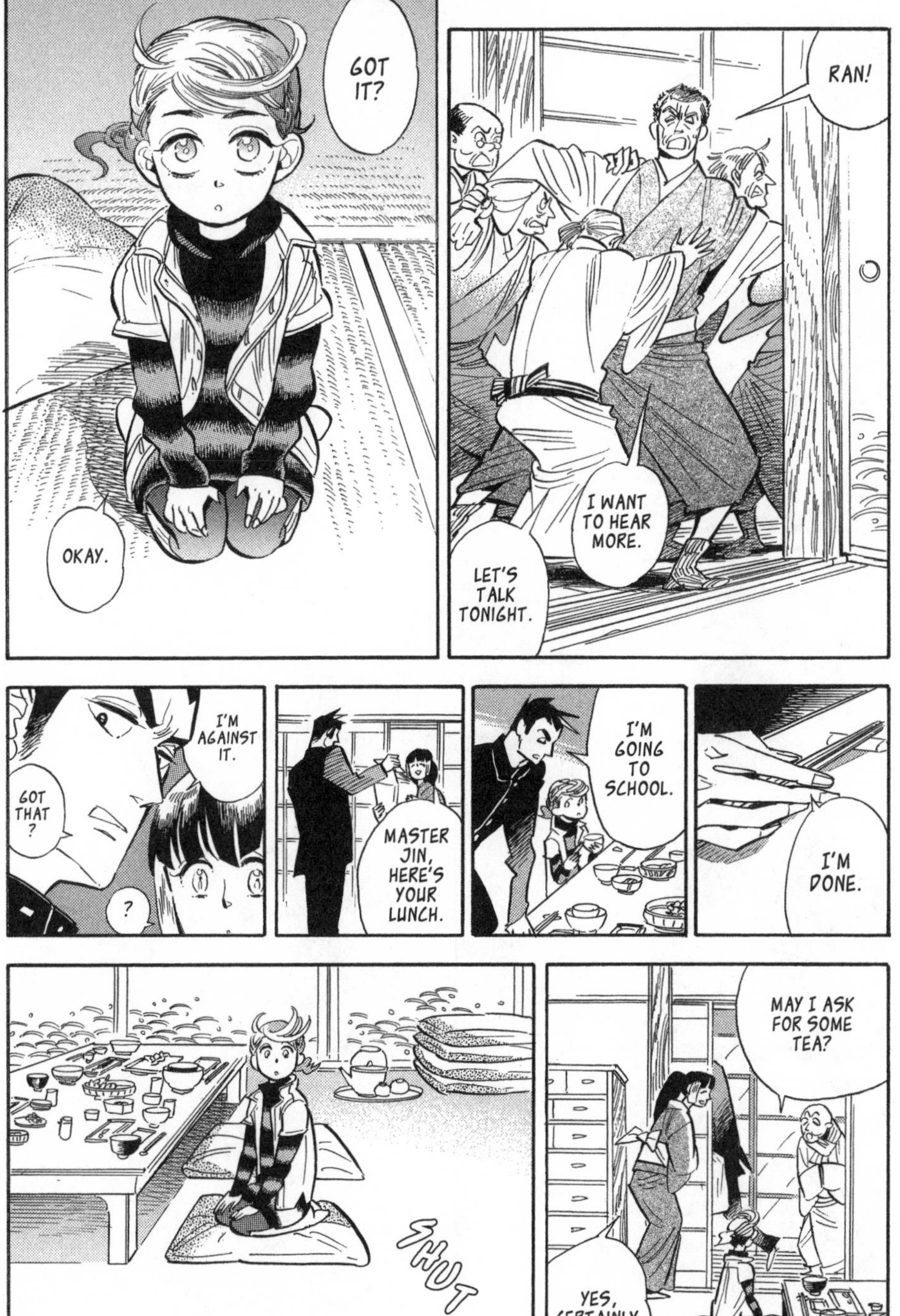
RAN!
I WANT TO HEAR MORE.
LET'S TALK TONIGHT.
GOT IT?
OKAY.
I'M DONE.
I'M GOING TO SCHOOL.
MASTER JIN, HERE'S YOUR LUNCH.
I'M AGAINST IT.
GOT THAT?
?
MAY I ASK FOR SOME TEA?
YES, CERTAINLY.
SHUT

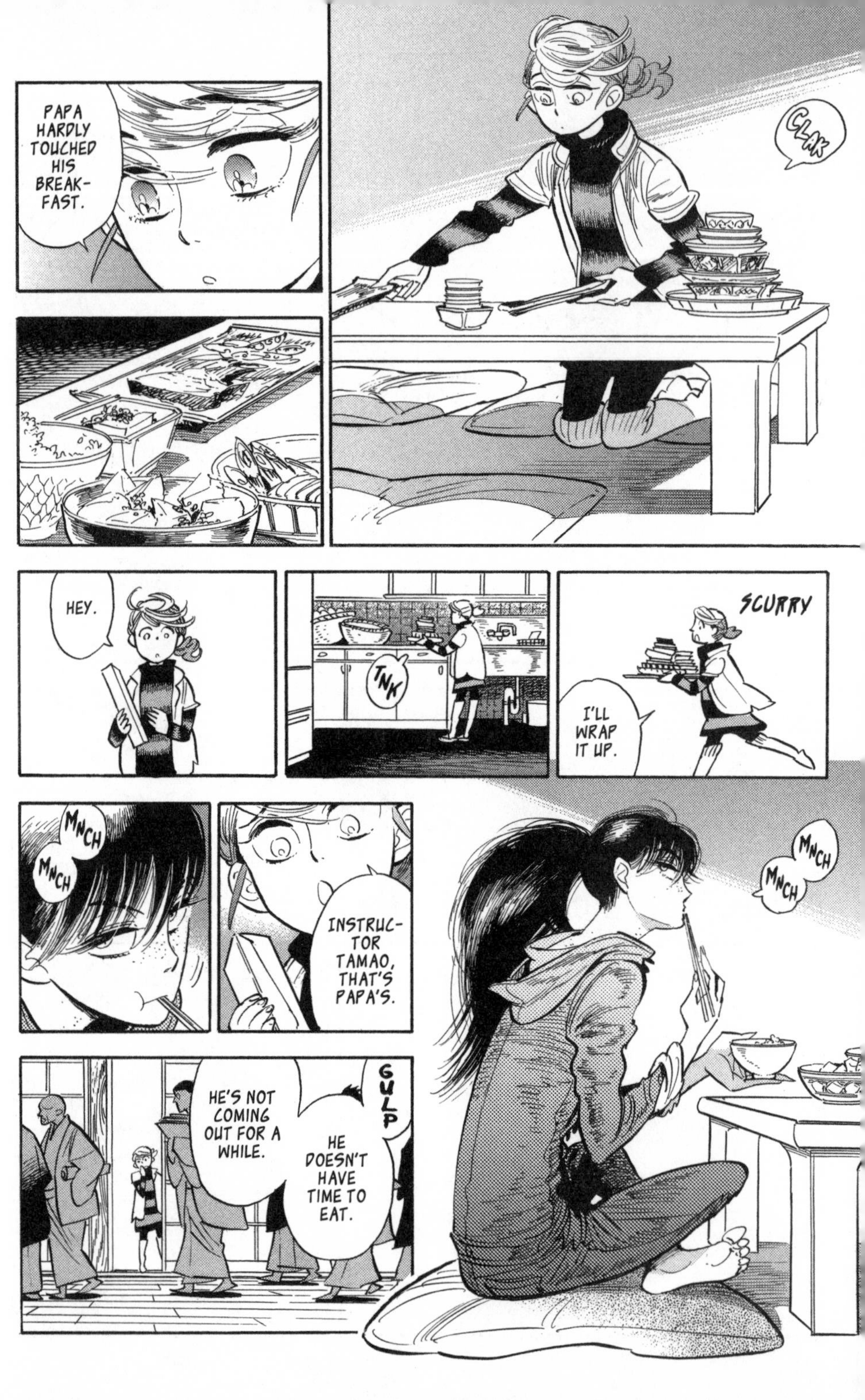
CLAK
PAPA HARDLY TOUCHED HIS BREAK-FAST.
SCURRY
I'LL WRAP IT UP.
TNK
HEY.
MNCH
MNCH
INSTRUC-TOR TAMAO, THAT'S PAPA'S.
MNCH
MNCH
GULP
HE DOESN'T HAVE TIME TO EAT.
HE'S NOT COMING OUT FOR A WHILE.

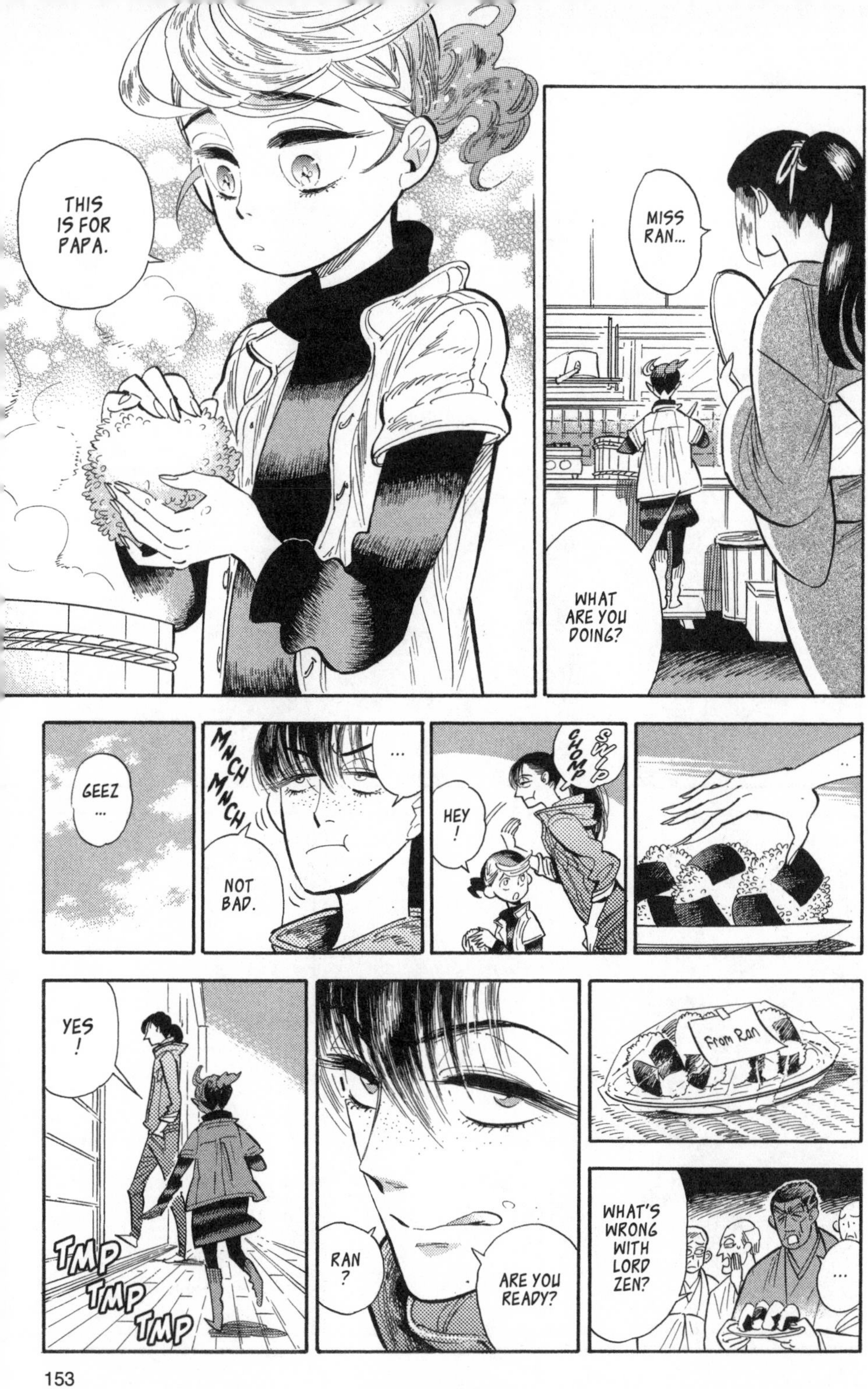
MISS RAN...
WHAT ARE YOU DOING?
THIS IS FOR PAPA.
..
SWIP
CHOMP
HEY!
...
MNCH MNCH
NOT BAD.
GEEZ...
From Ran
WHAT'S WRONG WITH LORD ZEN?
...
RAN?
ARE YOU READY?
YES!
TMP TMP TMP

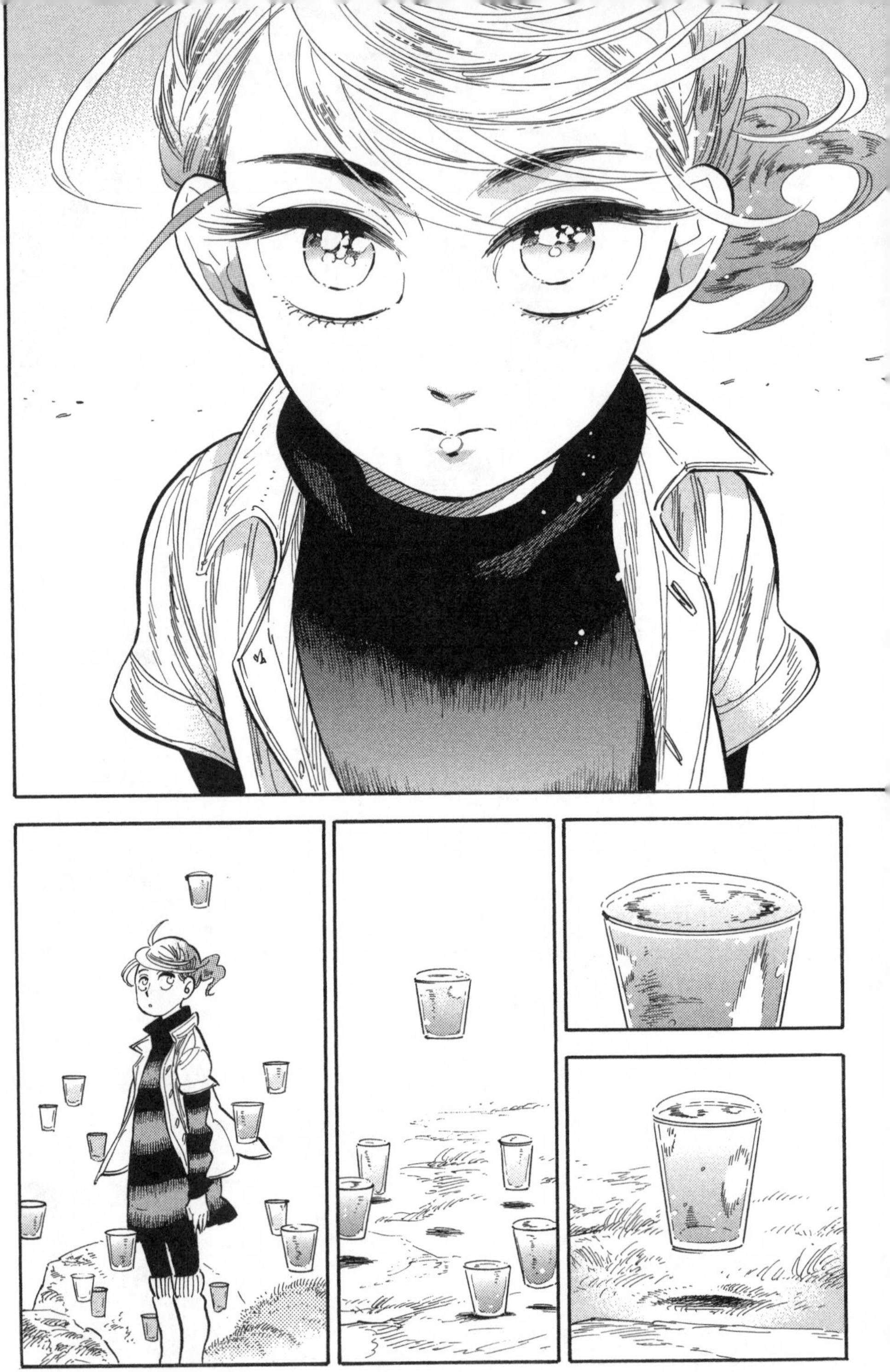

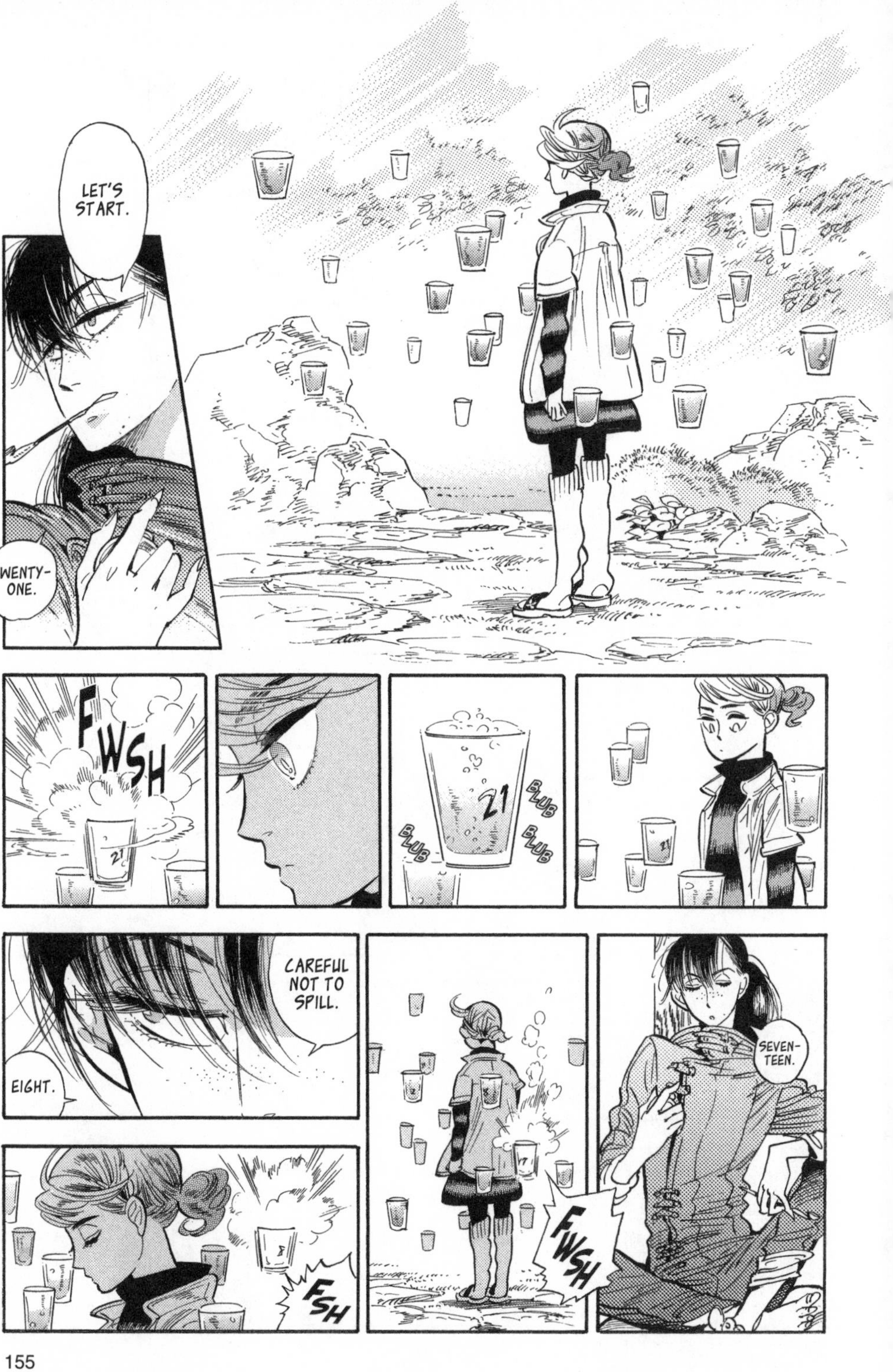
LET'S START.
TWENTY-ONE.
21
BLUB
BLUB
BLUB
FWSH
21
SEVENTEEN.
FWSH
CAREFUL NOT TO SPILL.
EIGHT.
FSH

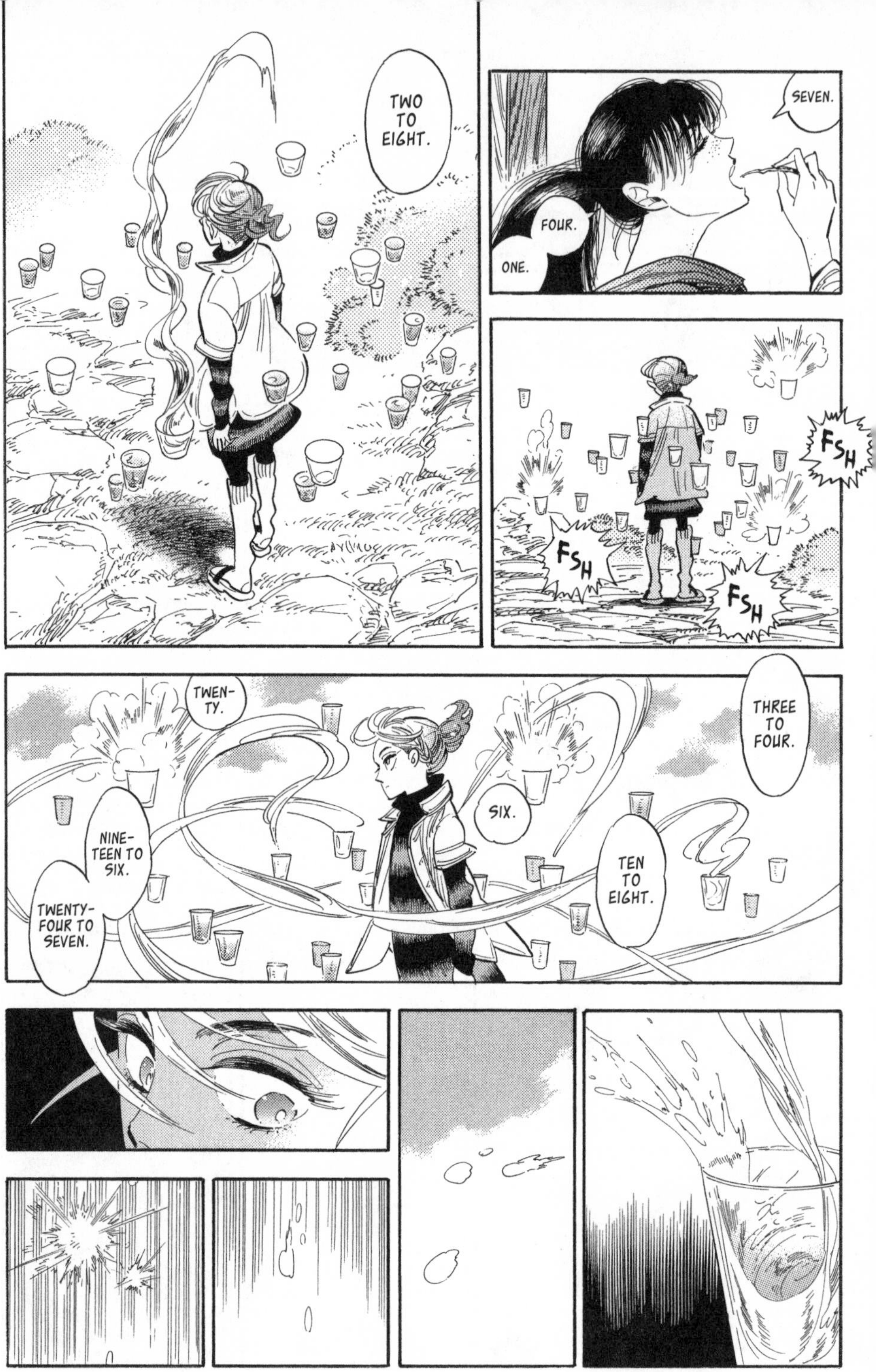
SEVEN.
FOUR.
ONE.
FSH
FSH
FSH
TWO TO EIGHT.
THREE TO FOUR.
TEN TO EIGHT.
SIX.
TWENTY.
NINETEEN TO SIX.
TWENTY-FOUR TO SEVEN.

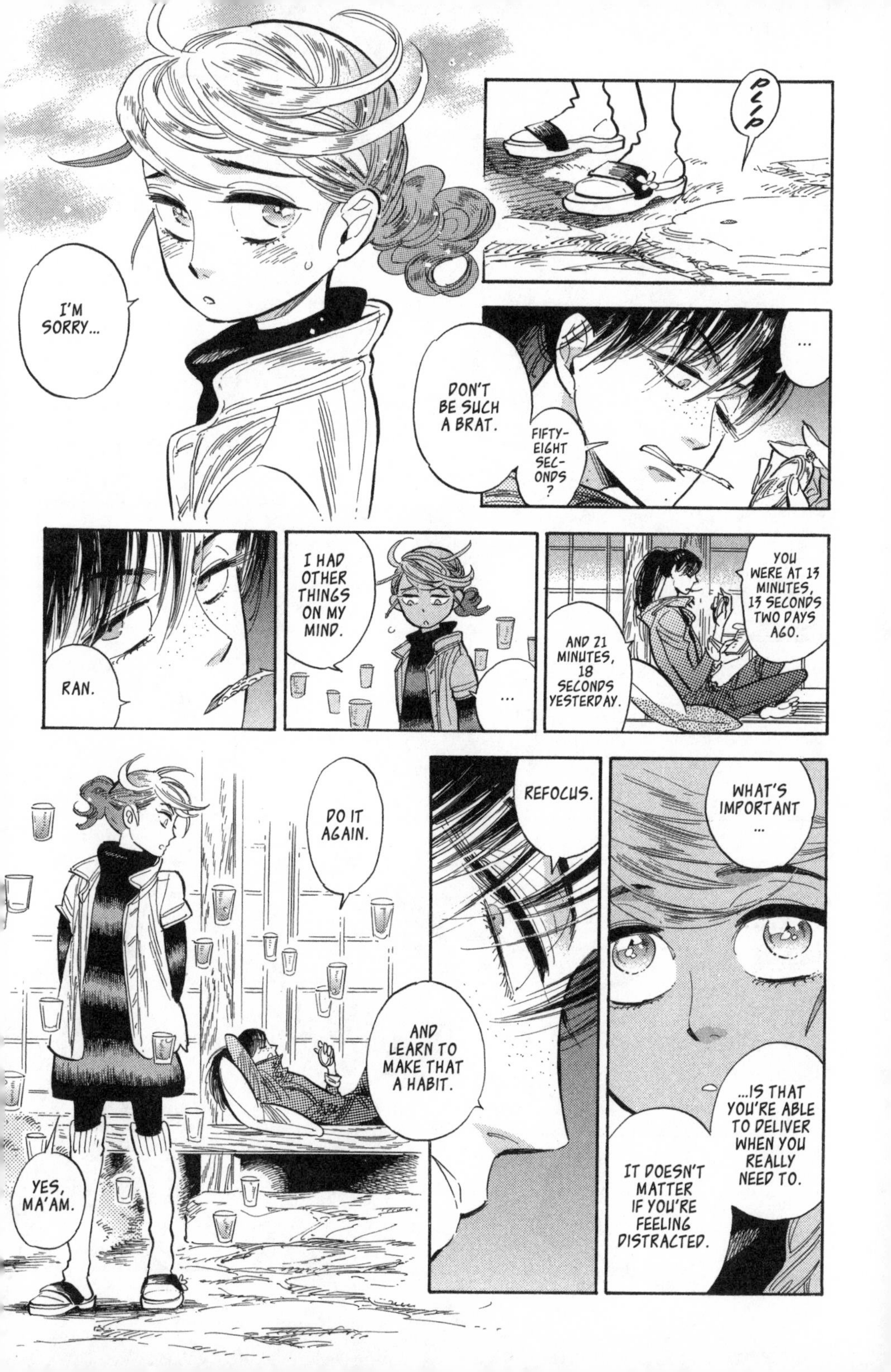
PLIP
...
FIFTY-EIGHT SECONDS?
DON'T BE SUCH A BRAT.
I'M SORRY...
YOU WERE AT 13 MINUTES, 13 SECONDS TWO DAYS AGO.
AND 21 MINUTES, 18 SECONDS YESTERDAY.
...
I HAD OTHER THINGS ON MY MIND.
RAN.
WHAT'S IMPORTANT ...
...IS THAT YOU'RE ABLE TO DELIVER WHEN YOU REALLY NEED TO.
IT DOESN'T MATTER IF YOU'RE FEELING DISTRACTED.
REFOCUS.
DO IT AGAIN.
AND LEARN TO MAKE THAT A HABIT.
YES, MA'AM.

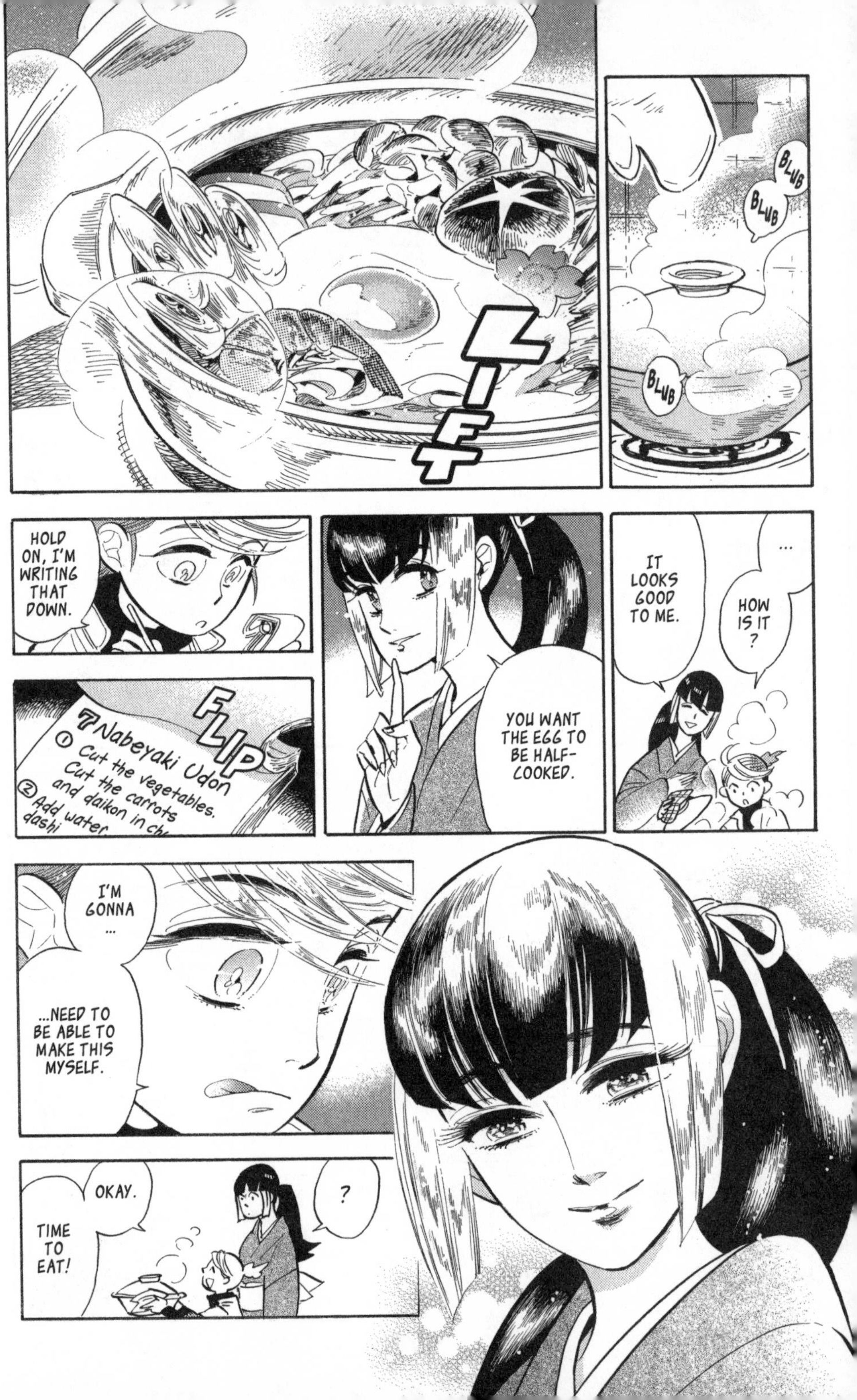
BLUB
BLUB
BLUB
LIFT
...
HOW IS IT?
IT LOOKS GOOD TO ME.
YOU WANT THE EGG TO BE HALF-COOKED.
HOLD ON, I'M WRITING THAT DOWN.
FLIP
7 Nabeyaki Udon
① Cut the vegetables.
Cut the carrots
and daikon in
② Add water.
dashi
I'M GONNA ...
...NEED TO BE ABLE TO MAKE THIS MYSELF.
?
OKAY.
TIME TO EAT!

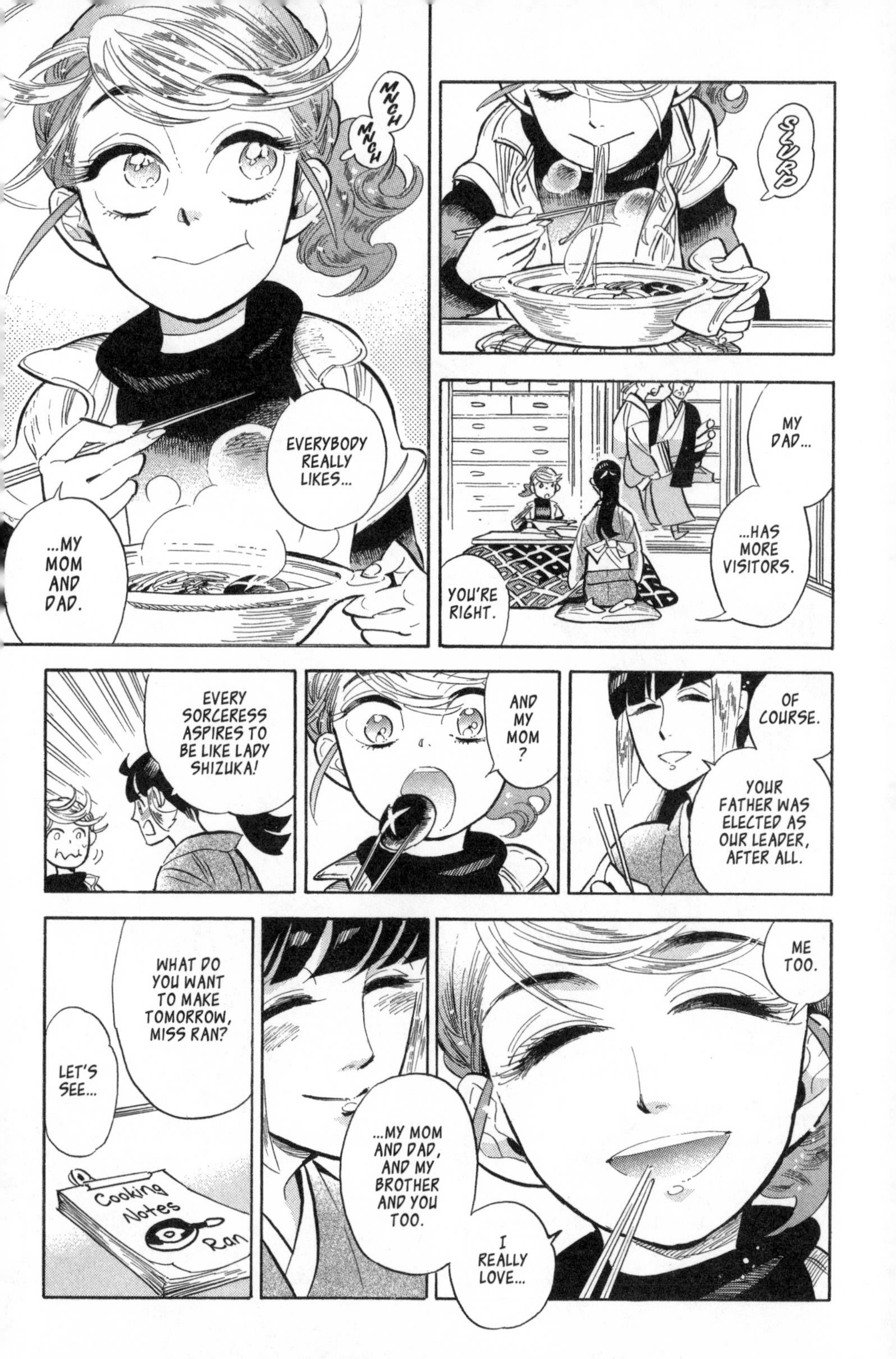
SLURP
MY DAD...
...HAS MORE VISITORS.
YOU'RE RIGHT.
MNCH MNCH
EVERYBODY REALLY LIKES...
...MY MOM AND DAD.
OF COURSE.
YOUR FATHER WAS ELECTED AS OUR LEADER, AFTER ALL.
AND MY MOM?
EVERY SORCERESS ASPIRES TO BE LIKE LADY SHIZUKA!
ME TOO.
I REALLY LOVE...
...MY MOM AND DAD, AND MY BROTHER AND YOU TOO.
WHAT DO YOU WANT TO MAKE TOMORROW, MISS RAN?
LET'S SEE...
Cooking Notes
Ran

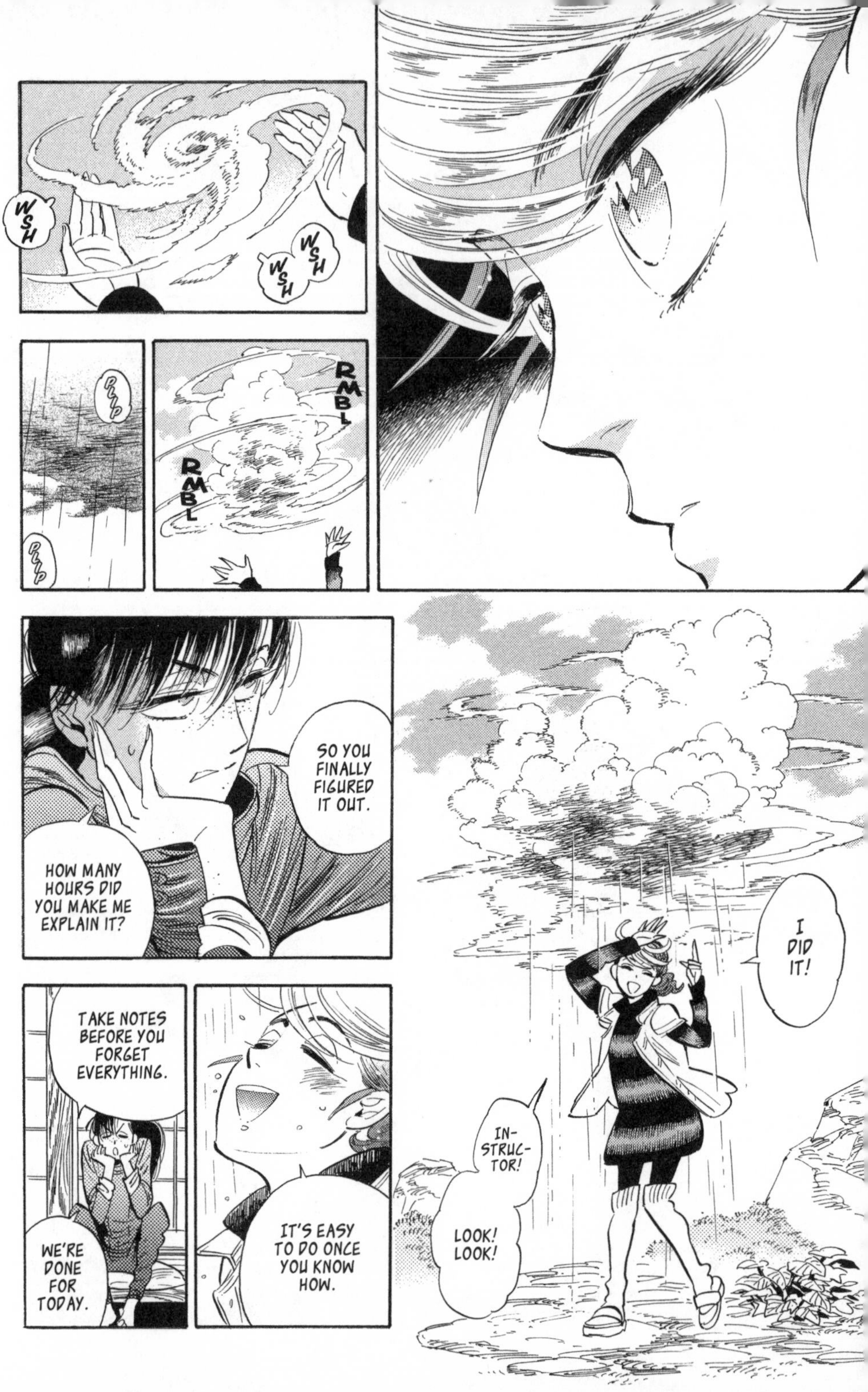
WSH
WSH
WSH
RMBL
RMBL
PLIP
PLIP
I DID IT!
INSTRUCTOR!
LOOK! LOOK!
SO YOU FINALLY FIGURED IT OUT.
HOW MANY HOURS DID YOU MAKE ME EXPLAIN IT?
IT'S EASY TO DO ONCE YOU KNOW HOW.
TAKE NOTES BEFORE YOU FORGET EVERYTHING.
WE'RE DONE FOR TODAY.

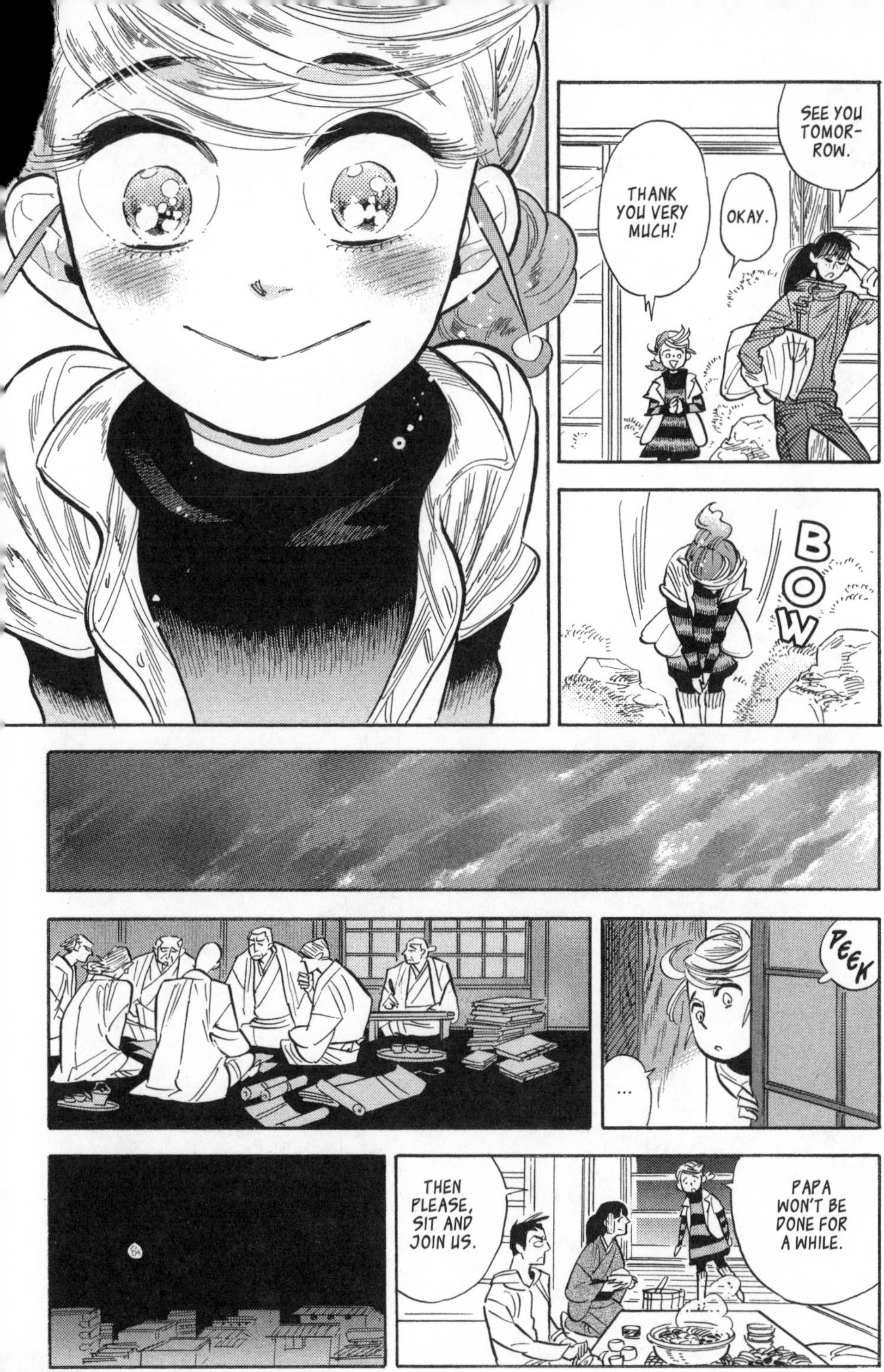
SEE YOU TOMOR-ROW.
OKAY.
THANK YOU VERY MUCH!
BOW
PEEK
...
PAPA WON'T BE DONE FOR A WHILE.
THEN PLEASE, SIT AND JOIN US.

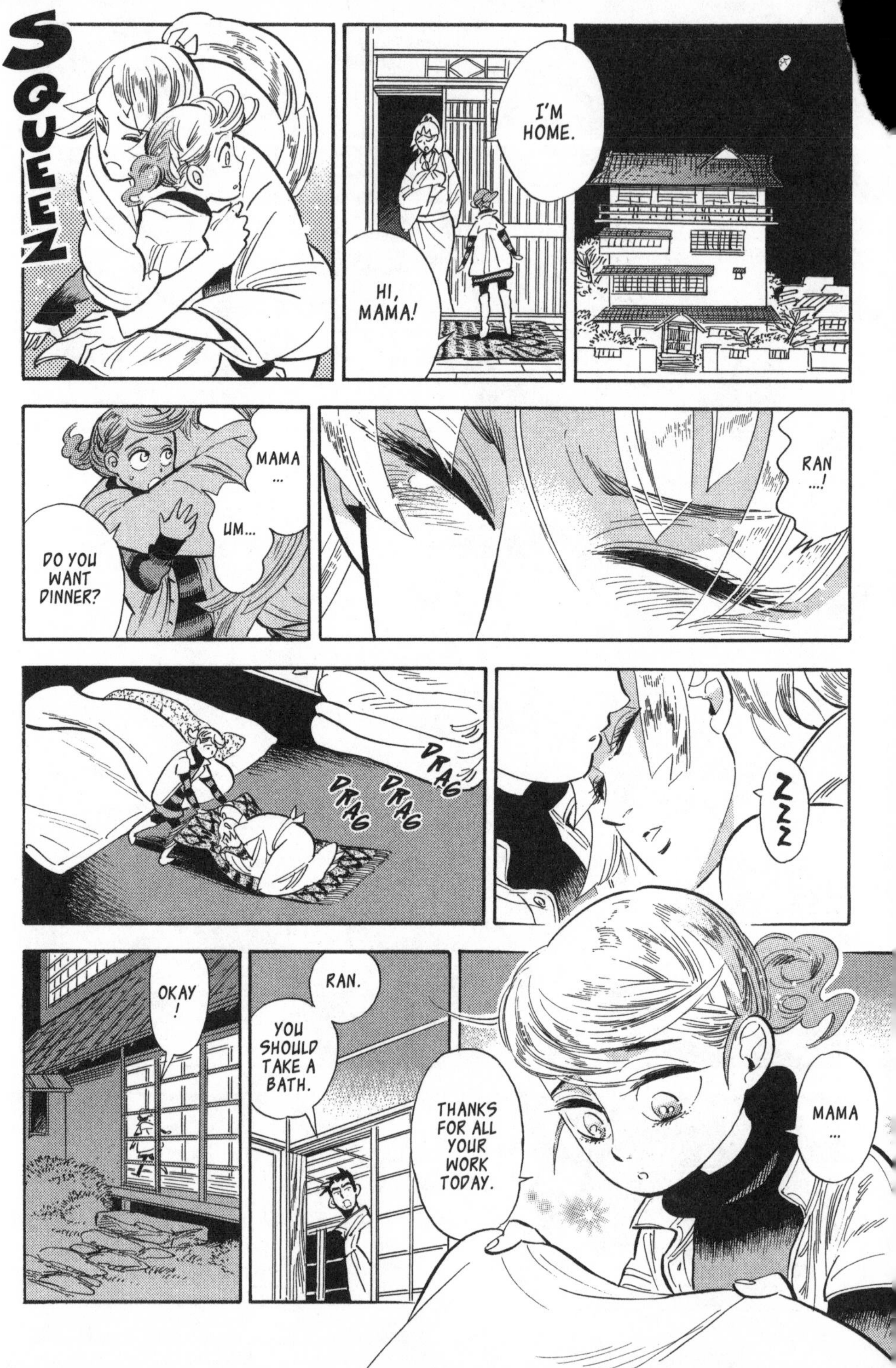
I'M HOME.
HI, MAMA!
SQUEEZ
RAN ...!
MAMA ...
UM...
DO YOU WANT DINNER?
ZZZ
DRAG
DRAG
DRAG
MAMA ...
THANKS FOR ALL YOUR WORK TODAY.
RAN.
YOU SHOULD TAKE A BATH.
OKAY!

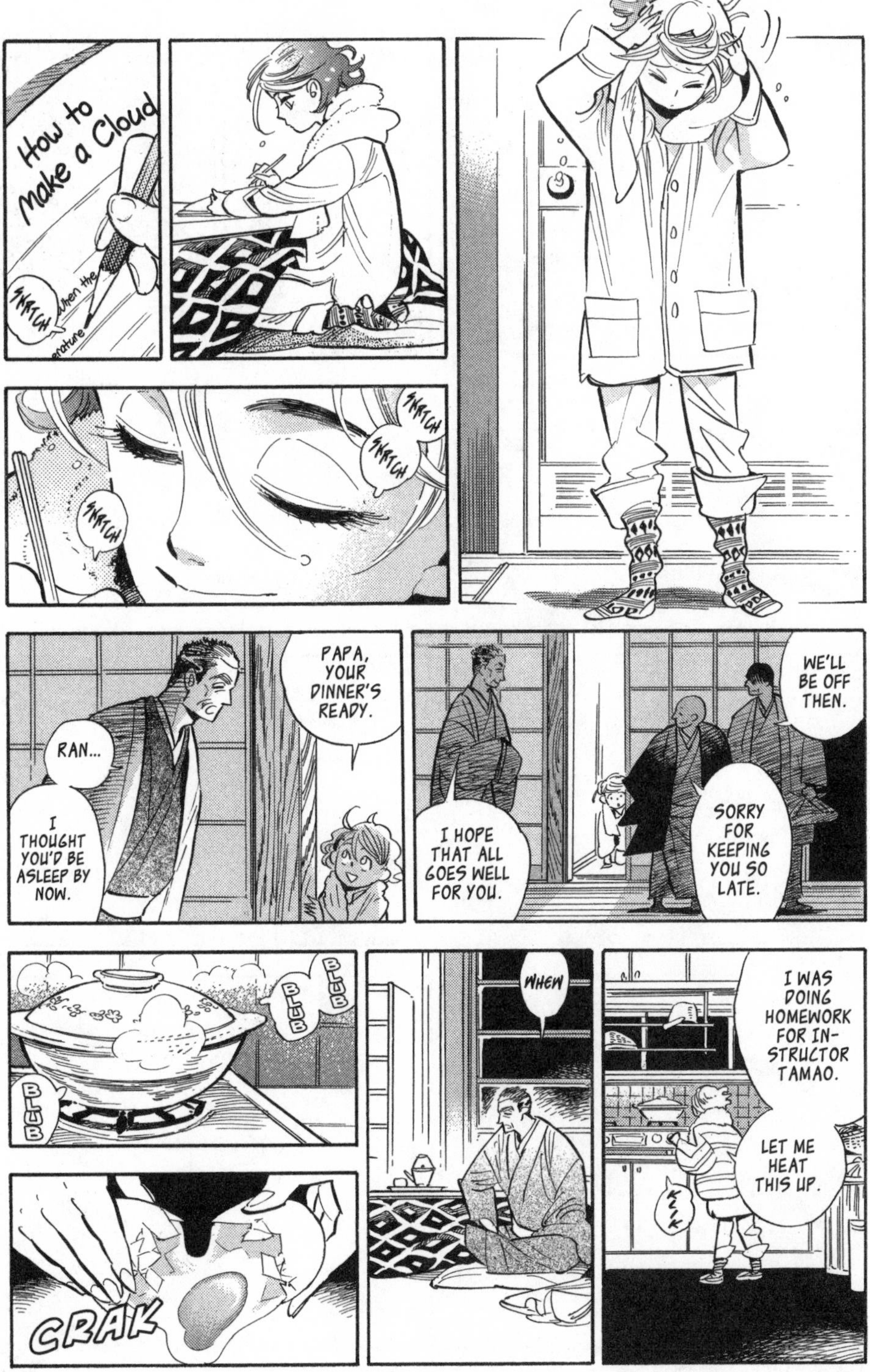
How to make a Cloud
When the
erature
SKRTCH
SKRTCH
SKRTCH
SKRTCH
WE'LL BE OFF THEN.
SORRY FOR KEEPING YOU SO LATE.
I HOPE THAT ALL GOES WELL FOR YOU.
PAPA, YOUR DINNER'S READY.
RAN...
I THOUGHT YOU'D BE ASLEEP BY NOW.
I WAS DOING HOMEWORK FOR IN-STRUCTOR TAMAO.
LET ME HEAT THIS UP.
KLIK
WHEW
BLUB BLUB
BLUB
CRAK

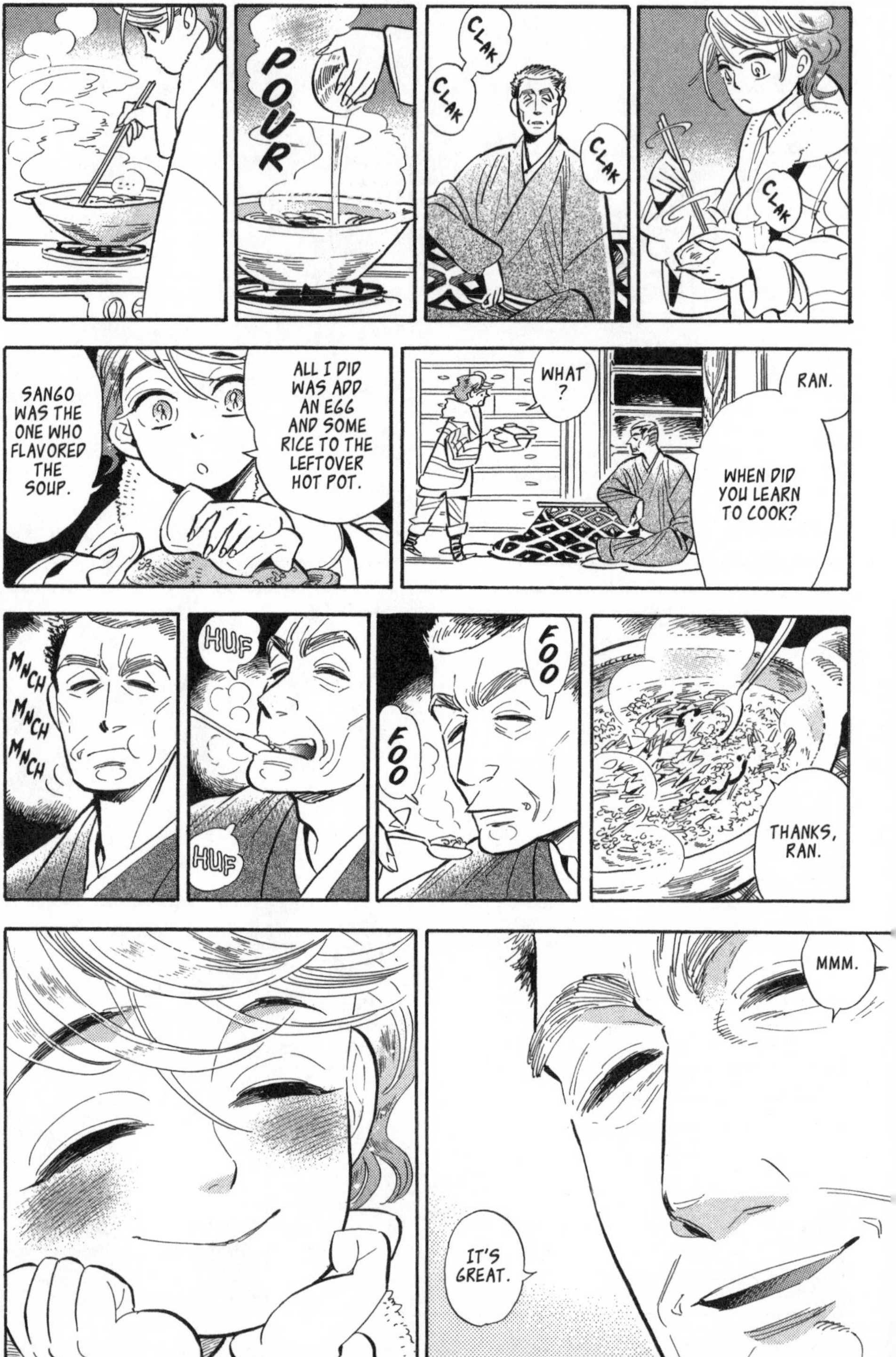
CLAK
CLAK
CLAK
CLAK
POUR
RAN.
WHAT?
WHEN DID YOU LEARN TO COOK?
ALL I DID WAS ADD AN EGG AND SOME RICE TO THE LEFTOVER HOT POT.
SANGO WAS THE ONE WHO FLAVORED THE SOUP.
THANKS, RAN.
FOO
FOO
HUF
HUF
MNCH
MNCH
MNCH
MMM.
IT'S GREAT.

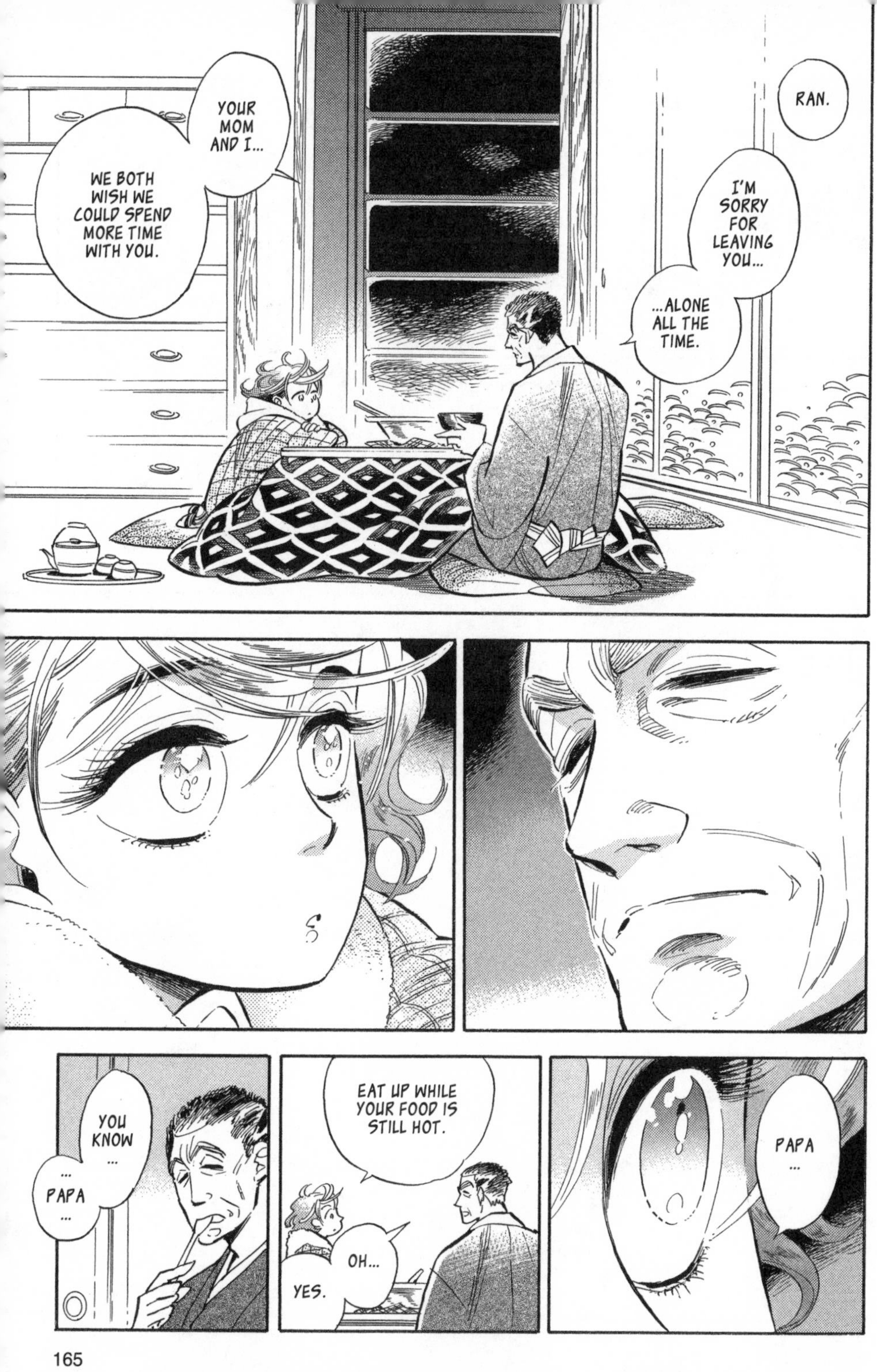
RAN.
I'M SORRY FOR LEAVING YOU...
...ALONE ALL THE TIME.
YOUR MOM AND I...
WE BOTH WISH WE COULD SPEND MORE TIME WITH YOU.
PAPA ...
EAT UP WHILE YOUR FOOD IS STILL HOT.
OH... YES.
YOU KNOW ...
... PAPA ...

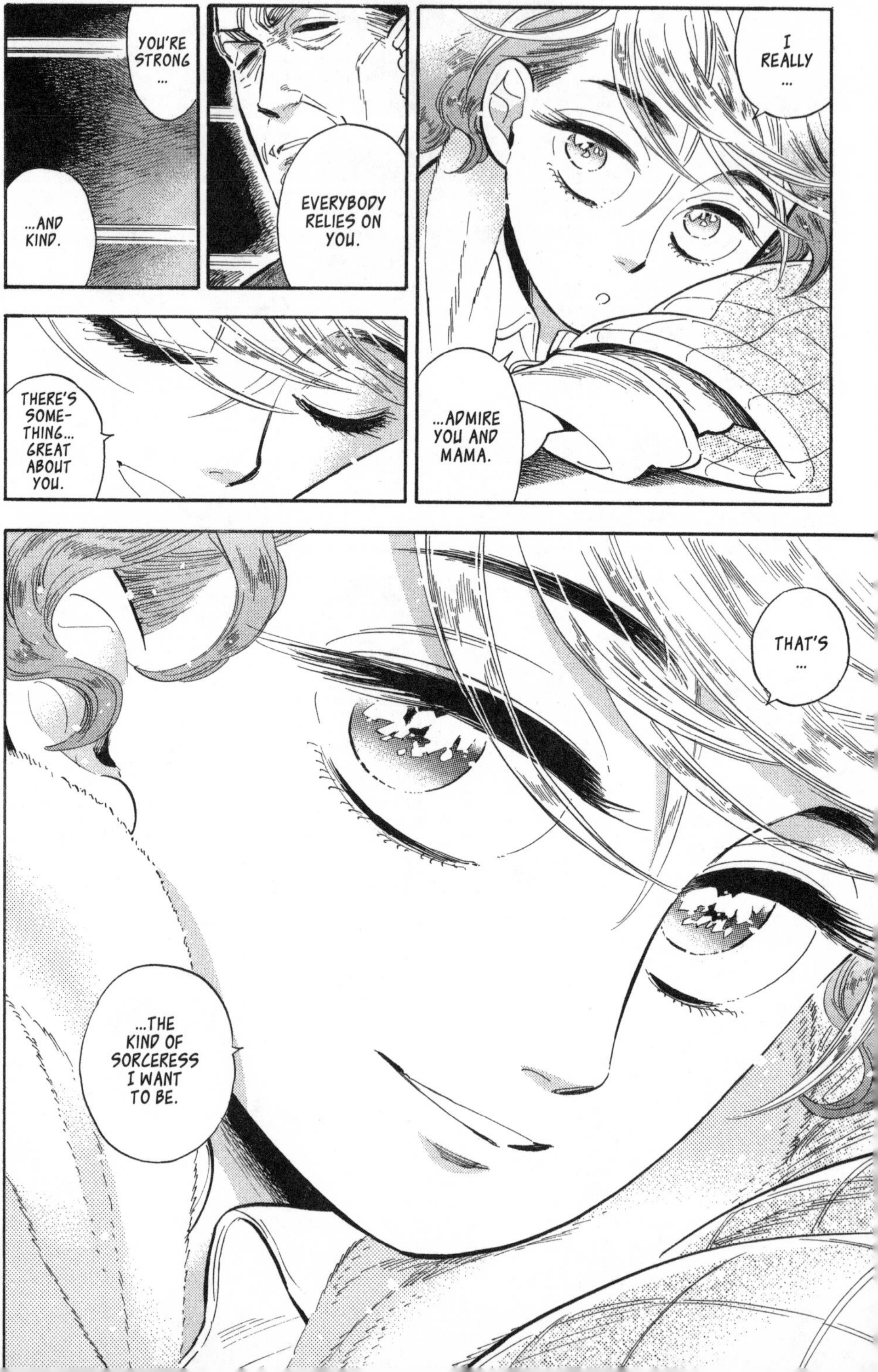
I REALLY ...
...ADMIRE YOU AND MAMA.
EVERYBODY RELIES ON YOU.
YOU'RE STRONG ...
...AND KIND.
THERE'S SOME-THING... GREAT ABOUT YOU.
THAT'S ...
...THE KIND OF SORCERESS I WANT TO BE.

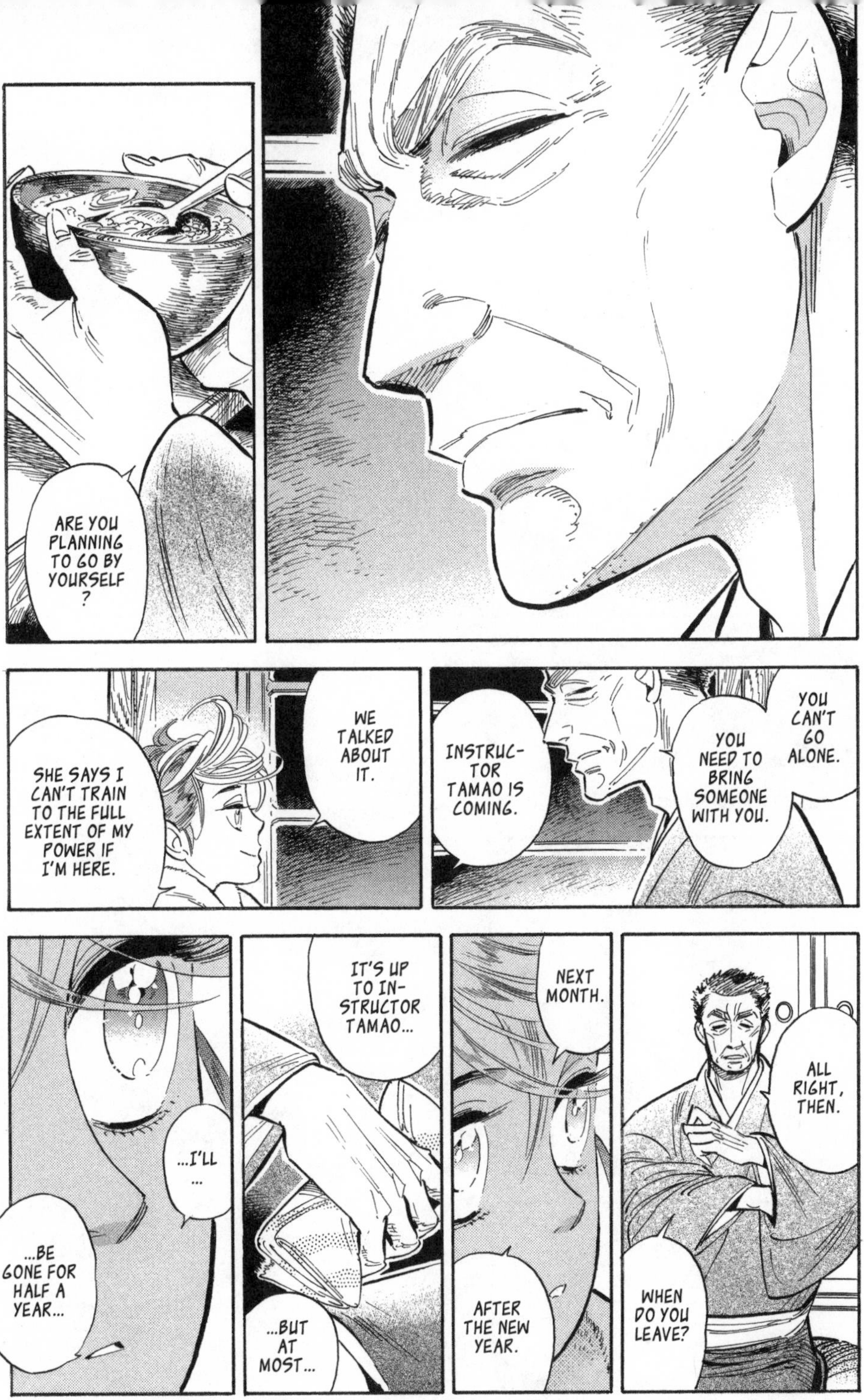
ARE YOU PLANNING TO GO BY YOURSELF?
YOU CAN'T GO ALONE.
YOU NEED TO BRING SOMEONE WITH YOU.
INSTRUCTOR TAMAO IS COMING.
WE TALKED ABOUT IT.
SHE SAYS I CAN'T TRAIN TO THE FULL EXTENT OF MY POWER IF I'M HERE.
ALL RIGHT, THEN.
WHEN DO YOU LEAVE?
NEXT MONTH.
AFTER THE NEW YEAR.
IT'S UP TO INSTRUCTOR TAMAO...
...BUT AT MOST...
...I'LL...
...BE GONE FOR HALF A YEAR...

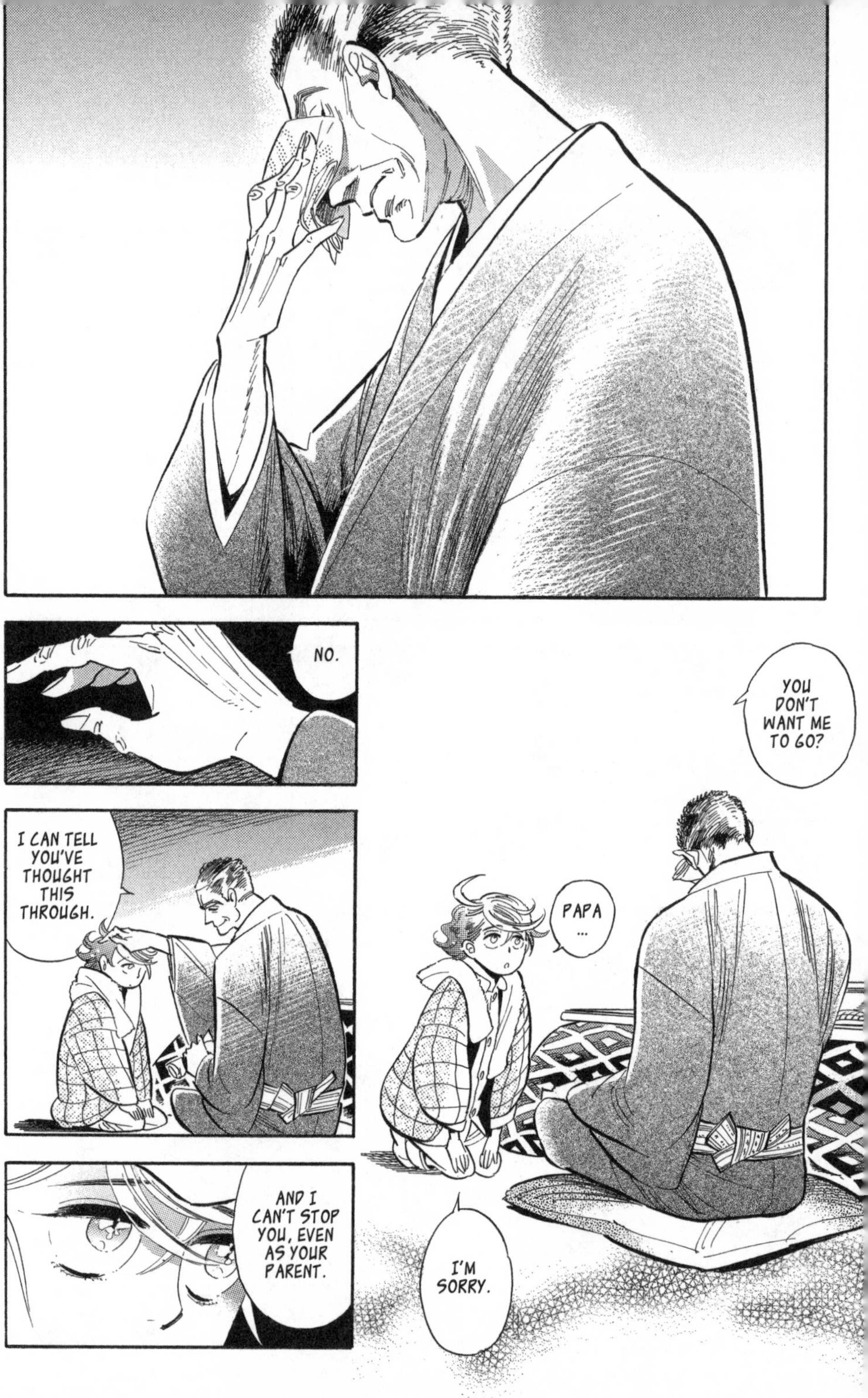
YOU DON'T WANT ME TO GO?
PAPA ...
I'M SORRY.
NO.
I CAN TELL YOU'VE THOUGHT THIS THROUGH.
AND I CAN'T STOP YOU, EVEN AS YOUR PARENT.

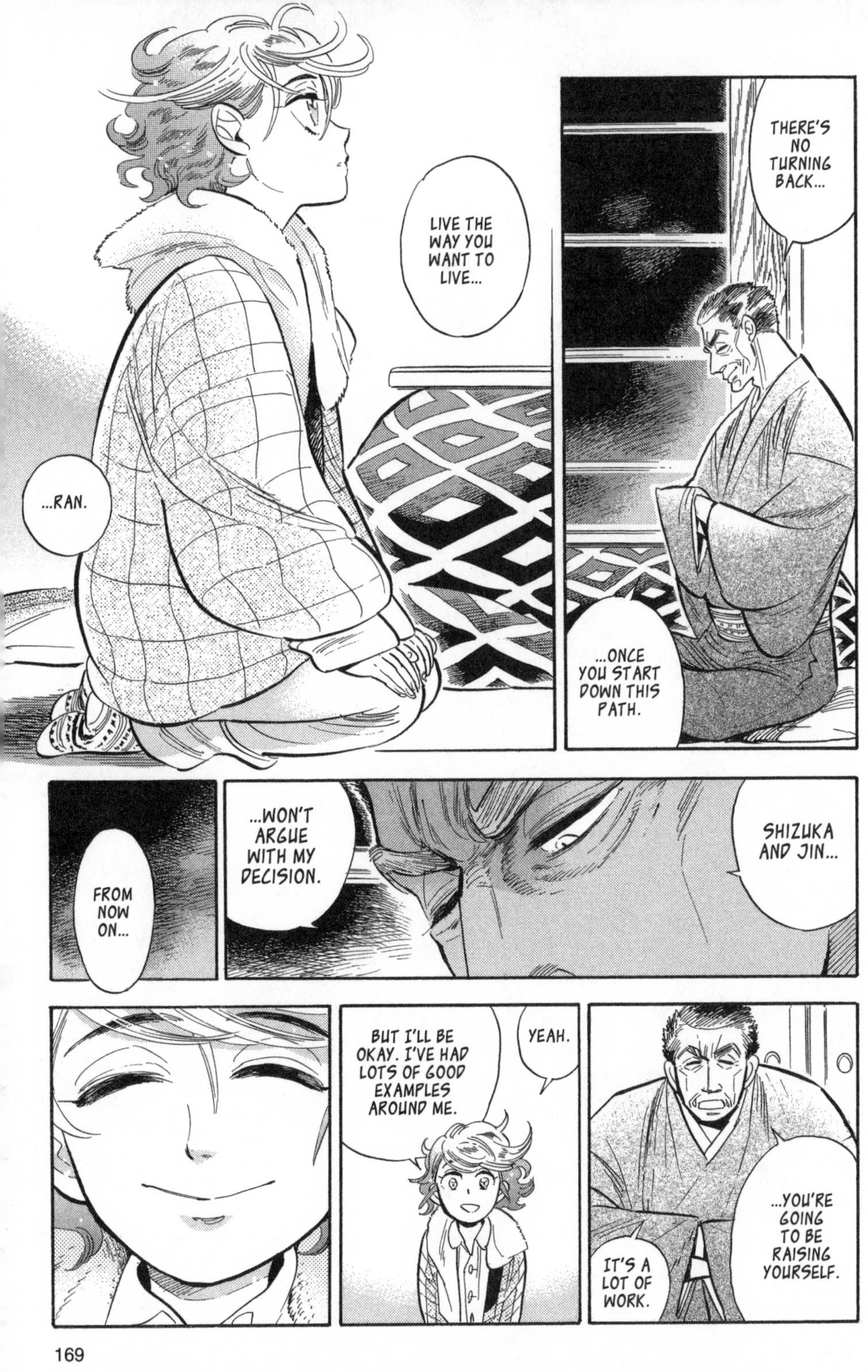
THERE'S NO TURNING BACK...
...ONCE YOU START DOWN THIS PATH.
LIVE THE WAY YOU WANT TO LIVE...
...RAN.
SHIZUKA AND JIN...
...WON'T ARGUE WITH MY DECISION.
FROM NOW ON...
...YOU'RE GOING TO BE RAISING YOURSELF.
IT'S A LOT OF WORK.
YEAH.
BUT I'LL BE OKAY. I'VE HAD LOTS OF GOOD EXAMPLES AROUND ME.

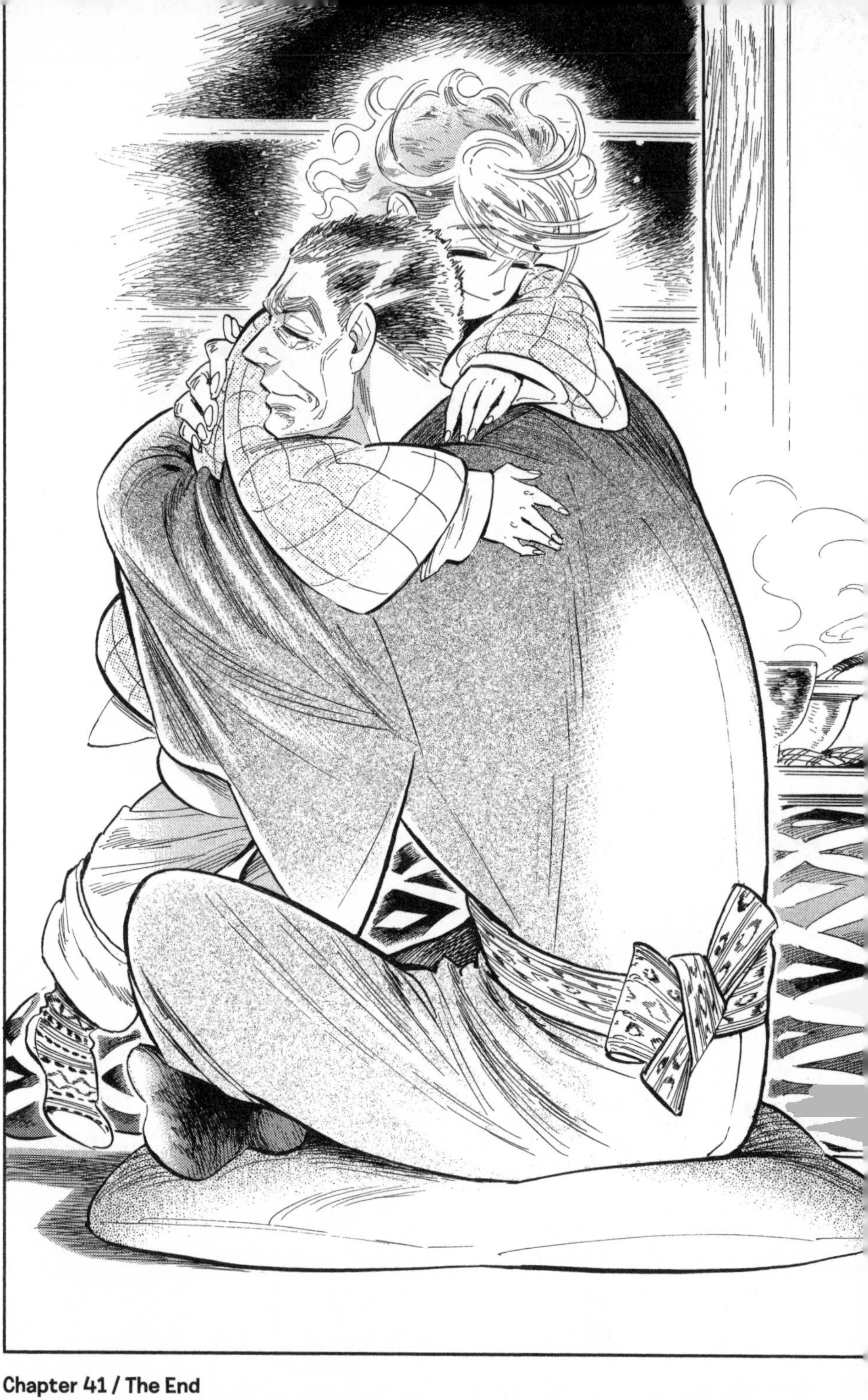

Chapter 41 / The End

Chapter 42
A Parting Gift and a Path to Spring (Part 1)

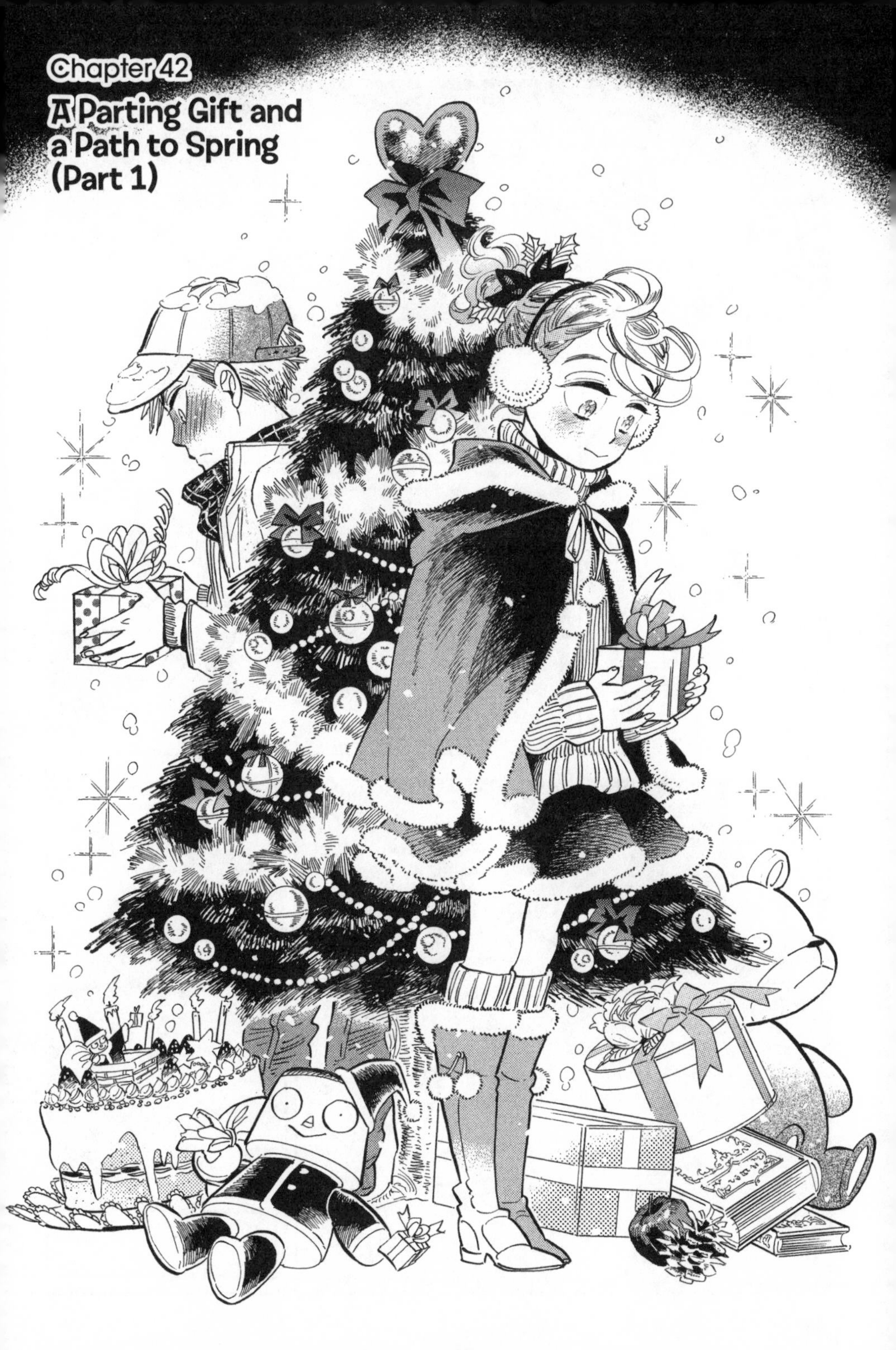

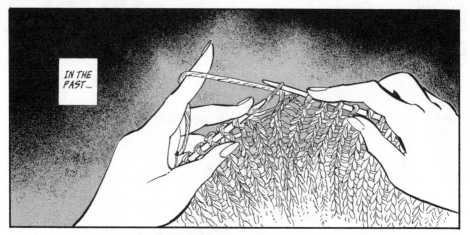

IN THE PAST...

...I SKIPPED STITCHES...

...HOW HARD I TRIED...

...NO MATTER...

I'D END UP LIKE THIS.

?

...AND KNIT...

...TOO TIGHTLY.

172

BUT NOW...

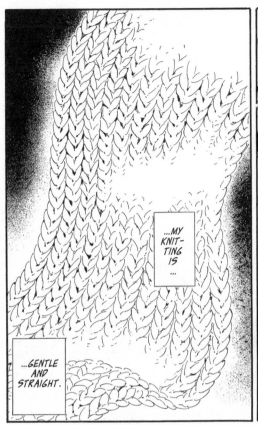

...MY KNIT-TING IS...

...GENTLE AND STRAIGHT.

TUG

...CHANGE?

...SUD-DENLY...

...DID I...

WHEN...

...FINISHED ON TIME.

I...

PHEW.

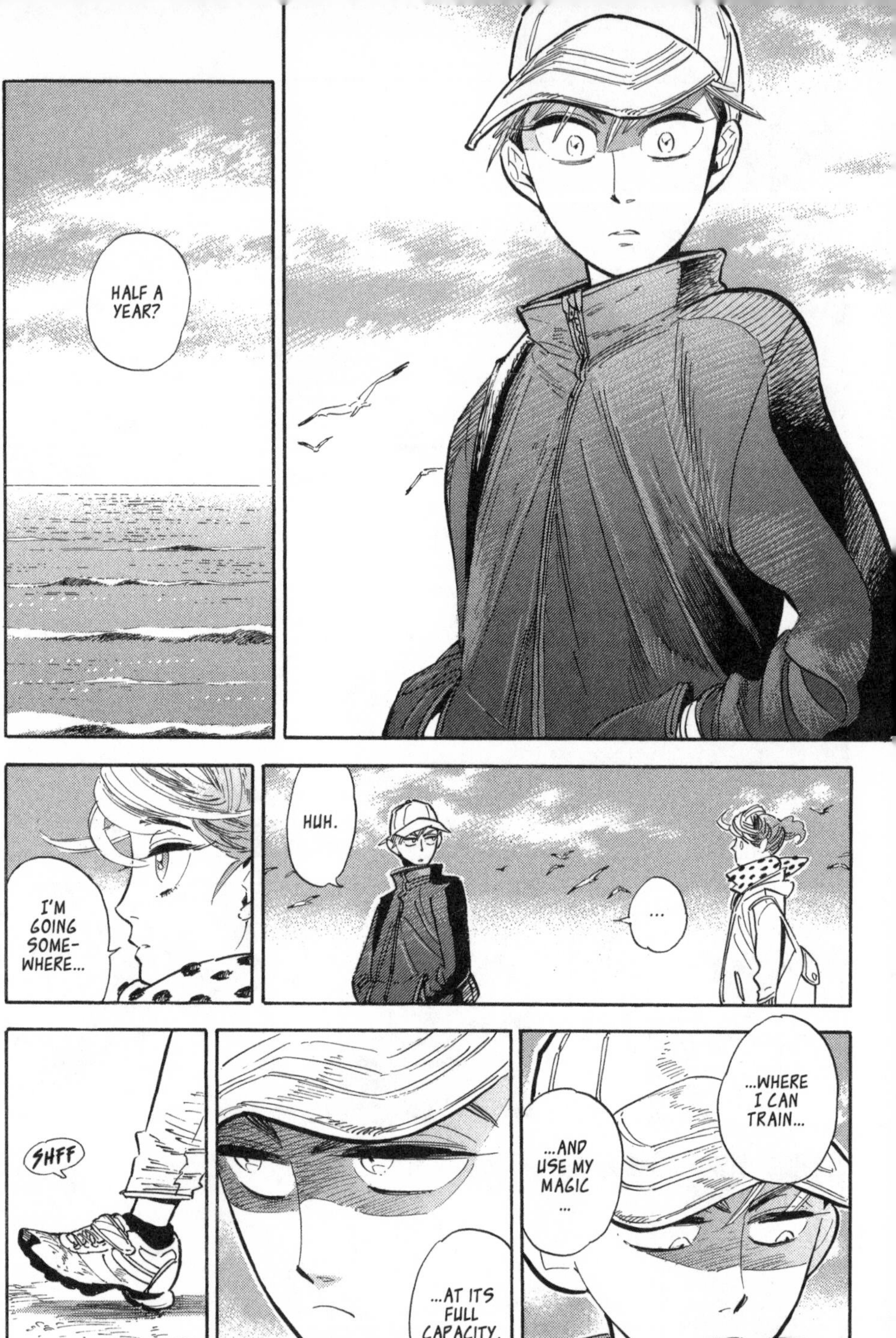
HALF A YEAR?
HUH.
...
I'M GOING SOME-WHERE...
...WHERE I CAN TRAIN...
...AND USE MY MAGIC ...
...AT ITS FULL CAPACITY.
SHFF

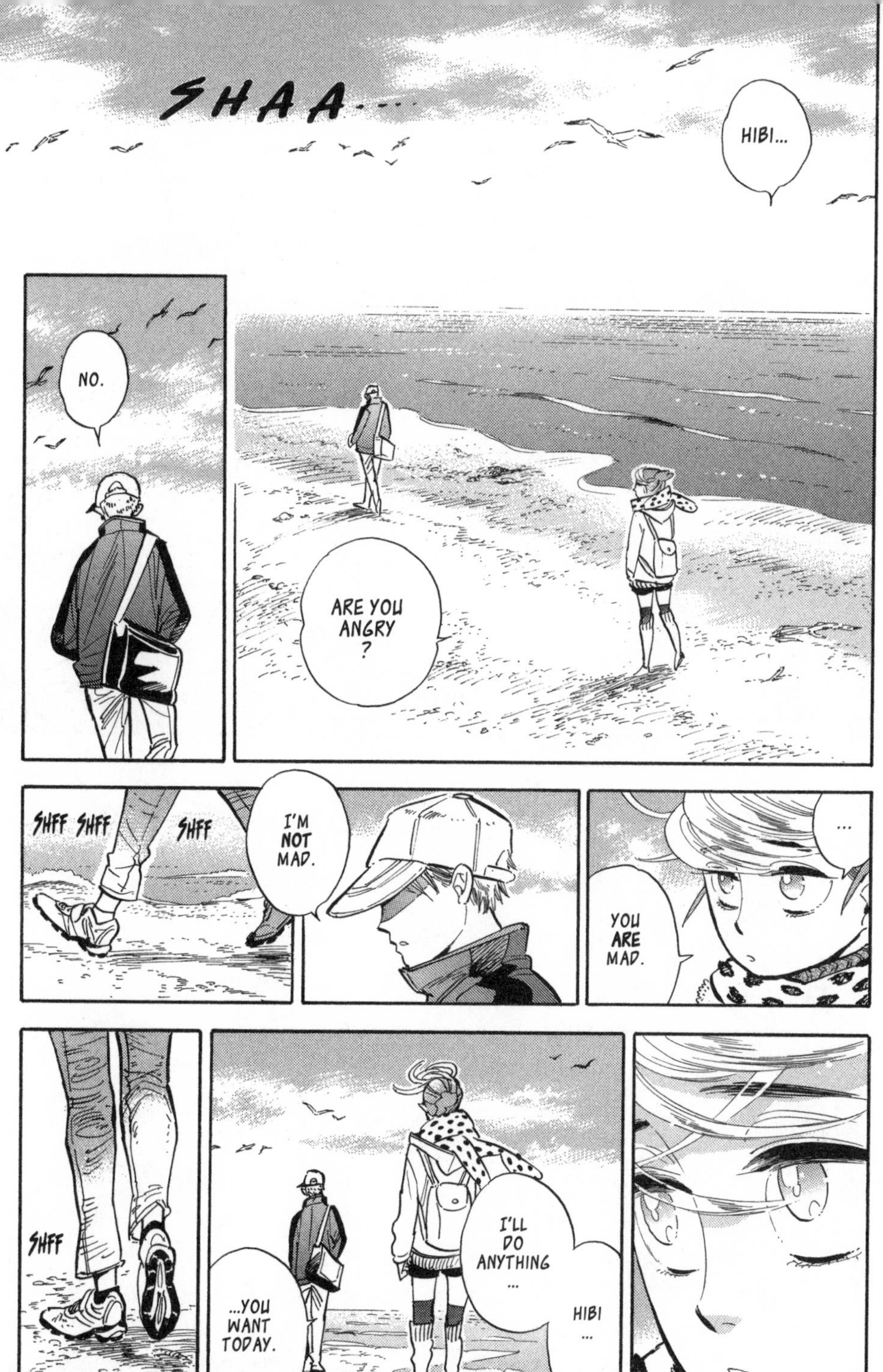
HIBI...
SHAA...
ARE YOU ANGRY?
NO.
...
YOU ARE MAD.
I'M NOT MAD.
SHFF SHFF
SHFF
I'LL DO ANYTHING...
HIBI...
...YOU WANT TODAY.
SHFF

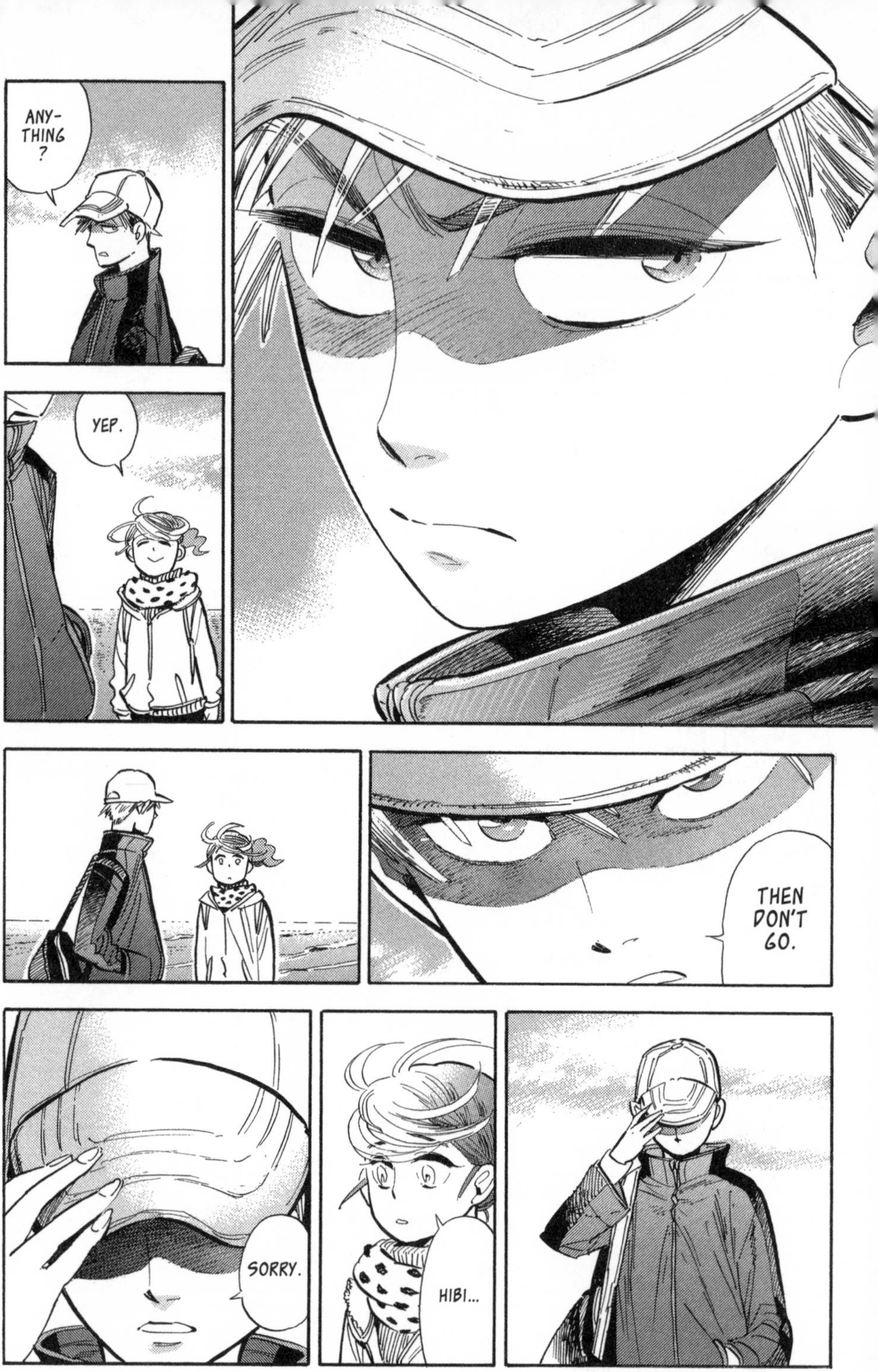
ANY-THING?
YEP.
THEN DON'T GO.
HIBI...
SORRY.

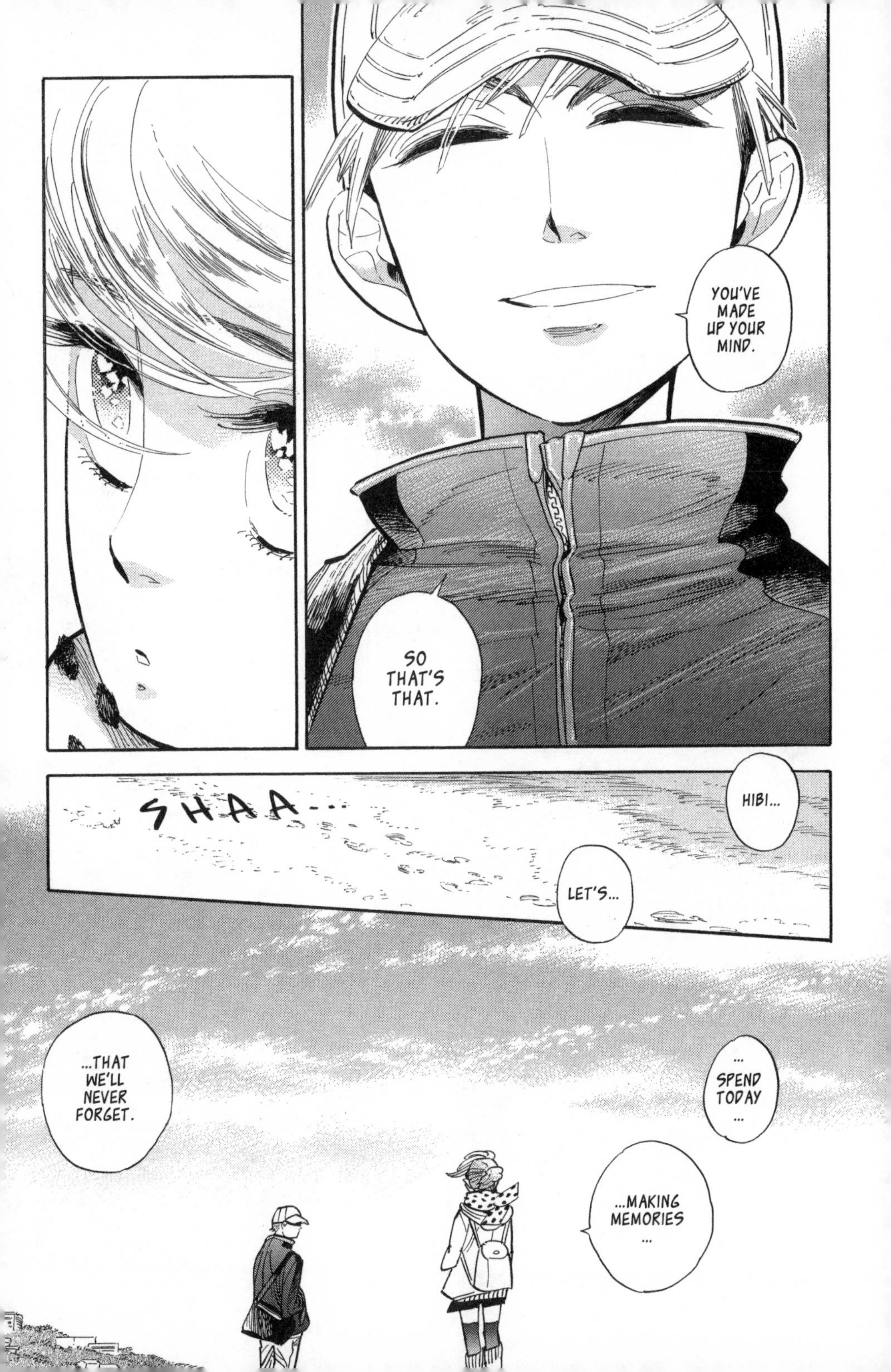
YOU'VE MADE UP YOUR MIND.
SO THAT'S THAT.
HIBI...
SHAA...
LET'S...
... SPEND TODAY ...
...MAKING MEMORIES ...
...THAT WE'LL NEVER FORGET.

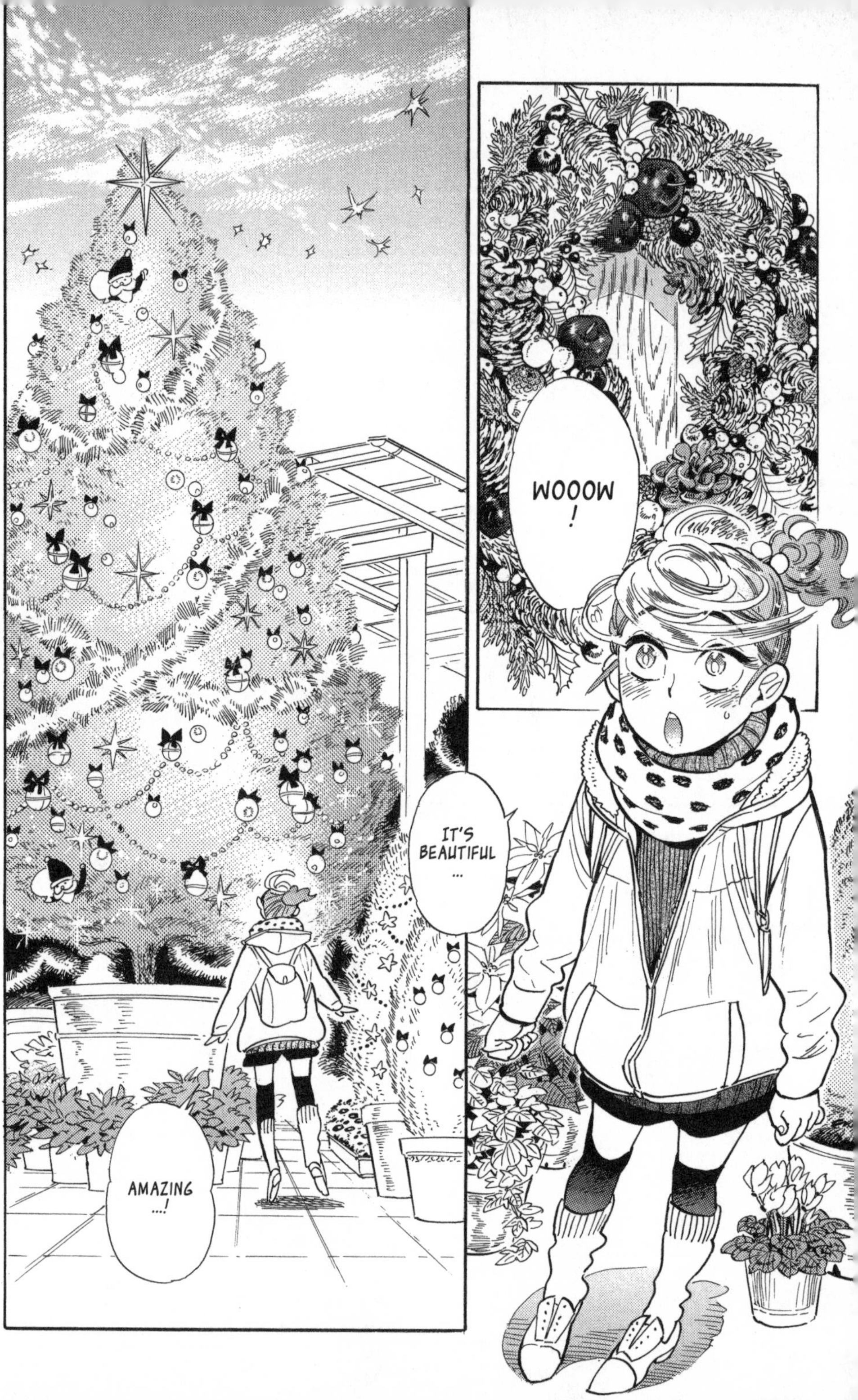
WOOOW!
IT'S BEAUTIFUL...
AMAZING...!

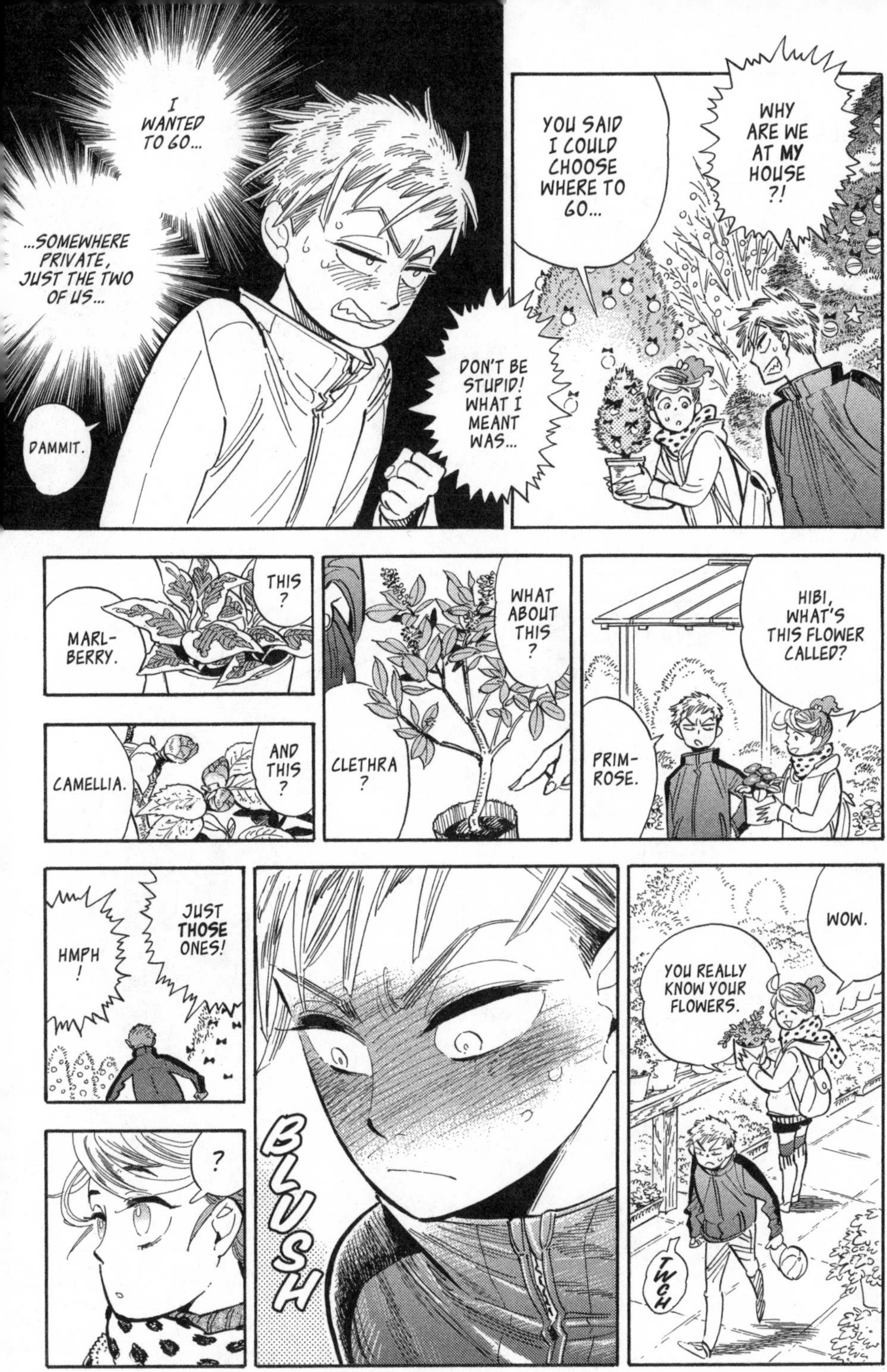
WHY ARE WE AT MY HOUSE ?!
YOU SAID I COULD CHOOSE WHERE TO GO...
DON'T BE STUPID! WHAT I MEANT WAS...
I WANTED TO GO...
...SOMEWHERE PRIVATE, JUST THE TWO OF US...
DAMMIT.
HIBI, WHAT'S THIS FLOWER CALLED?
PRIM-ROSE.
WHAT ABOUT THIS ?
CLETHRA ?
THIS ?
MARL-BERRY.
AND THIS ?
CAMELLIA.
WOW.
YOU REALLY KNOW YOUR FLOWERS.
TWCH
BLUSH
JUST THOSE ONES!
HMPH !
?

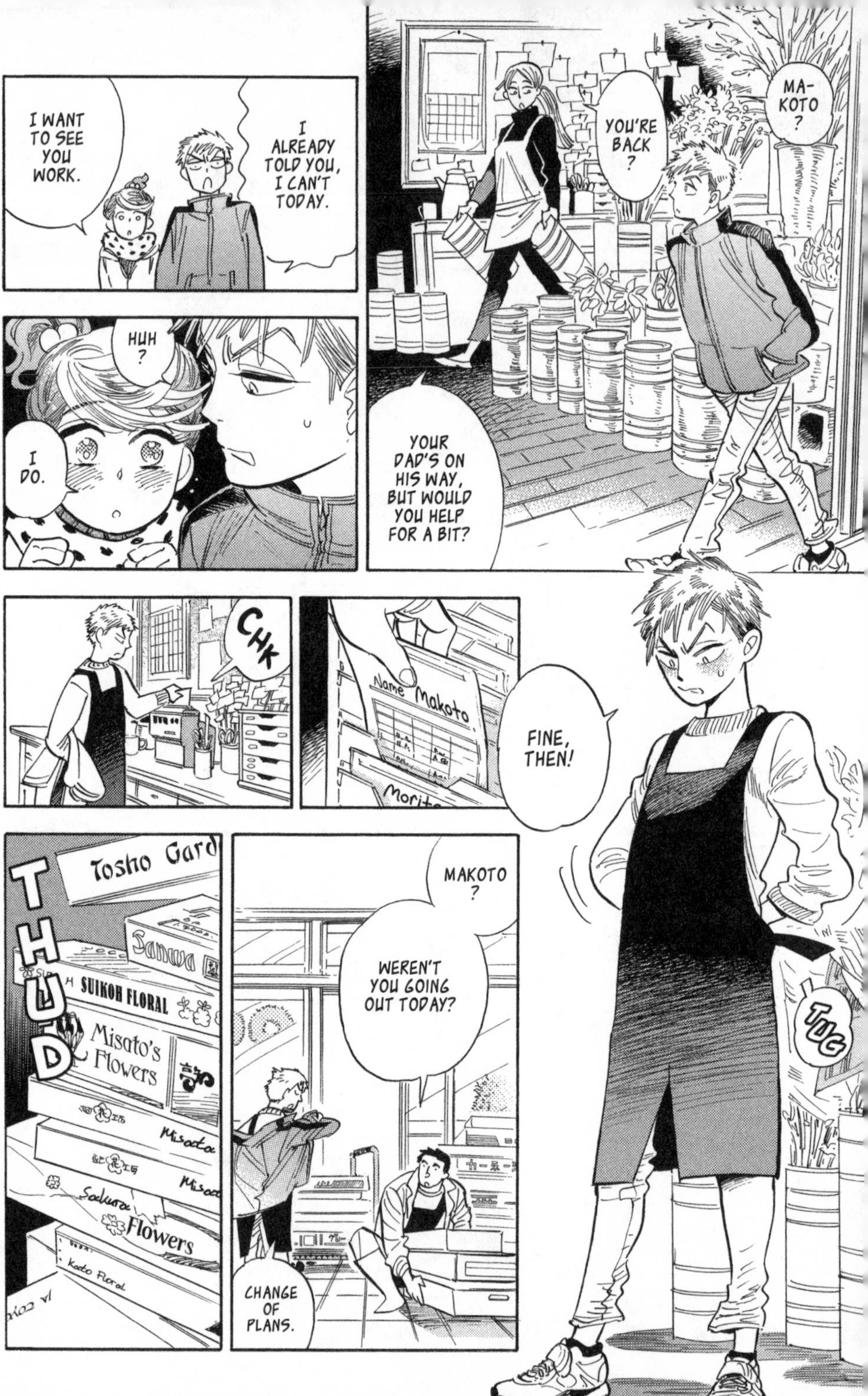

MA-KOTO?
YOU'RE BACK?
YOUR DAD'S ON HIS WAY, BUT WOULD YOU HELP FOR A BIT?
I ALREADY TOLD YOU, I CAN'T TODAY.
I WANT TO SEE YOU WORK.
HUH?
I DO.
FINE, THEN!
TUG
Name Makoto
CHK
MAKOTO?
WEREN'T YOU GOING OUT TODAY?
CHANGE OF PLANS.
Tosho Gard
Sanwa
SUIKOH FLORAL
Misato's Flowers
Misato
Sakura Flowers
Koto Floral
THUD

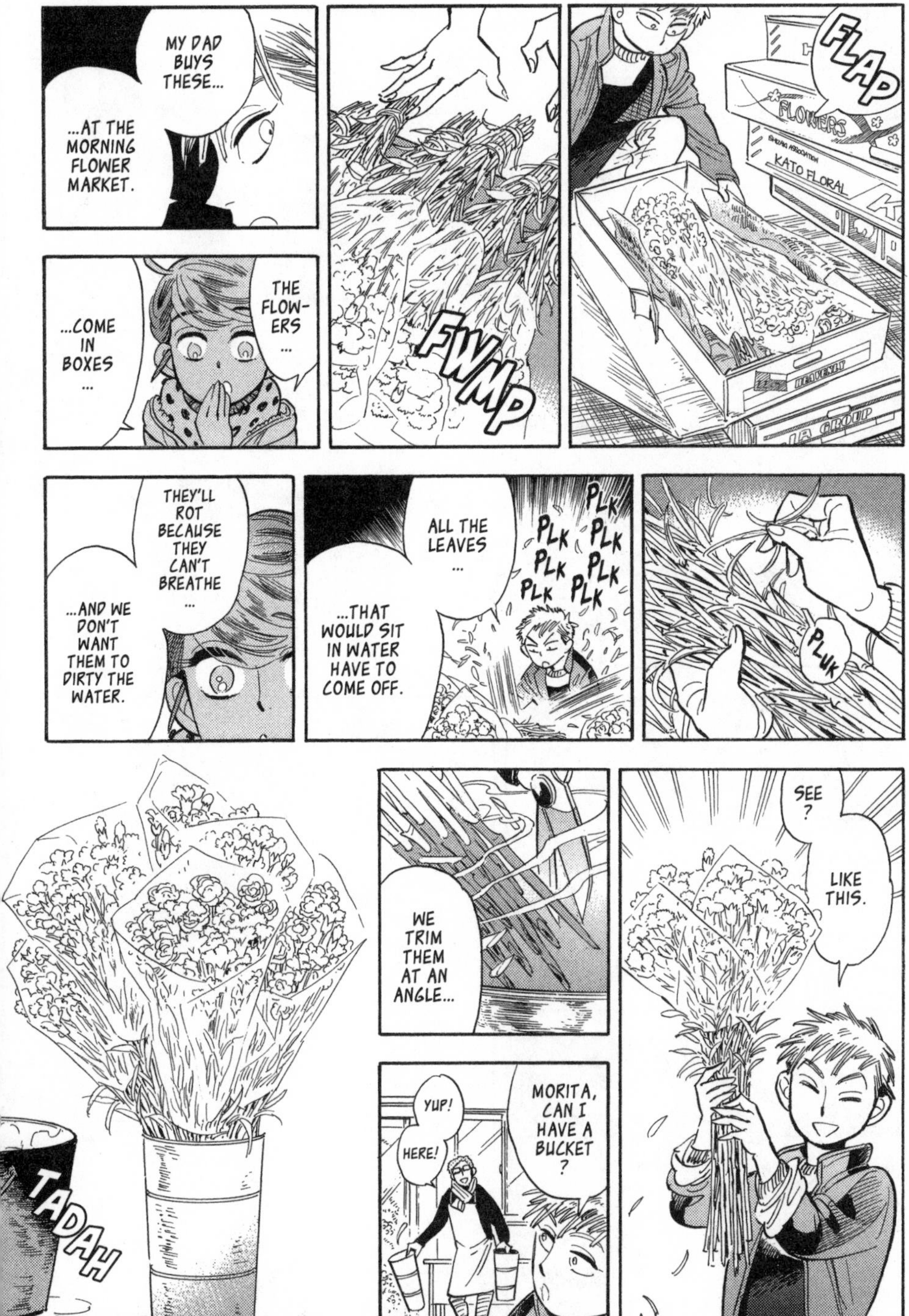
FLAP
FLOWERS
KATO FLORAL
HEAVENLY
FWMP
MY DAD BUYS THESE...
...AT THE MORNING FLOWER MARKET.
THE FLOWERS...
...COME IN BOXES...
PLUK
PLK PLK PLK PLK PLK PLK PLK
ALL THE LEAVES...
...THAT WOULD SIT IN WATER HAVE TO COME OFF.
THEY'LL ROT BECAUSE THEY CAN'T BREATHE...
...AND WE DON'T WANT THEM TO DIRTY THE WATER.
SEE?
LIKE THIS.
WE TRIM THEM AT AN ANGLE...
MORITA, CAN I HAVE A BUCKET?
YUP!
HERE!
TADAH

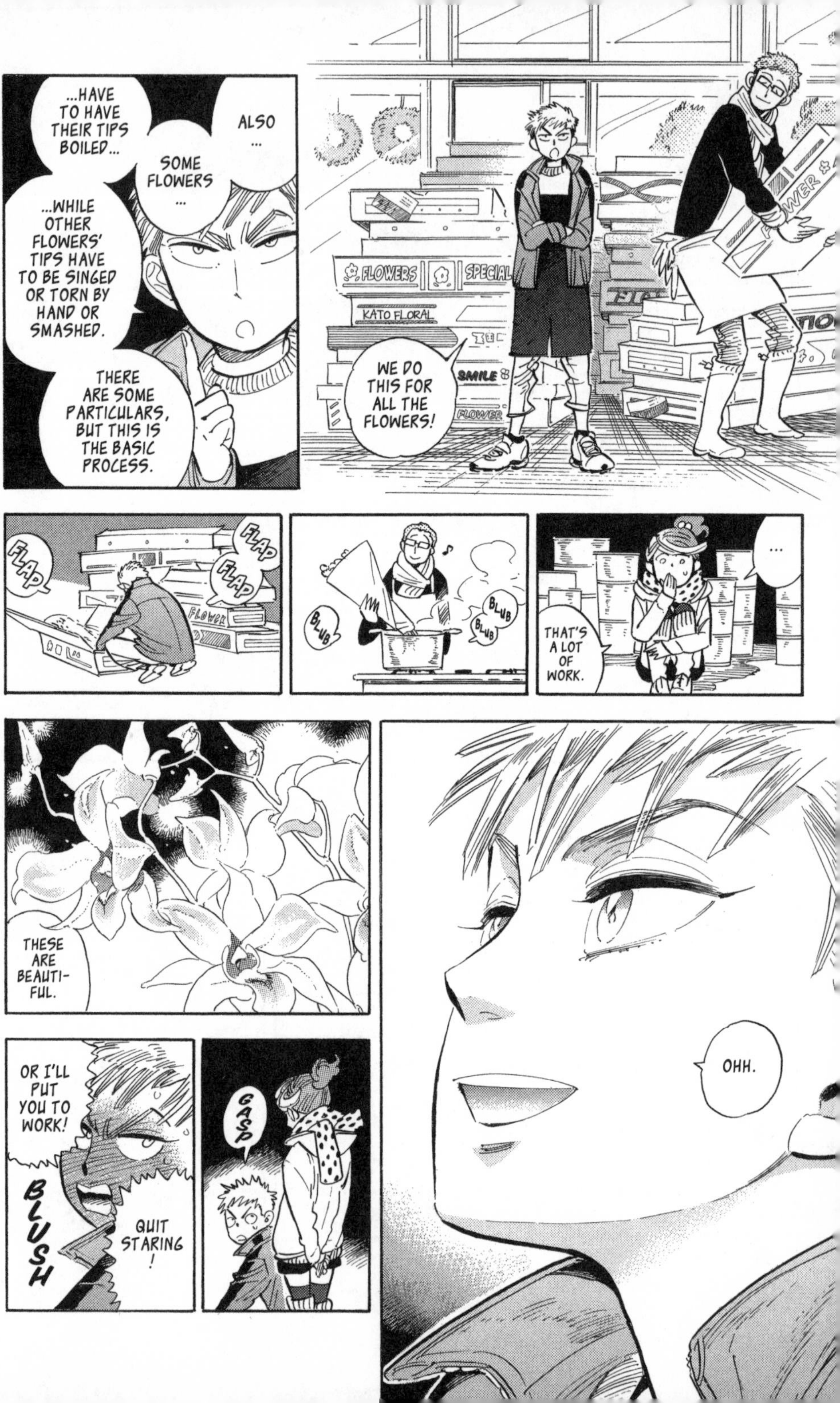
WE DO THIS FOR ALL THE FLOWERS!
ALSO ...
SOME FLOWERS ...
...HAVE TO HAVE THEIR TIPS BOILED...
...WHILE OTHER FLOWERS' TIPS HAVE TO BE SINGED OR TORN BY HAND OR SMASHED.
THERE ARE SOME PARTICULARS, BUT THIS IS THE BASIC PROCESS.
...
THAT'S A LOT OF WORK.
BLUB
BLUB
BLUB
FLAP
FLAP
FLAP
OHH.
THESE ARE BEAUTIFUL.
GASP
QUIT STARING!
OR I'LL PUT YOU TO WORK!
BLUSH

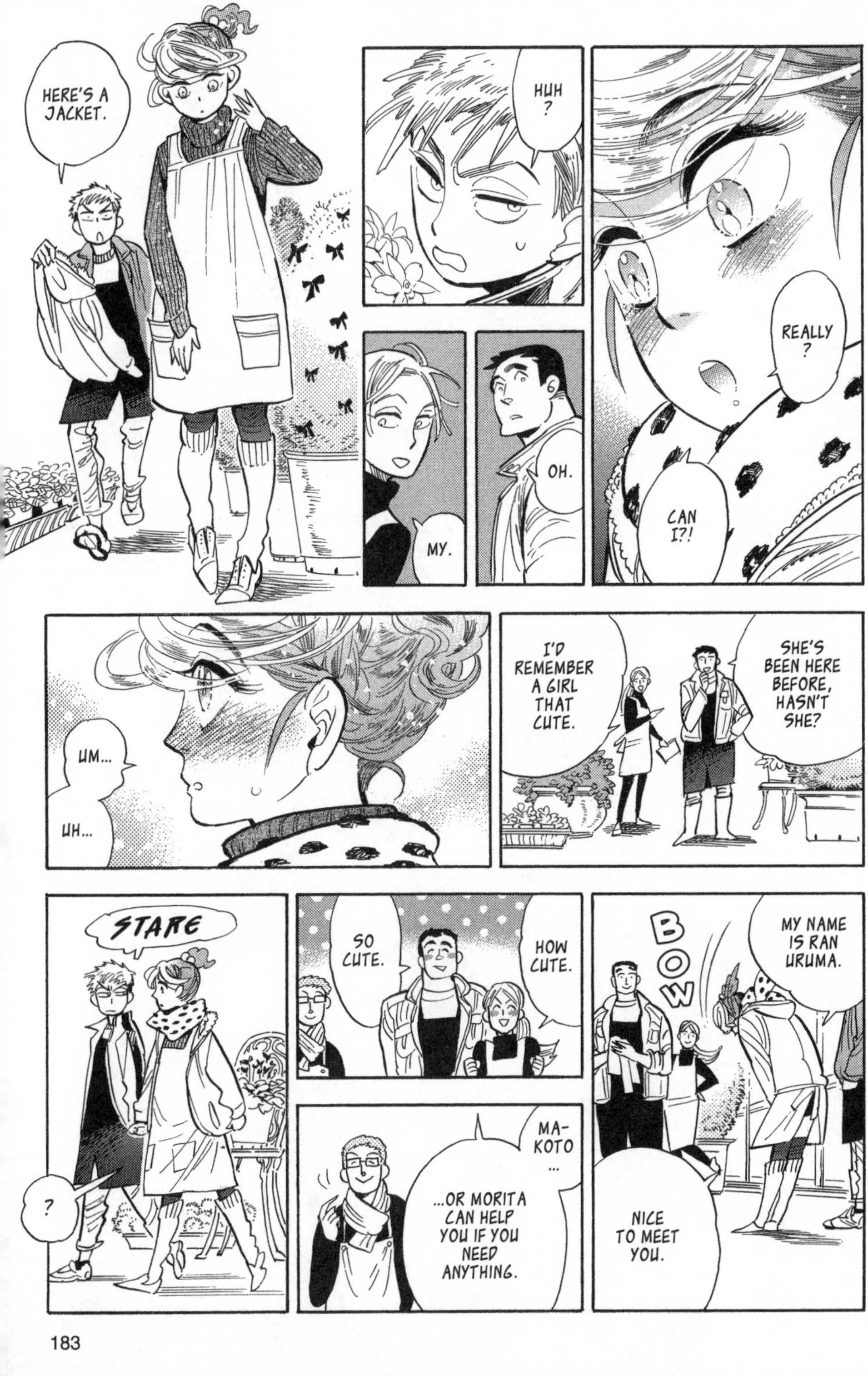
REALLY?
CAN I?!
HUH?
OH.
MY.
HERE'S A JACKET.
SHE'S BEEN HERE BEFORE, HASN'T SHE?
I'D REMEMBER A GIRL THAT CUTE.
UM...
UH...
BOW
MY NAME IS RAN URUMA.
NICE TO MEET YOU.
HOW CUTE.
SO CUTE.
MA-KOTO...
...OR MORITA CAN HELP YOU IF YOU NEED ANYTHING.
STARE
?

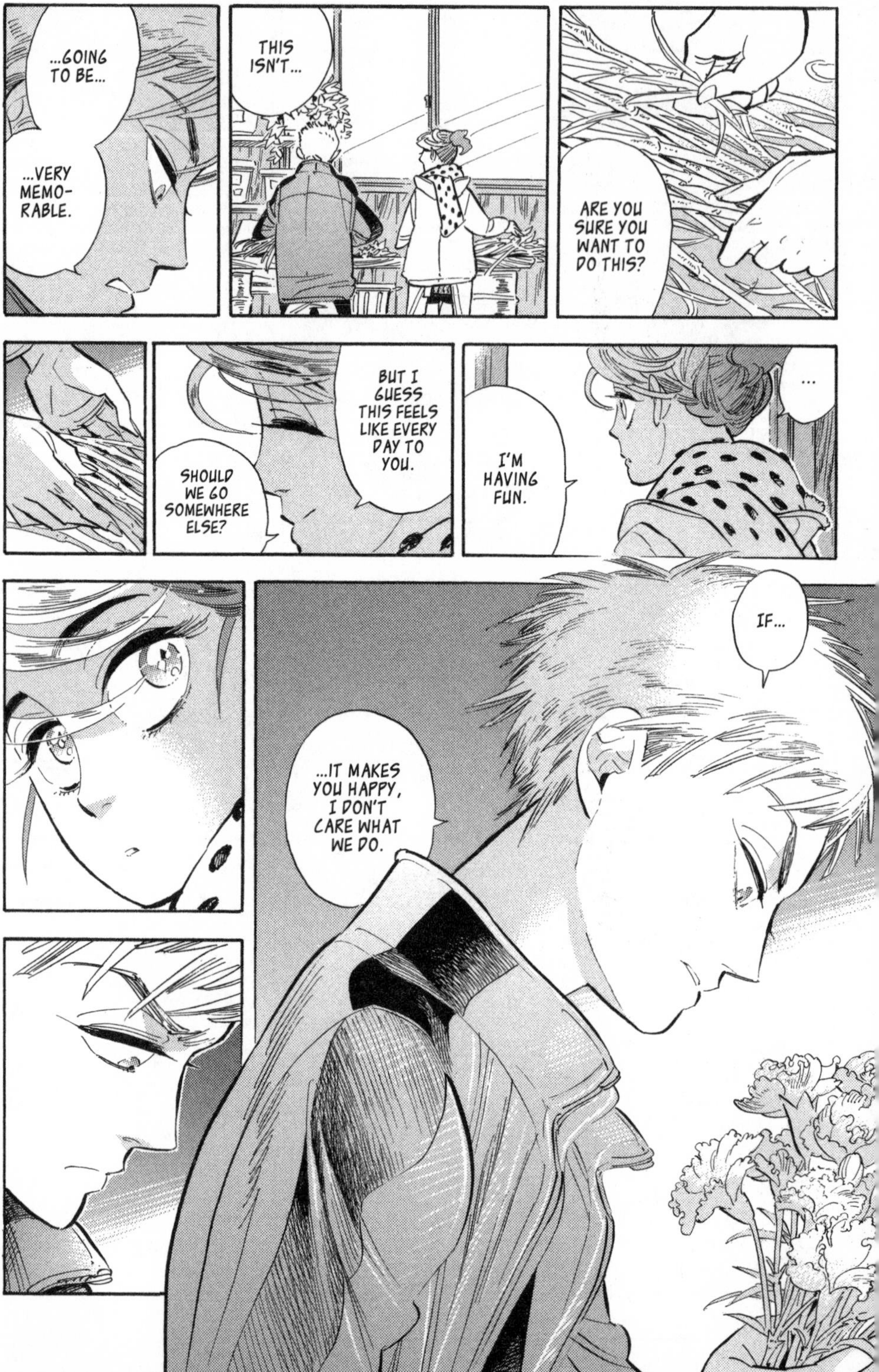
ARE YOU SURE YOU WANT TO DO THIS?
THIS ISN'T...
...GOING TO BE...
...VERY MEMO-RABLE.
...
I'M HAVING FUN.
BUT I GUESS THIS FEELS LIKE EVERY DAY TO YOU.
SHOULD WE GO SOMEWHERE ELSE?
IF...
...IT MAKES YOU HAPPY, I DON'T CARE WHAT WE DO.

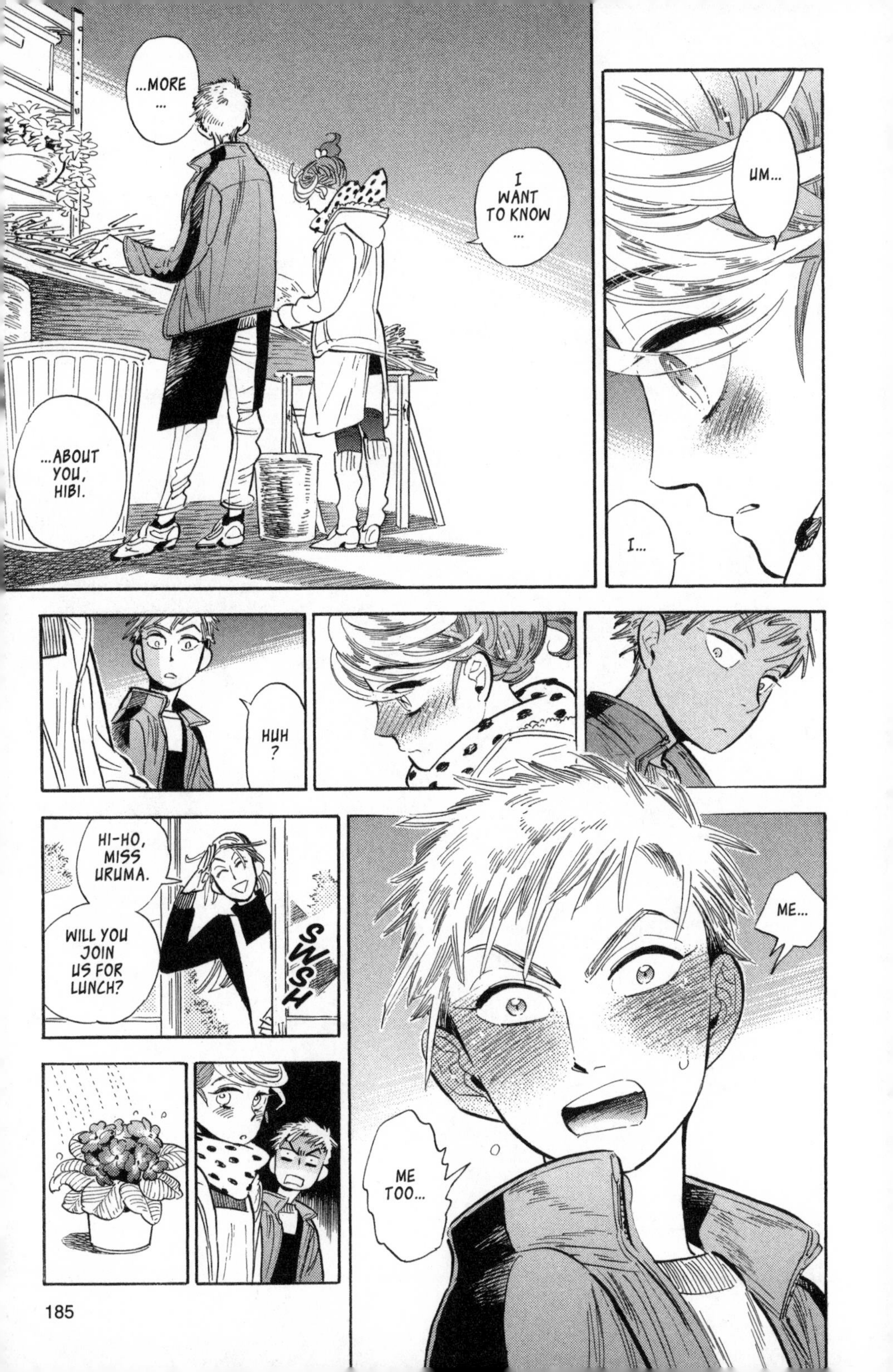
UM...
I...
I WANT TO KNOW ...
...MORE ...
...ABOUT YOU, HIBI.
HUH ?
ME...
ME TOO...
HI-HO, MISS URUMA.
WILL YOU JOIN US FOR LUNCH?
SWSH

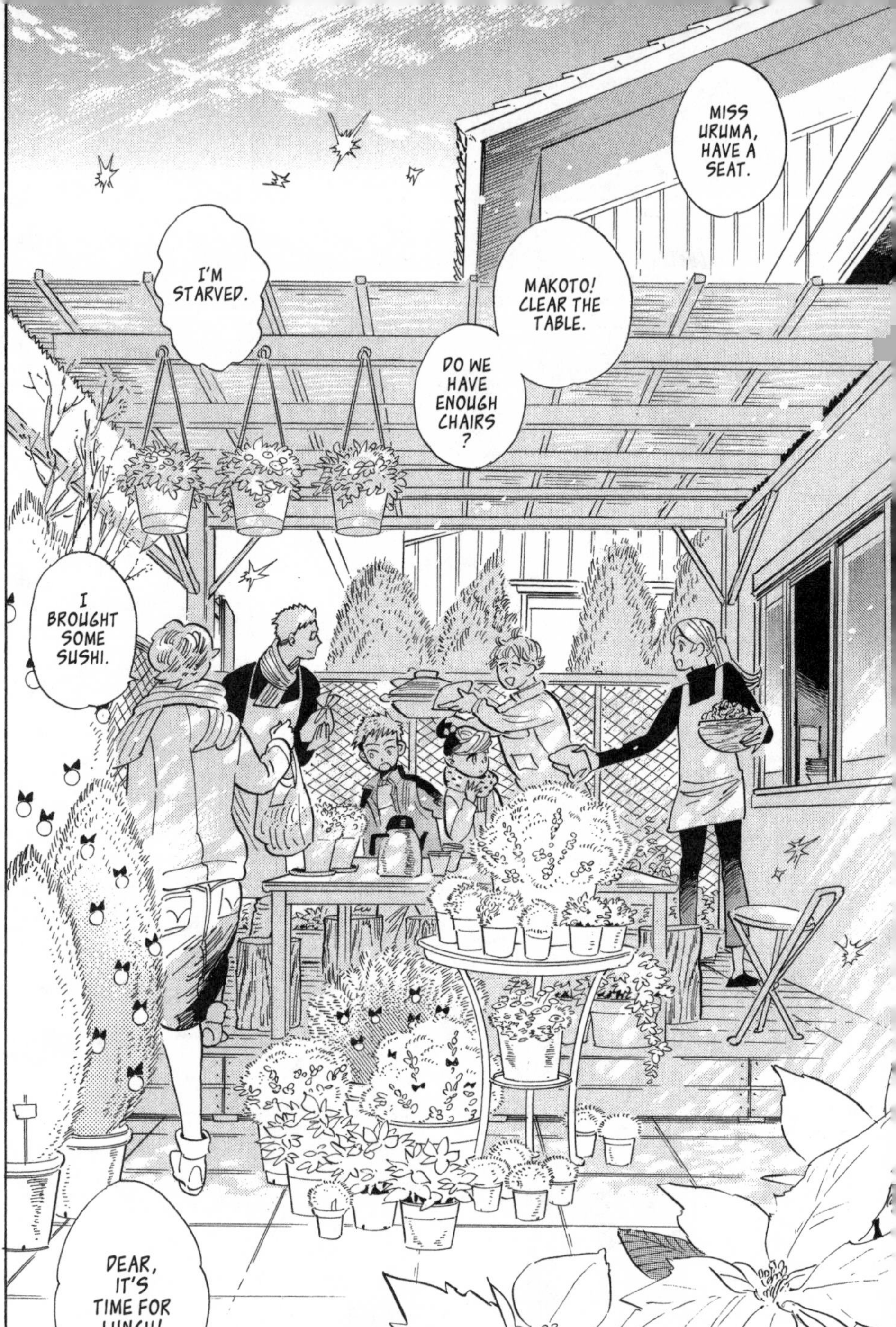
MISS URUMA, HAVE A SEAT.
MAKOTO! CLEAR THE TABLE.
DO WE HAVE ENOUGH CHAIRS?
I'M STARVED.
I BROUGHT SOME SUSHI.
DEAR, IT'S TIME FOR LUNCH!

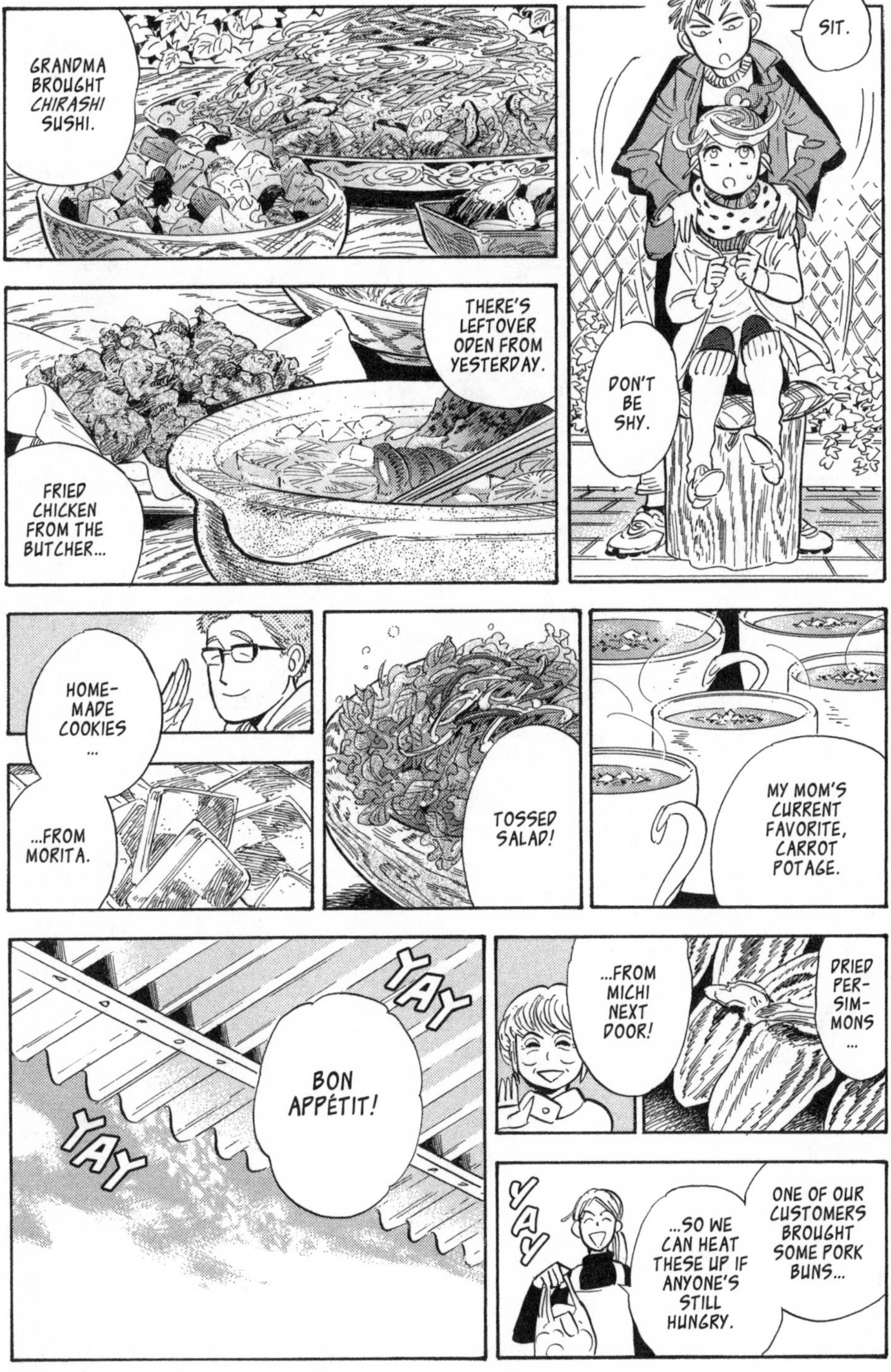
SIT.
DON'T BE SHY.
GRANDMA BROUGHT CHIRASHI SUSHI.
THERE'S LEFTOVER ODEN FROM YESTERDAY.
FRIED CHICKEN FROM THE BUTCHER...
MY MOM'S CURRENT FAVORITE, CARROT POTAGE.
TOSSED SALAD!
HOME-MADE COOKIES ...
...FROM MORITA.
DRIED PER-SIM-MONS ...
...FROM MICHI NEXT DOOR!
ONE OF OUR CUSTOMERS BROUGHT SOME PORK BUNS...
...SO WE CAN HEAT THESE UP IF ANYONE'S STILL HUNGRY.
YAY
YAY
BON APPÉTIT!
YAY

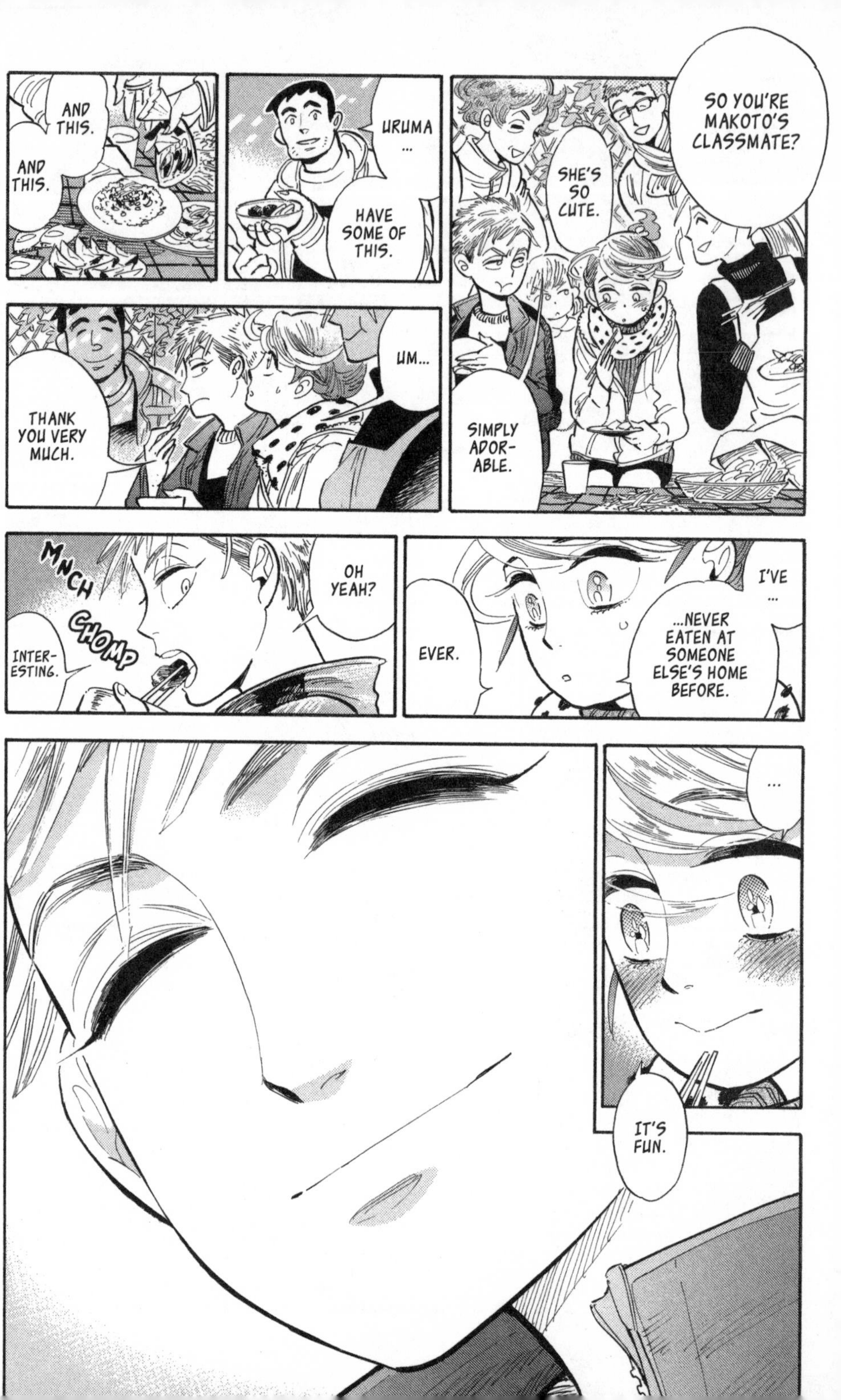
SO YOU'RE MAKOTO'S CLASSMATE?
SHE'S SO CUTE.
SIMPLY ADOR-ABLE.
URUMA ...
HAVE SOME OF THIS.
AND THIS.
AND THIS.
UM...
THANK YOU VERY MUCH.
I'VE ...
...NEVER EATEN AT SOMEONE ELSE'S HOME BEFORE.
EVER.
OH YEAH?
MNCH
CHOMP
INTER-ESTING.
...
IT'S FUN.

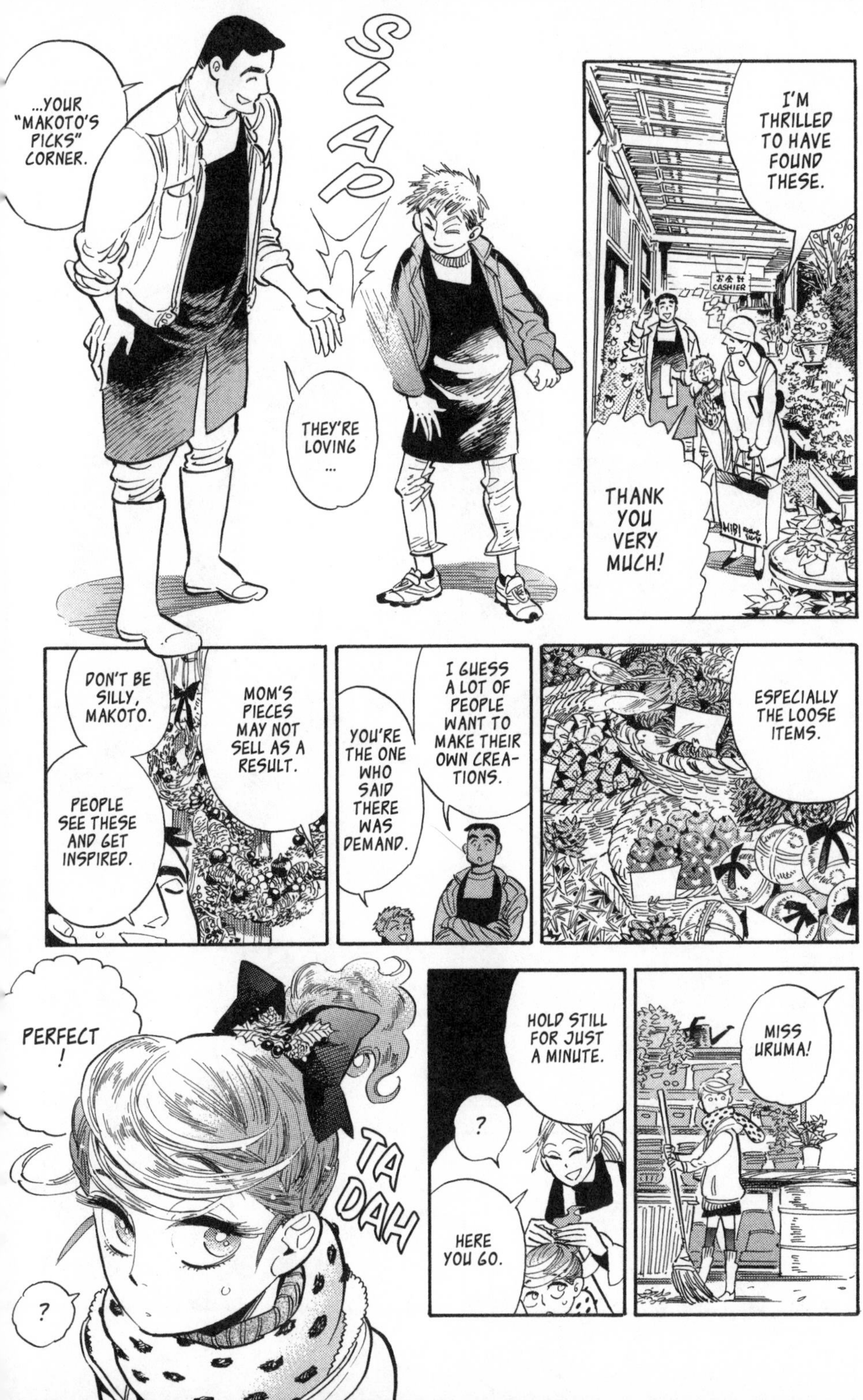
I'M THRILLED TO HAVE FOUND THESE.
THANK YOU VERY MUCH!
CASHIER
SLAP
THEY'RE LOVING ...
...YOUR "MAKOTO'S PICKS" CORNER.
ESPECIALLY THE LOOSE ITEMS.
I GUESS A LOT OF PEOPLE WANT TO MAKE THEIR OWN CREA-TIONS.
YOU'RE THE ONE WHO SAID THERE WAS DEMAND.
MOM'S PIECES MAY NOT SELL AS A RESULT.
DON'T BE SILLY, MAKOTO.
PEOPLE SEE THESE AND GET INSPIRED.
MISS URUMA!
HOLD STILL FOR JUST A MINUTE.
?
HERE YOU GO.
TA DAH
PERFECT!
?

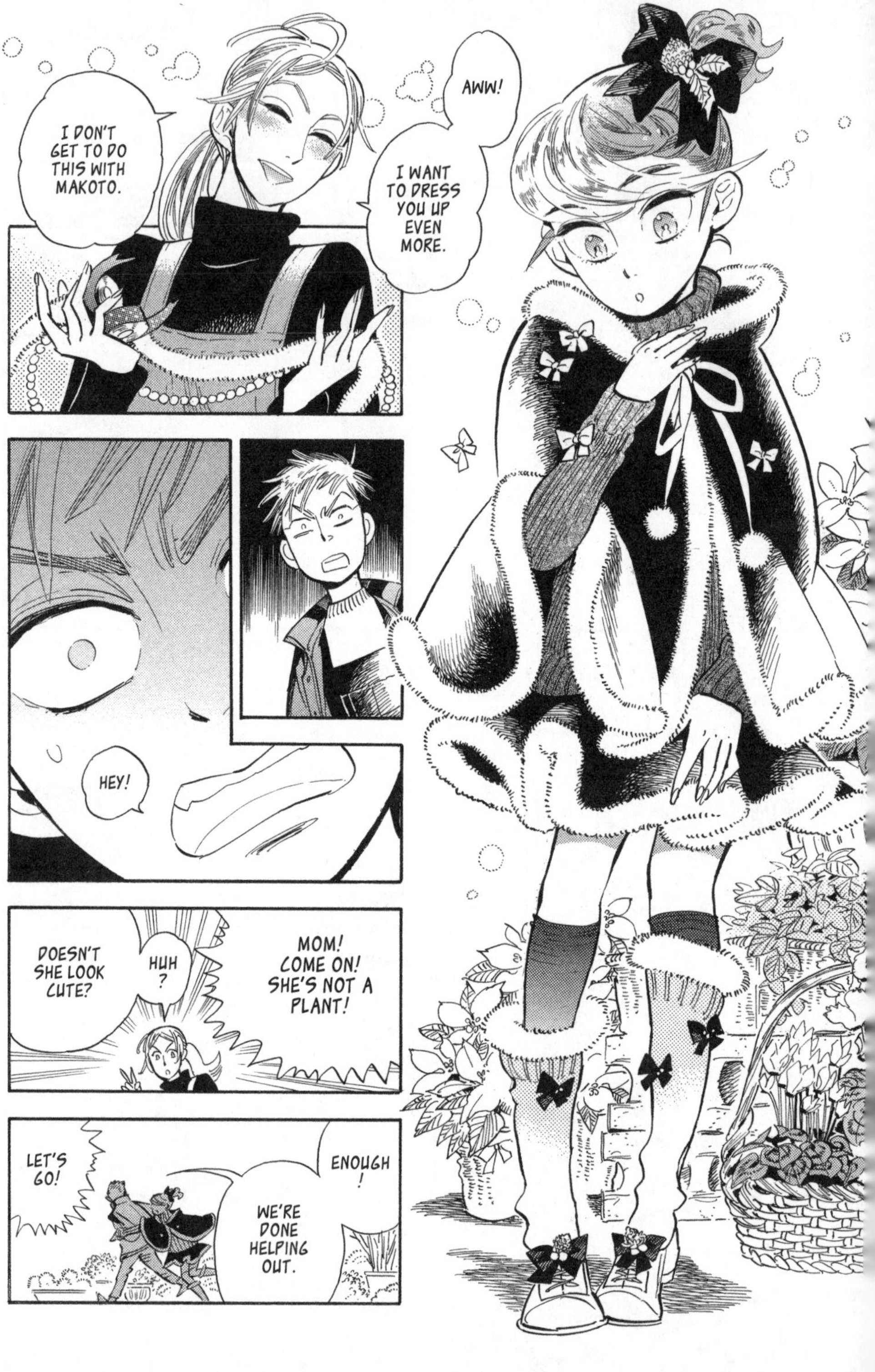
AWW!
I WANT TO DRESS YOU UP EVEN MORE.
I DON'T GET TO DO THIS WITH MAKOTO.
HEY!
MOM! COME ON! SHE'S NOT A PLANT!
HUH?
DOESN'T SHE LOOK CUTE?
ENOUGH!
WE'RE DONE HELPING OUT.
LET'S GO!

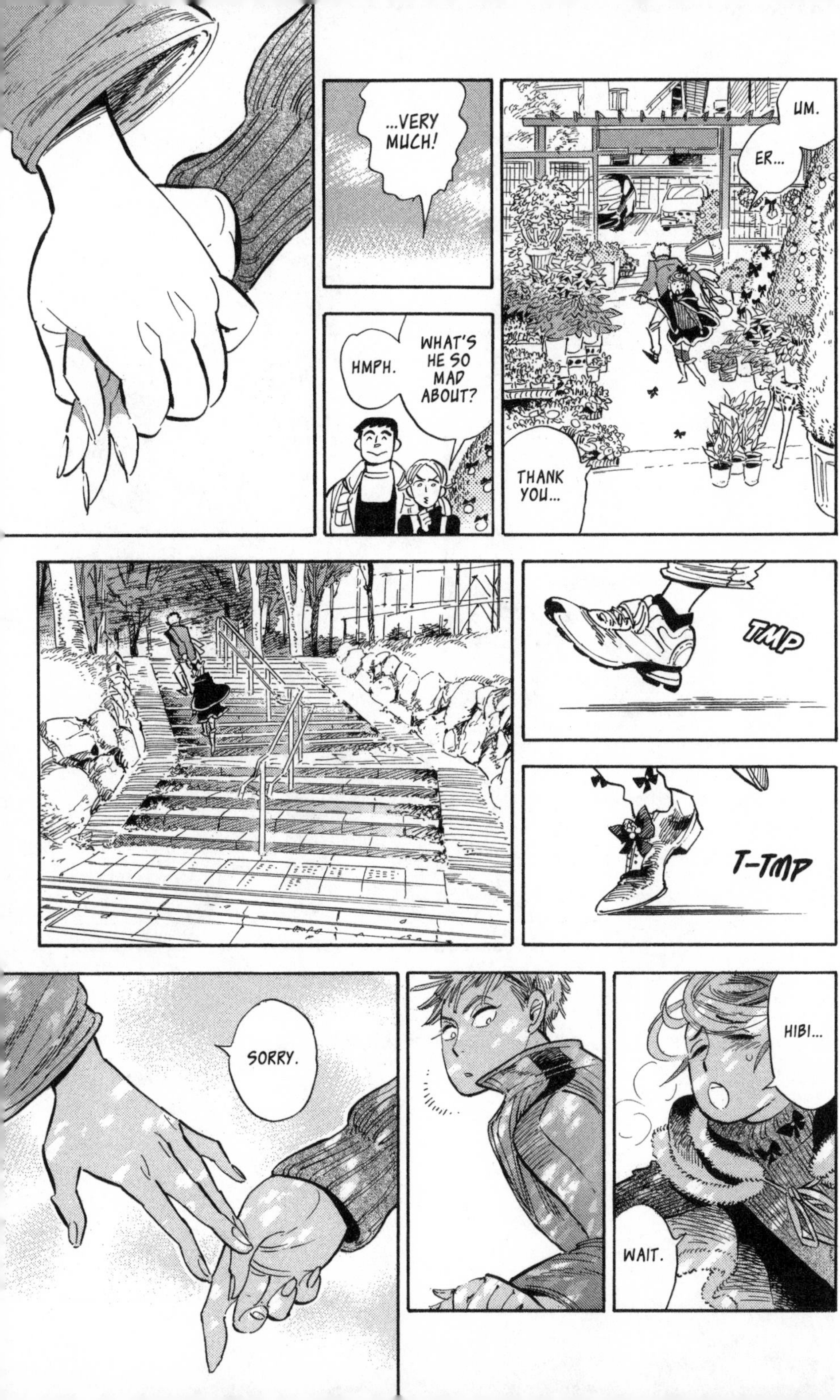
UM.
ER...
THANK YOU...
...VERY MUCH!
WHAT'S HE SO MAD ABOUT?
HMPH.
TMP
T-TMP
HIBI...
WAIT.
SORRY.

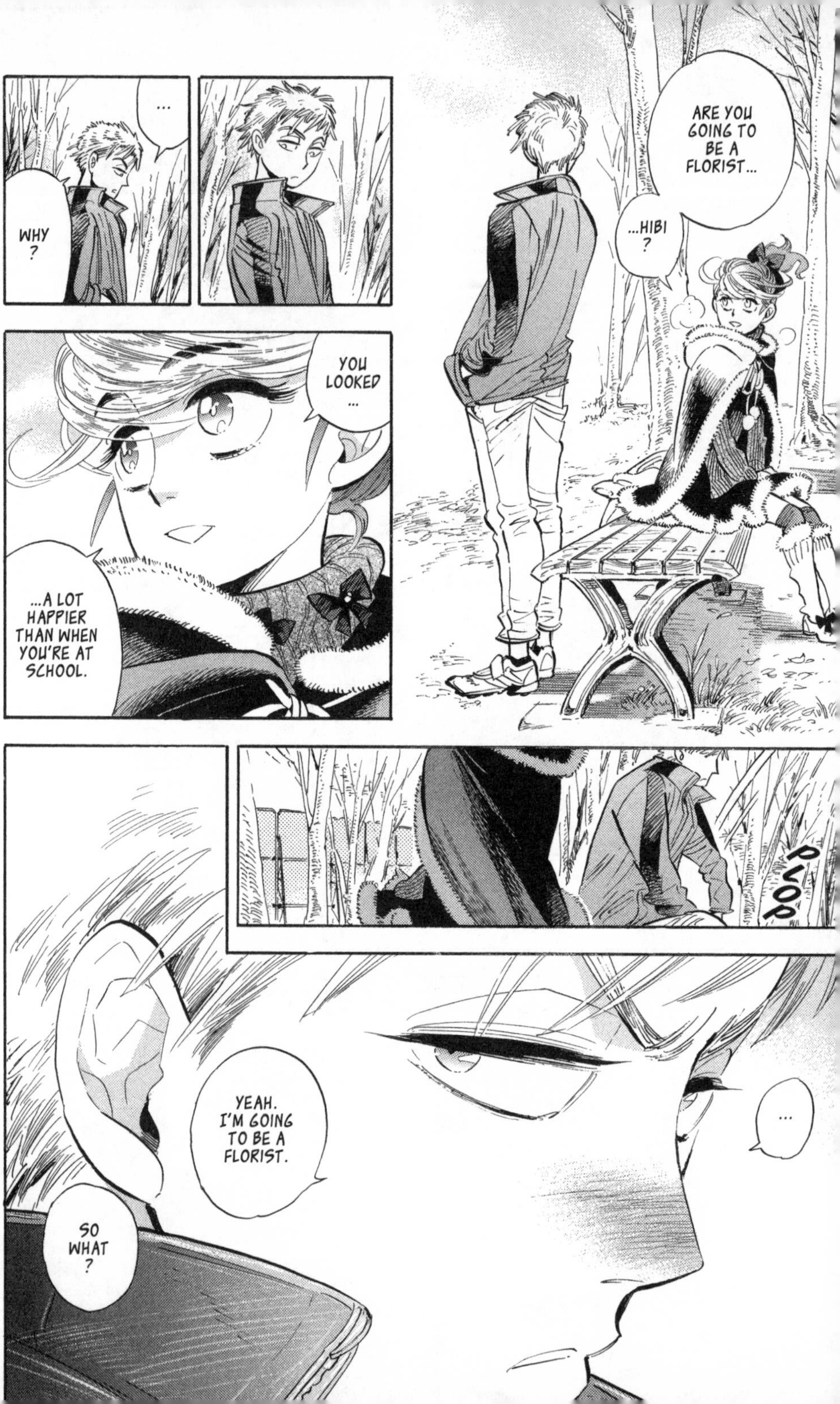
ARE YOU GOING TO BE A FLORIST...
...HIBI ?
...
WHY ?
YOU LOOKED ...
...A LOT HAPPIER THAN WHEN YOU'RE AT SCHOOL.
PLOP
...
YEAH. I'M GOING TO BE A FLORIST.
SO WHAT ?

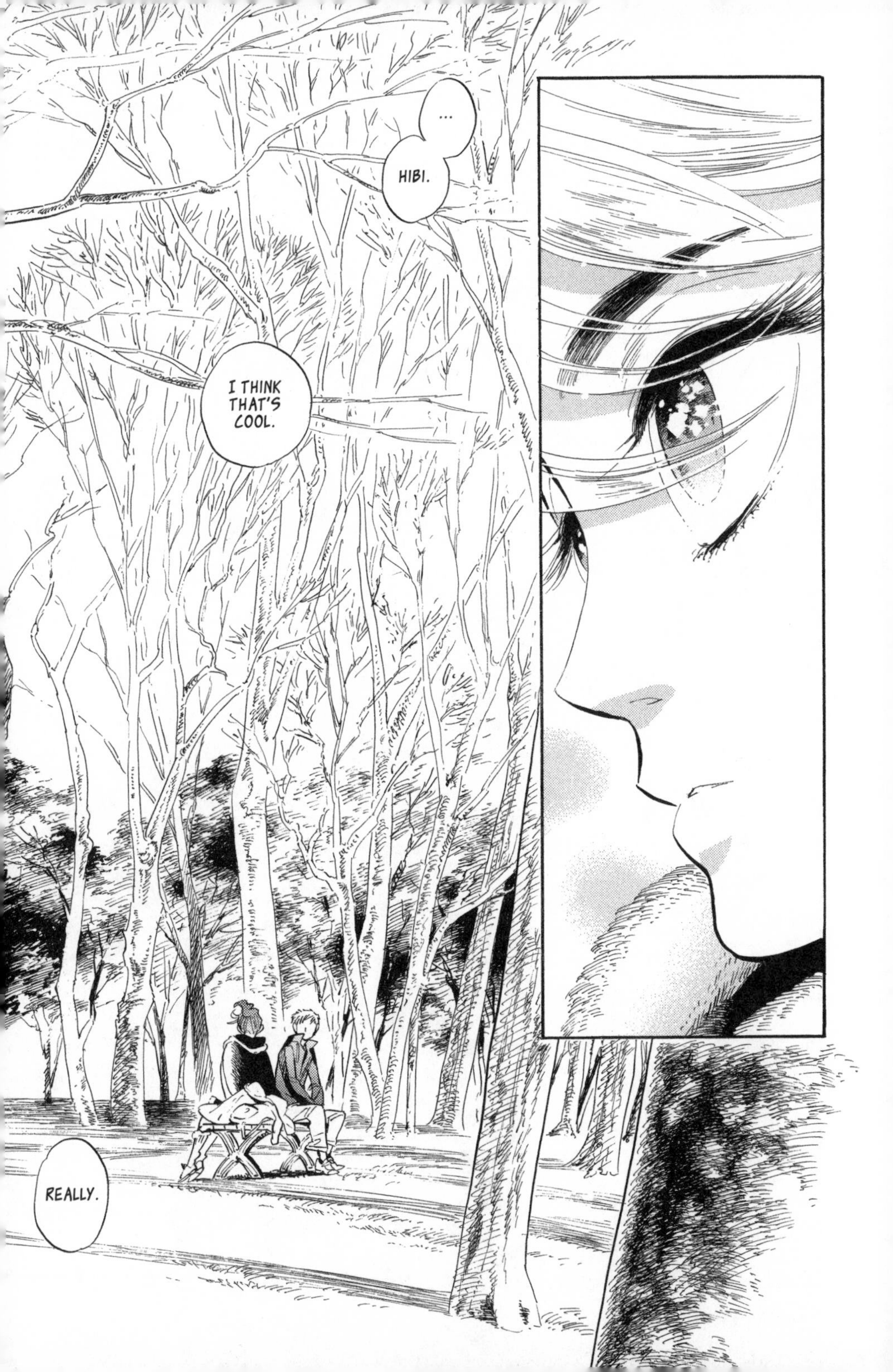
...
HIBI.
I THINK THAT'S COOL.
REALLY.

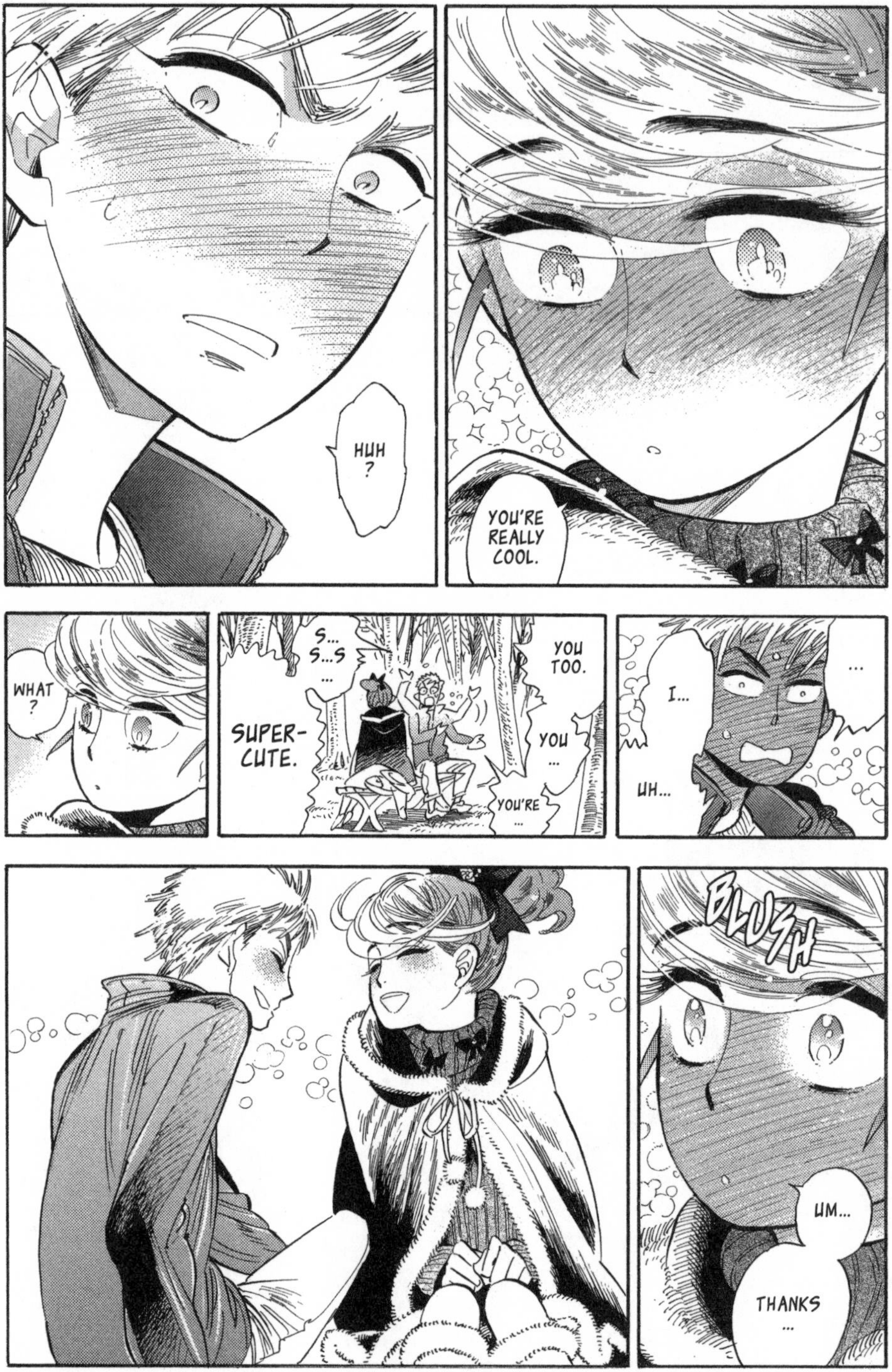
YOU'RE REALLY COOL.
HUH?
...
I...
UH...
YOU TOO.
YOU...
YOU'RE...
S... S...S ...
SUPER-CUTE.
WHAT?
BLUSH
UM...
THANKS...

Chapter 42 / The End

Chapter 43

A Parting Gift and a Path to Spring (Part 2)

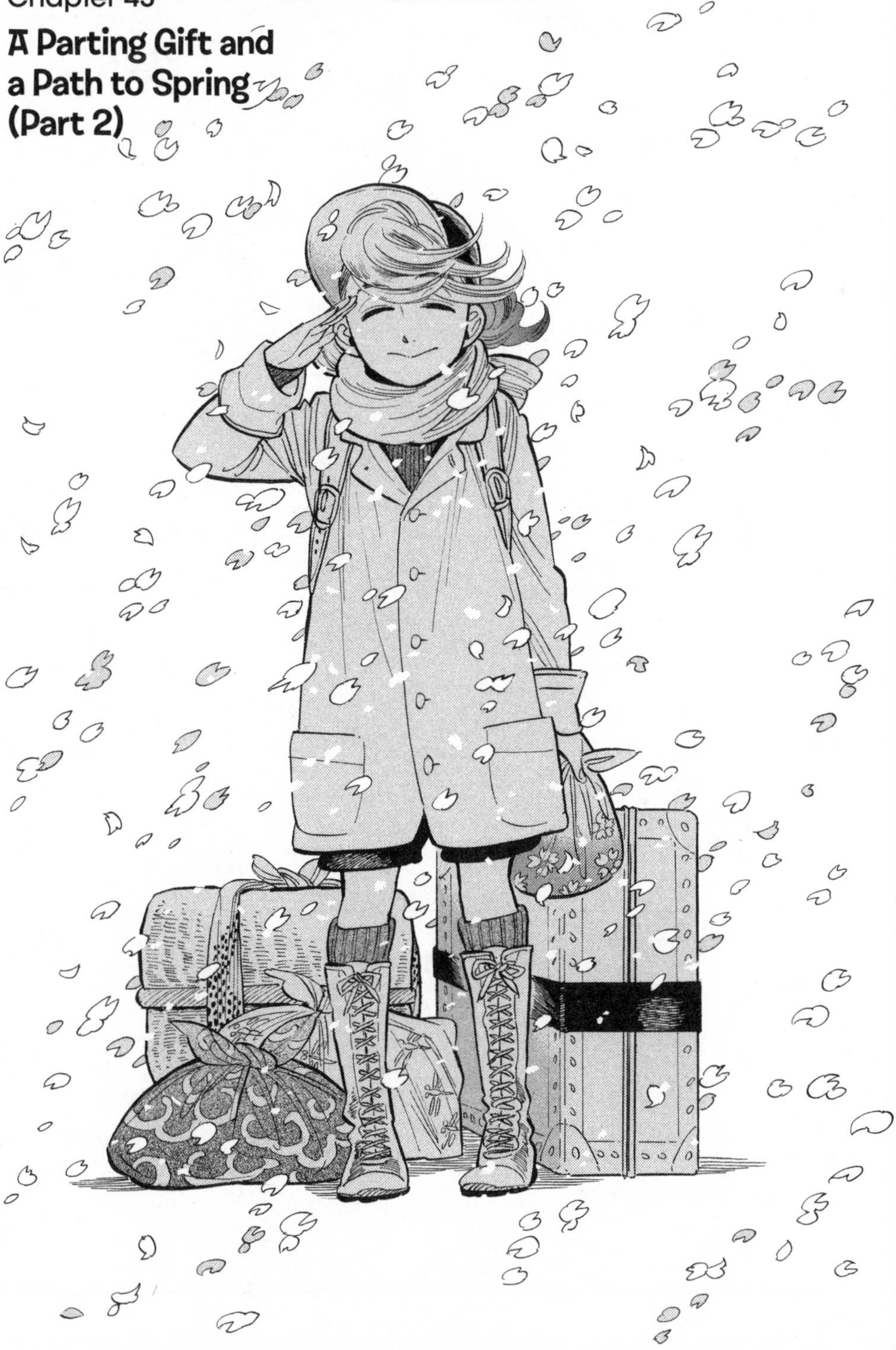

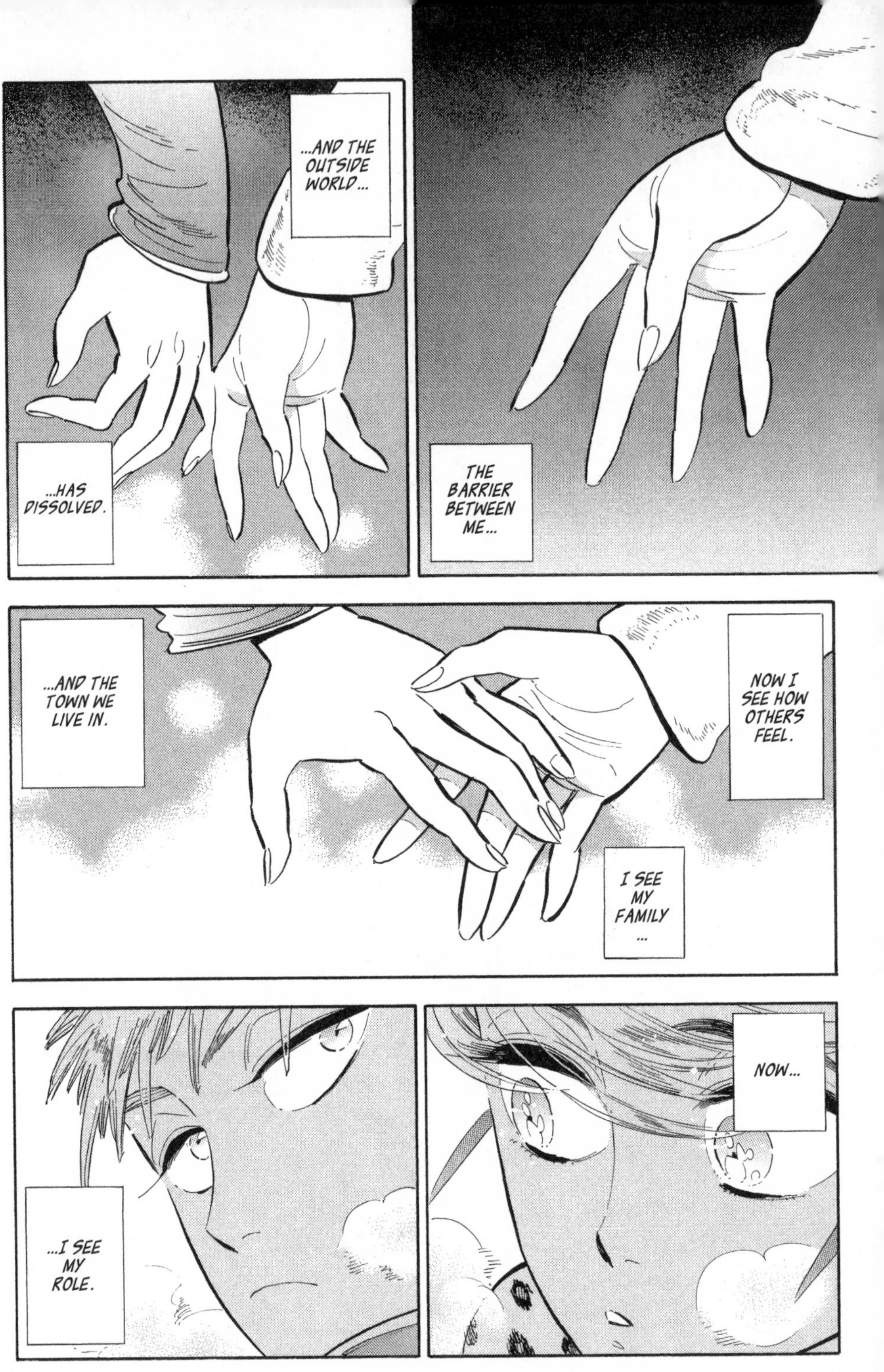
THE BARRIER BETWEEN ME...
...AND THE OUTSIDE WORLD...
...HAS DISSOLVED.
NOW I SEE HOW OTHERS FEEL.
I SEE MY FAMILY...
...AND THE TOWN WE LIVE IN.
NOW...
...I SEE MY ROLE.

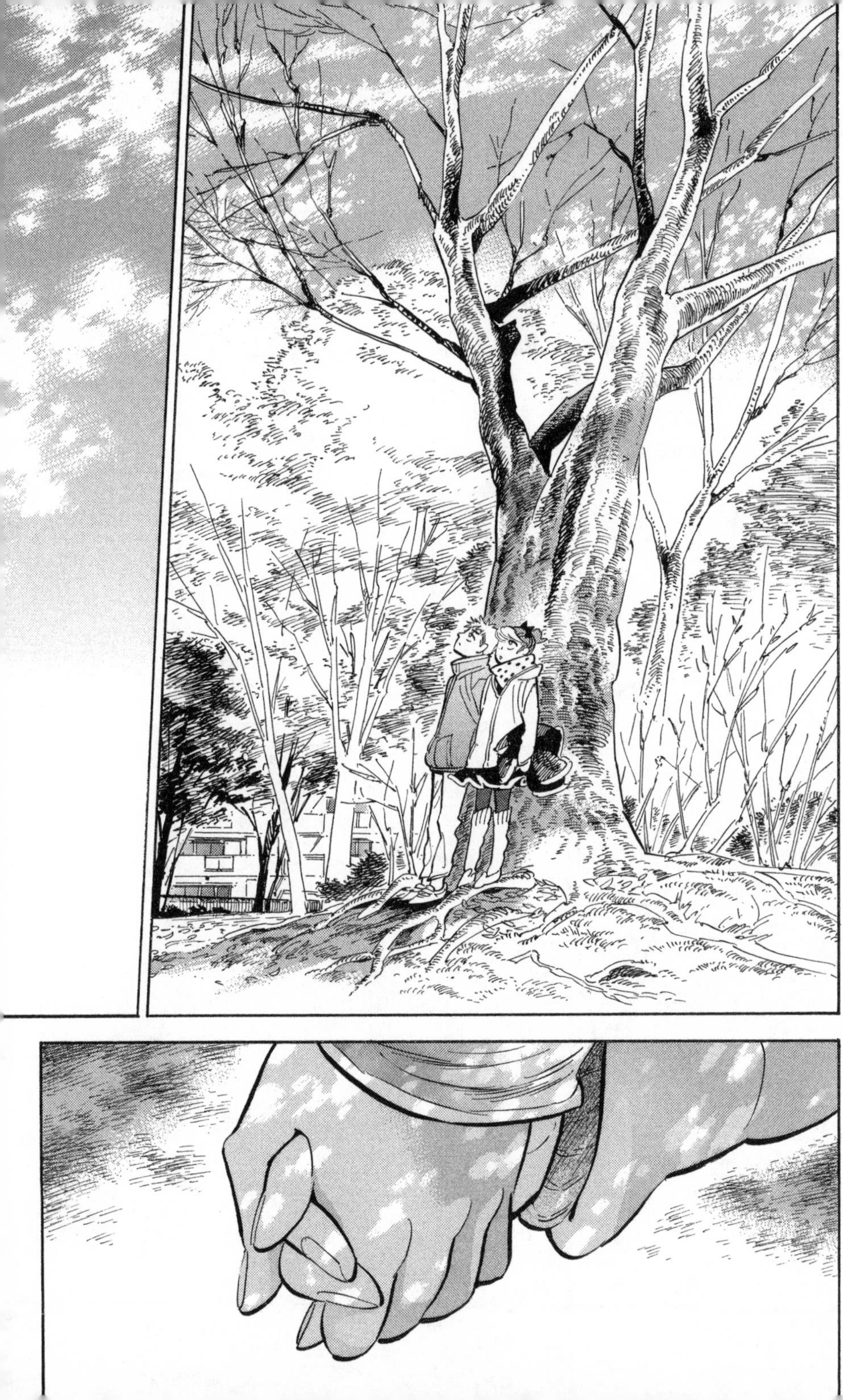

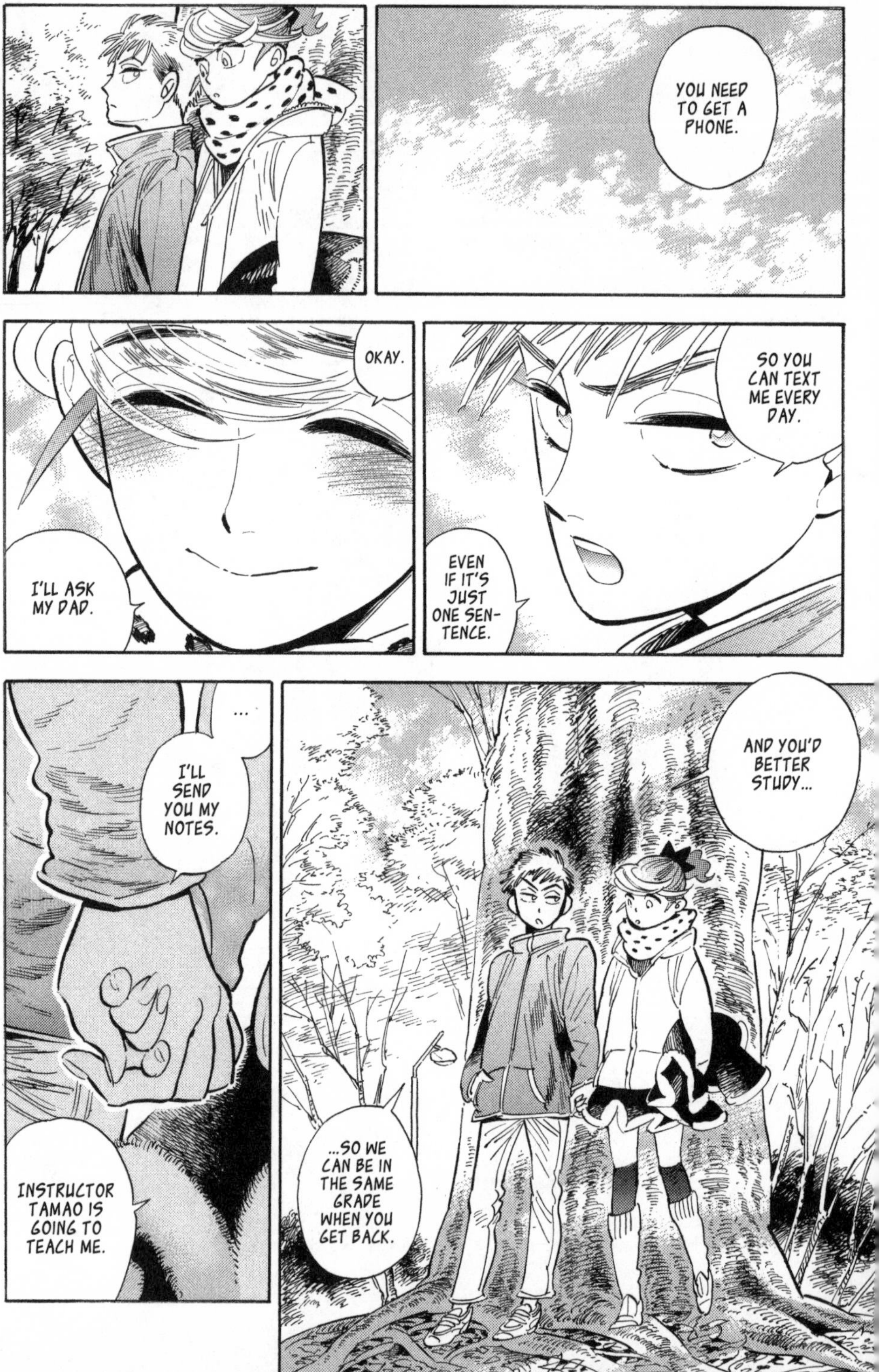
YOU NEED TO GET A PHONE.
SO YOU CAN TEXT ME EVERY DAY.
EVEN IF IT'S JUST ONE SEN-TENCE.
OKAY.
I'LL ASK MY DAD.
AND YOU'D BETTER STUDY...
...SO WE CAN BE IN THE SAME GRADE WHEN YOU GET BACK.
...
I'LL SEND YOU MY NOTES.
INSTRUCTOR TAMAO IS GOING TO TEACH ME.

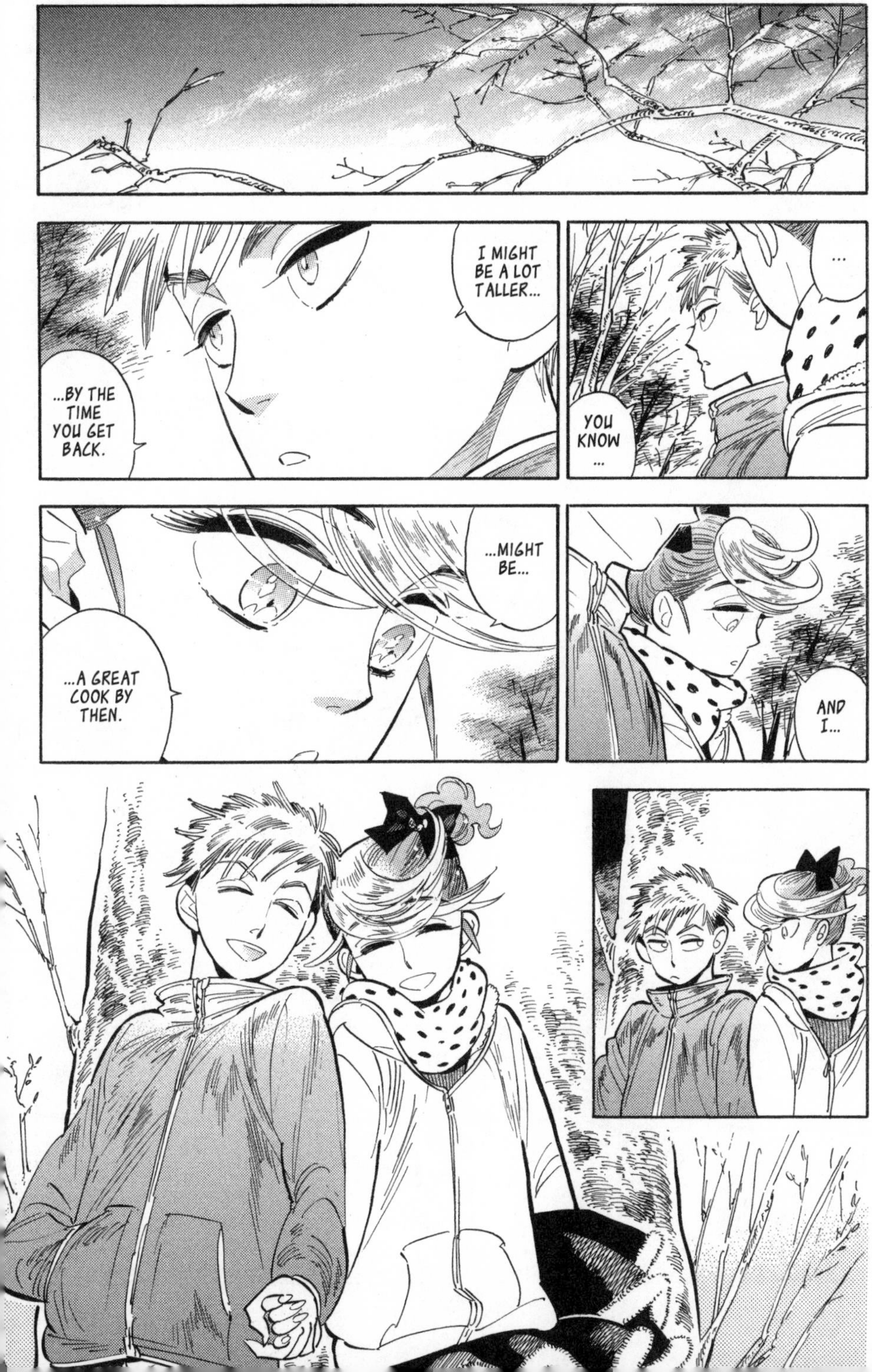
...
YOU KNOW ...
I MIGHT BE A LOT TALLER...
...BY THE TIME YOU GET BACK.
AND I...
...MIGHT BE...
...A GREAT COOK BY THEN.

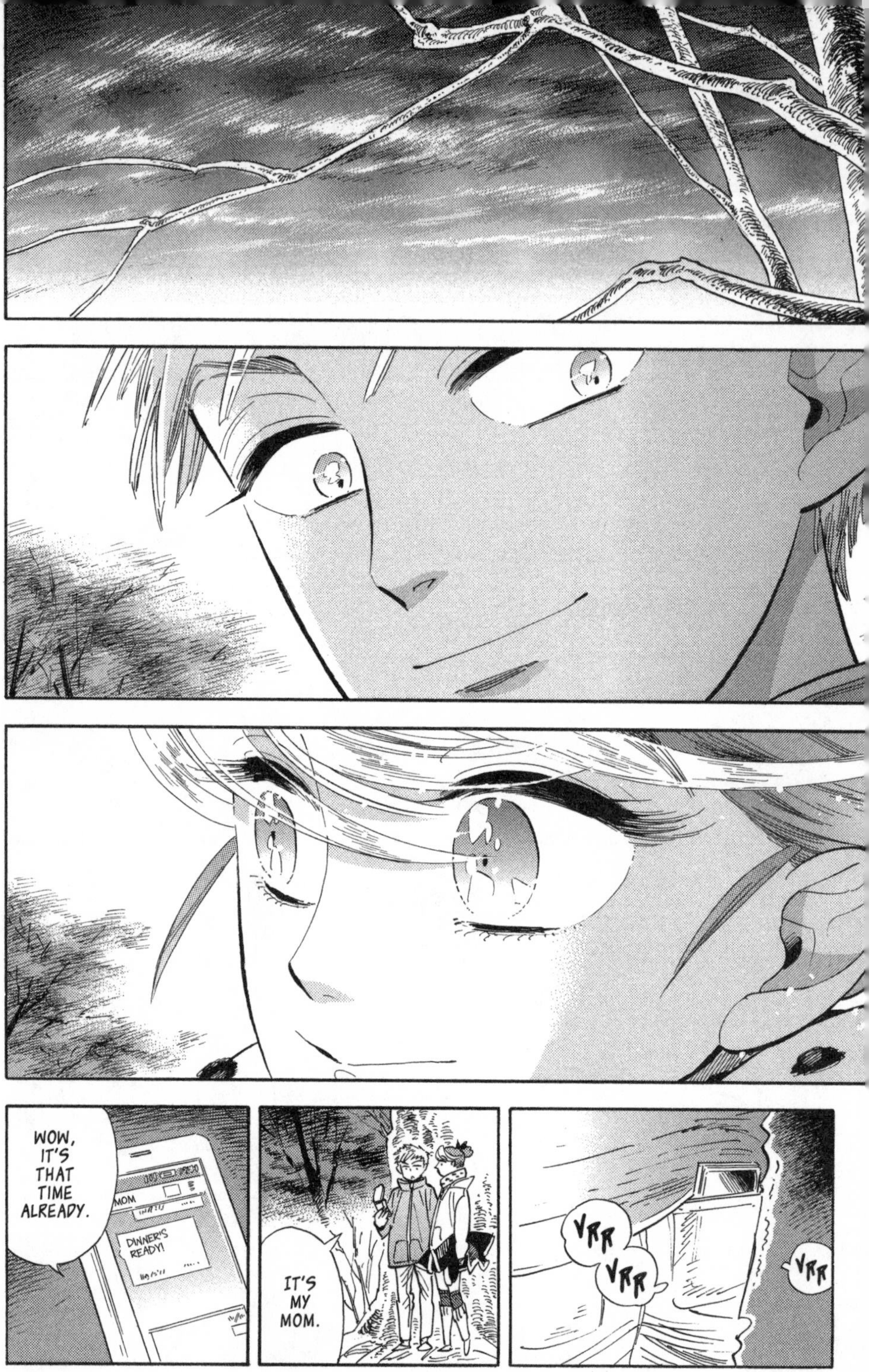
VRR
VRR
VRR
IT'S MY MOM.
WOW, IT'S THAT TIME ALREADY.
MOM
DINNER'S READY!

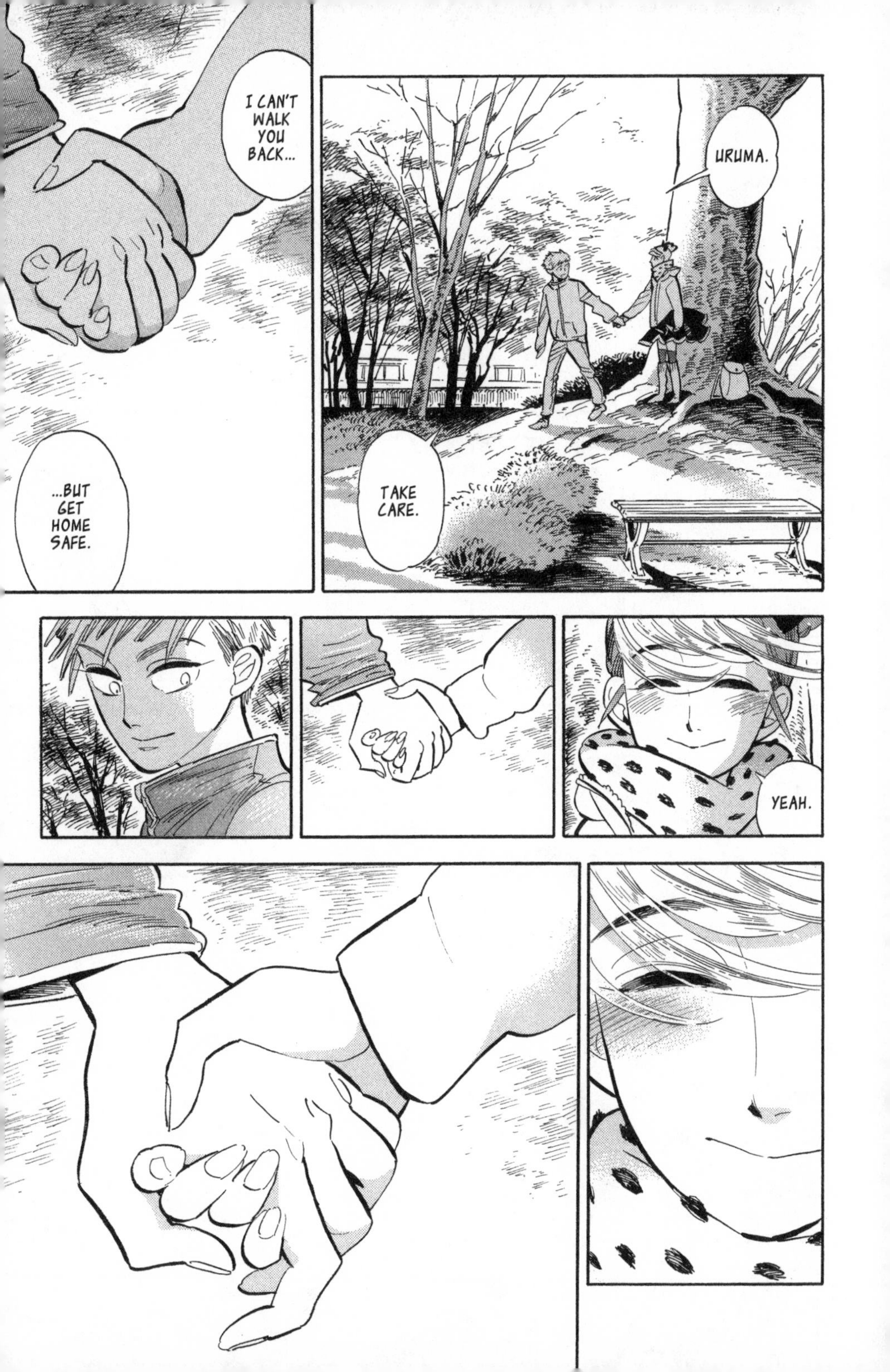
URUMA.
TAKE CARE.
I CAN'T WALK YOU BACK...
...BUT GET HOME SAFE.
YEAH.

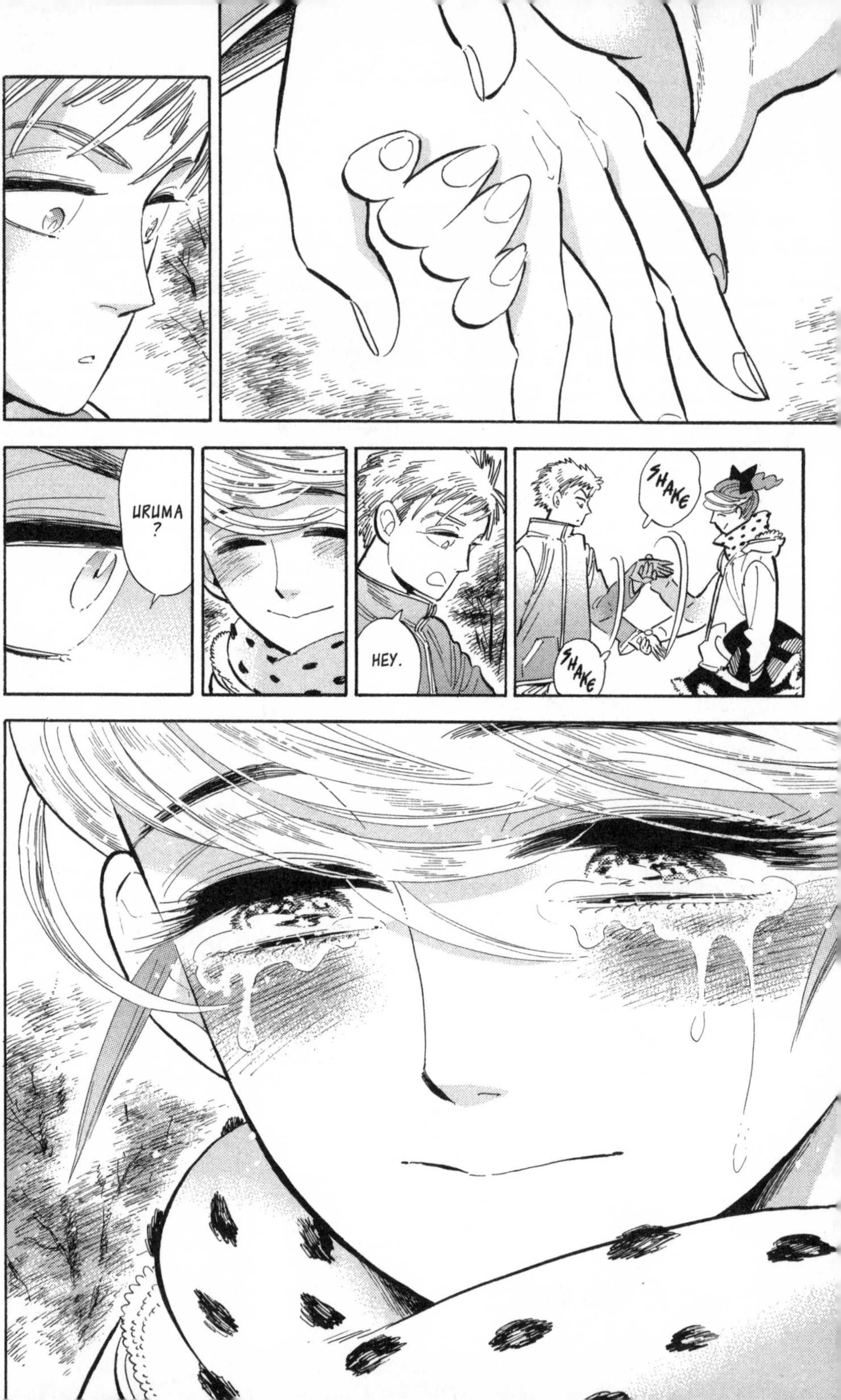
SHAKE
SHAKE
HEY.
URUMA ?

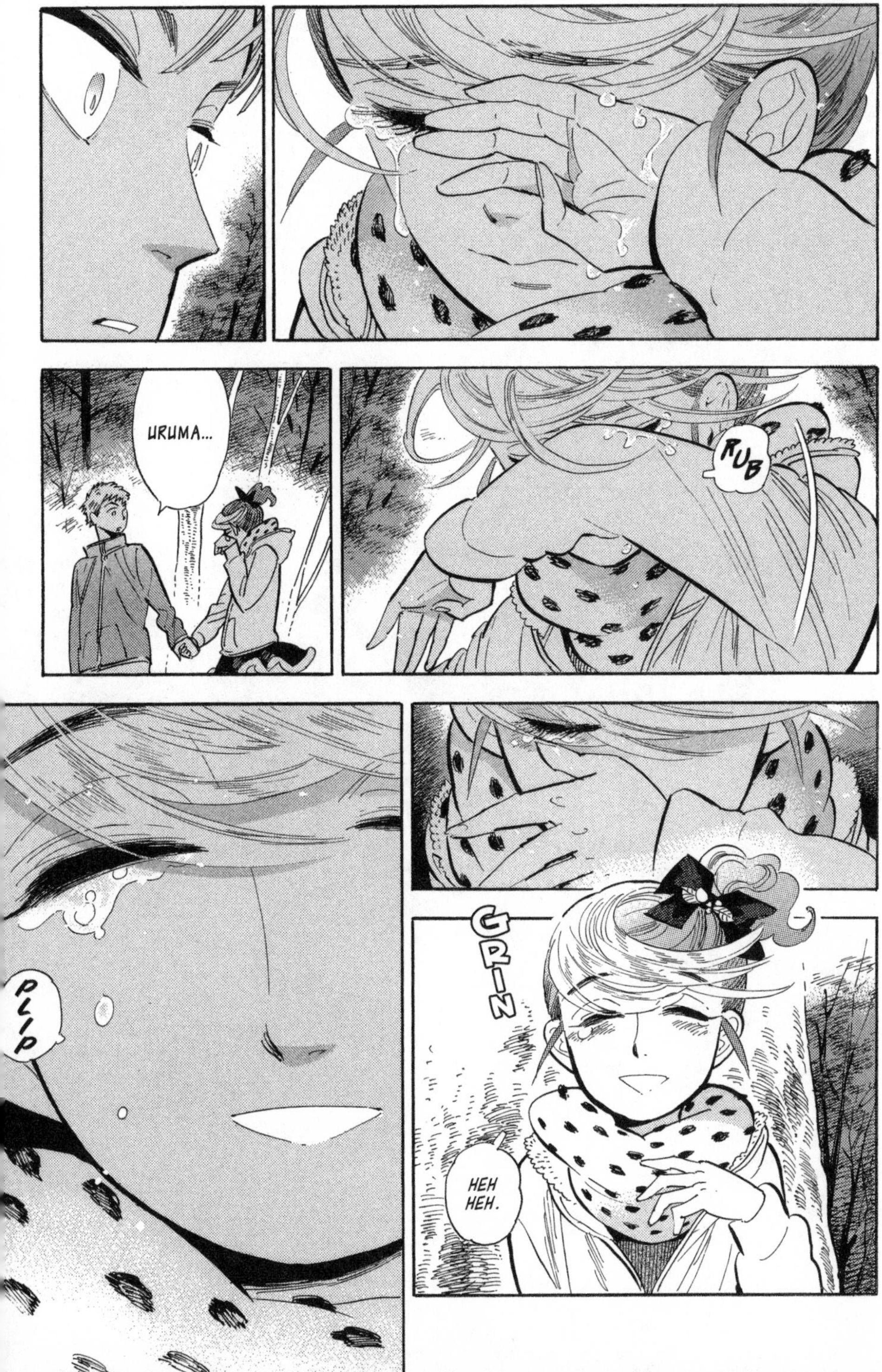
RUB
URUMA...
GRIN
HEH HEH.
PLIP

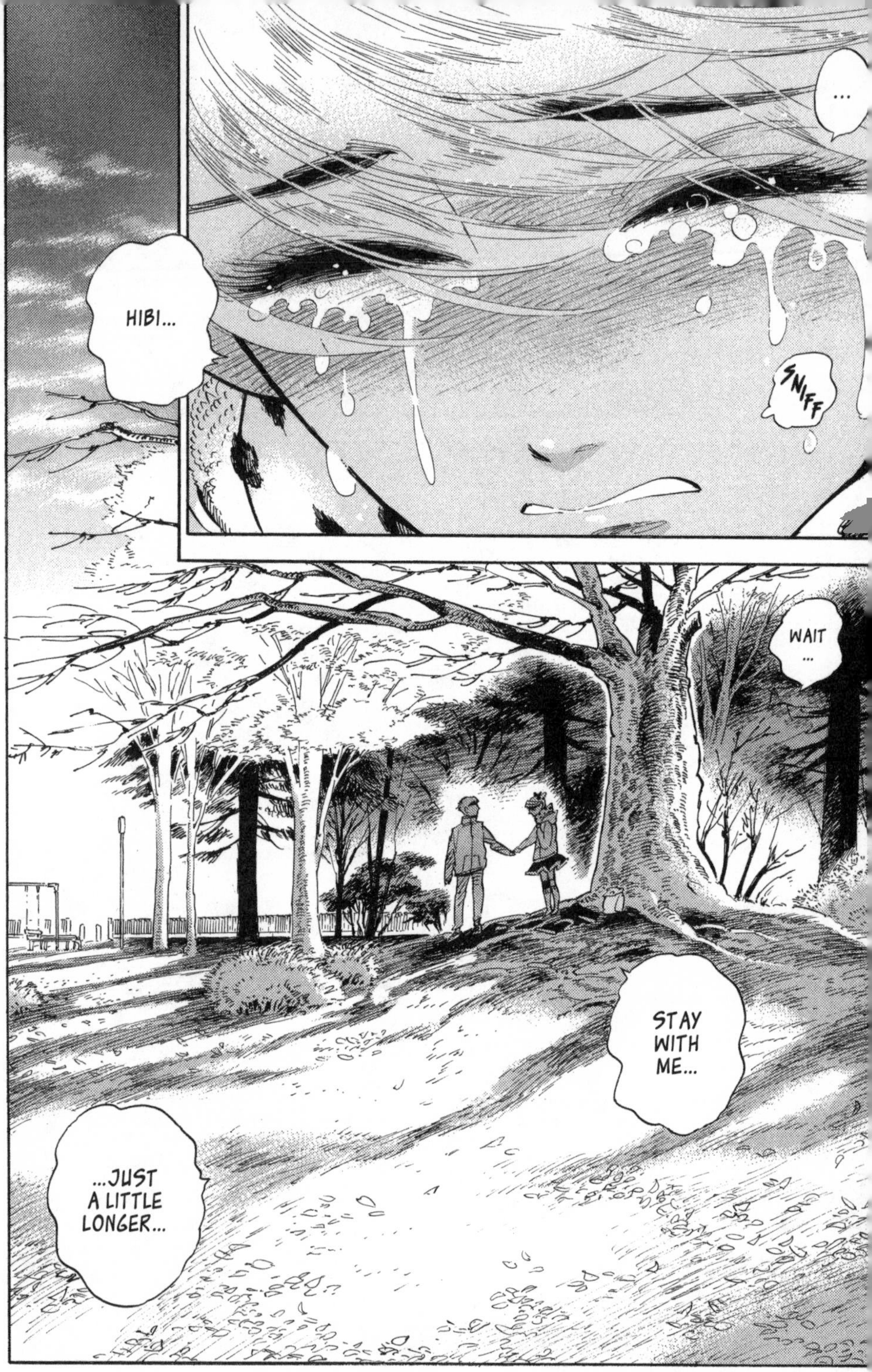
...
SNIFF
HIBI...
WAIT ...
STAY WITH ME...
...JUST A LITTLE LONGER...

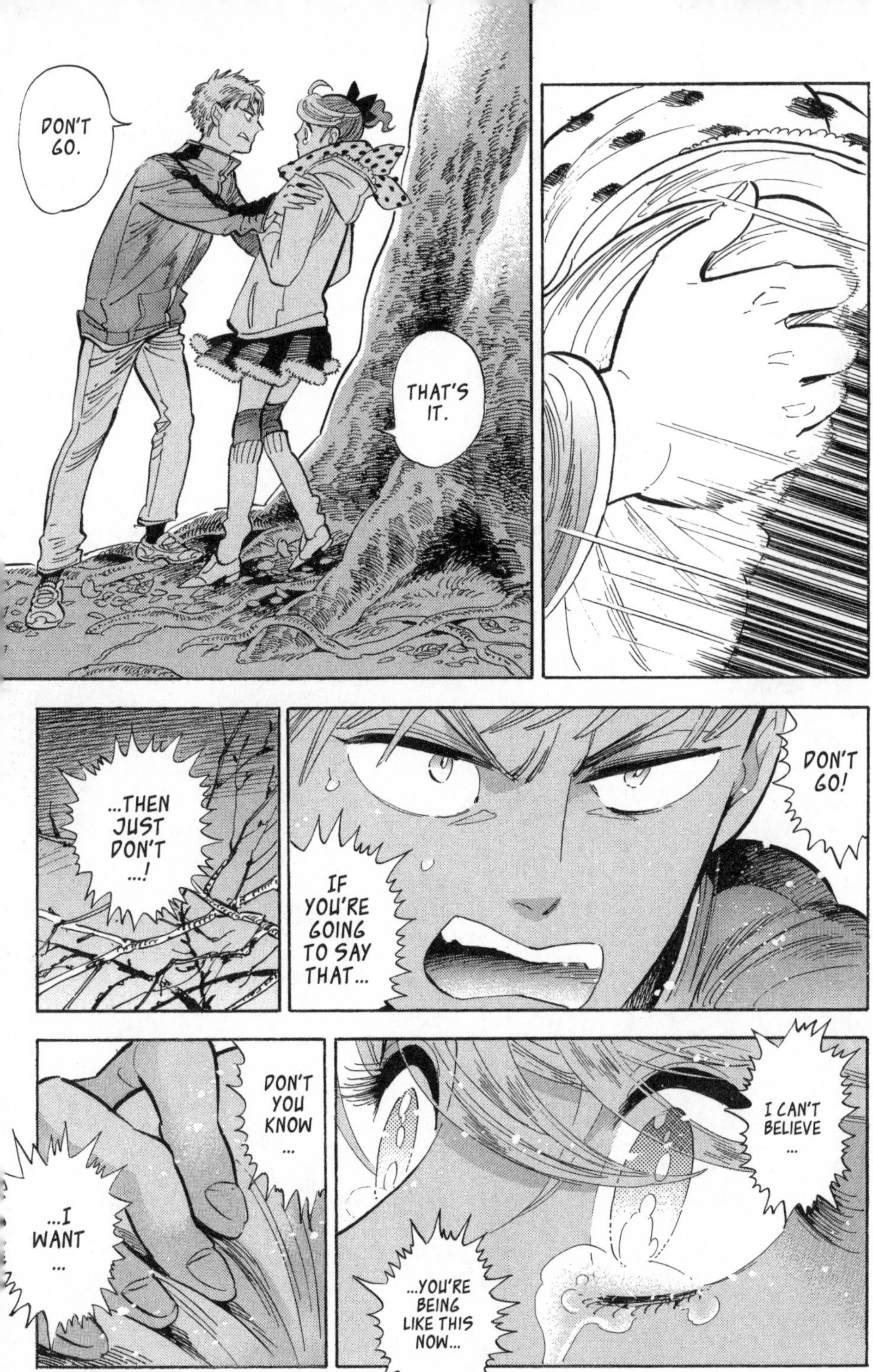
DON'T GO.
THAT'S IT.
DON'T GO!
IF YOU'RE GOING TO SAY THAT...
...THEN JUST DON'T ...!
I CAN'T BELIEVE ...
...YOU'RE BEING LIKE THIS NOW...
DON'T YOU KNOW ...
...I WANT ...

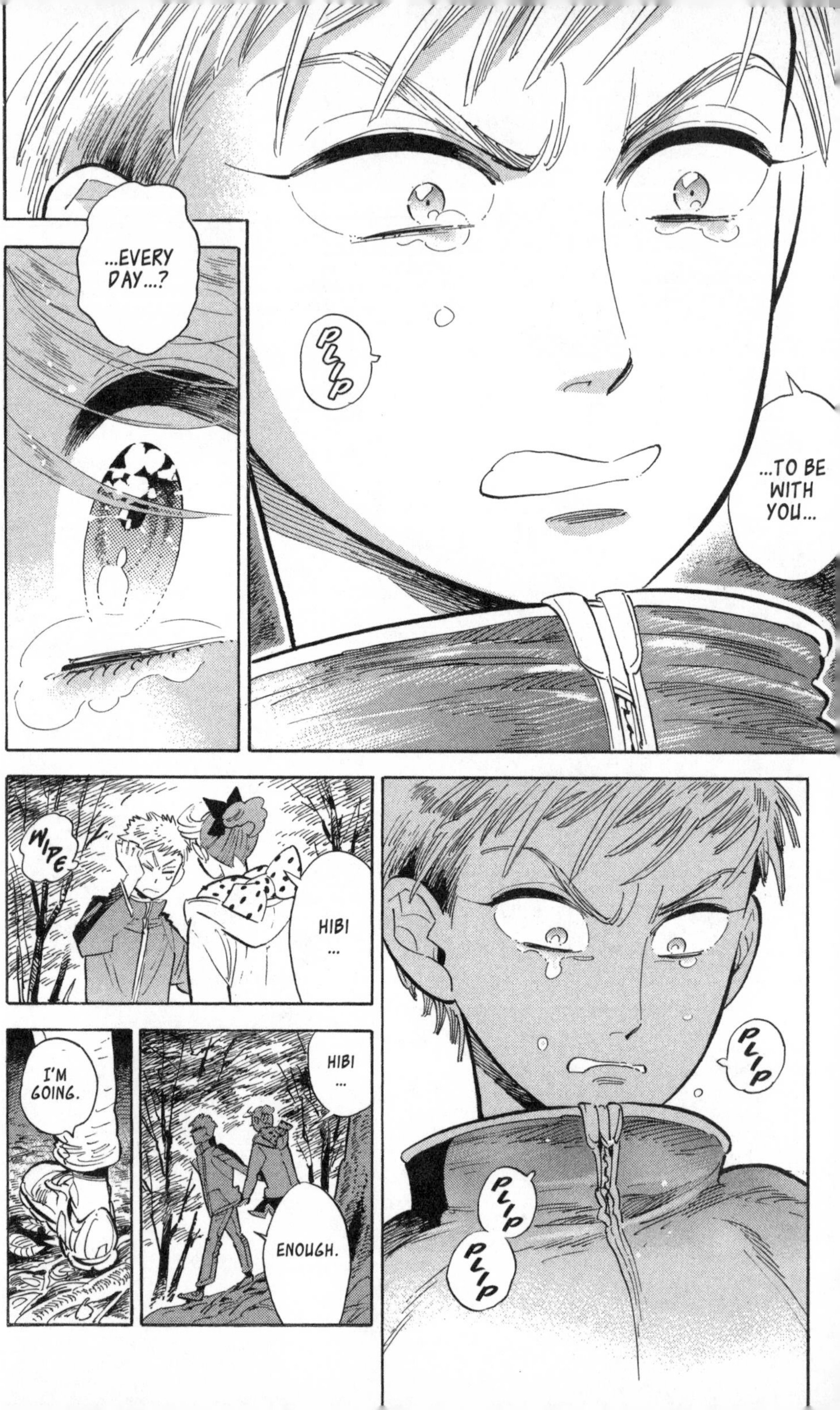

PLIP
...TO BE WITH YOU...
...EVERY DAY...?
PLIP
PLIP
PLIP
PLIP
HIBI ...
WIPE
HIBI ...
ENOUGH.
I'M GOING.

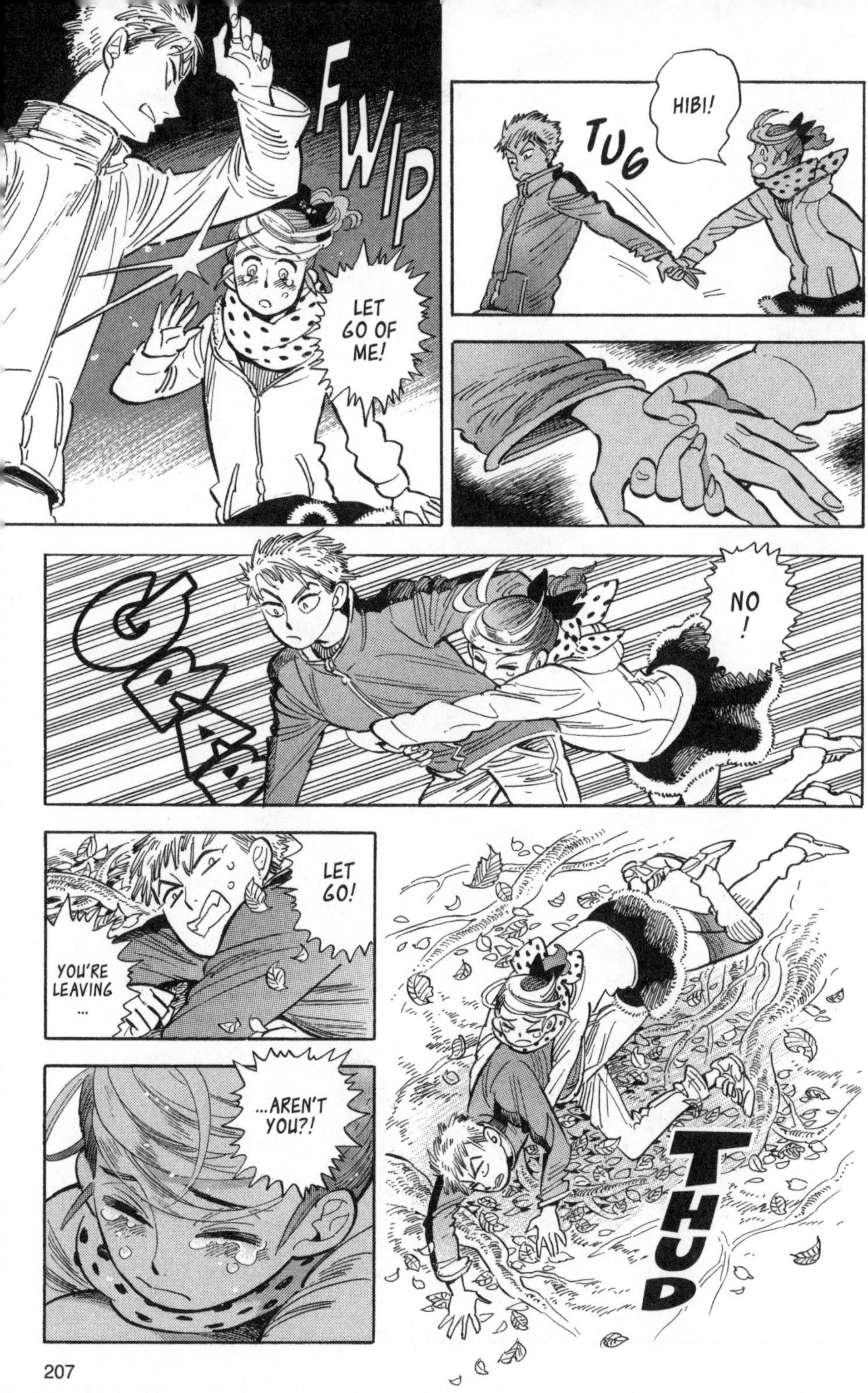
HIBI!
TUG
FWIP
LET GO OF ME!
NO!
GRAB
THUD
LET GO!
YOU'RE LEAVING ...
...AREN'T YOU?!

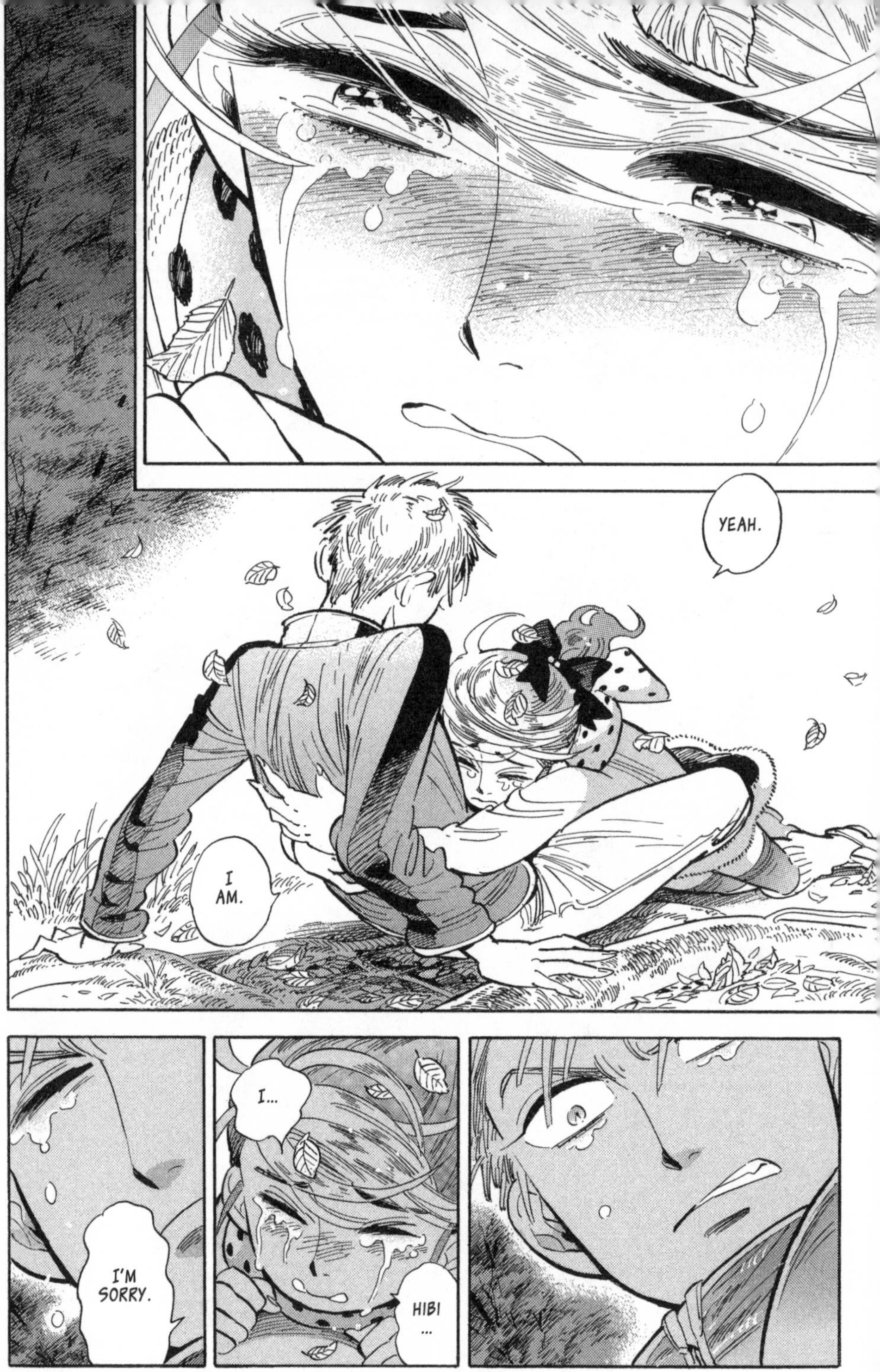
YEAH.
I AM.
I...
HIBI ...
I'M SORRY.

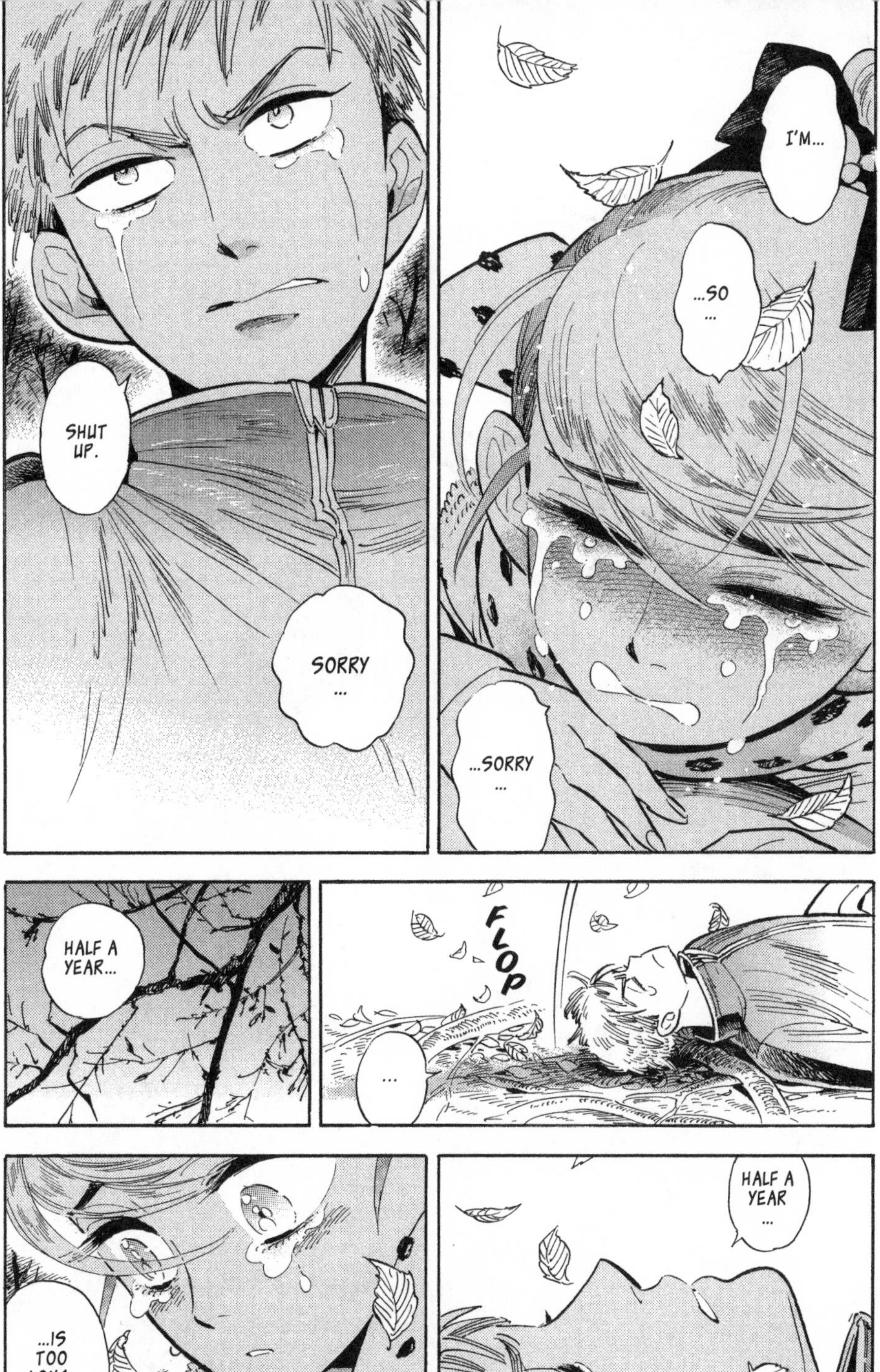
I'M...
...SO ...
...SORRY ...
SHUT UP.
SORRY ...
FLOP
...
HALF A YEAR...
HALF A YEAR ...
...IS TOO LONG.

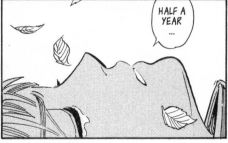

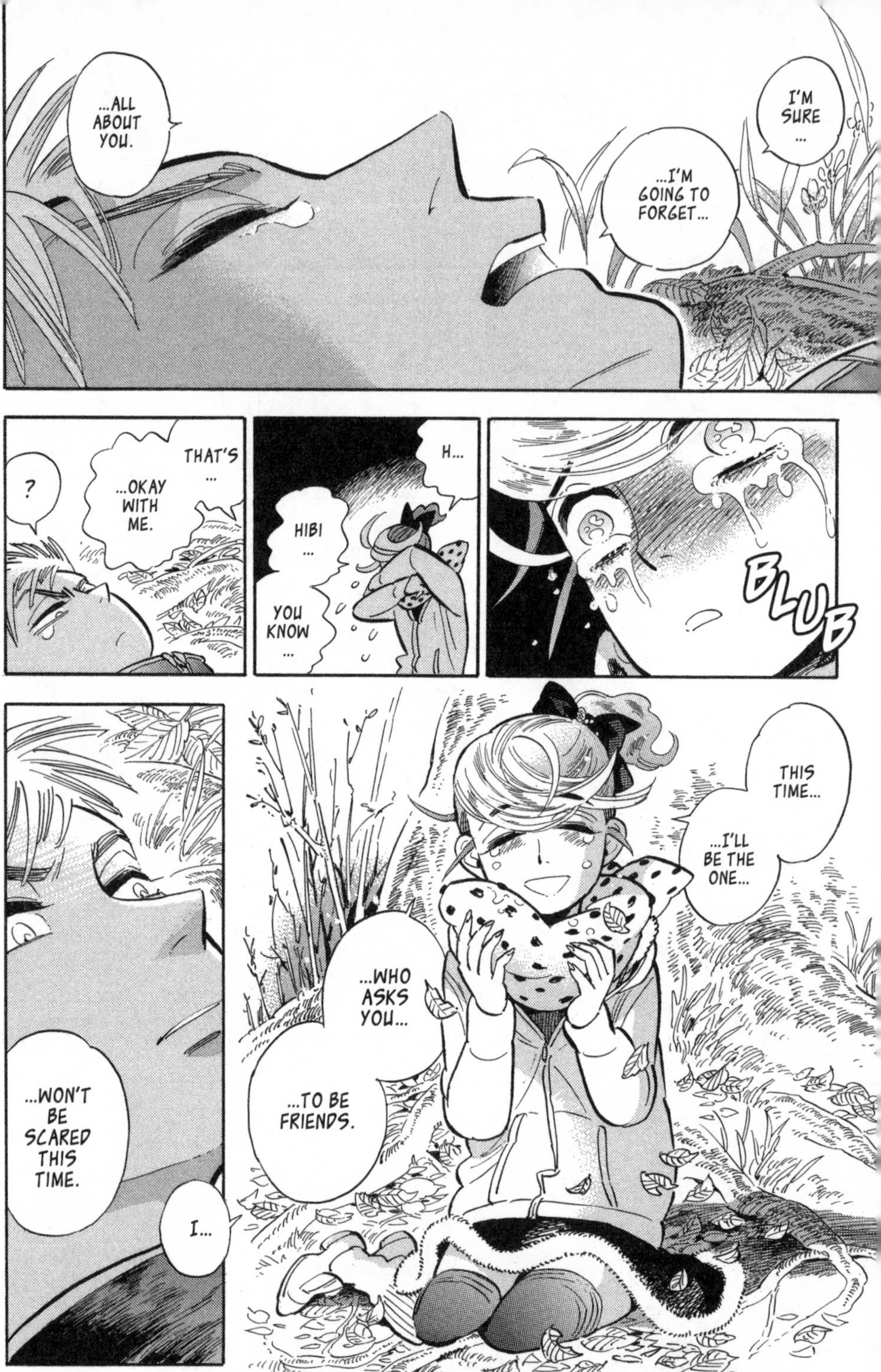
I'M SURE ...
...I'M GOING TO FORGET...
...ALL ABOUT YOU.
BLUB
H...
HIBI ...
YOU KNOW ...
THAT'S ...
...OKAY WITH ME.
?
THIS TIME...
...I'LL BE THE ONE...
...WHO ASKS YOU...
...TO BE FRIENDS.
I...
...WON'T BE SCARED THIS TIME.

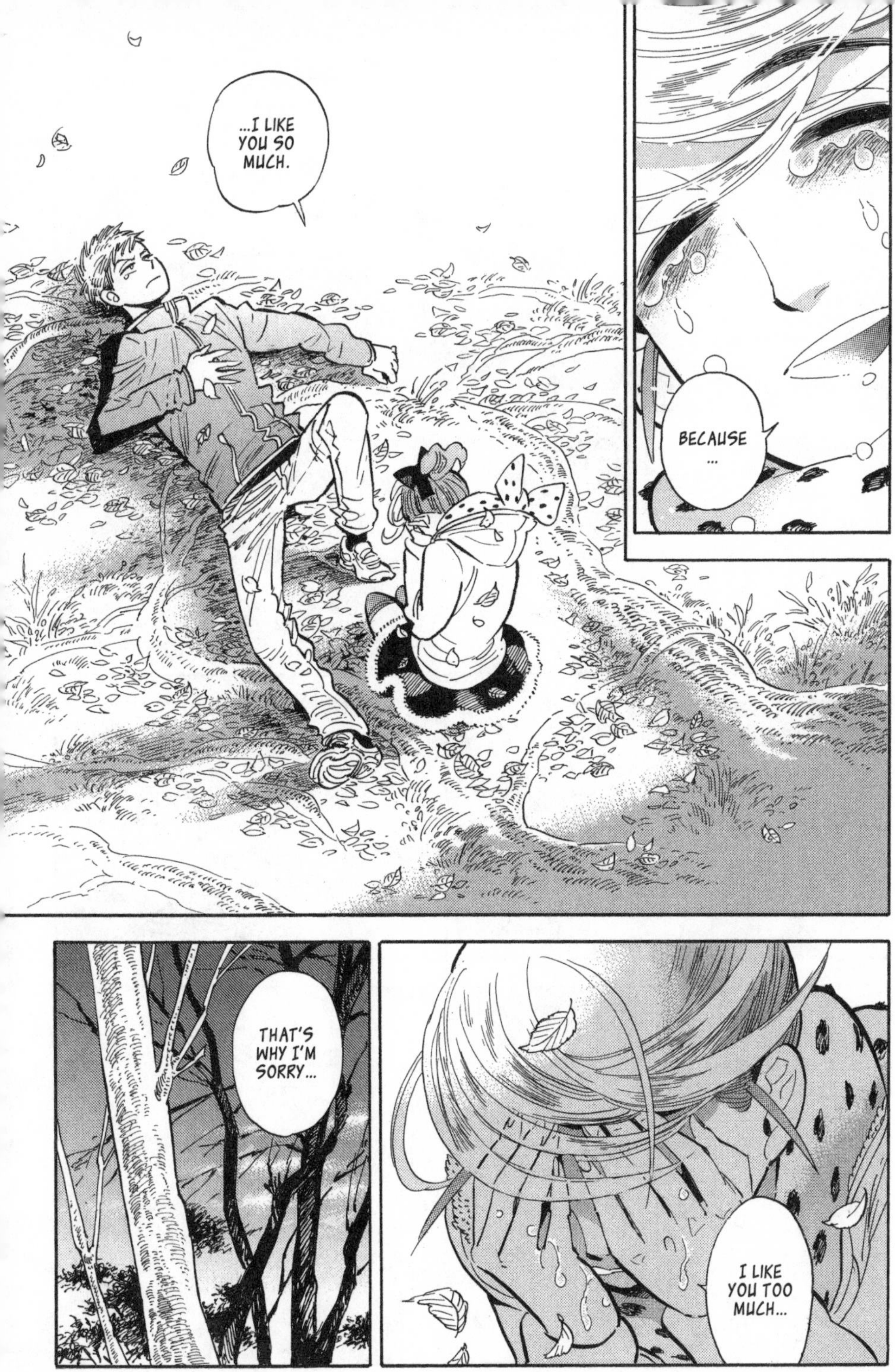
BECAUSE ...
...I LIKE YOU SO MUCH.
I LIKE YOU TOO MUCH...
THAT'S WHY I'M SORRY...

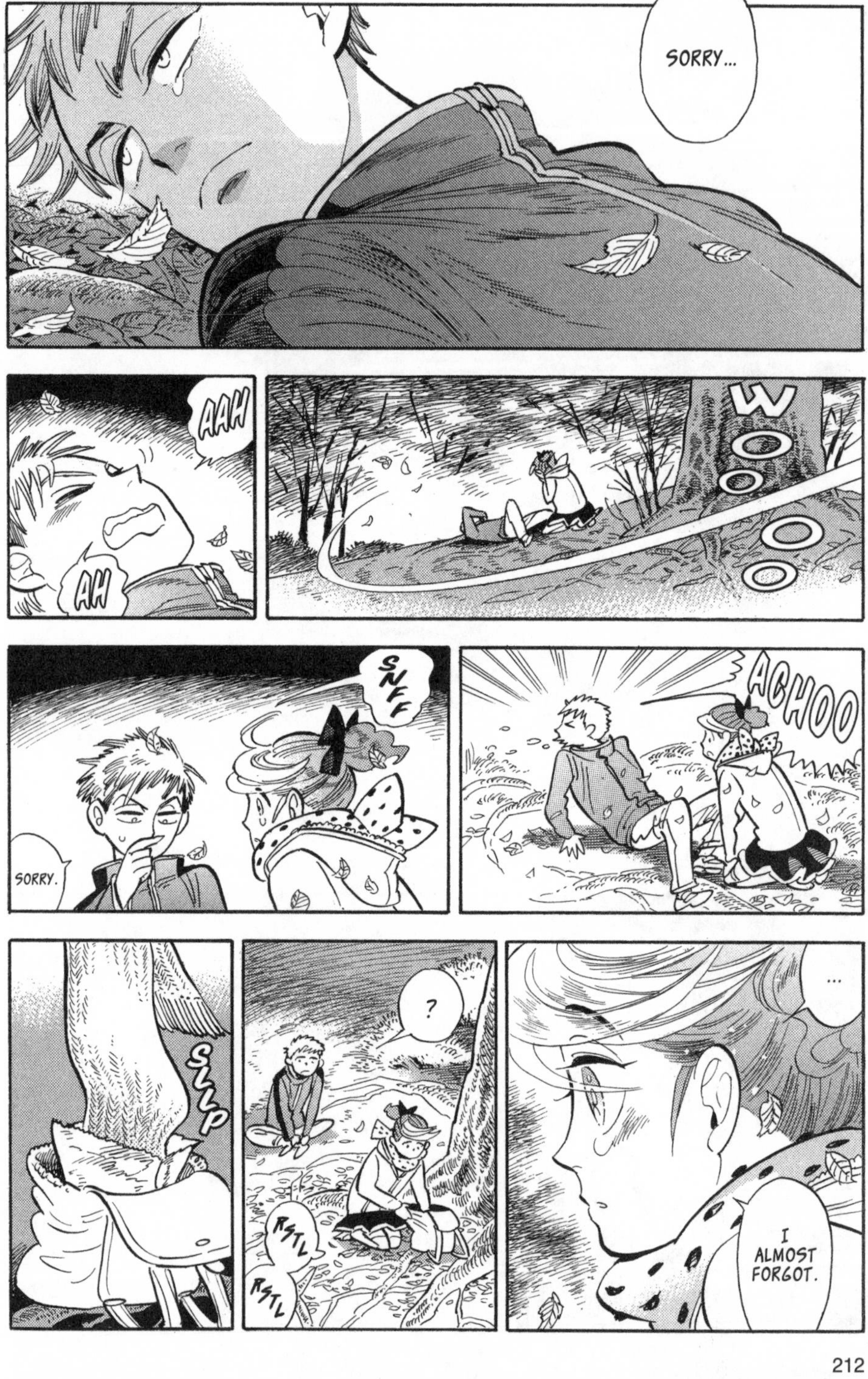
SORRY...
WOOOOO
AAH
AH
ACHOO
SNFF
SORRY.
...
I ALMOST FORGOT.
?
RSTL
RSTL
SLLP

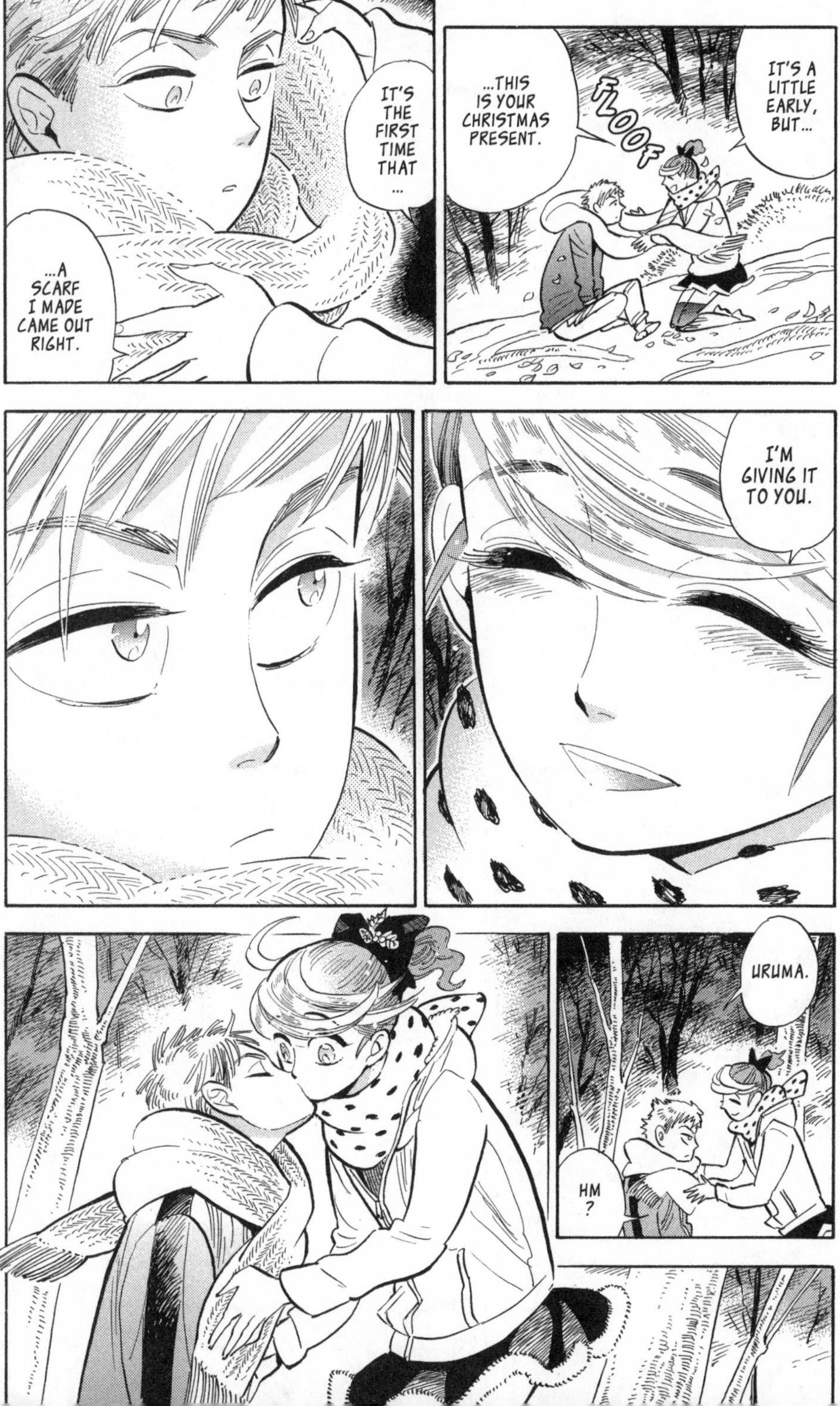
IT'S A LITTLE EARLY, BUT...
FLOOF
...THIS IS YOUR CHRISTMAS PRESENT.
IT'S THE FIRST TIME THAT ...
...A SCARF I MADE CAME OUT RIGHT.
I'M GIVING IT TO YOU.
URUMA.
HM?

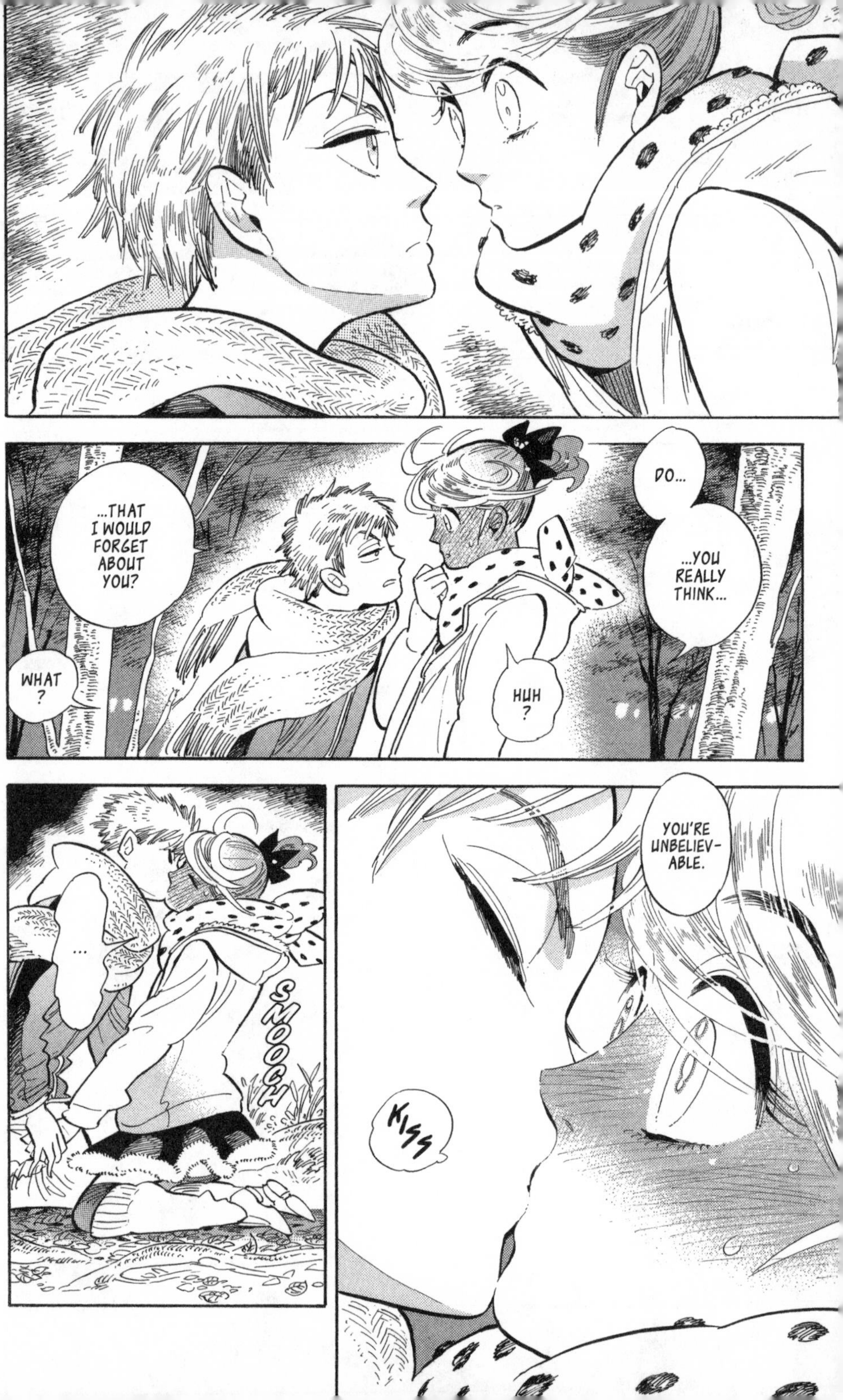
DO...
...YOU REALLY THINK...
HUH?
...THAT I WOULD FORGET ABOUT YOU?
WHAT?
YOU'RE UNBELIEV-ABLE.
KISS
...
SMOOCH

...NO WAY...

ABSOLUTELY NO WAY!

...I'D FORGET YOU.

GRAB

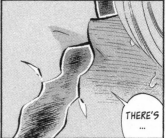

THERE'S ...

...ME EITHER.

SO DON'T YOU DARE ...

...FORGET ...

GOT IT?!

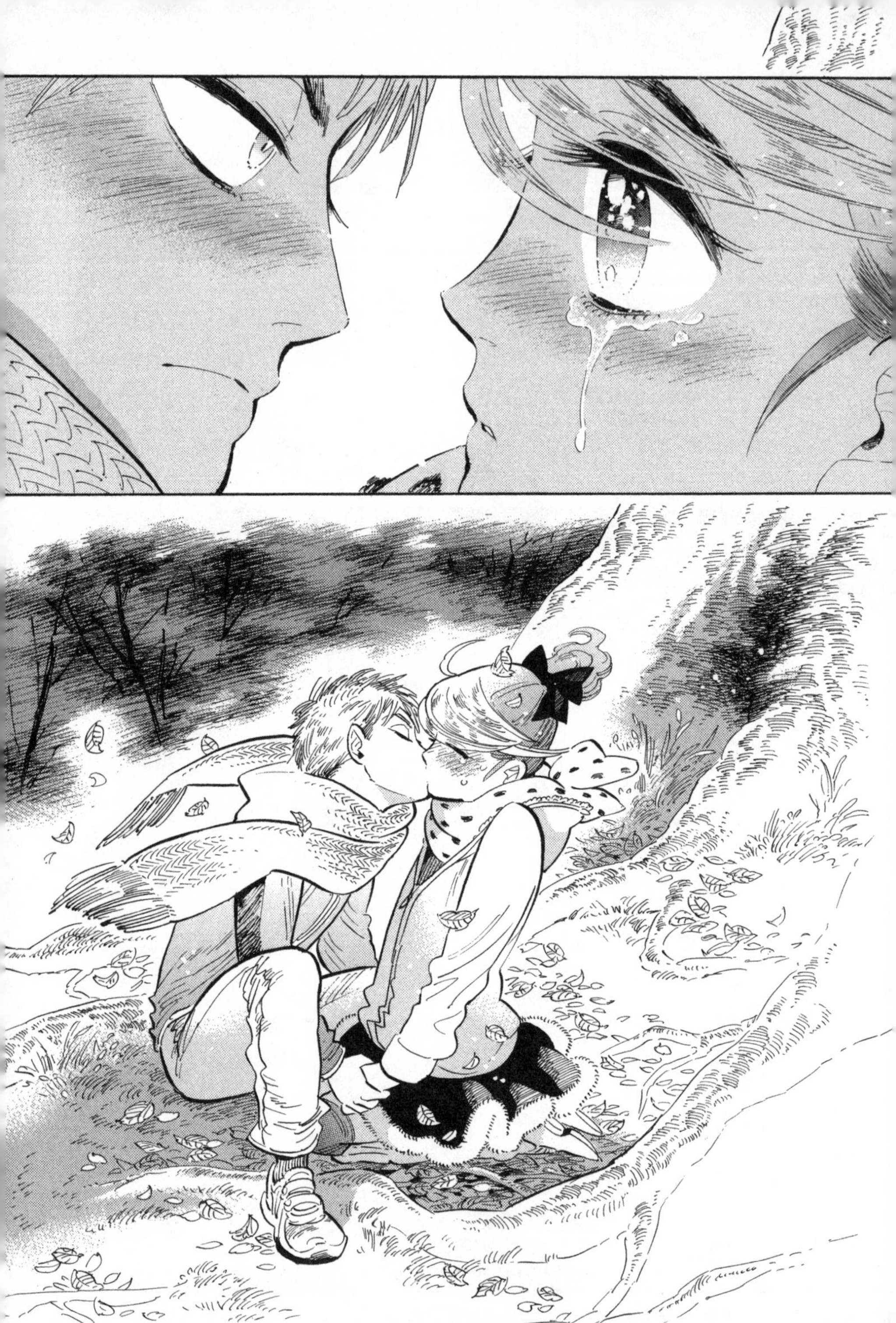

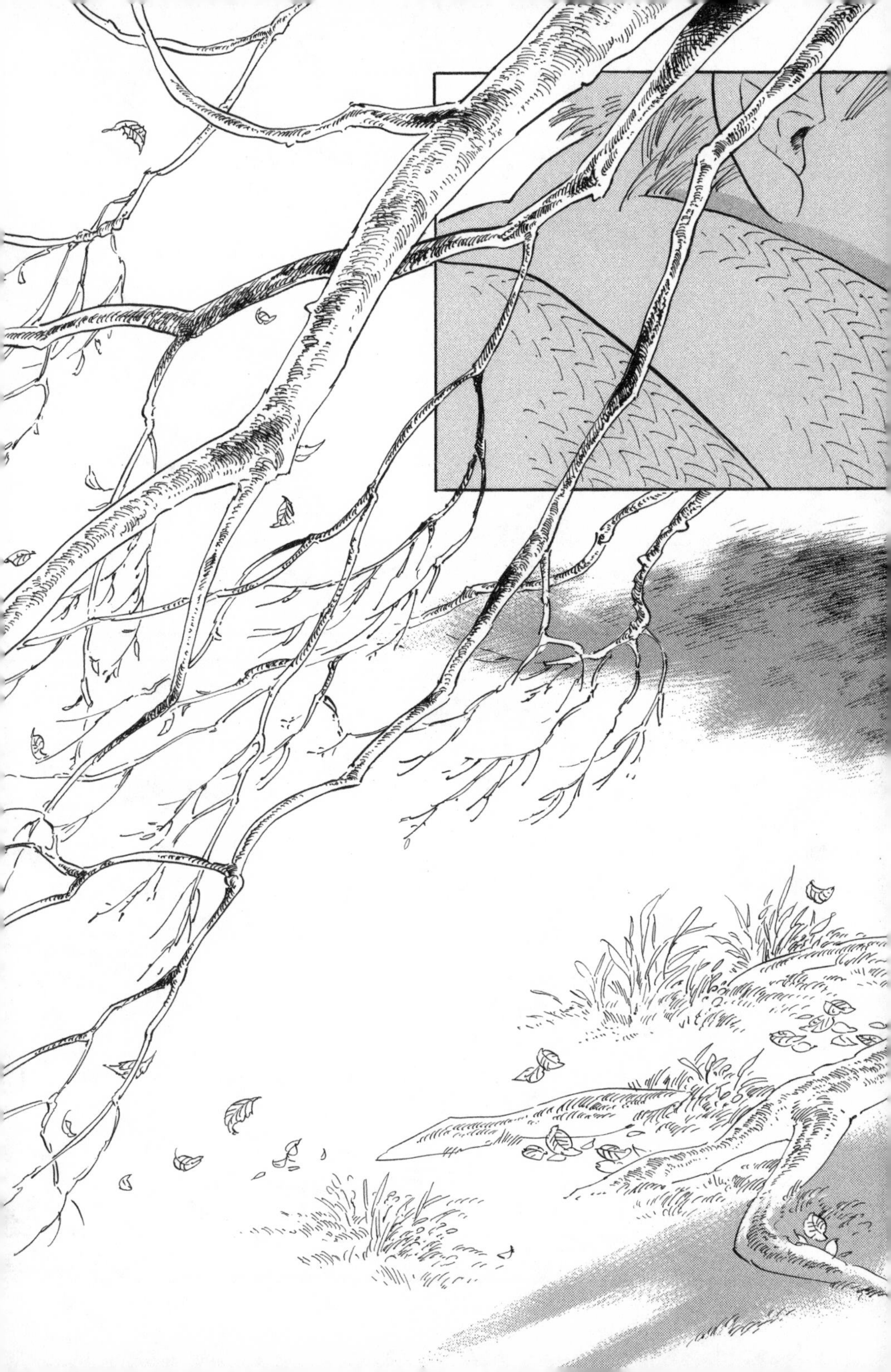

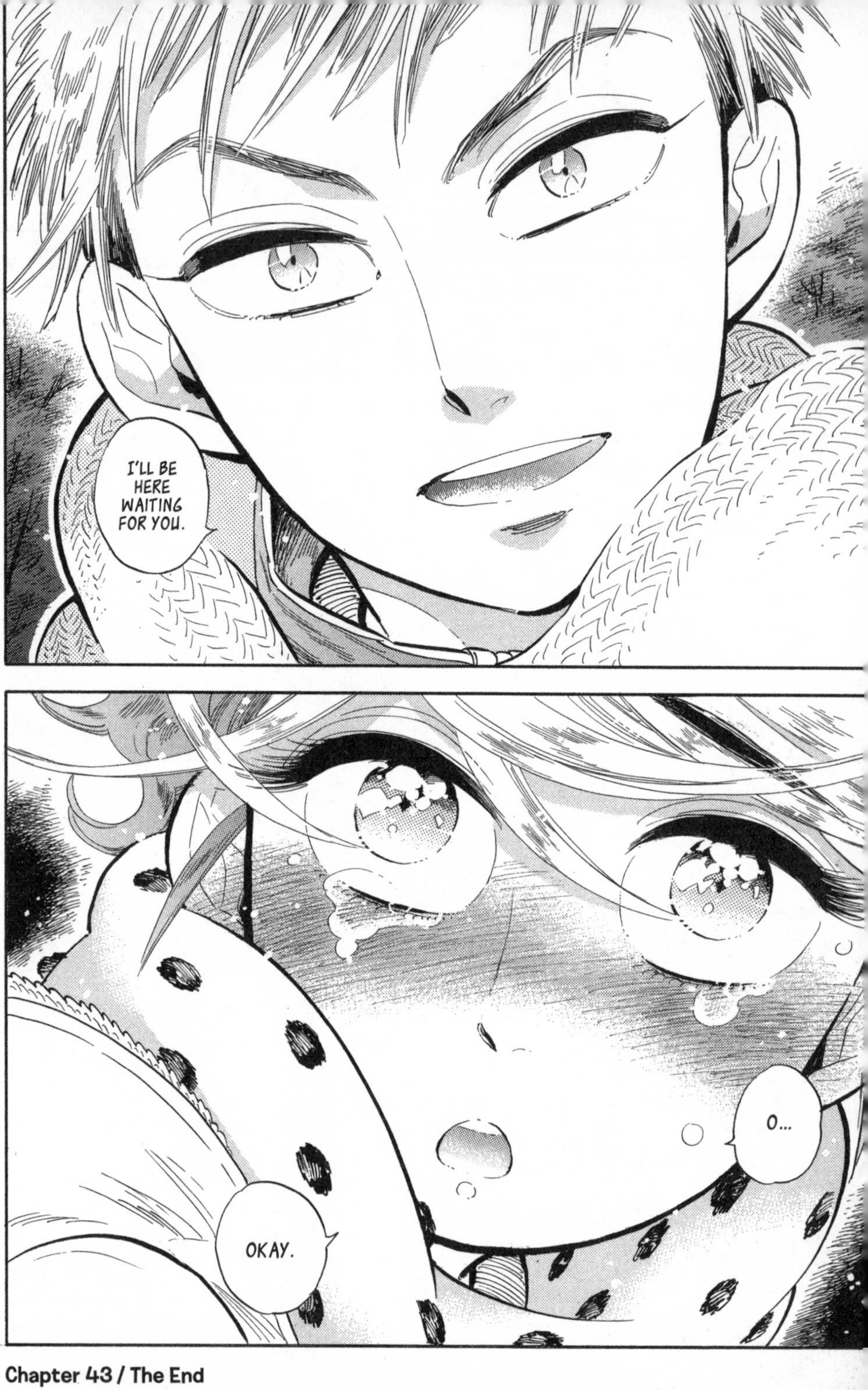
I'LL BE HERE WAITING FOR YOU.
O...
OKAY.

Chapter 43 / The End

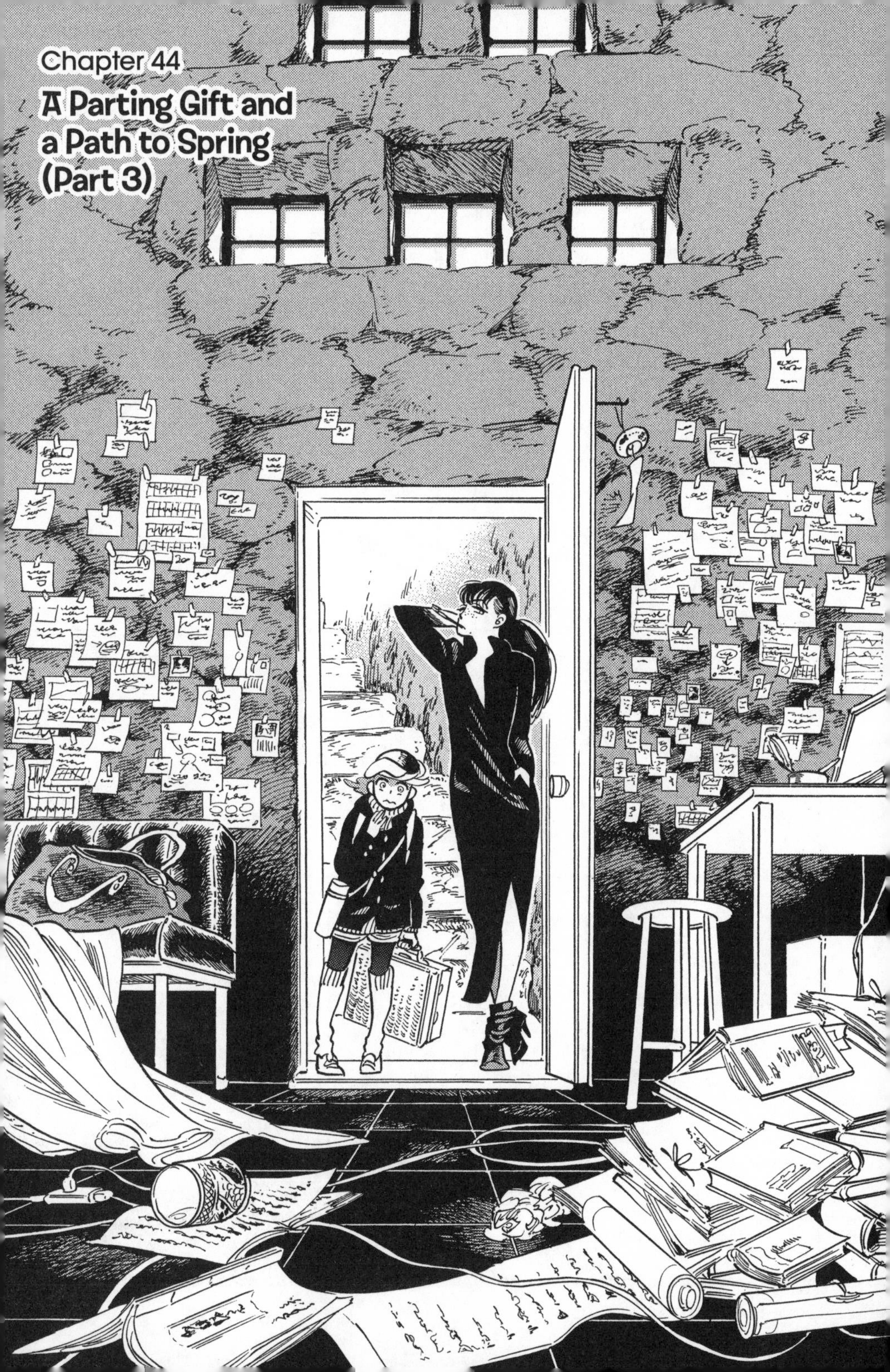
Chapter 44
A Parting Gift and a Path to Spring (Part 3)

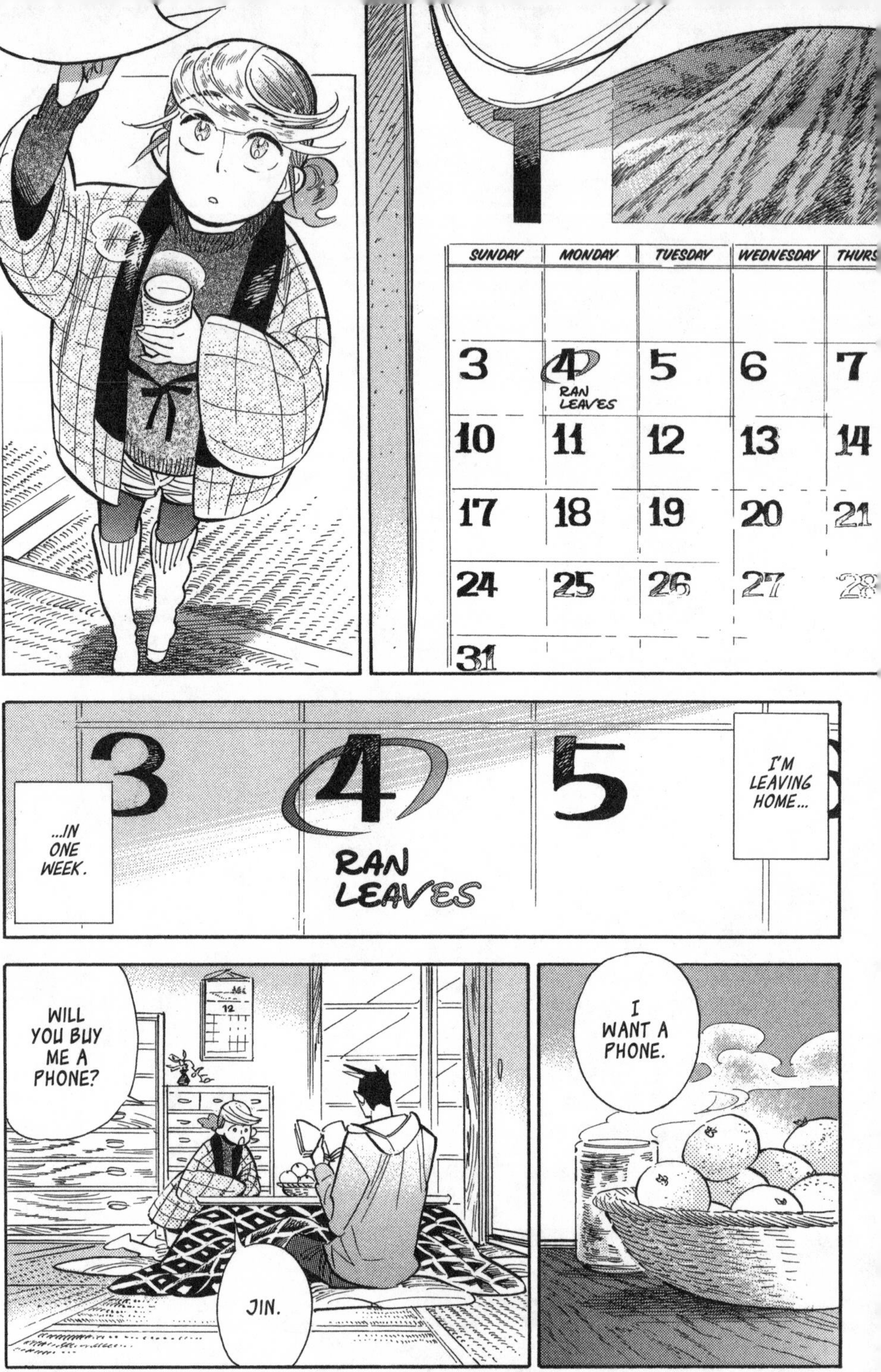
SUNDAY
MONDAY
TUESDAY
WEDNESDAY
THURS
RAN LEAVES
I'M LEAVING HOME...
RAN LEAVES
...IN ONE WEEK.
I WANT A PHONE.
WILL YOU BUY ME A PHONE?
JIN.

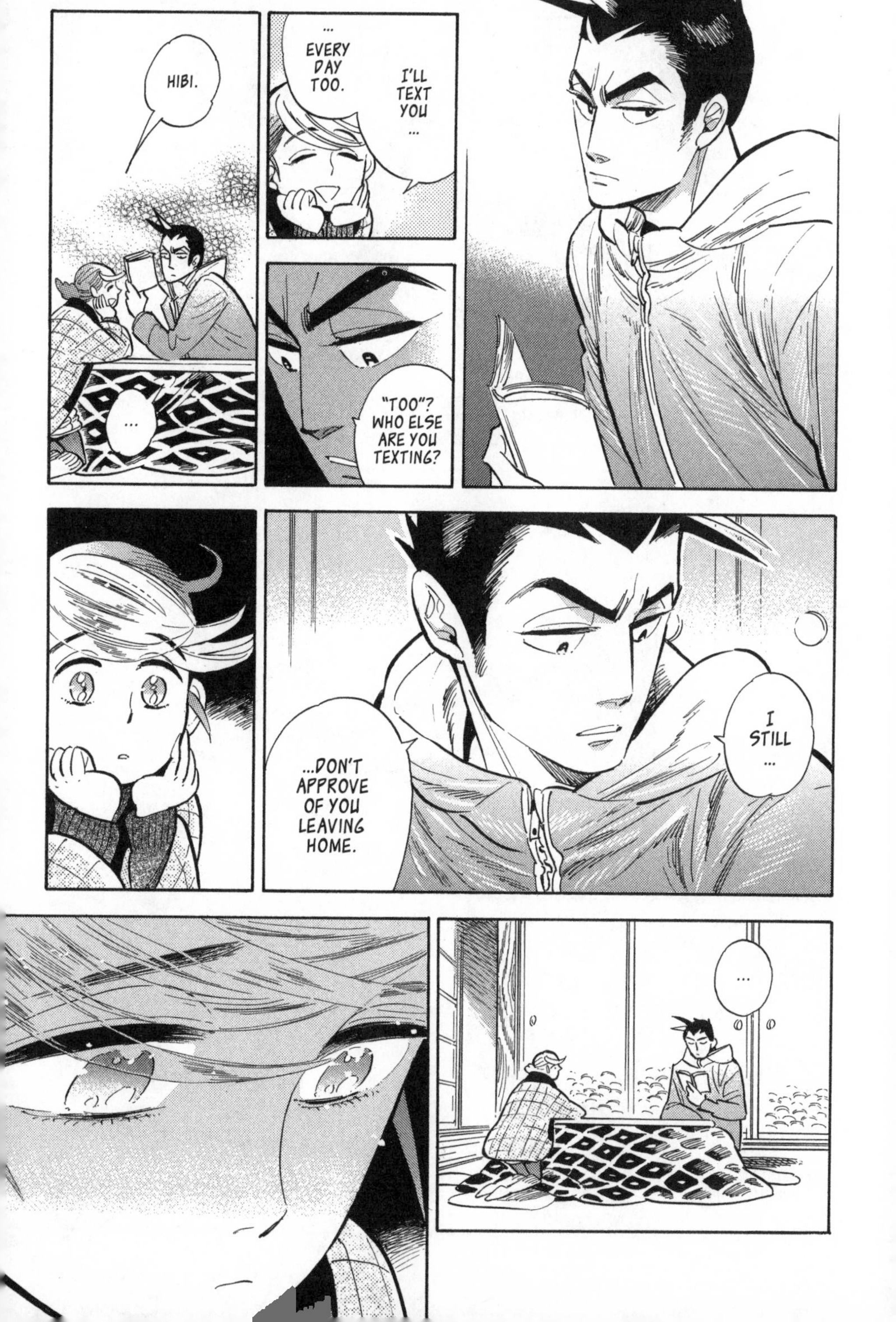
I'LL TEXT YOU ...
... EVERY DAY TOO.
"TOO"? WHO ELSE ARE YOU TEXTING?
HIBI.
...
I STILL ...
...DON'T APPROVE OF YOU LEAVING HOME.
...

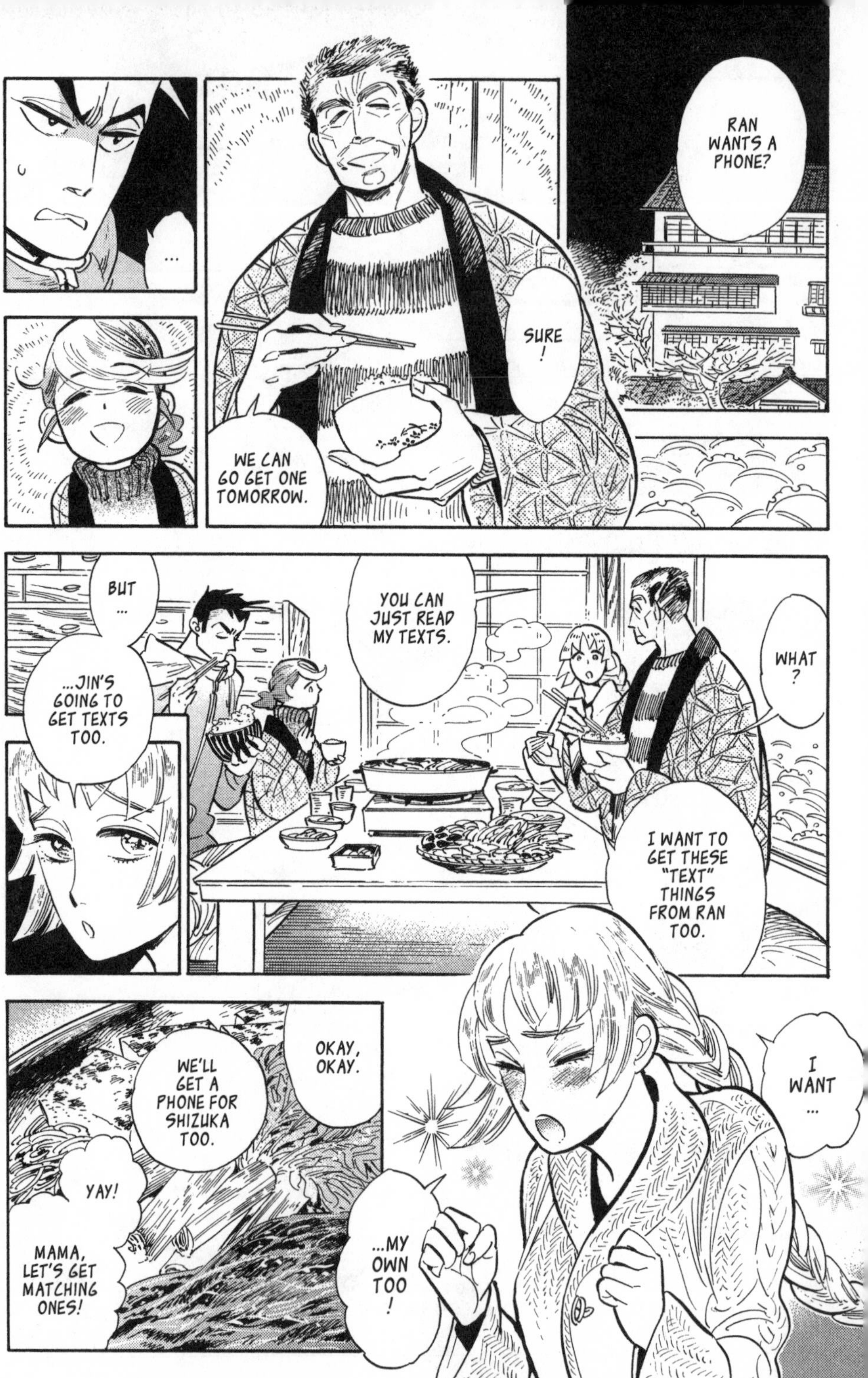
RAN WANTS A PHONE?
SURE!
WE CAN GO GET ONE TOMORROW.
...
WHAT?
YOU CAN JUST READ MY TEXTS.
BUT...
...JIN'S GOING TO GET TEXTS TOO.
I WANT TO GET THESE "TEXT" THINGS FROM RAN TOO.
I WANT...
...MY OWN TOO!
OKAY, OKAY.
WE'LL GET A PHONE FOR SHIZUKA TOO.
YAY!
MAMA, LET'S GET MATCHING ONES!

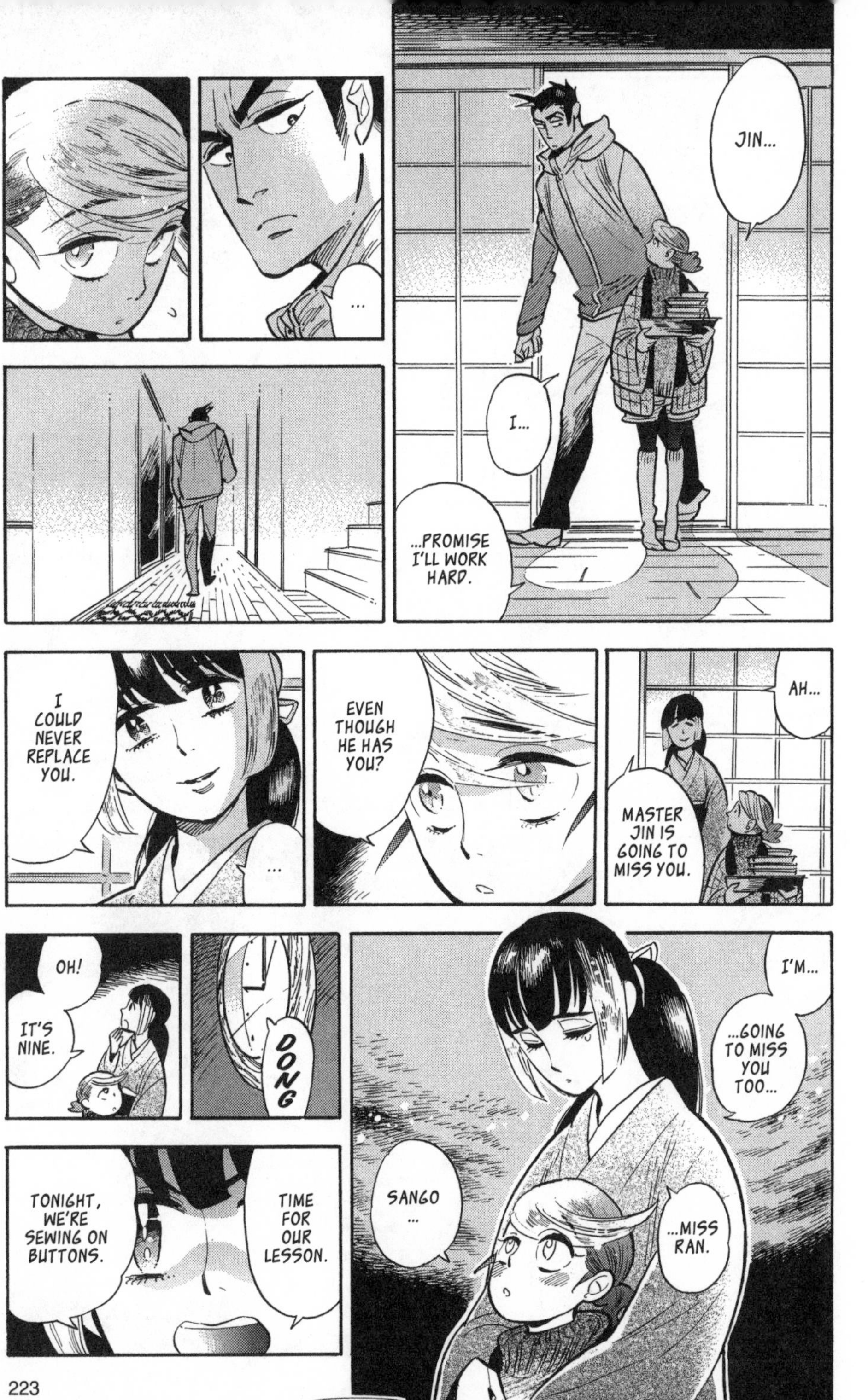
JIN...
I...
...PROMISE I'LL WORK HARD.
...
I COULD NEVER REPLACE YOU.
AH...
MASTER JIN IS GOING TO MISS YOU.
EVEN THOUGH HE HAS YOU?
I COULD NEVER REPLACE YOU.
...
I'M...
...GOING TO MISS YOU TOO...
SANGO ...
...MISS RAN.
DONG
OH!
IT'S NINE.
TIME FOR OUR LESSON.
TONIGHT, WE'RE SEWING ON BUTTONS.

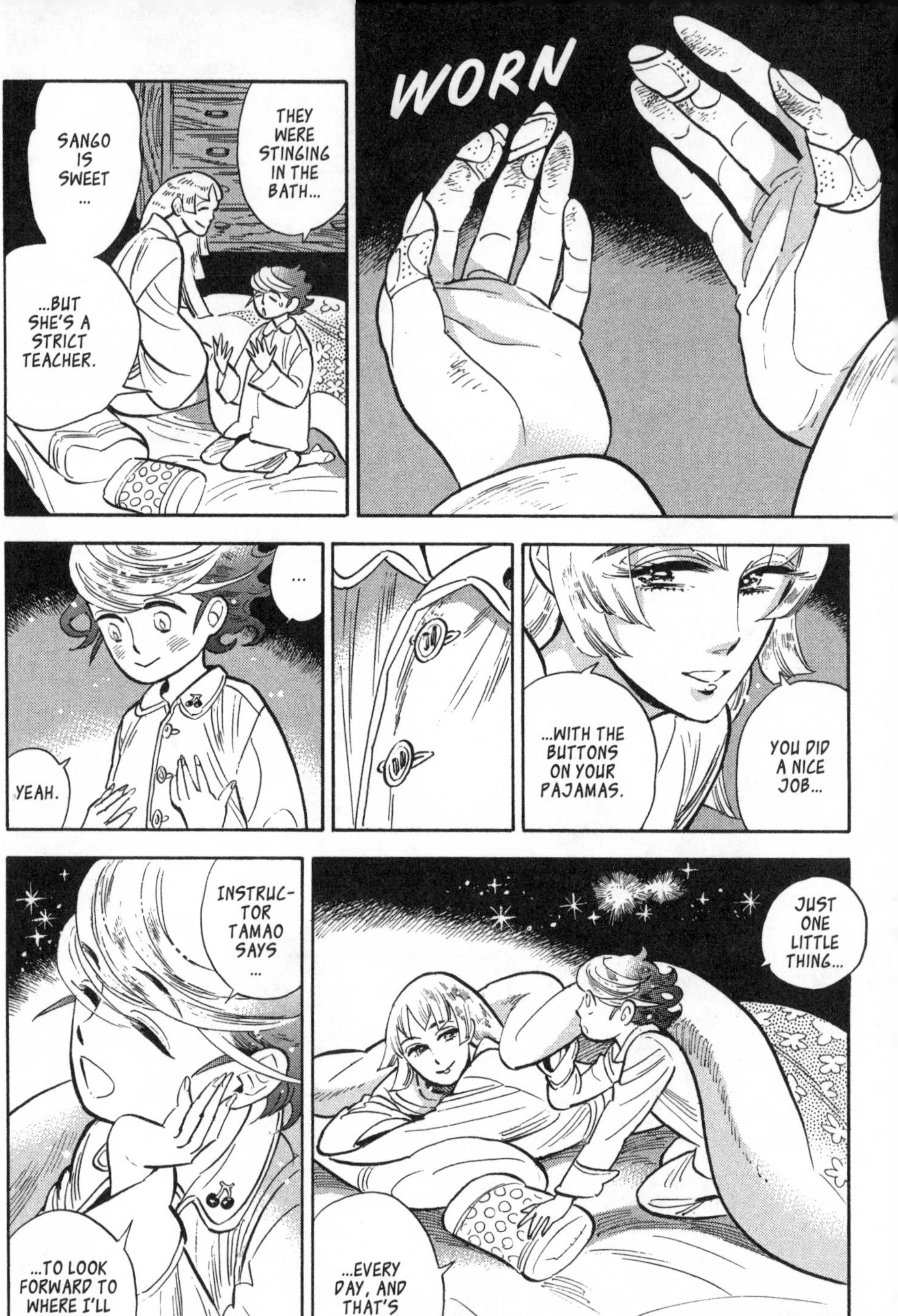
WORN
THEY WERE STINGING IN THE BATH...
SANGO IS SWEET...
...BUT SHE'S A STRICT TEACHER.
YOU DID A NICE JOB...
...WITH THE BUTTONS ON YOUR PAJAMAS.
...
YEAH.
JUST ONE LITTLE THING...
...EVERY DAY, AND THAT'S ENOUGH.
INSTRUCTOR TAMAO SAYS...
...TO LOOK FORWARD TO WHERE I'LL BE IN SIX MONTHS.

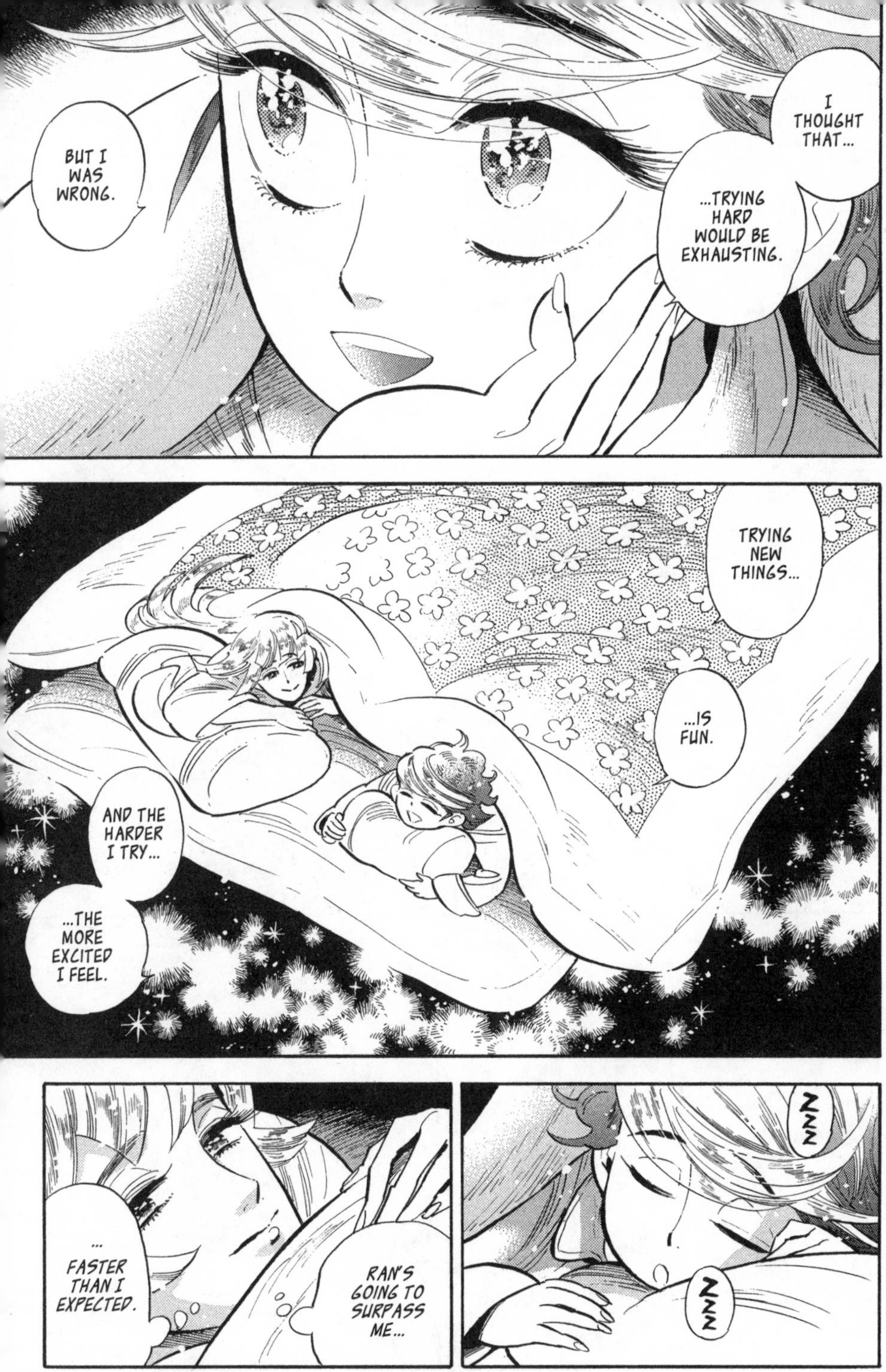
I THOUGHT THAT...
...TRYING HARD WOULD BE EXHAUSTING.
BUT I WAS WRONG.
TRYING NEW THINGS...
...IS FUN.
AND THE HARDER I TRY...
...THE MORE EXCITED I FEEL.
ZZZ
ZZZ
RAN'S GOING TO SURPASS ME...
... FASTER THAN I EXPECTED.

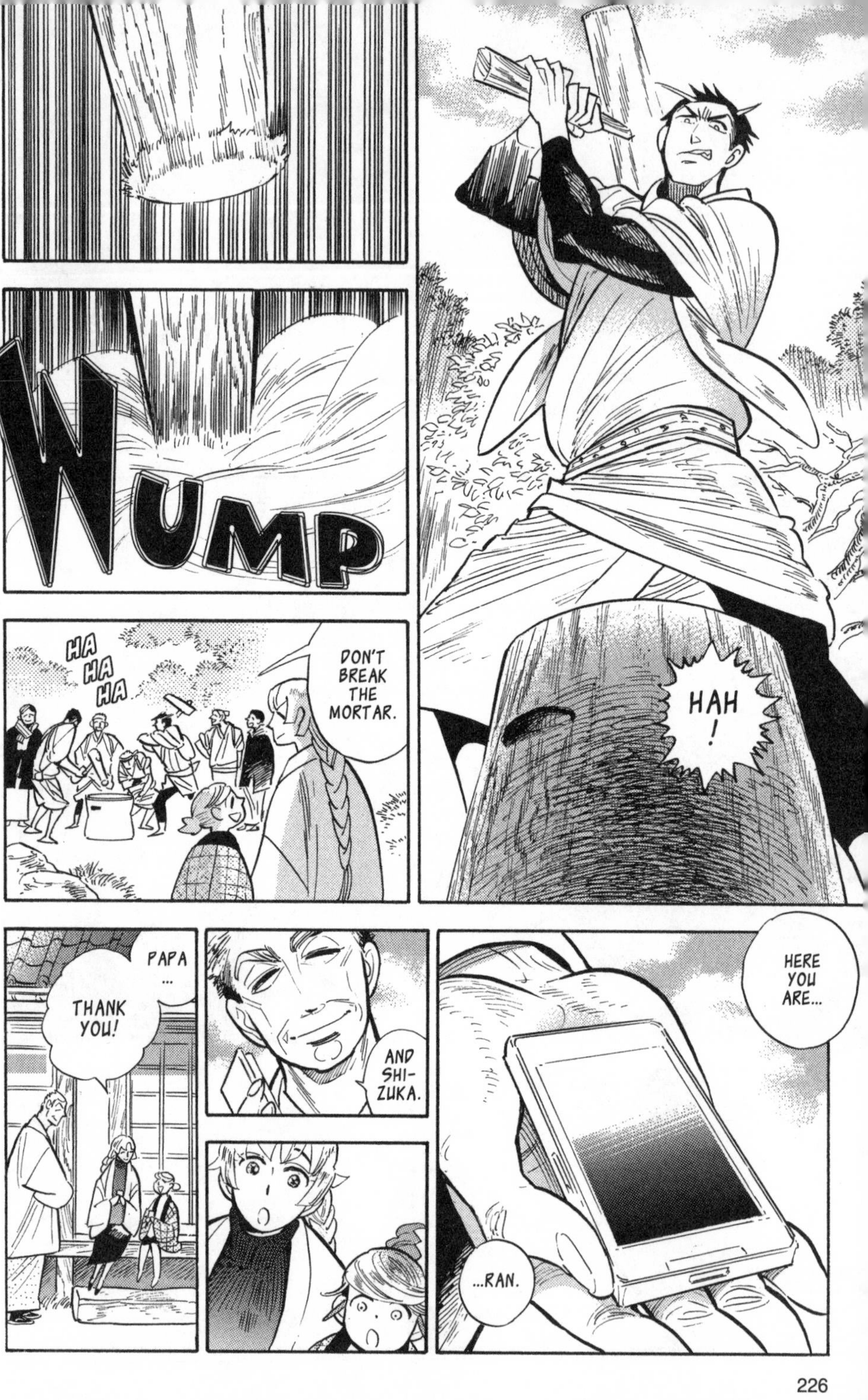
HAH!
WUMP
DON'T BREAK THE MORTAR.
HA HA HA
HERE YOU ARE...
...RAN.
AND SHI-ZUKA.
PAPA...
THANK YOU!

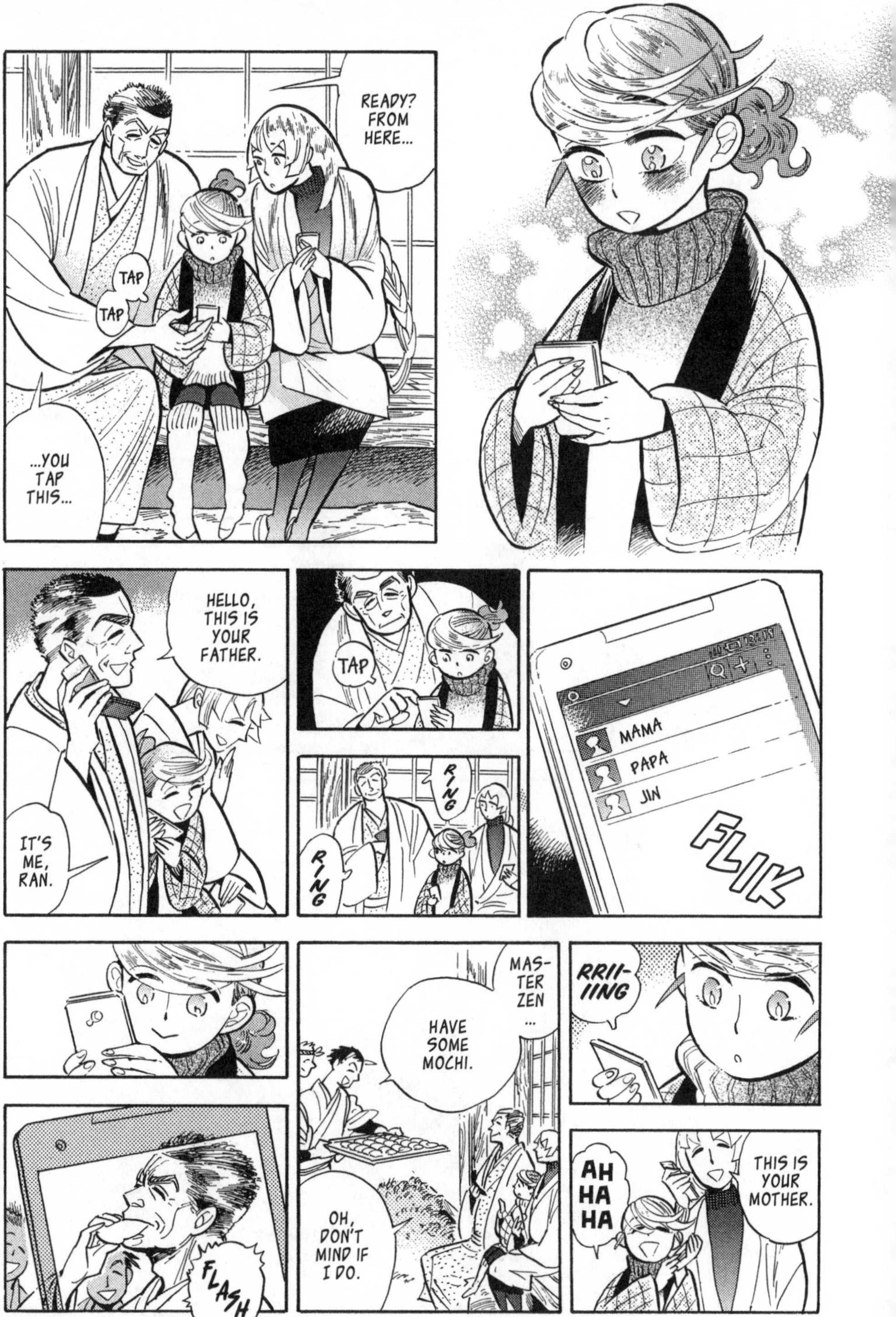
READY? FROM HERE...
TAP
TAP
...YOU TAP THIS...
MAMA
PAPA
JIN
FLIK
TAP
RING
RING
HELLO, THIS IS YOUR FATHER.
IT'S ME, RAN.
RRIIING
THIS IS YOUR MOTHER.
AH HA HA
MAS-TER ZEN ...
HAVE SOME MOCHI.
OH, DON'T MIND IF I DO.
FLASH

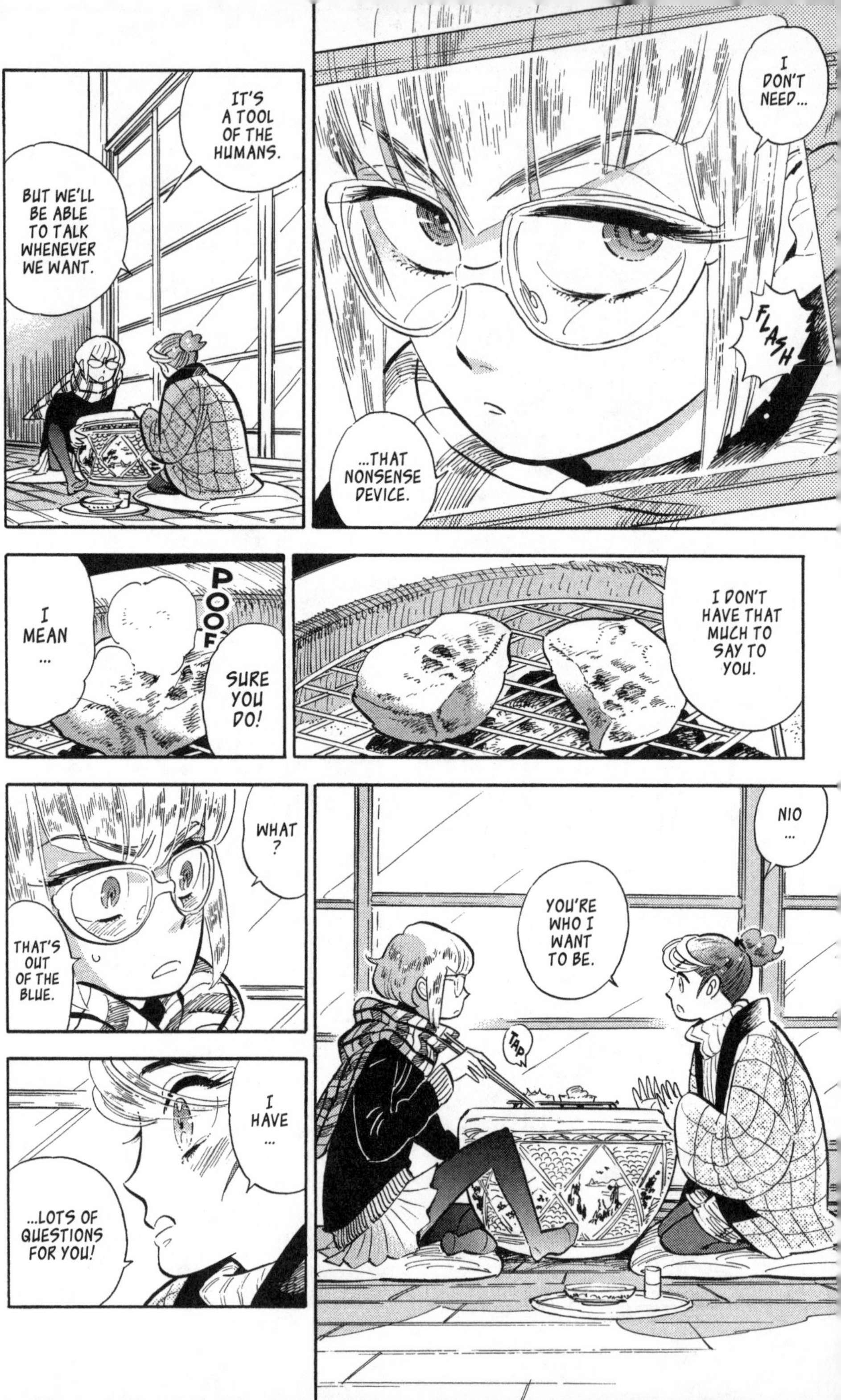
I DON'T NEED...
FLASH
...THAT NONSENSE DEVICE.
IT'S A TOOL OF THE HUMANS.
BUT WE'LL BE ABLE TO TALK WHENEVER WE WANT.
I DON'T HAVE THAT MUCH TO SAY TO YOU.
POOF
I MEAN ...
SURE YOU DO!
NIO ...
YOU'RE WHO I WANT TO BE.
TAP
WHAT?
THAT'S OUT OF THE BLUE.
I HAVE ...
...LOTS OF QUESTIONS FOR YOU!

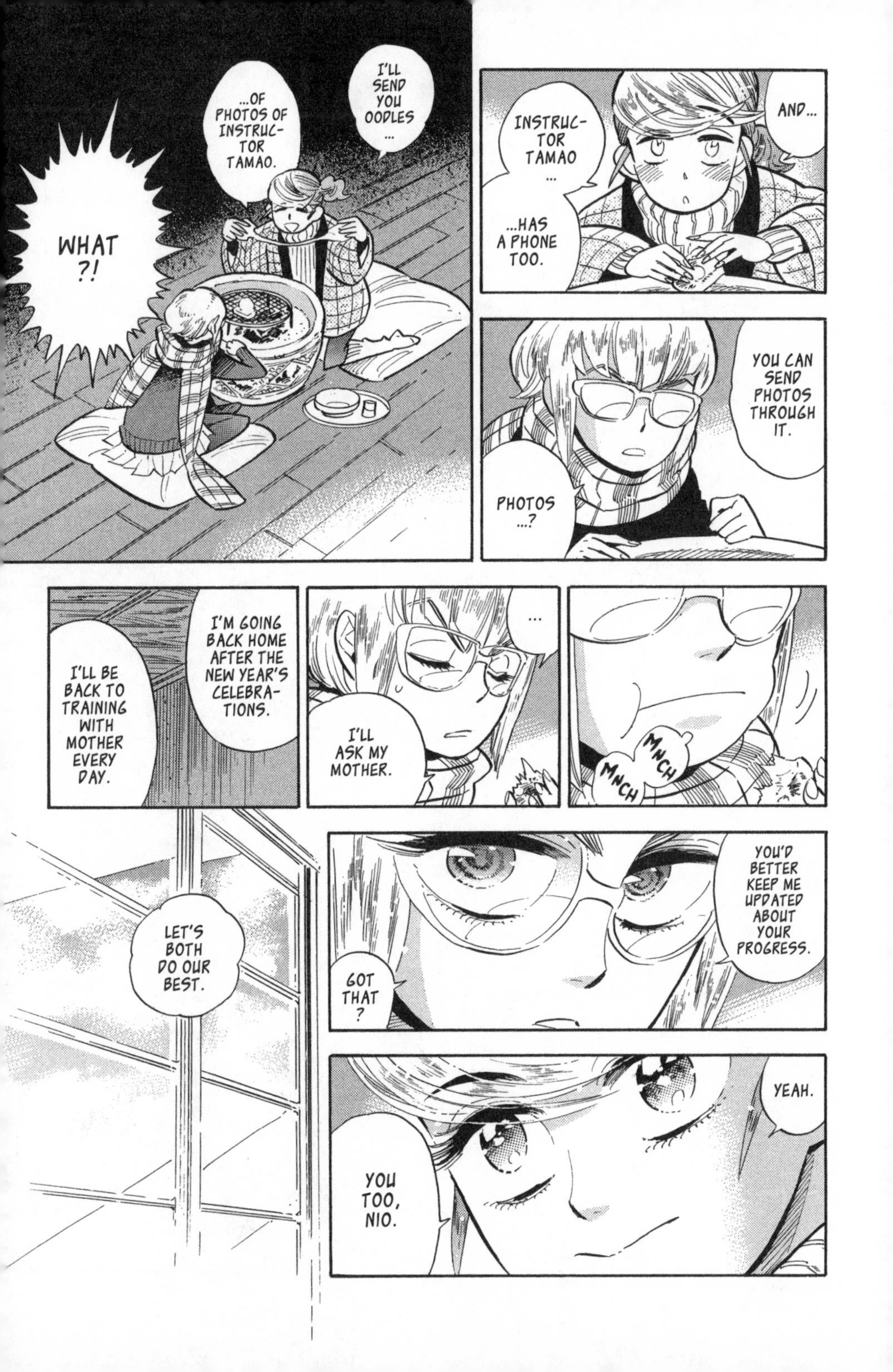
AND...
INSTRUCTOR TAMAO...
...HAS A PHONE TOO.
YOU CAN SEND PHOTOS THROUGH IT.
PHOTOS...?
I'LL SEND YOU OODLES...
...OF PHOTOS OF INSTRUCTOR TAMAO.
WHAT?!
MNCH MNCH
...
I'LL ASK MY MOTHER.
I'M GOING BACK HOME AFTER THE NEW YEAR'S CELEBRATIONS.
I'LL BE BACK TO TRAINING WITH MOTHER EVERY DAY.
YOU'D BETTER KEEP ME UPDATED ABOUT YOUR PROGRESS.
GOT THAT?
YEAH.
YOU TOO, NIO.
LET'S BOTH DO OUR BEST.

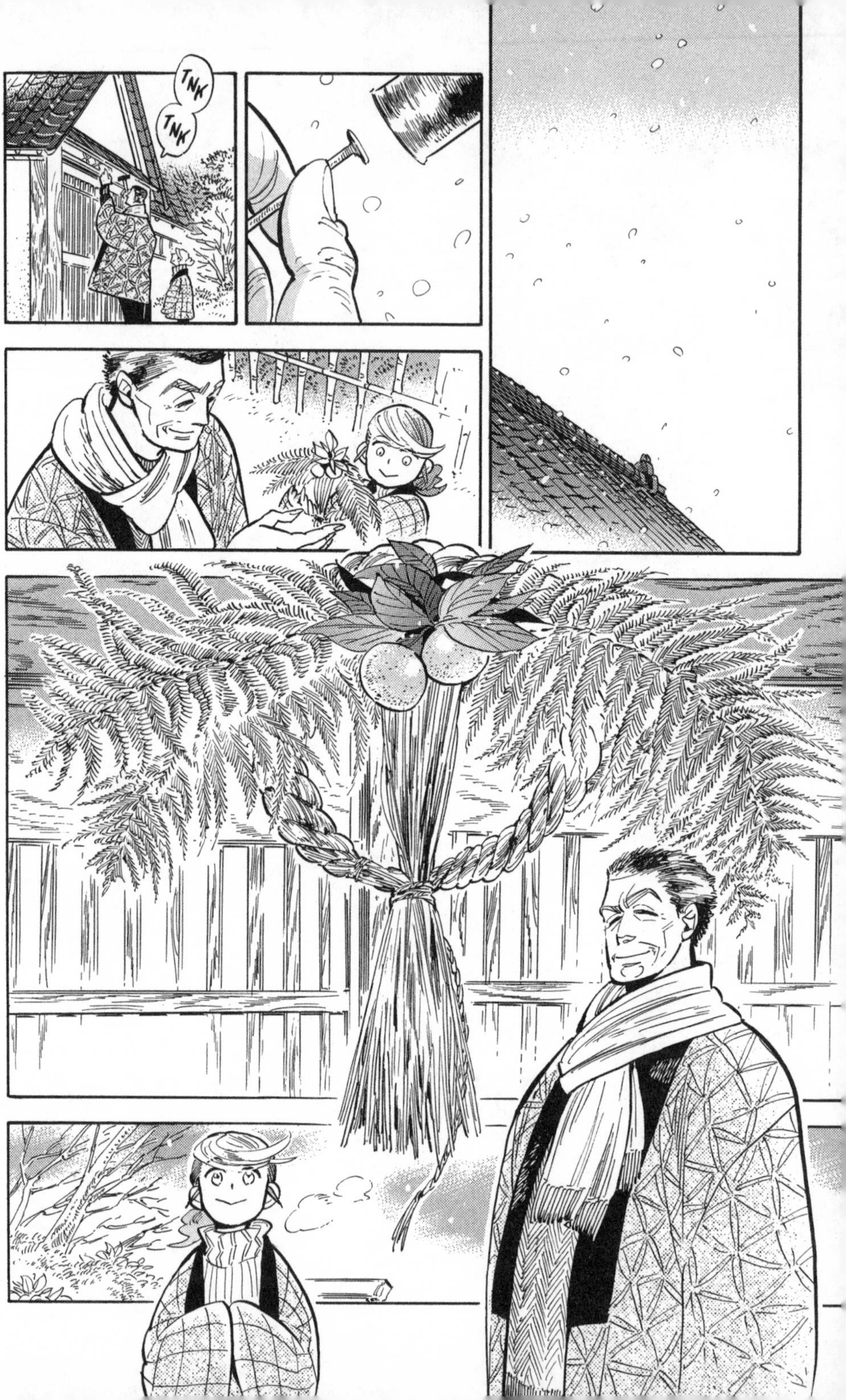
TNK
TNK

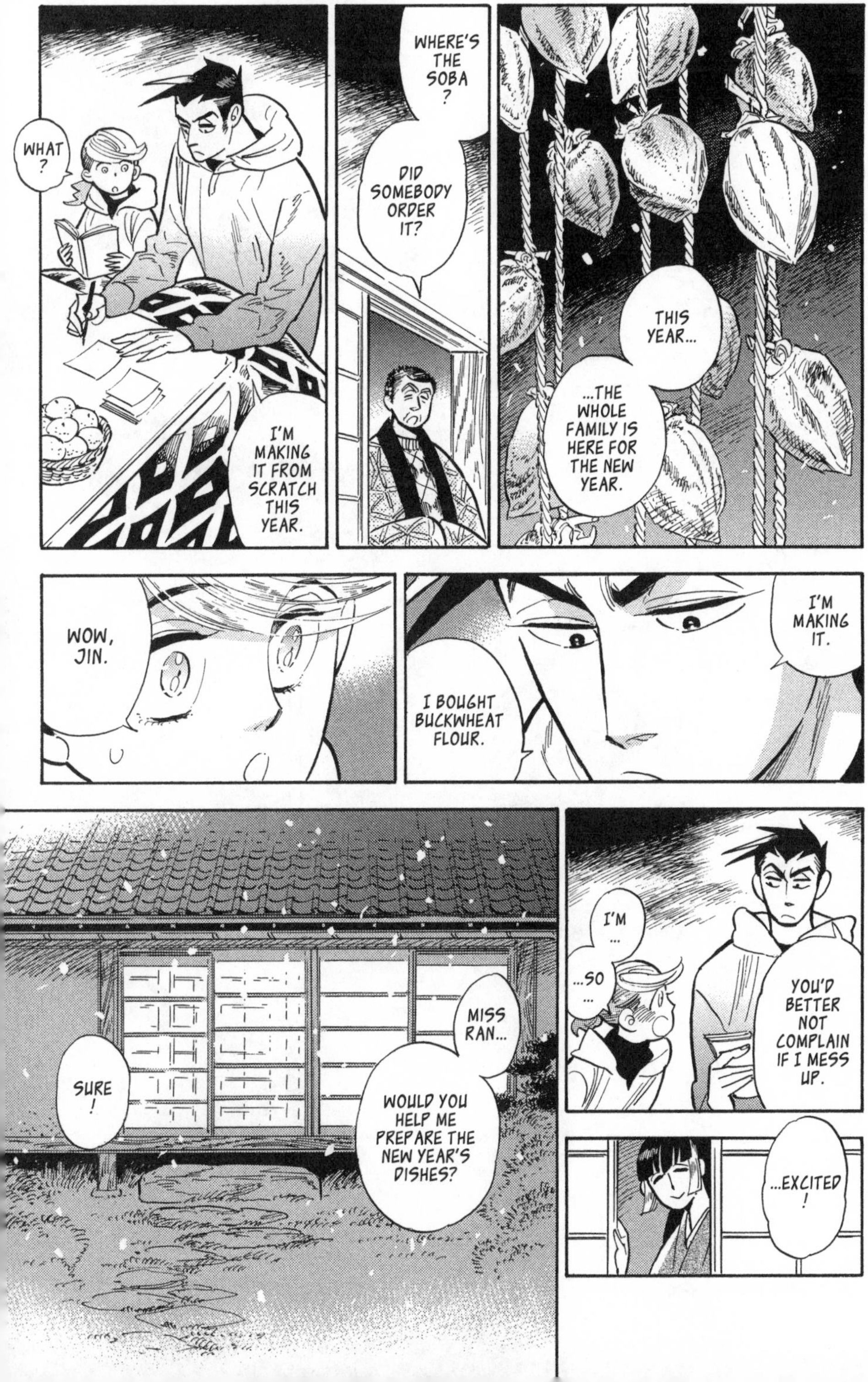
THIS YEAR...
...THE WHOLE FAMILY IS HERE FOR THE NEW YEAR.
WHERE'S THE SOBA?
DID SOMEBODY ORDER IT?
I'M MAKING IT FROM SCRATCH THIS YEAR.
WHAT?
I'M MAKING IT.
I BOUGHT BUCKWHEAT FLOUR.
WOW, JIN.
YOU'D BETTER NOT COMPLAIN IF I MESS UP.
I'M...
...SO...
...EXCITED!
MISS RAN...
WOULD YOU HELP ME PREPARE THE NEW YEAR'S DISHES?
SURE!

OKAY.

LET'S DO THIS.

AHH AHH HO HO OH

LOOKING GOOD.

OH.

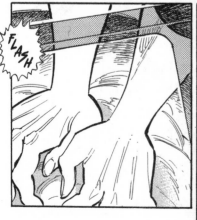

FLASH

FLASH

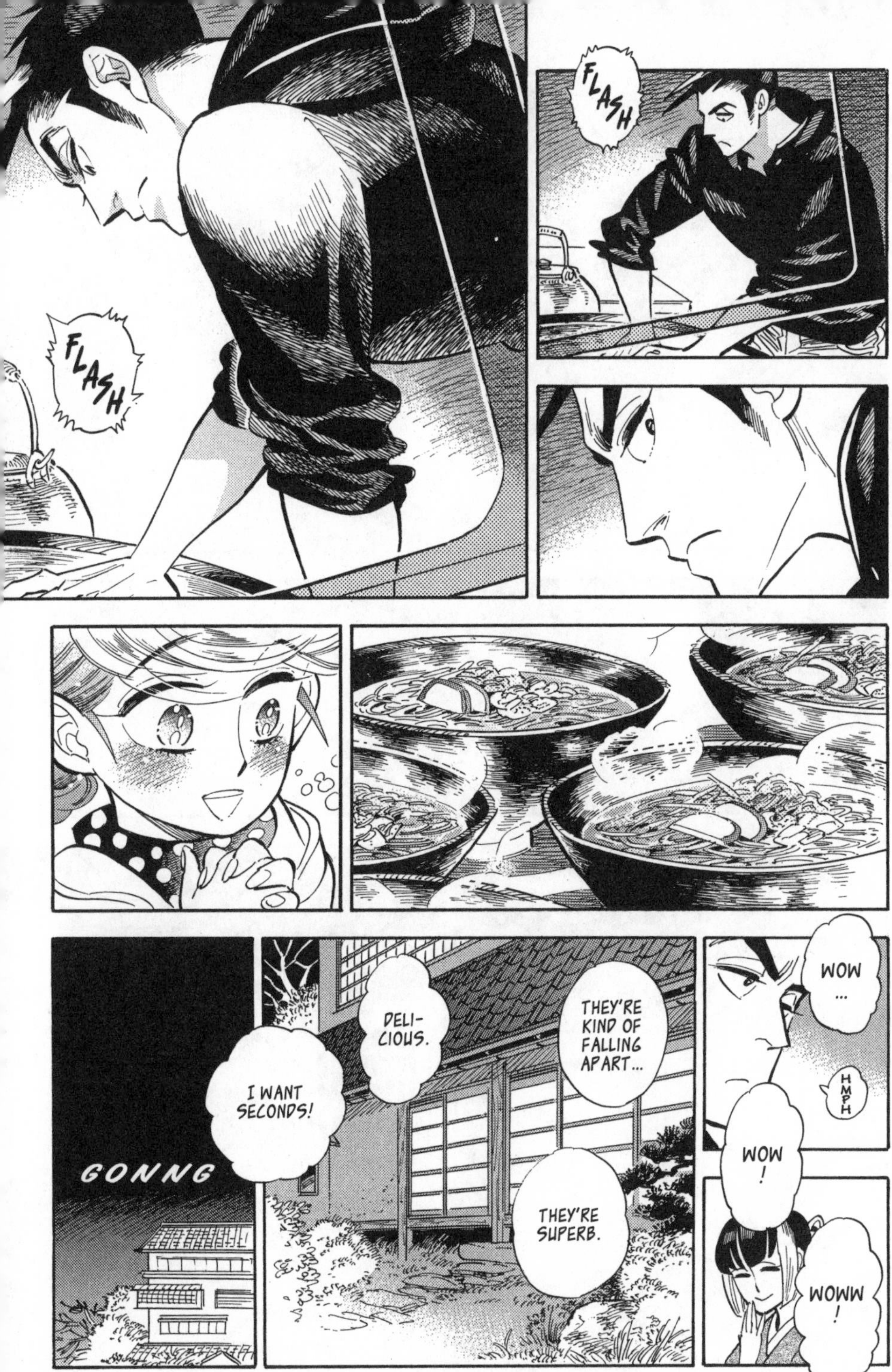
FLASH
FLASH
WOW ...
HMPH
WOW!
WOWW!
THEY'RE KIND OF FALLING APART...
DELI-CIOUS.
I WANT SECONDS!
THEY'RE SUPERB.
GONNG

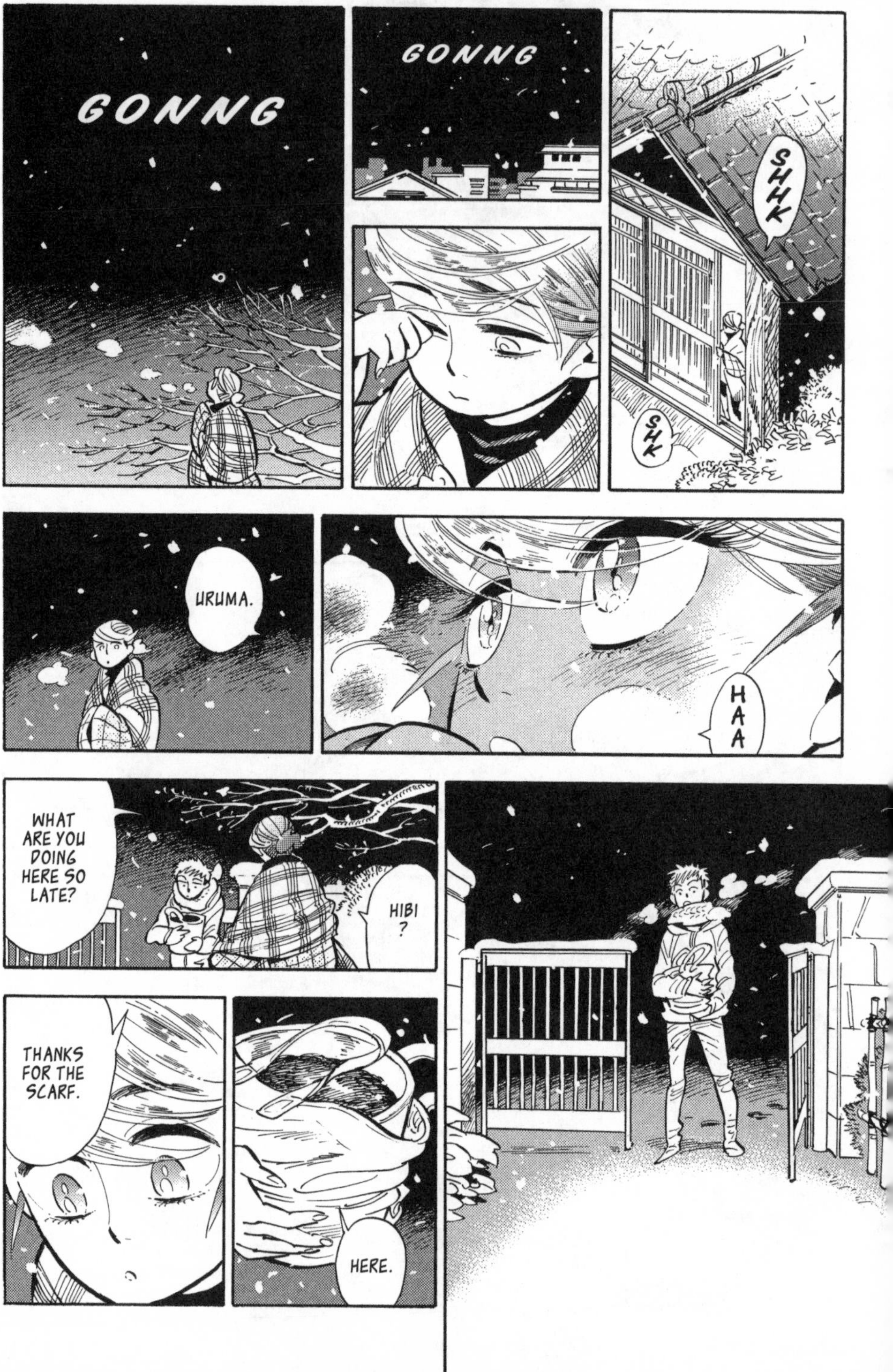
SHHK
SHK
GONNG
GONNG
HAA
URUMA.
HIBI?
WHAT ARE YOU DOING HERE SO LATE?
HERE.
THANKS FOR THE SCARF.

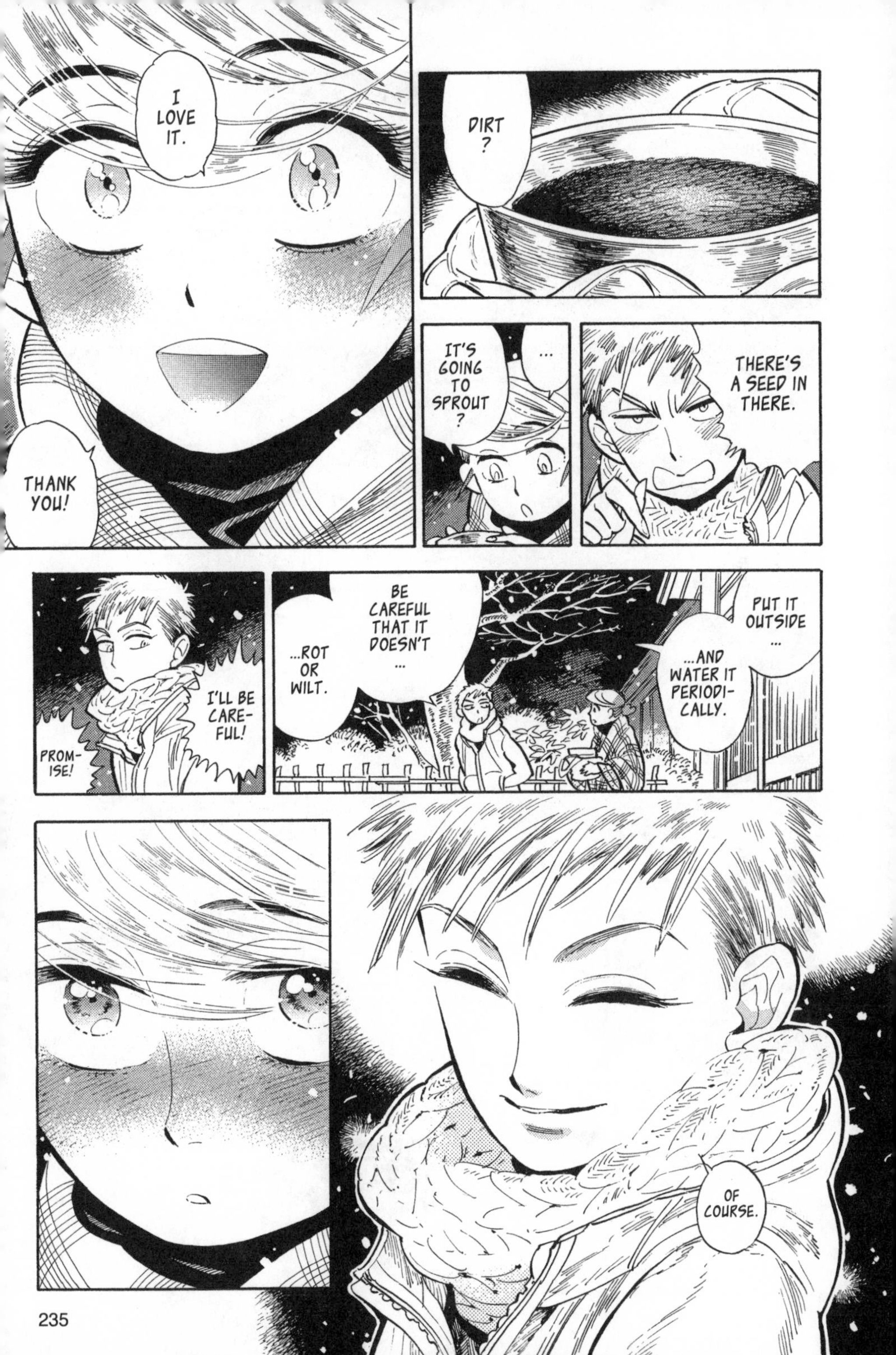
DIRT ?
THERE'S A SEED IN THERE.
...
IT'S GOING TO SPROUT ?
I LOVE IT.
THANK YOU!
PUT IT OUTSIDE ...
...AND WATER IT PERIODICALLY.
BE CAREFUL THAT IT DOESN'T ...
...ROT OR WILT.
I'LL BE CAREFUL!
PROMISE!
OF COURSE.

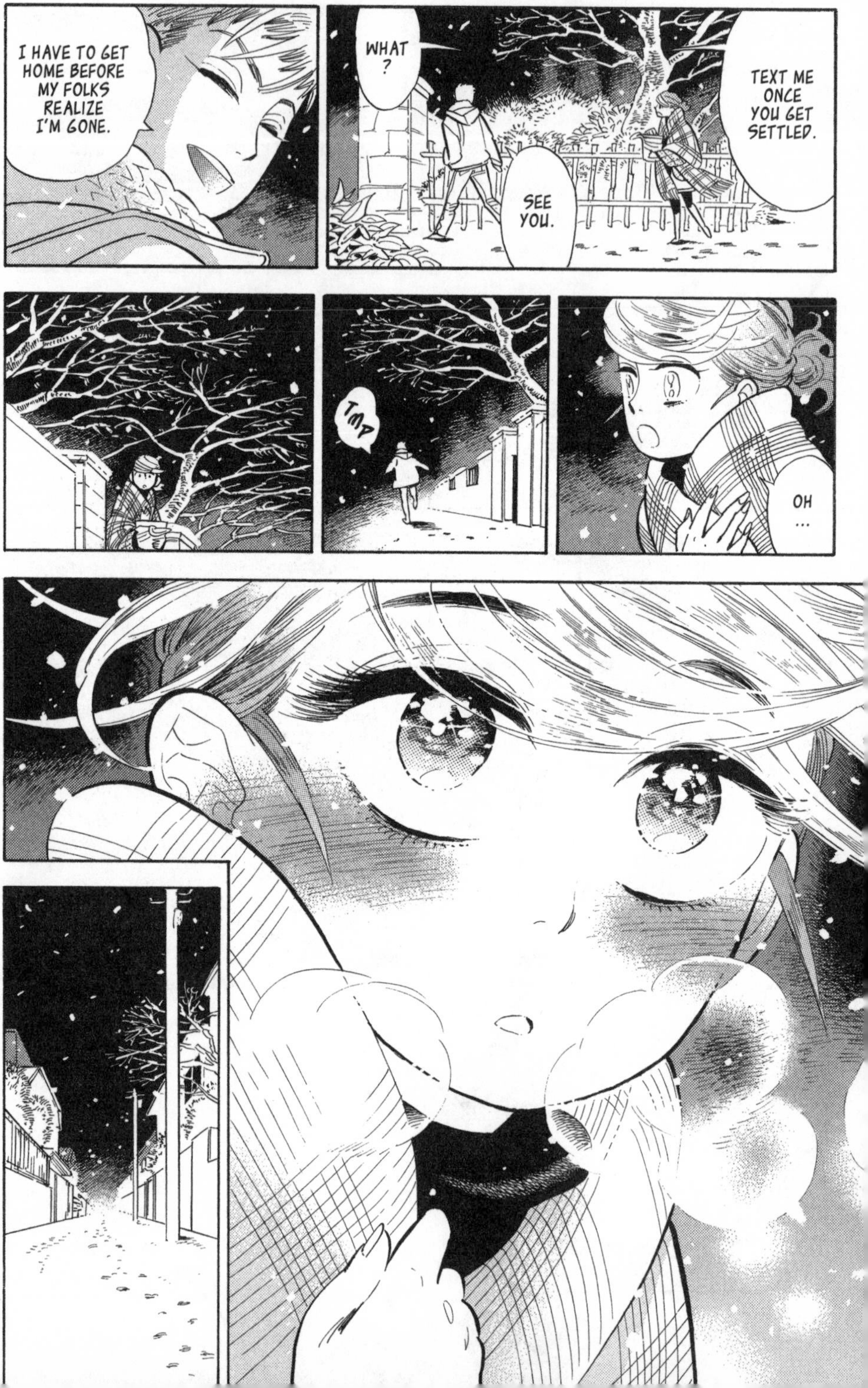
TEXT ME ONCE YOU GET SETTLED.
WHAT ?
SEE YOU.
I HAVE TO GET HOME BEFORE MY FOLKS REALIZE I'M GONE.
OH ...
TMP

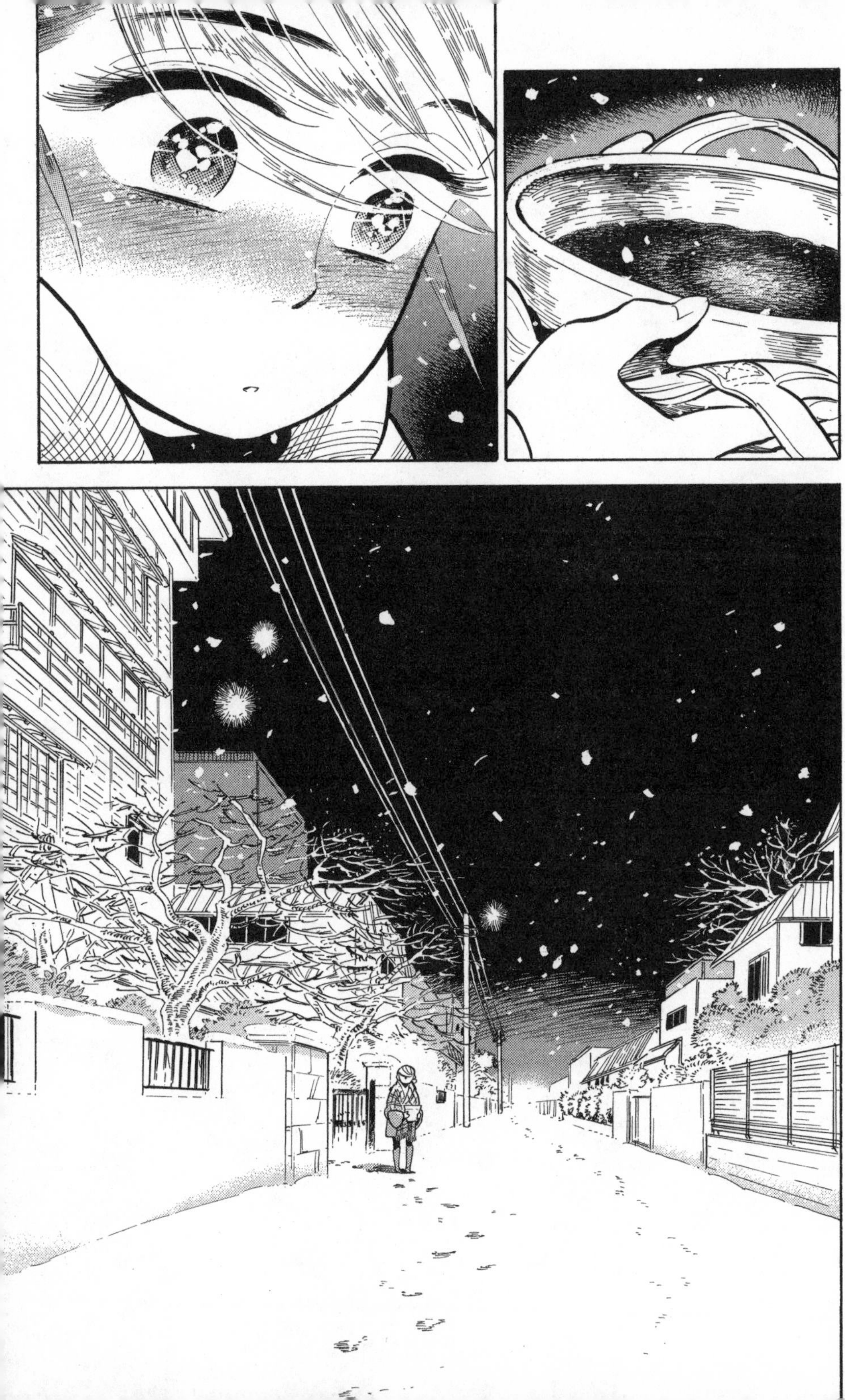

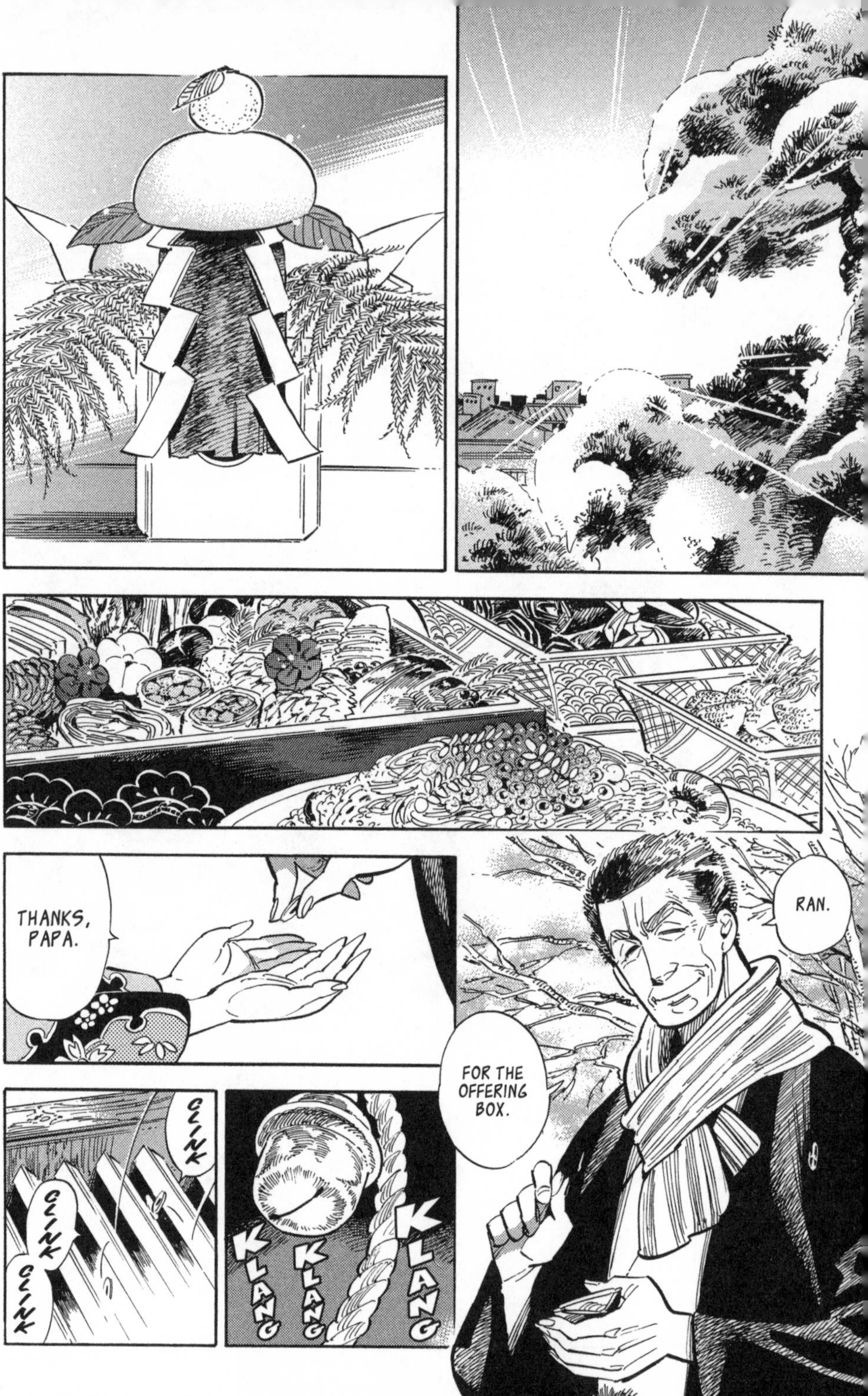
RAN.
FOR THE OFFERING BOX.
THANKS, PAPA.
KLANG
KLANG
KLANG
CLINK
CLINK
CLINK

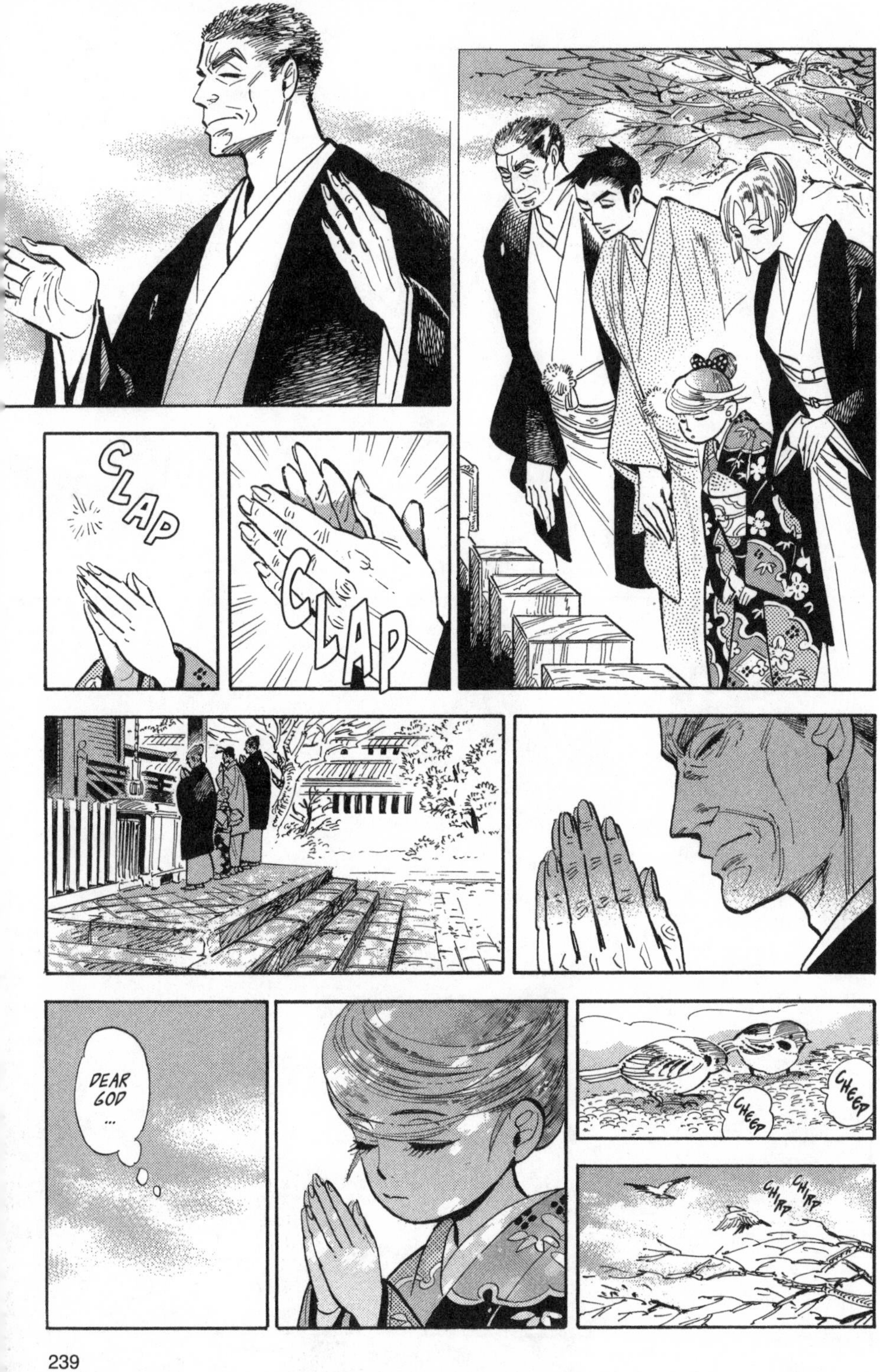
CLAP
CLAP
CHEEP
CHEEP
CHIRP CHIRP
DEAR GOD ...

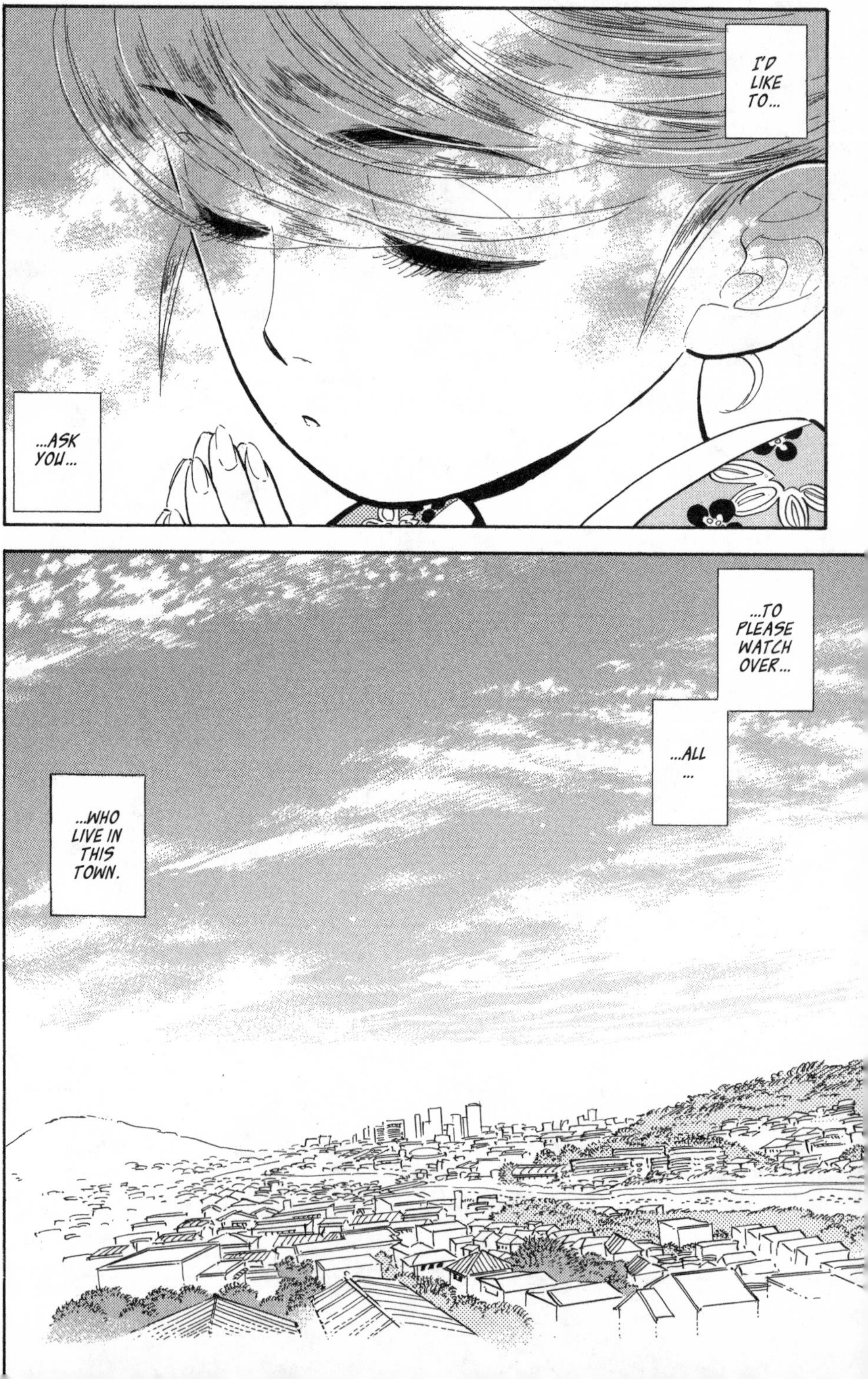
I'D LIKE TO...
...ASK YOU...
...TO PLEASE WATCH OVER...
...ALL ...
...WHO LIVE IN THIS TOWN.

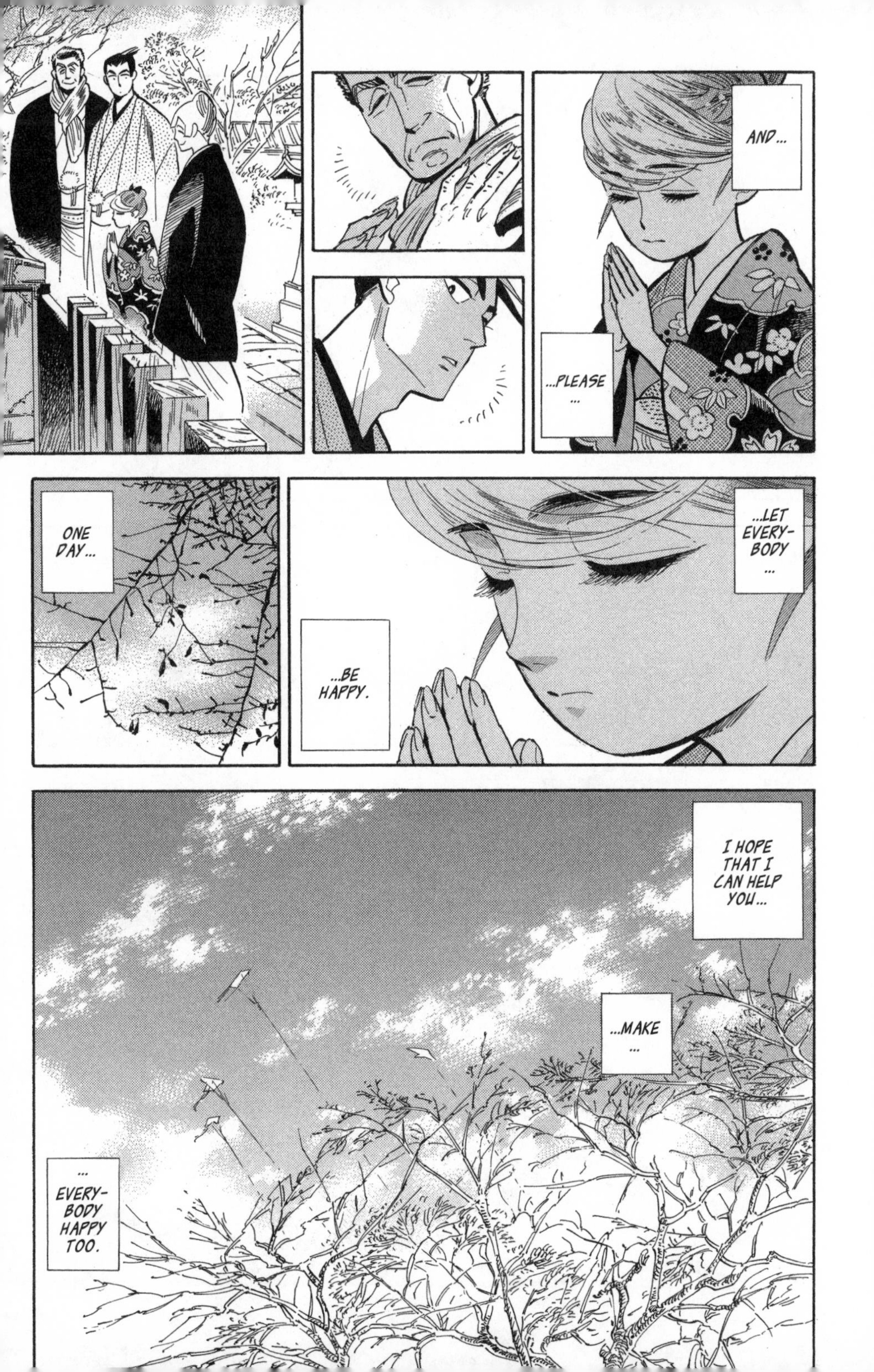
AND...
...PLEASE ...
...LET EVERY-BODY ...
...BE HAPPY.
ONE DAY...
I HOPE THAT I CAN HELP YOU...
...MAKE ...
... EVERY-BODY HAPPY TOO.

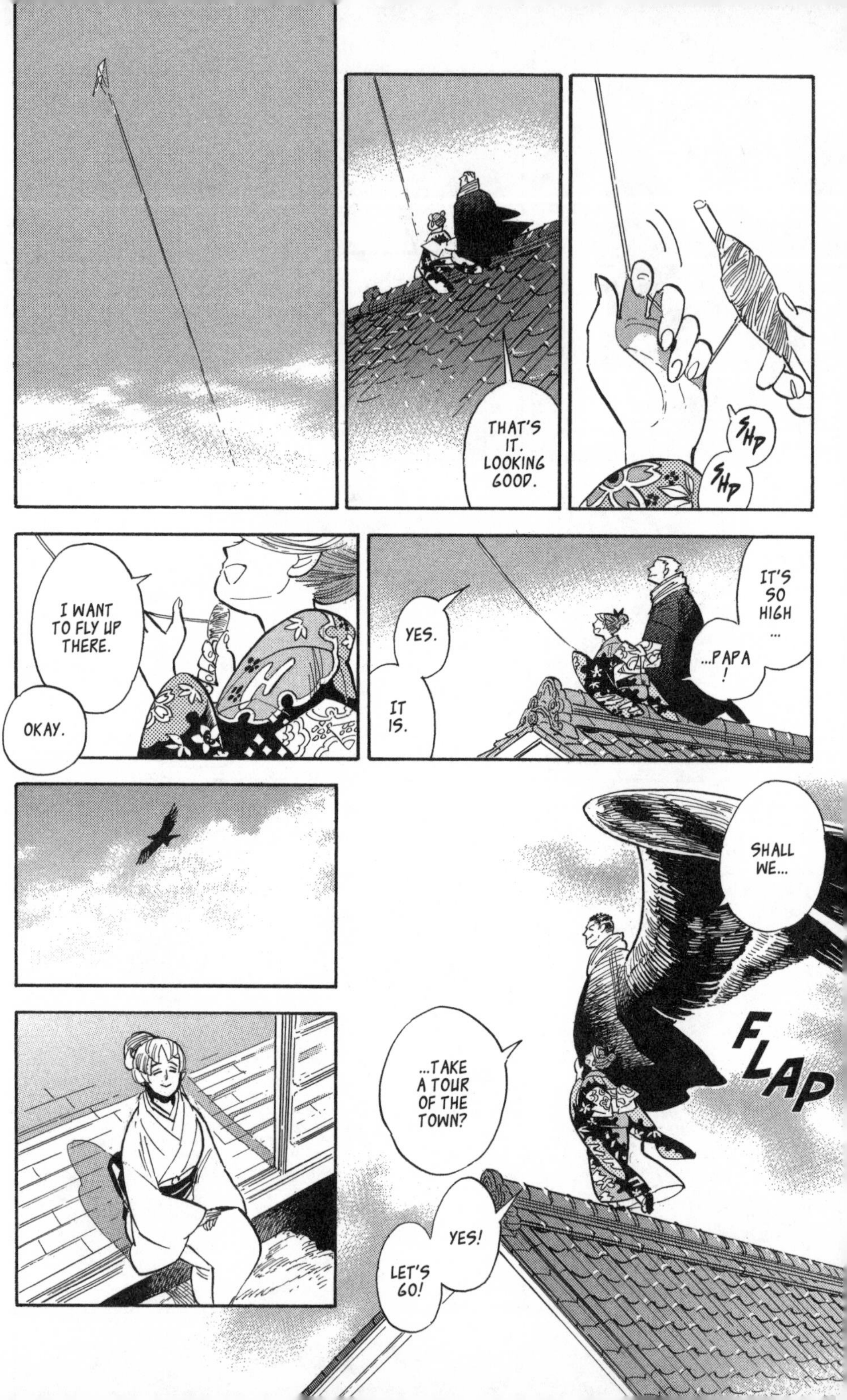
SHP
SHP
THAT'S IT. LOOKING GOOD.
IT'S SO HIGH...
...PAPA!
YES.
IT IS.
I WANT TO FLY UP THERE.
OKAY.
SHALL WE...
FLAP
...TAKE A TOUR OF THE TOWN?
YES!
LET'S GO!

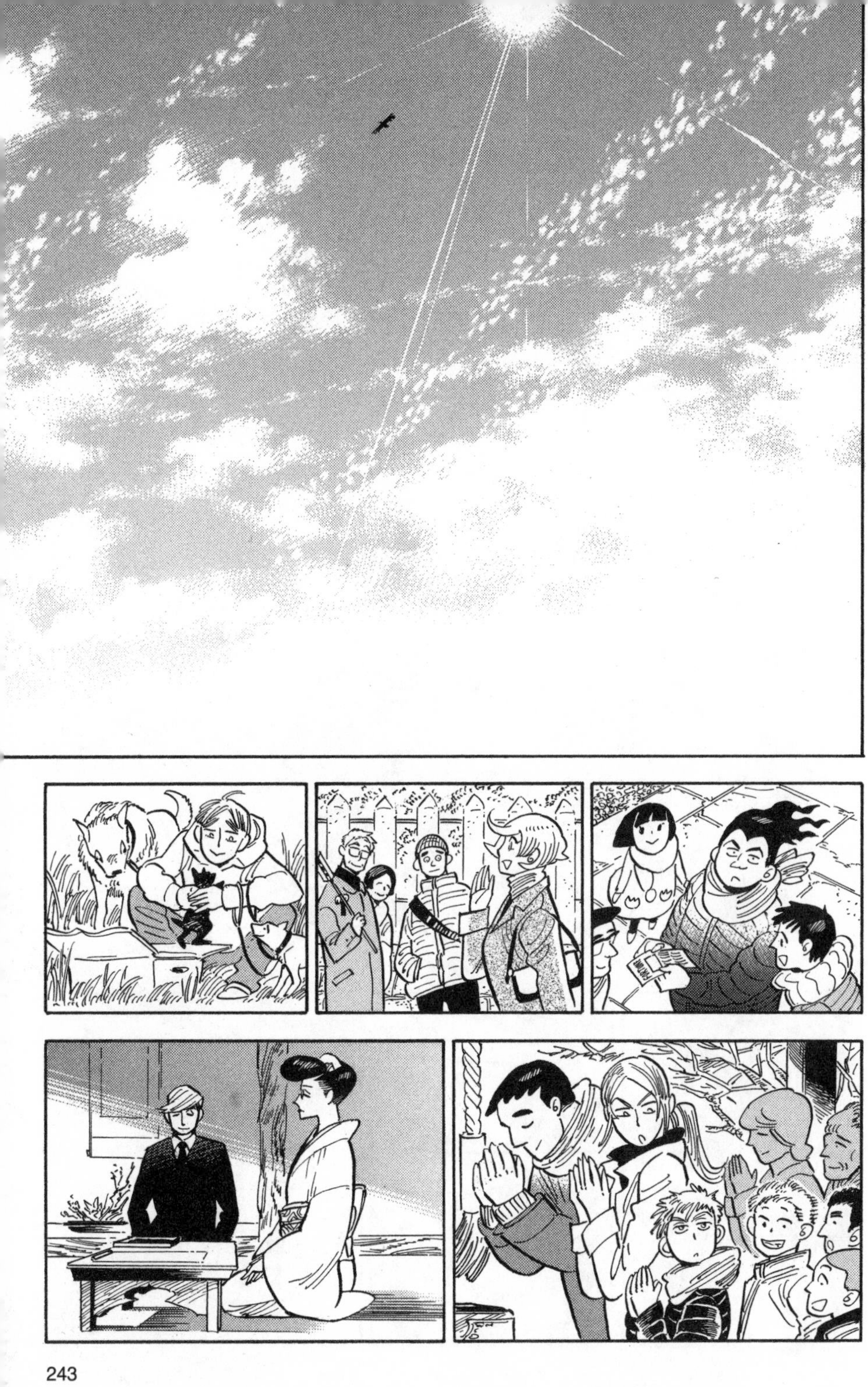

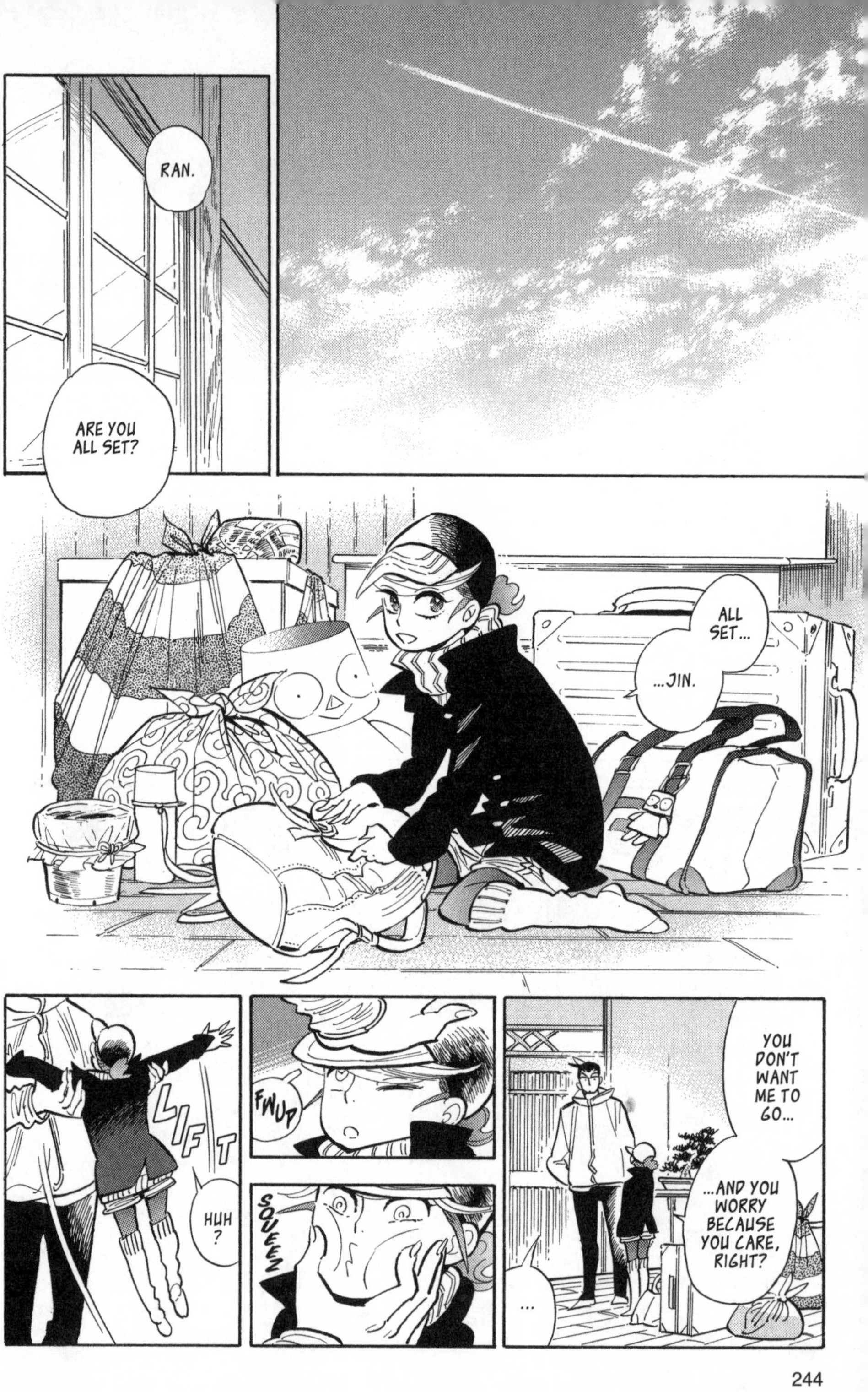

RAN.
ARE YOU ALL SET?
ALL SET...
...JIN.
YOU DON'T WANT ME TO GO...
...AND YOU WORRY BECAUSE YOU CARE, RIGHT?
...
FWUP
SQUEEZ
LIFT
HUH?

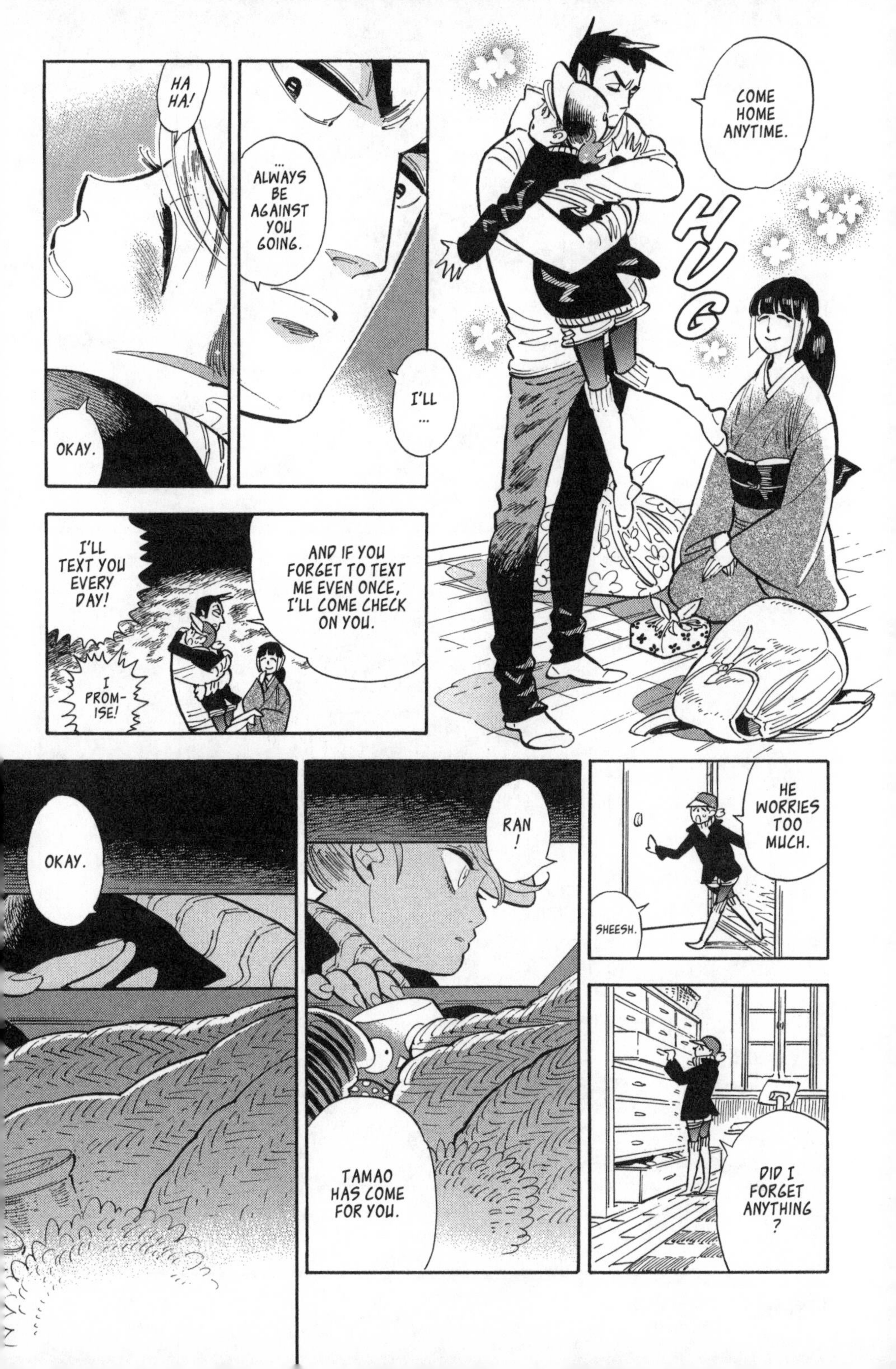
COME HOME ANYTIME.
HUG
I'LL ...
... ALWAYS BE AGAINST YOU GOING.
HA HA!
OKAY.
AND IF YOU FORGET TO TEXT ME EVEN ONCE, I'LL COME CHECK ON YOU.
I'LL TEXT YOU EVERY DAY!
I PROMISE!
HE WORRIES TOO MUCH.
SHEESH.
DID I FORGET ANYTHING?
RAN!
TAMAO HAS COME FOR YOU.
OKAY.

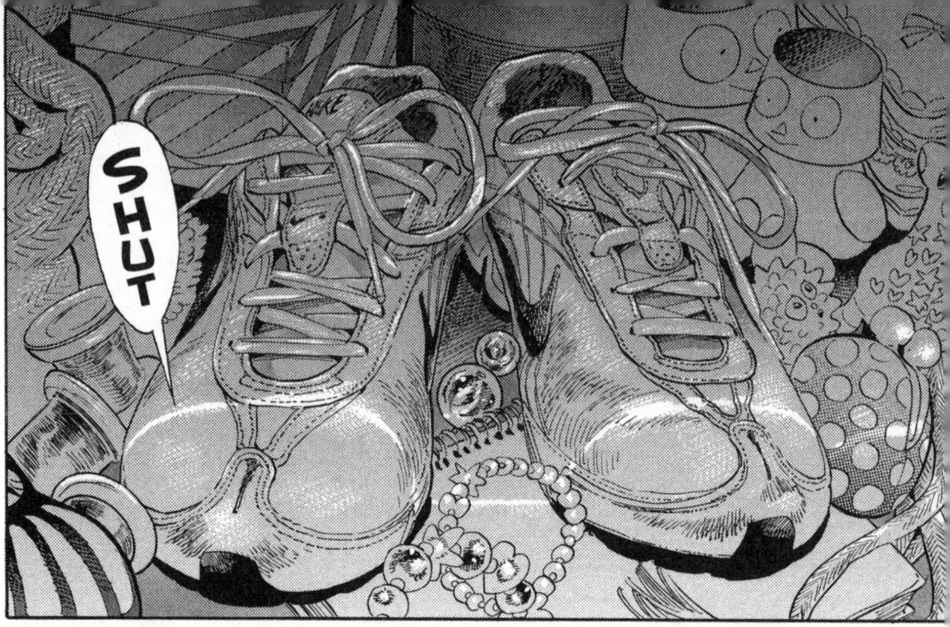
SHUT

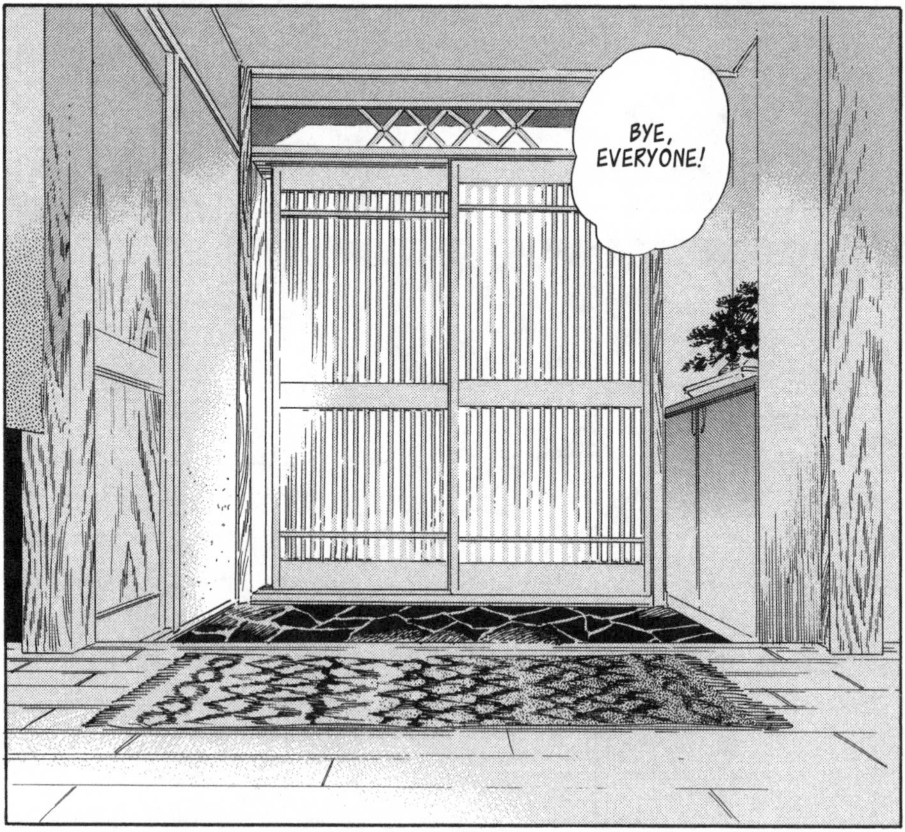
BYE, EVERYONE!

Chapter 44 / The End

Chapter 45

The Land of New Leaves

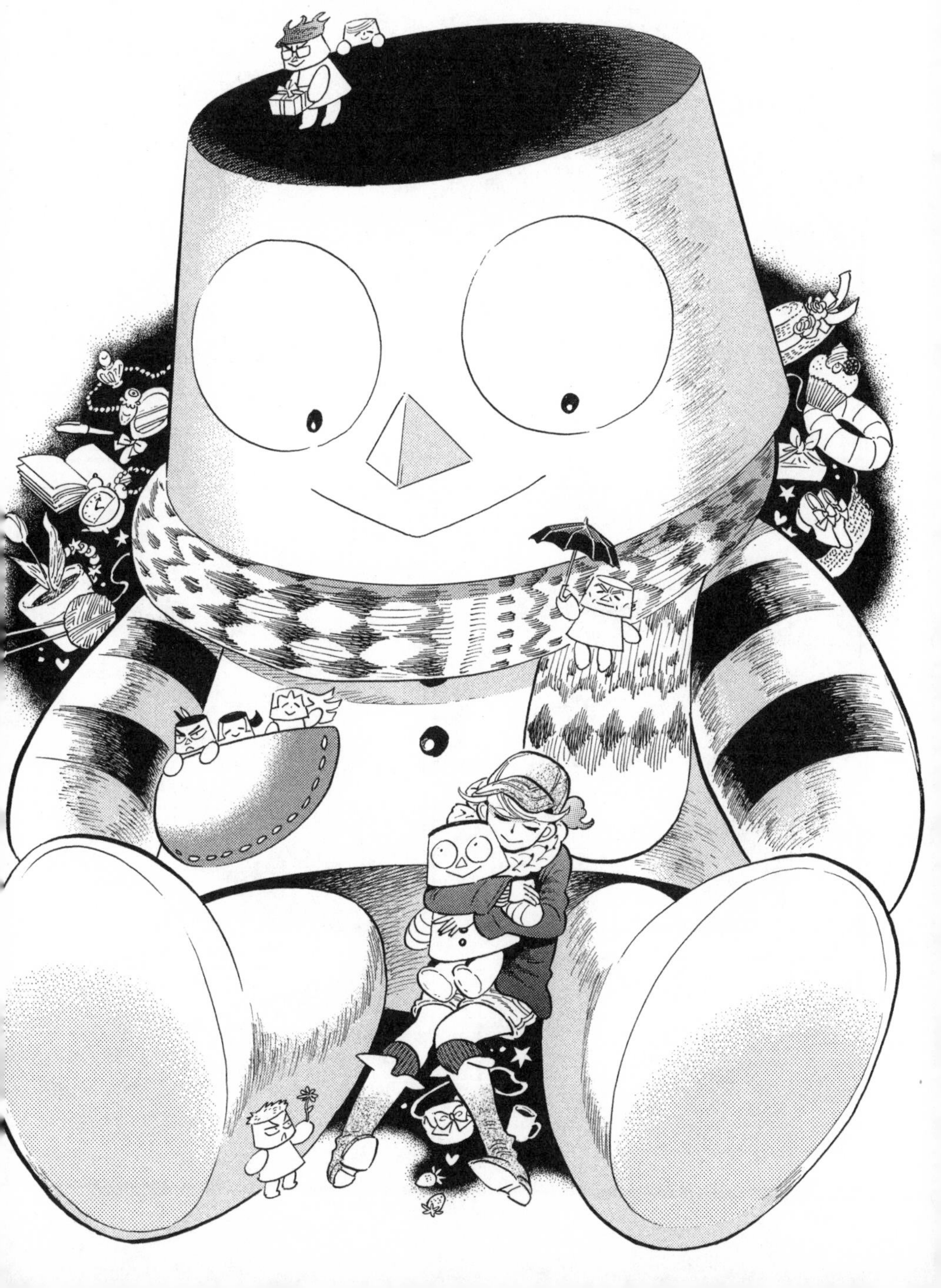

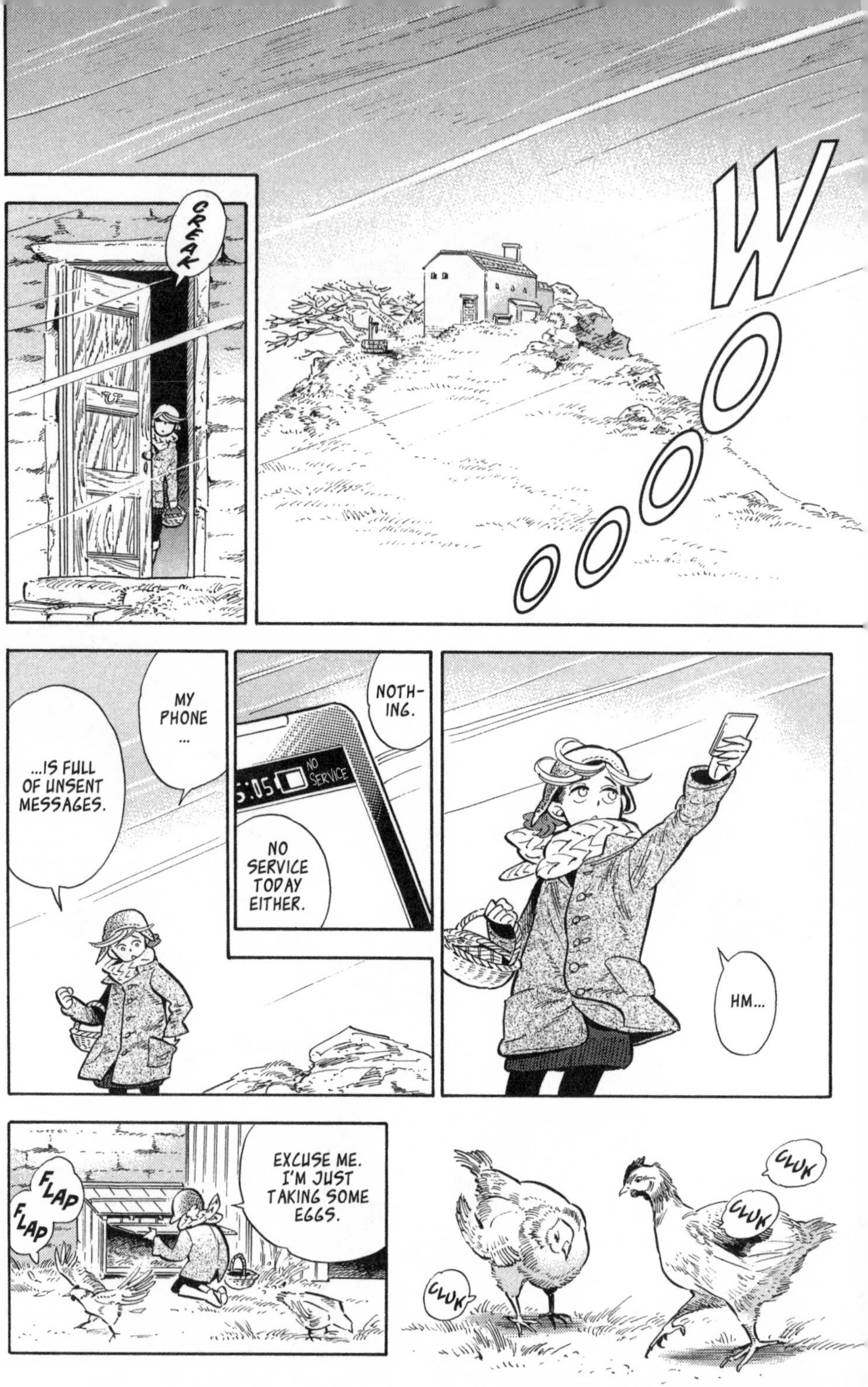
WOOOO
CREAK
HM...
NOTH-ING.
5:05 NO SERVICE
NO SERVICE TODAY EITHER.
MY PHONE ...
...IS FULL OF UNSENT MESSAGES.
CLUK
CLUK
CLUK
EXCUSE ME. I'M JUST TAKING SOME EGGS.
FLAP
FLAP

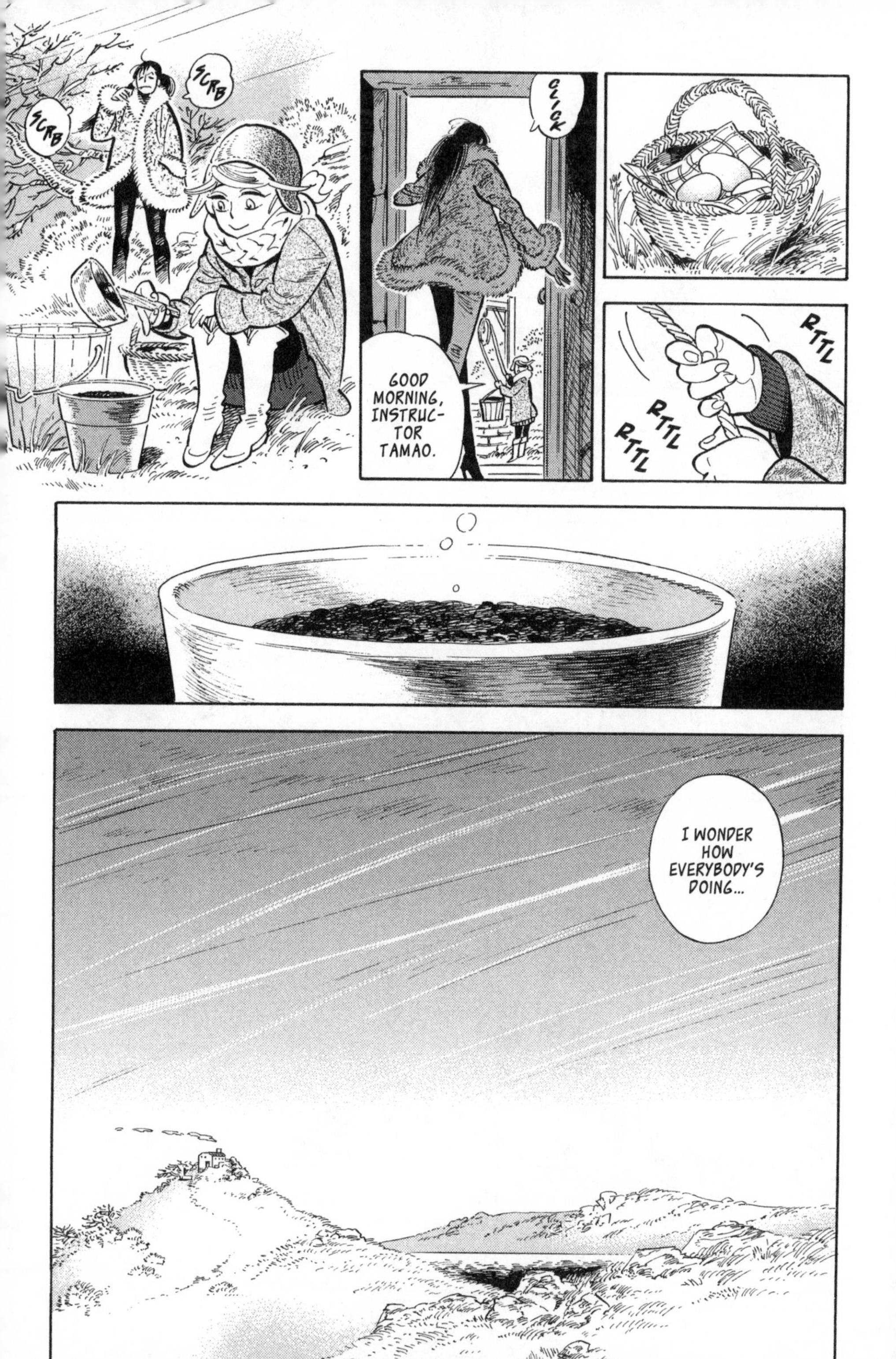
RTTL
RTTL
RTTL
CLICK
GOOD MORNING, INSTRUCTOR TAMAO.
SCRB
SCRB
I WONDER HOW EVERYBODY'S DOING...

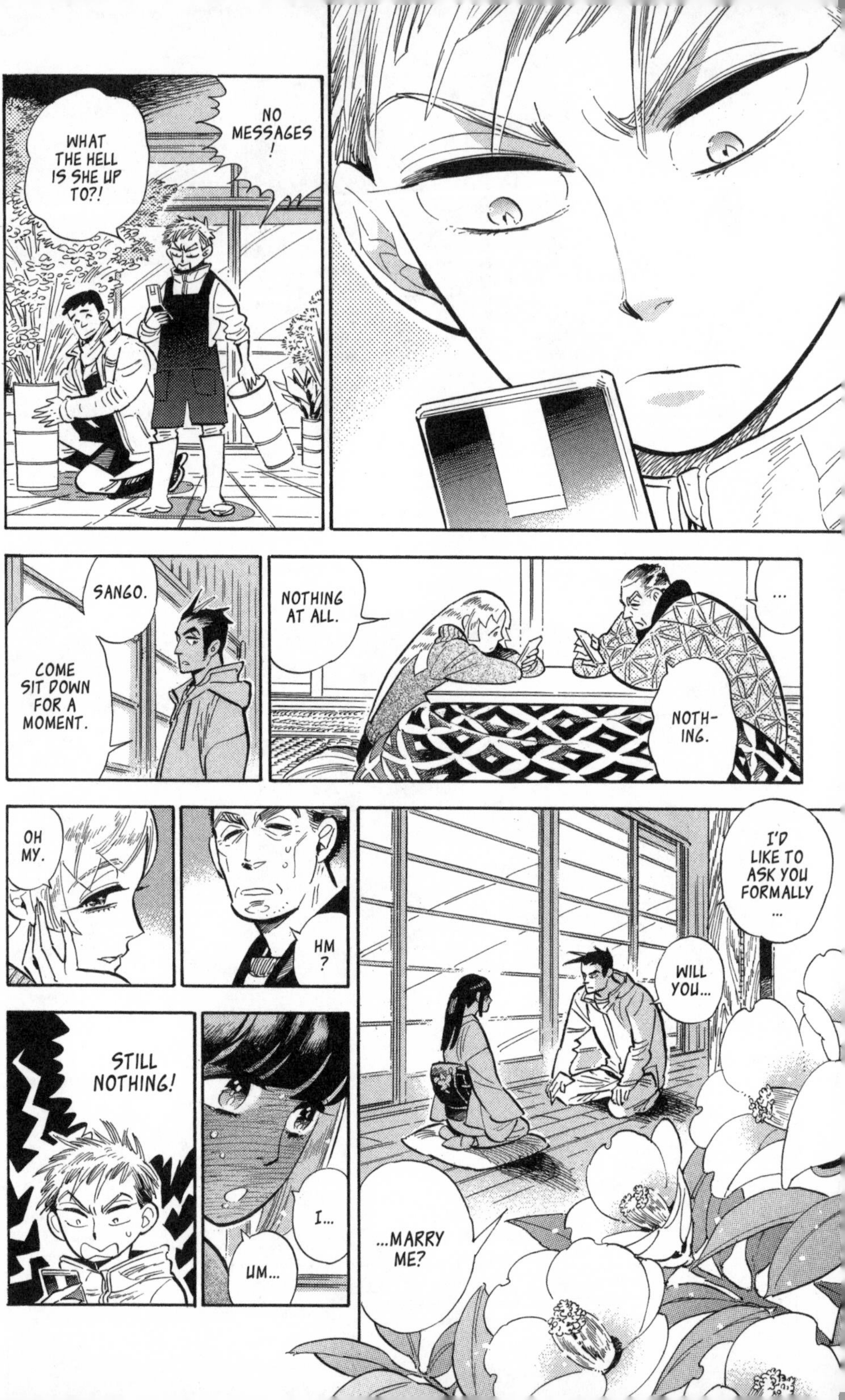
NO MESSAGES!
WHAT THE HELL IS SHE UP TO?!
...
NOTHING AT ALL.
NOTH-ING.
SANGO.
COME SIT DOWN FOR A MOMENT.
I'D LIKE TO ASK YOU FORMALLY...
WILL YOU...
...MARRY ME?
HM?
OH MY.
I...
UM...
STILL NOTHING!

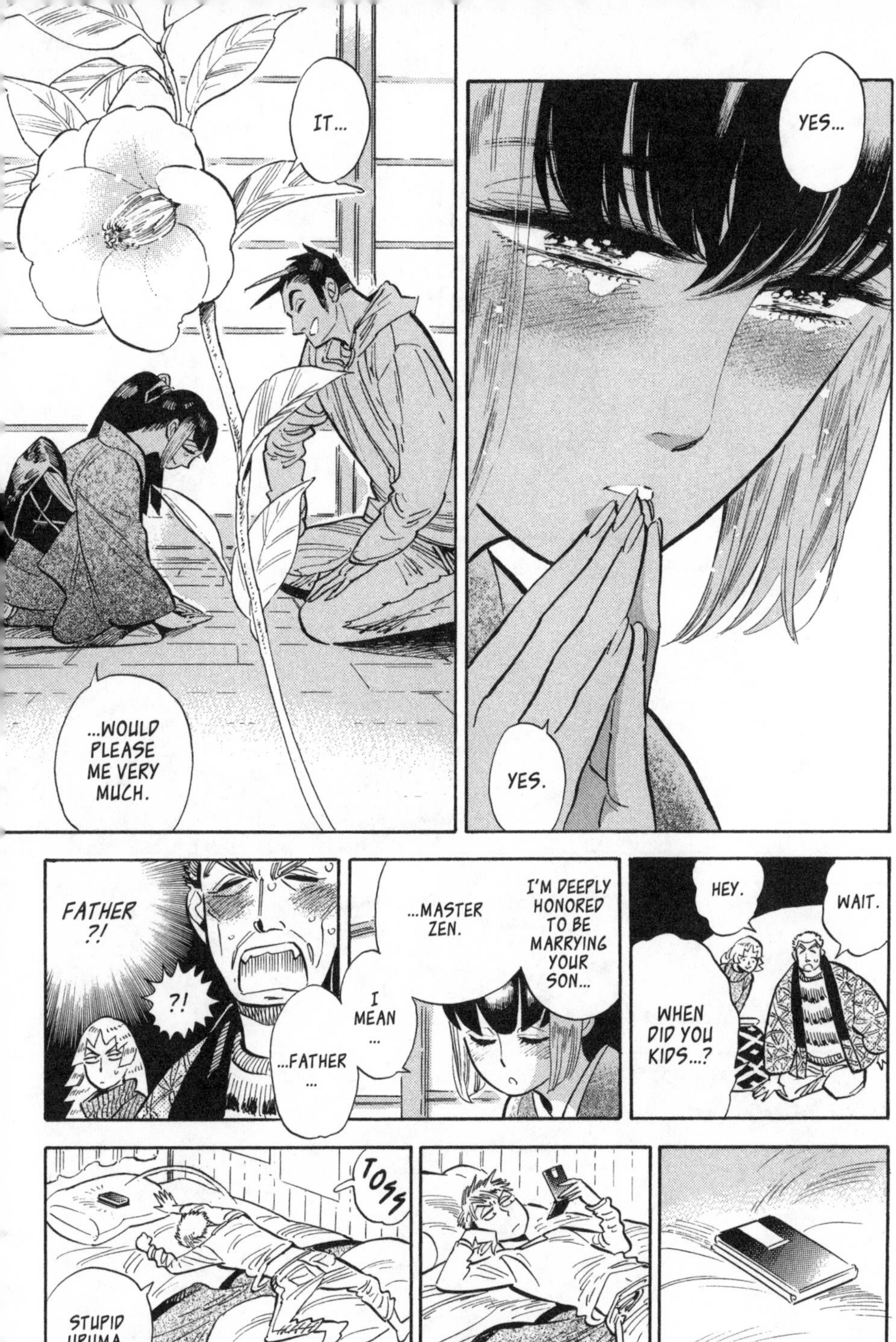
YES...
YES.
IT...
...WOULD PLEASE ME VERY MUCH.
WAIT.
HEY.
WHEN DID YOU KIDS...?
I'M DEEPLY HONORED TO BE MARRYING YOUR SON...
...MASTER ZEN.
I MEAN ...
...FATHER ...
FATHER ?!
?!
TOSS
STUPID URUMA.

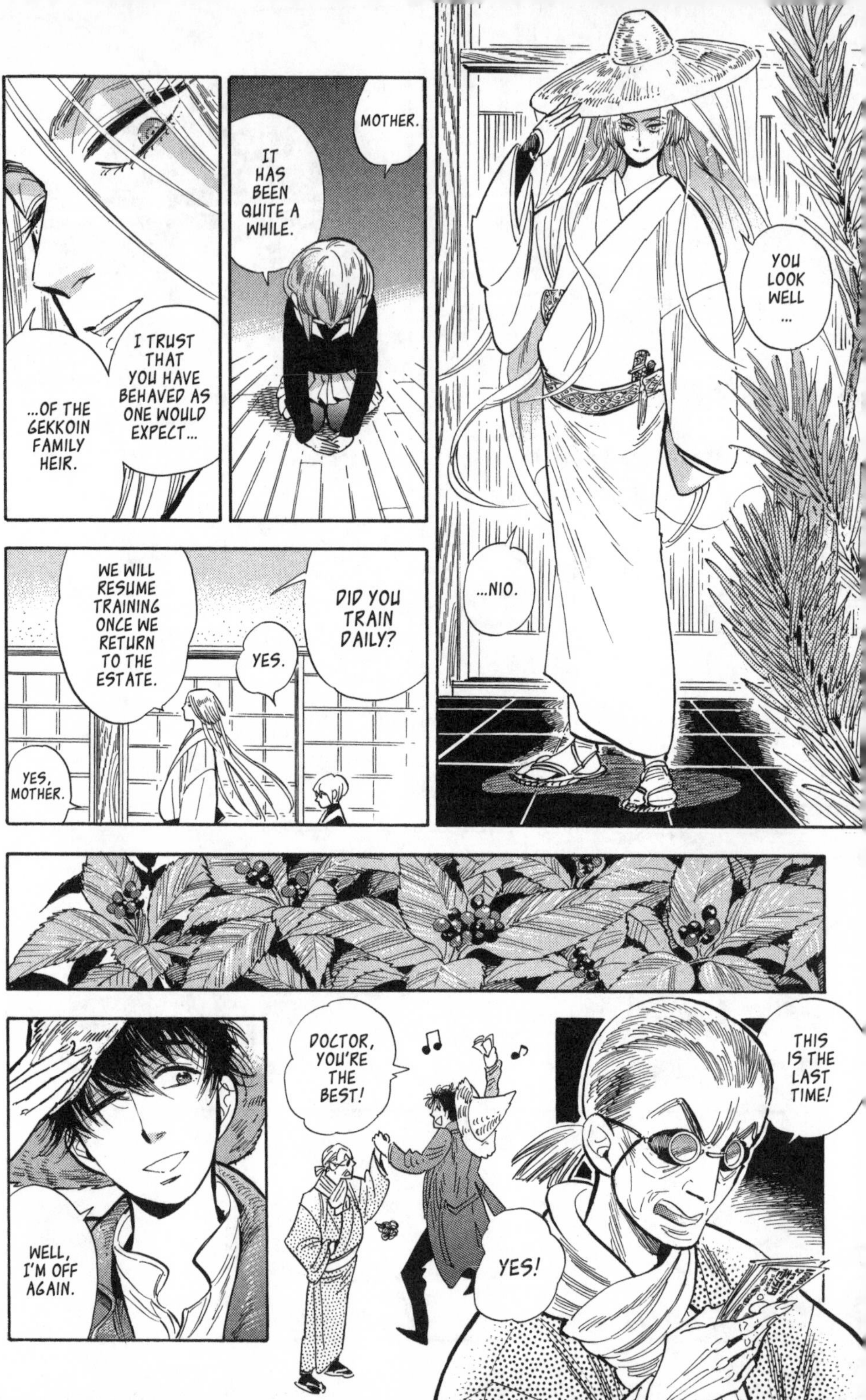
YOU LOOK WELL ...
...NIO.
MOTHER.
IT HAS BEEN QUITE A WHILE.
I TRUST THAT YOU HAVE BEHAVED AS ONE WOULD EXPECT...
...OF THE GEKKOIN FAMILY HEIR.
DID YOU TRAIN DAILY?
YES.
WE WILL RESUME TRAINING ONCE WE RETURN TO THE ESTATE.
YES, MOTHER.
THIS IS THE LAST TIME!
YES!
DOCTOR, YOU'RE THE BEST!
WELL, I'M OFF AGAIN.

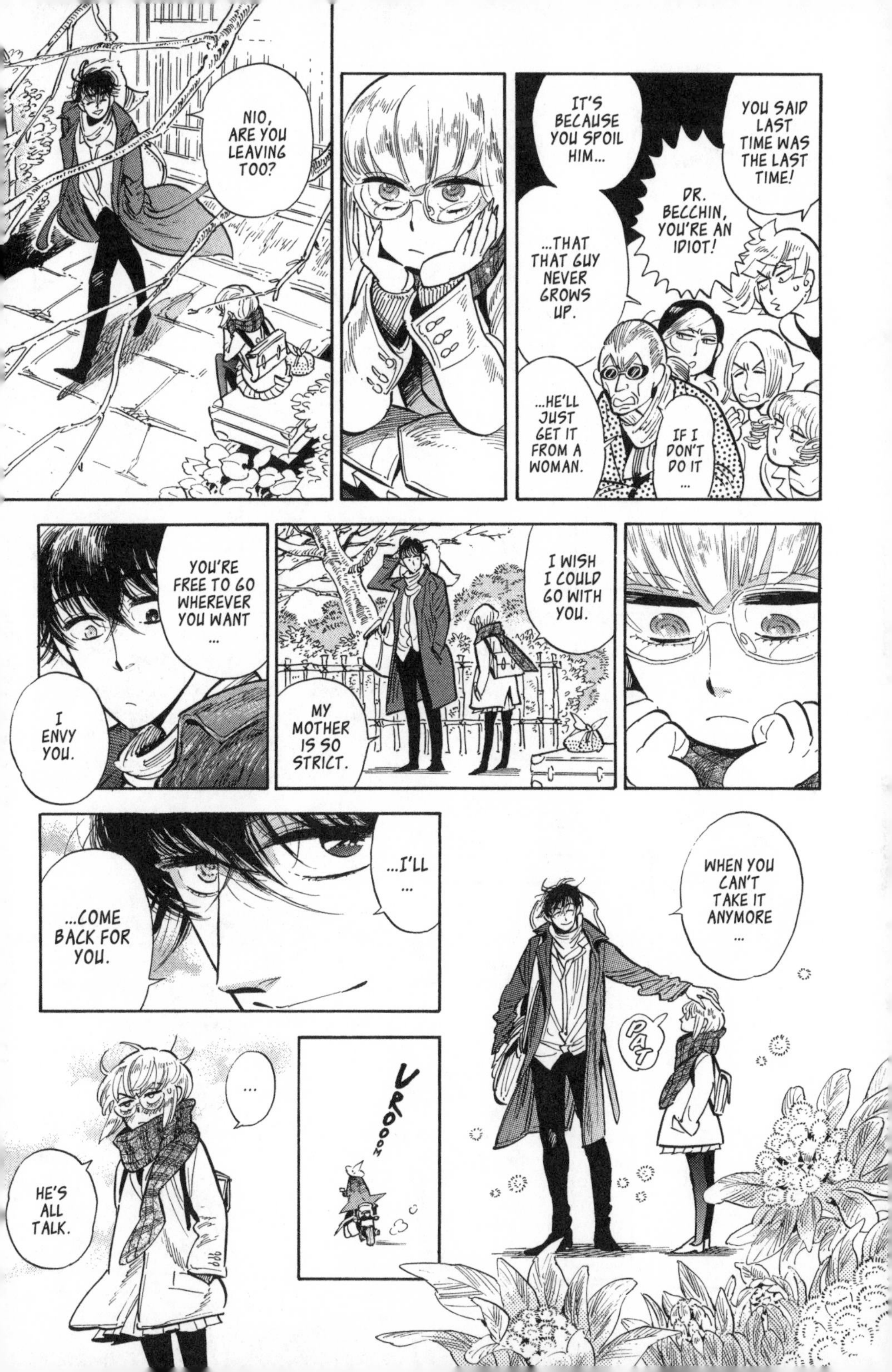
YOU SAID LAST TIME WAS THE LAST TIME!
DR. BECCHIN, YOU'RE AN IDIOT!
IT'S BECAUSE YOU SPOIL HIM...
...THAT THAT GUY NEVER GROWS UP.
IF I DON'T DO IT ...
...HE'LL JUST GET IT FROM A WOMAN.
NIO, ARE YOU LEAVING TOO?
I WISH I COULD GO WITH YOU.
MY MOTHER IS SO STRICT.
YOU'RE FREE TO GO WHEREVER YOU WANT ...
I ENVY YOU.
WHEN YOU CAN'T TAKE IT ANYMORE ...
PAT
...I'LL ...
...COME BACK FOR YOU.
VROOOOOM
...
HE'S ALL TALK.

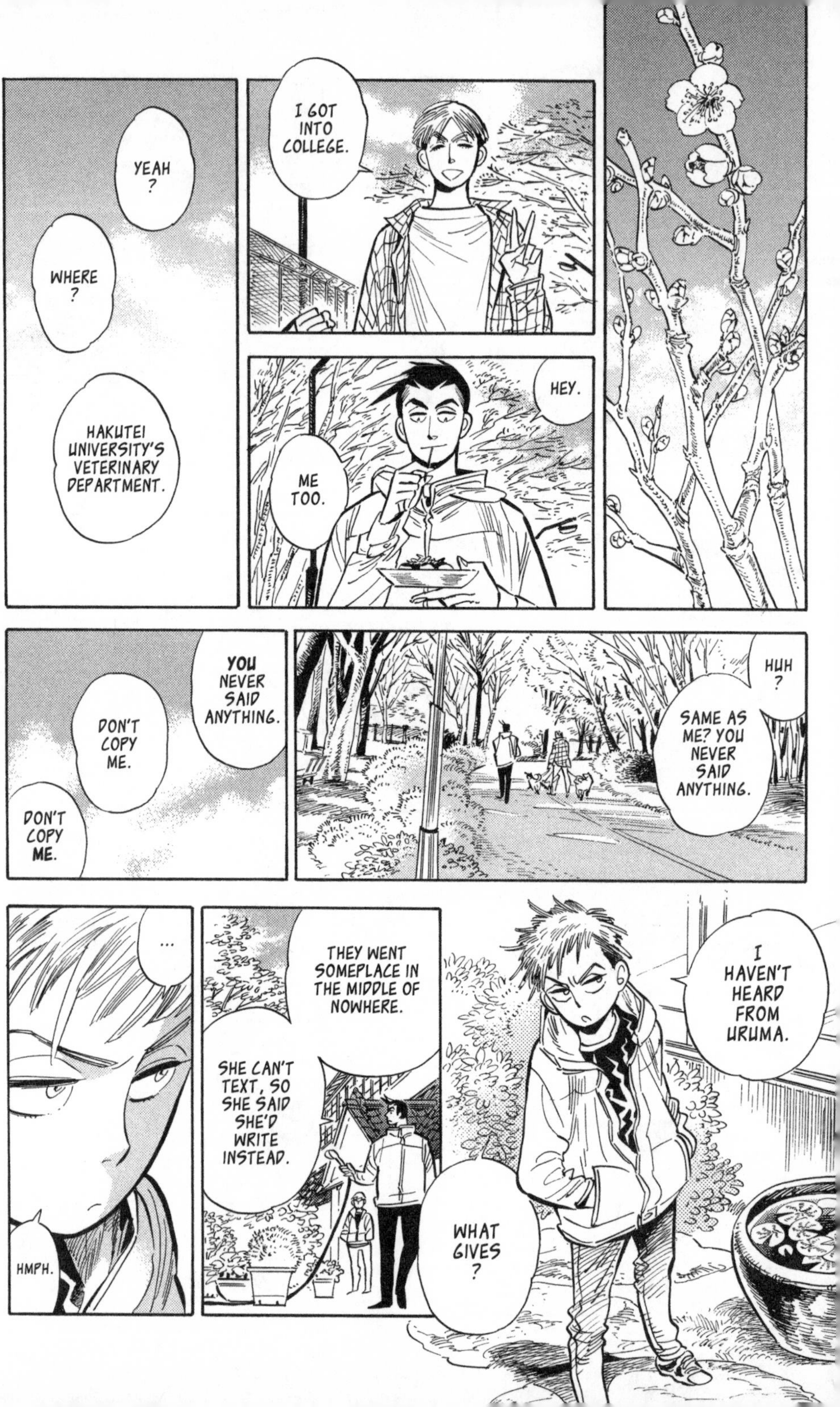
I GOT INTO COLLEGE.
HEY.
ME TOO.
YEAH?
WHERE?
HAKUTEI UNIVERSITY'S VETERINARY DEPARTMENT.
HUH?
SAME AS ME? YOU NEVER SAID ANYTHING.
YOU NEVER SAID ANYTHING.
DON'T COPY ME.
DON'T COPY ME.
I HAVEN'T HEARD FROM URUMA.
WHAT GIVES?
THEY WENT SOMEPLACE IN THE MIDDLE OF NOWHERE.
SHE CAN'T TEXT, SO SHE SAID SHE'D WRITE INSTEAD.
...
HMPH.

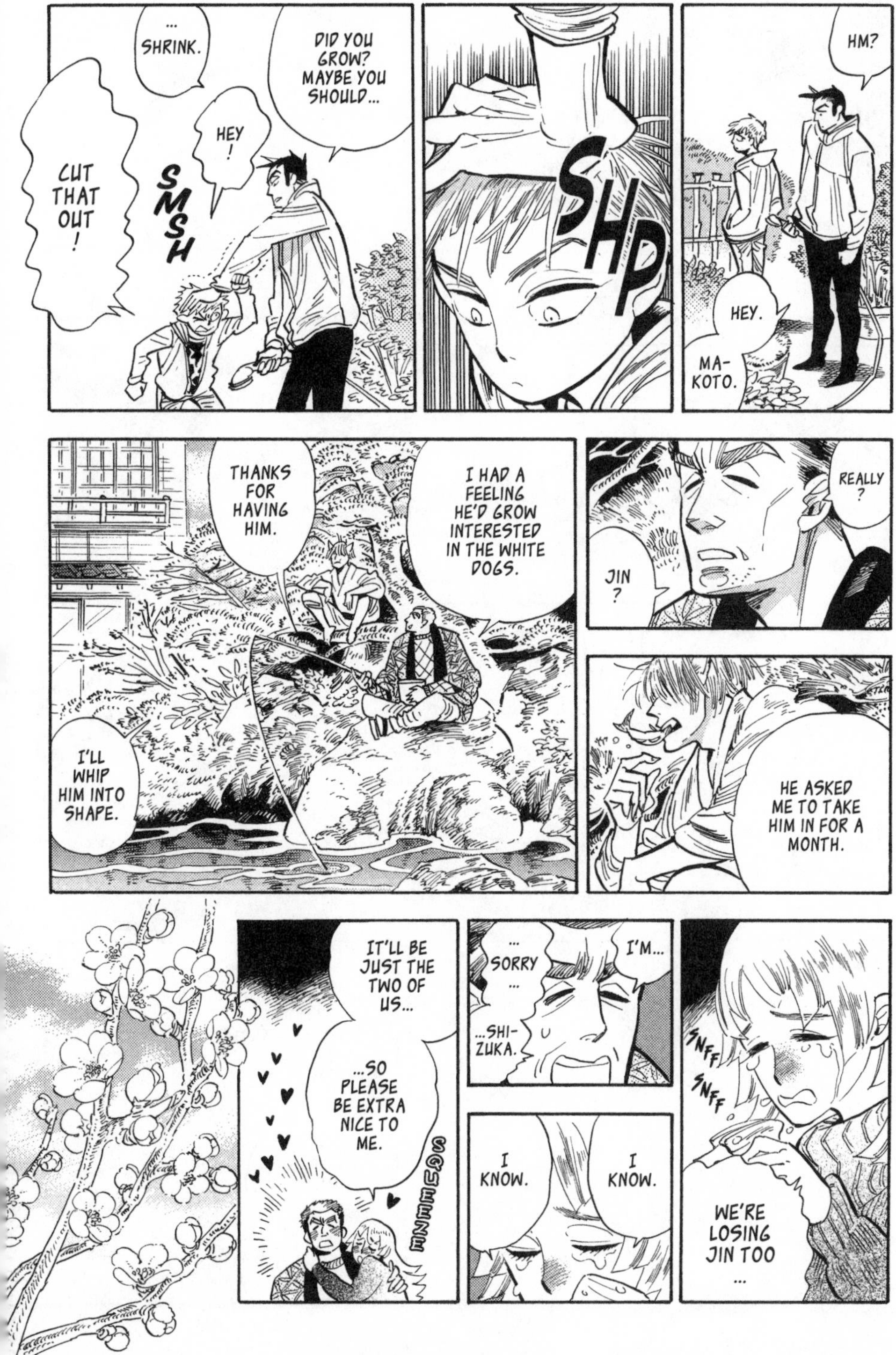
HEY.
MA-KOTO.
HM?
SHP
DID YOU GROW? MAYBE YOU SHOULD...
...SHRINK.
HEY!
SMSH
CUT THAT OUT!
REALLY?
JIN?
HE ASKED ME TO TAKE HIM IN FOR A MONTH.
I HAD A FEELING HE'D GROW INTERESTED IN THE WHITE DOGS.
THANKS FOR HAVING HIM.
I'LL WHIP HIM INTO SHAPE.
SNFF
SNFF
WE'RE LOSING JIN TOO...
I'M...
...SORRY...
...SHI-ZUKA.
I KNOW.
I KNOW.
IT'LL BE JUST THE TWO OF US...
...SO PLEASE BE EXTRA NICE TO ME.
SQUEEEZE

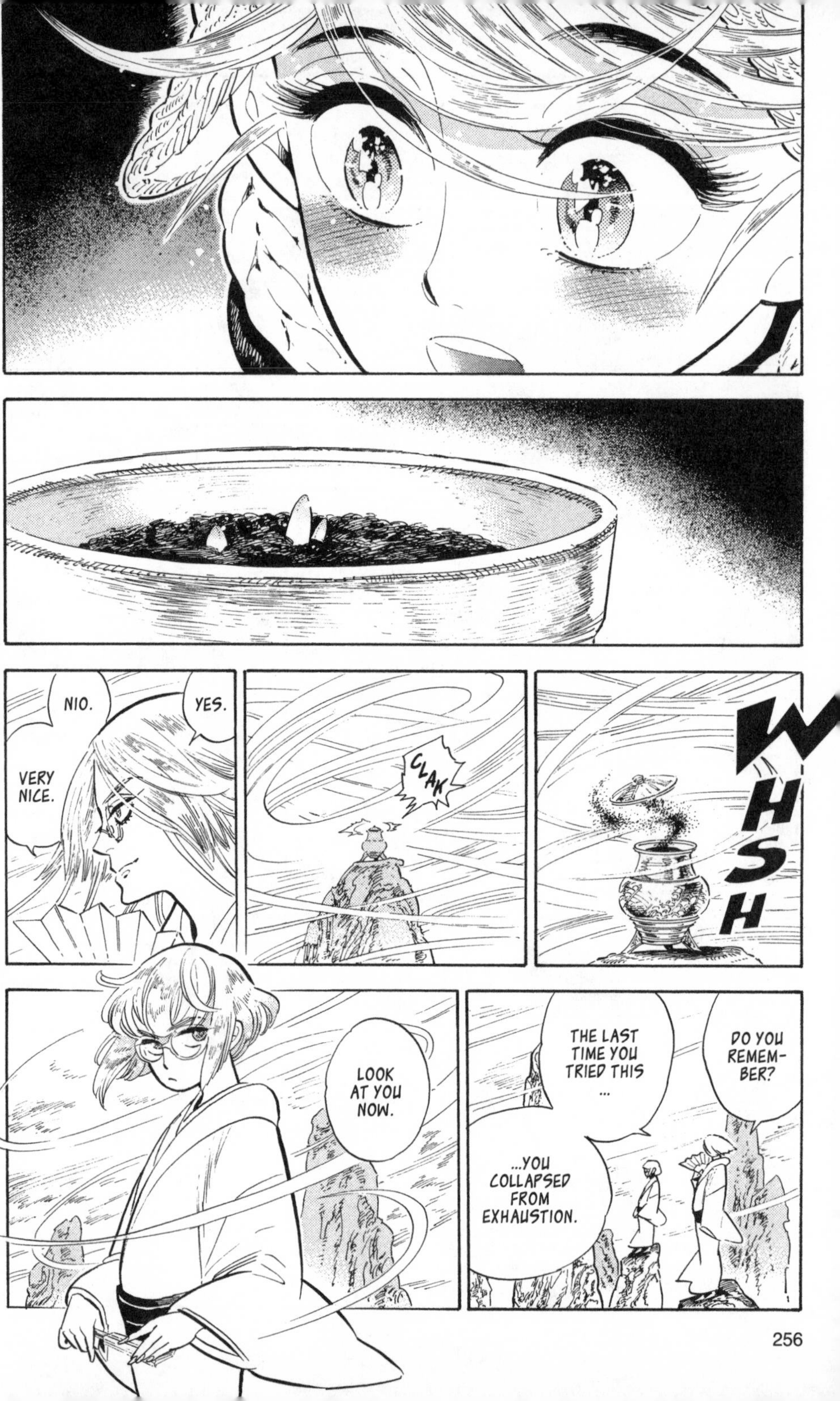

WHSH
CLAK
YES.
NIO.
VERY NICE.
DO YOU REMEM-BER?
THE LAST TIME YOU TRIED THIS ...
...YOU COLLAPSED FROM EXHAUSTION.
LOOK AT YOU NOW.

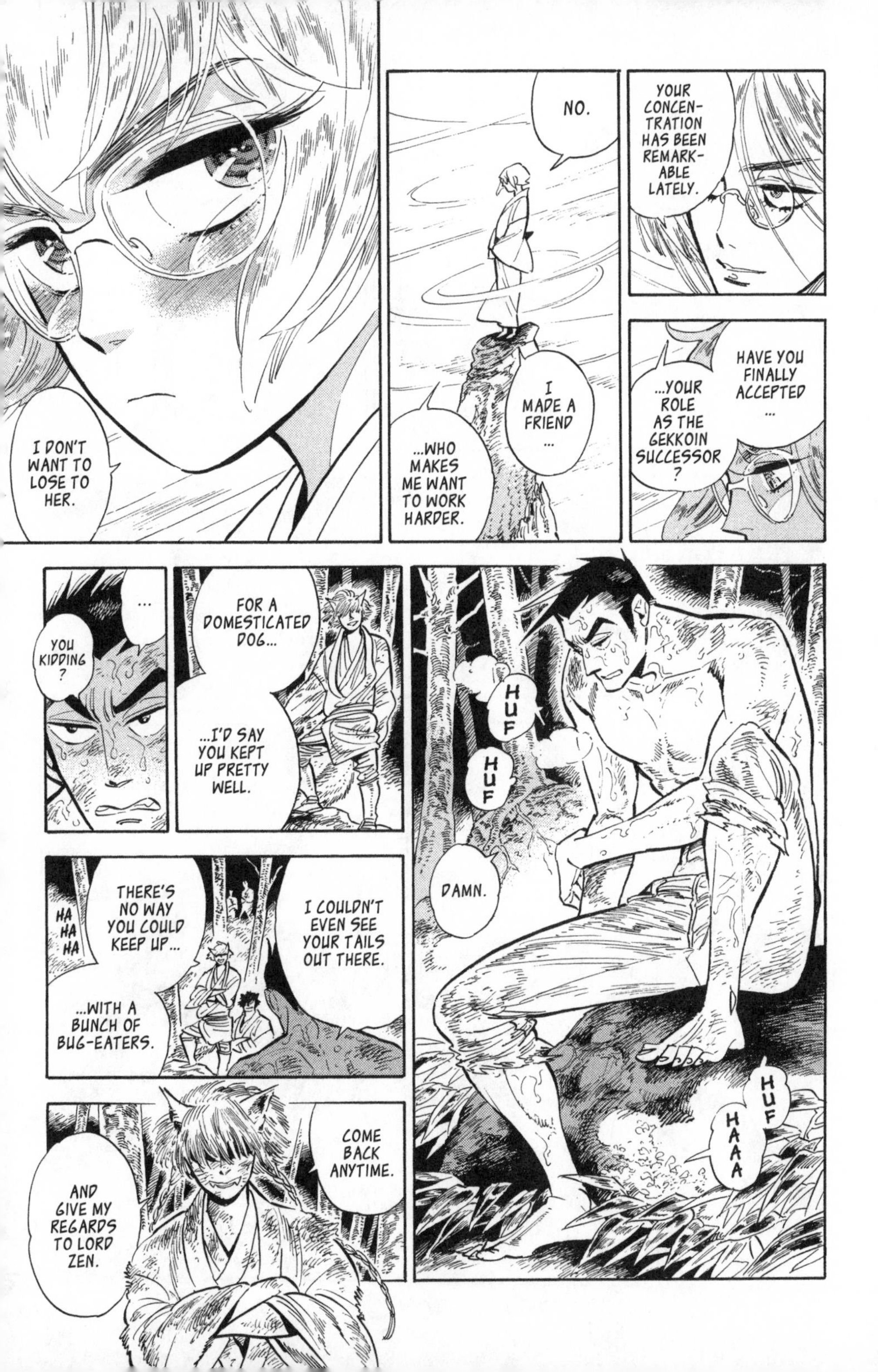
YOUR CONCENTRATION HAS BEEN REMARKABLE LATELY.
HAVE YOU FINALLY ACCEPTED...
...YOUR ROLE AS THE GEKKOIN SUCCESSOR?
NO.
I MADE A FRIEND...
...WHO MAKES ME WANT TO WORK HARDER.
I DON'T WANT TO LOSE TO HER.
HUF
HUF
DAMN.
HUF
HAAA
FOR A DOMESTICATED DOG...
...I'D SAY YOU KEPT UP PRETTY WELL.
...
YOU KIDDING?
I COULDN'T EVEN SEE YOUR TAILS OUT THERE.
THERE'S NO WAY YOU COULD KEEP UP...
HA HA HA
...WITH A BUNCH OF BUG-EATERS.
COME BACK ANYTIME.
AND GIVE MY REGARDS TO LORD ZEN.

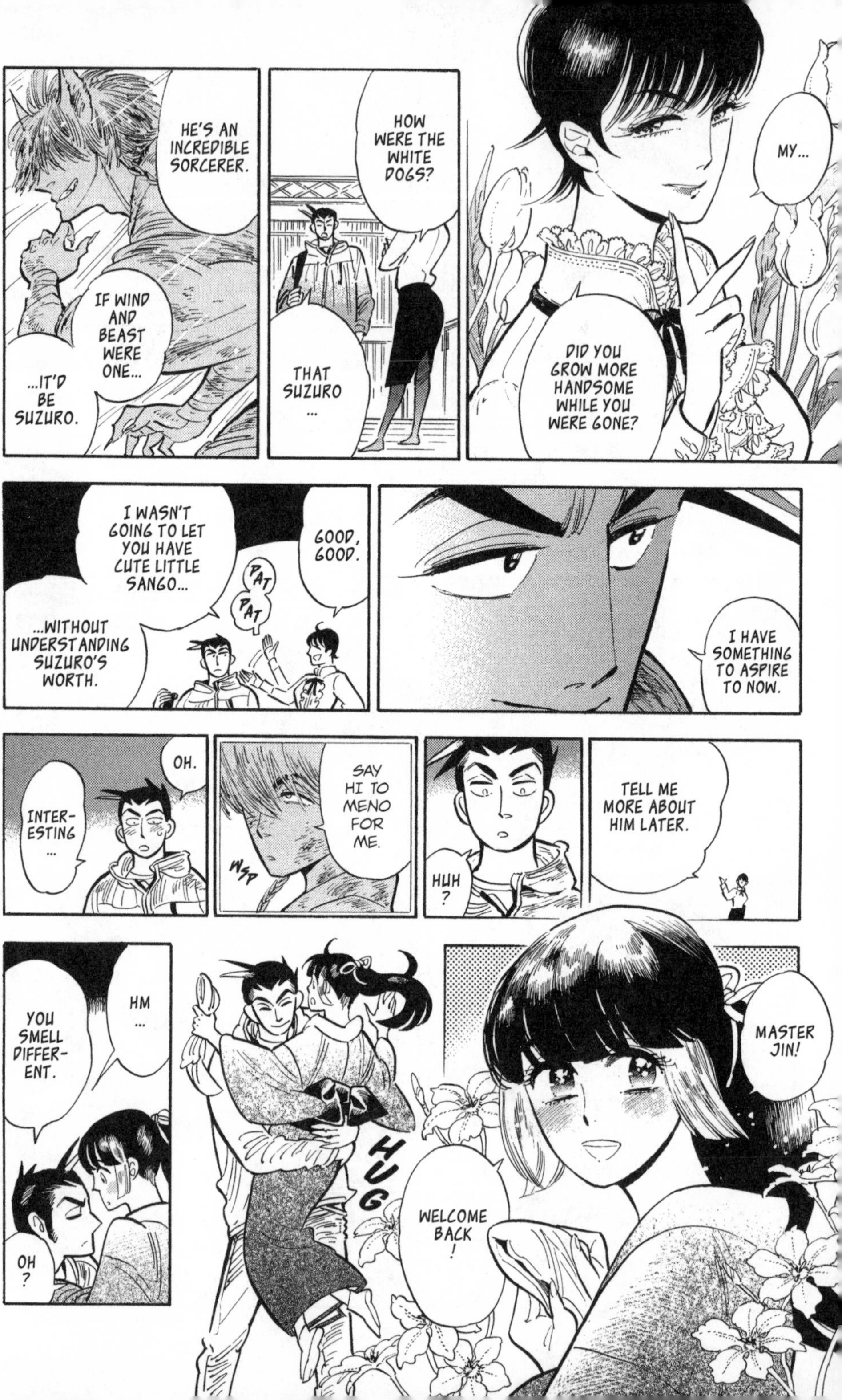
MY...
DID YOU GROW MORE HANDSOME WHILE YOU WERE GONE?
HOW WERE THE WHITE DOGS?
THAT SUZURO ...
HE'S AN INCREDIBLE SORCERER.
IF WIND AND BEAST WERE ONE...
...IT'D BE SUZURO.
I HAVE SOMETHING TO ASPIRE TO NOW.
GOOD, GOOD.
PAT
PAT
I WASN'T GOING TO LET YOU HAVE CUTE LITTLE SANGO...
...WITHOUT UNDERSTANDING SUZURO'S WORTH.
TELL ME MORE ABOUT HIM LATER.
HUH ?
SAY HI TO MENO FOR ME.
WSP
OH.
INTER-ESTING ...
MASTER JIN!
WELCOME BACK !
HUG
HM ...
YOU SMELL DIFFER-ENT.
OH ?

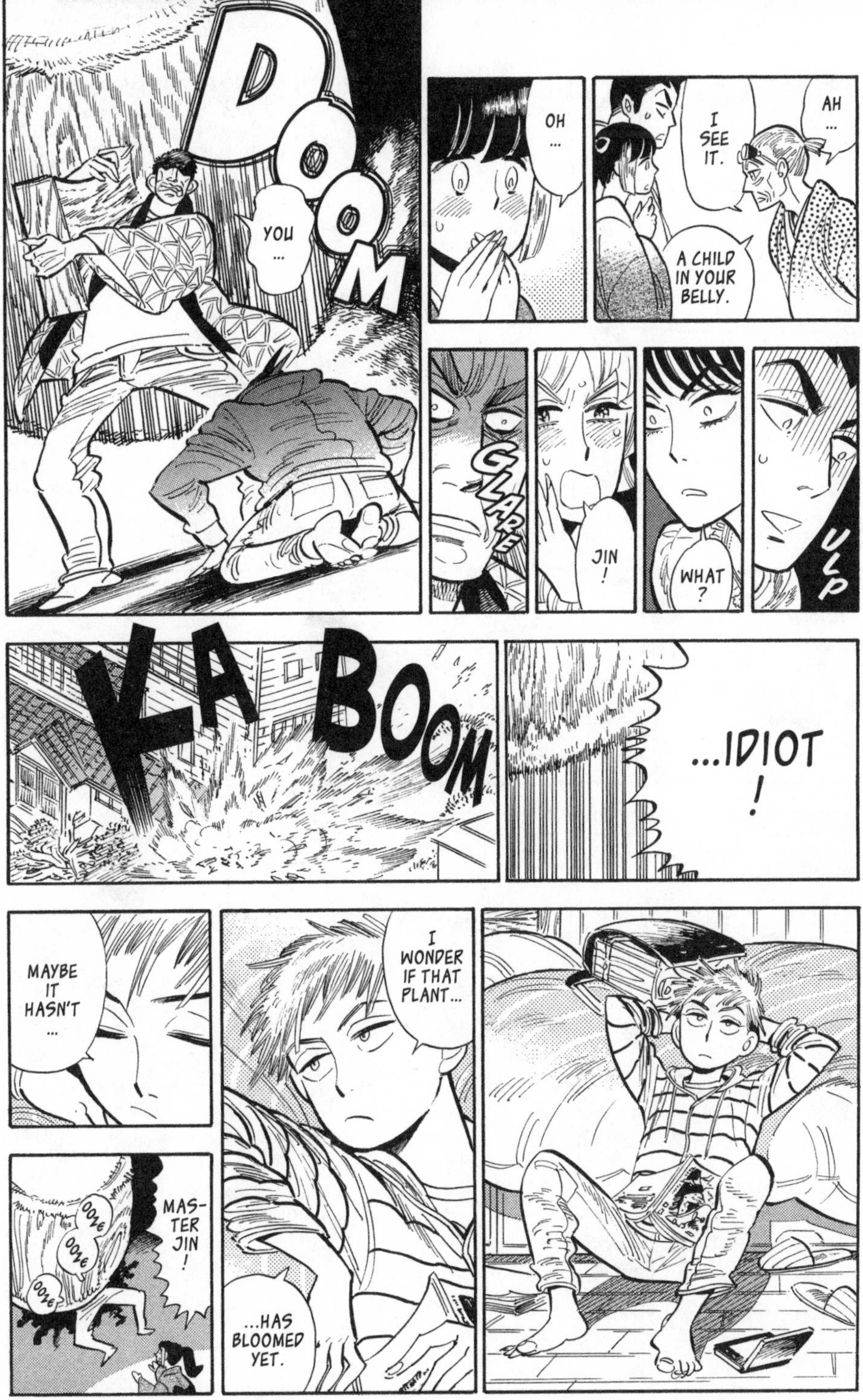
AH ...
I SEE IT.
A CHILD IN YOUR BELLY.
OH ...
ULP
WHAT?
JIN!
GLARE
DOOM
YOU ...
...IDIOT!
KA BOOM
I WONDER IF THAT PLANT...
...HAS BLOOMED YET.
MAYBE IT HASN'T ...
MASTER JIN!
OOZE
OOZE
OOZE

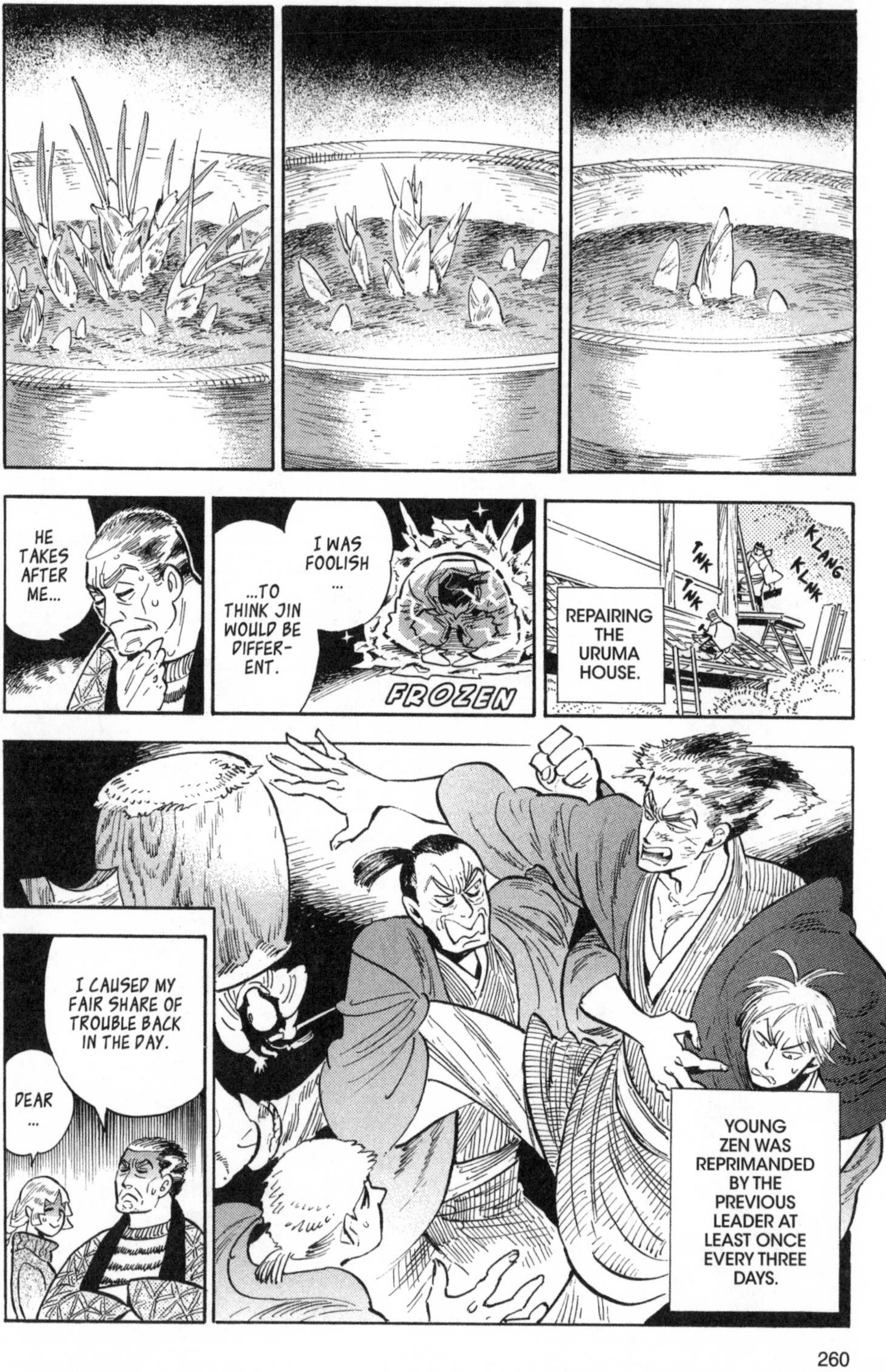
KLANG
KLNK
TNK
TNK
REPAIRING THE URUMA HOUSE.
I WAS FOOLISH ...
...TO THINK JIN WOULD BE DIFFER-ENT.
FROZEN
HE TAKES AFTER ME...
YOUNG ZEN WAS REPRIMANDED BY THE PREVIOUS LEADER AT LEAST ONCE EVERY THREE DAYS.
I CAUSED MY FAIR SHARE OF TROUBLE BACK IN THE DAY.
DEAR ...

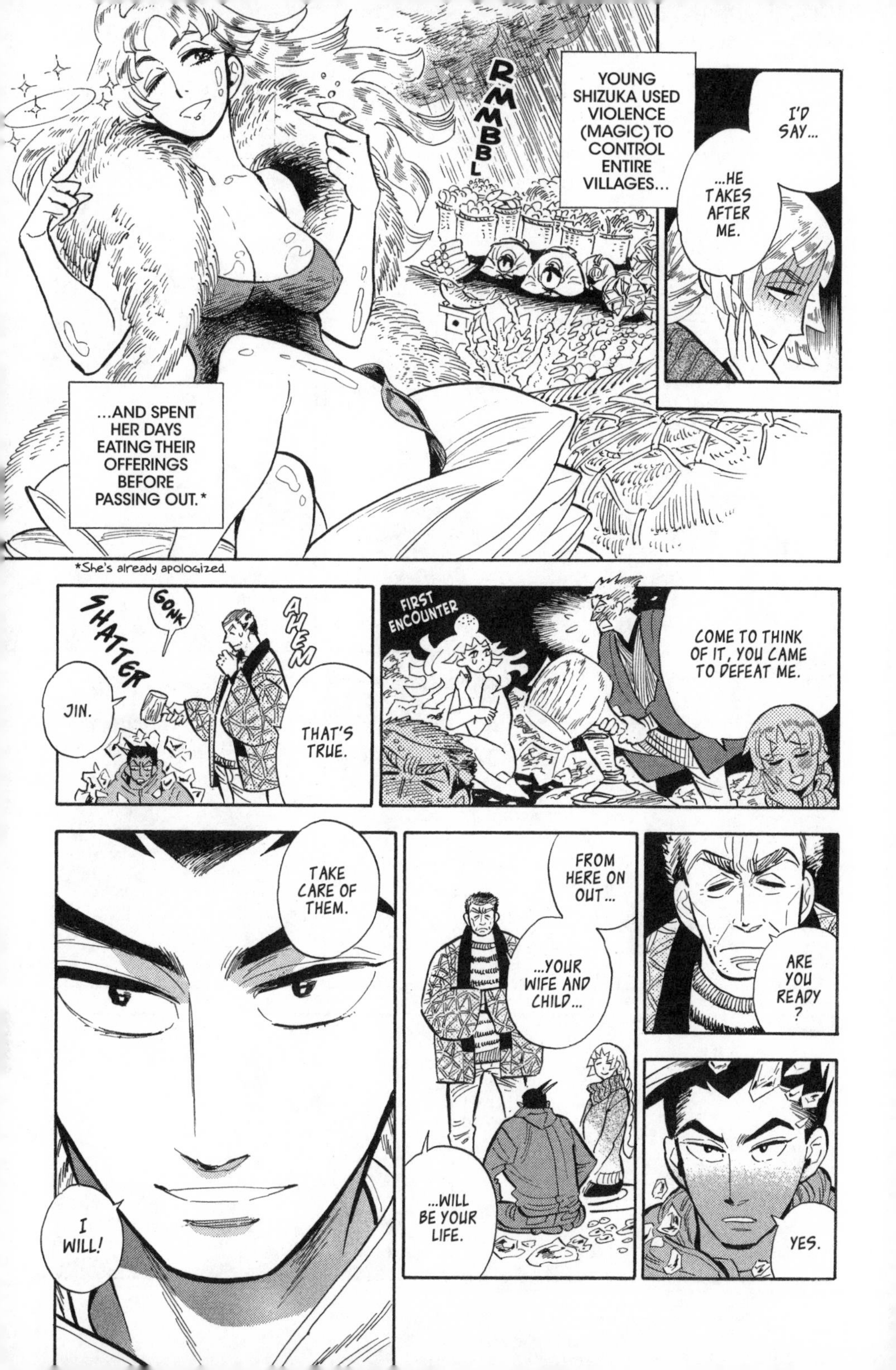
I'D SAY...
...HE TAKES AFTER ME.
YOUNG SHIZUKA USED VIOLENCE (MAGIC) TO CONTROL ENTIRE VILLAGES...
RMMBBL
...AND SPENT HER DAYS EATING THEIR OFFERINGS BEFORE PASSING OUT.*
*She's already apologized.
COME TO THINK OF IT, YOU CAME TO DEFEAT ME.
FIRST ENCOUNTER
THAT'S TRUE.
AHEM
GONK
SHATTER
JIN.
ARE YOU READY?
YES.
FROM HERE ON OUT...
...YOUR WIFE AND CHILD...
...WILL BE YOUR LIFE.
TAKE CARE OF THEM.
I WILL!

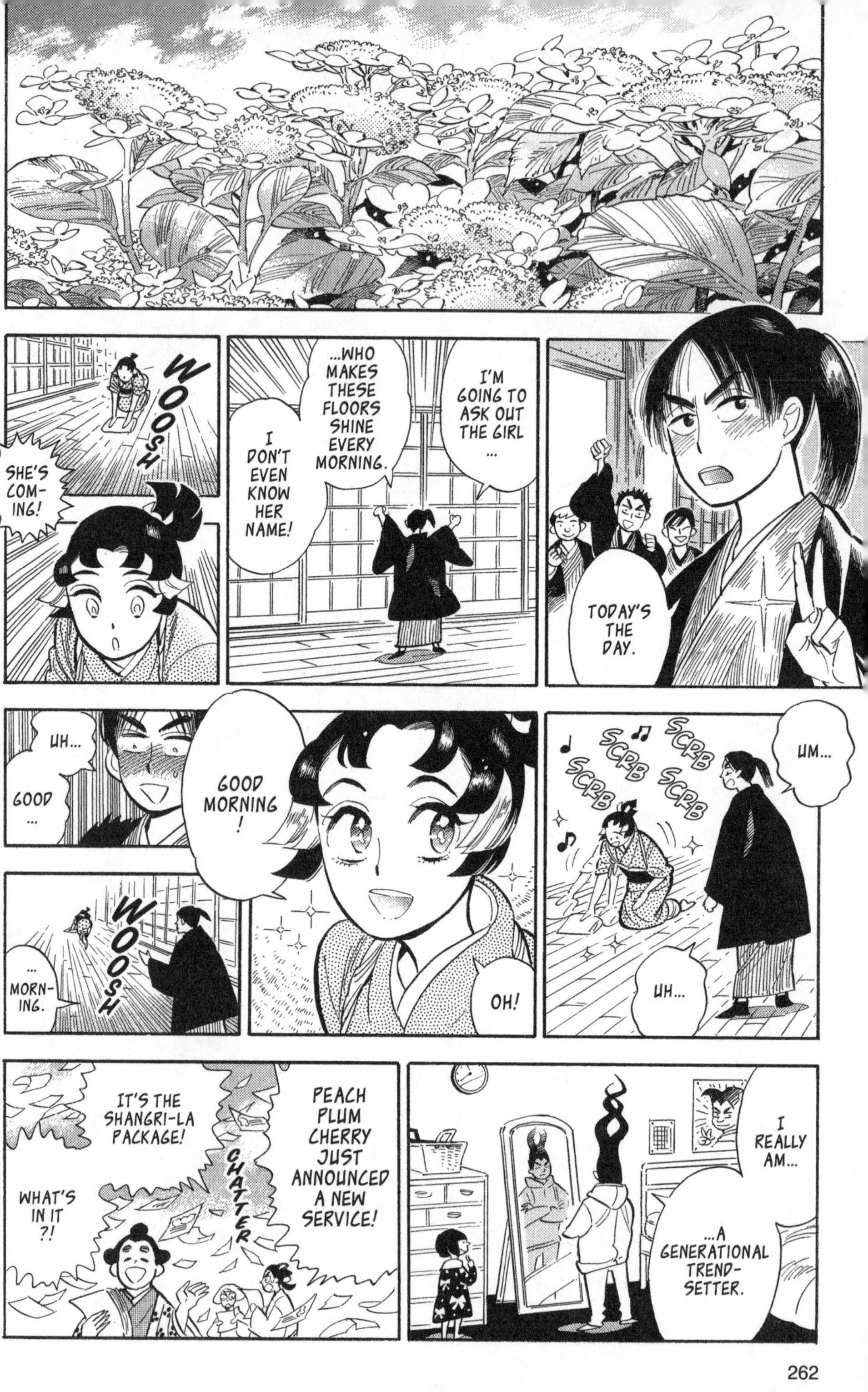
TODAY'S THE DAY.
I'M GOING TO ASK OUT THE GIRL ...
...WHO MAKES THESE FLOORS SHINE EVERY MORNING.
I DON'T EVEN KNOW HER NAME!
WOOOSH
SHE'S COMING!
UM...
SCRB SCRB SCRB SCRB
UH...
OH!
GOOD MORNING!
UH...
GOOD ...
WOOOSH
... MORNING.
I REALLY AM...
...A GENERATIONAL TRENDSETTER.
PEACH PLUM CHERRY JUST ANNOUNCED A NEW SERVICE!
IT'S THE SHANGRI-LA PACKAGE!
CHATTER
WHAT'S IN IT?!

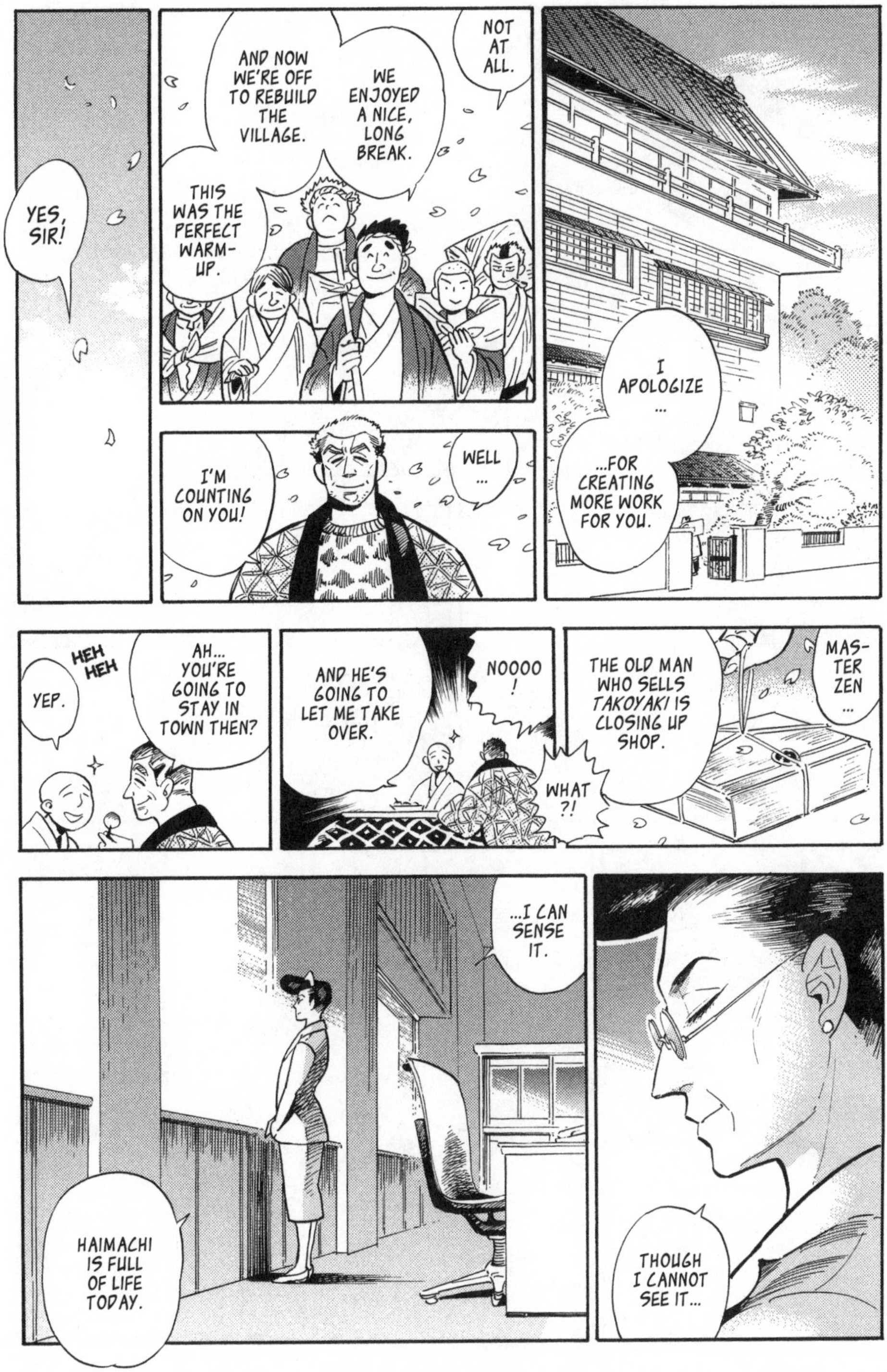
I APOLOGIZE ...
...FOR CREATING MORE WORK FOR YOU.
NOT AT ALL.
WE ENJOYED A NICE, LONG BREAK.
AND NOW WE'RE OFF TO REBUILD THE VILLAGE.
THIS WAS THE PERFECT WARM-UP.
WELL ...
I'M COUNTING ON YOU!
YES, SIR!
MASTER ZEN ...
THE OLD MAN WHO SELLS *TAKOYAKI* IS CLOSING UP SHOP.
WHAT ?!
NOOOO !
AND HE'S GOING TO LET ME TAKE OVER.
AH... YOU'RE GOING TO STAY IN TOWN THEN?
HEH HEH
YEP.
THOUGH I CANNOT SEE IT...
...I CAN SENSE IT.
HAIMACHI IS FULL OF LIFE TODAY.

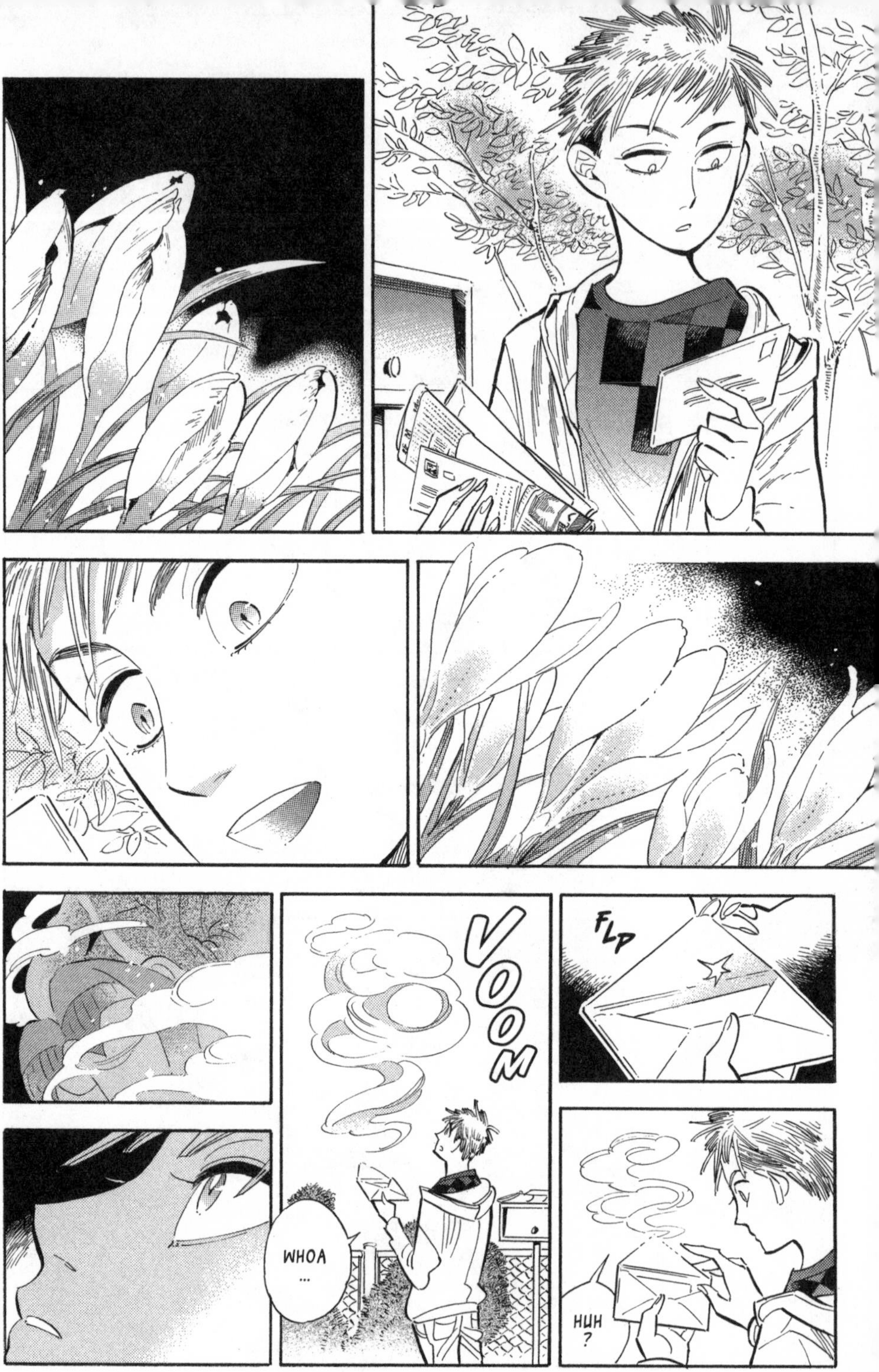
FLP
HUH ?
VOOM
WHOA ...

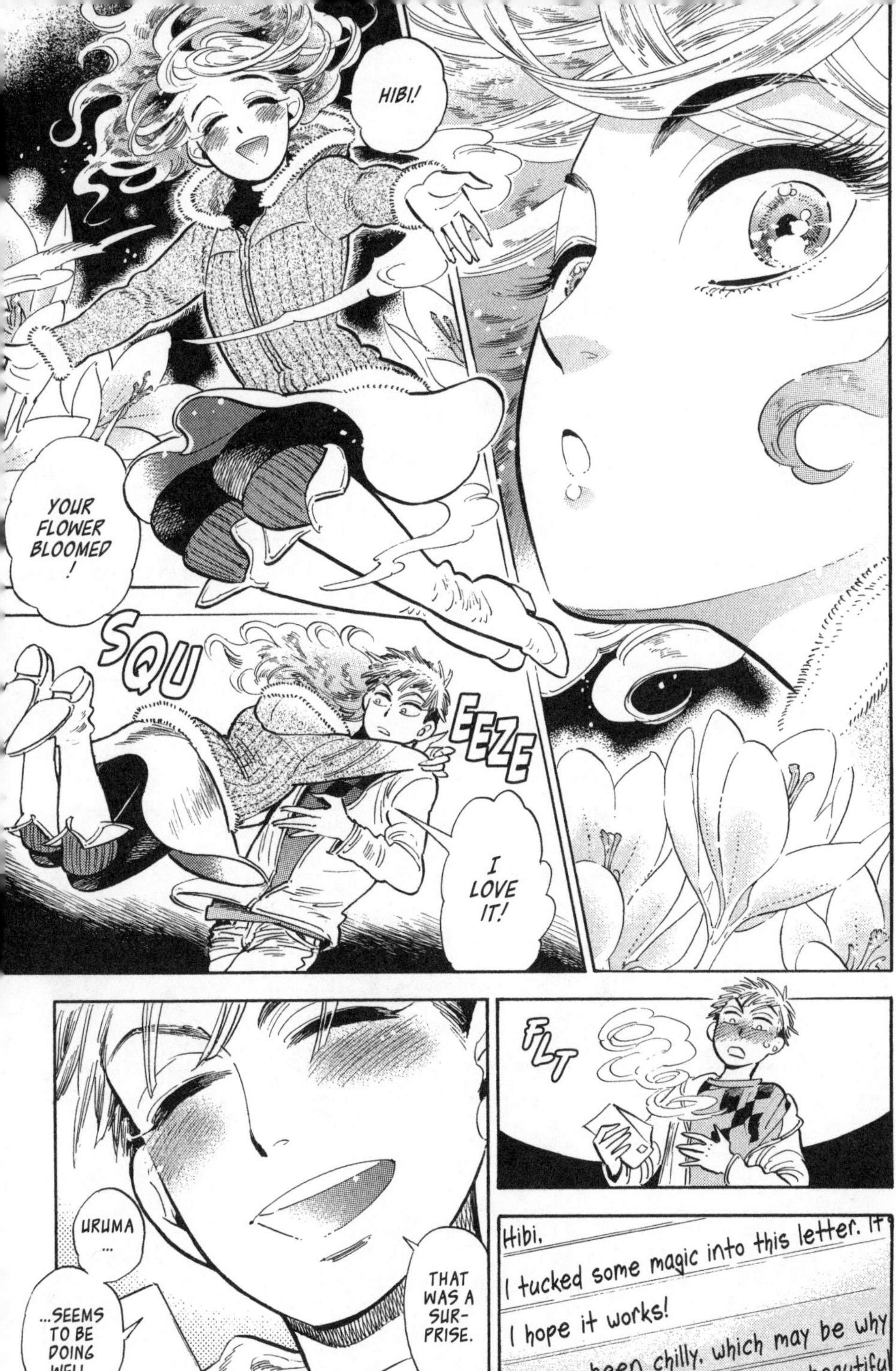
HIBI!
YOUR FLOWER BLOOMED!
SQUEEZE
I LOVE IT!
FLT
Hibi,
I tucked some magic into this letter.
I hope it works!
been chilly, which may be why
THAT WAS A SUR-PRISE.
URUMA...
...SEEMS TO BE DOING WELL.

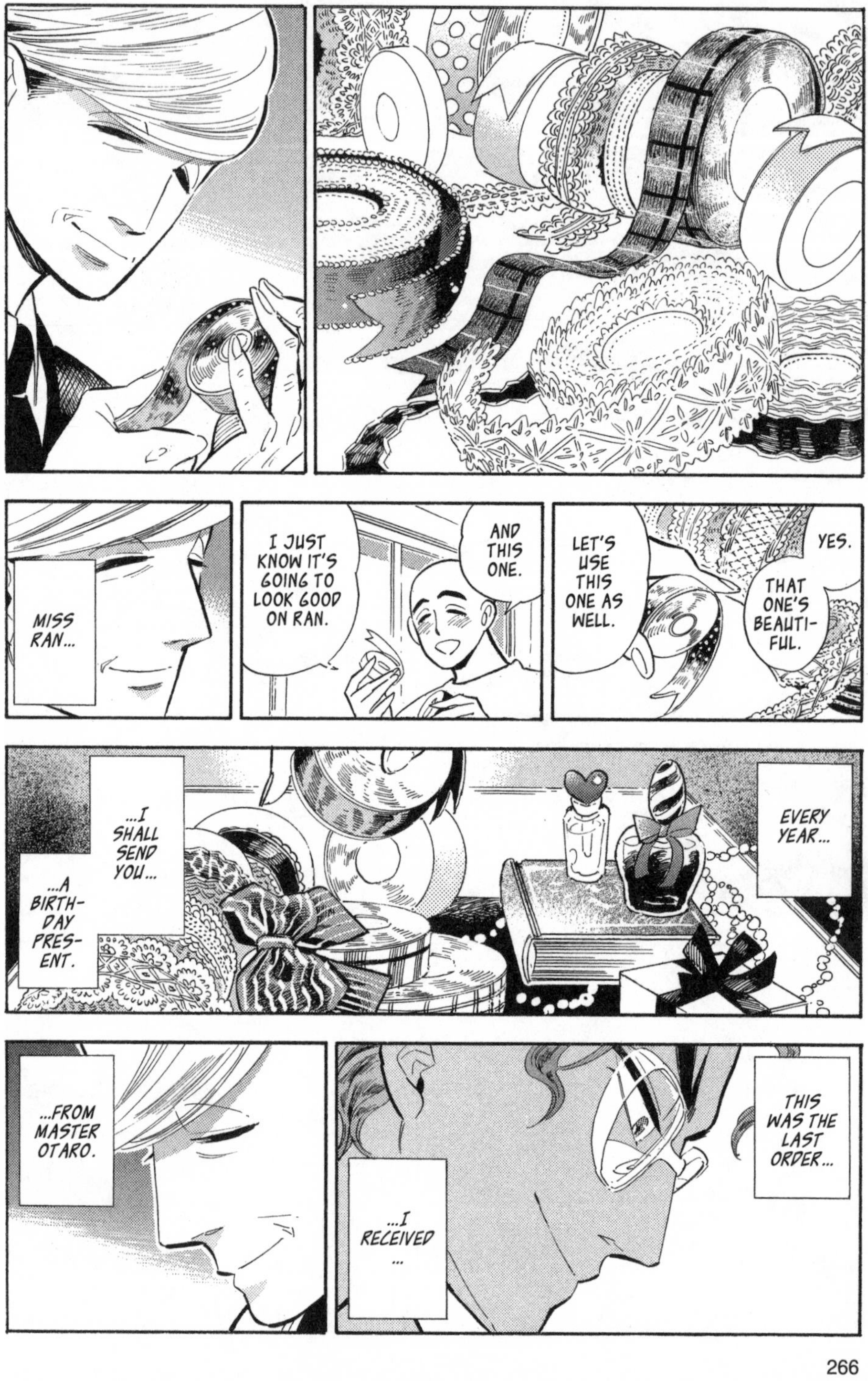
YES.
THAT ONE'S BEAUTI-FUL.
LET'S USE THIS ONE AS WELL.
AND THIS ONE.
I JUST KNOW IT'S GOING TO LOOK GOOD ON RAN.
MISS RAN...
EVERY YEAR...
...I SHALL SEND YOU...
...A BIRTH-DAY PRES-ENT.
THIS WAS THE LAST ORDER...
...I RECEIVED...
...FROM MASTER OTARO.

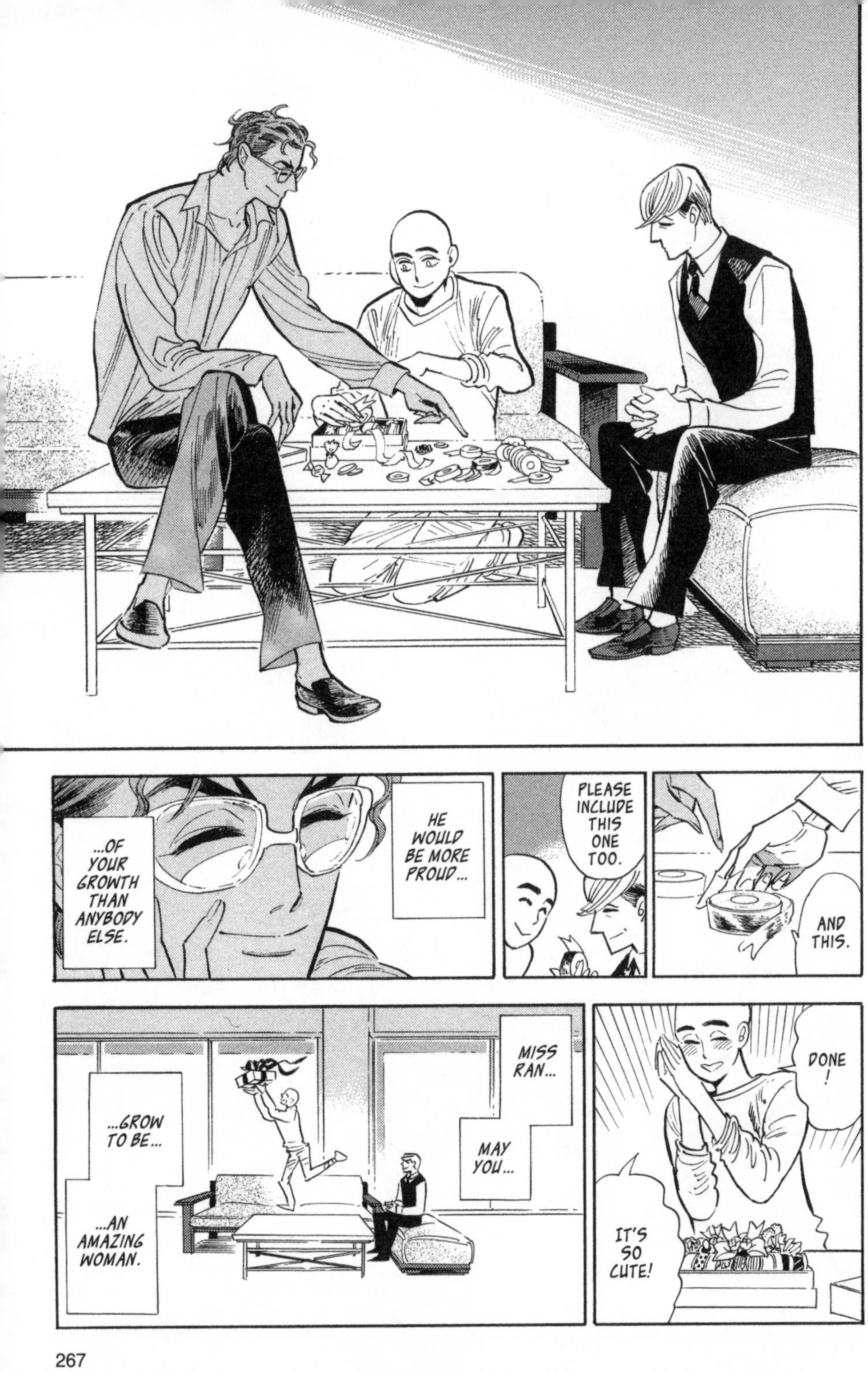
AND THIS.
PLEASE INCLUDE THIS ONE TOO.
HE WOULD BE MORE PROUD...
...OF YOUR GROWTH THAN ANYBODY ELSE.
DONE!
IT'S SO CUTE!
MISS RAN...
MAY YOU...
...GROW TO BE...
...AN AMAZING WOMAN.

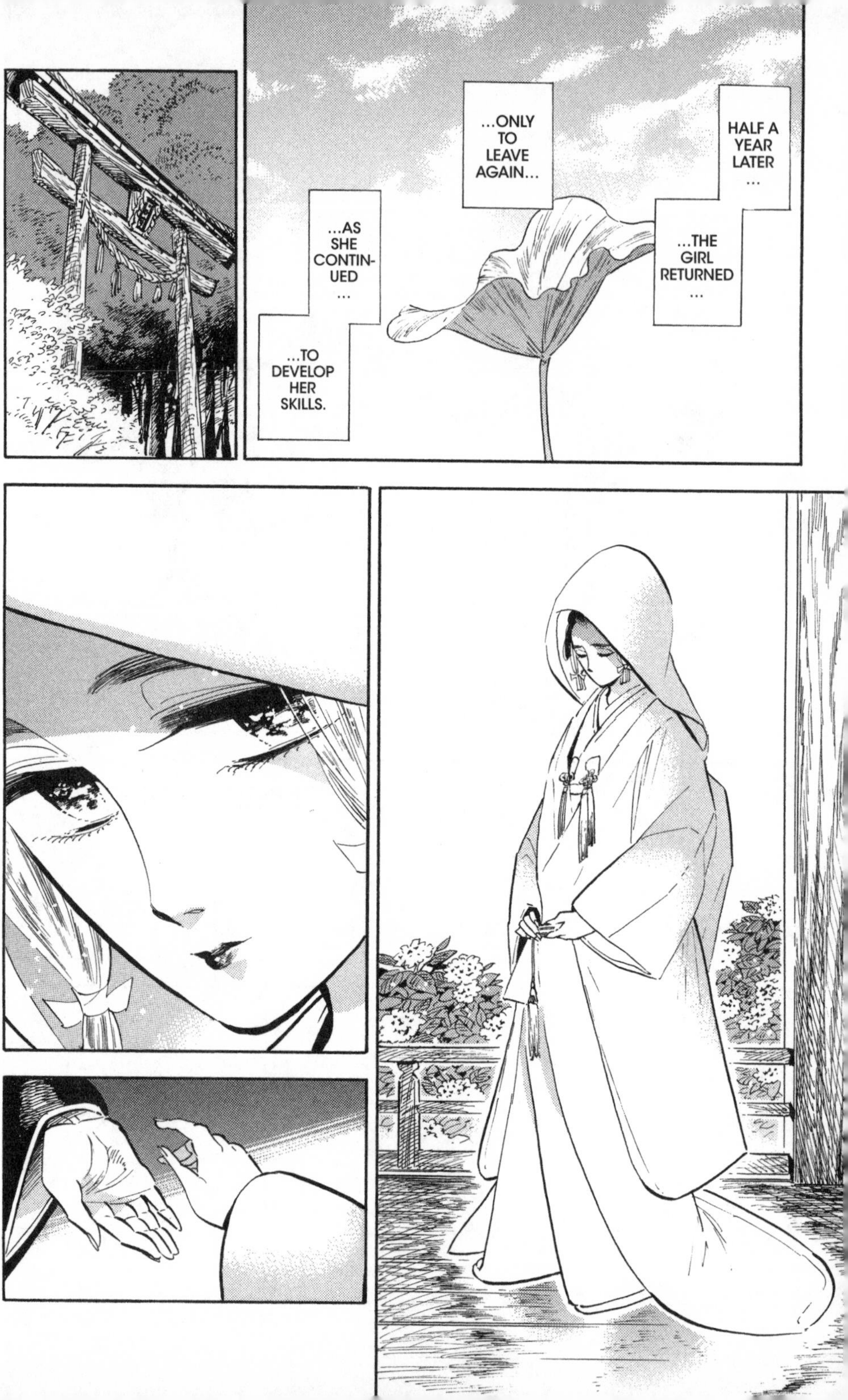
HALF A YEAR LATER …
…THE GIRL RETURNED …
…ONLY TO LEAVE AGAIN…
…AS SHE CONTIN-UED …
…TO DEVELOP HER SKILLS.

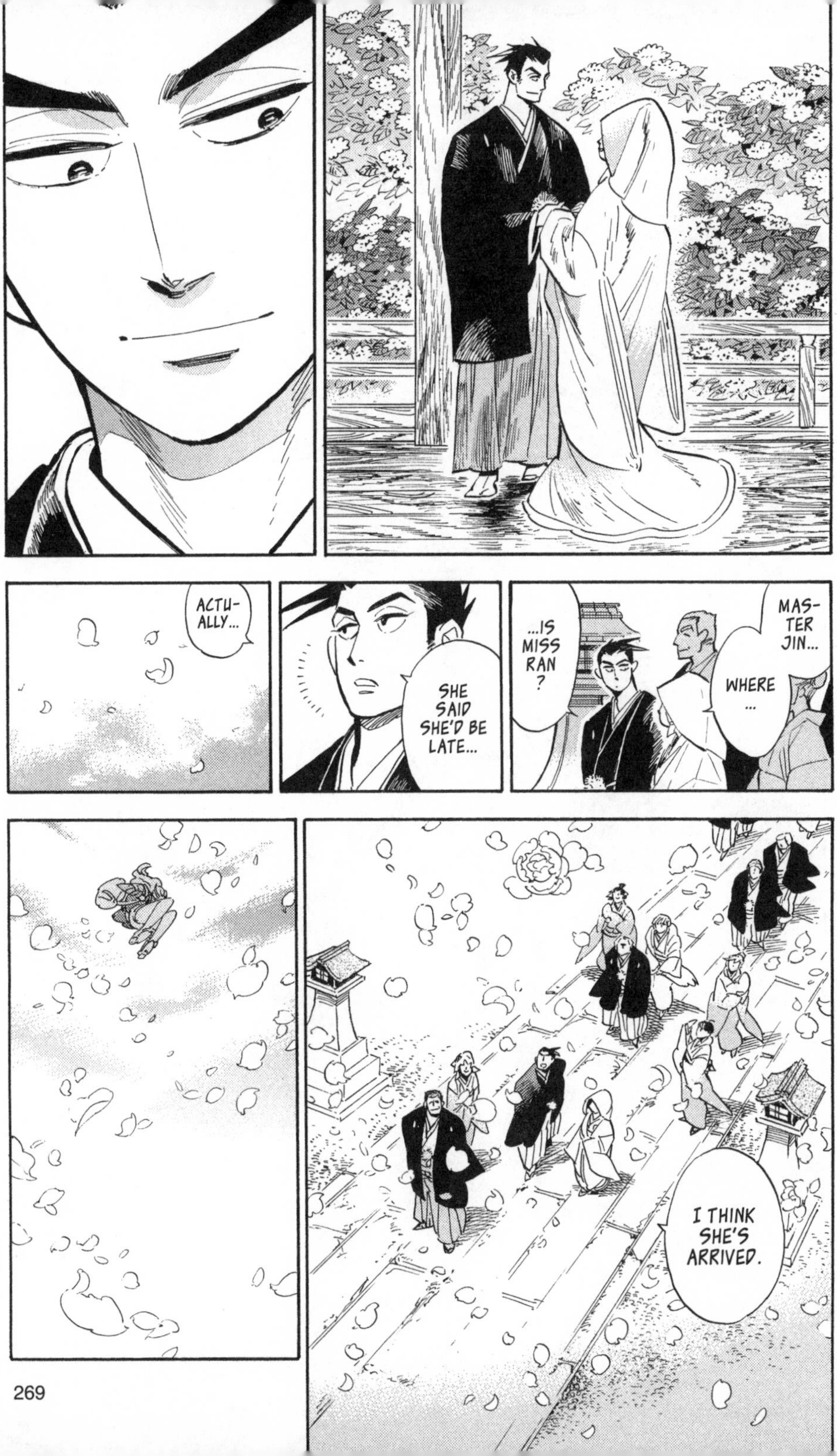
MAS-TER JIN... WHERE ...
...IS MISS RAN?
SHE SAID SHE'D BE LATE...
ACTU-ALLY...
I THINK SHE'S ARRIVED.

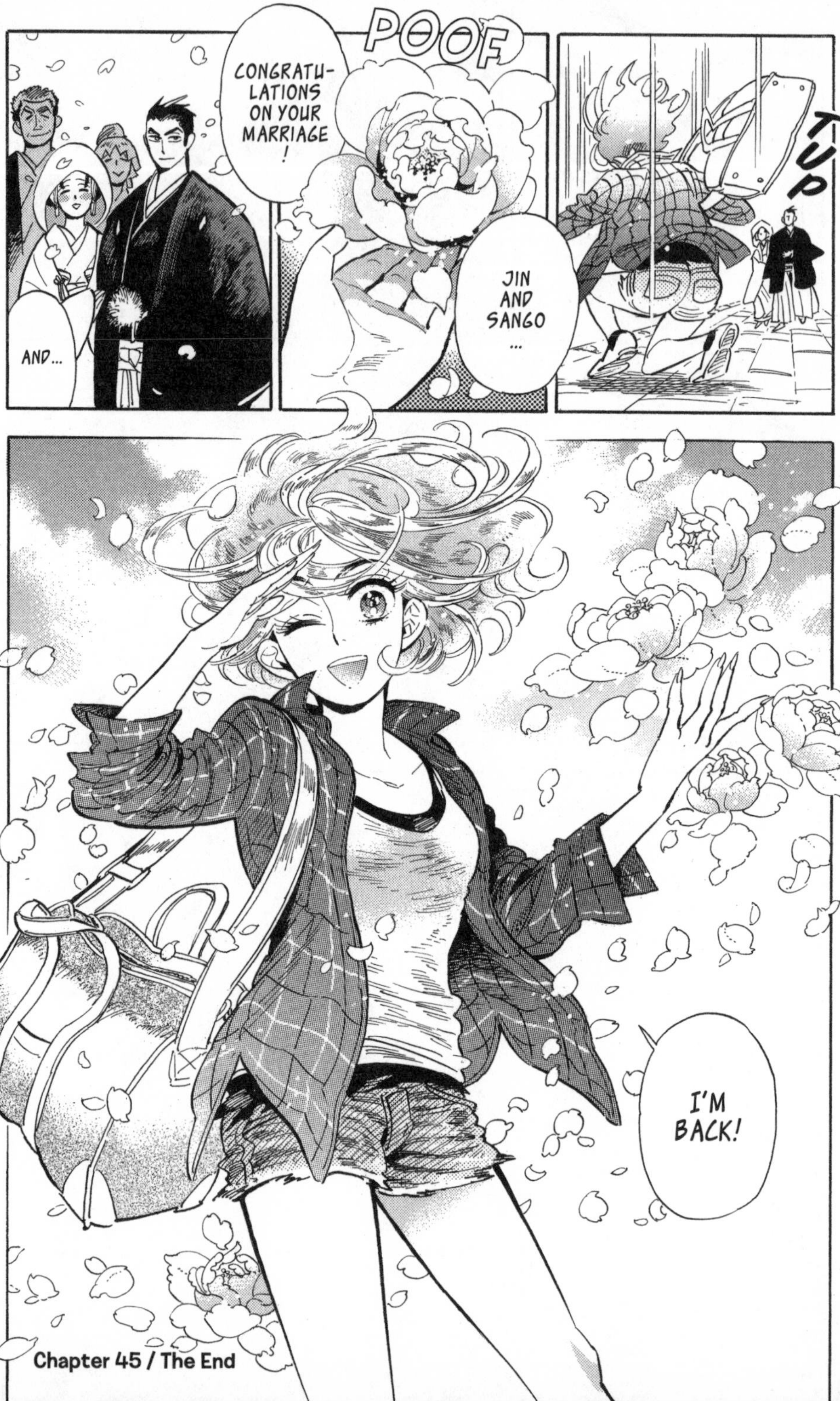
TUP
POOF
JIN AND SANGO ...
AND...
CONGRATULATIONS ON YOUR MARRIAGE!
I'M BACK!

Chapter 45 / The End

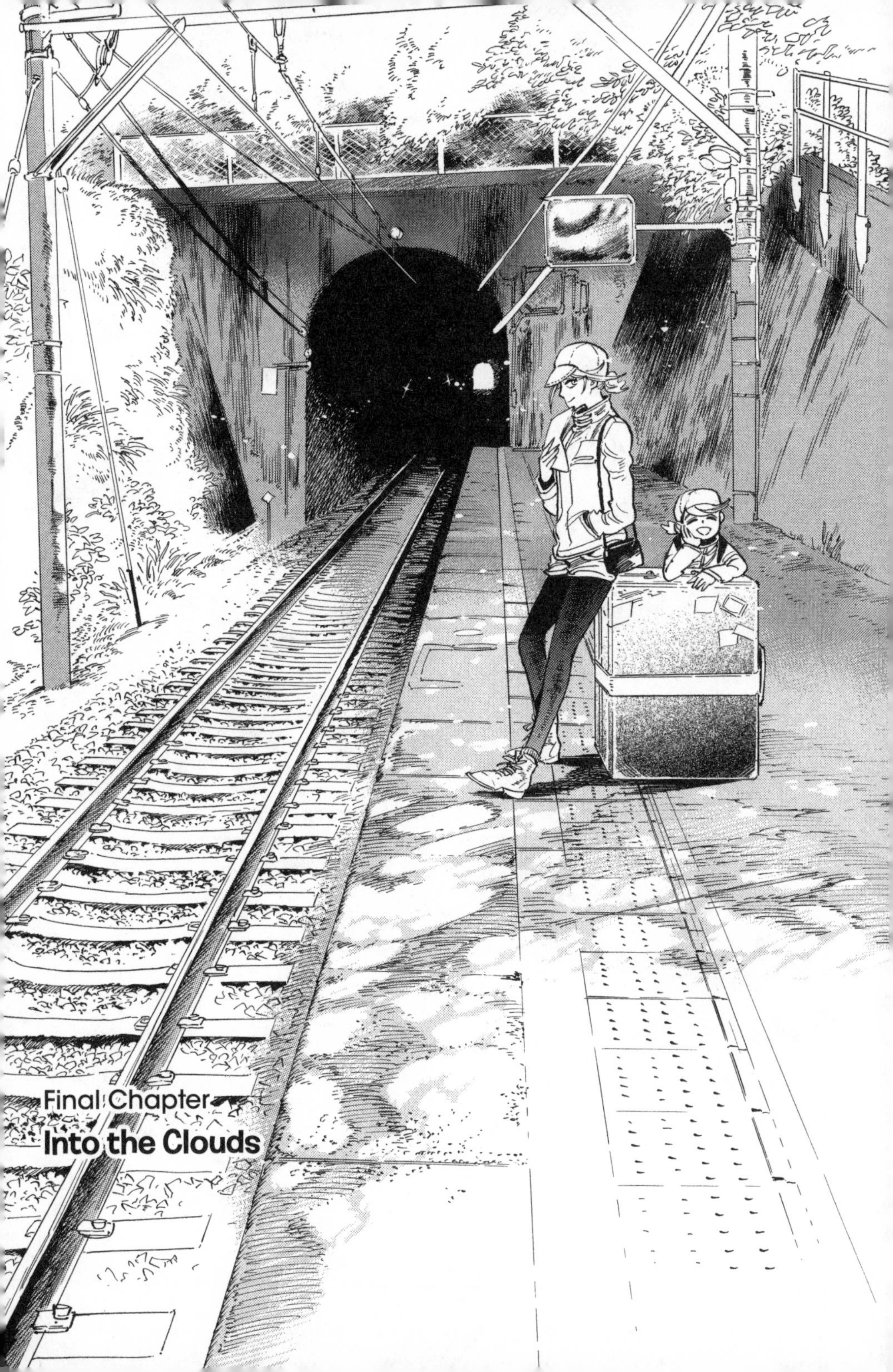
Final Chapter
Into the Clouds

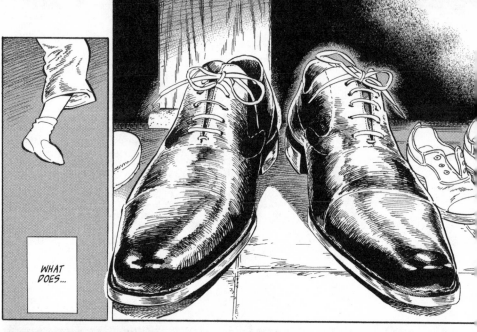

WHAT
DOES...

...IT
MEAN
...

...TO
GROW
UP?

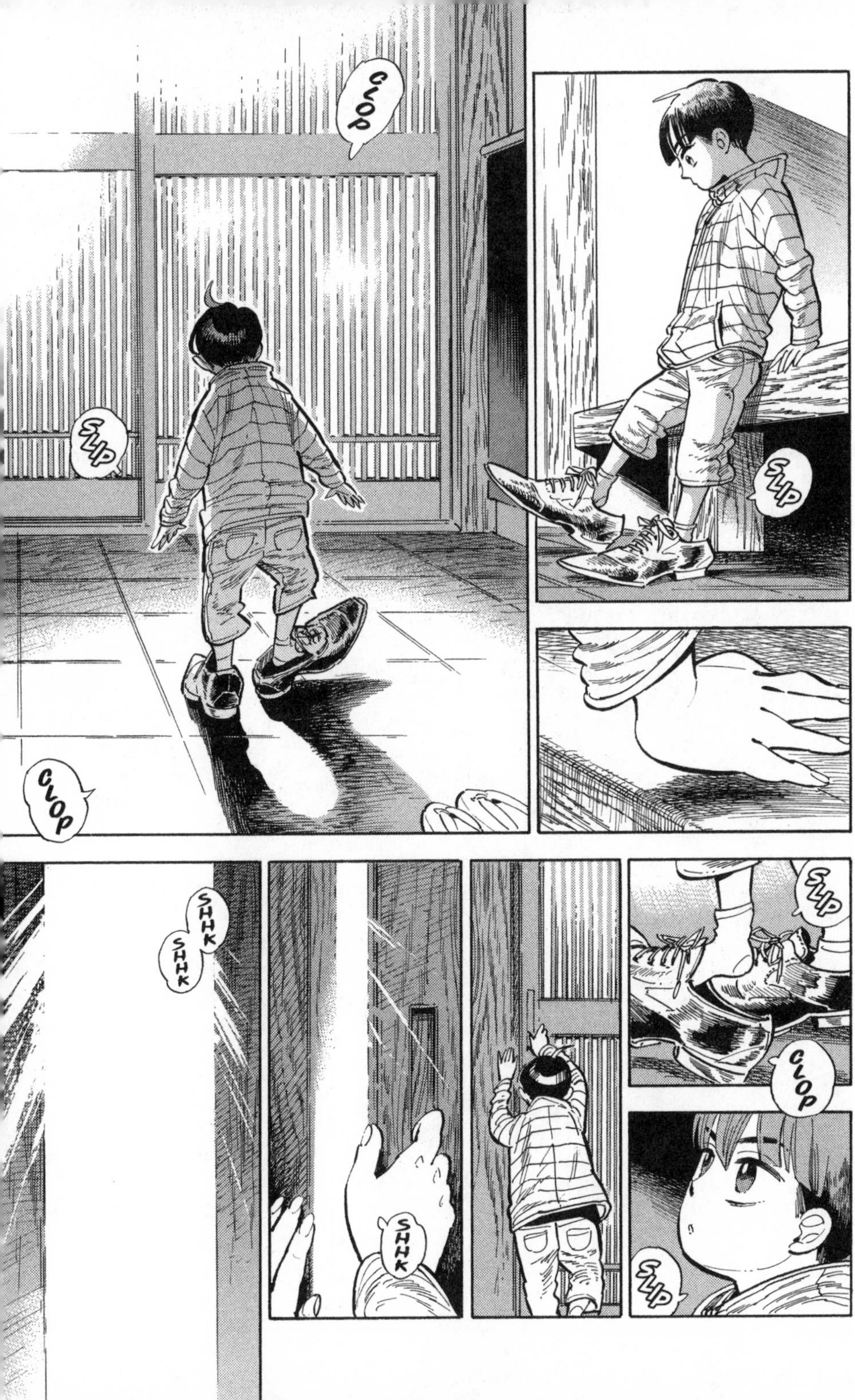
SLIP
CLOP
SLIP
CLOP
SLIP
CLOP
SLIP
SHHK
SHHK
SHHK

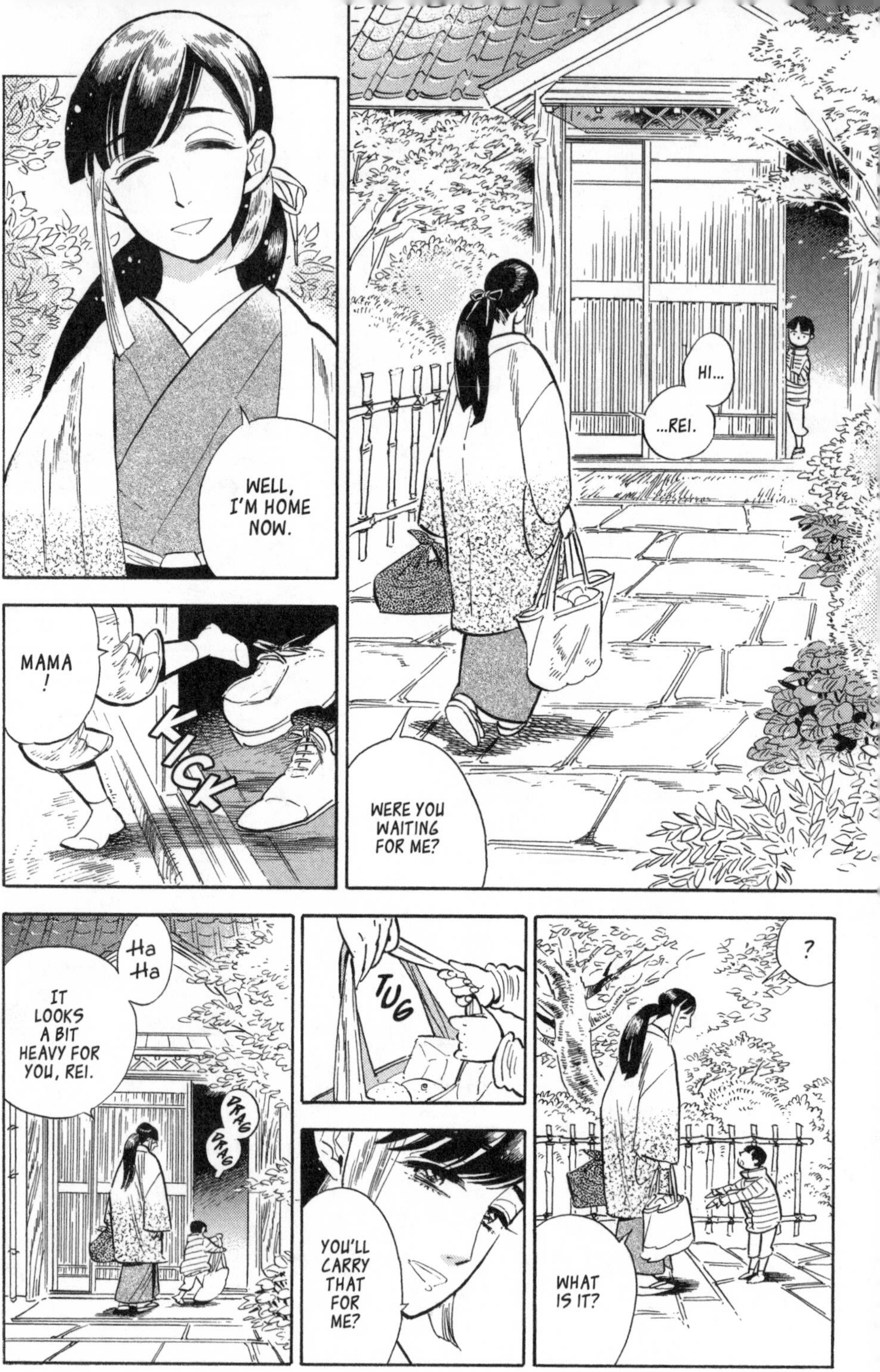
HI...
...REI.
WERE YOU WAITING FOR ME?
WELL, I'M HOME NOW.
MAMA!
KICK
?
WHAT IS IT?
TUG
YOU'LL CARRY THAT FOR ME?
Ha Ha
IT LOOKS A BIT HEAVY FOR YOU, REI.
DRAG
DRAG

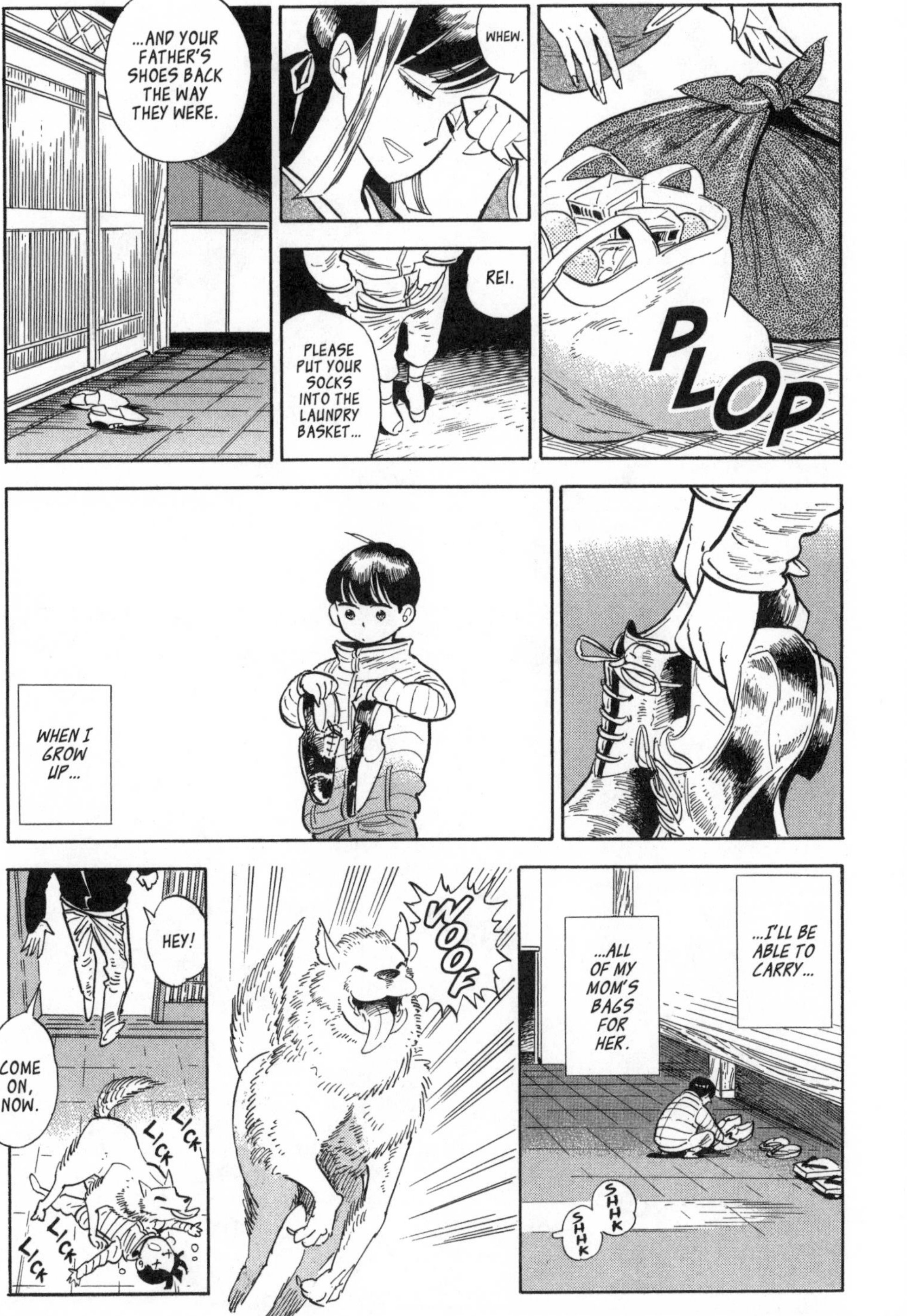
PLOP
WHEW.
REI.
PLEASE PUT YOUR SOCKS INTO THE LAUNDRY BASKET...
...AND YOUR FATHER'S SHOES BACK THE WAY THEY WERE.
WHEN I GROW UP...
...I'LL BE ABLE TO CARRY...
...ALL OF MY MOM'S BAGS FOR HER.
SHHK SHHK
WOOF
HEY!
COME ON, NOW.
LICK LICK LICK LICK

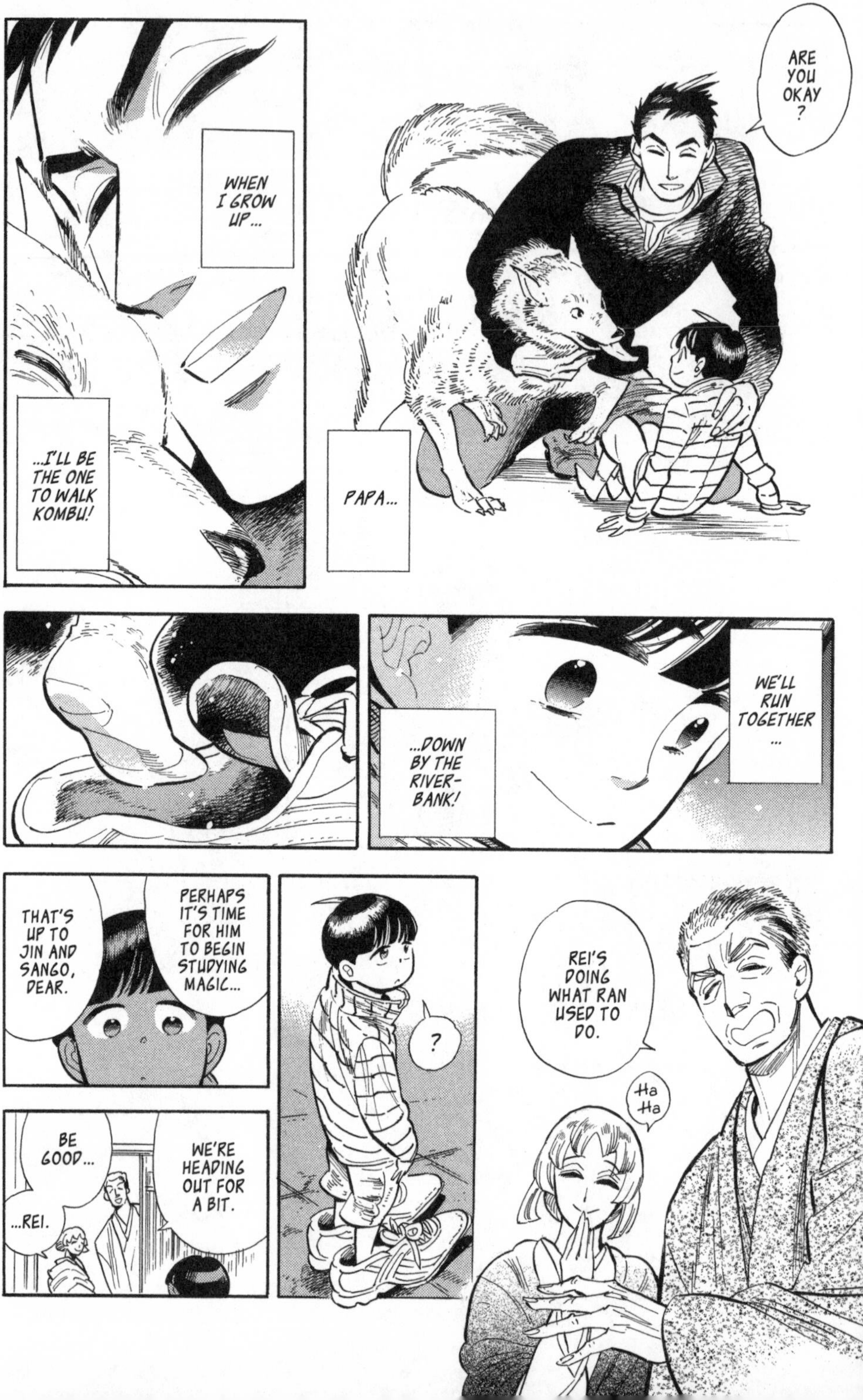
ARE YOU OKAY?
PAPA...
WHEN I GROW UP...
...I'LL BE THE ONE TO WALK KOMBU!
WE'LL RUN TOGETHER...
...DOWN BY THE RIVER-BANK!
REI'S DOING WHAT RAN USED TO DO.
Ha Ha
?
PERHAPS IT'S TIME FOR HIM TO BEGIN STUDYING MAGIC...
THAT'S UP TO JIN AND SANGO, DEAR.
WE'RE HEADING OUT FOR A BIT.
BE GOOD...
...REI.

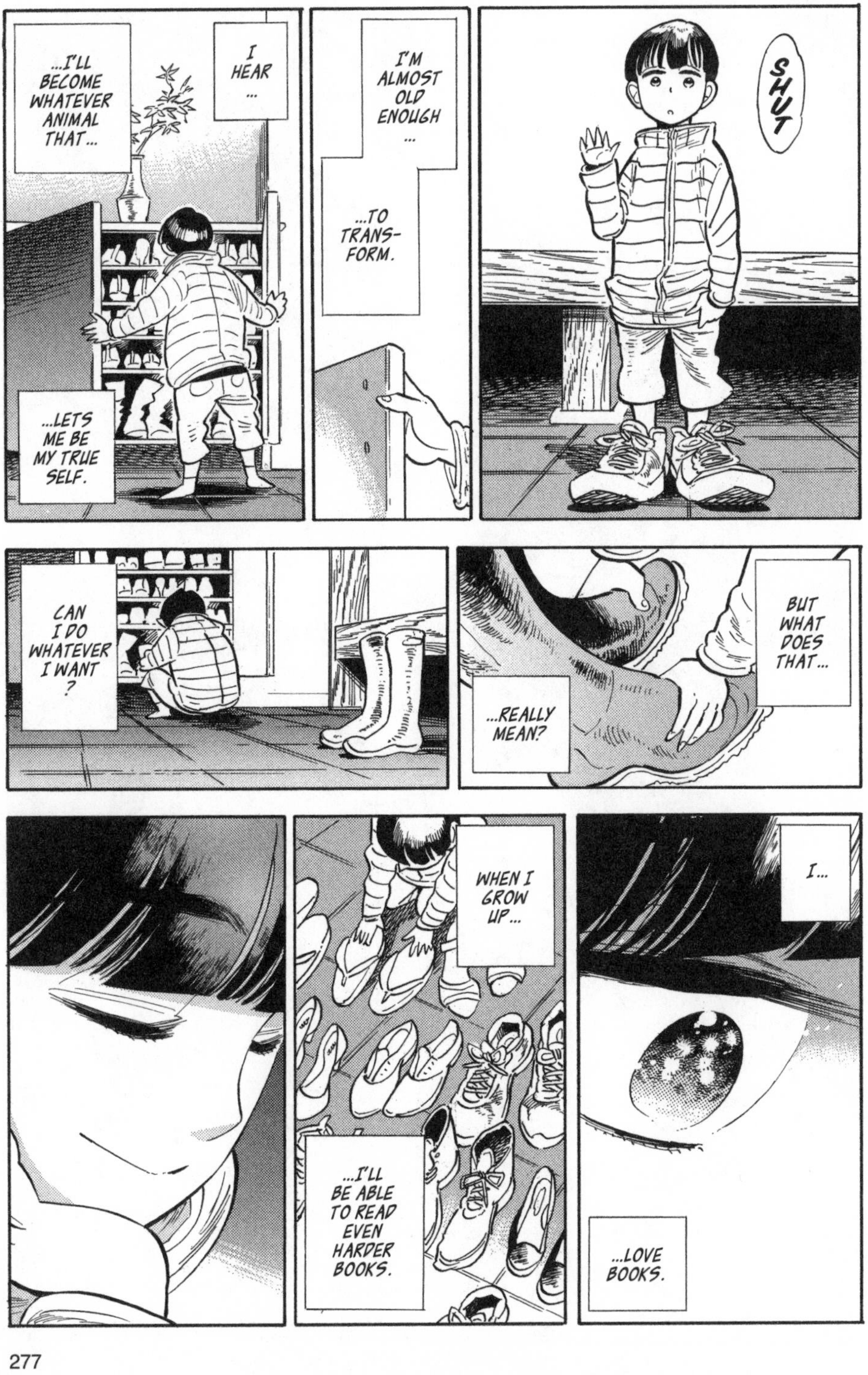
SHUT
I'M ALMOST OLD ENOUGH ...
...TO TRANSFORM.
I HEAR ...
...I'LL BECOME WHATEVER ANIMAL THAT...
...LETS ME BE MY TRUE SELF.
BUT WHAT DOES THAT...
...REALLY MEAN?
CAN I DO WHATEVER I WANT ?
I...
...LOVE BOOKS.
WHEN I GROW UP...
...I'LL BE ABLE TO READ EVEN HARDER BOOKS.

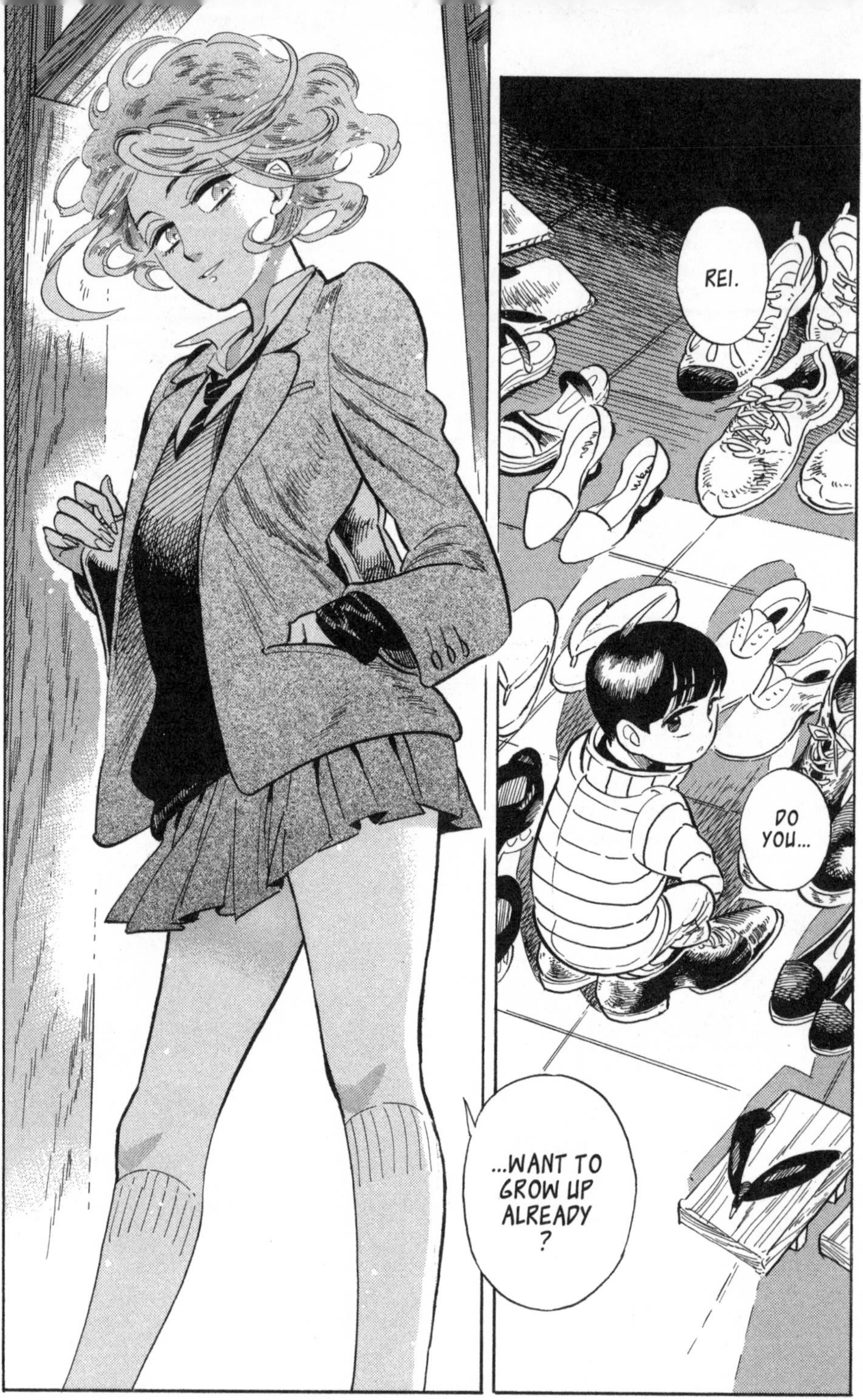
REI.
DO YOU...
...WANT TO GROW UP ALREADY ?

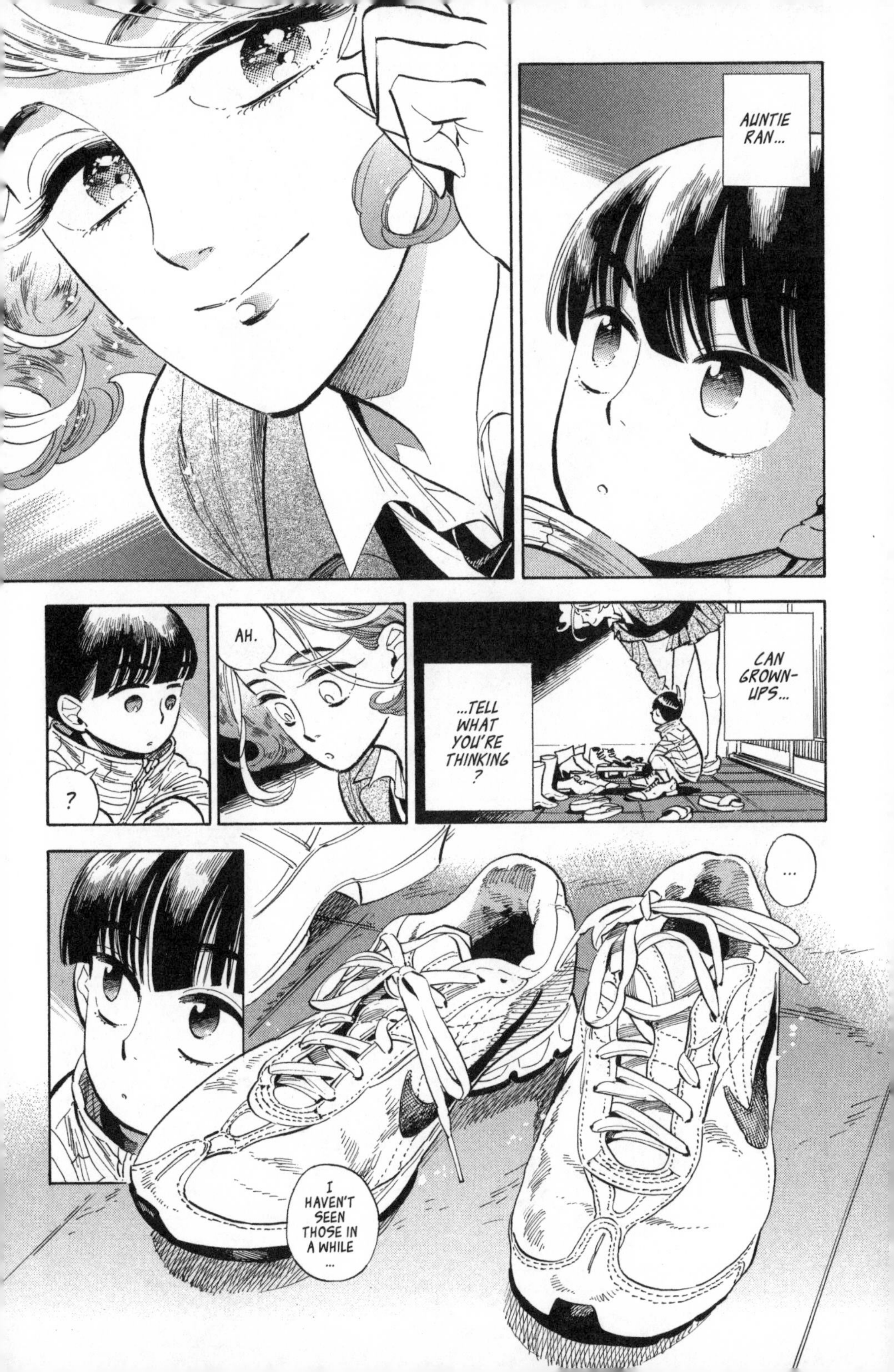
AUNTIE RAN...
CAN GROWN-UPS...
...TELL WHAT YOU'RE THINKING ?
AH.
?
...
I HAVEN'T SEEN THOSE IN A WHILE ...

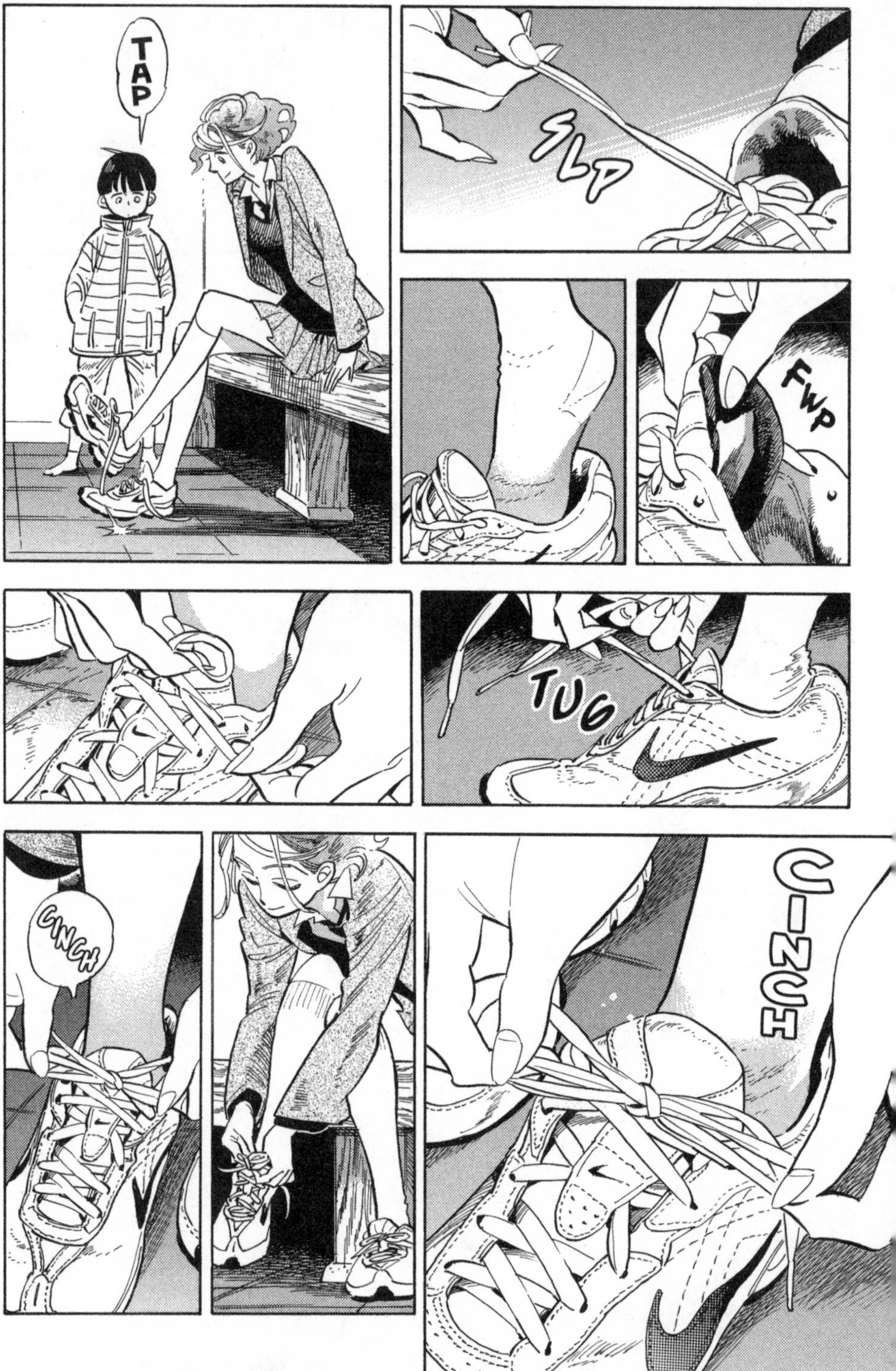
SLP
FWP
TAP
TUG
CINCH
CINCH

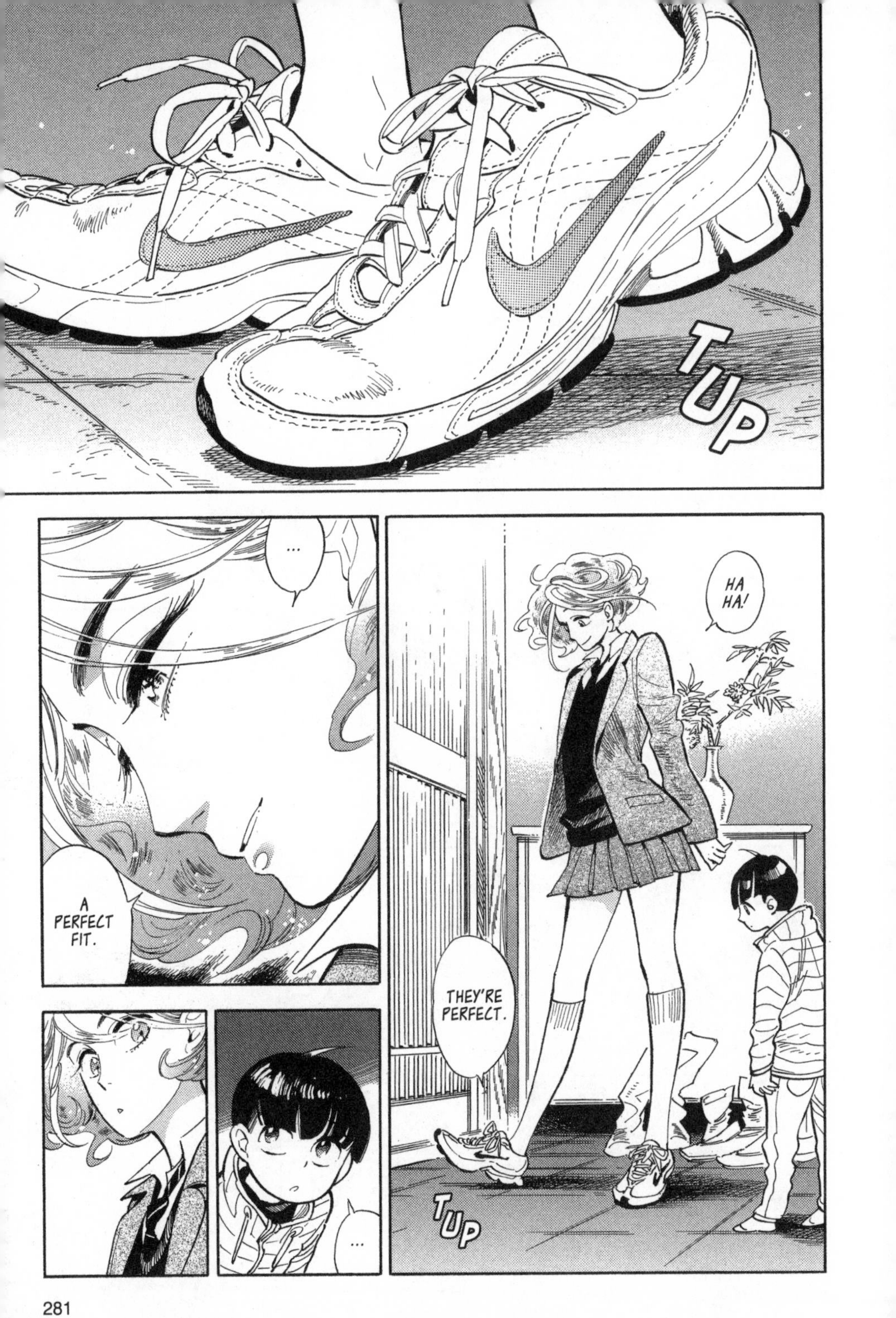
TUP
HA HA!
THEY'RE PERFECT.
TUP
...
A PERFECT FIT.
...

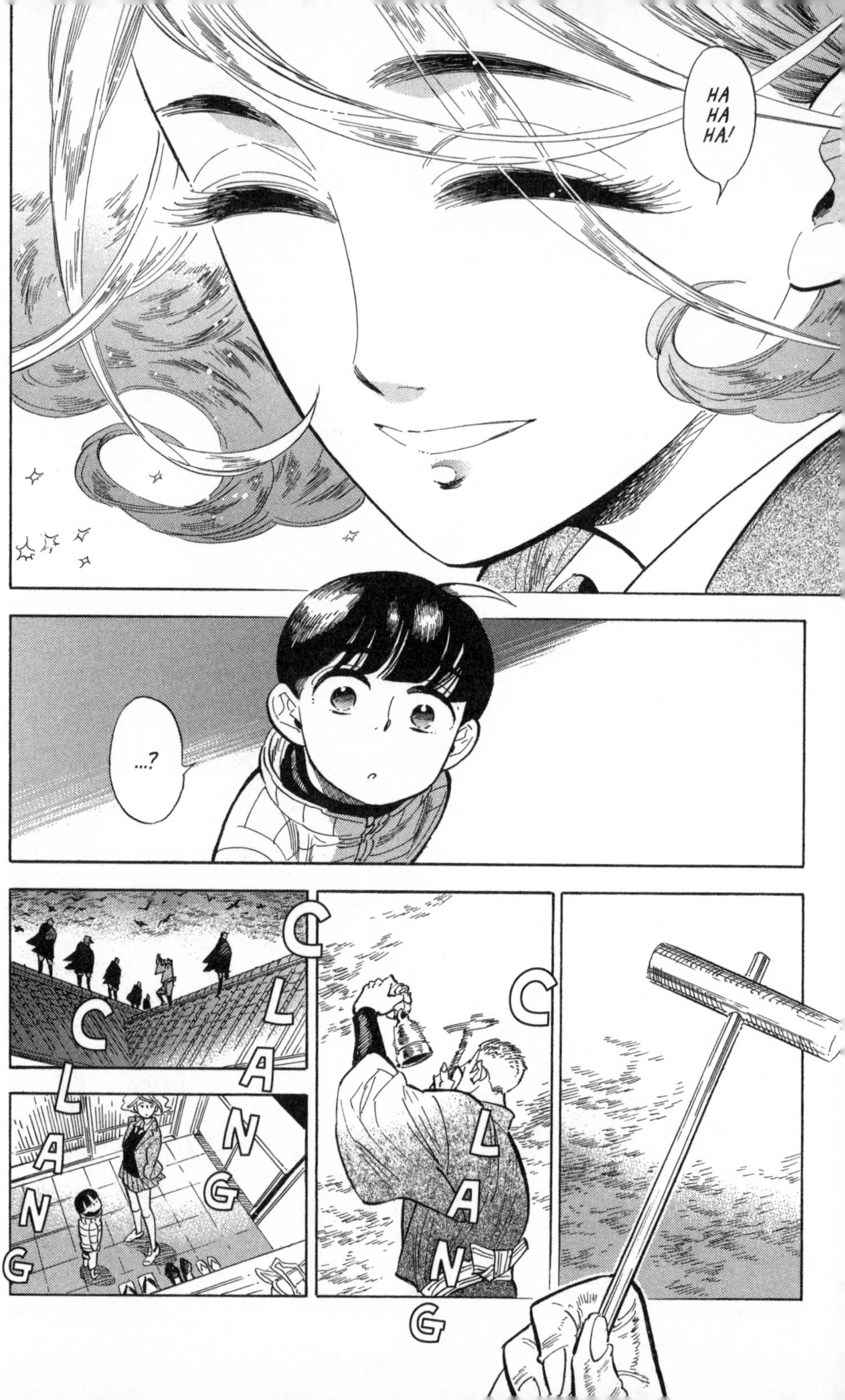
HA HA HA!
...?
CLANG
CLANG
CLANG

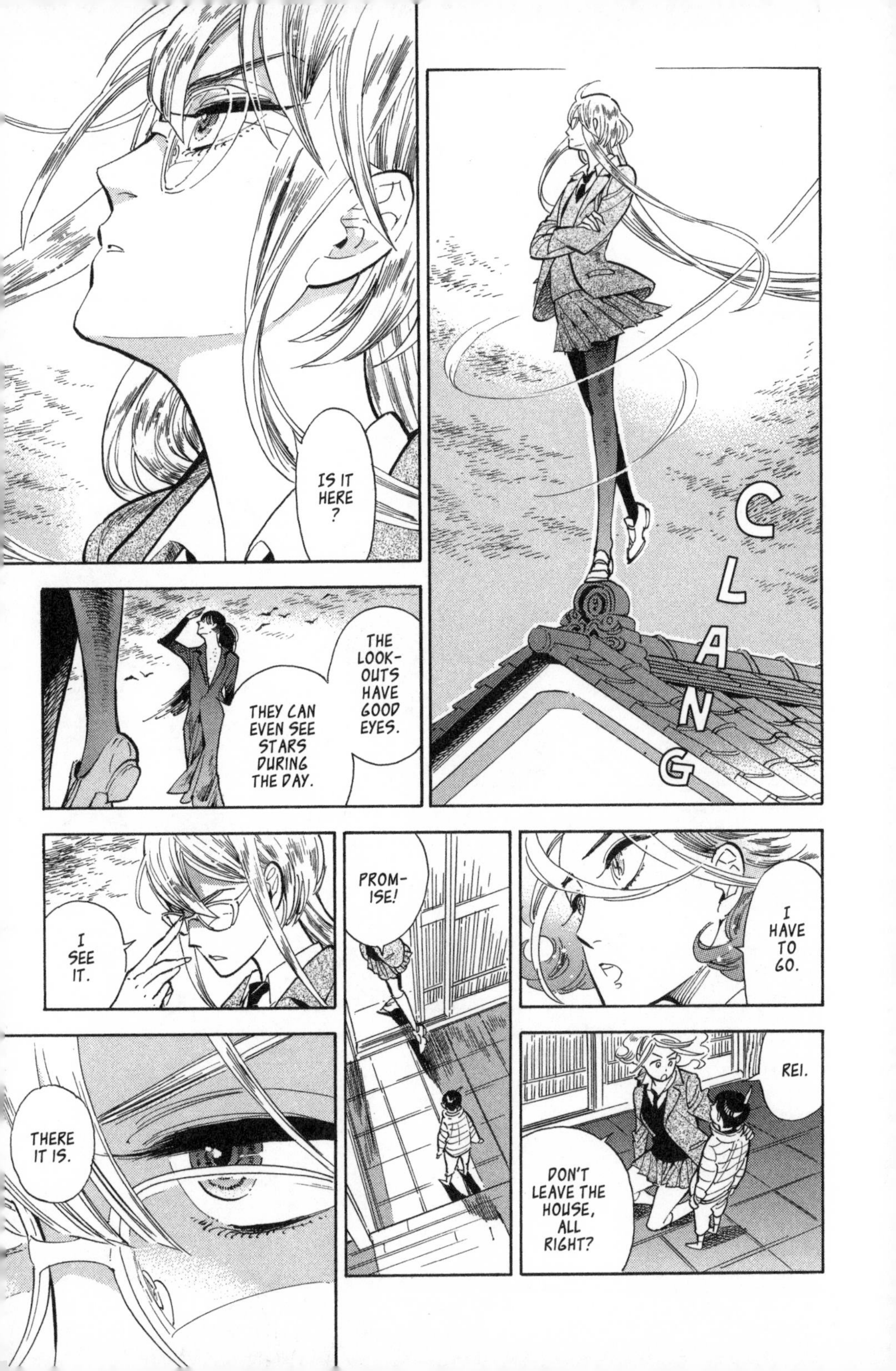
CLANG
IS IT HERE?
THE LOOKOUTS HAVE GOOD EYES.
THEY CAN EVEN SEE STARS DURING THE DAY.
I HAVE TO GO.
REI.
DON'T LEAVE THE HOUSE, ALL RIGHT?
PROMISE!
I SEE IT.
THERE IT IS.

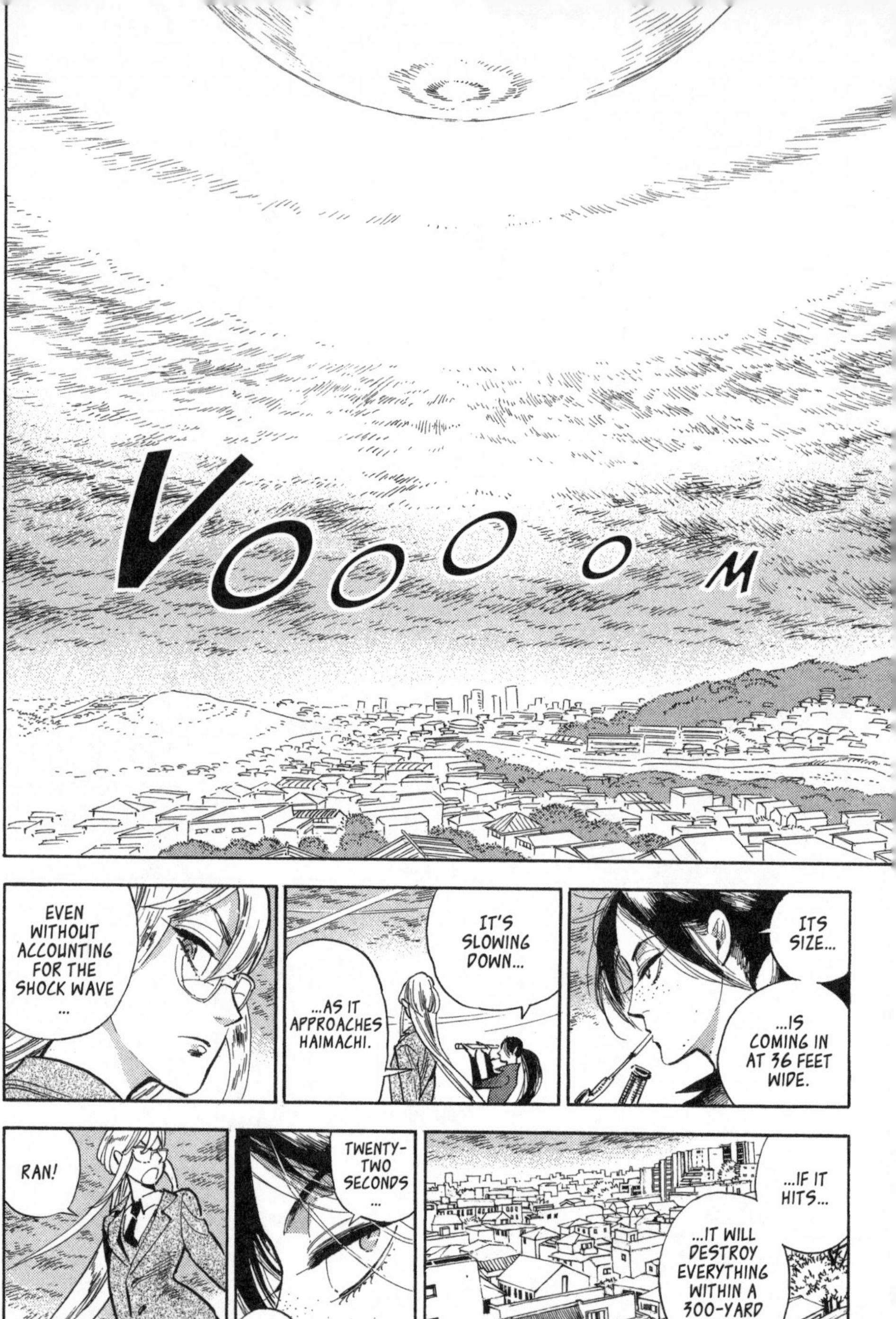
VOOOOM
ITS SIZE...
...IS COMING IN AT 36 FEET WIDE.
IT'S SLOWING DOWN...
...AS IT APPROACHES HAIMACHI.
EVEN WITHOUT ACCOUNTING FOR THE SHOCK WAVE ...
...IF IT HITS...
...IT WILL DESTROY EVERYTHING WITHIN A 300-YARD RADIUS.
TWENTY-TWO SECONDS ...
...TO IMPACT.
RAN!

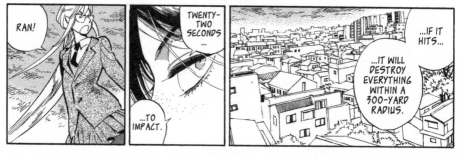

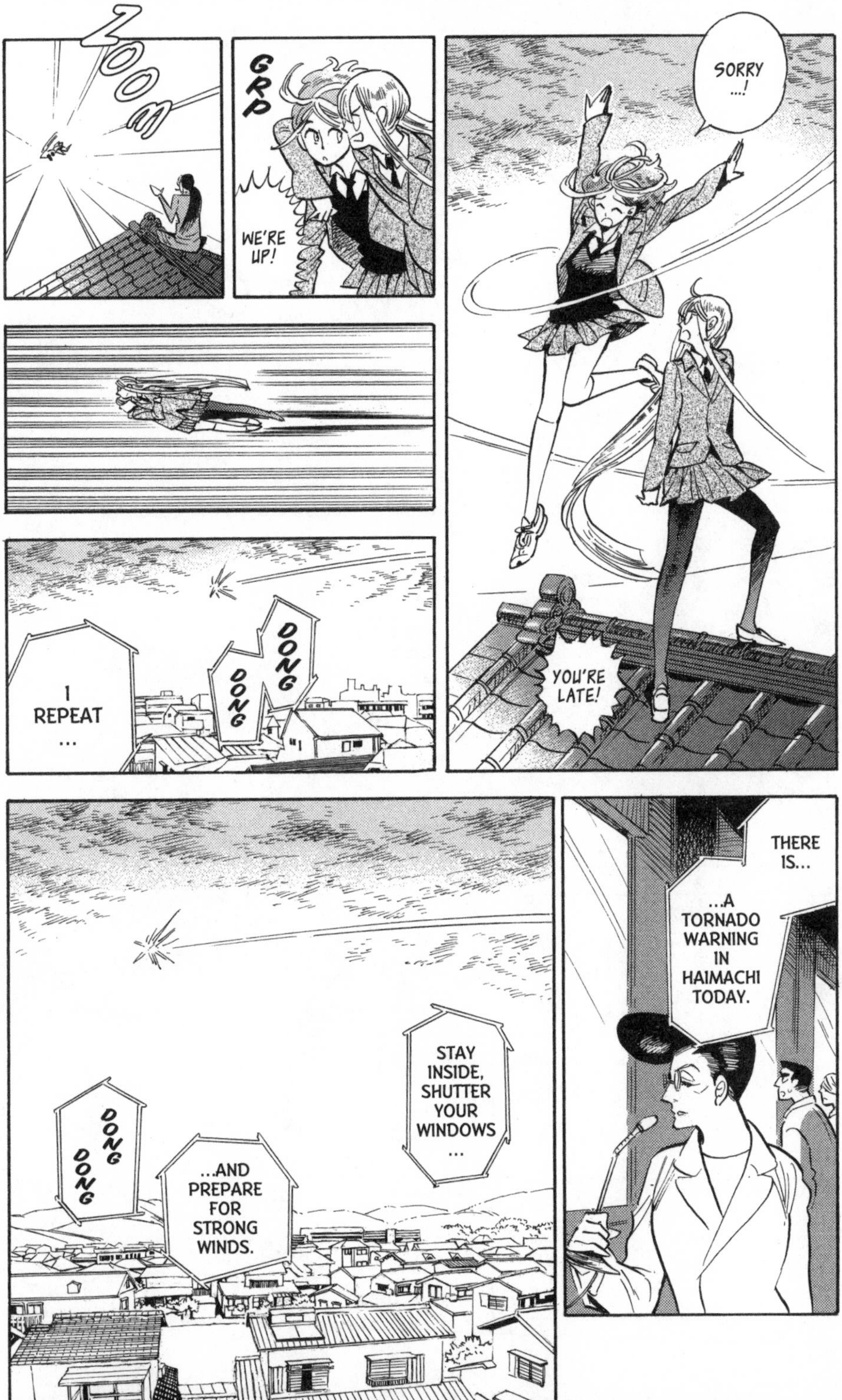
SORRY ...!
YOU'RE LATE!
GRP
WE'RE UP!
ZOOM
DONG DONG DONG
I REPEAT ...
THERE IS...
...A TORNADO WARNING IN HAIMACHI TODAY.
STAY INSIDE, SHUTTER YOUR WINDOWS ...
...AND PREPARE FOR STRONG WINDS.
DONG DONG

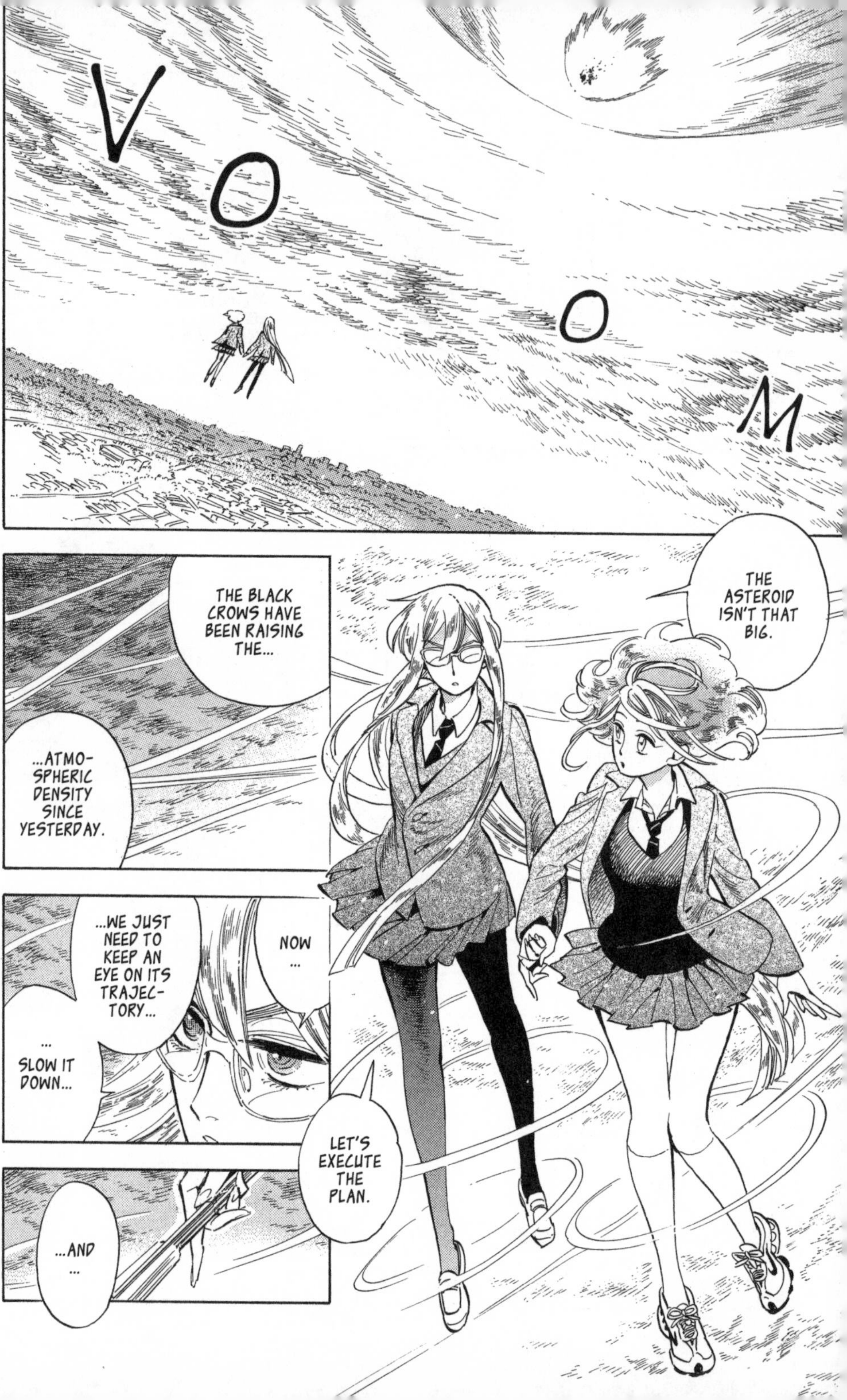
VOOM
THE ASTEROID ISN'T THAT BIG.
THE BLACK CROWS HAVE BEEN RAISING THE...
...ATMOSPHERIC DENSITY SINCE YESTERDAY.
NOW...
...WE JUST NEED TO KEEP AN EYE ON ITS TRAJECTORY...
... SLOW IT DOWN...
...AND ...
LET'S EXECUTE THE PLAN.

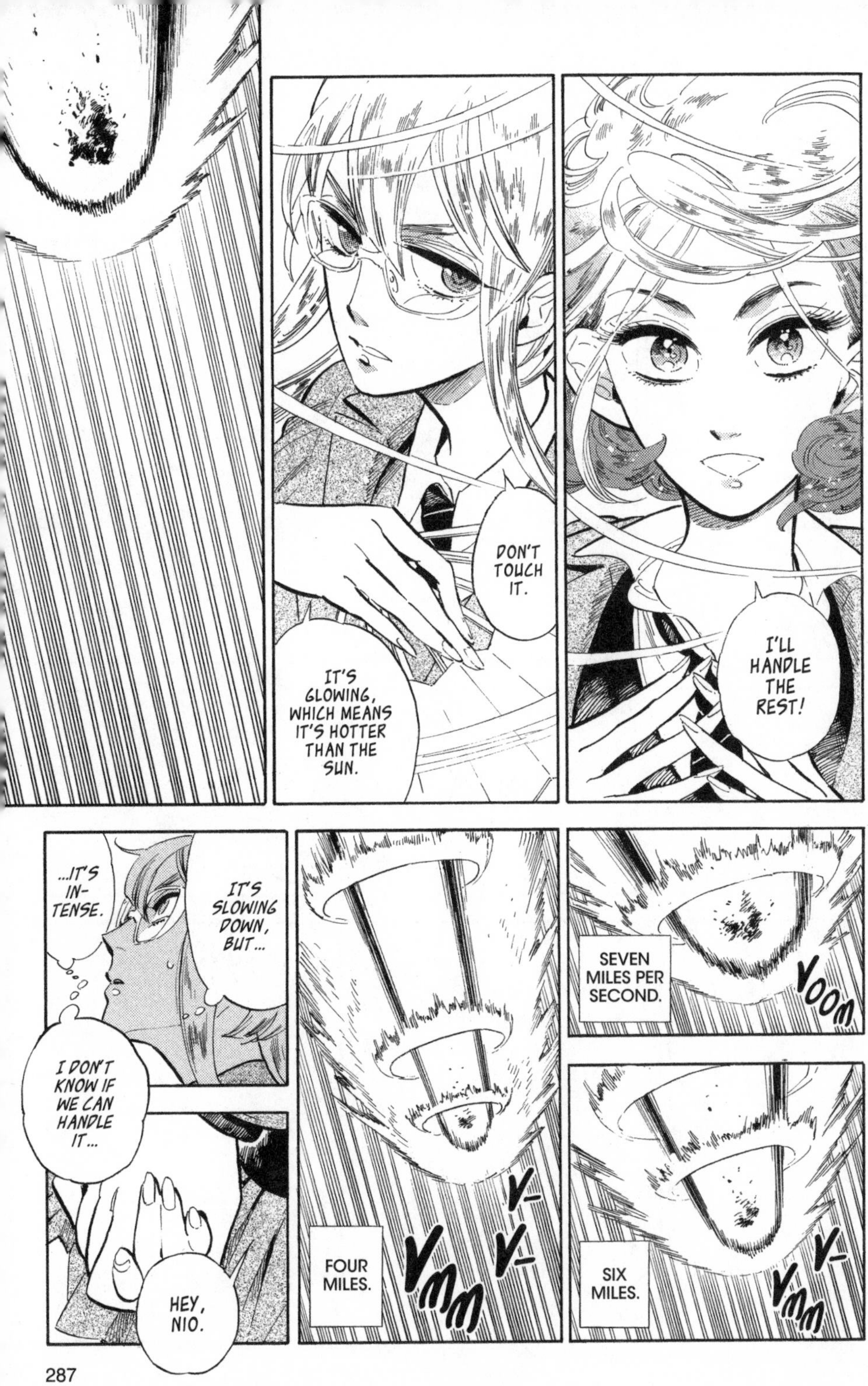

I'LL HANDLE THE REST!
DON'T TOUCH IT.
IT'S GLOWING, WHICH MEANS IT'S HOTTER THAN THE SUN.
SEVEN MILES PER SECOND.
VOOM
SIX MILES.
V— V— VMM
FOUR MILES.
V— V— VMM
IT'S SLOWING DOWN, BUT...
...IT'S IN-TENSE.
I DON'T KNOW IF WE CAN HANDLE IT...
HEY, NIO.

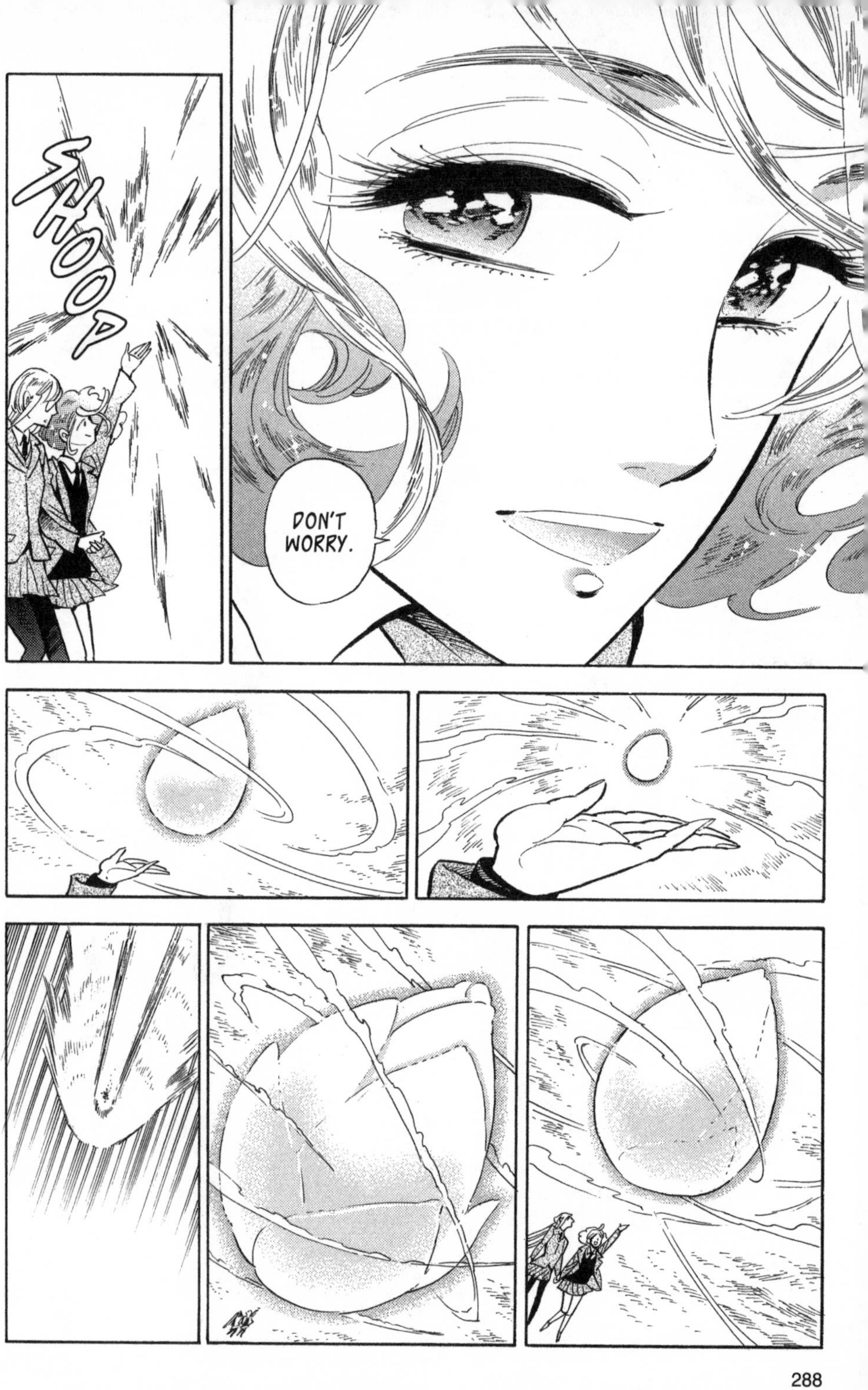
DON'T WORRY.
SHOOP

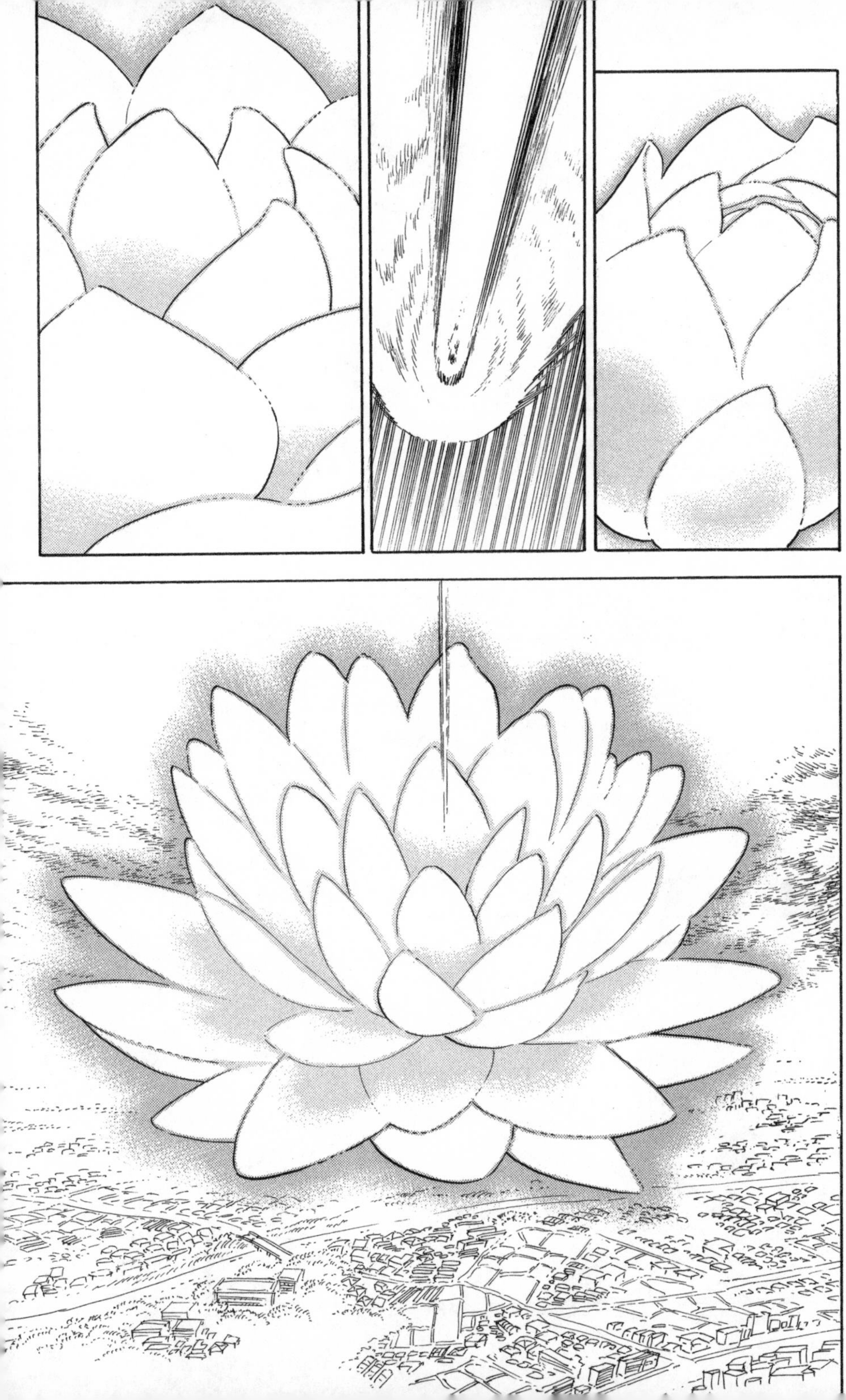

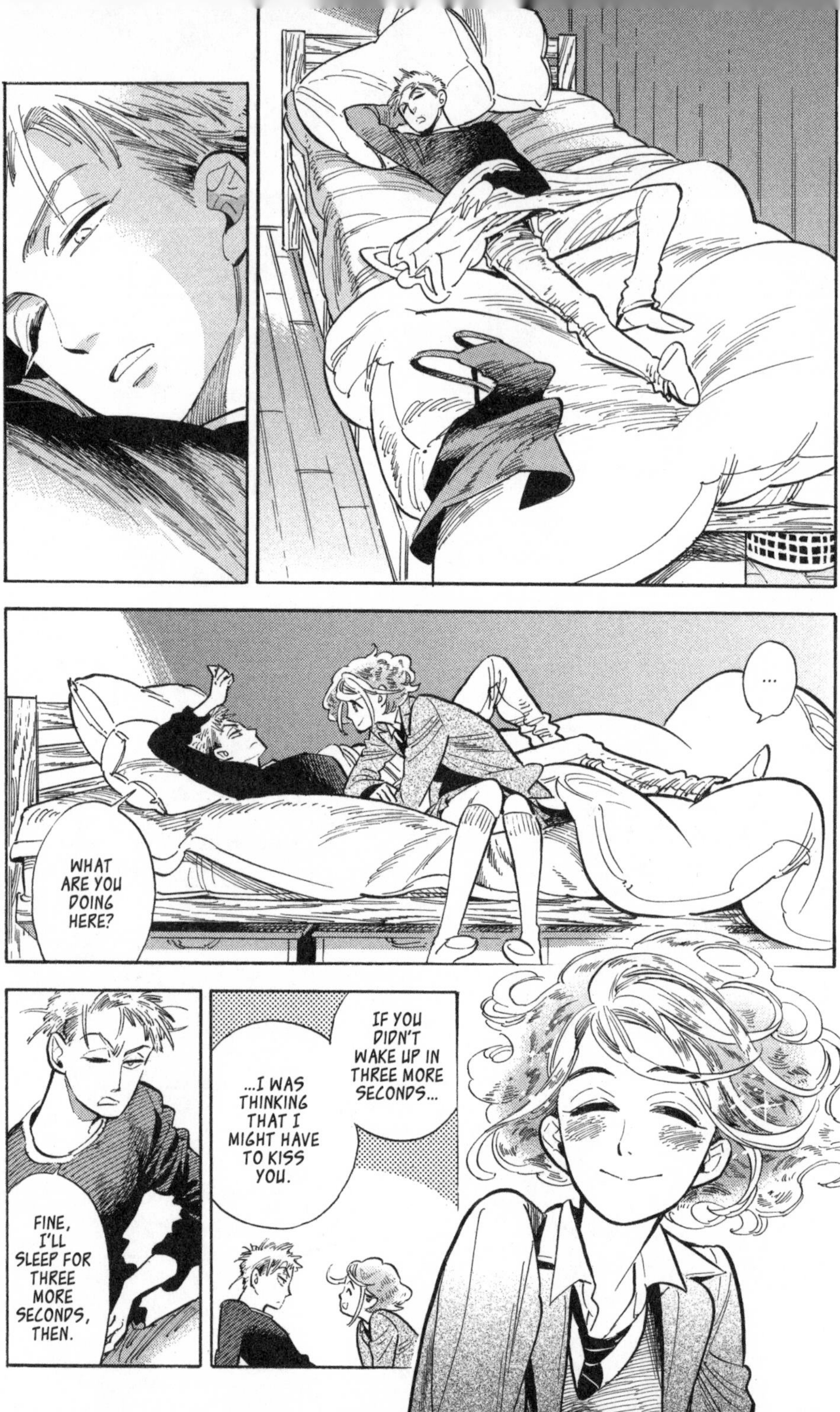
...
WHAT ARE YOU DOING HERE?
IF YOU DIDN'T WAKE UP IN THREE MORE SECONDS...
...I WAS THINKING THAT I MIGHT HAVE TO KISS YOU.
FINE, I'LL SLEEP FOR THREE MORE SECONDS, THEN.

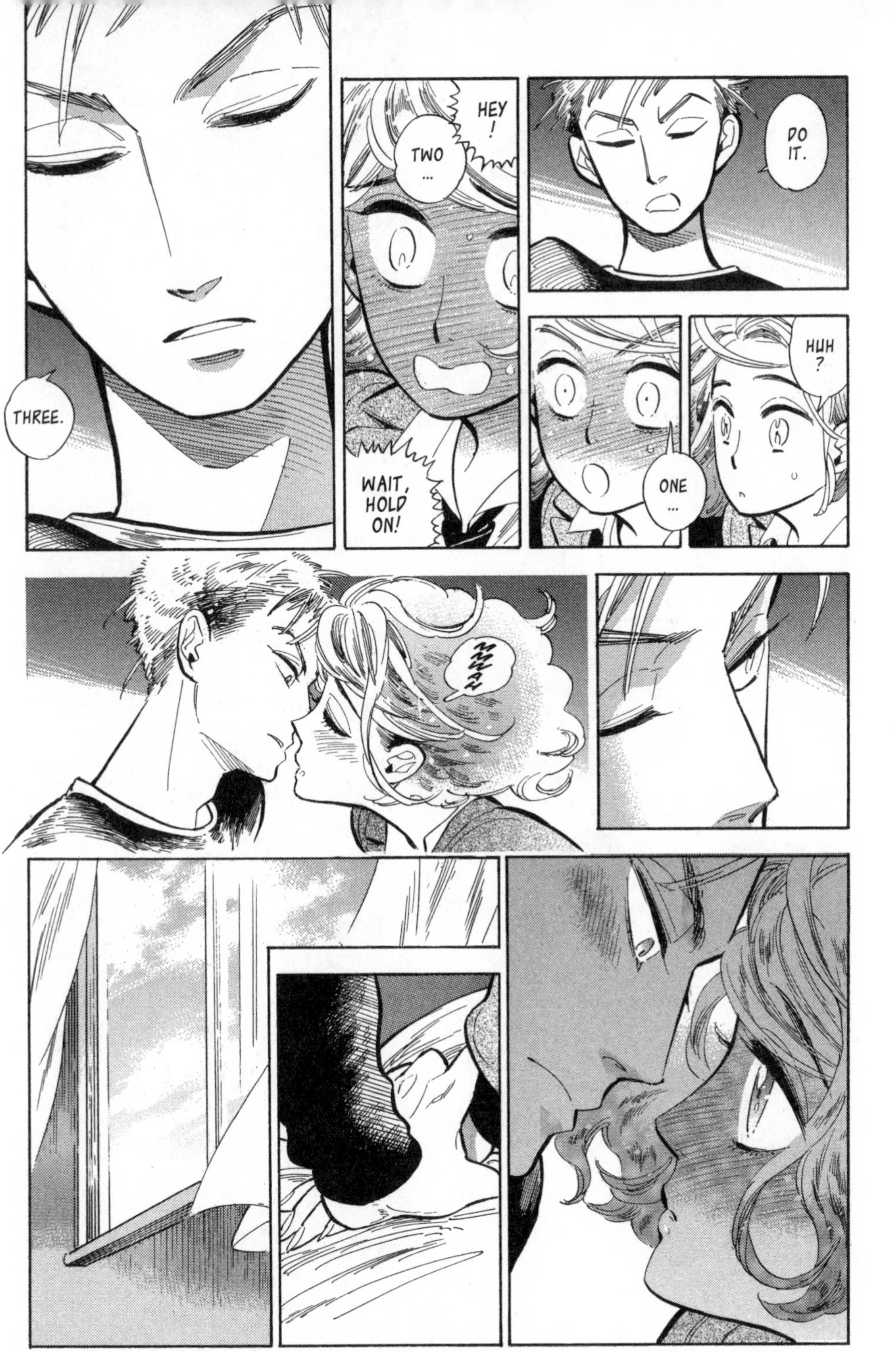
DO IT.
HUH?
ONE...
HEY!
TWO...
WAIT, HOLD ON!
THREE.
MMWAH

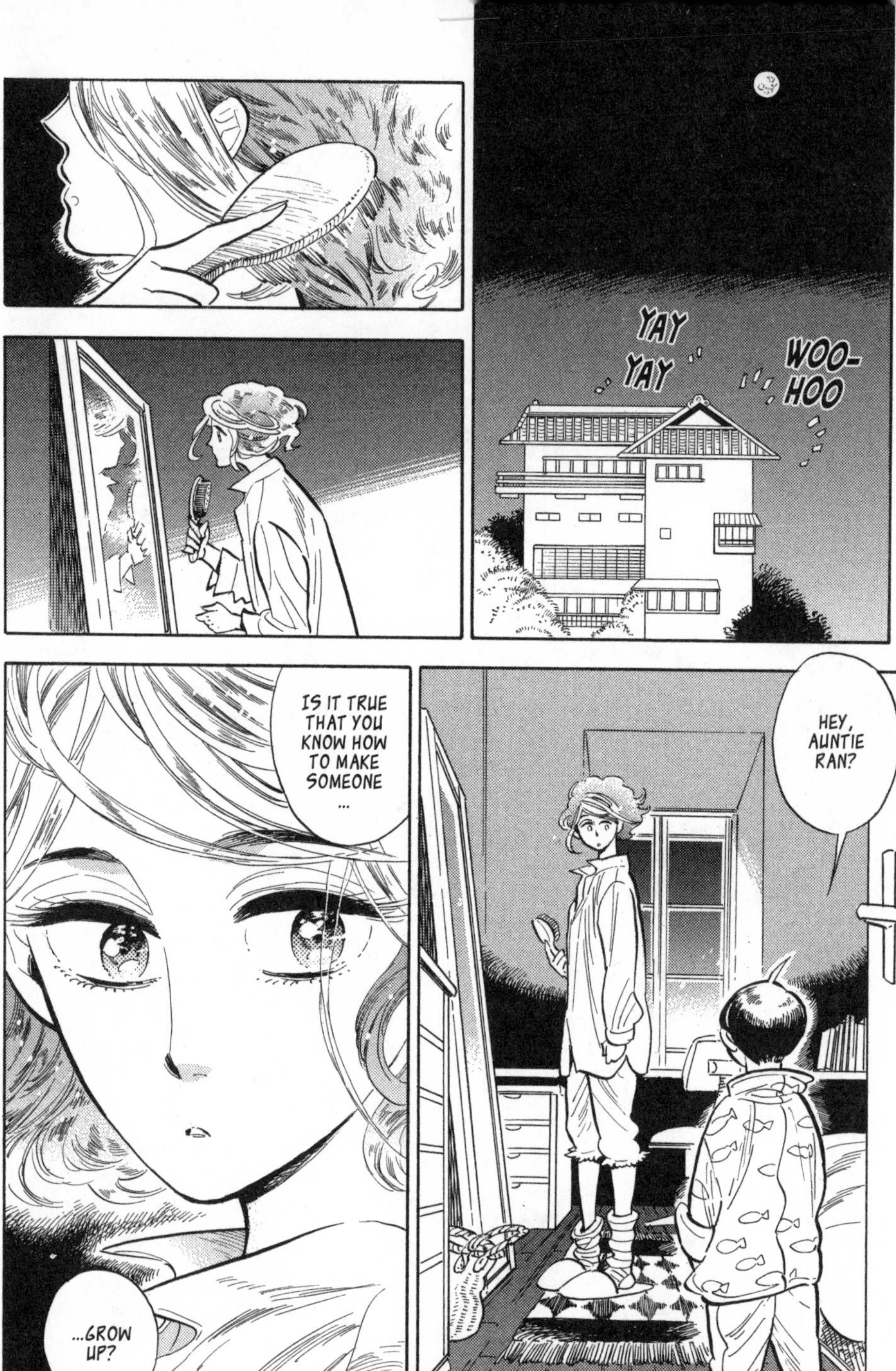
WOO-HOO
YAY YAY
HEY, AUNTIE RAN?
IS IT TRUE THAT YOU KNOW HOW TO MAKE SOMEONE ...
...GROW UP?

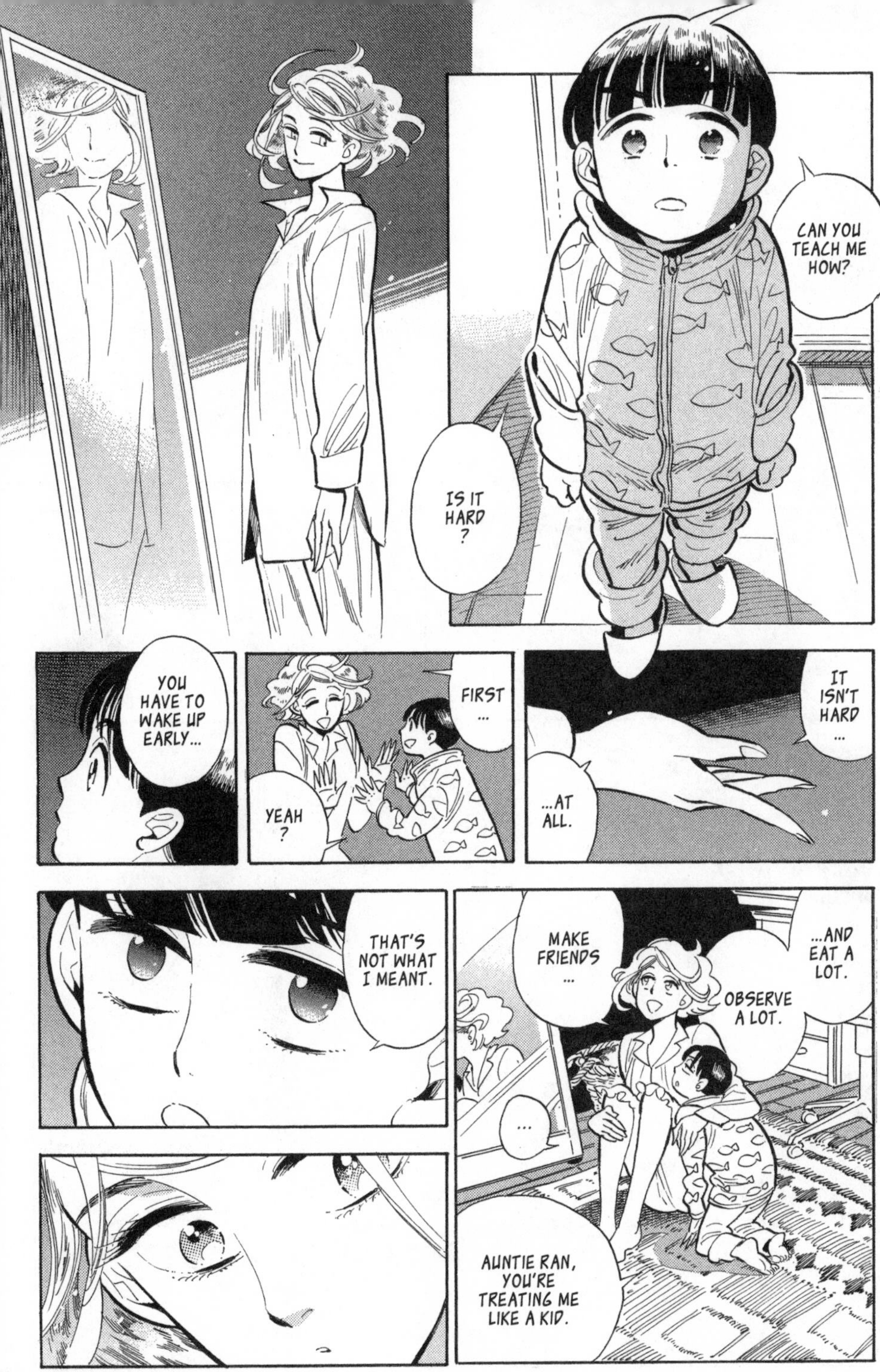

CAN YOU TEACH ME HOW?
IS IT HARD?
IT ISN'T HARD...
...AT ALL.
FIRST...
YEAH?
YOU HAVE TO WAKE UP EARLY...
MAKE FRIENDS...
OBSERVE A LOT.
...AND EAT A LOT.
...
AUNTIE RAN, YOU'RE TREATING ME LIKE A KID.
THAT'S NOT WHAT I MEANT.

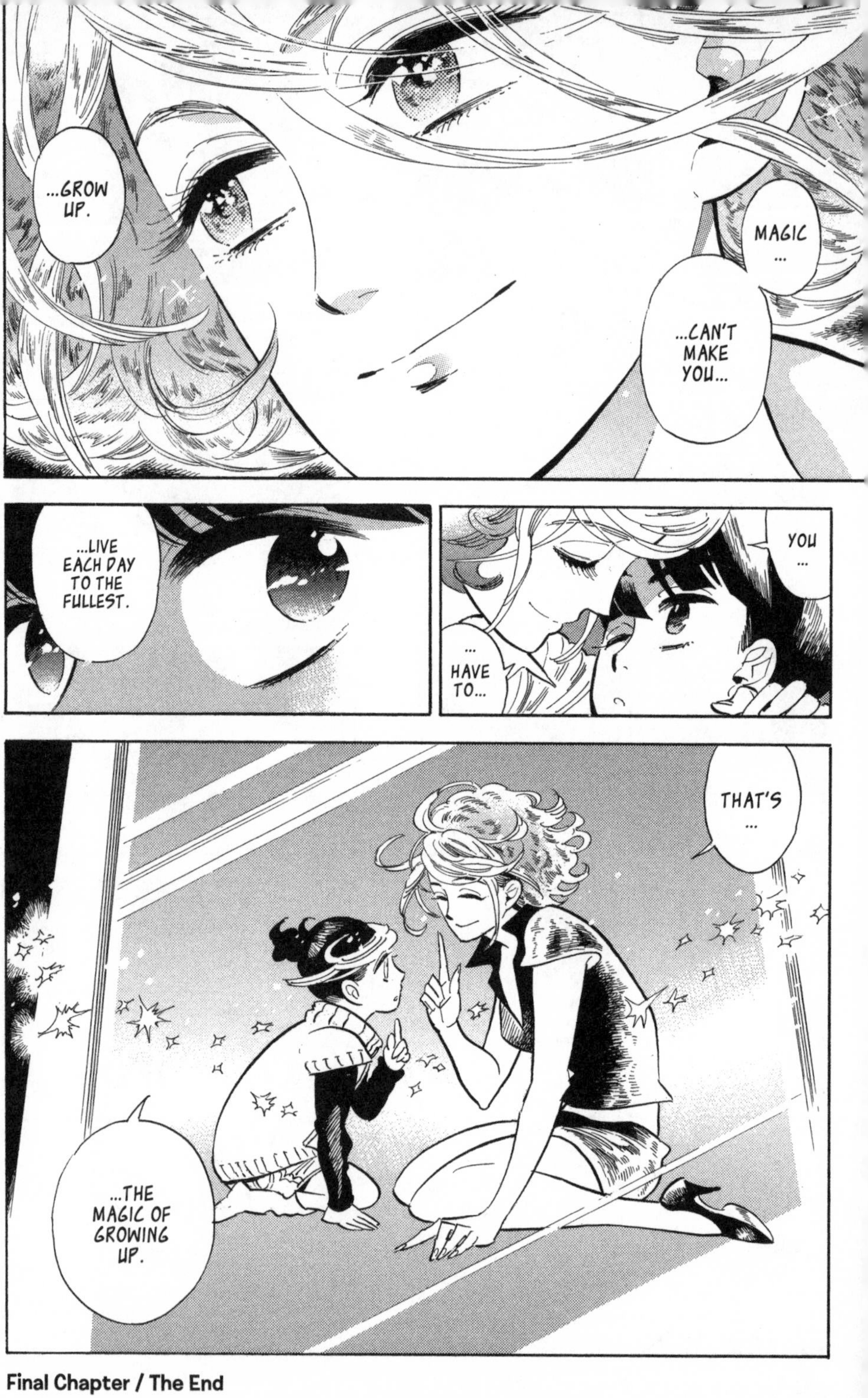
MAGIC ...
...CAN'T MAKE YOU...
...GROW UP.
YOU ...
... HAVE TO...
...LIVE EACH DAY TO THE FULLEST.
THAT'S ...
...THE MAGIC OF GROWING UP.

Final Chapter / The End

Afterword

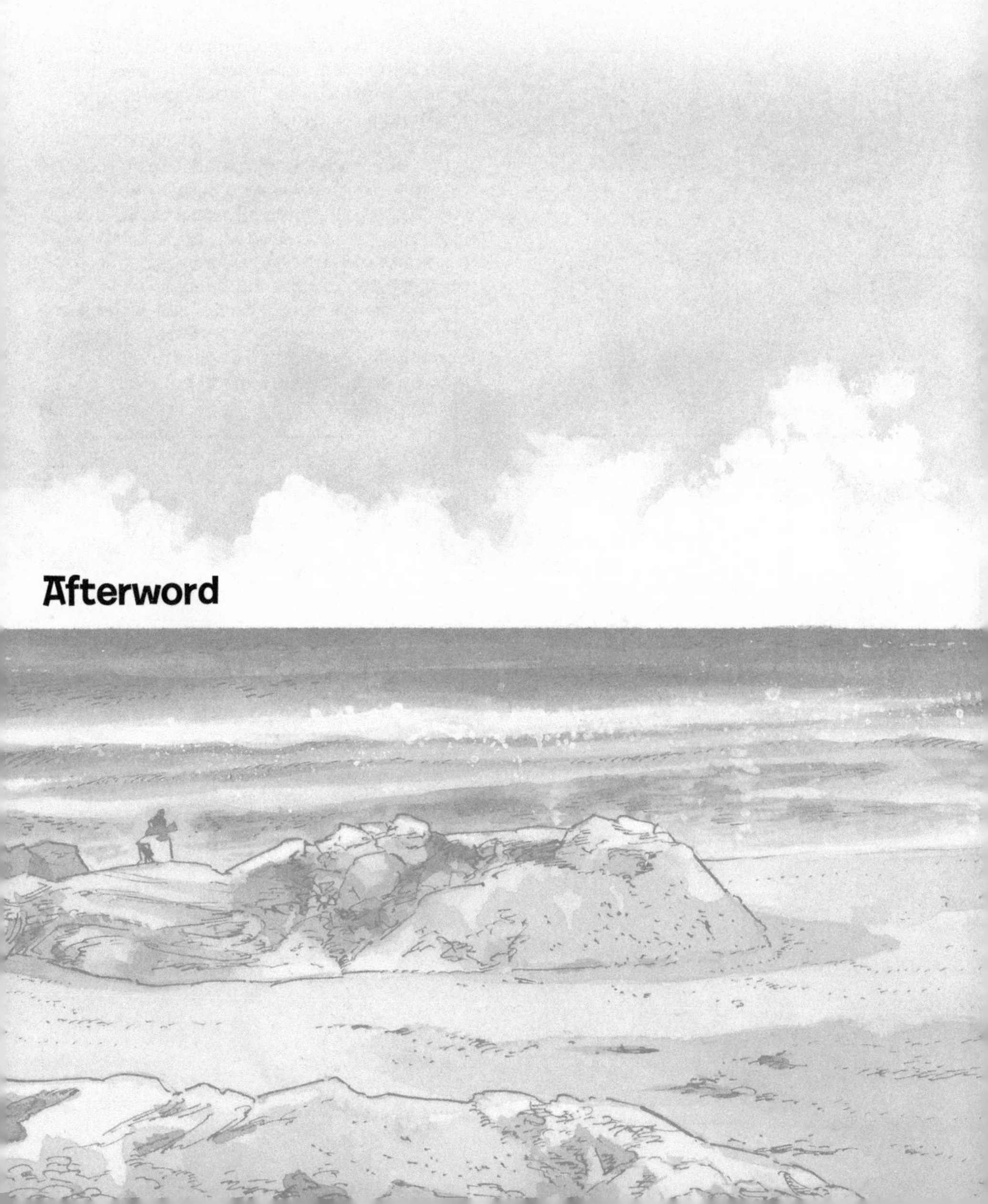

Do you remember when you were young?

I used to chase after my brother endlessly as he rode away on his bicycle. I covered the walls of my room with *Nausicaä* posters, and half of the space beneath my desk was occupied by my collection of foreign children's books that I'd read over and over again. I'd pull my mother's boots out from the shoe cabinet and try them on. And when I grew taller, rather than being excited, I'd become anxious that I wouldn't be able to wear my favorite dress anymore.

I don't remember if I imagined what it would be like to be an adult. As a child, I inhabited a vague space that was just steps before that moment when you suddenly have to find balance between living unattached to anything and discovering a reason for living. I think that space must be the gray world that Ran was slumbering through. Growing up is about both change and choice, and I'm relieved and proud to see the path Ran is heading down.

Thank you for reading along with me. I hope we'll meet again across another sheet of paper. Until then...

Aki Irie
May 2015

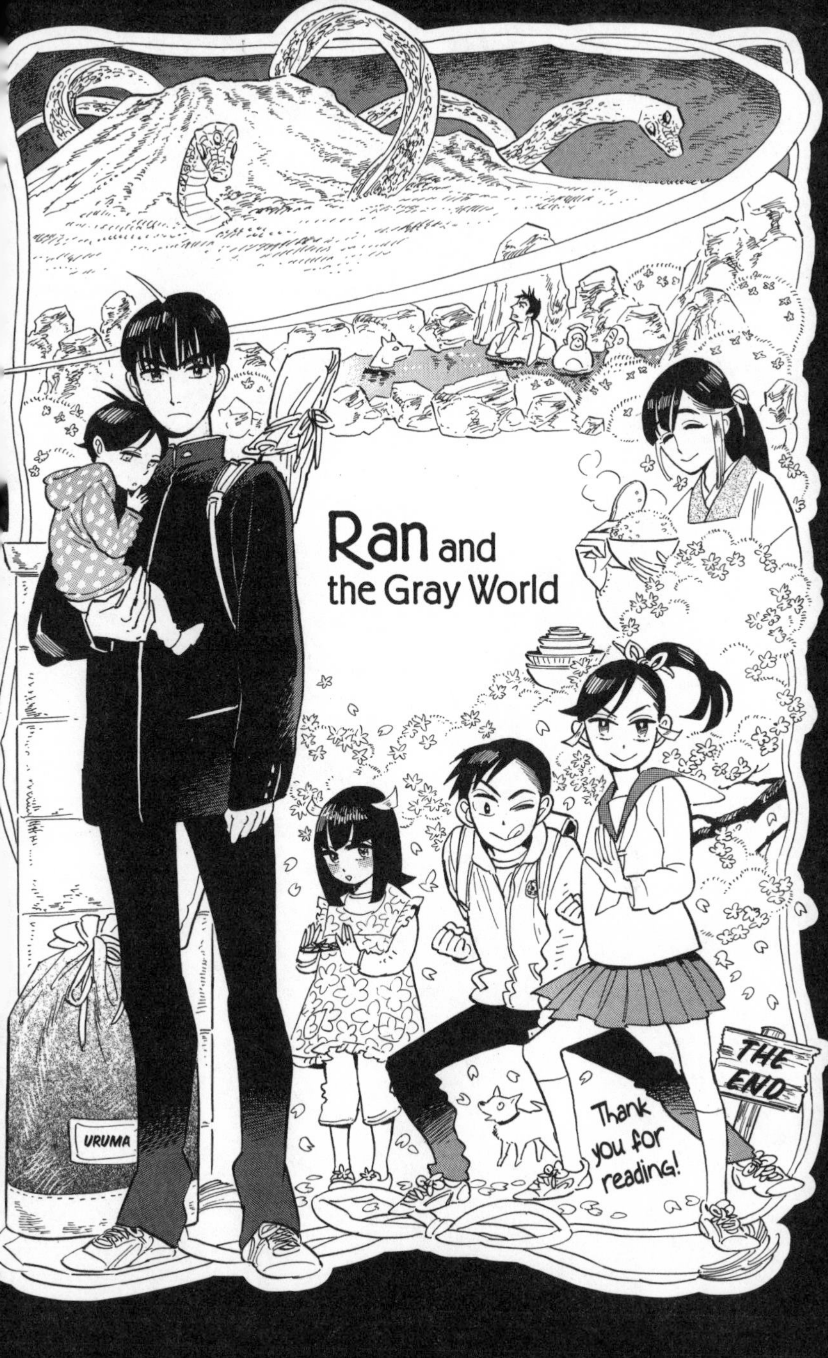
Ran and the Gray World
URUMA
THE END
Thank you for reading!

Aki Irie was born in Kagawa Prefecture, Japan. She
began her professional career as a manga artist in
2002 with the short story "Fuku-chan Tabi Mata Tabi"
(Fuku-chan on the Road Again), which was published in
the monthly manga magazine *Papu*. *Ran and the Gray
World*, her first full-length series, is also the first
of her works to be released in English.

RAN AND THE GRAY WORLD

VOL. 7

VIZ Signature Edition

Story & Art by

AKI IRIE

English Translation & Adaptation / Emi Louie-Nishikawa
Touch-Up Art & Lettering / Joanna Estep
Design / Yukiko Whitley
Editor / Amy Yu

Printed in Canada

Published by VIZ Media, LLC
P.O. Box 77010
San Francisco, CA 94107

10 9 8 7 6 5 4 3 2 1
First printing, May 2020

VIZ MEDIA
viz.com

VIZ SIGNATURE
vizsignature.com

ratings.viz.com RATED T+ OLDER TEEN

PARENTAL ADVISORY
RAN AND THE GRAY WORLD is rated T+ for Older Teen and is recommended for ages 16 and up. This volume contains brief nudity and suggestive themes.

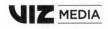

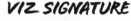

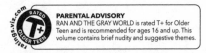

Ran and
the Gray World